Popular Science

Complete Book
of
Power Tools

Popular Science

Complete Book
of
Power Tools

By R. J. de Cristoforo

BLACK DOG
& LEVENTHAL
PUBLISHERS

Published by
Black Dog & Leventhal Publishers, Inc.
151 West 19th Street
New York, NY 10011

Distributed by
Workman Publishing Company
708 Broadway
New York, NY 10003

ISBN: 1-57912-026-1

h g f e d c b a

Library of Congress Cataloging-in-Publication Data

DeCristoforo, R. J.
     [Complete book of portable power tool techniques]
     Popular science complete book of power tools / by R.J. de Cristoforo,
          p.   cm.
     First work originally published: The complete book of portable
power tool techniques. 2nd work originally published: The complete
book of stationary power tool techniques. New York : Sterling Pub.,
©1985 and ©1986 respectively.
     Includes index.
     ISBN 1-57912-026-1
     1. Power tools. I. DeCristoforo, R.J. Complete book of
stationary power tool techniques. II. Title. III. Title: Complete
book of stationary power tool techniques.
TT153.5.D39 1998   98-11509
684' .083--dc21   CIP

Table of Contents

The Complete Book of
STATIONARY POWER TOOL TECHNIQUES

by R.J. De Cristoforo

to Mary

Preface

Over the past thirty years, R.J. De Cristoforo's work has had incredible impact in the home workshop field. He has helped thousands upon thousands of home craftsmen to do better and more imaginative work through his articles in *Popular Science,* other magazines, and his books. His clear, incisive writing and thoroughly illustrated techniques are universally admired. His inventiveness and versatility with jigs, guides, and other innovations to extend the uses of power tools are unsurpassed.

Now, his life-long experience with stand-alone home workshop tools is presented in these pages, freshly re-written, updated, and organized to give the reader a vast treasury of instructions and techniques for use with every kind of stationary power tool. No matter which kind of power tools you own—from the smallest 'benchtop' drill press to a heavy-duty thickness planer—there's valuable information here for you to study and emulate, or merely to page through and enjoy the wizardry of a true craftsman.

John W. Sill, Editorial Director
Popular Science Books

Introduction

Nothing irritates me more than the comment that individual craftsmanship is dead. The people I know, and many who have sent me snapshots of their projects, are surely not from another world. They live in every state—in apartments, private homes, and on farms. They live in countries I may never see, and some of them still use foot power to run a lathe.

Some are affluent, some are poor; some make bread-and-butter money working behind a desk, or turning screws on an assembly line, or by safeguarding a forest, or by mixing cement. They all have one thing in common: the desire to originate.

The urge to make something has not been destroyed by technology or mechanization, and more and more young people today are turning to craftsmanship as a means of self-expression.

I'm convinced that more creative talent goes unrecognized than is ever honored with a ribbon or museum acceptance. There is a universal beehive of creativity with cells in some highly unlikely places—a closet in an apartment, a carport, a mobile home, a corner in an attic, a basement, garage, tool shed; any place the worker can set up his tools.

Anyone can learn to use tools. If you start today, you will not be an expert by tomorrow, but the time will come more quickly than you might expect.

This book takes the reader's point of view throughout. If you are a beginner, start from page one in each chapter. If you've made a few projects, you can probably skip the basic information, but you should scan it, at least, since you can find a hint or a jig that will suggest a way to improve your work. If you are very knowledgeable about stationary power tools, you can be selective, but do be aware of all the information here. This book took over thirty years to produce and it is done *in depth*.

I'd like to stress the importance of safety in the shop. I've always been a little afraid of power tools; hence I still have all my fingers and no scars. That slight fear is healthy. If you allow yourself to become overconfident (as some craftsmen will attest) you will become vulnerable. You *are* the master of the tool and should have no qualms, but at the same time remember that the tool is disinterested in what it cuts.

Follow all procedures *carefully*, just as they are outlined. If you have never tried an operation before, be sure to read the instructions thoroughly. And don't be embarrassed to try a dry run before you flick the switch.

A lot of people deserve thanks for their help in producing this book: readers who have written to me through the years; editors, some gone, some still badgering me about deadlines and grammar; photographers; power tool manufacturers too numerous to list. All of them have my deepest gratitude.

R.J. De Cristoforo
Los Altos Hills, California

METRIC SYSTEM

UNIT	ABBREVIATION		APPROXIMATE U.S. EQUIVALENT		
Length					
		Number of Metres			
myriametre	mym	10,000	——————— 6.2 miles		
kilometre	km	1000	0.62 mile		
hectometre	hm	100	109.36 yards		
dekametre	dam	10	32.81 feet		
metre	m	1	39.37 inches		
decimetre	dm	0.1	3.94 inches		
centimetre	cm	0.01	0.39 inch		
millimetre	mm	0.001	0.04 inch		
Area					
		Number of Square Metres			
square kilometre	sq km *or* km²	1,000,000	0.3861 square miles		
hectare	ha	10,000	2.47 acres		
are	a	100	119.60 square yards		
centare	ca	1	10.76 square feet		
square centimetre	sq cm *or* cm²	0.0001	0.155 square inch		
Volume					
		Number of Cubic Metres			
dekastere	das	10	13.10 cubic yards		
stere	s	1	1.31 cubic yards		
decistere	ds	0.10	3.53 cubic feet		
cubic centimetre	cu cm *or* cm³ *also* cc	0.000001	0.061 cubic inch		
Capacity					
		Number of Litres	Cubic	Dry	Liquid
kilolitre	kl	1000	1.31 cubic yards		
hectolitre	hl	100	3.53 cubic feet	2.84 bushels	
dekalitre	dal	10	0.35 cubic foot	1.14 pecks	2.64 gallons
litre	l	1	61.02 cubic inches	0.908 quart	1.057 quarts
decilitre	dl	0.10	6.1 cubic inches	0.18 pint	0.21 pint
centilitre	cl	0.01	0.6 cubic inch		0.338 fluidounce
millilitre	ml	0.001	0.06 cubic inch		0.27 fluidram
Mass and Weight					
		Number of Grams			
metric ton	MT *or* t	1,000,000	1.1 tons		
quintal	q	100,000	220.46 pounds		
kilogram	kg	1,000	2.2046 pounds		
hectogram	hg	100	3.527 ounces		
dekagram	dag	10	0.353 ounce		
gram	g *or* gm	1	0.035 ounce		
decigram	dg	0.10	1.543 grains		
centigram	cg	0 01	0.154 grain		
milligram	mg	0.001	0.015 grain		

1. Working Safety

Recently, a friend came to visit, displaying a bandaged hand, damaged pride, and renewed respect for the woodworking tools he had been using for many years. His hand, luckily, was still whole but badly lacerated. As is often the case, the accident he described would not have happened if he had obeyed a rule he was thoroughly familiar with.

In this particular case, the operator was hand-holding a piece of wood that was much too small to be safely passed over a molding head. He thought that, this once, he could get away with it. He didn't. Ignorance of how tools function and of correct procedures can cause accidents, but overconfidence and carelessness can be just as deadly.

The point is that expertise does not keep you safe. Statistics indicate that as many, if not more, professionals are hurt using power tools as amateurs.

Another significant factor is the regard the worker has for the tool he is using. It's fairly common for the wise user of power tools to damage a finger when switching to hand work with a chisel or a hammer. You may do less damage with some tools, but if you're truly careful, there should be no damage at all.

On the whole, the damages in the workshop are no different from the potential hazards of everyday life. However, there is one important difference. Safety, when driving an automobile, depends as much on fellow drivers as it does on you. In the shop, you alone control the risk factor. Don't depend on the tool, or even its guards. These mechanical things can't think for you.

Safety rules, always printed in books and owner's manuals and magazine articles, are often ignored—we're so anxious to get on with the doing. I hope you don't ignore these. Safety admonitions that apply to power tools are as important to observe as the signs that advise about a possible avalanche or the unstable soil at a cliff's edge.

Tool Guards

Most power tools, especially stationary ones, are equipped with safety devices that should be mounted following manufacturer's instructions and maintained in good working order. On a radial arm saw, for example (Figure 1-1), the upper part of the guard is adjustable and locked in position for various sawing operations. The lower half-rings "float" to automatically ride the surface of the work during

a cut. I've seen operators remove these rings, which is not a wise thing to do. With the rings in place, it's more likely that you will keep your hands well away from the blade.

The rod, at the front of the guard, is an anti-kickback devise necessary for ripping operations. Leaving it mounted even for crosscutting is a good idea so long as the swiveling fingers at the end of the rod are situated above the workpiece.

The guard shown in Figure 1-2 is typical of many designed for table saws. The hood affair which covers the saw blade should be maintained so it lifts easily and allows work to pass while still covering the saw blade. The hood is mounted on a "splitter" whose job is to ride in the saw cut on ripping operations so the cut won't close and bind the blade. It's dangerous to work without the guard, yet many people do so.

Often, when a tool is designed for more than one job, the manufacturer makes available special guards to be used under particular circumstances. One, to be used for particular dadoing, molding head, and shaping techniques on a

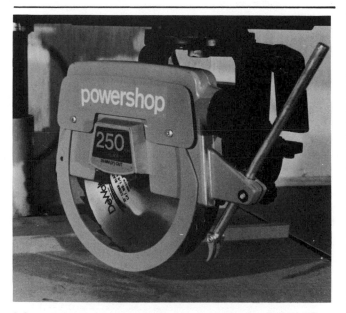

1-1.   The guard on a radial arm saw does a respectable job of covering the blade during and after the cut. The lower half-rings "float" so they automatically adjust to stock thickness.

radial arm saw is shown in Figure 1-3. These are usually extra cost items, but if you're going to take advantage of the multi-purpose facet of any tool it's critical to use any safety device that's recommended.

The design of some tools often makes it necessary for the maker to supply special guards. A case in point (Figure 1-4) is the multi-purpose tool where a good part of the saw blade is exposed beneath the table. This extra protection is supplied with the unit and should be mounted for all operations where it applies. With this and the upper guard in place, there is almost no portion of the saw blade exposed.

Many tools, the table saw being typical, have removable inserts through which the cutting tool pokes through (Figure 1-5). The purpose of the insert is to minimize the opening around the blade or cutter. The standard insert is for a saw blade but it is removable so other types of cutters like dadoing tools and molding heads can be substituted (Figure 1-6).

There are times when the insert you can buy is not ideal for the chore at hand. At such times, you should think of making special inserts that are exactly right for what you are doing. Such inserts, in size and shape and attachment methods, are customized using the standard insert as a pattern. Since situations like this will often occur, it is good practice to prepare a quantity of "blanks" (Figure 1-7), so you will be prepared for any eventuality.

An example of a custom-made insert that contributes to accuracy as well as safety is shown in Figure 1-8. It was made when a number of thin, almost ribbon-like strips of wood were needed. As you can see, the insert opening is only wide enough for the blade to come through. There is no chance for the ripped pieces to be pulled below the table by the saw blade. Later on we'll talk about how the openings in special inserts are cut.

Throughout this book there will be thoughts about accessories you can make that will help you work more safely and more accurately. An example is the special guard (Figures 1-9 and 1-10) you can make for a radial arm saw. The plastic shield provides front coverage without interfering with vision. The shield mounts on a metal angle which

1-2.   On a table saw, a typical guard has a swivel-mounted hood that rises and sits on the surface of the stock as the cut is made. The vertical piece to which the hood is attached is the "splitter."

1-4.   On multi-purpose tools, the manufacturer supplies a special guard to cover the part of the blade that is exposed beneath the table. The guard does double duty since it can be connected to a vacuum.

1-3.   Many tools have extra-cost guards that should be used with accessory operations. This radial arm saw unit covers cutters like dado heads, molding heads and shaper cutters.

1-5.   Tool inserts are secured to the main table and are meant to minimize the opening around the cutting tool. Take care to be sure they are flush with the worktable.

1-6.   Special inserts are available for particular operations. These units, from left to right, are for a saw blade, a dado cutter, and a molding head.

1-7.   Often, when the insert you can buy is not exactly right for the job on hand, make your own. The regular insert supplied with the tool serves as a pattern for the homemade ones.

1-8.   This special insert was made to provide only enough clearance for the saw blade. Cuts will be smoother and there is no chance that slim pieces will be pulled through the opening.

1-9.   This special shield you can make for a radial arm saw will cover the blade at the front without interfering with vision. It can be tilted and is adjustable vertically so it can be used with various types of work.

1-10.   Construction details of the special guard for a radial arm saw. The metal angle fits the split casting at the front end of the tool's guard and is secured with the same bolt that locks the anti-kickback device.

slips into the split casting at the front end of the tool's guard. The same bolt that locks the anti-kickback unit secures the special guard. The guard tilts and adjusts vertically so it can be set close to the saw blade while accommodating various stock thicknesses. Be aware though, that this guard is *not* a substitute for the anti-kickback device. Replace the anti-kickback for ripping operations.

Another do-it-yourself "gadget" that contributes to safer power tool operation is shown in Figure 1-11. This is a combination hold-down/pusher that should be used on ripping operations when using your hand would bring fingers too close to the cutting area. The hold-down/pusher keeps the work flat on the table and advances it past the saw blade so fingers are kept away from danger areas.

There are some useful safety products that are not supplied by the manufacturer of a tool but by independent companies. The following are examples:

1-11.   This combination hold-down/pusher is another example of safety tools you can make. It helps you do a narrow rip cut without allowing your hand to get close to the blade. Similar tools and plans for them will be detailed later on.

1-12.   The RIPSTRATE acts to keep work flat on the table and stable when making rip cuts. A pawl will lock the wheels should the work try to move backwards. This helps prevent kickback.

The RIPSTRATE (Figure 1-12) is a table saw safety tool employing two rubber wheels mounted on spring loaded arms so the wheels are angled slightly toward the fence. This action tends to press the work against the fence as it is moved forward. A pawl will lock the wheels should they try to reverse direction. This acts as an anti-kickback device. The arms supporting the wheels adapt themselves to stock thickness so that no adjustment is required between jobs involving different thicknesses of wood. The RIPSTRATE can be adjusted in various ways to accommodate different widths.

The BRETT-GUARD® table saw guard (Figure 1-13) is a transparent box-type shield that is supported by steel rods that attach to a heavy aluminum housing. In turn, the housing mounts on a special steel plate that is bolted to the edge of the saw table. An advantage of the guard is its flexibility. It covers the blade on routine operations like crosscutting and ripping and is thoroughly adjustable for use, for example, when dadoing, splining, grooving, and for advanced chores like the coving operation shown in Figure 1-14.

While the concept of the guard is universal, correct mounting requires that the buyer supply the manufacturer with particulars concerning this piece of equipment.

The BRETT-GUARD® bandsaw guard (Figure 1-15) provides additional protection during all normal bandsawing operations. The see-through, shatter-proof shield provides welcome illumination by means of a built-in bulb

1-13.   The BRETT-GUARD® table saw guard is a fully adjustable transparent shield that provides blade coverage without interfering with table saw operations.

which, if desired, can be wired into the on-off switch of the machine. The shield is useable within the full depth-of-cut capacity of the tool.

The SHOPMATE® SAFETY KIT (Figure 1-16) contains a push stick, push block, 'fence straddler', and featherboard. These are small hand tools or jigs that help keep your hands away from cutters and out of danger. For example, the push stick is used to guide small pieces of wood through a table saw or bandsaw. The push block holds wood down as you pass it over the jointer. The fence straddler rides on your rip fence and pushes very slender stock past a blade or cutter. Featherboards keep a workpiece pressed firmly against the rip fence and protect against kickback. You can also make these tools yourself— we'll talk more about them in later chapters.

Protection For Eyes, Ears, and Lungs

The safety items shown in Figure 1-17 should be standard equipment in all shops. There is much talk about safety goggles and face masks and it isn't difficult to convince most people to wear them. But it's often easy to overlook the effect of noise and dust.

Headphone-type hearing protectors are as important as any safety device. High frequencies can be generated by high-speed electric motors and some woodworking operations. The effects are cumulative; each exposure contributes to possible ear damage. Good ear protectors will screen out high frequencies while still allowing normal conversation,

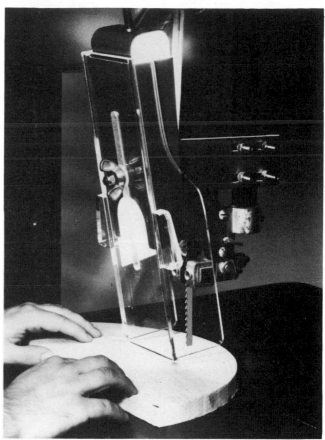

1-15.   This special bandsaw guard provides extra protection during all normal saw operations. It has a built-in light that can be wired into the tool's on-off switch.

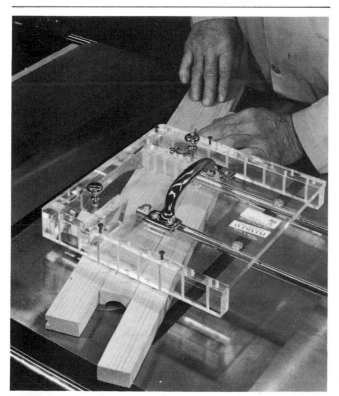

1-14.   The unique guard is useable on advanced operations like this cove-cutting technique. It can be adjusted for use with commercial jigs or special ones you might make yourself.

1-16.   The SHOPMATE® SAFETY KIT contains a push stick, push block, 'fence straddler', and featherboard—tools you need to keep your hands and fingers out of danger.

1-17.   Face mask, safety goggles, headphone-type ear protectors, dusk mask—all these items should be viewed as standard workshop equipment. Keep them handy and use them.

and they won't eliminate the woodworking noises you *should* hear.

Don't feel that a dust mask should be worn only when doing sanding chores. Many sawing, routing, shaping, and planing operations can produce particles best kept from your lungs. The filters in the masks should be kept clean and replaced as often as necessary.

Unauthorized Use

Power tools are tempting to children; even some adults love to flick a switch just to see what happens. Most modern power tools are designed so it's necessary to insert a key in the switch before the unit can be turned on. The system works, but not if you leave the key in the tool. Store locking devices or keys in a secret place.

Shop Dress and Shopkeeping

Have a special uniform to wear for shop work. Tight fitting shirt and trousers and heavy, nonslip shoes, preferably with steel toes, make sense. Don't wear gloves or a necktie or any loose clothing that might snag on a tool whether it's idle or in work. Don't wear jewelry. Rings, wristwatches, bracelets and other adornments are hazards. Cover your hair for safety and dust protection regardless of whether it is long or short.

Treat your shop as if it were a kitchen. Tables, benches, tools, accessories, and so on, should be maintained in pristine condition. Stop occasionally to remove sawdust from tool tables and workbenches. A neat helper is one of the new, small, cordless vacuum cleaners like the one shown in Figure 1-18. You hang it on the wall, plugged in so it's continually recharging; always ready to keep sawdust from accumulating.

Don't allow litter, wood scraps to clutter the floor. This creates dangerous hazards that can lead to a nasty slip or trip.

Keep tool surfaces in new-bright condition. If the work table is wood or a wood material, as with a radial arm saw, protect it from varying humidity conditions by occasionally applying a coat of penetrating sealer.

A dirty tool isn't nice to work with and work surfaces that are rough will make it harder to move workpieces. Wipe soil from tables, rip fences, and so on, and then apply paste wax rubbed to a polish. Don't use oil; this collects sawdust.

It's not wise to use a power tool in a damp or wet location or to expose it to rain.

The shop should be well lighted and, when possible, a power tool should have its own adjustable light to provide shadow-free illumination for any operation.

Shop Practice

Don't overreach, no matter what the operation or the tool. Don't struggle with work that is too large for you to safely handle. When necessary, get someone to help but be certain your assistant knows the procedure. Provide support for long pieces of work by having special stands. Many of these are available commercially (Figure 1-19), but you can make suitable stands yourself, as we will show.

Don't work with dull tools. You won't get good results. Also, dull tools require more feed pressure, which establishes a situation where your hands might slip.

Disconnect the tool when it's necessary to make an accessory change. Always check the on-off switch before plugging in. Don't leave a power tool running when you need to turn to another chore regardless of how little time is involved. It's prudent to wait for the cutting tool to stop turning before you move away.

Don't step on tools to get to high places. A serious injury can occur should you slip on a smooth surface, should the tool tip, or should you unintentionally make contact with a sharp cutting edge.

1-18.   A small, cordless vacuum you can hang on a wall and keep plugged in so it is continually charging, is handy for frequent, quick cleanups on tool surfaces and bench tops.

Be aware that something is wrong when you must force a cut. Usually, it means that the tool is dull or that you are trying to cut too deep. Most times, extra deep or oversize cuts must be accomplished by making repeat passes.

Don't mix shop work with socializing. Visitors should not be allowed when you are using tools. Politely advise friends and neighbors not to barge into the shop if they hear a tool running. You don't want them to startle you.

Stay alert; keep your mind on the job at hand. Don't do shop work when you are tired, upset, or have had an alcoholic drink.

Tool Practice

It's critical to know your tool especially if you are using it for the first time. Read and reread the owner's manual that is supplied with the equipment. Learn the machine's applications and, *especially,* its limitations. Don't use a tool for something it was not designed to do. Most tools, especially those designed for multi-purpose use, are secured in various attitudes by means of wrenches, knobs, levers, whatever. Make it a habit to recheck these devices before turning on the power.

Mount accessories by carefully following installation instructions. Don't use saw blades of a larger diameter than the tool can take. Check the maximum rpm of the blade. It should not be less than the tool's speed.

Don't work with damaged tools or tools with frayed cords. Know the correct alignment of components and be aware that excessive friction between moving parts might be dangerous or, at least, cause less than quality work.

Always move work so you are feeding against the direction of rotation of the blade or cutter. Be sure the cutting tool is mounted so it has correct rotation. Check frequently to be sure that components are in correct alignment.

Never try to work on a piece of wood that is too small to be safely held. When, for example, you need a small, shaped piece, do the work on a large workpiece and then cut off the part you need.

Don't work without the guards that are supplied with the tool. In many of the photographs in this book you will see operations performed without the guard in place or correctly adjusted. **THIS IS DONE FOR PHOTO PURPOSES ONLY. IF THE GUARD WERE IN PLACE YOU WOULD NOT SEE WHAT IS BEING DONE. ALWAYS USE SAFETY GUARDS WHEN USING THESE TECHNIQUES.**

Always be sure you know what you are going to do before you start an operation. If you preview the chore, you can plan how to feed the work and the safest hand placement. Often, and especially on operations you haven't tried before, it's wise to do a dry run. That is, go through the procedure but with the tool idle. Become "tool wise."

There are certain procedures in woodworking that are done without the standard guards in normal position. When involved with these, be extra cautious about how you proceed. Never, regardless of what you are doing, use your

1-19. Roller top stands that provide outboard support can help you work more safely when cutting long boards or large panels. This is one you can buy. Later we will show the plans for some you can make.

hands so they are too close to the cutting area.

One of the most important safety factors I know is this—**ALWAYS BE A BIT AFRAID OF THE TOOL.** Whether you are a beginner or an expert, remember that the tool can't think for you. To put it bluntly, a cutting tool can't distinguish between wood and flesh.

Electrical Considerations

Most power tools, double-insulated ones being an exception, must be grounded to protect the operator from electrical shock (Figure 1-20). Should a malfunction or a breakdown occur, the grounding system will provide a path of least resistance for the current. This reduces the risk of shock to the operator.

The electric cord on a tool that must be grounded has a grounding conductor and plug. For the system to work, the plug must be used in a matching outlet that is correctly installed AND GROUNDED in compliance with local codes and ordinances.

1-20.   Various methods of grounding. You're asking for trouble if you remove the grounding pin from a three-prong grounding plug. These ideas will work *only* if the connection is made to a CORRECTLY GROUNDED outlet.

If the tool is operable on less than 150V, the plug will look like the one shown in Figure 1-20A. The grounding pin, which must never be removed, engages with the third, specially shaped hole in the outlet.

An adapter, like the one shown in Figure 1-20B and mounted as in Figure 1-20C, can be used to accommodate a conventional two-prong plug. The lug on the adapter must be firmly attached to the outlet box. For this system to work, you must be sure that the box itself is CORRECTLY GROUNDED. Such adapters should be viewed as temporary measures for use only until a correctly grounded outlet box is installed, preferably by a qualified electrician. These adapters are not used in Canada.

Most tools designed for operation on 150-250V will have a plug like the one shown in Figure 1-20D. This must be used with a matching, correctly grounded receptacle that is wired to deliver the correct voltage. *Don't* use adapters with this plug design.

An amateur should not attempt to do any rewiring in a tool's electrical system. This is a job for the manufacturer's service center or a local, professional service person.

2. The Table Saw

The magic in a table saw is there for all to use. Anyone who has used a handsaw and then accomplished similar chores under power knows the value of this basic machine. The increase in production and the decrease in expended energy by no means covers its total usefulness. The gain in accuracy because the machine is organized to minimize the possibility of human error is more impressive.

Straight, square, and smooth cuts, made possible by modern saw blades, become automatic, allowing you to concentrate on the creative end. Anyone can flick the switch, and the tool will respond uninfluenced by whether the operator is an amateur or professional. The span between the novice and the expert is bridged by knowledge of the tool and its myriad practical applications and making fullest use of them.

General Characteristics

Types. All table saws have the same general characteristics (Figure 2-1). A saw blade is mounted on an arbor that is turned by a motor; the blade projects through a table on which the work is rested. The table is slotted to receive a miter gauge and is organized to accommodate a laterally adjustable rip fence. Blade projection, miter-gauge head and blade angularity are controllable.

The question of whether a table saw should operate with a tilting table or a tilting arbor doesn't have the importance it once did. For one thing, it's difficult to find a tool today, especially among those offered for home use, that does not provide the tilting arbor. Exceptions are found among the multi-purpose tools like the Shopsmith where the design does not allow for a tilting arbor. Anyway, the Shopsmith is a lot more than a saw so it shouldn't be judged on the basis of this one factor.

With a tilting *arbor* saw (Figure 2-2), the workpiece stays in horizontal position when doing cuts like cross-miters or bevels. When the *table* must be tilted for angular cuts such as bevels (Figure 2-3) the work is still held flat on the table but on the same plane as the tilt. A tilting arbor adds some convenience, but either way accuracy depends primarily on how carefully you adjust the settings and make the pass.

Other, more important factors to consider with individual saws are capacity, power, and physical machine size.

2-1.   The basic parts of a table saw. The "splitter," which is meant to keep the kerf from closing and so binding the blade, is the vertical part of the guard assembly on which the pivoting guard is mounted.

2-2.   Most individual saws have a tilting arbor. The workpiece stays flat on the table while the blade is tilted for jobs like cross-miters and bevels.

Today there is a wide variety of choices so you can judge a tool on the basis of the work you plan to do and available workshop space. Also, new, compact bench top power tools are becoming more accepted, indicating that we don't always need large machines. These products, all of which have a built-in power source, are not toys; they're capable sawing machines even though they may not have the capacity of their bigger brothers. The table saw shown in Figure 2-4 has a 2 hp motor that drives an 8-1/4″ blade so it can easily cut through 2″ stock.

When you get into a 9″ or 10″ machine (Figure 2-5) you increase overall capacity—larger tables that can be made even larger with extensions, greater depth-of-cut (as much as 3-1/2″), more table support in front of the blade, and so on.

A step up in capacity and, usually, in power are those machines that are considered industrial but which are just as happy in a home shop (Figure 2-6). To get the most from a tool like this it should be operated on 220v and with at least a 2 hp motor. The basic table provides a lot of work-support in front of and on both sides of the blade and with extra-cost extension rails has a better than 48″ capacity between blade and rip fence. You can slice a standard 4′ x 8′ panel in half along its long or short dimension.

Often, such tools can be fitted with unique accessories that provide convenience and accuracy on many standard saw cuts. An example is the sliding table unit that can be attached to Rockwell's Unisaw (Figure 2-7). The accessory and the workpiece move as a unit, relieving the operator from having to concentrate on keeping the workpiece stable. Later we'll show the design of smaller, similar units that you can customize for your own equipment.

Power tools are also beginning to be affected by electronic technology. An example is the Craftsman 10″ microprocessor-equipped table saw (Figure 2-8). The tool features programmable power blade elevation and bevel

2-3.   A tilting table is typical on machines like the Shopsmith Mark V. The work is still held flat on the table but on the same plane as the table-tilt. The cut-angle is determined by the tilt of the table, not that of the saw blade. *Sawguard removed for clarity. Always use guard in actual practice.*

2-4.   Bench top or "compact" power tools usually have built-in power sources. They are not toys. This one operates with a 2 hp motor that drives an 8-1/4″ diameter saw blade.

2-5.   Larger units, machines that drive 9″ or 10″ blades, provide larger work-support surfaces that can be extended even more with extensions and, usually, they have greater depth-of-cut.

2-6.   The Rockwell Unisaw is typical of those saws that span the gap between industry and home use; it is at home in either environment. A tool like this should be operated on 220v and with at least a 2 hp motor.

settings. A digital display on the touch control panel shows blade elevation to five-thousandths of an inch and bevel angles to one-tenth of a degree.

There will constantly be more mechanical and electronic innovations and we should welcome them. Anything that relieves us of mechanics will help us concentrate more on the creative end of power tool woodworking.

Overall, what is more important than the size of a machine, its capacities or its features, is the dedication of the person using it. All table saws will accomplish necessary operations. Fortunately, it is the operator who is most important. The painstaking craftsman working with a small, minimally-equipped machine can construct more impres-

sive projects than the casual, less dedicated super-saw owner.

Table saw safety. There are safety rules that apply generally and others that are peculiar to a particular machine. When we get into using the saw we'll point these out rather than filling pages of "do's" and "don't's" here. Yet, any approach to the subject must stress the responsibility of the operator. It's simply essential to accept as fact that any machine designed to cut wood can hurt you. Therefore, a constant respect for the tool is necessary for safe operation. Become professional but never so confident that you become nonchalant or fearless. Immediately mount, use and maintain the guard that comes with the unit (Figure 2-9).

2-7.   A nice accessory for the Unisaw is a sliding table unit that supports and moves with the work. It makes many operations easier to do and contributes to more precise cutting.

2-8.   Craftsman's (Sears Roebuck) new 10″ microprocessor-equipped table saw features programmable power blade elevation and bevel settings. A digital display tells blade projection and tilt angle. It's a sign of things to come.

2-9.   All modern table saws come equipped with guards that cover the saw blade. It's not always shown in place in this book but only because it would hide what's being done. In some cases, because of a particular operation, it *can't* be used. When it happens, recognize the situation and work accordingly.

There are particular techniques that don't allow the guard to be used in normal fashion. In such cases, know that you are exposed to a more hazardous situation and proceed accordingly or, if you are leary about trying the technique, determine whether you might be better off by using another tool or another method to accomplish the cut.

A correctly aligned, clean tool, used in a clean shop and turning *sharp* cutters contributes to safety. Carefully follow the rules outlined in the owner's manual. There may be thoughts that apply especially to the tool you have. Most important—always keep your hands away from the cutting area, no matter what (Figure 2-10). Proper hand positions, feed speeds, use of push sticks and similar devices, alignment of components, work supports, and so on, are vital to accomplishing the job in good fashion.

Adjustments. A table saw consists of parts bolted and screwed together. If any part slips, even just a bit, you lose the precision that was built into the machine. Therefore, any table saw should be checked thoroughly when it is new and regularly thereafter.

While methods of adjustment can vary from saw to saw, the correct relationship of components is the same. Doing the job is just a question of carefully following the instructions that are in the owner's manual that comes with the tool. Again, the beginner is on a par with the pro. There is no reason why a novice can't set up his machine just as accurately as anyone. However, his first problem may be an inability to analyze the reasons for getting poor results with his work.

There are checks you can employ as you work, and these will feed you a constant stream of information on how accurate the tool is. One of the most basic checks is to

2-10.   The table saw "arc of safety" is shown to make a point. Whether the guard is mounted or not, keep your hands away from the cutting area. On a rip cut, for example, exaggerate the height at which you bring your hand back to the front-table position. *Sawguard removed for clarity. Always use guard in actual practice.*

2-12.   After you are sure that the table slots are parallel to the saw blade, check the "0" setting of the miter gauge by using a square between it and a table slot. No allowances—settings are either right or wrong.

TABLE-SLOT-TO-BLADE PARALLEL ALIGNMENT

TABLE-TO-FENCE
TABLE-TO-BLADE &
TABLE-TO-MITRE-GAUGE
90° ALIGNMENT

MITRE-GAUGE-TO-BLADE
90° ALIGNMENT

2-11.   You must always be aware of the alignment rules that apply to any table saw. Unless you check these periodically, and maintain the correct relationships, the tool will not function efficiently.

2-13.   Distance between the rip fence and blade at "A" and "B" should be equal unless you offset a fraction at "B" so the blade will have some clearance at that point. This avoids having the "rear" teeth of the blade rubbing on the wood after the "front" teeth have cut.

frequently apply a square to a ripped edge or a crosscut end. If the square tells you the cut isn't right, you know you must check to find out why.

Another simple as-you-go check is to use a square to draw a crosscut line. If the blade doesn't stay on that line as you cut, it's probably the miter gauge that requires attention.

Three important alignment rules apply to any table saw (Figure 2-11). (1) The table slots, the rip fence and the saw blade must be all parallel. (2) The rip fence, the saw blade and the miter-gauge head must all be perpendicular to the table surface. (3) When the miter gauge is in the normal crosscut position, it must be at right angles to the blade and the rip fence. Assuming that you have already checked for parallelism between table slots and saw blade, the "0" setting of the miter gauge can be checked with a square as shown in Figure 2-12.

Since the blade, which is locked on the arbor, is the one thing over which you have no control, it's wise to start all alignment checks by determining whether the table slots are parallel to the saw blade. All other checks are made on the basis of this important relationship.

While the previous rules call for parallelism between the rip fence and the saw blade (Figure 2-13), it's not bad practice to be a bit generous at the rear of the blade so the "rear" teeth of the blade will not scrape the wood after the "front" teeth have cut. This offset kind of adjustment can reduce roughness in the cut and minimize feathering.

Since eliminating human error is an important factor in doing accurate work, it's wise to equip yourself with gauge tools. Tools you can make yourself are shown in Figures 2-14 through 2-17, but you must be most careful with the construction. The idea is to make them to perfection and to care for them so they will remain precise checking tools.

Gauge Tools That You Can Make Yourself

2-14.   An L-shaped block that snugs against the miter gauge can be used to set the miter gauge for most often-used cross-angular cuts. Precision is critical. Lay out the cut-lines on the guide block by using a protractor.

2-16.   Making special checking gauges for most commonly used miter gauge and saw blade settings is good practice. You can't always rely on the calibrations on tools. Also, gauges like this help to minimize the possibility of human error.

2-15.   This kind of gauge can be used to set blade tilt more precisely than you might be able to do merely by using the scales on the machine. Again, the cut-lines on the guide should be marked with a protractor.

2-17.   Check gauges must, of course, be precise. Best bet is to mark the cut lines with a protractor, make a rough cut close to the line, and then finish *exactly* by sanding.

2-18.   You can easily make this gauge which is used when setting projection of saw blades or dadoing tools. It's a block made by laminating stepped back pieces of 1/8″ plywood or hardwood. If you wish, you can include plies of 1/16″ material.

While blade projection is not an alignment factor, it's still a good idea to equip yourself with gauges that help accuracy, not so much for routine cutting where the blade projects through the work but for operations like dadoing, rabbeting, blind kerfing and so on, where the height of the blade above the table is less than the thickness of the stock.

One design for a blade height gauge is shown in Figure 2-18. The tool is made by laminating stepped back pieces of 1/8″ plywood or hardboard. Figures 2-19 and 2-19A show a more sophisticated version. The post is made of two pieces glued together after the groove is formed. Graduations are laid out on heavy paper which is then pasted to the side of the post or, if you have a damaged flex tape, you can cut off a section and put it in place with contact cement.

Saw blades. The blade that comes with the machine will be a combination type looking something like the example shown in Figure 2-20. Designed for both crosscutting and ripping, it will function efficiently for basic saw-

ing but will not be the best blade available for either type of cut.

It would be nice if one blade could do all sawing jobs with optimum results, but considering the characteristics of wood and the variety of materials we work with, the sawing jobs we have to do are so varied that it really isn't possible. An example of blade design as it relates to use is the difference between teeth that are shaped for crosscutting (sawing *across* the grain), and those that are designed for ripping

2-19.   This is a more sophisticated cutter projection gauge. It's certainly more accurate than sighting against a scale held against the blade. The gauge can be used with saw blades and dadoing tools, even with a molding head.

2-19A.   The post of the gauge is made of two pieces that are glued together after the groove is formed. Graduations are drawn on thick paper which is then glued to the side of the post. You can also use a section cut from a damaged flex scale.

2-20.   A typical all-steel, combination blade. It has set teeth separated by deep gullets; may be used for crosscutting and ripping, even mitering, but is not the *ideal* blade for any of the cuts.

2-21.   A special plywood blade is one of the cutters that does a good job on multi-layered material (example on right). Piece on the left was sawed with a combination blade.

(sawing *parallel* to the grain). Crosscut teeth should have sharp side-points that will sever wood fibers cleanly. The blade can have a lot of teeth, little hook angle, and small gullets. Ripping teeth have a flat top-grind so each tooth will work like a tiny chisel to remove a comparatively large chunk of wood. The blade will have fewer teeth, more hook angle, and deeper gullets than a crosscut blade. You can see the difference in the waste produced by the blades. The sawdust created by the crosscut blade will be much finer than that produced by the rip blade.

It would be expensive, and probably uncalled for, to equip yourself immediately with blades to meet all eventualities. It makes more sense to gradually increase your assortment of blades as you do more and more work and become more familiar with the table saw.

If you do a lot of work with plywood as most craftsmen do, you'll want to think immediately about getting a special plywood-cutting blade. This blade is designed to stand up under the abrasive action of the material while producing smooth cuts with minimum feathering (Figure 2-21). Without this special blade, you should work with a crosscut blade when cutting plywood. Its many small teeth will do a better job than the fewer, larger teeth of a combination blade.

In the area of special blades falls the "Grit-Edge" design (Figure 2-22), whose perimeter is coated with hundreds of particles of tungsten carbide. It can cut materials all-steel blades can't or shouldn't handle; like asbestos-cement, fiberglass, synthetic marble and so on. I keep one on hand to use when I don't want to abuse my conventional blades. It does a good job on plywood although it won't cut very fast and it's nice to have when you are confronted with that occasional piece of gritty, contaminated wood. Don't use it on soft wood and similar materials since they may gum up and clog the cutting edge. The blade will cut in any direction. You can extend its cutting life if you occasionally reverse it on the arbor.

Most all-steel blades have *set* teeth; alternate teeth are bent in opposite directions so the "kerf" (Figure 2-23) will be wider than the gauge of the blade. This is done to provide clearance so the blade won't drag in the cut and cause burning that can harm the blade and the wood.

2-22.   Perimeter of "Grit-Edge" blade is coated with hundreds of particles of tungsten carbide. It can be used to saw materials all-steel blades, even carbide-tipped blades can't handle.

2-23.   The "kerf" is the slot formed by the saw blade. Its width will differ depending on the style, gauge, and amount of set on the teeth of the blade. *Sawguard removed for clarity. Always use guard in actual practice.*

2-24.   A hollow-ground blade is specially ground to reduce blade-gauge in an area that runs from the points of the teeth to somewhere near its center. Arrow points to area that is full gauge.

2-25.   The hollow-ground blade needs more projection above the work than other blade styles. This prevents the teeth from rubbing in the wood which would cause the blade or the wood, or both, to burn.

2-26.   Safest way to work is with minimum blade projection. High projection may be more efficient because it shortens the cutting angle, but it's more dangerous. Many operators work so the blade barely pokes through the wood.

An exception is the hollow-ground blade which is made without set teeth so it will cut smoother (Figure 2-24). That's why the blade is often used for miters and similar cuts where smooth-as-possible results are desirable. The kerf width at the points of the teeth is the same as the blade gauge. It gets clearance because of a special concave grinding that runs from the teeth toward the blade's center. The part of the blade that is in the workpiece during the cut is thinner than the true gauge. That's why this type of blade should get more projection (Figure 2-25). If it doesn't, it will burn itself and/or the work. Too little projection will most certainly dull it faster.

The projection of conventional blades during normal use has to do with efficiency and safety. There is less resistance when blade projection is high since fewer teeth are in the work (Figure 2-26), but more of the blade is exposed above the workpiece. Minimum projection creates more drag because of the longer cutting angle but it reduces blade exposure. Many operators work so the blade barely pokes through the work. A generally accepted rule that regards both efficiency and safety is to set projection to not more than the deepest gullet on the blade.

Carbide-tipped blades.   One of the major advantages of a carbide-tipped saw blade is that, if correctly used and maintained, it will stay sharp longer than a steel blade. The teeth of carbide blades cut a kerf that is wider than the blade's gauge, so no set is involved. Generally, they cut smoother than steel blades. However, despite some popular thinking, no carbide-tipped blade is any more "all-purpose" than a single steel blade. Actually, there is as much variety in carbide blades as in steel blades. Some are combination blades that do a respectable job of crosscutting and ripping and even some mitering. Others are designed specifically for particular applications.

Carbide-tipped saw blades are expensive so be careful when you buy. Some of the facts to consider are shown in Figure 2-27. Some of these factors such as gullets, pitch and hook angle apply to steel blades as well.

One of my pet carbides (Figure 2-28) is a new design with about as many teeth as you can get on the rim of a steel disc—80 on a 10″ blade. The plate has a baked-on, self-lubricating, anti-grip material so tooth clearance can be minimal. A unique, concave configuration behind the teeth helps to remove waste and to keep the blade running cool. Crosscuts, miters, cuts on plywood, even rip cuts made with this blade have, literally, burnished surfaces. However, the blade should not be abused by running it overlong on ripping operations. It's an excellent blade to use on a powered miter box.

No matter what blade you use, some attention to how fast you feed the work can result in better cuts. A slow feed is always better. You can prove this simply by making two crosscuts on the same piece of stock, one very quickly, the other very slowly. The slow feed will allow more teeth to pass over a given area of the wood, and the result will be smoother. The slow feed is especially important at the end of the cut when the blade breaks through (Figure 2-29). It will minimize splintering and feathering.

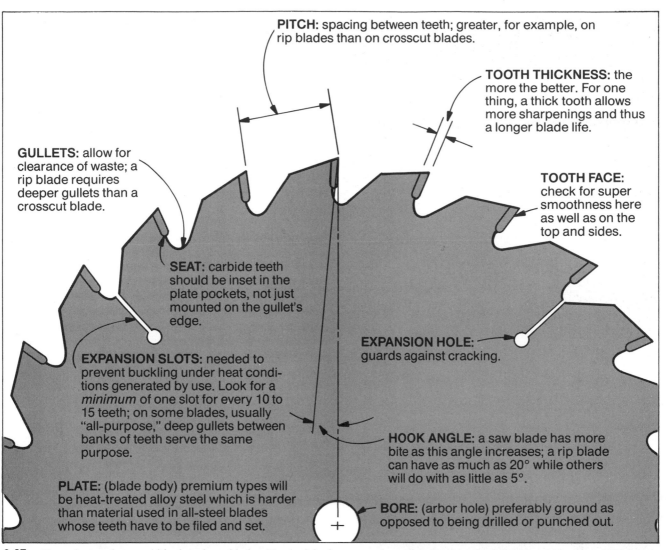

PITCH: spacing between teeth; greater, for example, on rip blades than on crosscut blades.

TOOTH THICKNESS: the more the better. For one thing, a thick tooth allows more sharpenings and thus a longer blade life.

GULLETS: allow for clearance of waste; a rip blade requires deeper gullets than a crosscut blade.

TOOTH FACE: check for super smoothness here as well as on the top and sides.

SEAT: carbide teeth should be inset in the plate pockets, not just mounted on the gullet's edge.

EXPANSION HOLE: guards against cracking.

EXPANSION SLOTS: needed to prevent buckling under heat conditions generated by use. Look for a *minimum* of one slot for every 10 to 15 teeth; on some blades, usually "all-purpose," deep gullets between banks of teeth serve the same purpose.

HOOK ANGLE: a saw blade has more bite as this angle increases; a rip blade can have as much as 20° while others will do with as little as 5°.

PLATE: (blade body) premium types will be heat-treated alloy steel which is harder than material used in all-steel blades whose teeth have to be filed and set.

BORE: (arbor hole) preferably ground as opposed to being drilled or punched out.

2-27.   Facts that apply to carbide-tipped saw blades. Many of the factors, such as pitch, hook angle, gullets, apply to all-steel blades as well.

2-28.   New design comes as close as possible to being the "All-purpose" saw blade. It does a super job when crosscutting or mitering, even when ripping, but it should not be over-used on the latter application.

2-29.   How fast you feed the work affects the quality of the cut. Splintering and feathering at the end of the cut will result even with a super carbide-tipped blade when you try to work too fast. *Sawguard removed for clarity. Always use guard in actual practice.*

2-30.   Blade sharpening is a job for experts. They do the job right and at reasonable prices. Cleaning the teeth, however, is something you can and should do frequently. An old toothbrush can help.

I don't recommend that blades be sharpened in a home workshop, certainly not those that are carbide tipped. Sharpening is a job for professionals who have the proper equipment, and the prices they charge are reasonable. Keeping the blade and its teeth clean between sharpenings, however, is a chore you can and should do. All blades will accumulate some residue on teeth and in gullets (especially when sawing softwoods) and this will interfere with smooth cutting. Keep an old toothbrush on hand and use it with a solvent such as lacquer thinner on both sides of the teeth and in the gullets (Figure 2-30). Wipe the body of the blade and then dry it with a lint-free cloth.

Store blades very carefully. Often, they are placed on hooks. That's okay, but a better way is to provide a special storage facility like the case shown in Figures 2-31 and 2-31A. Sections can be assembled with just glue and clamps, or you can glue and nail separate sections as you go along to build up the stack. In making the cover, note that you need two 3-1/4″ x 5-1/4″ sections 3/4″ thick for the front and back. Cement a pad of thick foam rubber inside the cover to bear down on the blades when the case is closed.

Sawing Procedures

The table saw is used for much more than crosscutting and

2-31.   A saw-blade "safe" is not difficult to make and will provide good storage for your saw blades. This one is designed for six 10″ blades.

2-31A.   Construction details for the saw-blade "safe."

ripping. All of the cuts shown in Figure 2-32 can be done with a regular saw blade. Some, like the taper cuts, require a special jig that is used to guide the work. Others, like the rabbet, call for a two-pass procedure with work position changed for each.

When you substitute a dadoing tool or a molding head for the same blade or use one of the special techniques we will describe, you can produce all the forms shown in Figure 2-33. As you see, the tool's functions are not limited to basic sawing. Forms for joints, surface and edge decorating, cove shapes, and more; all are possible.

Crosscutting. A simple crosscut is made by placing the good edge of the stock against the miter gauge and moving both the gauge and work past the saw blade (Figure 2-34). Most times, the miter gauge is used in the left-hand slot; the right hand moves the miter gauge, the left hand snugs the work. Your position should be almost directly behind the miter gauge so you will be out of line with the saw blade. Feed the work slowly, without pausing, until the cut is complete; then return both work and gauge to the starting position.

There will be variations of this basic procedure because of work size and types of cuts, but the important factors such as slow feed, good hand position for safety and proper support of the work should not change drastically. The size of the table and whether you have a table extension

CROSSCUT   RIP   MITER

CROSS BEVEL   RIP BEVEL   COMPOUND MITER   CHAMFER

TWO-SIDE TAPER   FOUR-SIDE TAPER   COMPOUND RIP BEVEL

KERFING (DECORATIVE & WOOD BENDING)   KERFING (FOR INLAY)   RABBET (TWO-PASS)

2-32.   All of the cuts shown here can be accomplished with a regular saw blade.

on one side of the blade or the other can influence in what slot you use the miter gauge. Your judgment should be based on what position provides the most support for the work.

Don't use your free hand to push against the cutoff end of the workpiece. This can cause binding and will result in a kickback. The free hand can be used for extra guidance, maybe even for support on long stock, but never to force the work forward. Also, don't remove the cutoff, especially if it's a short one, until you have turned off the machine and the blade has stopped turning.

Many professionals will use the miter gauge backwards when the work width is greater than the distance between the blade and the front table-edge (Figure 2-35). This means that one hand will be holding the miter gauge (or an attached extension) against the forward edge of the work

DADO GROOVE (PLOUGHING) HOLLOWING END RABBET EDGE RABBET

NOTCHING TONGUE AND GROOVE STUD TENON SLOT THROUGH SLOT TRUE TENON

COVE EDGE COVE SURFACE CUTS FINGERLAP DOVETAIL SPECIAL GROOVE

MOLDED EDGE COVED EDGE MOLDINGS

2-33.   These cuts are also done on a table saw with dadoing tools or a molding head or by employing a special technique.

while the other hand is pushing against the opposite edge. You must be especially careful when working this way since you and your hands will be in strange positions. Sometimes, depending on the width of the work and the amount to be cut off, such jobs can be done in better fashion by ripping instead of crosscutting.

Miter gauge extensions provide additional support for the workpiece and, when used for crosscutting, help to keep the work square to the blade. After the extension is secured and moved past the saw blade, the kerf that is formed (Figure 2-36) is a guide for accurate crosscutting. A line, marked on the work with a square, is aligned with the kerf so you'll know exactly where the cut will be.

Most miter gauges are designed to accept extensions. The means of attachment may be wood screws or nuts and bolts through a set of holes or slots in the gauge head. The extension can be a simple, straight piece of wood, as most commercial ones are (Figure 2-37), or a more sophisticated version that you make yourself. The one shown in Figures 2-38 and 2-38A, can be used in straightforward fashion or with the sliding block to gauge the length of multiple, similar pieces.

2-34.   Simple crosscut is accomplished by placing the work flat on the table and snug against the miter gauge. Blade projection does not have to be as high as this. *Sawguard removed for clarity. Always use guard in actual practice.*

2-35.   Many workers will use the miter gauge backwards when the work is too wide to cut in normal fashion. Be careful if you work this way since you and your hands will be in strange positions. *Sawguard removed for clarity. Always use guard in actual practice.*

2-36.   An extension can be a straight piece of lumber or plywood. A kerf in the extension will serve as a location point when placing work for crosscutting.

2-37.   Most miter gauges are designed to accept extensions. Attachment may be by means of screws or nuts and bolts through a set of holes or slots in the gauge's head.

2-38.   A special miter-gauge extension you can make provides a stop block that can be set to gauge cut-off length when you need multiple, similar pieces. *Sawguard removed for clarity. Always use guard in actual practice.*

Often, a special design can be used to facilitate certain kinds of cutting. The example shown in Figure 2-39 was made for production work when a number of workpieces of specific lengths were required. The stop block fits any of the dadoes in the extension and is set to gauge the length of the particular pieces.

There's no point in trying to anticipate the number and types of extensions you should have. However, a simple, straight extension and the adjustable one are units you should get to pretty quickly; others as the need for them arises.

Many times an extension is used when the work is long and calls for extra support. In such cases, don't use a hand to push against the free end of the work. This can close the kerf, bind the blade, and result in a kickback that can be dangerous. We repeat, if you have a hand on the free end of the work, use it only as a guide or for additional support.

Crosscutting to length. Unless you are just squaring off the end of a board, crosscutting is usually done to size a workpiece to a certain length. Many times it's done to get duplicate pieces. In such cases, it's important to create some sort of mechanical setup so the length of the pieces will be

2-38A.   How to make a special extension for a miter gauge.

2-39.   Extensions can be made as production tools for special jobs. This dadoed one provides for cutting off specific lengths. The stop block is a tight fit in any of the dadoes in the extension. *Sawguard removed for clarity. Always use guard in actual practice.*

2-40.   Crosscutting to exact length can be accomplished by working with a commercial miter-gauge stop rod or an extension that is fitted with a stop block. *Sawguard removed for clarity. Always use guard in actual practice.*

gauged automatically. This can be done with commercial miter gauge stop rods (Figure 2-40), special extensions you make, or with stop blocks.

It is critical that you NEVER use the rip fence as a stop to gauge the length of cutoffs. The work will be captured and twisted between the fence and the blade, and it can be thrown up or back at you. The fence can be part of the setup but only if you also employ a stop block. The stop block doesn't have to be more than a block of wood that is placed against the fence at the forward edge of the table well ahead of the saw blade (Figure 2-41). The rip fence is positioned so the distance from the edge of the block to the saw blade equals the cutoff length. The setup provides room in excess of the cutoff length so the workpieces won't bind between rip fence and blade.

While the any-piece-of-wood stop block works, there are those you can make to keep on hand as permanent accessories. An advantage here is that you will always know where to lock the rip fence to compensate for the thickness of the stop block. For example, if the cutoffs must be 4″ long and the stop block is 1-1/2″ thick, then you set the rip fence 5-1/2″ from the blade.

There are two types of permanent stop blocks you can make. One (shown in Figures 2-42 and 2-43) assumes that the rip fence has holes through it or that you will do the job of providing the holes. Its most useful position will be at the forward end of the fence. The other (Figures 2-44 and 2-45)

2-43.   The stop block is secured with a bolt that passes through the rip fence. *Sawguard removed for clarity. Always use guard in actual practice.*

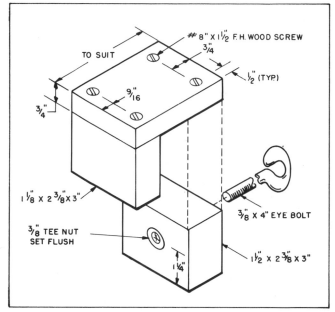

2-44.   This stop block is designed so it can be secured at any point on the fence.

2-41.   The rip fence is set so the block of wood is the gauge that determines the thickness of the pieces being cut. Stop blocks should be positioned well forward of the saw blade. NEVER USE THE RIP FENCE ITSELF AS A STOP FOR CUTOFF WORK. *Sawguard removed for clarity. Always use guard in actual practice.*

2-42.   You can make stop blocks, like this one, to keep on hand as permanent accessories.

2-45.   The movable stop can be used any place on the rip fence. It isn't necessary to overtighten the eye bolt that secures the stop.

2-46. An example of how you can work with two miter gauges. *Sawguard removed for clarity. Always use guard in actual practice.*

2-47. Here is a double "miter gauge" you can make, and it includes an adjustable stop to use when crosscutting to length. It's not designed for angular cutting.

is designed so it can be locked any place along the rip fence. In addition to being used to gauge cutoff lengths, it can be situated at the rear of the blade to limit cut-lengths; for example, a stopped kerf or dado.

Using two miter gauges. As you learn more woodworking techniques, the addition of an extra gauge is something to consider. In crosscutting, for example, you could make an extension longer than the width of the saw table and back it up with a gauge in each slot. This can take care of two work extremes, the overly long piece that can use a great deal of support and the very small piece that can't be held safely without special consideration.

The two-gauge idea is also good for other work. Making miter cuts, when the job calls for frequent readjustment of a single miter gauge to make mating cuts, is an excellent example (Figure 2-46). This will occur when the stock is so shaped that it can't be flipped over.

Construction details for a double "miter gauge" you can make are shown in Figure 2-47. This design is only for crosscutting but it includes an adjustable stop so it may be used for, among other things, sawing multiple pieces of the same length. The size and location of the twin guide bars must be customized to suit your equipment.

Extra long work. Good work support is important for both accuracy and safety. To crosscut very long work you must think in terms of providing more support than the main table can provide. Some machines, like the Unisaw shown in Figure 2-48, can be equipped with accessory rip fence bars that increase work support as well as capacity. The area between the outboard legs and the main table is filled in with a plywood panel. While the operation shown involves the rip fence, you can see that the additional support surface will also be useful for simple crosscutting.

When the machine can't provide necessary support even with extensions, you can seek help from another per-

son or use an extension stand. If you get a person, be sure to explain what will occur and how support should be provided. In fact, going through the procedure with the power off and the blade set below the table—a dry run—would be good practice.

Extension stands can be purchased or made. A good commercial version, one that can be used for crosscutting and ripping and is height-adjustable, is shown in Figure 2-49.

A practical one you can make, which is also height-adjustable, is shown in Figure 2-50. The straight roller-top is used for ripping operations, while the roller-cluster provides good support for crosscutting. The individual rollers do not have to be handmade. You can substitute ready-made ones of plastic, metal, or wood, even if they are not exactly the 2″ diameter the drawing indicates. Just be sure they project above the U-shaped frame when you mount them.

2-48. Some machines can be equipped with extra-long rip-fence bars to greatly increase the work-support surface.

2-49. A type of extension stand you can buy. Its height is adjustable and it can supply outboard support when crosscutting or ripping.

ROLLER 2″ D. x 17″

PINS—2½″ BOLTS MAY BE USED

½″

(2) 1″ x 2″ x 3″

(1) 1″ x 3″ x 20″

(2) 1″ x 3″ x 3″

(1) 1″ x 3″ x 26″

ROLLERS (9) 2″ DIA. x ⅞″

(1) 1″ x 3″ x 20″

¼″ BOLTS AND WINGED NUTS

(4) 1″ x 3″ x 20″

GLUE—USE F.H. SCREWS FOR ASSEMBLY

Ⓐ

(2) 1″ x 3″ x 26″

¼″ SLOT

(2) 1″ x 8″ x 20″

(2) 1″ x 3″ x 20″

(2) 1″ x 2″ x 20″

½″

2¼″ CENTER

USE ¼″ DRILL ROD FOR PINS—SHOULD BE TIGHT FIT IN ROLLERS

2-50. An extension stand you can make. Its height is adjustable and, with separate tops, can be used for ripping or crosscutting operations.

Figure 2-51 shows another version of a stand-top. Plate-type casters which can swivel in any direction will supply support for either crosscutting or ripping. Some workers prefer a non-adjustable stand, matching its height to that of the saw. A unique one is shown in Figure 2-52. By including a sheet of perforated hardboard and using standard hangers, the stand does the extra job of holding many of the accessories that are nice to have close by. The "roller" top on this stand is achieved by using ball roller glides.

The advantage of a stand that is height-adjustable is that it can be used with other tools; for example, a bandsaw or radial arm saw.

2-51.   Another type of support top you can make for an extension stand. The casters are plate-mounted and can swivel in any direction.

2-52.   Another version of extension stand has a fixed height but provides for storage of accessories that are nice to have close by. The top is studded with ball roller glides.

Ripping. Sizing a workpiece to correct width, whether it is lumber or a panel material, is done by passing the work between the blade and the rip fence (Figure 2-53). Often, the procedure is described as being a cut made parallel to or *with* the grain of the wood. This applies to lumber, but when sawing plywood, for example, you may be cutting *across* the surface grain. So it's best to view ripping merely as a cutting-to-width operation.

The essential factors are these: The rip fence is located by measuring between it and the saw blade (Figure 2-54). When the blade has set teeth, be sure to measure from a tooth that slants toward the fence. If you are using an offset fence alignment, measure from the front of the blade.

A basic rip cut is done by placing the work on the front edge of the table, flat down and snugly against the fence. Use your left hand at the front edge of the table, well away from the saw blade, to maintain the work's position against the fence, and your right hand to feed the work forward. When your right hand approaches the fence, hook your fingers over it to continue the pass. This is a precaution that helps keep your hand where it should be. Your left hand

2-53.   A rip cut is made by passing the work between the rip fence and the saw blade. The "splitter," which keeps the kerf open, is the vertical part of the guard assembly which supports the pivoting blade-cover.

2-54.   The rip fence is set by measuring between it and the saw blade. When the blade has set teeth, be sure to measure from one that points toward the fence.

maintains its original position, snugging the work against the fence. Feed the work until it is well past the blade. There is no return on a rip cut. When work-size permits, feed until the overhang at the rear of the table causes the back end of the work to tilt up into the palm of your hand. Then grip tightly and lift it completely clear of the cutting area. The length of the workpiece has a bearing on how you finish the cut. If it's very long, you can allow it to tilt down so it will angle from the table to the floor or, preferably, to an outboard support such as an extension stand. A stand is especially wise when you are sawing heavy stock (Figure 2-55) or large panels.

This procedure is fairly standard as long as you have ample room to move your hand safely between the fence and blade. When cuts are narrow enough to place your hands in a danger zone, substitute a push stick for your hand.

Too often, a push stick is nothing more than a strip of wood salvaged from the scrap heap. That's certainly better than fingers, but it's wiser to buy or make special ones that will be permanent accessories. A commercial one, of plastic, notched so it can ride the top edge of the work is shown in Figure 2-56. Similar, simple ones, can easily be made

(Figure 2-57). A cute trick, used by many woodworkers, is to separate a wooden clothes hanger at the center joint to get two pieces which, after being notched, serve pretty nicely as pushers.

Variations of the pusher idea are shown in Figures 2-58 and 2-59. Both these units do double duty. In addition to moving the work forward, they also help to keep it flat on the table.

2-57. Simple pusher sticks are easy to make and are a must if you are safety minded, as you should be.

2-58. This is how you can make a tool that is a combination push stick and hold-down.

2-55. It's always wise to use an extension stand when sawing extra-long pieces, especially when the stock is heavy. *Sawguard removed for clarity. Always use guard in actual practice.*

2-56. Don't neglect to use a push stick whenever one is needed. Never work so that your hands get close to the cutting area. Note the special insert. *Sawguard removed for clarity. Always use guard in actual practice.*

2-59. Another version of a combination push stick and hold-down. The tool keeps the work flat on the table as it moves it forward. *Sawguard removed for clarity. Always use guard in actual practice.*

In some situations, especially when the pieces you need are very narrow, it's wise to design pushers that will straddle the rip fence. I have two versions in my shop. One (Figures 2-60 and 2-61) has a spring-powered hold-down/pusher so it can be used on various stock thicknesses. The springs should be fairly strong to supply the hold-down action needed. The other (Figures 2-62 and 2-63) has an adjustable hook so it too can be suited to various thicknesses of wood. The hook is screw-tightened after it has been set to accommodate the stock.

An important point is that, often, you can do a job more accurately, or faster, or safer, by employing a jig; a device you make simply because it isn't available commercially or must be designed exclusively for the job on hand. An example, for a ripping operation, is shown in Figure 2-64. Assuming you have a number of similar pieces that must be ripped in half, it would be better, instead of handling them as routine rip cuts, to make a jig you could clamp to the rip fence. The jig would be a long block of wood with a work-size, U-shaped opening centered over the saw blade. The work would be fed into the front end of the "U" and pulled out the other. Two identical pieces would emerge and you could continue the process until you have as many pieces as you need.

Extra-thick stock. You must follow a two-pass procedure when the stock is thicker than maximum blade projection (Figure 2-65). Make the first pass with blade projection slightly higher than half the stock-thickness. Feed the work slowly to give the blade a chance to cut without undue heating since it will be buried in the wood. Then, keeping the same surface of the stock against the fence, invert the stock and make a second pass. This same procedure can be followed when you need to crosscut extra-thick workpieces.

The squaring board. There are times when a piece of stock doesn't have an edge straight enough to ride the rip fence. Maybe it's left over from a jigsaw or bandsaw job.

2-60. This push stick/hold-down straddles the rip fence and employs springs so it can be used on various stock thicknesses. *Sawguard removed for clarity. Always use guard in actual practice.*

2-62. This type of fence-straddling pusher works with an adjustable hook. The hook is secured with the screws after it's been adjusted to accommodate the stock-thickness. *Sawguard removed for clarity. Always use guard in actual practice.*

2-61. How to make the spring-powered pusher/hold-down.

2-63. Construction details for the hook-type pusher.

The squaring board lets you mount it for ripping to get a straight edge. The jig is just a platform with a saw-table-slot guide fastened to its underside (Figure 2-66). The cleat, secured to the forward edge of the platform, is at right angles to the saw blade. You butt the work against the cleat and push the whole assembly past the saw blade (Figure 2-67). Of course, there is a size limit to work that can be handled on the jig.

Very large pieces can be done by tack-nailing a straight, narrow piece of wood to the underside of the work. This is to be used as a guide along the edge of the saw table. (Figure 2-68). Where you place the guide strip determines how much of the rough edge will be cut off. Another technique is to nail the guide to the top edge of the work along the rough edge. Then, the guide rides the rip fence as you make the cut to remove the bad edge.

The spring stick.   Also called a "fingerboard," this is an accessory you can make to help on jobs other than ripping (Figure 2-69). It's actually a horizontal hold-down that helps to hold work firmly against the fence as you make the pass. Such units can be made in various widths and lengths. The fingers are the result of parallel cuts made with a regular saw blade. In use, it is clamped to the table so the fingers

2-64.   Special setups help to do many jobs. This jig, clamped to the rip fence, is grooved to receive pieces that must be sawed in half. The work is pushed into the front of the jig and pulled out the rear.

FIRST CUT

RIP FENCE

FIRST PASS

SECOND PASS

2-65.   Two passes are required when maximum blade projection won't get you through a thick piece of stock in a single operation.

2-66.   A squaring board makes it possible to saw a straight edge on pieces that can't be moved along the rip fence.

STOP (¾" THICK)

PLATFORM (1½" THICK)

WORK

PATH OF BLADE

HARDWOOD BAR SHOULD BE SLIDE-FIT IN TABLE SLOT

USE WHEN WORK HAS NO STRAIGHT EDGE TO RIDE AGAINST RIP FENCE

2-67.   The work is butted against the cleat on the squaring board and the whole assembly is moved past the saw blade. *Sawguard removed for clarity. Always use guard in actual practice.*

2-68.   Another way to get a straight edge on stock that can't ride the rip fence. The guide strip, which is clamped or tack-nailed to the work, rides the edge of the table. *Sawguard removed for clarity. Always use guard in actual practice.*

bear against the work. Don't situate it so it tends to force a board against the saw blade. We'll show other uses for the device as we go along.

Mitering.   Few jobs in woodworking can be as frustrating as cutting a good miter joint. The actual cutting is simple, but accuracy must be perfect. You can be the least bit off when making the cut and the two parts will mate perfectly, but the angle formed by the two parts will not be 90°. Multiply the error by eight times and you can visualize the result when you try to assemble four frame pieces, each of which was cut at each end. This is discouraging on jobs that run from picture frames to case goods to face-framing, and so on. The only solution is accuracy.

Examples of miter cuts and the angles required are shown in Figure 2-70. A point to remember is that the *cut* angle is always half the *joint* angle; a 90° turn requires two 45° cuts. The formula for any number of sides is, divide

2-69.   The "spring stick" is a horizontal hold-down that will help to hold work against the fence as you make the pass. The fingers are the result of parallel saw-blade cuts. Uses for it will be shown as we go along.

2-70.   Examples of miter cuts and the angles required for various forms.

360° by the number of sides and then divide the answer by 2.

Make it a rule to mark the cut line on the work. You'll know immediately whether you are getting the accuracy you want (Figure 2-71). Be aware that the blade, cutting in a forward direction, tends to pull the work so that it "creeps" along the miter gauge. Also, there is a pivoting action where the work and the forward edge of the miter gauge meet (Figure 2-72). Positive holding action of the work against the miter-gauge head throughout the pass is absolutely necessary.

You can get help in holding the work against the gauge head by using a miter-gauge extension; even more helpful is facing the extension with sandpaper. Make the pass even more slowly than you do normally. Needless to say, machine alignment has to be perfectly accurate.

A good way to work, even though it does waste some wood, is to cut frame parts to overall size to begin with and then miter the ends by using a stop block on the rip fence to gauge the cutoff (Figure 2-73). Another method is to use one of the miter-gauge extensions that has been shown, employing a stop block on the extension to gauge the length of the work (Figure 2-74).

Simple miter jigs.   Part of the problem of cutting true miters is the difficulty of matching left- and right-hand cuts, This is most critical when the work is shaped so that it can't be flipped because it means having to work on both sides of the blade. To do that, you also have to change the miter-gauge setting for mating cuts. You can avoid most of these problems by making some sliding tables.

2-71.   Wise precaution when doing angle cuts is to mark the cut-line on the work. Thus you will know right off if the cut is accurate. Mark the lines with a square or protractor. *Sawguard removed for clarity. Always use guard in actual practice.*

2-73.   Easy mitering system calls for cutting frame pieces to overall size and then working like this for the miter cuts. The stop block gauges the amount of material that will be removed. *Sawguard removed for clarity. Always use guard in actual practice.*

2-72.   Accuracy on miters can be spoiled simply because of the cut action. The work tends to pivot about the front edge of the miter gauge. It will also "creep." Firm work support is essential. *Sawguard removed for clarity. Always use guard in actual practice.*

2-74.   An extension with a stop block may also be used to gauge the length of pieces that require mitering. When stock is flat, pieces may be cut in sequence by flipping the work after each pass.

FOR MITERING AT END OF STOCK

FOR MITERING AT ANY POINT ALONG BOARD

PLATFORM: 1/2" PLYWOOD

GUIDES: 1/2" PLYWOOD

GLUE SANDPAPER STRIPS ALONG EDGES

SAW SLOT

BARS—TO FIT MITER GAUGE SLOTS (HARDWOOD)

GUIDE BLOCK: 3/4" PLYWOOD

PLATFORM: 1/2" PLYWOOD

BARS TO FIT MITER GAUGE SLOTS (HARDWOOD)

2-75.   Construction details of two types of sliding tables for miter cuts. The one on the left requires that frame pieces be pre-cut to length. The other is for cutting consecutively from a single length of work; essential when the stock can't be flipped. *Sawguard removed for clarity. Always use guard in actual practice.*

2-76.   This mitering-jig design is made for use as a miter-gauge attachment. Frame pieces are cut to overall length before they are miter-cut. It's a procedure that wastes some wood but the advantage is a gain in accuracy. *Sawguard removed for clarity. Always use guard in actual practice.*

2-77.   Instead of being a sliding table or a miter-gauge attachment, this jig is designed with its own miter-gauge "bars."

These sliding tables are no more than platforms guided by twin bars that ride the slots in the saw table (Figure 2-75). Attached to the platforms are guides that position the work for the cut. If these sliding tables are made accurately and cared for, they will function in good style for as long as you care to use them.

In constructing the sliding tables, cut the platforms first, sizing them to suit your table. Then cut the bars so they will ride smoothly in the slots. Put the bars in the slots, and after lowering the blade, set the platform so it lines up with one edge of the saw table. Tack-nail through the platform into the bars, and while holding down the platform, raise the saw blade so it cuts its own slot. The position of the guides on the platform should be made by layout from this slot.

Two other types of jigs that will help you work more accurately when cutting miters are shown in Figures 2-76 and 2-77.

2-78.   Bevel cutting is done by tilting the saw blade or, if the tool is so equipped as shown here, by tilting the table. Of course, beveling is often done with the stock flat on the table. *Sawguard removed for clarity. Always use guard in actual practice.*

FOR OCTAGON, SET FOR BEVEL OF 22½°

SEGMENT

FOR SQUARE, SET FOR BEVEL OF 45°

FOR HEXAGON, SET FOR BEVEL OF 30°

SEGMENT

SEGMENT

2-79.　How to set up for various types of bevel cuts. Accuracy is critical if segments are to join correctly.

Beveling.　Most bevels are cut using the rip fence as a guide, while the blade (or the table) is tilted to the angle required (Figure 2-78). Sometimes, usually on narrow work, the miter gauge is used to make the pass. When two such cuts are mated, the joint is called a miter. For the sake of clarity, we'll call such cuts bevels from here on. Be aware though, that many times, a "bevel" made across the grain, a job usually done with the miter gauge, is called a "cross-miter." Examples of bevel-cut assemblies are shown in Figure 2-79.

There is more of a tendency on this type of cut for the work to move away from the fence, so use extra care to keep it snug throughout the pass. A chamfer (beveled edge) is done like a bevel, but you don't cut away as much stock (Figure 2-80). In either case, should you require the cut on all four edges or two adjacent edges, do the cross-grain cuts first. It's more likely that feathering will occur at the end of these cuts, so you rely on the final with-the-grain pass to re-

move the imperfection.

You can do bevel cutting on a number of pieces so that after assembly they will turn a corner (Figure 2-81). A circle is formed when the total included angles of all the pieces equal 360°. Determining the correct angle is simple. Divide 360° by the number of pieces you want in your circle to find the total angle that each piece will have. Then divide this in half to get the angle at which each side of the pieces should be cut.

Accuracy is very important. Part of a degree doesn't seem like much of an error, but multiply it by 20 and then picture the gap when you fit in the last piece. The same idea applies to flat work; the difference is that you use the miter gauge to do the cutting.

Tapering.　A taper is a saw cut made at an oblique angle across the work. When work-size permits, the cut can be made with the miter gauge set at the required angle, but most times it will be more convenient and you will work

2-80.　A chamfer is accomplished by beveling, but it's a cut that only removes a corner of the stock. *Sawguard removed for clarity. Always use guard in actual practice.*

2-81.　Accurately cut, beveled pieces, can turn corners or form full circles. Remember that the cut-angle is always one half of the joint angle.

2-82. A taper is a saw cut that is made at an oblique angle across the work. Most times, a special taper-cutting jig that you can make is needed. *Sawguard removed for clarity. Always use guard in actual practice.*

more accurately if you make a special taper-cutting jig (Figure 2-82). Construction details for several jigs are shown in Figure 2-83.

What the jigs do is provide a straight side that can ride the rip fence and an adjustable side that you can set for the degree of taper you need. When you make the adjustable jig, keep the legs clamped together when attaching the hinge. The crosspiece that is used to secure the setting can be made of sheet metal or hardwood. Mark a line on both legs 12″ in from the hinged end. By opening the jig and measuring between these two marks, you can determine how much taper per foot you are setting for.

To use the jig, set the straight side against the fence and place the work against the opposite leg. Advance both jig and work past the saw blade (Figure 2-84). If you require the same taper on both edges of the stock, open the jig up to twice the original setting before making the second cut.

There will be a tendency here for the work to move away from the jig as you cut, so be sure to set the work correctly at the beginning and keep it in place throughout the pass.

The jig, when combined with a blade tilt (Figure 2-85), can also be used to guide compound angle cuts when the size of the stock makes it inconvenient to work in standard

2-83. There are various types of taper jigs you can make. The variable one at the top left is the most useful for general work. You can use the guide method when work is too large to be handled with a jig.

fashion. More about compound angle cutting to come.

It's also possible to use notched jigs to accomplish taper cuts. These are no more than pieces of wood with parallel sides. What you do is recess one side to match the shape and size of what you wish to remove—or the shape you need—and then, with the work set in the notch, move jig and work as if you were making a rip cut (Figure 2-86). The distance from the rip fence to the saw blade matches the width of the notching jig. Notched jigs are good to use when the job calls for a setting that might be too extreme for the variable jig and for very small pieces like wedges (Figure 2-87). They are also good for production runs since they eliminate resetting and thus reduce the possibility of human error.

Compound angles. Many projects have compound angle joints—peak figures, structures with sloping sides (Figure 2-88), picture frames with sides that slant toward or away from the wall, truncated pyramid shapes, and so on.

Some cuts require a miter-gauge setting, others a blade tilt. The compound angle requires both at the same time. Accuracy is essential. Settings must be done carefully and checked out on scrap before the good stock is cut. This type of cutting will often require alternating the miter gauge in the table slots. Of course, this means changing the miter-gauge setting, which offers another opportunity for error. There really is no reason why you can't cut a good compound miter in the basic fashion; it's just important to impress you with the need for precision.

2-84. The taper jig moves the work forward for the cut. The taper angle is determined by measuring across the 12″ marks on the legs of the jig. The gap between the legs at that point gives the taper in inches, per foot of length. *Sawguard removed for clarity. Always use guard in actual practice.*

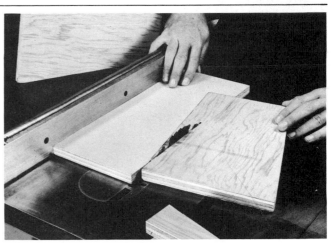

2-86. A notched jig may be the solution to a taper cut that might be difficult to do with standard means. The notch in the jig can be for the part to be removed or the part you need. *Sawguard removed for clarity. Always use guard in actual practice.*

2-85. The jig, when combined with a blade tilt, is used for compound angle cutting; especially useful when the size of the work makes it inconvenient to work in standard fashion. *Sawguard removed for clarity. Always use guard in actual practice.*

2-87. A notched jig is often the smart way to go when you require tapered pieces, like wedges, that are too small to be cut safely using conventional cutting techniques. The blade does not have to be this high, and you should use the guard.

2-88.   Examples of assemblies that require compound angle cuts.

You can work from the accompanying chart that supplies the settings for 4-, 6-, and 8-sided work (Figure 2-89), but there is a much overlooked factor in this area of woodworking. The slope angle, as far as the appearance of the work is concerned, is very seldom critical. Any person who judges, for example, your shadowbox picture-frame project on the basis of whether the slope angle should have been a couple of degrees more or less is being needlessly critical.

If you use something to hold the work at the slope angle you want instead of keeping the work flat on the table, the job is done like a simple miter cut, but you produce a compound angle. This will occur regardless of the slope angle. Naturally it has limitations that are imposed mostly by work size and the capacities of your machine. But if the jigs and ideas shown in Figures 2-90 through 2-97 can't solve the immediate problem, you can always use the chart.

In any event, use a blade that will produce a smooth cut, and be sure that it is sharp. Make all passes very slowly, and keep a firm grip on the work throughout.

Dadoing.   If you set a regular saw blade to less than the stock thickness and make repeat passes to widen the normal kerf, you get a U-shaped cut that is a dado when done across the grain, a groove when done with the grain. You may even hear the word "ploughing," but this is the same as grooving.

The saw-blade, repeat-pass technique is fine for an occasional groove or dado. But since such cuts are needed quite often, then purchase a dado tool accessory because it makes such work easier and faster to do (Figure 2-98). When you have many similar cuts to make, you'll know each will be alike once you've set this special tool. Also, this accessory can be used for a wider range of jobs than the basic U-shaped cuts. Those shown in Figures 2-99 and 2-100 don't begin to tell the story.

Dadoing tools.   There are two basic types of dadoing tools. One is an assembly that consists of two outside blades and a set of chippers (Figure 2-101). Cut width is determined by the size and number of chippers you use. These are always mounted between the blades and situated so the swaged cutting edges are aligned with blade gullets (Figure 2-102). Often, to get a more precise width-of-cut, paper washers are mounted on the arbor along with the chippers. Most units can be used for cuts that run from 1/4″ (blades only) to better than 3/4″ (all chippers). The blades may be flat-ground or hollow-ground. Hollow-ground ones are

WORK SLOPE	BUTT JOINT (4 sides)		(4 sides)		MITER JOINT (6 sides)		(8 sides)	
	A	B	A	B	A	B	A	B
5°	1/2	85	44-3/4	85	29-3/4	87-1/2	22-1/4	88
10°	1-1/2	80-1/4	44-1/4	80-1/4	29-1/2	84-1/2	22	86
15°	3-3/4	75-1/2	43-1/4	75-1/2	29	81-3/4	21-1/2	84
20°	6-1/4	71-1/4	41-3/4	71-1/4	28-1/4	79	21	82
25°	10	67	40	67	27-1/4	76-1/2	20-1/4	80
30°	14-1/2	63-1/2	37-3/4	63-1/2	26	74	19-1/2	78-1/4
35°	19-1/2	60-1/4	35-1/2	60-1/4	24-1/2	71-3/4	18-1/4	76-3/4
40°	24-1/2	57-1/4	32-1/2	57-1/4	22-3/4	69-3/4	17	75
45°	30	54-3/4	30	54-3/4	21	67-3/4	15-3/4	73-3/4
50°	36	52-1/2	27	52-1/2	19	66-1/4	14-1/2	72-1/2
55°	42	50-3/4	24	50-3/4	16-3/4	64-3/4	12-1/2	71-1/4
60°	48	49	21	49	14-1/2	63-1/2	11	70-1/4
"A" = tilt of saw blade				"B" = miter gauge setting				

2-89.   Table saw settings for compound angle joints.

2-90.   A slope angle jig, secured to the miter gauge like an extension, lets you make compound angle cuts without having to tilt the blade. A strip, nailed along the top of the base, positions the work at the angle you select. The thickness and location of the guide strip determines the slope angle. *Sawguard removed for clarity. Always use guard in actual practice.*

2-93.   The sliding table fixture eliminates even the miter-gauge setting and lets you work on either side of the blade. Once it is set up accurately for the cut you need, there are no outside factors to mar getting good joints. *Sawguard removed for clarity. Always use guard in actual practice.*

2-91.   The adjustable tilt jig also works with the miter gauge. The jig provides the slope angle so the blade doesn't have to be tilted; the cut is made like a simple miter. *Sawguard removed for clarity. Always use guard in actual practice.*

2-94.   The slope angle is determined by the distance between the slides and the miter guides. Be sure to make this setting exactly the same on both sides.

2-92.   This is how you can make the adjustable tilt jig.

2-95.   A limitation is work width. This becomes negligible as the slope angle decreases. The sliding table will handle 80 to 90 percent of the compound angle cuts you're likely to need. *Sawguard removed for clarity. Always use guard in actual practice.*

2-96. You can cut similar pieces from one length of stock simply by flipping it over for each pass. For molded shapes that can't be flipped, you have to make alternate cuts, working on each side of the blade. *Sawguard removed for clarity. Always use guard in actual practice.*

2-98. A dadoing tool, in this case a dado assembly, is used to make U-shaped cuts. They are called "dadoes" if formed across the grain, "grooves" if cut with the grain.

2-97. Construction details of the sliding table jig for compound angle cutting. It can be used for simple miters too; just keep the workpieces flat.

2-102. Chippers are *always* used between the blades. The swaged cutting edges of the chippers that abut the blades are situated in the blade's gullets.

2-99. A dado tool can do quickly what would require many repeat passes to accomplish with a saw blade. Dadoes, grooves, rabbets, and tenons are just a few examples of what can be done.

2-100. By making repeat passes you can do hollowing jobs; actually extra-wide grooves. A good, well-jointed dado will leave a nice flat bottom on jobs like this.

2-103. Adjustable dado allows infinite settings between its minimum and maximum cuts. Width-of-cut adjustments are made by using the central hub.

2-101. A dado assembly consists of two outside blades and a set of chippers. Number and size of chippers used with the blades determines the cut-width.

more expensive but they provide more clearance in the cut and so are less likely to burn themselves or the wood. There are also assemblies with tungsten carbide teeth on chippers and blades. These are top of the line products and are costly but they cut cleaner, faster and smoother and with good care will stay sharp for impressive periods of time.

Another type (Figure 2-103), is an infinitely adjustable unit. Any cut-width is possible between 1/8" and 15/16". Adjustments are made by rotating the inner dial. This causes the single blade to, in effect, move from side to side, thus forming a particular cut-width. Another product that works in similar fashion has individual cutters mounted on a central hub instead of a saw blade (Figure 2-104). Both types are available with tungsten carbide or steel cutting teeth. The major advantage of adjustable dadoing tools is that they can be so precise. They can, for example, be set perfectly for a piece of lumber or plywood that's a fraction over or under a specific thickness.

All dado cuts remove much more material than a simple saw cut, so slow up on the feed to avoid choking the tool. Like blades, dado teeth are designed to remove so much wood at a given rate of feed. Don't force them to do more. On very deep cuts, especially on those wider than 3/8", set the projection for less than you need on the first pass. Then, increase the projection and make a second pass, even a third one if necessary. Tool power will also affect this cutting process; if the work chatters or the tool slows up, you'll know you are cutting too deeply.

Dadoing tools require special inserts simply because they make wider cuts than a saw blade (Figure 2-105). On some jobs, this can result in an opening that is wider than needed around the cutter. When this seems like an unsafe

2-104.   Another type of infinitely adjustable dadoing tool. This one works with individual cutters. All types of dadoing tools are available with all-steel or carbide-tipped teeth.

2-106.   A facing, which is a nice, straight length of wood that is clamped or bolted to the rip fence, will be useful for many dadoing operations. The text explains how to form the arch that provides clearance for the cutter.

2-105.   Dadoing tools are always set to make a wider cut than you can accomplish with a saw blade. Therefore, a special insert, that you buy as an accessory, must be used in place of the standard table insert.

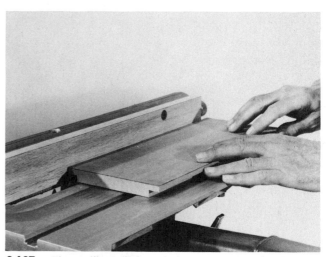

2-107.   The auxiliary rip-fence facing is a practical aid when, for example, using a dadoing tool to form rabbets. The width of the rabbet is determined by the distance from the facing to the outside blade of the cutter.

situation, make a special insert using plywood or hardboard. Use the regular insert as a pattern. Put the new insert in place with the dado at zero projection. Then, unless the insert is secured with screws, situate the rip fence over the insert, clear of the cutter, and use shims under the fence to keep the insert secure. The final step is to very slowly raise the dado so it will form its own slot. The opening in the new insert will be just enough for the cutting tool to poke through.

Another good idea is to make a wooden facing for the rip fence. This facing is no more than a good, straight piece of wood attached with screws through the fence (Figure 2-106) or secured with clamps. After it is in place you can situate it over the cut area and slowly raise the cutter to form a clearance arch. Typical applications that can be done easier and more accurately by using the auxiliary wood facing are shown in Figures 2-107 and 2-108.

Tenoning jig. It's often necessary to make cuts across the end of narrow stock. Sometimes they can be accomplished by using the miter gauge. Other times they're done best by holding the stock on end. The latter method should never be attempted freehand. So the job will be safe and accurate to do, make and use the tenoning jig that is shown in Figures 2-109 and 2-109A. The jig is basically a U-shaped affair, designed so it can straddle the rip fence and hold the work securely in relation to the cutter. The work, situated against the vertical guide, can be clamped in place or held by hand as the jig is moved forward to make the cut. Clamping or hand-holding can be judged on the basis of work size and cut size. Generally, clamping is safer and more accurate.

2-108.   Cuts made across narrow pieces should always be supported by the miter gauge. Don't ever attempt to do jobs like this by working freehand.

2-109A.   Construction details of a basic tenoning jig. Be sure that the vertical face is exactly 90° to the table's surface.

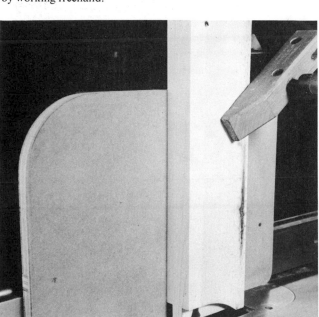

2-109.   A tenoning jig that straddles the rip fence should be used so jobs like grooving, tenoning, rabbeting done on the ends of narrow stock, can be accomplished accurately and safely. For duplicate cuts on opposite ends of the stock, just invert the workpiece and cut again.

2-110.   You can form slots by lowering the work *very* slowly over the turning cutter. Here, a clamp provides a point against which you can brace the work for starting the cut. An alternate method is to secure the work flat on the table and then raise the cutter until it projects through. Work with care, *always*.

Forming slots. You can form slots with a dado but the technique is very special and must be done with extreme care. The idea is to lower the workpiece over the cutter while it is turning (Figure 2-110). ALWAYS use a stop block or a clamp on the rip fence to act as a gauge and a brace point against which you can secure the work as you slowly lower it. Also, don't try this method with small workpieces. The motion is pivotal, from the brace point to where the stock rests flat on the table. At this point, the cutter should barely poke through the work; then you move the work to lengthen the slot. To determine slot length, use two stop blocks. Figures 2-111 and 2-111A show a rip-fence stop jig you can make. The jig may also be used when stopped cuts are made with the stock on edge. An example application would be forming limited-length grooves in stock edges for insertion of a blind spline. The stop jig will also be useful on some molding head applications.

Extensions. Miter-gauge extensions are as useful for dado work as they are for saw cuts. They help to keep the work square; they provide support for long stock; and they can be organized to do special jobs. An extension with a stop will accurately gauge dado location on multiple, similar pieces. When one is organized as shown in Figure 2-112, it automatically gauges the distance between cuts. The guide strip, which is glued in a notch cut into the extension, is sized to suit the width and depth of the dado and is positioned from the cutter the distance required between cuts. Each cut made is set over the strip to position the work for the following cut. This is a good way to work when, for example, you need matching dadoes for a bookcase that will have evenly spaced shelves.

2-112. A guide strip, nailed and glued into a notch that is cut in a miter-gauge extension, serves to automatically position the work for following cuts—one way to work when you need equally-spaced dadoes.

2-111. Stop jig, attached to the rip fence, has slots its full length so the hardwood stop blocks can be positioned for controlling length of cut. The blocks are secured with bolts and wing nuts. Start the cut by bracing the work against the front stop. The cut is completed by advancing the work until it butts against the rear stop. Be very careful when making initial contact with the cutter.

2-111A. This is one way you can make an adjustable stop jig that can be secured to the rip fence.

2-113. Spring-type fingers bear against the work to keep it flat on the table and snug against the fence. This commercial unit can be used on any table saw so long as you equip the rip fence with a wood facing.

Helpers. There are products you can buy and items you can make that help you work more accurately and, many times, more safely. A commercial one, which is an assortment of clamps, rods and spring-type fingers is shown in Figure 2-113. The springs keep the work flat on the table and snug against the fence. When the cut nears completion, you substitute a pusher for your fingers. Always situate the springs so they can't interfere with the pass or snap down on the cutter.

A variation of the spring stick that you make that we have already mentioned is shown in use in Figure 2-114,

2-114. Spring sticks can be made in various widths and lengths. Once made, they can be retained for use on various power tool operations. Position them so they keep the work snug without forcing it against the cutter.

2-115. Examples of surface cuts you can form by working with a molding head. The knives you use can be blank or have a profile shape. It depends on the pattern you wish to produce.

helping to secure work against the rip fence during a grooving operation. Note that the spring stick is positioned so it will snug work against the fence but not force it against the cutter.

Molding heads. Adding a molding head to your table-saw equipment and accumulating a nice assortment of knives will enable you to create many standard and original molding designs. You can also form edge joints, cabinet-door lips, and do unique things like surface "carving" (Figure 2-115). Many of these operations, and others, would normally require the use of an individual shaping machine.

There are several kinds of molding head designs on the market, some of which are shown in Figure 2-116, but they all work the same way on a table saw. The knives, usually in sets of three, are locked into slots equally spaced about the perimeter of the head. The head is mounted on the saw arbor between washers just as you would install a saw blade or dado tool. Do be sure (and this will relate to the length of the arbor on the tool you have) that there will be enough thread for the locking nut to seat securely. It's possible you may have to use a molding head of particular thickness, but your owner's manual will tell you that.

You can be bewildered by the number of molding knives available (Figure 2-117), but the fact is, you can get by in good fashion with a few basic types to start with and add others as you rely more on molding-head work. What to start with depends on current work and interests—decorative edges, tongue and groove joints, cope cuts for

2-116. Different types of molding heads. Many are designed so bushings can be used for mounting them whether the table-saw arbor is 1/2″ or 5/8″. Usually, the head is slotted for mounting a three-piece set of knives.

2-117. There is a vast assortment of knives that you can use in a molding head. It's best to start with a few that you can use immediately. Add others as the need comes up.

2-118. Typical molding knives. Study these profiles to determine which will be most useful for you to start with.

frames, reeding or fluting? The examples shown in Figure 2-118 will help you decide.

It's important to remember that knives, like the 1/4″, 1/2″ quarter round, are combination types that produce different shapes depending on what portion of the profile you use, or do a specific job, like the glue joint cutter, and require that the full profile be employed. Other cutters usually used for a full-profile shape are panel insert, sash, tongue, groove. However, no rule says you can't use part of or the entire profile of *any* cutter if the shape that results suits your purpose. There is a lot of flexibility even with a single knife. All of the shapes shown in Figure 2-119 were produced with a single cutter. Variations in shapes were due to changes in, mainly, work position and cutter projection.

Much of what has been said about dado use applies to the molding head. Unlike a saw blade, which removes a minimum amount of material, the molding cutter takes a big bite. Never force the work to try to cut too deeply. On very deep cuts, make several passes, adjusting the height of the knife after each one to attain the full depth of cut required. If the machine slows up drastically, vibrates, makes it hard to hold the work steady, throws out chunks of wood

instead of fine shavings, or stalls, chances are you are feeding too fast or cutting too deeply.

Immediately after using them, clean the knives of gum and dirt and coat them with a light oil to prevent rust. Store them so the cutting edges will be protected. The head should also be cleaned, especially the slots in which the knives fit. Never leave knives locked in the head.

No matter how good your equipment is, you won't get optimum cuts unless the setups that you make are accurate. So spend a few extra seconds to check such things as knife height and rip-fence settings. It's wise to make trial cuts in scrap wood before cutting actual parts. This practice is especially important when you are using matched sets of cutters. For example, one set of knives will cut the tongue; another set will cut the groove for a tongue-and-groove joint. Forms shaped by the mating cutters must line up perfectly or the joints will be spoiled.

It's a good idea to cut or to draw on stiff cardboard the full profile shape of each knife as you acquire it. The cut can then be "filed" for reference. By doing this, you can easily tell, without making a trial cut, what knife or what part of the knife you need to do the job.

Generally, as far as handling is concerned, molding head operations don't differ too much from dado work. The results are completely different, of course, but such factors as a rip-fence facing, special inserts when required, slow feeds, the advisability of a tenoning jig, and so on, apply to each.

Many of the operations you can do with a molding head are shown and explained in Figures 2-120 through 2-132.

Coving. Oblique sawing is what makes it possible to get arched shapes with a regular saw blade (Figure 2-133). By working so, you can form coves, troughs, do decorative work, even make special pieces for turning corners (Figure 2-134). The basic procedure is to clamp a guide strip, or two, to the table at some angle to the saw blade. The blade is set so it barely pokes above the table, and the work is

2-119. It's important to remember that the shapes you can produce with molding knives depend, in great part, on the position of the work and the projection of the cutter. All of these forms were made with a single set of knives.

Molding Head Operations

2-120.   Like dadoing tools, the molding head should be used with a special table insert.

2-121.   Don't neglect to make special inserts when the operation calls for minimizing the opening around the cutter. It's a wise general rule to remember for safer, more accurate cutting.

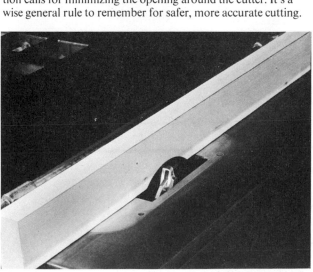

2-122.   Auxiliary wood facing, like the one suggested for dado work, is also needed for molding head operations. Make the clearance arch by raising the cutter very slowly after you have positioned and locked the rip fence. The arch doesn't have to be more than about 1″ deep.

2-123.   An example operation that proves the value of a rip-fence facing, and also shows that a molding head can be for more than decorative cuts. Here, a blank knife is used to form a tongue.

2-124.   Work can be held on edge and fed across the cutter. How deep you can cut in one pass will depend on tool power, wood species, and so on. Chances are that you are trying to cut too deeply in the single pass if you must force the work across or if it chatters.

2-125.   You can shape across the ends of narrow pieces but such jobs must always be done by using the miter gauge for work support. *Don't ever* do this kind of job with only your hands to feed the stock.

Molding Head Operations (cont'd.)

2-126.   Cuts on narrow stock can also be made with the work on edge BUT, for safety and accuracy, the work must be supported by a tenoning jig, like the one shown for dado work.

2-127.   A jig like this is a must if you wish to shape pre-cut, narrow work. The guide block, rabbet-cut to suit the work, is clamped or nailed to the wood facing. Feed the workpieces in the front end and pull them out the rear.

2-128.   Surface cuts can produce many decorative effects. Accurate spacing of cuts is required when doing this kind of repeat-pass operation.

2-129.   Blank knives with the cutter or the table tilted can produce faceted surfaces. You must be very precise when setting up for cuts that must match. Note the use of the pusher/hold-down.

2-130.   It's also possible to do shaping cuts on assembled projects like this square-to-begin-with picture frame. Slow up drastically as you approach the end of each cut.

2-131.   A V-block trough makes it possible to do longitudinal cuts on cylinders. The cutter pokes through the base of the jig which is secured to the rip fence. You must be very careful not to turn the work as you make the pass.

2-132.   A matching pair of V-blocks, shaped like these and clamped to the rip fence, serve as guides when you wish to shape the perimeter of circular pieces. The work is very slowly fed into the cutter and then, as slowly, rotated in the direction indicated by the arrow.

moved very slowly along the guide. Many passes are needed with blade projection increased about 1/16″ for each pass. How much you increase projection for each pass will depend on the nature of the wood and the pass-angle you have decided on, but, since the action is pretty much a scraping one, it must never be extreme. If it's difficult to move the work without forcing or if the work moves away from the guide, you probably are trying to remove too much material in one pass.

By making a parallel rule (Figure 2-135), you can come close to predetermining the shape you will get. To use it, adjust the legs so the distance between them equals the diameter of the cove you want. Set the saw blade height to equal the radius of the cove. Place the parallel rule over the saw blade so opposite inside edges of the legs just touch the front and rear teeth of the blade. This is the angle at which you should clamp the guide strips.

Edge-coves can be accomplished in similar fashion

2-133.   Oblique sawing is the technique that makes it possible to produce arched shapes with a regular saw blade. The action is mostly a scraping one, so depth of cut for each pass must be slight, and passes must be made slowly.

2-135.   How to make a parallel rule that you can use to gauge cove cuts. Note, in the top detail, that a lot of the waste can be removed by making saw cuts before doing the coving.

2-134.   Some examples of things you can do by using the coving technique.

(Figure 2-136) but always be certain the work has sufficient body to seat solidly on the table. Should you need a slim piece, form it on a wide board you can safely handle and then remove the coved edge by making a rip cut. Another way, especially if you need more than one coved-edge piece, is to form a full cove in standard fashion and then rip-cut the workpiece in half.

To form twin coves or a series of troughs, work as shown in Figure 2-137. Just turn the stock end-for-end after each pass. You'll find that the work will go faster if you use a blade that has set teeth; a combination blade is good. Don't work with a smooth cutter like a hollow-ground blade. You can also work with a dadoing tool or a molding head that is equipped with blank blades (Figure 2-138). With these cutters, especially, rate of feed must be very slow, and depth of cut for each pass, very slight.

In all situations, no matter how much material you can remove by the repeat shaping passes, the final pass should be made with the blade barely touching the wood so the end result will be as smooth as possible.

Coves produced in this fashion are not a true arc but they can come close enough so that if perfection is essential, you can finish the job with a drum sander or by hand. The more oblique the cutting angle, the closer you get to a true arc.

Notching jigs. There are times when a part can't be sawed accurately or safely using the rip fence or the miter gauge only. The part may be too small to be held safely or too oddly shaped to be done conventionally. A notched jig is often the solution (Figure 2-139).

The jig is a piece of wood with parallel sides. The notch can be the shape of the part you wish to keep, or it

2-138.   The molding head, or a dadoing tool, may also be used for coving. Note, that with a blank cutter, the cove has a flat bottom. Keep cuts very, very light. The guide used here is an extension that is locked to the miter gauge. The miter gauge must be locked or clamped in place.

2-139.   Remember, when using notching jigs, that the cut in the jig can be the shape of the part you need or the waste you wish to remove. *Sawguard removed for clarity. Always use guard in actual practice.*

2-136.   Edge coves can be formed in similar fashion. The stock must always have enough bearing surface to sit solidly on the table. You can form a full cove and then saw the piece in half to get two edge-coved parts.

2-137.   Twin coves on a single workpiece are formed by turning the stock end-for-end after each pass. Coving cuts are not true arcs but can be made so by drum or hand-sanding after the table-saw work.

2-140.   Notched jigs often make it possible to work more safely and accurately on workpieces that are too small or too oddly shaped to be done in conventional fashion. *Sawguard removed for clarity. Always use guard in actual practice.*

can be the shape of the waste piece. Usually, the jig will ride the rip fence and act as both carrier and gauge. It allows you to position the work precisely, even when unusual shapes are involved (Figure 2-140).

Making generalizations about the use of notched jigs is difficult because, in most cases, they are employed for very special jobs. In a few general situations, however, notched jigs can be very helpful. Think about using them when the part is so small or so oddly shaped that it can't be hand held safely, the cut is such that the piece can't be held in the nor-mal manner with the rip fence or the miter gauge, or you need many identical parts so that making a special setup is justified.

Of course, the jigs must be made accurately. This may be too much trouble when you need only a piece or two. At such times, if accuracy is really critical, it may be better to lay out the workpiece, cut just outside the line, and then fin-ish the job on a belt or disc sander.

Ideas for notching jigs are shown in Figures 2-141 through 2-146.

Notching Jigs

2-141.   Small wedges are easier to cut when you use a notch-ing jig. In all cases, the jig is first cut to width, sized to provide enough room between the fence and blade, and then the notch is shaped at an appropriate point. *Sawguard removed for clarity. Always use guard in actual practice.*

2-144.   This type of notching jig facilitates cutting duplicate discs from a wood round. The depth of the notch determines the thickness of the discs. Return the jig to starting position before removing the disc that was cut. Make the jig long enough so your hand doesn't have to come near the blade. *Sawguard removed for clarity. Always use guard in actual practice.*

2-142.   This jig, notched on its underside to suit the size of the work, was made to produce a large number of thin, narrow pieces that will be used as splines. Note the finger hole in the jig. *Sawguard removed for clarity. Always use guard in actual practice.*

2-145.   This jig was designed so a large number of dowels of equal length could be cut accurately. Note the finger hole in the jig. *Sawguard removed for clarity. Always use guard in actual practice.*

2-143.   Jobs like cheek cuts for tenons can also be accom-plished by using a special type of notched jig. This method is safer than trying to hold down narrow stock.

2-146.   This is the jig to work with when you need to form slots in the end of dowels or rounds. The jig is moved forward and returned with one hand while the other hand holds the workpiece.

Multi-blade work. Two, or even more, saw blades turning on a single shaft speed the production on thousands of industrial duplicating jobs. In limited fashion, the same method can be employed by home craftsmen (Figure 2-147). All you need are extra saw blades and some suitable washers.

The basic idea is to mount the extra saw blades on the arbor and use the washer to hold them the desired distance apart (Figure 2-148). With one pass of the stock through the blades, you have two or three accurately spaced cuts. With this setup you can double or triple your output on all sorts of repetitive sawing chores that call for parallel cutting. As will be shown, you can also use the idea with dadoing tools.

The limitations of this setup should also be mentioned. The spacing of the multiple cuts is restricted by the length of the saw's arbor and the width of the saw slot in the table. Fortunately, most circular saws have a fairly long shaft and a removable table insert. This prompts a word of caution.

It's not possible to use the regular insert when you mount more than one blade. Maybe you can substitute a dado insert, but it's usually necessary to provide maximum support around the cutting area by making special inserts (Figure 2-149). Be certain, if you use this technique, that the saw's arbor is long enough to provide sufficient thread-length for the locking nut after the blades and washers are mounted.

With most saws there is not much cause to be concerned about power. If the tool will drive a dado assembly or a molding head, it will drive more than one saw blade. If you do experience some drag on any of the operations, simply slow down the rate of feed. Jobs like this should be done at a slower-than-usual pace anyway.

Running off a large number of identical strips or slats or forming multiple slots (Figure 2-150), are obvious situations where extra blades mounted on the arbor can be very useful. With the rip fence gauging the width of the first piece, you'll get as many strips, for example, in one pass as there are blades on the arbor. Similarly, you can make

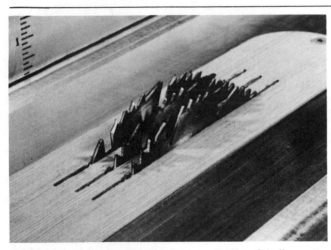

2-147. Three-blade setup can triple production of similar parts. Be sure the saw arbor is long enough to take such an assembly while still leaving ample thread for the lock nut.

2-149. A substitute insert that you can make of plywood or hardboard is needed for multiple blade sawing. When necessary, the new insert can be installed by pressing it into place over blobs of thick, adhesive putty. On many saws, the regular insert is secured with screws. The same screws can be used to secure the special insert that you make.

2-148. Washers, which are available in various thicknesses, are used as spacers between blades.

2-150. Forming multiple slots is an obvious example of when extra blades mounted on the arbor can be helpful. Starting the cut involves easing the work down on the turning blades, so extra care is required. You can saw to marks on the work or, better still, use stop blocks on the rip fence.

repetitive kerfs or grooves on the undersides of strips or panels that are to be curved as will be shown in the following section on wood bending.

When you mount blades of different diameters, you can saw through a board for an end cut and at the same time make a shallow cut that will be the shoulder of a rabbet. The width of the rabbet will be determined by the spacing between the two blades.

Two saw blades can be employed to make both cheek cuts for a tenon at the same time (Figure 2-151). By making repeat passes and using the setup shown in Figure 2-152, you can quickly form twin grooves like those needed in case-work facing for sliding doors.

When you substitute dadoing tools for saw blades, you can do many standard jobs, like those shown in Figures 2-153 through 2-155, faster and more accurately.

Bending wood by kerfing. Almost any species of wood can be made flexible enough, usually by a special steaming process, so it can be tied into knots. Once it has

dried, the wood will retain its new shape forever. The bending systems employed by industry are not usually suitable for home workshop use, yet it's often necessary to reshape wood to conform to a particular design. You may need a circular apron on projects like drum tables and stools, or an arched top for a doorway or garden arbor. If you can't, or choose not to use a steaming method, then what? There are two solutions. One—use the kerfing method which, in essence, reduces the stock thickness in a prescribed pattern so the material can be bent back on itself or, two—removing much of the wood in the bend area so what remains will be thin enough for bending (Figures 2-156 through 2-158).

The kerfing technique involves no more than making a series of equally-spaced cuts in one face of the stock which, in effect, allow the opposite face to be more flexible. It's like forming a veneer with the material remaining between the kerfs acting like reinforcing ribs.

The closer you space the kerfs and the deeper they are, the more sharply you can bend the wood. However, mak-

2-151. A double-blade setup makes both cheek cuts for a tenon in a single pass. Work with a tenoning jig when the part is too narrow to be hand-held. Use a special insert.

2-152. By making repeat passes and adjusting the fence position after each, you can form twin grooves accurately and pretty quickly. A nice way to go when you need twin grooves for sliding doors.

2-153. A tongue is produced in a single pass when you work with two dado cutters. Washers are used between the cutters to obtain the necessary gap. The length of the tongue is determined by the projection of the cutters.

2-154. Use the same setup to produce in one pass what would require repeat passes if done with regular saw blades.

2-155. Here, the same type of setup produces a pair of matching dadoes with just one pass.

ing too many kerfs will waste time, and cutting too deeply will weaken the stock needlessly. To gauge how to space the kerfs and how deep to make them for any given radius, make a test kerf in a scrap of wood that is the same species and thickness as the material you wish to bend. The depth of the kerf is an important factor, but it's good practice, at least to start with, to leave 1/8″ of solid stock above it. Next, clamp the stock to a flat surface, and on the free side of the kerf, measure out the distance of the desired curve radius. Then, lift the test piece until the kerf closes. The

height from the bench top to the underside of the test piece at the radius mark is the kerf spacing and depth you should start with (Figure 2-159).

The kerfing is done best by working with a miter gauge fitted with an extension (Figure 2-160). To make the job go faster and to be sure that kerf-spacing is uniform, fit the extension with a guide pin as shown in Figure 2-161. The distance from the pin (which can be just a headless nail) to the adjacent side of the blade, equals the kerf spacing. Each cut is placed over the nail to position the stock for the next cut.

2-156.   A kerfed piece can be bent in different directions as demonstrated by the cut-away view of a chair seat. Glue blocks support the piece in required shape and provide extra strength.

2-157.   The closer kerfs are spaced and the deeper they are, the more flexible the wood. The technique is like forming a veneer with the solid wood between the kerfs supplying needed strength.

2-158.   You can use these methods to bend wood without the need of steaming equipment. Note that bending can also be accomplished by using the thinning-out technique.

If you make a special extension like the one shown in Figure 2-162, you will be able to adjust settings for various kerf spacings. The extension is slotted so it can be moved laterally to change the distance between guide pin and blade. Kerfing will go much faster if you employ the two-blade technique we have already discussed (Figures 2-163 and 2-164).

When parts are to turn an outside corner and there is room to back them with glue blocks, you may find it easier to reduce the entire bend area to veneer thickness. When stock size permits, the job is done best on a jigsaw or band saw. Otherwise, you can work by making repeat passes with a dado head or even a molder with blank knives (Figure 2-165). The thinned section should be a couple of inches longer than the true length of the bend. This extra length will provide for a smooth and stress-free transition from a straight to a curved wood strip.

When you are ready to bend, do it slowly. On stubborn woods you can wet the unkerfed side. When it's necessary to hide the kerfs, you can do it by gluing on some

2-159.   Use this system to make a test kerf. Be sure that the sample piece is the same material you will use in the project.

2-162.   This miter-gauge extension, made for kerfing, is designed so it can be used for various kerf spacings. The extension is adjustable laterally because of the slots that are cut into it.

2-160.   It's a good idea to work with a miter-gauge extension when cutting the kerfs. Work with a smooth-cutting blade.

2-163.   Kerfing is one operation where a multi-blade setup is very practical. Note the special table insert.

2-161.   Fit the extension with a guide pin and you'll automatically get equal kerf-spacing. Each cut is placed over the pin to position the work for the next cut.

2-164.   The arrow indicates the guide pin that positions work for successive cuts. It should be installed in the miter-gauge extension whether you work with one or several blades.

2-165.   You can thin out material by working with a molding head fitted with blank blades, or even by using a dadoing tool but, as will be shown later on, you can do such work faster on a band saw.

2-166.   First step in pivot cutting is to make tangent cuts to remove the bulk of the waste stock. The pivot is a nail that passes through the work into a hardwood bar that rides the table slot. *Sawguard removed for clarity. Always use guard in actual practice.*

2-167.   After the waste is removed, clamp the hardwood bar so the work centerline is near the front of the blade. Rotate the work very slowly in the direction indicated by the arrow. Blade projection doesn't have to be more than is adequate for the stock thickness. Pivoting operations should be done with the guard in place.

veneer. Kerfs that show on board edges can be filled with a thick mixture of wood putty. Most times, however, the kerfing is hidden by other project components.

Sawing circles.   It may be strange to think of forming perfect circles using a saw blade designed for straight cutting, yet it's feasible if you use the pivot-cutting technique. The work is mounted either on an improvised miter-gauge bar you can make of hardwood or on a special platform designed for the purpose. The platform is a sheet of 1/4" or 3/8" plywood fitted with a hardwood strip that rides in the table slot like a miter-gauge bar.

The trick is to remove the bulk of the waste stock by making multiple tangent cuts first (Figure 2-166). The more waste you remove, the easier it will be to do the actual circle-forming. After the waste is removed, clamp the platform or bar to the table so the center line of the work is near the front edge of the blade. Then, rotate the work very slowly against the direction in which the blade is rotating (Figure 2-167). Your first impression may be that the cut is coved. There will be a resemblance, but you will discover that this occurs only on the waste side. The good edge of the stock will be square.

You use the bar or the platform for both the tangent cuts and for the final pivot pass that produces the true circle. Throughout the operation, the work is mounted on a nail-pivot, driven through the work and into the carrier (Figure 2-168). Smoothest cuts will result when you do enough tangent cutting to leave a minimum of material for removal by the final rotation pass.

Although the idea was devised specifically for forming circles, it can also be used for shaping bevels and coves on circular edges (Figures 2-169 and 2-170). If you substitute a dadoing tool for the saw blade, you can even form rabbets on the perimeter of discs (Figure 2-171). All of these operations must be done slowly and with care. Although it is not shown in the photographs for the sake of clarity, there is no reason why you should work without the saw guard in place.

2-168.   The pivot-cutting technique can be used for circles of almost any diameter. Here, a platform, nailed to the hardwood bar, is being used. Radius of the circle is the distance between pivot point and saw blade. *Sawguard removed for clarity. Always use guard in actual practice.*

Spirals. The table-saw technique that will be discussed is used mostly to lay out a spiral pattern and to remove much of the waste stock that is ordinarily filed away. Of course, if square-shouldered spirals are acceptable, then the same technique can be used for a full job. A dado is shown doing the job, but a regular saw blade may be used instead.

The angle at which the miter-gauge head is set determines the "lead" of the spiral, so you can determine beforehand whether the grooves will be close or far apart. Determine the depth of cut by the position of the miter gauge which should be clamped in position, and the projection of the cutter. A low projection is safer.

To start the cut, hold the stock firmly against the miter-gauge, fitted with an extension, and lower it slowly over the turning cutter. When the stock rests solidly on the table, turn it slowly toward the cutter. If you turn slowly and hold firmly, the work will automatically lead to the correct pitch (Figure 2-172). There are no limitations to the length or the diameter of the work you can handle in this fashion.

Pattern sawing. The rip-fence jig shown in Figures 2-173 and 2-174, permits cutting any number of odd-shaped pieces exactly alike. First, cut one of the parts you want to exact shape and size. Rough-cut all other pieces to approximate this shape and size. Drive two nails through the pattern just far enough so they project slightly. Then, press the pattern down on each workpiece as you go. The pattern rides the guide that is clamped to the rip fence so the saw blade slices off the workpiece to match.

The forward edge of the rip-fence guide must be in line with the outside edge of the saw blade. Jobs like this are best done with a smooth-cutting blade. When you work carefully, all the pieces you produce will be exactly alike.

Special Joint Techniques

There is more to a woodworking project than meets the eye; the joints that keep components together, often hidden, have everything to do with the quality and permanence of the project. This doesn't mean that everything you do must be knitted with intricate joinery. After all, some types of projects shouldn't be done with more than a butt joint, and a butt joint, correctly done, can last a long, long time.

2-169.   Bevels are possible if you tilt the saw blade AFTER the circle is fully formed with the saw blade in vertical position. Bevels will be flat if you do a final, minimum-cut pass, with the centers of work and blade on a common line. *Sawguard removed for clarity. Always use guard in actual practice.*

2-170.   You can even cove circular edges if you work with the blade tilted and the workpiece positioned almost in front of the blade. Make repeat passes, raising the blade a fraction after each. You can get different cove shapes by changing the position of the work or the tilt of the blade. *Sawguard removed for clarity. Always use guard in actual practice.*

2-171.   You can form a rabbet on a circular piece by using the pivot technique with a dado assembly. Repeat passes are required. How deep you can cut each time must be judged on the job. However, don't ever work so that you must force the cut.

2-172.   Spirals can be formed by limiting the cutter's depth of cut and rotating the stock as you hold it securely against a slanted guide. You must feed very slowly. The cutting action will automatically hold the "pitch" of the spiral which is established by the angle of the guide.

In any event, regardless of whether the joint is simple or complex, careful, precise cutting is required. In this section we will discuss many of the joints you can accomplish on a table saw working with either a saw blade or a dadoing tool. Many of the joints, and some of their applications, are shown in Figures 2-175, 2-176, and 2-177.

The finger lap. Finger-lap joints are often found on old works of enduring excellence. These joints are exposed in some areas to denote a good degree of craftsmanship and are used in some hidden areas because of their strength. Structurally, the appeal of a finger-lap joint lies in the unusual amount of gluing surface it provides (Figure 2-178). The resulting strength is recommendation enough for using the joint on moving components like drawers and on frequently handled items like boxes. If it were done by hand, it would be a tiresome chore, but with a table saw and the jigs shown, you can turn out finger-lap joints precisely and quickly.

The generalization that the cut width should equal the stock thickness is not always a good rule to follow in making these joints. Being more flexible can lead to better looking joints on many projects. Consider the following ideas.

A 3/8″ finger looks quite good on stock that ranges from 3/8″ to 3/4″ thick. A 1/4″ finger is effective on stock that ranges from 1/4″ to 1/2″ thick. If you ever work on material that is less than 1/4″ thick, match the cut to the thickness of the material or just a bit less.

Three types of jigs for making finger-lap joints are shown in the accompanying photos. The independent jig (Figure 2-179) is good to use because its double miter-gauge bars provide firm support on both sides of the cutter. It might be especially appealing to owners of small saws. The second type of jig is just an extension, screw-attached to the miter gauge (Figure 2-180). The adjustable jig (Figures 2-181 and 2-181A) is designed primarily for those who anticipate frequent reliance on this type of joint and wish to be flexible in finger-size selection.

To make the guides in the jigs, saw the extension to size and then replace the saw blade with a dado. Set the dado for the cut thickness you want and its projection to equal the stock thickness. Screw the extension to the miter gauge so you can make a pass close to the center of the extension. Make this cut and then a duplicate cut spaced a groove width away. The guide block is glued and nailed in the second cut.

Follow the accompanying photos (Figures 2-182, 2-183, 2-184) for the sequence of the cuts. Precision is fine, but don't work toward making the tongue and groove so snug that you must mate them with a mallet. A slip fit is more practical.

The simplest method of using the jig provides for a full-size groove at one edge of the assembly. Make the first cut in one piece, spacing it from the guide block with a strip of wood sized to match the groove width. Remove the strip of wood and butt the first piece against the guide block. Put the second piece in place, also butting it against the guide block. Proceed with the cutting, placing each formed groove over the guide block to position the work for the next pass.

A second method provides for equalizing partial cuts at each edge of the assembly. Make a vertical line midway between the facing edges of the guide block and groove. Make a second vertical line on the center line of the groove. Place one part in line with the first mark, the mating part in

2-174.   The outside of the saw blade and the edge of the guide are on the same plane. The pattern is moved along the guide: the blade saws off waste material from the workpieces.

2-173.   The pattern sawing technique allows you to saw any number of similar pieces with perfect accuracy. The pattern, which is the shape of the parts you need, is tack-nailed to rough-cut workpieces.

2-175. These are some of the more common woodworking joints you can form on a table saw by using a regular saw blade or a dado.

BUTT JOINTS

RABBETED

MITERED

OTHER CORNER JOINTS

2-176. These joints are commonly used on drawers, boxes, and similar projects. The finger lap, at lower right, is not difficult to do if you work with the special jig that will be shown.

DRAWER CONSTRUCTION

THIS OR THIS

SECTION A·A

CUTTING DOWN SIDES
REDUCES FRICTION

ATTACH TO DRAWER

ATTACH TO
DRAWER RAIL
FRAME

OR THIS

SIDE OF DRAWER

OR THIS

ROUNDED

TREATMENT FOR
DRAWER FRONTS

BEVELED

DRAWER GUIDES

RABBET

ATTACHING DRAWER
RAIL FRAME TO SIDE
OF CABINET

TYPICAL
DRAWER RAIL
FRAME

GUIDES

SECTION A·A

BUTT

POSTS

RABBET

PANEL

DOWELED

2-177.   Joints like this are often used in assemblies of case goods and drawers.

2-178. The finger-lap joint is attractive, and has much strength because the interlocking fingers provide a lot of glue area. Accuracy is important but easy to achieve if you do the cutting with a special jig.

2-180. This finger-lap jig is an extension that is screw-attached to the miter gauge. The guide block, spaced a groove-width away from the cutter, is glued in the notch cut into the extension.

2-179. The independent jig is a miter-gauge substitute with twin bars to ride both table slots. Back up the "head" with braces nailed and glued to both the jig and the bars.

2-181. The adjustable jig is slotted so it can be moved laterally to change the distance between the guide and the cutter. Work is positioned by butting cuts against the side of the hardboard stop.

2-181A. This is how an adjustable finger-lap jig can be constructed.

2-182.   Cuts are made by holding parts firmly against the extension and snug against the guide block. How to start cutting depends on how you want the finger-lap assembly to appear. The text describes various methods.

2-183.   Place the first cut *over* the guide block and butt the mating piece against it. The work, held securely against the jig, is advanced to make the second cut. At this point you can use a clamp to hold the two pieces together.

2-184.   The cuts that are formed are placed over the guide block to position the work for the cuts that follow. Pull the work well away from the cutter when you make changes. Make the passes very slowly.

2-185.   The finger lap doesn't have the locking action of a dovetail so loosening can occur if the glue should fail. You can guard against this if you wish, by drilling through the assembled joint and inserting a dowel.

2-186.   The finger lap can be a swivel joint if you shape the fingers for clearance that will allow the turning action. A dowel, or something similar, serves as an "axle."

2-187.   How to do a corner-lock joint. All the cuts are made with a dado set to cut a 1/4"-wide groove. Work slowly; accuracy is critical.

line with the second mark. Cut the two pieces together and butt them against the guide block for the following cut.

Finger lap joints don't lock like a dovetail joint, so loosening can occur should the glue fail. To guard against this, you can drill a hole through the assembled joint and insert a dowel (Figure 2-185). You may have to use an extension drill to accomplish this.

The finger lap can also be designed as a swivel joint. All you have to do is round the fingers after they are formed to provide clearance for the turning action (Figure 2-186).

Corner-lock joint. The advantages of this type of joint (Figure 2-187), are that it has interlocking forms that contribute to strength if only because of increased glue area, and it will stay together even if the glue should fail. The example procedure, done on stock that is 1″ thick, is typical. All cuts are made with a dadoing tool that is set to cut a groove 1/4″ wide. The first cut, on part "A", is made with the stock on edge so be sure to work with a tenoning jig, especially if the workpiece is narrow. The second cut on part "A" and all the cuts on part "B" are done by using the miter gauge and with the stock flat on the table. As with all joints, being precise with settings is critical.

2-188. Work from this formula when you design rabbet-miter joints.

Rabbet-miter joints. Aside from picture-frame moldings and some other cases where it is the *only* suitable connection, the classic miter joint is popular for one major reason: it enables you to join components along an edge or an end without exposing unsightly, hard-to-conceal edge or

Making a "Simple" Rabbet Miter

2-189. An example of the simple rabbet-miter joint. How to work is shown in the following illustrations.

2-191. Set the rip fence so the distance from it to the *outer* face of the blade equals the thickness of the stock.

2-190. Set saw blade projection at half the stock's thickness. Mark a piece carefully so you can use it as a gauge for other settings. Check by cutting a kerf and measuring it. Accuracy is *everything* in this job.

2-192. With the work against the miter gauge, butt the squared end against the fence, and make the first pass. When more than one joint is involved, be sure to make the same cut on similar pieces.

Making a "Simple" Rabbet Miter (cont'd.)

2-193.   Make a second cut on the same piece but with the work pulled away from the rip fence so the cut is *more than* halfway to the end of the work. It's important that you cut beyond the halfway point.

2-196.   With the new settings established, butt the end of the *mating* piece against the rip fence and advance it with the miter gauge to form the kerf.

2-194.   Make repeat passes to remove the material between the two kerfs. Although it's done here with a saw blade, there's no reason why you can't use a dado assembly to speed this part of the job.

2-197.   Set the saw blade at 45° and make the miter cut on the same piece. The miter cut and the inside bottom corner of the kerf must just meet. Blade projection is important so raise it a bit at a time until it is perfect.

2-195.   Leave the blade projection as is, and, using the same piece, reset the fence so distance from it to the outer face of the saw blade equals *half* the stock thickness. This setup will be used to make a cut on the *mating* workpiece.

2-198.   The same miter cut is made on the mating piece with the contact point at the very corner of the work. Saw-blade projection for this step is not so critical.

2-199.   The result of accurate work is two pieces that mate perfectly to form the joint.

end grain. This is a fine way to go but the joint really doesn't have any advantages as far as strength is concerned. The diagonal cut doesn't provide much more glue area than you have in a simple butt joint, and it's not the easiest joint to assemble in any woodworker's book.

Variations of the miter, to increase its strength and ease of assembly, are shown in this section. All of them look like a miter; what can't be seen is the additional "togetherness" you have provided. The joints are not difficult to make, but accuracy is critical. Work with a sharp, smooth-cutting blade. Take your time, re-check settings, make test cuts

when necessary, and be sure your table-saw components are in correct alignment.

Procedures are shown in a step-by-step sequence. Before doing any of them, study the general-application formula in Figure 2-188. If the examples don't suit a particular situation, you can use the formula to customize.

To do the "simple" rabbet-miter, follow figures 2-189 through 2-199. Steps to take for the more intricate "locked" rabbet-miter are demonstrated in Figures 2-200 through 2-206. Cuts to make to accomplish a "housed" rabbet-miter, are shown in Figures 2-207 through 2-210.

Making a "Locked" Rabbet Miter

2-200. This is the *locked* rabbet miter. The following illustrations show how it is done.

2-201. It pays to draw a layout of the joint on a test piece. Here, blade projection is half the stock thickness. This also applies to the distance from the fence to the *outer* face of the blade.

2-202. After the first cut on the *mating* piece, the groove is formed with the stock on end. The distance from the fence to the *inside* face of the blade equals *half* the stock thickness. Cuts like this, on narrow stock, should be made with a tenoning jig.

2-203. Set the blade projections to *equal* stock thickness. Form the groove by making repeat passes or by working with a dado. The width of the groove should equal the thickness of the tongue formed on the mating part. Work with a tenoning jig.

2-204. The miter cuts on the parts of the locked design are made exactly as if the joint were a simple rabbet miter. Here, the miter cut is shown being made on the same parts used in the first series of photos.

2-205. The mating part (the one already grooved) gets its miter cut as shown here. Through this whole operation it would pay to make trial cuts on scrap material similar to the good stock.

2-206. This is how the parts of the locked rabbet miter should join.

Splines and feathers. Splines and feathers are reinforcing, slim strips of wood set into grooves that are cut in the edges of mating pieces. Splines are often used to assemble miter joints (Figure 2-211), but they should not be limited to this application. Edge-to-edge joints, for example, gain a lot of strength and are easier to assemble when these special pieces are added (Figure 2-212). One good rule is to cut the strips so the grain of the wood runs across the narrow dimension. This gives them greater strength since it's more difficult to crack wood across the grain than with the grain. You can have ready-made splines if you work with thin plywood, which has a crossgrain pattern, or hardboard which has no grain at all.

Splines can be used on beveled joints whether they are simple or compound (Figure 2-213). They not only add strength, they make it a lot easier to put the pieces together correctly. Splines must enter at right angles to the work-edges. It's a little tricky to accomplish this if you work freehand, so make a guide-jig like the one shown in Figure 2-214. This is clamped to the rip fence and the work is moved between the legs of the jig to make the cut. The legs are cut to match the bevel angle on the work; blade projection should be one half the width of the spline.

The "feather" is like a spline, but triangular in shape and used most often across the edge of miter joints in, for example, picture frames. It's a good idea to cut feathers oversize so that, after the glue has dried, you can trim and sand them flush to adjacent surfaces. The best way to cut grooves for feathers is to make a fence-straddling jig (Figure 2-215). You'll know the grooves will be aligned since mating pieces are cut simultaneously. Mark the workpieces so you'll know which surface to place against the jig each time you cut.

Feathers can also be used *across* compound miter joints. This calls for a special V-jig which is secured to the miter gauge and used as shown in Figure 2-216. The work is positioned by the V-cut and is held securely in place as the cut is made.

The dovetail. Making dovetails is not really a table-saw operation, but the need for the application could arise for some special purpose such as a dovetail slot too large to be handled by more conventional means.

The idea is to make outline cuts with the saw blade slanted to the angle needed. Then, with the blade vertical, clean out the stock between. Blade slant, accuracy of cut, good depth-of-cut settings are all very important (Figure 2-217).

Decorative work. There are three techniques I use to do ornamental work using only the table saw. I call them, "weaving," "doodling," and "piercing." The methods are

Making a "Housed" Rabbet Miter

2-207. The *housed* rabbet miter is a good design for joining pieces that are different in thickness.

2-209. The miter cut on the thick stock starts exactly at the corner and just meets the bottom inside corner of the shoulder cut. Blade projection is critical.

2-208. Start with the thicker part. The blade projection equals the thickness of this part *minus* that of the thinner one. Fence distance to blade's *outer* surface equals the thickness of the thinner workpiece.

2-210. Final cut, on the thinner part, is a simple miter. When you have many similar cuts to make, it pays to clamp a block to the table that can be used as a stop to position the work for the cut. *Sawguard removed for clarity. Always use guard in actual practice.*

2-211.   Splines are, usually, slim strips of wood that fit into matching grooves that are cut in the edges of mating pieces.

2-213.   Splines can be used in beveled or compound miter joints. In addition to supplying strength, they make it easier to assemble components.

2-212.   Splines are strongest when they are cut so the grain direction runs across the narrow dimension. They can be used in assemblies other than miter joints.

2-214.   This type of jig makes it easier to form spline grooves in bevel cuts. Grooves for splines are always perpendicular to the bevel.

2-215.   Feathers are like splines but they are triangular in shape and installed across the corner of the assembly. Grain direction should be from the base to the point of the triangle. The best way to cut grooves for feathers to be used in miter joints is to work with this kind of fence-straddling jig.

practical, and the results can be rewarding, especially when you desire something different and exclusive for items like doors, room dividers, screens, and so on.

The "woven" technique calls for making multiple, stopped rip cuts inside a panel. When the material is flexible enough (and almost any material can be made flexible if you do enough cutting), it's easy to interweave with thin, wooden slats or another material (Figures 2-218 and 2-219). This procedure is a good place to employ the multiple-blade cutting technique (Figure 2-220).

"Doodling" produces workpieces like those shown in Figures 2-221 and 2-222. The technique calls for making matching cuts across opposite surfaces of a piece of lumber and then assembling strips that are rip-cut from the board. The strips are bonded edge-to-edge with contact cement or glue. Often, if the strips are thick enough or will be secured in a frame, you may not even have to do that. Some methods of cutting you can do with either a saw blade or a dado are shown in Figures 2-223 through 2-225; variations are unlimited.

Be sure to use a push stick when ripping the strips (Figure 2-226). Make and use a special insert if the strips are very thin to avoid having them pulled beneath the table by the action of the saw blade.

The third technique is "piercing," a term usually associated with the jigsaw. You make cuts on one side of a panel with the cutting tool projecting a bit more than half the panel's thickness. Then you turn the panel over and make opposing cuts (Figure 2-227). Openings are created where the cuts cross. These can be almost any shape depending on

2-216.   You can form feather-grooves in compound angle joints if you work with a V-jig like this one. The jig is attached to the miter gauge. The work is moved past the saw blade, or other cutter, while it is held securely in the V-jig.

2-217.   Dovetail joints are best cut on other tools, for example, a portable router, but you can follow this procedure if you wish to produce some on a table saw.

2-218.   Multiple, parallel saw cuts make it possible to "weave" panels so they can be used decoratively in many ways.

2-219.   The more saw cuts you make and the closer they are spaced, the more flexible the material becomes. The weaving strips can be similar material or something that contrasts like, for example, colorful plastic.

2-220. The multiple saw blade technique certainly finds good application for this kind of work. Use an outboard support when the stock you are cutting is very long. *Sawguard removed for clarity. Always use guard in actual practice.*

2-221. Surface cuts on wide pieces that are then strip-cut produce slats that can be assembled edge-to-edge to produce decorative panels. The designs that you can produce are infinite.

2-222. The cuts on the basic block (that was strip-cut into individual slats to form this panel) were not made with a conventional blade, but a smooth-cutting one.

2-223. The patterns you get depend on how you make the initial cuts. Here, by flipping the stock to make opposing cuts, you produce both V's and thin slots.

2-224. Cuts made with a tilted dado are the start for this pattern. You can gauge distance between cuts by first marking guide lines on the work.

how you plan the design and, to some extent, what cutting tool you use. The examples shown in Figure 2-228 were done with a regular saw blade.

Special Jigs

Anyone who can turn a key or push a button has the potential of a power tool at their disposal. The key word is "potential." To fully utilize a machine, one must advance even beyond what the manufacturer planned for it, and that's where special jigs come in. Some jigs help you do standard operations better, or faster, or more accurately and, often, in safer fashion. Some jigs save you money because, by making them, you avoid having to buy a commercial unit. Still others permit unique operations that can't be done with the tool alone. In some cases, the method can't be performed with normal guards in place. When this is so, be aware of the situation and use extreme caution. I like doing different things with tools and so will you, but safety must always be of paramount concern.

All of the jigs shown in this section, in fact throughout the book, are made, re-made, and thoroughly tested. The final prototype remains as a permanent accessory in my own shop.

2-227.   "Piercing" is done by making cuts on one side of the stock with cutter projection a bit more than half the stock's thickness. Then, other cuts are made after the stock has been inverted. A dado tool is used here. Note the use of the notched jig.

2-228.   A sample of the effects you can create when doing table-saw piercing with a regular saw blade. It's best to work with a saw blade that cuts smoothly.

2-225.   Invert the stock after the first cuts so you can make opposing cuts on the opposite surface.

2-226.   After the "shaping" operation the workpieces are strip-cut into slats that are then joined edge-to-edge to form a panel. Get the work past the blade by using a push stick.

2-229.   This jig, mounted on its own sliding table, vastly improves safety and accuracy on any kind of cut where it is necessary to hold work on end, especially if the workpiece is narrow.

2-230. Construction details of the all-purpose jig.

2-231. Cheek cuts on tongues and tenons can be made after the shoulder cuts are produced in conventional manner with the work flat on the table and moved with the miter gauge. One advantage of the jig is shown here, where work would fall into the insert slot if it were not supported.

2-232. Miter guides are attached to the face of the jig for positioning stock with angle-cut ends. Here, a spline groove is formed in a 45° miter cut.

2-233. Making the groove for a feather that will reinforce a 45° frame joint. You don't have to worry about the groove being exactly centered since both parts of the joint are cut at the same time.

All-purpose jig. This jig is mounted on its own sliding table (Figure 2-229), improves safety and accuracy on any cut where the stock must be held on its small edge. This includes tenons, grooves, tongues, and molding-head returns. The design is basically that of a tenoning jig, but because it's mounted on its own table, it's about as sophisticated as you can get without spending money for a commercial type.

Unless you own a very small table saw, the dimensions given in Figure 2-230 should be suitable. Do check the width of the sliding table against the distance between saw blade and table slot. If necessary, you can reduce the width or relocate the wooden bar that rides the slot. Leaving about 1-1/2″ between the left edge of the sliding table and the blade works quite well.

The position of the crosspiece on the table is critical. The angle between it and the saw blade must be 90°. The face piece of the carrier assembly must be 90° to the saw-table surface. The handsaw-type handle is very convenient, but the clamp carriage is optional. If you have a good variety of conventional woodworking clamps, you can get by without it.

You will get the maximum use out of this jig if you visualize it as a holder and carrier for stock that requires being held on a small edge in order to be cut. Setting up is just a matter of situating the carrier face in relation to the cutter

2-236.   A true tenon takes four passes after the shoulder cuts are made. If you work with a dado assembly, you can skip the shoulder cuts since the dado can do the whole job.

2-234.   This panel-raising operation is accomplished with greater accuracy and far more conveniently because of the special jig.

2-235.   Another job for the jig—chamfering the top of a 4x4. When the cuts you need prevent the bottom edge of the work from resting on the table (as here), use a piece of wood to establish work height before clamping it to the jig.

2-237.   Grooves of any width can be accurately centered by making two passes, reversing and clamping the work after the first pass. If stock remains after the first two passes, you can clear it away by making additional passes.

and the cutter projection in relation to required depth of cut.

Typical applications are demonstrated and explained in Figures 2-231 through 2-237.

A vertical table. This jig will do many of the jobs described for the all-purpose jig, but it's a unit you attach to the rip fence rather than a table of its own (Figure 2-238). Also, it has its own miter gauge so angular settings can be infinitely variable between extremes. Construction details are shown in Figure 2-239.

Be careful of the setback at the base of the platform

(the rabbet formed by the bottom miter-slide guide and the backup board). Determine this by the height of the rip fence; just a fraction less than the total rip-fence height is fine since you don't want the jig scraping the table when you position the fence.

2-238. A vertical table, made this way, is pretty much like having a workable miter gauge on a plane that is 90° to the saw table. It's like a tenoning jig but has a movable head that can be adjusted for angular work.

2-240. Cutting tenons is a typical job for the vertical table. The slide, with attached "miter-gauge" head, is moved horizontally, carrying the work with it.

2-239. Construction details of a vertical table you can make for your table saw.

The top edge of the bottom slide guide must be parallel to the table surface. Your best bet here, after the rabbets are cut, is to clamp this piece in position against the fence and clamp the backup board to it while you then fasten the two pieces together with screws. After that, you can remove the two pieces, put the miter slide in place, and screw on the top slide guide. The top slide guide should be fitted fairly snugly but not so tightly that the miter slide won't move easily. A coating of paste wax will help solve that problem.

Figures 2-240 and 2-241 show two of the jobs that can be done with the vertical table but this, as they say, is just the tip of the iceberg.

The "thingamajig." For lack of a better term, we'll label this device a "thingamajig." It's a strange looking table-saw accessory, but there are times when it functions in fine style on jobs inconvenient to do any other way. It can be used in either table slot or against either edge of the saw table. It will handle odd-angle cuts or tapers (Figures 2-242 and 2-243), or it can be used parallel to the saw blade for ripping or crosscutting small stock.

Make the guide (Figure 2-244) from 5/8" hardboard-surfaced plywood or a good hardwood. The arms are straight pieces 1-1/2" wide x 16-1/2" long. First cut the tenon on the end of each piece. This should be a snug fit in the slot cut in the guide. Repeat saw cuts will form the slots in the arms. The slight radius left by the saw blade at the ends of the cuts is not objectionable. Be sure that you hold the parts together when drilling the hole for the pivot. This should be a tight fit for a 1/4" bolt. Use hardwood for the table-slot bar and size it very carefully. Make it as tight a fit as possible without interfering with the sliding action. Be sure to recess the Tee-Nuts for a flush fit.

A master jig for the table saw. A sliding table is a super aid for anyone doing table saw work. Sawing is easier and accuracy increases since the work and the table move together. When the table has its own attachments for precise crosscutting, mitering, feathering, splining, tenoning, slotting, and many other standard (and some not so standard) operations, it becomes an accessory you'll keep on the saw for a hefty percentage of the work you do (Figure 2-245). It may even increase your work-scope and professionalism since it paves the way for some advanced cuts. All of the forms and cuts shown in Figure 2-246 can be accomplished with the master jig, once you have trained yourself to work with it.

The jig can't be a quickie job; consider it a lifetime investment and work accordingly. Accurate construction is important although we've built in some tolerances. For example, holes in the attachments are 5/16" even though they are secured with 1/4" locking hardware that threads into 1/4" T-nuts. This provides 1/16" of adjustment so when

2-241.   Since the head is adjustable, you can position and feed angular-cut pieces without having to add extra guides.

2-242.   I've used the thingamajig for jobs like tapering stock to be used as furniture legs. Make cuts on two adjacent sides and then reset the jig for the last two cuts. *Sawguard removed for clarity. Always use guard in actual practice.*

2-243.   Cuts on wide stock can be done this way, with the thingamajig riding the edge of the saw table. The jig may be used in either table slot or against either edge of the saw table. You can also turn it around and use it backwards. The jig does not prevent the use of the saw guard.

2-244. This is how you can make a thingamajig.

you add an attachment, say, the right angle guide to the vertical work support, you can use a square to be sure the bearing edge of the guide is 90° to the table.

Construction details for the jig and its accessories as well as material lists for parts and hardware are shown in Figures 2-247, 2-248, and 2-249. Although it is not shown in the photographs, the master jig is equipped with a special guard (Figure 2-250). The guard is adjustable vertically and horizontally so the blade and the cut being made will always be covered by the plastic shield. Adjust the height of

the guard so that it's always between 1/4″ and 1/2″ above the blade. The width of the shield keeps your hands away from the cutting area.

The guard should be used for all operations with the sliding table. It's not for use with the vertical work-support system, but with that accessory, hands never have to be placed in a hazardous position.

The prototype is being used on a Rockwell 10″ Unisaw that has a 27″ x 36″ table. We've checked many other 9″ and 10″ machines (the most popular sizes) and found that, with

2-245. The master jig is probably one of the most sophisticated accessory tools you can make for the table saw. It's basically a sliding table but with attachments that help you do standard, and some not so standard, operations safely and more accurately.

2-246. Once you become fully acquainted with the master jig, you can use it to cut all the forms and shapes that are shown here.

LOCKING HARDWARE

$\frac{1}{4}$" WING NUTS (8 REQ)

$\frac{1}{4}$" FLAT WASHERS (8 REQ)

2" LENGTHS OF $\frac{1}{4}$" THREADED ROD (8 REQ)

3"

4"

5$\frac{1}{2}$"

12"

1$\frac{1}{2}$"

$\frac{5}{16}$" X 9" SLOT

$\frac{3}{4}$" X 8" X 24"

1$\frac{1}{2}$"

4$\frac{1}{2}$"

4$\frac{1}{2}$"

2$\frac{3}{4}$"

1$\frac{7}{8}$" RAD.

#10 X 1$\frac{1}{2}$" F.H. WOOD SCREW (TYPICAL)

4$\frac{1}{2}$"

4$\frac{3}{4}$"

1"

10$\frac{1}{2}$"

3"

1$\frac{1}{2}$"

3$\frac{1}{2}$"

4$\frac{1}{2}$"

1"

3$\frac{3}{4}$"

1$\frac{1}{2}$"

5$\frac{3}{4}$"

8"

$\frac{3}{8}$"

1"

5$\frac{3}{4}$"

$\frac{1}{4}$" PRONGED T-NUT 6 REQ. DRILL $\frac{5}{16}$" HOLES FOR T-NUTS

DETAIL A

$\frac{5}{16}$"

$\frac{1}{4}$" PRONGED T-NUT SET FLUSH

$\frac{3}{4}$" RAD. (TYPICAL)

$\frac{5}{16}$" HOLE

1$\frac{1}{2}$" X 3$\frac{1}{2}$" X 24"

$\frac{1}{4}$" X 2" BOLT (2 REQ)

FLAT WASHER

8"

2$\frac{3}{4}$"

8"

1$\frac{1}{2}$"

2$\frac{1}{2}$"

1$\frac{1}{4}$"

1$\frac{5}{8}$"

12"

10$\frac{3}{4}$"

2$\frac{3}{4}$"

3$\frac{5}{8}$"

3"

6"

6"

3"

2$\frac{1}{2}$"

2$\frac{1}{4}$"

ALUMINUM

2$\frac{3}{4}$"

3$\frac{5}{8}$"

SEE DETAIL A

SAW KERF

1"

10$\frac{3}{4}$"

3"

4"

2"

TO SUIT

ATTACH BARS WITH 5 NO. 8 X $\frac{3}{4}$" F.H. WOOD SCREWS

$\frac{1}{2}$" X 26" X 28"

1$\frac{7}{8}$" RAD.

2-247. Construction details of the master jig. It's not a job to do quickly. You will defeat its purpose if you don't make and assemble the parts in good style.

1⅞" RAD.

1½"

4½"

3"

¾"

½" X 6" X 8"

3"   1¾"

1½"

5/16" HOLE CENTERED

RABBET
½" DEEP
¾" WIDE

6"   2½"   3"

½" X 12" X 26"

⅜ X 10" SLOT

1¼"

½" X 2¼" X 4½"

3"   3"   3"   3"   3"   3"

5/16" (TYPICAL)

FLAT WASHER

HOLD-DOWN

¼" X 4"
BOLT

1½" X 6½" X 14"

9¼"

90°

TO SUIT

⅜ X 4½" SLOT

NOTCHING JIG

¼" X ¾" F.H.
BOLT
(2 REQ.)

3"

13"

2¼"

11½"   ¾"
1¾"

9"

CIRCLE
CUTTING GUIDE

½" X 15" X 18"

12"

9"

3"   4"

10¾"

¾"

2"

90°

CUT KERF AFTER
GUIDES ARE INSTALLED

5/16" HOLES

TABLE
MITER
GUIDE

LEFT AND RIGHT
VERTICAL MITER
GUIDES

1⅞" RAD.

45°

5½"

1"

½"

¾"

¾"

5¾"

8"

5/16" (TYPICAL)

#10 X 1½" SHEET
METAL SCREW

¼" WASHER 3 REQ

1"   1¼"

4⅞"

4⅛"   3"

ADJUSTABLE
STOP

3/16" SLOT

2"

¾" X 1½" X 34"

1" RAD.

PART	NO. PCS.	SIZE	MATERIAL
Sliding Table			
Main table	1	1/2″ x 26″ x 28″	Cabinet grade plywood
Table cover	1	26″ x 28″	Aluminum sheet
Bars	2	3/8″ x 3/4″ x 36″	Hardwood
Crosscut fence	1	1-1/2″ x 3-1/2″ x 24″	Hardwood
Vertical Work Support			
Base	1	3/4″ x 12″ x 24″	Cabinet grade plywood
Face	1	3/4″ x 8″ x 24″	Cabinet grade plywood
Brace	2	1-1/2″ x 5-1/2″ x 12″	Hardwood
Table Miter Guides			
Guides	2	3/4″ x 12″ x 16″	Cabinet grade plywood
Adjustable Stop			
Bar	1	3/4″ x 1-1/2″ x 34″	Cabinet grade plywood or hardwood
Stop	1	1-1/4″ x 3″ x 4-7/8″	Hardwood
Circle Cutting Guide			
Platform	1	1/2″ x 15″ x 18″	Cabinet grade plywood
Taper Guide			
Platform	1	1/2″ x 12″ x 26″	Cabinet grade plywood
Stop	1	1-1/2″ x 1-3/4″ x 3″	Hardwood
Clamp pad	1	1/2″ x 2-1/4″ x 4-1/2″	Hardwood or plywood
Vertical Miter Guides			
Guides	2	1/2″ x 5-1/2″ x 8″	Cabinet grade plywood
Right Angle Guide			
Guide	1	1/2″ x 6″ x 8″	Cabinet grade plywood
Hold-Down			
Bar	1	5/8″ x 1-1/2″ x 18″	Hardwood
Example Notching Jig			
Guide	1	1/2″ x 6-1/2″ x 14″	Cabinet grade plywood

2-248.   These are the materials you will need to make the master jig for the table saw.

Sliding Table
9	1/4″ pronged Tee-Nuts
10	#8 x 3/4″ fh wood screws
2	1/4″ x 2″ bolts
2	1/4″ flat washers

Vertical Work Support
6	1/4″ pronged Tee-Nuts
13	#10 x 1-1/2″ fh wood screws

Adjustable Stop
3	#10 x 1-1/2″ panhead sheet metal screws
3	1/4″ flat washers

Circle Cutting Guide
2	1/4″ x 3/4″ fh bolts

Hold-Down
1	1/4″ x 4″ bolt
1	1/4″ flat washer

Locking Hardware
8	1/4″ wing nuts
8	1/4″ flat washers
8	1/4″ x 2″ lengths of threaded steel rod

Guard
2	5/16″ Tee-Nuts
6	5/16″ flat washers
6	5/16″ nuts
2	5/16″ x 6″ lengths of threaded steel rod

2-249.   Hardware requirements for the master jig.

2-250. This guard was especially designed to be used with the master jig.

extensions, table areas are pretty similar, so the dimensions in the drawings are generally applicable for those saw-sizes. It won't matter if your saw has a larger table but, sized as shown, the master jig might be too big on, for example, a very small 8″ tool and will have to be scaled down so it won't be unwieldy.

The thickness of the sliding table does reduce maximum blade projection but since this is normally anywhere from 2-3/4″ to about 3-1/2″, depending on the saw, reducing it by 1/2″ isn't critical for the kind of work you'll do with the jig. The only customizing needed is on the dimensions of the bars and their placement on the main table. These slide in the table slots and the position of these varies from saw to saw.

Use a good grade of maple or birch plywood for the sliding table and, after the part has been sized and the corners rounded, use fine sandpaper to smooth surfaces and edges. Cut a sheet of aluminum (Reynolds Do-It-Yourself®

aluminum works fine) to match and bond it to the table with contact cement.

Next, shape the bars. They are listed as 3/8″ x 3/4″, which seems right for most saws, but check on your own equipment. Sand the bars so they will slide easily in the table slots but without wobble. Put the bars in position and then place the sliding table so it is centered over the saw blade and so its edges are parallel to the table slots. Use C-clamps at one end to hold the bars in position and then drive a small brad to secure them. Repeat this procedure at the opposite end of the table and then permanently attach the bars with #8 x 3/4″ fh wood screws. Be sure to drill shank holes for the screws. If you don't, driving the screws may spread the bars and cause them to fit too tightly in the table slots.

The next step is to form the saw kerf. Work with a

2-251.   Built-in adjustments allow components to be locked in correct relationships. Here, a square is used to be sure the fence is 90° to the saw blade before it is locked in place.

2-253.   The vertical right-angle guide is used for end cuts such as slots and tenons. Before locking it in position, check with a square to be sure guide's bearing edge is 90° to the table.

2-252.   The table miter guides are more than guides for miter cuts. Here, they position round stock for slotting. Use the same system to find centers of round or square stock. Use minimum blade projection and make cuts at right angles: center is where the shallow kerfs intersect. Don't do this kind of thing on stock that is too small to be held safely.

2-254.   To form a slot in narrow work, set the vertical work support to the width you want the shoulder of the slot to be. Make a pass, reverse the stock and make another—the slot will be centered. If waste remains between the two cuts, remove it by making additional passes.

good, smooth-cutting blade: one you will always use with the master jig. *Don't* use a conventional hollow-ground blade. A high-quality, carbide-tipped combination blade is a good way to go. With the machine off, set the blade to its lowest point and put the sliding table in place. Then turn on the machine and very slowly raise the blade until it cuts through the sliding table. Keep your hands well away from the cut-area when you do this and as you move the table to lengthen the kerf.

Very carefully mark the locations for all the T-nuts that are needed in the table. Work with a scriber but mark lightly so you don't mar the aluminum. Mark the hole locations with a sharp punch and then drill a 1/16″ hole at each place. Use a 3/4″ brad-point bit on the underside to form a 1/16″ counterbore, and then, from the top side, enlarge each hole to 5/16″. Install the 1/4″ T-nuts by tapping them

into place with a hammer. They must be flushed with, or slightly below the surface of the plywood.

Shape the crosscut fence and then drill the 5/16″ holes for the bolts that are used to secure the fence to the table. The three hole locations on the top edge of the fence are for the screws that hold the adjustable stop when it is used.

The table miter guides are two pieces rather than a one-piece V-block for this reason. Use both pieces when mitering parts that have been pre-cut to length. Use either the left- or right-hand guide (with crosscut fence removed) when making consecutive miter cuts on a single length of stock.

Mark the 45° angle on each guide by using a combination square. Saw *approximately* to the line and finish by sanding *exactly* to the line. Lock them on the table so the short ends abut and the joint is centered over the kerf. Then move the table so the saw blade, in effect, cuts them apart. When the guides are mounted, use a triangle to be sure they

2-255. To form tenons, first make shoulder cuts and then use the jig this way for the cheek cuts. For each cheek cut you just reverse the stock's position. Use same-size scrap under the free end of the hold-down.

2-257. To be sure a spline groove is centered, make two cuts, the second after reversing the stock. If you cut both pieces of the joint at the same time, it isn't critical for the groove to be *exactly* centered. If you are cutting four pieces, mark each so the same surface of the parts will be placed against the jig when cuts are made.

2-256. To set the vertical miter guides correctly, first lock one into place, checking with a triangle to be sure bearing edge is 45°. Secure the mating guide while checking with a square as shown here.

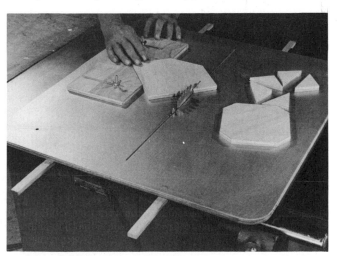

2-258. Notching jig can be used to form odd-shaped pieces or strange cuts that would be difficult to do in standard fashion. The shape of notching jigs must be custom-designed, according to what you need to do with it. *Sawguard removed for clarity. Always use guard in actual practice.*

are in correct alignment with the saw kerf.

When you make the vertical work support, you must be sure that its face will be 90° to the table. First make the base—the slots can be formed by making repeat passes with a saw blade—and then add the braces. Check with a square to be sure the front edge of the braces are 90° to the base.

Shape the face and carefully lay out locations for the T-nuts. Here, the T-nuts do not have to be set flush so all

you need do is drill a 1/16″ pilot hole and then enlarge it to 5/16″.

Mark the 45° angle on the vertical miter guides by using a combination square. Again, make an approximate saw cut and then sand exactly to the line. Here, as in other attachments, the installation holes are 5/16″ even though the locking hardware is 1/4″.

The right angle guide is pretty straightforward. Just be

2-259.   Forming circles with the master jig doesn't differ from the circle-cutting technique already described. With the jig, the platform on which the work rests is locked to the sliding table. The whole table is moved to make the tangent cuts. The table is clamped in position when the work is rotated for the final cuts. *Sawguard removed for clarity. Always use guard in actual practice.*

2-260.   The work guides for the rotajig are all the same in outer diameter, but differ in inside shape since this must be customized to suit the work. The guides must not wobble, yet be free enough to turn without being forced.

2-261.   Construction details on the rotajig.

sure its base and forward edge form a 90° angle.

Construction details for an adjustable stop, hold-down, circle cutting guide, taper guide, and an example notching jig, all of which are attachments for the master jig, are shown in the drawing. To form the long slot in the adjustable stop, first drill 3/16″ end-holes and then cut between them with a coping saw or on a jigsaw. The slots in the other attachments can easily be formed by making repeat passes on the saw.

Do the construction work carefully and be especially persnickety when marking locations for the T-nuts. Remember that whatever alignment adjustment is possible is due to the oversize holes in the attachments. Sand all parts to super smoothness before any assembly work. Apply several coats of sanding sealer, with a light sanding between coats and after the final one, to assembled components and to separate pieces. Apply paste wax, rubbed to a polish, to the saw table and to the bars and underside of the sliding table.

Typical applications and methods of adjusting the master jig are shown in Figures 2-251 through 2-259.

The rotajig. With this unusual tool you can form both round and square tenons on square or round stock, and you can do this work on the table saw using a saw blade or dado. The rotajig (Figure 2-260) connects to the miter gauge and works like an extension of the gauge, permitting conventional-type cross or miter passes.

Work guides (Figure 2-261) can be made to hold almost any odd-shaped piece so further cutting can be done accurately and safely. Each work guide you make becomes a permanent part of the setup for future use on similar applications. A critical dimension is the distance from the center of the holes in the guide holders to the table surface. As shown in the drawing, this tool is very good for a 10″ blade with about a 3″ projection. If your maximum blade projection is considerably less, you should probably adjust that one dimension to get maximum depth of cut on work held in the jig.

So that they will retain the work guides, make the holders from two pieces of stock with the hole in the thin piece a bit smaller than the hole in the thick piece. Then glue the two together. Use a fly cutter or hole saw to form the holes. If you don't have one of these tools, do the job on a jigsaw but make the cuts undersized so you can finish with a drum sander. This also applies to the retainers.

The work guides must fit well in the holders. Make them from the same material used for the holders and then reduce the thickness just a fraction by sanding. The kind of opening you make depends on the work, a square opening for square stock, a round opening for round stock (Figures 2-262 and 2-263), or a diamond-shaped, cross, quarter-round, or rectangular opening to correspond to the particular work shape. In some situations, guides can do double-duty. For example, if you have guides with a 1″ square opening, they can be used to work 1″ dowels.

Be sure that you provide for the slot in the miter-gauge connection piece since this makes it possible to situate the jig close to the cutter for maximum work support.

Figure 2-264 shows another use for the rotajig, one you can utilize if your machine permits substituting a sanding disc for the saw blade.

2-262.   How the rotajig is used. The work, positioned in the guides, is held very firmly and slowly rotated against the cutter's direction of rotation. Work very carefully and keep depth of cut to a minimum.

2-263.   You can form spirals with the jig if you lock it to the miter gauge which is clamped in place at the angle you need. Rotate the work very slowly. It will feed itself to maintain the "pitch" of the spiral.

2-264.   If your table saw can be equipped with a sanding disc, you can use the rotajig to do sanding operations on the end of round or square stock. Here, the end of a dowel is being shaped to a conical point. The dowel is rotated as it is moved toward the disc.

Lathe Work on the Table Saw

"Turning" bowls. By using quite a variation of the coving technique, you can form projects like the one shown in Figure 2-265, right on the table saw. Instead of an oblique feed (as in coving), the action here is rotary with the work jig-positioned over the saw blade. When the work and the saw blade are on the same centerline, the depression you create by making repeat passes is a true arc.

Be extra cautious! You can't use the regular guard when working with the jig shown in Figures 2-266 and 2-267, and even though the work covers the blade when you are doing inside cuts, a miscalculation might bring it through. So, always calculate the maximum projection you can use for the thickness of the stock.

You *can* use the guard for outside cuts even though it is not shown mounted in Figure 2-268. Even so, keep your hands well away from the cut area. The bulk of the work should be between you and the saw blade.

The overhead pivot jig is used for inside shaping; the simple bottom-pivot jig (Figure 2-269) is used for perimeter cuts. With the two you can accomplish complete bowl turning. The jigs must be securely clamped in position when they are being used. Overall dimensions of the jigs are not critical. If necessary, change them to suit your equipment.

2-267.   Work of any shape can be held by the pivot bolt. Form a slight depression in the center of the work by using a countersink. Then place the work and turn the pivot downward until it rests snugly in the countersink.

2-268.   Perimeter shapes are formed with the work pivot-mounted on a platform. Shapes you get will vary depending on the distance from the center of the work to the blade, blade height, and blade tilt. All shapes are produced with very light, repeat passes. The saw guard should be used on operations of this nature.

2-265.   You can use a variation of the coving technique to form bowl projects on the table saw.

2-266.   How to make the overhead pivot jig.

2-269.   The flat jig is simply a platform with twin bars that fit the table slots. Clamp it in place after you have decided its position on the saw table.

2-270.   Methods that allow varying the shapes produced by inside cuts. Some of these ideas can also be used to produce larger bowls.

2-271.   Some ideas on how to do the outside shaping. Note that different types of cuts can be combined to contribute to shape variety.

2-272.   Construction details of the fence jig that is used for spindle work.

The thickness of the platforms, in effect, reduces the maximum blade projection so don't make them thicker than 1/4″. Be sure the pivot support bar is well above the maximum blade-projection height. The distance between the vertical supports limits the size of the stock you can turn between them. However, this distance can be increased if you wish.

It's difficult to be precise about how much to raise the blade after each pass. Too little is much better than too much. Actually, you will know when you are trying to cut too deeply because you'll have to force the work, and this should never be necessary.

There is considerable freedom in designing, as shown in Figures 2-270 and 2-271. The complete design is based on the pivot point of the work as it relates to the centerline of the saw blade.

2-273. Reeding and fluting, two of the common "after" jobs in lathe work, can be accomplished on the table saw by using the fence jig. Repeat passes are made over the cutter after the work has been mounted between centers in the jig.

Fence jig for spindle work. Strangely enough, many intriguing lathe effects can't be accomplished on the lathe itself or by using conventional turning tools. Most longitudinal details—cuts like reeding and fluting—require a specially mounted and powered cutter, with the lathe—if it is used at all—merely a holding device for the work. Switching these functions to the table saw is really a logical alternative.

The rip fence is a ready-to-use guide. You have built-in depth-of-cut adjustments, and you can work with a molding head and its vast assortment of knives, a dado, or even a saw blade. Combine these assets with the fence jig, and you have a complete tool that is adjustable for work length and diameter. This jig also has mounting centers that can operate independently (Figure 2-272).

With the fence jig, you can make reeding or fluting cuts on stock that has been preshaped in the lathe or on ready-made cylinders such as large dowels or closet poles (Figure 2-273). In addition, by using a regular saw blade, you can "turn" square stock into round and, by working with offset centers, form a tapered leg from square or round stock (Figures 2-274 and 2-275). Once you have become familiar with the tool, many other possibilities than the ones illustrated will occur to you.

Follow the construction details for the jig very carefully. Use a good grade of hardwood or a hardboard-surfaced plywood for the parts.

When adjusting the jig for work length, first set the adjustable end in an approximate position and lock it in place with small C-clamps; then use the adjustable center for the final setting. Take up on the screw enough so the work will be held securely between centers.

Adjust the pivot arms for work height and lock in place. Set the rip fence so the centerline of the work will be directly over the cutter. Raising or lowering the cutter gives you the depth of cut you want.

2-274   You can "turn" square stock into a cylinder by making successive passes with a regular saw blade. The more passes you make, turning the work just a bit for each, the closer to "round" you get. Work carefully, with hands well away from the cut area.

2-275.   Using the same technique but with the work mounted on off-centers, you can saw tapers. Again, repeat, light-cut passes are needed. I've used this technique to form table and chair legs.

2-276. Construction details of the jig needed for circumference work.

2-277. Using the jig to form perfect beads without the need of lathe chisels. The beads are formed by the knives mounted in a molding head. A sure grip away from the cutting area, very slow feed, repeat passes against the cutters rotation, light cuts—all are essential.

2-278. Edge-shapes on a rectangular block can be left as decorative details or, another idea, the edges can be ripped off and used as half-round moldings.

At all times, be sure that the work is locked in position, that all jig locks are tight, and that you feed very slowly and with your hands well away from the cut area.

Jigs for circumference work.   With this table-saw jig you can turn a workpiece against an arbor-mounted cutting tool to achieve precise profiles that will rival the best efforts of a skilled woodturner (Figures 2-276 and 2-277).

The jig can be used with various cutters like saw blades, molding heads, and dadoing tools. If you work with a molding head, the "turning" patterns needn't be limited by a meager assortment of knives. By utilizing portions of knife profiles and even by combining separate cuts, you can extend the basic shapes considerably. When you use the jig with a dado tool, which allows wider cuts, you can produce cylinders from square stock and do many other jobs such as forming round tenons on either square or round workpieces. Example operations are shown in Figures 2-278 through 2-280.

If you remove the "miter-gauge bars," you can use the same jig along the rip fence to do fluting and reeding (Figure 2-281). Spacing of cuts can be judged, but for precision make an indexing disc like the one shown in Figure 2-282, which can be attached to the workpiece before it is mounted in the jig. A nail, inserted through the jig, engages successive holes in the indexing disc to position it for the cut and to keep it from turning during the pass.

An upside-down trolley version of the jig, shown in Figures 2-283 and 2-284, can be used for small-diameter work. The jig rides in the table's slots and uses the rip fence as a stop. To space cuts, you relocate the rip fence for each.

Don't try to make deep cuts in a single pass. Set the cutter, initially, so it barely touches the work. Obviously, when you are using the circumference jig, the action of the cutter will tend to spin the workpiece, so you must keep a firm grip and with hands well away from the cut area. *Don't ever* attempt to use these jigs with pieces so small that your

2-279.   Round tenons on square stock can be formed by making repeat passes. Here, the job was done with a regular saw blade. A dado assembly will make the job go faster.

2-280.   Tapered legs or spindles are "turned" by mounting work as it would be in a lathe—with a true center at one end and an offset center at the other. Be sure the work is secure and that the jig is clamped in position.

2-281.   If you wish to use the jig for reeding or fluting, you can remove the miter-gauge strips so the jig can be run along the rip fence. You can hand-hold the cylinder and judge spacing by eye but it's much better to work with the indexing device shown in the next illustration.

2-282.   An indexing disc is nailed to one end of the cylinder. A nail, inserted through the jig, engages successive holes in the disc to space the cuts and to keep the work from turning during the pass.

hands have to be placed near where the cutting is taking place. If you ever need a short piece, form it on a safely-handled long piece, and then cut off the section that serves the purpose. Remember, with a saw blade or a dado that is set to produce a narrow groove, you can make deeper cuts than you should ever attempt with a shaper knife that is mounted in a molding head. After you have made the starting cut, raise the cutter ever so slightly for each of the repeat passes that will eventually result in the form you need. The work is *always* rotated *against* the direction of rotation of the cutting tool.

For all of the jobs done with the circumference jig, unless it is being used along the rip fence, and for the trolley jig, the jigs must be securely clamped in place.

Trouble shooting. The chart shown in Figure 2-285 should be checked whenever an operation you are doing doesn't seem exactly right. It doesn't point out mechanical faults, those that have to do with the machine and which should be examined by reading the owner's manual. It does point up operational faults and, for example, those faults that might be caused by misalignment of components.

2-283.   Upside-down trolley is another version of the cylinder jig. The jig rides in the table slots and uses the rip fence as a stop for the work. You must be very careful on operations like this not to form sections so thin that the work can break apart as you are cutting. Always be very cautious on this and similar operations.

2-284.   How to make a cylinder jig for small diameter stock.

2-285.   A trouble-shooting chart for the table saw.

THE PROBLEM	POSSIBLE CAUSES	WHAT TO LOOK FOR OR DO
WHEN RIPPING		
Work is narrower than you need	Measuring from wrong side of blade	Always measure from side of blade nearest fence and from teeth set toward fence
Cut edge is not square	Blade-to-table angle is not correct Distorted stock	Check alignment—reset 0° auto-stop Material may have to be surfaced before ripping
Inaccurate bevels	Alignment or wrong settings	Check settings carefully—make trial cuts—check 45° auto-stop
Sides of cut gouged—excessive tooth marks	Blade chatter Poor work-handling Bad blade	Feed more slowly—be sure blade is sharp Keep work against fence throughout pass Replace or recondition

(Continued on next page)

THE PROBLEM	POSSIBLE CAUSES	WHAT TO LOOK FOR OR DO
WHEN RIPPING (Cont'd)		
Blade stalls—sides of cut show burn marks	Dull blade	Replace or sharpen
	Feeding too fast	Take more time to make cut
	Tough wood	Feed slowly—make repeat passes for deep cuts
	Accumulation of wood residue on blade	Clean blade
	Incorrect projection on hollow-ground blade	Hollow-ground blades require more projection than conventional blades
Kerf closes and binds blade	Moisture content in wood	Be sure to use splitter—use wedge in kerf if necessary
Work moves away from fence—work jams between fence and blade	Misalignment	Table slots should be parallel to blade—fence should be parallel to table slots
	Poor work-handling	Keep work against fence throughout pass
	Distorted stock	Edge that rides rip fence must be true
Work won't pass splitter	Misalignment	Be sure splitter lines up with saw blade
Kickback	Misalignment	Be sure anti-kickback fingers are adjusted
	Pass not completed	Be sure work is moved completely past the saw blade
WHEN CROSSCUTTING		
Cuts aren't square	Misalignment	Check miter gauge—reset 90° auto-stop
Work jams	Miter gauge square to slots but slots not parallel to blade	Be sure table slots are parallel to saw blade
Inaccurate cuts	Misalignment	Check miter gauge setting—make trial cuts—reset auto-stops
	Poor work handling	Keep work secure when making pass—use miter gauge hold-down if available
Cut has slight bevel	Misalignment	Be sure blade is square to table—check blade-tilt 0° auto-stop
Miter gauge binds in slots	Poor tool-keeping	Clean table slots and miter gauge bar—apply paste wax and rub to polish
Blade binds in kerf	Dull blade	Replace or sharpen
	Excessive work-overhang	Provide adequate support so work will level
WHEN DADOING/ MOLDING		
Bottom of dado or groove uneven	Dado chippers uneven—outside blades poorly matched	Chippers and blades should be jointed and sharpened as a set and kept in prime condition
	Inconsistent placement on saw arbor	Mark blades and chippers—line up marks each time units are mounted
Chatter—tool stalls	Cutting too fast—cutting too deep	Use a slow feed—make repeat passes for very deep cuts
	Dull tools	Be sure dado units, molding knives are sharp
Dado units, molding knives, wood, burn	Feeding too fast or cutting too deep	Slow up feed—make repeat passes
	Accumulation of wood residue on cutters	Clean—maintain in prime condition
	Dull cutters	Sharpen, and keep sharp
Excessive splintering or feathering at end of cut	Breaking out of cut too fast	End cut by feeding very slowly especially when cutting cross grain
Dado width inaccurate	Poor setup	Set adjustable dadoes carefully—dado assemblies sometimes require paper shims for exact width settings—make trial cuts
Molded edges not uniform	Poor work-handling	Keep work firmly down on table—or against fence—throughout pass

3. The Radial Arm Saw

If you combine the rigidity of a large stationary tool with the flexibility of the portable circular saw, you get a fairly good picture of what a radial arm saw is (Figure 3-1). Of course, with this machine you always bring the work to the tool; but the fact that you can swing, tilt, raise and lower or adjust the cutting direction of the blade makes the tool-work relationship comparable to hand-held saw applications.

When the tool is ideally situated, it's easy to trim off the ends of 20′ long pieces of 2″ stock or to reduce such material to shorter lengths. This capability is a great feature of the radial arm saw and explains why the original model was generally a contractor's tool. The saw's table was extended to the left and the right to provide a total length of as much as 20′ (Figure 3-2). Such support for long pieces that had to be crossed, mitered, and so on, made the tool ideal for people involved in house framing.

In modern versions, especially those designed for laymen's use, the tool still performs these basic applications well, but other features have been added and a wider range of applications devised so the inherent flexibility of the design is fully utilized. As a result, the radial arm saw enters the shop-in-one-tool category.

General Characteristics

Capacities. Radial arm saws differ in features and size and, sometimes, in the assortment of accessories that can be used with them. So, when shopping, it's wise to check out more than the basic tool. If the unit is to be your major power tool, then you want to be able to do as much as possible with it. It's difficult, these days, to find a unit that's specifically designed to work with less than a 9″ saw blade. Homeworkers usually do with a 9″ or 10″ machine while industry and contractors get involved with tools that are powered to turn blades that are 12″, 14″, 16″, even 18″ in diameter (Figures 3-3 and 3-4). However, this doesn't mean that if you have a 10″ product, you can't, when necessary, use it to turn a smaller diameter cutting tool: a 9″ or an 8″ blade or a 6″ dadoing tool.

With all modern saws you can mount dadoes and molding heads, do shaping and routing, accomplish many drilling and sanding chores, use it as a power source to drive flex shafts, and, sometimes, complement "individual" tools. An example of how a radial arm saw can be transformed

into another tool is shown in Figure 3-5. With this unique attachment, the saw becomes a stroke sander that can smooth pieces of any length and up to 30″ wide. Other interesting accessories for radial arm saws include a saber saw attachment and a special arbor-mount for a portable router.

Electronics are starting to affect, not so much what you can do with the tool, but the ease with which you can use it. The 10″ tool shown in Figure 3-6, features programmable blade height and power elevation. The touch control panel includes a digital display showing blade elevation to five one-thousandths of an inch, and bevel and miter angles to one-half degree. That "one-half degree" can pose a problem, especially if you are making eight cuts say, for a picture frame. You still want to do a test to be sure the setting is *perfect*. Happily, tools can't get by without US!

3-1.   The modern radial arm saw is used for more than sawing. With accessories, and special jigs you can make, it will do drilling, sanding, shaping, even saber sawing and routing.

3-2.   Contractors and industry set up the saw so it will provide support for long work-pieces. You can do the same. This is a large, turret arm model.

3-3.   Most machines for home use work with a 9″ or 10″ saw blade, but you can work with smaller diameter cutting tools; molding head, 6″ dado assembly, and so on.

3-5.   Unique accessories are available for some model saws, like this add-on that allows surface-sanding on long and wide material.

3-4.   Bigger machines handle bigger blades. Blades 18″ in diameter, even more, are not uncommon in, for example, lumberyards where cutting large timbers is routine.

3-6.   New electronic radial arm saw features programmable blade height and power elevation. Digital display shows blade elevation and bevel and miter angles; makes the machine easier to use, but YOU are still the boss.

As far as sawing is concerned, the big difference between the radial arm and the table saw can be demonstrated with a simple crosscut. On the table saw, you hold the work against the miter gauge and advance both the gauge and the wood past the blade to make the cut. On the radial tool, the work is set on the table and against a fence. The saw blade is pulled through to make the cut (Figure 3-7). Obviously, this procedure can have advantages in some areas—typically, on some angular cuts where a stationary workpiece can help achieve accuracy.

Tool capacities (Figure 3-8) are listed as maximum crosscut, which has to do with how wide a board can be cut in a single pass, maximum rip cut, which tells how far away from the fence you can set the blade, and maximum depth of cut, which tells the thickest piece of stock you get through with one cut.

Features. Design details may differ, but all radial arm saws have the same controllable features shown in Figure 3-9. The motor, which usually has a *main* and an *auxiliary* arbor, is cradled in a yoke which hangs from an overhead carriage that is movable to and fro along an arm that extends over the table.

Figure 3-10 shows a basic cut action. You pull the motor unit toward you to make the cut, away from you to a position behind the fence to complete the pass action. The motor, the yoke, and the arm are all adjustable, and each component can be locked in a particular position to situate the saw blade for any cut you wish to make. For a miter,

3-7.   Crosscutting is done by securing the work and pulling the saw blade through to make the cut. Hand holding the work must always be well away from the cut-path.

3-9.   Basic nomenclature of a radial arm saw. Features may differ from machine to machine but all will have these essential components. Many units have all controls at the front of the arm.

3-8.   Tool capacities are listed as maximum crosscut, maximum rip, and maximum depth of cut. Even "small" units will cut through 2″ stock at 90° and 45°.

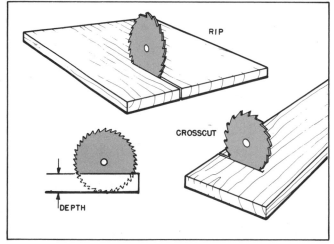

3-10.   Basic cut action of the radial arm saw. The blade turns clockwise so it tends to keep the work down on the table and against the fence.

you simply swing the arm. For a cross-miter, you tilt the blade. When you do both, you get a compound cut (Figure 3-11).

The rotation of the saw blade is away from you. In essence, its action is to hold the work down on the table and against the fence as you make the cut by pulling the blade toward you. If you feed too fast, the blade will tend to "walk," much like a tractor tread. So feed speed is critical. For smoother cuts and safety, it's better to feed a little too slowly than too rapidly.

The yoke can swivel 360° (Figure 3-12). A 90° turn will place the blade parallel to the fence; this is the rip position. For ripping, you secure the blade in a particular position and move the work for the cut. When you turn the blade 90° toward the column, you set up for "in-ripping."

When you turn the blade 90° away from the column, you organize for "out-ripping." The latter position is used for extra-wide rip cuts (Figure 3-13).

On rip operations, you feed the work against the blade's rotation. Therefore, the blade tends to fight feed pressure. This can cause kickback if you neglect to use the anti-kickback "fingers." This safety item (Figure 3-14), is mounted on a rod that is situated in the saw guard. The fingers do not interfere with normal pass direction, but they dig in if the blade tries to fight you. It only takes seconds to set them up regardless of stock thickness.

It's normal on the radial arm saw for the blade to cut into the table; it has to in order to get through the stock. Each time you change the saw-blade position, for a miter or a rip cut or whatever, you make a new cut in the table (Figure 3-15). These cuts, which shouldn't be more than about 1/8″ deep, shouldn't bother you since it's a routine procedure. Those you will need most often are for crosscutting, 45° mitering, and basic ripping, but don't form them in a new machine until you have gone through component-alignment procedures.

When you do a lot of experimental cutting that might distress the table beyond normal needs, or when you must cut a kerf in the table for one-time use, you can protect it with a thin material that takes the abuse. This covering can

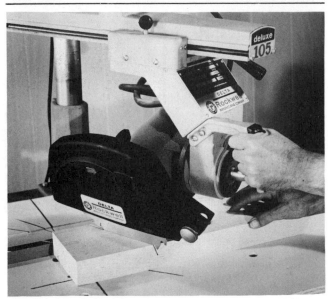

3-11. To set the blade in mitering position, you swing the arm. If you add a blade-tilt, you will have a compound-angle cut.

3-12. The motor unit can turn a full circle and tilt through 180°. It's this flexibility that provides almost unlimited relationships between cutting tool and work position.

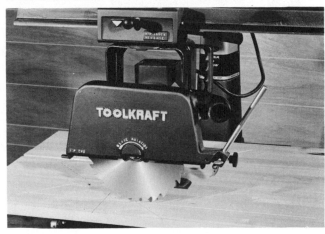

3-13. Ripping is done with the blade set parallel to the fence. This is the out-rip position shown on a turret arm machine.

3-14. Anti-kickback fingers, situated like this, must always be used on ripping operations. They don't interfere with the pass, but will dig in should the blade try to move the work back toward the operator.

be a sheet of plywood that you tack-nail in place or, preferably, a special unit that you can slide into position whenever you have need for it (Figure 3-16).

Consider the fence an expendable item. If you use the saw for nothing but crosscutting, one fence might last forever. But when many other saw cuts and different non-sawing operations are involved, the fence will be punished and should be replaced when necessary. Also, there will be times when you wish to alter the fence to suit a particular technique. Happily, the fence is nothing but a straight piece of wood. It's a good idea to make several fences (Figure 3-17) to be ready to use when needed. Many times, a fence designed for a particular use should be retained for future, similar applications.

Work Support

One of the major advantages of the radial arm saw is the ease with which you can make cuts on long pieces of material. But this feature must be developed to make it wholly operational. Supplying more work support than you get from the tool's table is the answer whether the machine is on casters so you can move it about or whether you place it in a fixed position.

A common work support is a roller-top floor stand, much like the ones that are usable with a table saw. When used with the radial arm saw, a stand can be positioned to provide outboard support whether you are crosscutting or ripping. One that you can buy is shown in Figure 3-18, supporting a wide panel on a ripping operation. The construction ideas for one that you can make are detailed in Figure 3-19. Since the height of the units is adjustable, these floor stands may be used with other tools.

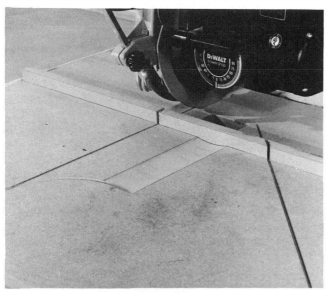

3-15. Cuts like this in the saw's table are normal. They should be made after the tool has been checked for correct relationship of components.

3-17. It's a good idea to have spare fences on hand. Those made for a special application should be retained for future use.

3-16. An auxiliary table can protect the regular table from abuse. This one slides into place when needed.

Labels in figure 3-16: SAW TABLE · 1/4" PLYWOOD · RABBET FITS TABLE EDGE · 2" x 2" STOCK

3-18. An extension stand you can buy will provide extra support for large workpieces. It can be used when crosscutting or ripping.

Contractors, who normally set the tool up outdoors and have no space limitations, and lumber-supply people, who also have no space problems, usually use fixed, roller-type extensions. When the tool is so equipped, it's no chore to square off the ends of pieces that are 20' or more long. That example may seem extreme, but it is a fact that you may need a similar setup even if the lengths you ordinarily work with are only 6, 8 or 10 feet long.

Beyond the freestanding roller-top unit, there are other work-supports you can make. They can be considered permanent attachments but are easy to remove when necessary. For example, the roller-type extension which is seen in Figure 3-20 can be knocked down by removing a few screws. The hinged versions, one of which is expandable (Figure 3-21), swing down when not being used so they add little to the floor space required for the saw. Also, the hinged extensions won't interfere with mobility if you have the tool on a stand with casters.

Figure 3-22 gives specific dimensions for the roller type, but these dimensions can be changed to suit your own requirements. Two of these units, attached at either side of a 3' saw table, will give you over 11' of work support. If you want to make them longer, just supply more leg assemblies. If you work regularly with heavy structural lumber, you may prefer a stronger frame by substituting 2 x 4's for the 5/8" side pieces shown.

Suitable material for the rollers can range from antenna masts to seamless tubes. Just get something with enough wall thickness to be strong and with at least 1-1/2" O.D. You can cut the plugs for the tube ends with a hole saw. Cut the plugs just enough oversize so they will fit tightly. The hole saw will also provide an accurate center hole. The bolt "axles" must be secured before the plugs are inserted.

For the hinged versions, the length of the extension table must be related to the distance from the saw-table surface to the floor. This is necessary so the extensions can be tilted down to storage position. This does impose limitations since the length of the extension must accommodate the table-to-floor dimension. You can get around this nicely if you make the project as shown in Figure 3-23. This unit incorporates a slide so the extension can be lengthened much like a dining table. If you make it as shown, with one extension attached on each side of the main table, you can get 13' of work support without sacrificing space-saving advantages.

3-20. You can make a roller-top extension that works like those produced commercially. You can easily remove it, when necessary, since it is secured to the table with just a few screws.

3-21. Extensions can also be attached with hinges. You swing them down out of the way when they are not needed. This one is designed to be expandable—like a dining table.

3-19. Here is a roller-top extension stand you can make. Its height is adjustable so it can be used on tools other than the radial arm saw.

3-22.   How to make the roller type extension table.

3-23.   The expandable extension, designed to be hinged to the tool's table, is made this way.

Start this project by shaping the guides and the block that attaches to the table. Follow with the slides but dress down the dimensions just enough so they will move freely in the guide grooves. Attach the guides to the block by using 3″ T-hinges and set this assembly on a flat surface.

After you cut the extension table to size, use clamps to hold it to the slides. Then, put this in place on the guides and make any necessary adjustment to be sure the table will move freely. Make the assembly permanent by using #8, 1-1/2″ fh wood screws in place of the clamps. When you locate the extension table, be sure its forward edge lines up with the forward edge of the saw table.

Then you can cut and attach the cleat to the outboard end of the inner slides. When you make the leg assembly, adjust the height to match the distance from the saw-table surface to the floor. Attach to the cleat with 1-1/2″ butt hinges.

Hold the block to the saw table with clamps and then drill for, and drive home, the #12, 2″ screws that secure it.

If you prefer not to get involved with the sliding action you can make a similar extension by working as shown in Figure 3-24. To assure that the extension will be level with the tool's table, make the upper part first and attach it with the two hinges. Then you can make and attach the leg assembly, sizing its total length to suit. Adjustment is possible in the area on the drawing marked "A", or by changing the leg-length.

3-24. If you would rather skip the extra work involved in making the expandable extension, you can duplicate this idea.

A Complete Shop for a Radial Arm Saw

The design shown here (Figure 3-25) is a permanent part of my workshop. It's a very practical concept and is suitable whether the radial arm saw is to be your only tool or one of many.

The plan is designed for efficient use of the tool and easy construction. It doesn't require more than 40 square feet of floor space yet it provides ample storage facilities for the tool and its accessories as well as for a good assortment of portable tools and the items used with them.

Actually, it isn't difficult to organize ideally for the radial arm saw since the average machine requires less than 3 square feet of space and is perfectly efficient when backed against a wall. Little maneuvering space is required in front of it, but it's nice to have space on each side. The base cabinets in the shop act as extensions of the tool's table so you get good support for oversize workpieces. The length of work you can handle is not limited by the length of the shop, not if you cut an access door through an adjacent wall. Extra-long boards simply poke through the side of the building! Due to the access door, just about any length material can be handled in a shop that is little more than 10' long.

Putting the shop together is not a difficult chore but it's certainly not a one-evening project. Your best bet, with the tool on its own stand, is to begin by framing the base cabinets. Then the tool will be usable for whatever you wish to do with it, and you choose when and how much time to devote to finishing the shop.

Construction information is contained in Figures 3-26 through 3-42.

3-25.   A shop designed specifically for a radial arm saw. Base cabinets are also support areas on each side of the tool. There is a generous amount of storage area for accessories and other tools.

3-27.   If you cut carefully when you form the access, you can make the door by using the cutaway material. The bottom of the opening should be a bit below the surface of the bench.

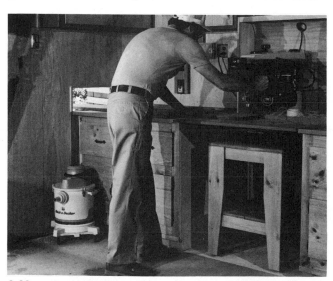

3-26.   An opening through the wall at the end of the base cabinet allows working on extra-long stock. The work simply pokes through the side of the building.

3-28.   A friend uses a special little building as a radial arm saw shop. His access door is better than 4' wide. Thus, he can slip in full size panels.

3-31. The workshop will be nice to look at because the framing is "veneered" with a good grade of plywood. I used knotty pine. Install runners for drawers before you install the bench tops.

3-29. When you cut through a wall, you must install a header to compensate for the strength that is lost when the studs are cut. This should be done in line with local building codes.

3-32. Cabinets are rather easy to install if you work this way. A frame, covered with perforated hardboard, around which you add other components.

3-30. Framing material for the base cabinets doesn't have to be fancy, but it should be dry.

3-33. The perforated hardboard allows the use of standard hangers.

3-34.   Use perforated hardboard on the backs of cabinet doors. Mount the hardboard on strips so there will be space for inserting the hangers.

3-35.   Design the inside of some of the cabinets for storage of other tools. There is more than enough room for a full set of portable equipment.

3-36.   This is how the shop was constructed. Parts are keyed to the materials list. Some dimensions are oversize so you can trim to fit. Of course, sizes can be modified, if necessary, to suit available space.

NO.	NO. PCS.	SIZE	MATERIAL
1	1	3/4 x 2 x 122-1/2	Fir lumber
2	2	3/4 x 2 x 45-1/4	Fir lumber
3	2	3/4 x 2 x 24-1/2	Fir lumber
4	1	3/4 x 2 x 39-1/4	Fir lumber
5	1	3/4 x 2 x 36	Fir lumber
6	1	3/4 x 2 x 36	Fir lumber
7	1	1/8 x 24-1/2 x 46-1/2	Perforated hardboard
8	1	1/8 x 17-3/4 x 36	Perforated hardboard
9	1	1/8 x 24-1/2 x 40	Perforated hardboard
10	1	1/8 x 24-1/2 x 48	Perforated hardboard
11	1	3/4 x 10 x 113-3/4	Pine lumber
12	2	3/4 x 10 x 47-1/4	Pine lumber
13	2	3/4 x 10 x 26	Pine lumber
14	1	3/4 x 10 x 46-1/2	Pine lumber
15	2	3/4 x 10 x 6	Pine lumber
16	1	3/4 x 10 x 37-1/2	Pine lumber
17	1	3/4 x 10 x 40	Pine lumber
18	6	3/4 x 2 x 26	Pine lumber
19	3	3/4 x 2 x 24	Pine lumber
20	1	3/4 x 2 x 18	Pine lumber
21	2	3/4 x 2 x 34	Pine lumber
22	2	3/4 x 2 x 30	Pine lumber
23	2	3/4 x 2 x 36	Pine lumber
24	2	3/4 x 2 x 46	Pine lumber

Left-Hand Floor Unit

NO.	NO. PCS.	SIZE	MATERIAL
25	4	2 x 4 x 40	Fir lumber
26	2	2 x 4 x 31-1/4	Fir lumber
27	1	2 x 4 x 36	Fir lumber
28	1	2 x 4 x 32	Fir lumber
29	2	2 x 4 x 27-1/4	Fir lumber
30	2	2 x 4 x 29-1/4	Fir lumber
31	1	2 x 4 x 28-1/4	Fir lumber
32	2	2 x 4 x 27-1/4	Fir lumber
33	2	2 x 4 x 25	Fir lumber
34	2	2 x 4 x 33-1/8	Fir lumber

Right-Hand Floor Unit

NO.	NO. PCS.	SIZE	MATERIAL
35	1	3/4 x 32 x 48	Fir plywood
36	1	1/8 x 32 x 48	Tempered hardboard
37	1	3/4 x 31-3/4 x 48	Fir plywood
38	1	1/4 x 2 x 48	Pine
39	1	3/4 x 4 x 48	Pine
40	1	3/4 x 4-3/4 x 48	Pine
41	1	3/4 x 3 x 48	Pine
42	2	3/4 x 2 x 26	Pine
43	1	3/4 x 4 x 44	Pine
44	1	3/4 x 2 x 14	Pine
45	1	3/4 x 2 x 12	Pine

Right-Hand Floor Unit

NO.	NO. PCS.	SIZE	MATERIAL
25	4	2 x 4 x 48	Fir lumber
26	2	2 x 4 x 31-1/4	Fir lumber
27	1	2 x 4 x 44	Fir lumber
28	1	2 x 4 x 40	Fir lumber
29	2	2 x 4 x 27-1/4	Fir lumber
30	2	2 x 4 x 29-1/4	Fir lumber
31	1	2 x 4 x 28-1/4	Fir lumber
32	2	2 x 4 x 27-1/4	Fir lumber
33	2	2 x 4 x 25	Fir lumber
34	2	2 x 4 x 33-1/8	Fir lumber

Left-Hand Floor Unit

NO.	NO. PCS.	SIZE	MATERIAL
35	1	3/4 x 32 x 40	Fir plywood
36	1	1/8 x 32 x 40	Tempered hardboard
37	1	3/4 x 31-3/4 x 40	Fir plywood
38	1	1/4 x 2 x 40	Pine
39	1	3/4 x 4 x 40	Pine
40	1	3/4 x 4-3/4 x 40	Pine
41	1	3/4 x 3 x 40	Pine
42	2	3/4 x 2 x 26	Pine
43	1	3/4 x 4 x 36	Pine
44	1	3/4 x 2 x 14	Pine
45	1	3/4 x 2 x 12	Pine
46	3	1/4 x 32 x 36	Fir plywood

3-37. Materials list for the radial arm saw shop. Bench tops are hardboard over plywood but you can substitute 1″ dense particleboard.

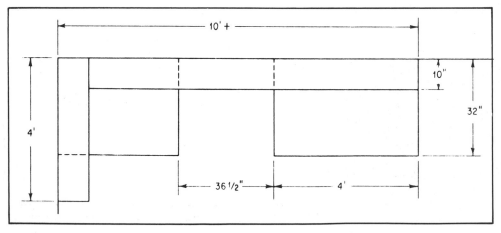

3-38. Floor plan of the shop. Any changes will affect the sizes listed in the bill of materials.

3-41.   This sawdust catcher was designed especially for the shop. It just sits on the back structure of the machine so it can be removed when necessary.

3-39.   Construction details of an all-plywood stand you can make for a radial arm saw. This is the design of the stand used in the shop.

3-40.   A plastic shield, which is easy to attach to the saw, will catch most of the sawdust that is thrown back during crosscut operations.

3-42.   Construction details of a sawdust catcher you can make.

Alignment

To get the most out of your machine, check it immediately, and periodically thereafter, to be sure all components are in correct relationship. All machines have built-in adjustment features so corrections can be made, when necessary, to maintain a high level of accuracy. How this is accomplished can vary from tool to tool, but the end result must be the same. Check your owner's manual for adjustment procedures to accomplish the following.

On a simple crosscut, the line of the blade must be 90° to the fence. Check by marking a wide piece of wood with a square and then cutting on the line (Figure 3-43). If the blade doesn't follow the line for the full length of the cut, you know adjustment is required. You can also check with a carpenter's square. Place the short leg against the fence and the long leg on the line of cut. Raise the blade to just clear the table and then, while pulling for a crosscut, see if the blade follows the line of the square (Figure 3-44).

The cut must be square to the work edge placed against the fence, but it must also be square to adjacent surfaces. This will occur if the vertical plane of the saw blade is 90° to the table surface. Use a square to check for this after you remove the saw guard (Figure 3-45). Be sure to place the blade of the square between set teeth on the saw blade.

When the "back" teeth of the blade do not cut on the same line as the "front" teeth, you get an undesirable result called "heeling." Check for this by crosscutting a wide piece

of 2″ stock; halt the blade just short of leaving the stock (Figure 3-46). Check at the back teeth to see if there are pronounced radial marks on the cut edge. If there are, then adjustment is required. Adjustment is simply a matter of pivoting the blade a bit to the left or to the right. Heeling is something you can feel and see during normal cutting. The blade will seem to drag and cut edges will not be as smooth as they should be.

To check the angular settings—those for which the machine has auto-stops—work as you did for the crosscut. Mark the line on the work with a protractor and check to see if the blade follows the line as you make the cut (Figure 3-47). Actually, you could make gauge blocks from wide pieces of wood and keep them on hand for just this purpose.

Be sure, after making any adjustments for angular settings, those controlled by an auto-stop, that they are compatible with readings taken from the tool's miter scale (Figure 3-48).

The table surface must be parallel to the arm. A good way to check is as follows. With the tool unplugged, remove the saw guard and anything that is mounted on the arbor. Elevate the tool's arm so the motor can be tilted enough, counterclockwise, to place the arbor in a vertical position. Place a small, smooth block of wood under the arbor and then lower the arbor until it barely touches the wood. The

3-45.   Use a square this way to see if the blade is perpendicular to the table. Be sure to set the blade of the square between set teeth.

3-43.   To get square cuts, the saw blade must travel on a line that is 90° to the fence. You can check this out by crosscutting a wide board on which the cut line has been marked with a square.

3-44.   Another way to check for correct crosscut action. Elevate the square on strips of wood. The points of the saw blade's teeth should barely touch the leg of the square throughout the crosscut travel.

3-46.   If there are pronounced radial marks on the work in the area indicated by the arrow, the blade is "healing": "back" teeth are not cutting on the same line as the "front" teeth.

wood should be movable: you will be using it like a thick feeler gauge.

Release the miter lock. Then, swing the arm and move the motor to and fro to various points on the table as you use the wood block to check between the arbor and the table's surface. The table will require adjustment if there is variation in the distance between arbor and table. This is usually accomplished by loosening nuts and bolts that secure the table to the tool's base frame. After adjusting, retighten the nuts in the series a bit at a time so you don't disturb the new setting.

Check the auto-stop settings for bevel cuts by actually making the cuts and then checking them with a protractor—or—first mark the work with a protractor and then see if the blade follows the line as you make the cuts.

All settings should be checked periodically, even as you work. Once in a while, use a square or protractor to check the cut you have made, or mark the work *before* making the cut, to be assured that you are working accurately. Machines do get out of alignment even during routine work sessions, and it's better to know quickly that a negative situation exists.

Saw Blades

Everything said about saw blades in the chapter on table saws applies to blades for the radial arm machine, even feed speed as it affects smoothness of cut, and choice of blade for a particular cut or material. However, if I had to choose one blade for all-purpose work on the radial arm saw, it would be the one shown in Figure 3-49. It has deeply gulleted, carbide-tipped teeth: 24 of them on a 10″ diameter unit. Teeth are arranged in banks of six, separated by expansion slots that end in a smooth hole to guard against cracking. There is one raker tooth for every two ATB (alternate top bevel), slight hook angle (about 7°), and the teeth have a special back clearance. All the factors add up to easy feeding and little vibration. It can be used for crosscutting and ripping and does a nice job on miter and bevel cuts.

No matter what blade you use, forcing the feed will always result in a rougher cut than the blade will normally produce. If you want proof of this, make two cuts with the same blade. Feed as fast as possible on one without stalling the motor; feed easily and steadily on the second. When you compare the two cuts, the effect of feed speed will be obvious (Figure 3-50).

On the radial arm saw it's not possible to get the free projection normally recommended for a hollow-ground blade. You can get around this, when you feel it's necessary, by placing a wide piece of plywood on each side of the cut line. This will raise the work and provide clearance under it for the blade. Place the plywood "elevators" so the gap between them is not much more than the normal kerf width.

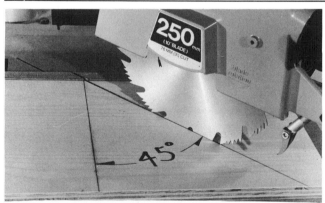

3-47. Check the accuracy of the machine's miter-cut auto-stops by marking the cutline with a protractor. The blade must cut on the line for the full length of the pass.

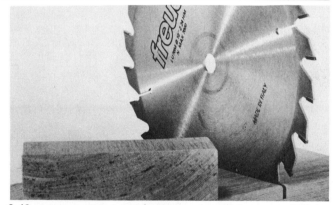

3-49. A type of blade I like to use on the radial arm saw. I find that its special back clearance and hook angle reduce vibration and improve feeding when crosscutting or ripping.

3-48. Check the miter scale to be sure its readings are compatible with miter-cut settings. The scale should be reset, if necessary, after making the alignment check.

3-50. How fast you try to work will affect the cut no matter what blade you use. The sample on the left was done with a fast feed; the other, at a slower pace.

Crosscutting

When you start a crosscut, the saw blade should be behind the fence in "neutral" position. After you have placed the workpiece snugly against the fence, you can turn on the machine and pull the blade toward you to make the cut (Figure 3-51). This completes the *cut,* but the total *operation* is not finished until you have returned the blade to its starting position behind the fence. Your left hand, situated well away from the cut line, secures the work. Your right hand, on the tool's handle, controls saw-blade motion. This is a good way to operate and is not difficult even for left-handed workers.

It's usually a good idea to mark the cut line on the work. This provides a point you can align with the kerf in the fence (Figure 3-52), and is an on-going, visual means of checking the accuracy of the cut while it is being done. Remember that the kerf has width and should occur on the waste side of the stock (Figure 3-53).

Always keep your left hand away from the cut line. If the workpiece is so small that holding it places your hand in a hazardous position, you'd think twice about how to make that particular cut. If necessary, nail or clamp the work to the table and keep your hand in your pocket. When the work *is* held by hand, keep the hand in correct position until the blade has been returned to its neutral place. Don't pick cutoffs from the table until you have turned off the machine and the blade has stopped spinning.

You can do crosscutting on extra-wide stock by making two passes. First, mark the cut line completely across the stock. Place the work in normal position and crosscut to the point that is a little more than half the stock's width. Return the blade to neutral position. Turn the stock so the opposite edge is against the fence and with the marked cut line correctly positioned with the fence kerf. Then do a second cut to meet the first one.

You can also use a stop block on the fence as a gauge. Place the work in position against the fence and stop block and make the first cut. Then, turn the work, reposition it against fence and block, and make the second cut. Be sure that the same edge of the work bears against the stop block for each cut.

Stock that is thicker than the maximum depth of cut of the saw blade can also be crosscut by making two passes. Your best bet is to use a square to mark the cut line on opposite surfaces of the work. After you have made the first cut, flip the stock, line up the saw blade with the cut mark, and make the second pass (Figure 3-54).

When work size permits, you can do "gang cutting" to produce many similar pieces in one pass. Just butt the parts together and place them against the fence as if they were a solid piece. Then simply crosscut as you would normally.

Another way to produce similar pieces is to use a stop block on the fence. The stop can simply be a clamp, or a commercial stop you buy (Figure 3-55), or special stops that you make yourself (Figures 3-56 and 3-57). Place the stop so it determines the length of the cutoff. Position the work against the stop and then cut. Avoid letting sawdust pile up against the stop, for the accumulation can throw off the ac-

3-51.   The basic crosscut—left hand, away from the blade, holding the work, right hand moving the saw blade. Always move the blade back to neutral position before considering the operation completed.

3-53.   The kerf has width so be sure to situate the stock so the cut occurs on the waste side of the material.

3-52.   Make the guide cut in the fence after the fence has been locked in position. Thereafter, lining up a mark on the work with this cut places the work in correct position.

3-54.   Crosscut extra-thick stock by making two passes. Mark the work so the second cut, being done here, will match with the first one.

curacy of your setting. On this kind of work you'll probably be tempted to leave the saw blade running as you position the work for each new cut. If so, be more alert than ever!

With the blade set up for normal crosscutting, you can use a repeat pass technique to accomplish dadoes and rabbets (Figure 3-58). Elevate the blade above the table so the depth of cut will equal the depth of the dado or rabbet you need. When a lot of this work is required, it's best to use a dado assembly so you can accomplish the job faster and more accurately on similar cuts. But when you need just one or two, you can save setup time by staying with the saw blade and repeat passes.

Lastly, you can be guided by marks that you place on the work, or you can use stop blocks to gauge the outline cuts and then clean away between them.

Ripping

Ripping is done by swinging the motor so the saw blade can be locked in a position parallel to the fence. Then the work is fed *against* the direction of rotation of the blade (Figure 3-59). Because the motor unit can be rotated in either direction you can set up for "in-ripping," which positions the blade on the column side of the table, or for "out-ripping," where the blade is swung away from the column. Width of cut settings are made by measuring between the fence and the side of the blade that faces it. All radial saws have scales

3-55. Use a stop block on the fence as a gauge when you must cut to a specific length. This is the way to work when you need many similar pieces.

3-56. How to make a stop block. The thumbscrew is force-threaded into an undersize hole.

3-57. This type of stop block will extend farther out from the fence. On some types of cuts, it will be more useful than the first one.

3-58. You can form dadoes with a regular saw blade by making repeat passes. Form the outline cuts first and then clean away the waste that remains between them. You can also use the repeat-pass idea to shape rabbets.

3-59. Ripping is done by feeding the work against the direction of rotation of the saw blade. This is the in-rip position; the blade is on the column side of the machine.

3-60. The arm of the machine has a scale which is usable for either in-ripping or out-ripping. Check settings by actually measuring between the blade and the fence.

and indicators that can be used for rip-cut settings (Figure 3-60). However, it's good practice to use the scales only as a guide. Make the final adjustment by actually measuring with a rule. When the blade has set teeth, be sure to measure from the tip of a tooth that points toward the fence.

Always adjust the anti-kickback fingers so they rest on the surface of the work (Figure 3-61). They will not interfere with the feed, but will dig in to hold the work should the blade's rotation tend to move the work back toward you. Tilt the guard so the end you face from the feed position is not more than about 1/4″ above the surface of the work. Set this way, the guard will cover most of the "front" edge of the blade, and it will be positioned to capture most of the sawdust.

You'll find the in-rip position most convenient for average cuts. Work with care since the hand feeding the stock will be between the blade and fence. ALWAYS use a push stick when the width of cut isn't sufficient to permit a safe hand feed, but don't rely on just any piece of scrap. It's much wiser to make a special tool for permanent use. The one being used in Figure 3-62 and which is detailed in Figure 3-63 works quite well. It straddles the fence so it can't slip and it is long enough so you can get work past the saw blade without using your fingers hazardously.

Another good push-stick design is shown in Figure 3-64. It can be used on rip cuts of various widths and is made so that when the part marked "A" hits the guard, the work will have passed the saw blade. At that point you pull back the pusher and shut down the machine. Because the pusher has spaced legs, the saw blade won't cut into it.

When you are in-ripping, the feed direction will be right to left. For out-ripping (Figure 3-65), you will be moving the work from left to right. Use the out-rip position for extra-wide cuts.

3-61.   Always do ripping with the anti-kickback fingers positioned correctly. The guard is tilted so it almost touches the work on the side from which you are feeding.

3-63.   Construction details of the fence-straddling push stick.

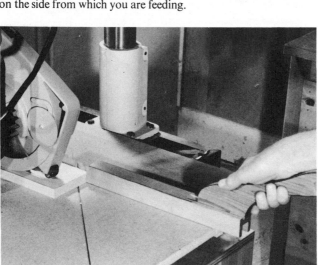

3-62.   It's critical that you use a push stick when ripping narrow pieces. You must never place your hands in a hazardous position. This push stick is designed to straddle the fence.

3-64.   This push stick can be used on cuts of various widths. Because of the spaced legs, it won't be damaged by the saw blade.

Make two passes to rip-cut stock that is thicker than the maximum depth of cut of the blade. Raise the blade high enough to get clearance between the bottom of the motor and the surface of the stock. Make a pass as you would for any rip cut. The cut-depth on this first pass should be a bit more than half the stock's thickness. Then flip the stock and make a second pass. Since you are using the fence to guide the work, the cut marks recommended for a similar operation when crosscutting are not needed here. Just be sure you have the same side of the work against the fence for each of the passes.

You can do a rip cut on workpieces that lack a straightedge to ride the fence by clamping or tack-nailing a guide strip to the work's underside and then making the pass with the guide strip riding the outboard edge of the table (Figure 3-66). The width of the cut, or the amount of material you remove, is determined by where you place the guide strip on the work and the location of the saw blade. Always make the setup so there will be ample table surface to support the work. Usually, jobs like this are done with the blade in the out-rip position. Be sure to keep the guide strip snugly against the edge of the table throughout the pass.

By making repeat passes, you can use the ripping set-up to form grooves (Figure 3-67). The depth of the groove will be determined by how high above the table you set the blade. If you need a 5/8″-deep dado in 1″ stock, then the distance between table and blade should be 3/8″. You can do this kind of measuring with a rule but you'll work more conveniently and accurately if you add a height gauge to your equipment (Figure 3-68).

Best procedure for repeat-pass grooving is to make the outline cuts first and then clean out between them. Be sure to lock the blade's position for each cut.

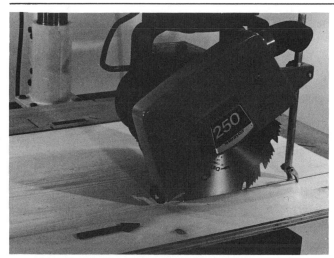

3-65. This is the out-rip position, usually used for extra-wide cuts. The blade points *away* from the column. Feed direction is left to right. Note the position of the guard and anti-kickback fingers.

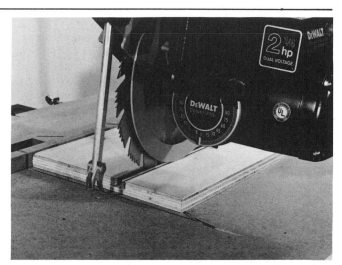

3-67. You can work in the rip position and do repeat passes to form grooves. Be sure to secure the rip lock for each pass that you make.

3-66. A technique to use when a workpiece does not have a straight edge to ride the fence. The cut is guided by the clamped-on, or tack-nailed strip that bears against the edge of the table.

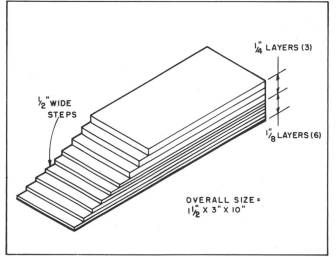

3-68. How to make a height block. It can be used when you need to set a cutting tool at a particular height above the table.

Miter Cuts

A miter cut is accomplished with the saw blade in normal position but with the arm of the tool swung to the angle required (Figure 3-69). The angle that you must use depends on the number of sides in the project. Remember that the *cut* angle is always one half of the *joint* angle (Figure 3-70). On most machines, common angles such as 45° will have auto-stops. Settings for angles between the automatic stops have to be gauged by using a miter scale usually situated at the top of the column. Since the joining of miter cuts in good fashion relates directly to how accurately the cuts are made, it's good practice to check the first cut with a protractor before you proceed to cut all the pieces. In a picture frame, for example, being "off" just a second or two will result in quite a gap when you try to assemble all four pieces.

Hold the stock firmly against the fence and make the pass even more slowly than you usually do. On the radial arm saw, you don't have the amount of movement from the cut line that you can encounter on a table saw. Even so, many professionals use a special fence as an aid in keeping the work stationary. This special fence is more than a regular fence with nails or screws driven through from the back so the points protrude just a bit at the front. These protrusions help to hold the stock still as you pull the blade through. Another special mitering fence that will help in similar fashion is one that is faced with sandpaper.

Making miter cuts at each end of the stock is no problem when the material is flat and can be flipped for alternate cuts (Figure 3-71). This is not the case when mitering moldings. Then you must make both left- and right-hand cuts which means swinging the blade to achieve the positions. Therefore, you have twice as much room for error, which calls for being specially careful when setting up the machine and for making test cuts to prove the settings.

One possible method is to cut the frame pieces to overall size first and then miter the ends. This will waste some material, but you have to judge the cost of the waste in terms of better accuracy. The use of a stop block makes the procedure even simpler. Cut the first piece and use it as a gauge for setting the stop block on the fence. The stop then positions other pieces correctly so the cuts will be duplicated.

You can also make and use special mitering jigs like the one shown in Figures 3-72 and 3-72A. Although the jig is a two-part affair, it should initially be assembled in one piece. Then it can be separated by making a crosscut on its centerline. This is done so the jig can be used two ways. Use half the jig when cutting consecutively along a single length of stock. Use the entire jig for mitering pieces that have been precut to exact length. Since either arm of the jig can be used to position the stock, it won't matter if the stock is flat, in which case it can be flipped over for cuts at opposite ends of the piece, or contoured. In any case, the cut is made like a simple crosscut. When both parts of the jig are used, separate them by the width of the saw kerf.

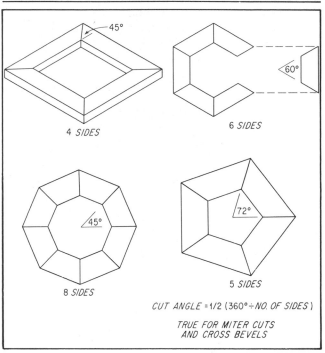

CUT ANGLE =1/2 (360° ÷ NO. OF SIDES)

TRUE FOR MITER CUTS AND CROSS BEVELS

3-70.   Remember that the miter CUT angle is always one half of the JOINT angle.

3-71.   When the stock is flat and can be inverted for opposite cuts, you can make all of the cuts with the saw blade at one setting.

3-69.   Miter cutting is done by swinging the arm to the angle you need and then making the pass as if you were crosscutting. Accuracy is critical.

Bevel Cutting

Bevels, whether they are made across or parallel to the grain of the wood, are made by tilting the blade to the required angle. Whenever it is necessary to tilt the blade, raise it above the table and set it to the correct angle. Lower it until it just misses touching the table and then, with the motor turned on, lower it just a bit more so it will form the necessary table kerf. As with miter cuts, settings will be critical. It pays to make a test cut in scrap stock before cutting good material.

A cross bevel (often called a cross miter) is made with the stock positioned as it would be for a simple crosscut (Figure 3-73). Because of the blade tilt, you'll want to be even more careful with hand position. Make the pass slowly and return the blade to neutral position after the cut. Allow the blade to stop before removing workpieces.

When you need the same cut on a number of pieces, you can place them together as shown in Figure 3-74 and then saw as you would a solid piece. Use a stop block on the fence or a clamped piece of wood as a gauge.

You can use the same type of setup to form spline grooves in cross bevels (Figure 3-75). The thickness of the splines you use must match the kerf width of the saw blade. Be sure the spline groove is perpendicular to the angle of the bevel.

3-72. A special mitering jig. You can use it for flat or shaped stock. Since the work-angle is established by the guides, the cut is done like a simple crosscut.

3-73. A cross bevel, or cross miter, is done in crosscut position. The blade is tilted to the angle you need.

3-74. Use the gang-cutting technique when you require the cut on a number of pieces.

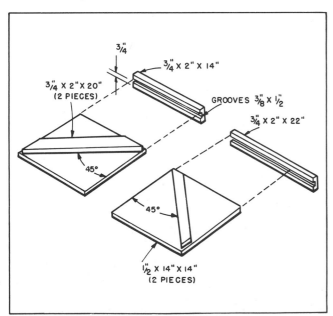

3-72A. How to make the mitering jig. It is made as one unit and then separated as explained in the text.

3-75. This is how you can use a saw blade to form a spline groove in a cross bevel. It's okay to use splines whose thickness matches the width of the saw kerf.

The rip bevel (often called a rip miter, even a bevel miter) is accomplished with the machine in rip position but with the blade tilted to the angle required (Figure 3-76). Follow all the rip-cut rules concerning anti-kickback device position, guard setting, and, especially, safe hand placement. Feed the stock through as you would for a rip cut but be even more careful about keeping it snug against the fence throughout the pass. Use a push stick instead of your hands to get the work past the saw blade. Remember, as in simple ripping, you must always feed the stock *against* the blade's direction of rotation.

Chamfer cuts. The chamfer cut is just a partial bevel. You can make it along an edge or across an end. When working on an edge, set the saw up for a rip-bevel operation. However, since you won't remove the entire edge of the stock, keep the blade elevated above the table (Figure 3-77). When the chamfer is across an end, set up as you would for a cross bevel.

V-grooves. Do V-grooves by setting up for a rip bevel but adjust the blade height to provide for the groove depth required. Two cuts are required for each groove. When the "V" is in the center of the board, you can turn the stock end for end to make the second pass (Figure 3-78). When it's located elsewhere, you must reset the blade in order to mate the second cut with the first cut.

Compound miters. You cut a simple miter when you swing the arm but keep the blade in a perpendicular position. If you swing the arm and also tilt the saw blade, you get a compound angle cut (Figures 3-79 and 3-80).

Compound miters are probably the toughest kinds of cuts to make simply because of the perfect accuracy they require. Everything we said about care when doing the simple miter has double the emphasis here. Work slowly, double-check each setting before you make the cuts, and test the setting by cutting first on scrap stock. Blade tilt and arm swing settings for compound angle joints are shown in Figure 3-81.

Sometimes, when you are cutting parts of similar length consecutively from one long board, you can use the first piece cut as a template for making the succeeding cuts. Flip the first piece over and place it on the board so you can mark the cut line with a very sharp pencil (Figure 3-82). Place the stock so the next cut you make will just remove the pencil line.

You can work in similar fashion by using a stop block to gauge the length of the pieces (Figure 3-83). First cut one end of the stock, then invert it and use it as a gauge to position the stop block. The stock must be turned over for each of the cuts that follow.

Being able to flip the stock will allow you to work exclusively with right-hand cuts. Other times, you must change the settings and make half the cuts on the right side and half the cuts on the left side. This situation should make it more obvious than any number of words that care in setting up is the primary factor.

If you first establish the slope angle of the work by making bevel cuts on the edges, you can use the miter jig to do compound cutting. The work is put in position against

3-76.   To rip bevels, set up for ripping but work with the blade tilted to the angle you need. Follow all the safety rules that apply to simple rip cuts.

3-77.   Chamfers are formed like rip bevels. The difference is that the blade is elevated so only the top corner of the stock is removed.

3-78.   Two passes are required to form V-grooves. Work position must be perfect for each pass so the two cuts will meet exactly at the bottom of the V.

3-79.   A compound angle results when you combine a miter-cut setting with a blade tilt.

3-80. A typical compound-angle joint. The cuts must be precise in order for the frame pieces to join correctly.

WORK SLOPE	BUTT JOINT (4 sides)		MITER JOINT					
			(4 sides)		(6 sides)		(8 sides)	
	A	B	A	B	A	B	A	B
5°	1/2	5	44-3/4	5	29-3/4	2-1/2	22-1/4	2
10°	1-1/2	9-3/4	44-1/4	9-3/4	29-1/2	5-1/2	22	4
15°	3-3/4	14-1/2	43-1/4	14-1/2	29	8-1/4	21-1/2	6
20°	6-1/4	18-3/4	41-3/4	18-3/4	28-1/4	11	21	8
25°	10	23	40	23	27-1/4	13-1/2	20-1/4	10
30°	14-1/2	26-1/2	37-3/4	26-1/2	26	16	19-1/2	11-3/4
35°	19-1/2	29-3/4	35-1/4	29-3/4	24-1/2	18-1/4	18-1/4	13-1/4
40°	24-1/2	32-3/4	32-1/2	32-3/4	22-3/4	20-1/4	17	15
45°	30	35-1/4	30	35-1/4	21	22-1/4	15-3/4	16-1/4
50°	36	37-1/2	27	37-1/2	19	23-3/4	14-1/4	17-1/2
55°	42	39-1/4	24	39-1/4	16-3/4	25-1/4	12-1/2	18-3/4
60°	48	41	21	41	14-1/2	26-1/2	11	19-3/4
	"A" = tilt of saw blade			"B" = arm swing				

3-81.   How to combine arm setting and blade tilt for various types of compound-angle joints.

3-82.   When doing compound-angle cuts on flat stock, you can use the first piece as a template for marking those that follow. The following cut must be precise enough to just remove the pencil line.

the guide but resting on the bevel. The blade is set in normal crosscut position and pulled through in the usual fashion. The cut is compound simply because the work is tilted to begin with.

Another "easy" way to do compound miters, so long as you are not persnickety about the slope angle, is to work with a modified mitering jig like the one being used in Figure 3-84. The work is placed between the leg of the jig and the triangular guide. The distance between the leg and the guide determines the slope angle. The blade is pulled through as if you were doing a simple crosscut but the result is a compound angle. Construction details for a typical jig of this type are shown in Figure 3-85.

Dadoing Operations

Dadoing tools, like those described in the chapter on table saws, are not used to sever stock, so they are always elevated above the table surface to form U-shaped cuts that are *dadoes* when formed across the grain, *grooves* when done with the grain. The cut depth can be gauged by marking it on an edge of the stock and then adjusting the cutter height to match, or by using the height gauge that we have already described. Many of the shapes that can be formed with a dado are shown in Figure 3-86. Some are pretty basic; others require special techniques.

The dado assembly is used much like a saw blade. However, since it removes considerably more wood, the feed speed should be minimized. If you feed too fast, the dado will tend to "climb" and "walk" along the work instead of cut. While the normal feed direction is the same as for a saw blade, there are times when pushing the cutter through instead of pulling it may be better. This means that you position the dado at the front of the table instead of behind the fence and, after the work is placed, push the dado toward the rear of the machine to make the cut. However, this should not be adopted as standard procedure.

No matter which way you feed, across the grain or with it, make all dado cuts at a speed that will permit the cutting edges to do their job without clogging. As with all cutting tools, one rule concerning good feed speed and pressure is paramount: keep the tool cutting constantly but without strain.

Since dadoing makes cuts that are wider than the kerf of a saw blade, it's a good idea for the tool to have its own fence (Figure 3-87). The simple dado is done with the machine in crosscut position (Figure 3-88). Start with the cutter behind the fence. Then, as in crosscutting, pull the cutter slowly toward you and return it to neutral position when the cut is complete. Some operators reverse the pass procedure when making deep cuts or working on hardwood. The cutter is pulled away from the fence before the work is positioned. Then the pass is made by moving the cutter to its neutral position (Figure 3-89). The motive is to minimize any tendency of the cutter to climb the stock. It works, but it also eliminates the cutter's tendency, which occurs in a normal pass, to keep the work flat on the table and against the fence. Anyway, it's the exception, not the rule, of radial arm saw work.

3-83. You can work in similar fashion by using a stop block on the fence to set the position of the pieces. The stock must be turned over for each cut.

3-84. Make compound-angle cuts by using this jig, so long as you are not persnickety about the slope angle of the project. Slope angle is set by the distance between the guide and the leg of the jig.

3-85. This is the jig you can make for positioning pieces for compound-angle cuts. The pass is a simple crosscut, but since the work is at an angle, the result is a compound angle.

(1) DADO	(6) NOTCHING	(11) SLOT	(16) SPECIAL GROOVES
(2) GROOVE	(7) TONGUE	(12) THROUGH SLOT	(17) ANGLE RABBET
(3) HOLLOWING	(8) GROOVE	(13) COVE	(18) CORNER MOLD
(4) EDGE RABBET	(9) STUD TENON	(14) EDGE COVE	(19) DECORATIVE SURFACE GROOVES
(5) END RABBET	(10) TRUE TENON	(15) V GROOVE	(20) BLIND GROOVE

3-86. These are the kinds of forms you can produce by working with a dadoing tool. Some are routine; others require special procedures.

3-87. It's a good idea to have a special fence for dadoing operations.

3-88. Make the pass for a basic dado cut as you would for a simple crosscut. Feed more slowly though, since the dado must get through more material than a saw blade is faced with.

3-89. Some operators prefer to push the blade rather than pull it for a dado cut. It's okay, but remember it's the exception, not the rule, of radial arm saw work.

When the same dado is required on many pieces, it's wise to use a stop block on the fence to gauge the position of the cut (Figure 3-90). This method is much better than marking the pieces individually and then gauging each cut by eye. A stop block may also be used when you need extra-wide cuts. First set the stop to position the work for one side of the cut (Figure 3-91). Then reset the stop for the second side (Figure 3-92). Any material that remains between the outline cuts is cleaned out by making repeat passes. When the same cut is required on many pieces, be sure to make the first cut on each piece before setting up for the second one.

A kind of "gang cutting" may be employed to assure accuracy of dadoes on mating pieces. For example, in dadoing opposite sides of a case for horizontal shelves, cut the first dado in each of the pieces, butt them edge-to-edge, and use a piece of the shelf material in the dadoes already formed (Figure 3-93). This will hold the parts in correct alignment for the following cuts. Often you can combine this technique with a stop block on the fence for faster, more accurate work.

When the pieces to be dadoed are too wide to be ganged, cut them individually but use stop blocks to position them. Make the first cut in each of the parts before going on to the others.

The "stopped" or "blind" dado is a cut that doesn't go across the full width of the stock. It's useful, for example, when you use a dado to install a shelf but wish to conceal the U-shape at the front edge. One way to operate is to mark the work to indicate where the dado must end and then cut to that point (Figure 3-94). This is okay when you don't mind the U-shape appearing at one edge. If you don't

3-90. When you need the same dado on many pieces, use a stop on the fence to position the workpieces.

3-93. Use a kind of gang-cutting when you need equally-spaced dadoes on similar pieces. A dado-sized piece of wood placed in the first cuts holds the parts in correct alignment for following cuts.

3-91. When you need extra-wide dadoes, set the stop to position the work for one side of the cut. If you need the same cut on many pieces, make this first one on all of them.

3-92. Reset the stop so the work will be positioned for the other side of the cut. The material between the two cuts is removed by making additional passes.

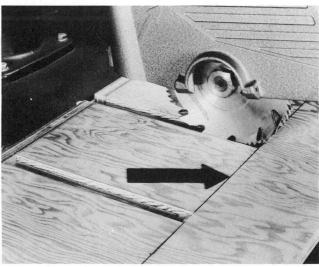

3-94. For stopped dadoes, make the pass to a line marked on the work, or use a stop on the tool's arm that will limit how far forward you can pull the cutter.

want it to show at either edge, you can follow the procedure demonstrated in Figure 3-95. The cutter is elevated before the work is positioned. Then it is lowered very slowly to start the cut and pulled through to where you want the dado to end. Be very careful when making the initial contact: the work must be held firmly, or clamped.

You can judge the length of such cuts by eye but it's better to use stops on the arm of the tool to control the distance the cutter will travel. You can do this with a stop block you can buy (Figure 3-96), or simply by using C-clamps (Figure 3-97).

Since dadoes formed in this manner end in a radius, you must modify them by squaring the end of the cut with a chisel and then notching the shelf to suit, or by shaping the shelf to match the curve (Figure 3-98).

To form grooves, organize the saw in its ripping mode and feed the stock into the cutter as you would for simple ripping. To get the correct depth of cut, work as explained for dadoing. Obey all the rules that apply to safe ripping; proper hand position, use of push sticks, placement of guard and anti-kickback device, and so on.

Try to work with the machine in in-rip position. Feed steadily but, since the dado must remove more wood, more slowly than you would when ripping. For grooves that are wider than you can accomplish in a single pass, use the repeat pass technique, overlapping the cuts so you'll get a smoother bottom in the groove. To do stopped grooves, use a stop block on the fence to limit the length of the cuts (Figure 3-99). After you hit the stop block, turn off the machine and when the cutter is still, retract the work. Remember, for cuts of this nature, the motor is locked in position as when ripping.

3-95.   For blind dadoes, which start and stop between the edges of the stock, you need two stops on the tool's arm. The text explains how this kind of cutting should be done.

3-96.   A stop you can buy is a U-shaped clamp that locks on the tool's arm. The stop controls how far you can move the cutting tool.

3-97.   You can improvise stops by using C-clamps. Use thin scrap wood to protect the tool.

3-98.   Blind and stopped dadoes end in a radius so you must shape the insert piece accordingly.

3-99.   To form grooves with a dadoing tool, work with the machine in rip position. For stopped grooves, make the pass to a stop on the fence. Doing blind grooves is like doing blind dadoes. The difference is that here you move the work while the cutter is in a fixed position.

When you need dadoes that run at an angle across the stock, situate the machine as you would for miter cutting.

Cutting rabbets. The dadoing tool is fine to use when you require a number of rabbet cuts that are too many to be done by the repeat-pass regular saw blade method. When the rabbet is required across the end of the stock, use the crosscut position (Figure 3-100); when it follows a long edge, use the rip position. Procedures are approximately the same as for dadoing; the difference is simply in the shape you produce.

Variable-depth cuts. You can use this technique on both dado and rabbet cuts when, for example, you want the side members of a bookcase to slope inward. How much slope you can get will depend on the thickness of the stock you are using. To do the job, tack-nail a strip of wood under one edge of the work or to the saw table so the top surface of the workpiece is no longer parallel to the table.

Since the cutting tool moves on a parallel plane, the cut will be deeper at one end of the stock (Figure 3-101). The difference in depth from one end of the cut to the other is controlled by the thickness of the elevating strip.

Using a V-block. You can form notches across a corner post by using a V-block to situate the work and pulling the cutter across as you would for a simple dado (Figure 3-102). The block doesn't have to be more than a length of 2x4 with a "V" cut down its center. When you need such a cut on many pieces, it's a simple matter to tack-nail a strip across the "V" for use as a stop. In such cases, it's probably a good idea to secure the V-block to the table or to the fence. Your concern will then be to hold the work still as you make the cut.

Other uses for dadoing tools will be shown later in this chapter.

Shaping on the Radial Arm Saw

Shaping operations on the radial arm saw are done with a molding head. The various types of heads illustrated in chapter two, an example being shown in Figure 3-103, can be mounted on the arbor of the radial arm machine. Some manufacturers offer special units which, while being generally useful, are especially good for particular non-molding operations (Figure 3-104). This one, because of its heavy

3-100.   Work in the crosscut position when you need to form a rabbet on the end of stock. Make repeat passes if the rabbet must be extra-wide. Rabbets on long edges are formed by working in the rip position.

3-102.   A V-block lets you position square stock for cross-corner dadoes. The work is done with the machine in crosscut position. You can even use the V-block to form a dado in a cylinder. The work must be held or clamped firmly.

3-101.   You can form a variable-depth rabbet, or dado, if you make the pass with the work tilted with a height block.

3-103.   The molding head locks on the arbor just like a dadoing tool. Some heads work with three knives, others with two. Some typical molding knives are shown.

body construction, can handle jointing knives that are 2″ wide and almost 1/4″ thick. Thus it can be used to joint edges on stock up to 2″ thick (Figure 3-105). Always, when you have an accessory in mind, you must be sure it can be correctly mounted on the tool you own. The only way to ascertain this is to read the literature that is supplied with the tool. Be sure the thickness of the accessory leaves enough thread on the arbor for the lock nut to seat securely. Don't experiment. What is right for one tool, may not be for another. Also, while the regular saw guard can be used on some molding head operations, it is not suitable for everything that can be done with the accessory. Therefore, be sure to acquire any special guarding equipment that is offered. An example, on a Rockwell tool, is shown in Figure 3-106. Sometimes, due to a unique situation, you have to create a guard. It's important, as always, to plan for safety as well as results.

The flexibility of the radial arm saw increases the usefulness of a molding cutterhead. When you consider the variety of knives that are available (Figure 3-107), each one being capable of providing various shapes, and the posi-

3-104. Two-knife head is extra-heavy; can handle jointing knives that are 1/4″ thick and 2″ wide.

3-105. The two-knife head can smooth edges on stock up to 2″ thick. The guard, at the left, is not mounted, only so the cut can be seen.

3-106. Many manufacturers offer special guarding equipment for molding-head operations. It's not wise to work without it.

CLOVER LEAF

THREE BEAD

5/16″ COVE AND QUARTER ROUND

FLUTE AND QUARTER ROUND

WEDGE GROOVE

1″ FLUTE

BASE MOLD

3/16″ AND 3/8″ QUARTER ROUND AND 1/4″ BEAD

OGEE

1/4″ AND 1/2″ COMBINATION QUARTER ROUND

GLUE JOINT

DOOR LIP

FLUTE AND COVE

5/8″ COVE

CUPBOARD-DOOR LIP

WEDGE TONGUE

FLUTE

PLAIN

3-107. A typical assortment of molding knives and the cuts you can make with them. Any knife can be used for a full or a partial cut.

tioning of the head, which can be vertical, horizontal or at an angle, you realize the infinite number of cut possibilities. Some knives are designed for a special form, others are combination cutters, but *any* knife can be used wholly or partially. The best way to judge the cut is to hold the knife against the edge of a board. Thus you can preview the results (Figure 3-108).

Some molding head cuts remove the entire edge of the stock, others only part of it. These two factors bear on the type of fence you must use in order to get the work correctly past the cutter. When the cut is partial, the "infeed" side, where the pass is started, and the "outfeed" side, where the cut ends, can be on the same plane. When the entire edge of the stock is removed, then one of the fences must be offset to compensate for the material that is cut away (Figure 3-109). The rule is simple—the work must be supported *before* and *after* the cut.

One type of fence you can make for use on straight cuts that do not remove the entire edge of the stock is shown in Figure 3-110. This is locked in place like the regular fence. Sometimes, especially when doing partial cuts, it's necessary to allow the cutter to form a slight arc in the table. Other times, the cut is such that you can work with the cutter above the table (Figures 3-111 and 3-112).

A molding head fence you can make, which is usable for partial cuts and also adjustable for full cuts, is shown in Figures 3-113 and 3-114. Note that this jig has its own work-support platform. When you must adjust cutter height so it is below the surface on which the work rests, you'll cut into the platform, not the tool's table.

3-108.   You can see what a knife will do if you hold it against an edge of the stock.

3-110.   You can make a fence like this for use on all straight-line cuts that do not remove the entire edge of the stock.

3-109.   Fences can be on the same plane, or offset by using shims. It depends on whether you are removing the entire edge of the stock or just part of it.

3-111.   Sometimes, so you can use a specific part of the profile on a knife, it's necessary to cut slightly into the table.

3-112.   At other times, depending on the cut, the knife can be high enough so it doesn't touch the table at all.

$3/4'' \times 2 5/8'' \times 15 3/4''$

$3/4'' \times 2 5/8'' \times 14 3/4''$

$3/4'' \times 3/4'' \times 14 3/4''$

$3/4$

$3/4$

DO NOT ATTACH
THIS SECTION
OF FENCE

$3/4'' \times 12'' \times 36''$

3-113.   How to construct a special shaper table that can be used for full or partial cuts.

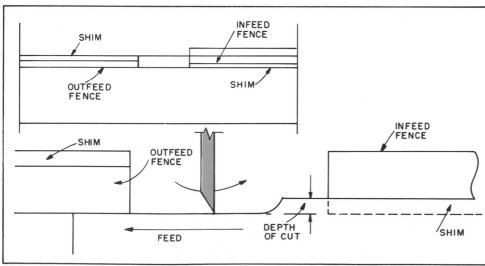

SHIM

INFEED
FENCE

OUTFEED
FENCE

SHIM

SHIM

OUTFEED
FENCE

INFEED
FENCE

DEPTH
OF CUT

FEED

SHIM

3-114.   Shims are used when it is necessary to offset the infeed fence. The thickness of the shim determines the depth of the cut.

Lastly, as far as special fences are concerned, some manufacturers offer units especially designed for shaping operations. The one shown in Figure 3-115 is locked in place like a regular fence and has a screw-adjustable infeed fence so the accessory is usable for whole or partial cutting. Often, as you will see in some of the illustrations, shaping work can be done using only the regular fence.

To make the cut, hold the work flat on the table and snug against the fence throughout the pass. Move it slowly to engage the cutter and keep the feed action steady until the cut is complete. Position hands at all times so they don't get near a danger zone. Most molding cuts, like dadoes, remove a lot of material, so don't force the feed. Most times, when the cut is deep or wide, you'll get better results by making several passes to get to the final result. You'll *always* get smoother results when the cut action is with the grain (Figure 3-116). When this isn't possible, make the passes even slower than usual. This will allow the knives to take smaller bites, and they will pass over a given area of the wood a greater number of times.

When you must shape all four edges of a workpiece, or two adjacent edges, do the cross-grain cuts first. The final with-the-grain cuts will remove the end-area imperfections that are almost inevitable on cross-grain passes. Don't feed narrow stock using only your hands. For one thing, it will be difficult to keep the work square to the fence; for another, the cutter's action, combined with lack of support for the work, can cause bad things to happen to the work and to you. It's better to use a wide block to back up the work, moving both pieces past the cutter as if they were one, or to make a "miter gauge" like the one shown in Figure 3-117. The project is two pieces of wood, nailed and glued together to form a 90° angle. One edge backs up the work, the other rides the edge of the table. Don't work on stock that is so narrow even a backup block or a miter gauge won't help. In such cases, it's better to do the job on a wide piece and then remove the part you need by sawing.

Narrow moldings. When you need just one piece, you can work by shaping the edge of a wide board and then ripping off the width you want.

To turn out narrow moldings in quantity, it's best to pre-rip pieces to the size you want and then run them through a special fixture. This is no more than a long, heavy piece of stock in which you form a rabbet to suit the size of

3-115.   Some manufacturers offer a special shaper fence. The infeed fence is adjustable so the unit can be used for whole or partial cutting.

3-117.   Never try to cut crossgrain, especially on narrow stock, by hand-holding the material. Use a substantial backup block or make a special "miter gauge."

3-116.   Cuts will always be smoother when the pass is made *with* the grain of the wood. When you need to shape four edges or two adjacent edges, do the crossgrain cuts first.

3-118.   How to shape slim pieces. The work is moved in one end of the guide block and pulled out the other. The rabbet in the block is sized to match the dimensions of the work, with just enough clearance so the work can get through.

the basic strips. The block is clamped in place to cover the cutter; the work is fed into one end (the infeed side) and pulled out the other (Figure 3-118). To avoid chatter as you make the pass, be sure the L-shaped cut in the block matches the size of the precut strips quite closely.

Circular work. You can shape the perimeter of circular pieces if you use V-blocks to position the work and as guides as you turn the work for the cut. One way to make the jig is shown in Figure 3-119. Here, each triangular piece is attached to a strip that is locked in the tool's table as if it were a fence. The second method (Figure 3-120), has the blocks attached to vertical pieces which can be clamped to a shaper fence. In both cases, the two pieces of the jigs can be situated to suit the size of the workpiece. The centerline of the jig, after its parts have been secured, should be on the centerline of the cutter.

Ease the work in slowly to make initial contact and, when the piece is firmly settled in the V, rotate it slowly against the direction of rotation of the cutterhead. Keep the work flat on the table. If you allow it to lift, the cutterhead will dig in and cause damage.

Irregular work. To shape the edges of workpieces with irregular curves, you must make a special guide which acts pretty much like the depth collars used on the spindle of a regular shaping machine. The machine you work on will influence how to design the guide, but one of the two that are shown, possibly with some modifications, should serve the purpose. The one detailed in Figure 3-121 is attached to a strip that is secured in the table in place of the fence. The pointed piece acts like a fulcrum pin does on a shaper. The procedure is started with the work held firmly against the fulcrum. Then the work is slowly advanced until it has contacted the cutter and is firmly against the guide.

3-120.   Another way to provide V-blocks for circular work. These guides have vertical pieces so they can be clamped in place. Either method is practical.

3-119.   A V-block setup lets you shape the rim of circular pieces. The work is turned counterclockwise after contact with the cutter. The two-piece fence permits adjustment to suit the size of the work and to minimize the gap around the cutter. You need one left- and one right-hand guide.

3-121.   One way to provide a guide that will allow you to use a molding head for freehand shaping. The pointed piece is a "fulcrum." The text explains its use.

At this point you can swing the work free of the fulcrum but this is not a rule. If bearing against the fulcrum helps you keep the work steady, do it. You won't have the support at the end of the cut but by that time the job will be almost complete. At any rate, keep the work flat on the table and bearing against the guide throughout the pass (Figure 3-122). Depth of cut is controlled by the relationship between the knives in the cutterhead and position of the guide. Since the guide, and the fulcrum, are adjustable, there is much latitude in what you can do.

The second guide design is shown in Figure 3-123. This one has a fixed position but depth of cut adjustments can be made by moving the cutterhead. If you don't have a commercial guard to use for safety, you should make a unit like the one shown in the same illustration. The cut is made in normal fashion, with the pass made very slowly and the work bearing against the guide at all times (Figure 3-124).

Always place your hands so they don't get near the cut area. Don't ever try to shape pieces you feel are too small to be safely hand-held. Do the work on a large piece and then saw off what you need.

Shaping across the grain. You can do shaping cuts across the grain by working with the machine set up in crosscut position. All such work must be done with a very slow feed and by making many repeat passes to achieve the final shape (Figure 3-125). You can keep the work in position and lower the cutter about 1/16″ for each of the passes, or, set the cutter at the depth of cut you need and then move the work from left to right just a bit for each pass you make. You might be tempted to rush because of the number of passes required and that would be bad for two reasons. The cut won't be as smooth as it should, and you might become careless. Note for jobs like this that the regular saw guard is used. Be sure that the knives have ample clearance in the guard.

The same technique can be used to surface-"carve" material which can then be ripped to form slim moldings (Figure 3-126). To space the cuts, you can mark the work for each cut line and align the marks with a point on the fence, or you can make a special fence to keep on hand for this kind of work. The fence should have a series of equally spaced holes in which a nail can be placed for use as a stop. The end of the work is butted against the nail; the nail is moved to the next hole to position the work for the following cut.

Surface cuts. If you use the machine in rip position and move the stock as if you were doing a rip cut, you can do the kind of work shown in Figure 3-127. Obey all the rules that apply to ripping operations—correct placement of guard, anti-kickback fingers, use of push sticks, and so on. You can use the rip scale on the arm to space cuts but be sure to secure the rip lock after each change.

It's not usual for decorative work of this nature to require deep cuts, but if it's ever necessary, use the repeat pass idea to achieve full cut depth.

The rip setup can also be used for shaping edges (Figure 3-128), but you must be extremely careful feeding the stock. If you allow the work to move away from the

3-122. The pass is started by bracing the work against the fulcrum and then advancing it to engage the cutter, at which point it should be seated firmly against the guide. Keep the work against the guide throughout the pass.

3-123. Another way to make a guide for freehand shaping and a cover to go with it that will provide some extra protection.

fence, the cutter will dig in; the work will be marred and there will be more possibility of kickback. It's not shown in the photograph, but on this type of work it's a good idea to tack-nail a strip to the table, spacing it from the fence the width of the workpiece. Then the pass can be made with the work moving between fence and strip. After edges are shaped, you can saw them off—another way to obtain long strips of slim molding.

Scallops. If you move the workpiece directly into the cutters you'll form decorative scallops like those in Figure 3-129. A stop or a clamp on the fence serves as a gauge for spacing the cuts and also as a brace for starting the operation. Place the work flat on the table, angled away from the cutter and with one corner against the stop. Then slowly swing it in until it rests firmly against the fence. Reverse the pivoting action to move the work away. Many interesting effects are possible, depending on the knives you select.

3-126. You can "carve" pieces by making crossgrain surface cuts. The pieces can be used as is, or they can be strip cut into slim moldings. *Use the guard in actual practice.*

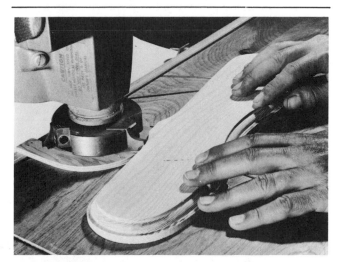

3-124. Freehand shaping is necessary when the work has even or irregular curved edges. Keep the work flat on the table and against the guide throughout the pass. The guard is not shown in this photo so you can see the cut.

3-127. You can do surface "carving" by working in the rip position. Be sure to secure the rip lock for each of the passes you make. Cuts are smoothest when the knives work *with* the grain of the wood.

3-128. You can use the ripping position for shaping long edges. Don't allow the work to move away from the fence or the cutter will dig in and cause damage.

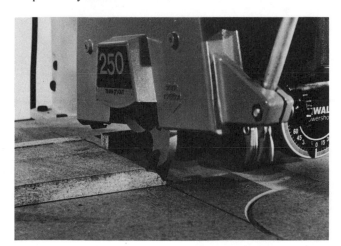

3-125. You can shape edges by working in the crosscut position. The stock must be held or clamped very firmly. Don't try to make very deep or very wide cuts in a single pass.

3-129. How to form scallops. The work is braced against a stop and then swung in to engage the cutter. Many shapes are possible. It all depends on the knives you mount in the molding head.

Special Surface Cuts

Planing. You can do some amount of surface planing by using blank knives, BUT ONLY if the knives are sharpened on their sides as well as the front edge. The heavy, two-knife shaper head is ideal for the purpose. Work with the machine in shaper position with the knives set above the table to cut about 1/16″ into the stock. Pass the work in normal fashion, with a feed-speed that will allow the knives to keep cutting without strain (Figure 3-130). To surface wide stock, you adjust the position of the cutterhead and make more passes. This kind of work can be done with a regular fence, with a cutout, if necessary, to provide clearance for the cutter.

Louvers. This work is done with the machine in horizontal shaping mode but with the head tilted from 5° to 15° (Figure 3-131). Depth of cut shouldn't be more than about 1/4″. Use the rip scale to gauge the spacing and be sure to secure the rip lock after each adjustment. Work so you are cutting *with* the grain of the wood and with the work snug against the fence throughout the pass. Don't do

this kind of thing on small pieces. Keep your hands away from the cutting area. Use push sticks when necessary.

Panel raising. The two-knife cutterhead, with blank knives, is a good tool to use for this purpose (Figure 3-132). Tilt the cutter to an angle of 10° to 15° and adjust its height so the cut will leave a slight shoulder. How far the cutter projects in front of the fence determines the width of the cut. It's wise, on jobs like this, to test the setup on scrap stock. Make the crossgrain cuts first.

Panel raising can also be done with a regular saw blade (Figure 3-133). Adjust the height of the blade so its gauge determines the height of the shoulder. Since the blade is tilted, the shoulder will have a slight angle. If you wish to avoid this, make shoulder cuts first (just shallow kerfs) using regular sawing methods. Then, for the panel raising, adjust the saw blade so it cuts just to the bottom of the kerfs.

Forming flutes or reeds. If you make a jig like the one shown in Figure 3-134, you can mount round or square stock, even pieces that have been lathe-turned, and use a molding head to decorate them with flutes or reeds. The jig,

3-130.   The heavy-duty two-knife cutter head is a good tool to use for some surfacing. This work is possible because the knives are sharpened on three edges.

3-132.   The cutter is tilted 10° to 15° and its height is adjusted so the cut will leave a slight shoulder. Do the crossgrain cuts first.

3-131.   Form louvers by working this way. Tilt the cutter from 5° to 15°. It isn't necessary to cut deeper than about 1/4″.

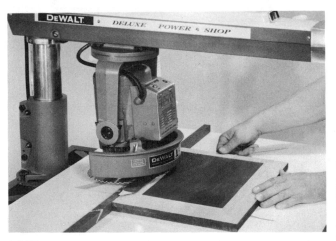

3-133.   You can also do panel raising with a regular saw blade. How far the blade projects at the front of the fence determines the width of the cut.

made to cradle the work, must provide for the length of the project plus the guide block. The guide, which is nailed to the work, is critical since it is clamped to one end of the jig to keep the work secure while the cut is made. The height of the cutterhead must be set so the cutting portion of the knives will be on the horizontal centerline of the work. The depth of the cut is determined by where the motor is locked on the tool's arm.

After the work is mounted and secured by clamping the guide block, the jig is moved along the fence to make the cut (Figure 3-135). A stop block, or a clamped piece of wood, is used on the fence to determine where the cut will end. After each pass, the work is rotated for the following cut. Cut-spacing can be marked on the work before it is mounted, or you can design the guide block as a spacing gauge. Form it as a disc and mark it in degrees; 10°, 20°, whatever. Then the degree marks can be set to the alignment mark that you make on the jig.

The shape you get depends on the knife you use. Beading knives, a bead-and-cove cutter, the groove cutter off a tongue-and-groove set, are examples of what you can try. You can even form flats on a round if you work with blank knives.

Taper Cuts

There are several ways to cut tapers on the radial arm saw, and each of them calls for a special arrangement that will position the work for the cut. You can make a step jig to suit the job or a variable jig that can become a permanent accessory for use on just about any tapering job.

The step jig can be a production tool, used when you require many similar cuts. It has an advantage in that the steps, which determine the taper, are fixed. Any number of pieces you cut will be exactly alike. When the taper is required on opposite edges or on all four edges of a piece of stock, the jig must incorporate two steps. For four edges, the first step in the jig will position the work for cuts on adjacent sides. The second step, which doubles the first setting, sets the work for the two remaining cuts (Figure 3-136).

FLUTING JIG

3-134. By making this jig, you can mount work so it can be decorated with flutes or reeds.

3-135. The work must be mounted securely in the jig and then moved along a fence to make the cut. A stop block on the fence determines how long the cut will be.

3-136. This is how you can make a fixed taper jig. If the work is square you only need two steps in the jig even if the cut is required on four sides of the workpiece.

A single step jig can also be designed to suit various tapers. For example, you may have a project, or projects, that call for different angular cuts on various components. Once made, the jig is available for all the cuts (Figure 3-137).

A variable jig, which you can make by following the diagram in Figure 3-138, will, of course, allow you to organize for most any taper cut as the need arises. If you make matching marks on the legs 12″ from the hinged end, you can predetermine the amount of taper per foot by measuring between the legs at the mark lines (Figure 3-139).

Make taper cuts approximately the same way you do ripping. The work is snugged in the jig; both the jig and the work are moved past the blade for the cut. The distance between the fence and the blade should equal the width of the jig plus the width of the work where the taper begins.

Notched guides (Figure 3-140) are also possibilities for taper cuts. Since these are used with the machine in crosscut position, the work length will have to be within the crosscut limits of the machine.

Figure 3-141 shows how you can make a taper cut on material that is too large to be handled with a jig. A guide strip, tack-nailed to the under side of the work, is positioned to be parallel to the cut. The cut is guided by keeping the guide strip against the edge of the table. This kind of cut is usually better to do with the machine set for out-ripping.

Pattern Sawing

Pattern sawing is a fast method of cutting any number of odd-shaped pieces. It's a good method because it sets up a mechanical means of gauging cuts; therefore, the size and the shape of the workpieces are determined by the pattern. All pieces will be exactly alike, since the pattern is a precise example.

The stock is first roughly cut to approximate size and then, for the cutting, each piece is tack-nailed to the pattern (Figure 3-142). Feeding is done by guiding the pattern along a guide block that is secured to the table in line with the saw blade (Figure 3-143). The blade cuts the work so that it matches the pattern.

3-138.   How to make a variable taper jig.

3-139.   Make a mark on the legs of the jig 1″ away from the hinged end. Measure across at this point to set the jig for the amount of taper per foot.

3-137.   The jig, which is held against the fence, and the work are moved together to make the cut. The taper is determined by which step in the jig is used.

3-140.   A notched jig can also be used for taper cutting. The jig determines the angle of the cut and how much material will be removed.

3-141.   You can work this way when you need a taper cut on large pieces. The guide strip, which is clamped or tack-nailed to the work, is parallel to the cutline. Keep the strip bearing against the edge of the table throughout the pass.

3-142.   The work is tack-nailed to the pattern, or you can use screws that are just long enough to project through the pattern as anchor points.

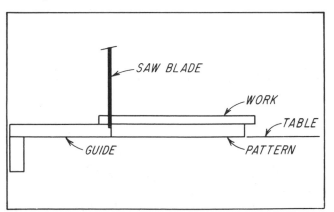

3-143.   This is how pattern sawing is done. The guide is nailed to a strip that is used in place of the fence. The cut is made with the pattern bearing against the guide. It's a good idea for pattern and guide thicknesses to be equal.

Kerfing for Bending

The techniques described in Chapter 2 for kerfing wood so it may be bent without having to go through a steaming process, apply to the radial arm saw (Figure 3-144). The difference is that, on the table saw, the blade is under the work. On the radial arm, the blade is topside, so the depth of the cut is determined by the distance between the blade and the table. The cuts are made with the machine in cross-cut mode.

So you can space the cuts accurately, drill a hole through a regular face and install a nail to serve as a spacing gauge (Figure 3-145). The distance between the nail and the fence-kerf will be the spacing between cuts. This you can determine, at least to begin with, by following the test procedure shown in Figure 3-146. Each cut you make is positioned over the nail to place the work for the next cut.

The thinning-out technique also applies to the radial arm saw. Instead of kerfing the wood, you work with a dado assembly to reduce the thickness of the stock in the area to be bent so what remains is a flexible "veneer." Most times, it's wise to use glue blocks to reinforce the thinned area (Figure 3-147).

3-144.   The technique called "kerfing" is used so wood can be bent without steaming. The cutting must be done carefully and with correct spacing so the wood will bend easily but without breaking.

3-145.   A regular fence can be used to space the kerfs if you install a nail as a stop.

Kerfing for Moldings

The same kind of kerfs made for wood bending, and variations of them, can be used to produce many types of distinctive moldings. The idea is to strip cut the pieces after they have been kerfed to produce the design you have in mind.

Since you are not concerned with bending the wood, the depth and even the width of the kerfs can be varied arbitrarily to suit your design (Figure 3-148).

A sample variation is to flip the stock for each cut or after each two cuts. You can use a dado for this kind of work, or you can combine saw kerfs with dado cuts.

Since spacing for this kind of cutting is variable, work with a fence like the one in Figure 3-149. The nail-stop can be used in any of the holes so you are set to automatically space different types of cuts.

Coving

Coving is a unique operation in that you use a saw blade designed for straight cutting to produce semi-circular shapes (Figure 3-150). Whether the cut is on an edge or down the center of the stock depends on the relationship between blade and work as the cut is made. The technique works because the cutting tool is set obliquely to the line of cut and the shape is formed by making many passes that scrape rather than cut. The repeat pass procedure is mandatory, with the depth of cut increased by no more than 1/16″ to 1/8″ for each. Actually, the less you try to cut in a pass, the easier it will be to feed the stock.

Coving is done with the tool locked in rip position but with the blade tilted and swung as if for a compound angle cut. The greater the angle at which the blade is set, the wider the cove will be. The depth of the cove will be determined

3-146.   This test will help you determine kerf spacing for the job on hand. Lift the wood until the sample kerf closes. Then measure from the bottom of the work to the table surface. It's not fool-proof, but a good way to start.

3-147.   You can also bend wood by using the thinning-out method. The "veneer" left after cutting should be as thick as possible while still being flexible enough for the bend.

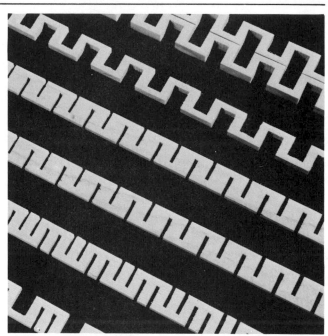

3-148.   Use the kerfing method to produce distinctive moldings. Workpieces are strip-cut after the kerfing is done. Top sample shows results you can achieve by joining pieces edge-to-edge.

3-149.   A guide fence like this one can be used to gauge various spacings between kerfs.

by the number of passes you make (Figure 3-151). To get an idea of what the cove will be like before you start to cut it, make and use the parallel rule shown in Figure 3-152. To use the rule, set the distance between the long arms to equal the width of the cove you want. Swing the saw blade so the "front" and "back" teeth just touch the arms. This must be done on the blade at a point that is on the same plane as the surface of the stock *after* you have adjusted the blade for cove depth. If you are going to center the cove, be sure the centerline of the work is on the centerline of the cutter.

Feed the work very slowly past the blade as if you were making a rip cut. Be sure to hold the work snugly against the fence throughout the pass. The procedure must be repeated many times, with the blade lowered a bit for each cut, until the form is satisfactory (Figure 3-153). Cove shapes will differ depending on the angles at which you tilt

and swing the blade. A true arc will occur if you lock the blade in crosscut position but tilted about 10° or 15° as demonstrated in Figure 3-154.

Don't be in a hurry if you do this kind of work; the procedure takes time and care. Never get your hands close to the cutter. Make the final pass with the blade barely touching the work; this will result in the smoothest finish.

Cutting Circles

You can cut circles with a regular saw blade if you set the machine for out-ripping and use a pivot-guide system so the work can be rotated *against* the blade's direction of rotation (Figure 3-155). The nail, used as the pivot, should be on the blade's centerline. The distance from the nail to the blade determines the radius of the circle. Start with the blade above the work. Then, while holding the work, lower the

3-150. You can produce shapes like this by using the coving technique.

3-151. The angle at which the blade is set determines the width of the cove. Its depth depends on how many passes you make.

3-152. Making a parallel rule and using it as described in the text will help you determine the size of the cove.

3-153. Coving requires many passes with a slight increase in depth-of-cut for each. Work carefully. This is not the kind of work you can do quickly.

3-154. The closer the blade comes to being 90° to the line of cut, the truer the arc will be. Always remember this is a scraping action. Feed must be slow.

blade so it will make a cut about 1/16″ deep. Rotate the work until you have a complete circle. Repeat the procedure as often as necessary, lowering the blade about 1/16″ for each cut.

Figure 3-156 shows how the same technique can be used to form a circular cove. The only difference is that the pivot nail is not on the blade's centerline.

When the work is very large, you can establish a pivot point off the table by using a sawhorse or by improvising a stand.

Another way to form circles is shown in Figure 3-157. Here, the machine is in crosscut position. The pivot-mounted work is turned for each cut. When the bulk of the stock has been removed, continue to make passes, turning the work just a few degrees for each. If you don't wish to go through the entire procedure, you can easily bring the work to the point where a little sanding will produce the final result.

Some Decorative Cuts

Piercing. When you cut kerfs in one surface of the stock with cut-depth a bit more than half the stock's thickness, and then repeat the procedure on the opposite surface but following a different pattern, you create openings at all points where the cuts cross (Figure 3-158). The openings can be square, oblong, diamond-shaped, some can be wider or longer than others; it all depends on how you do the cutting. The openings will be square when the cuts are at right angles to each other and of equal width. Diamond shapes will occur when you make the cuts at an angle.

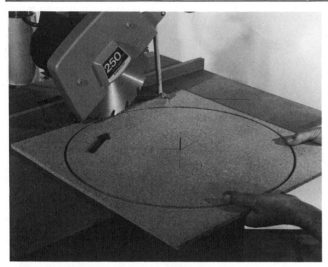

3-155. How to set up a pivot method so you can cut circles with a regular saw blade. Feed slowly and make repeat passes.

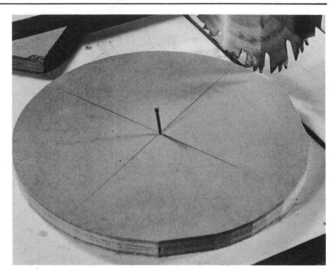

3-157. You can actually cut a disc by working in the crosscut position and turning the pivot-mounted board for each pass you make. Make the final passes by turning the wood just a few degrees for each.

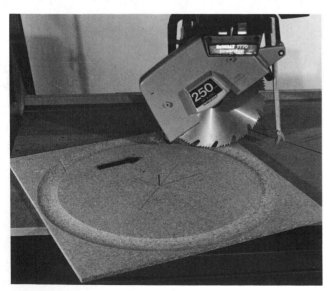

3-156. If the pivot point and the centerline of the saw blade are not on the same line, the pivot-sawing technique will result in a cove.

3-158. Piercing is done by cutting kerfs on both sides of the work. Kerfs are a little deeper than half the stock's thickness. Openings occur where the kerfs cross each other.

The cutting can be done with a saw blade to get delicate effects (Figure 3-159), or you can work with a dadoing tool (Figure 3-160). In any case, the possibilities are so infinite that it pays to do some experimenting to test various patterns. Also remember that the kerfs or grooves are part of the design so you must include them when visualizing results.

Cutting "diamonds". Diamond-shaped pieces that can be assembled into multi-pointed star shapes (Figure 3-161), can be cut by using the following technique.

First, bevel the stock so that a cross-section would be an isosceles triangle. Actually, any bevel may be used, but the given method that produces certain results is best to start with before you attempt variations (Figure 3-162). Once the stock is so formed, a series of compound angle cuts are done to form the individual pieces. If you swing the arm to 45° and tilt the blade to the same angle used to cut the bevel, you'll get an eight-point star. If you want a specific number of points, divide the number required into 360° and set the arm to this figure.

Make the first cut on the end of the stock with the work positioned on the left-hand side of the blade. Then move the work to the right-hand side of the blade and make a second cut to mate with the topmost point of the first cut.

Return the work to the left-hand side and again make a cut; then return the work to the right side of the second cut. The piece cut off when the work is on the left side of the blade is scrap (Figure 3-163). Continue the procedure until you have the number of pieces you require.

3-159. Piercing can be done with a saw blade. You must plan bearing in mind that the kerfs are part of the pattern.

3-160. Piercing can also be done with a dado. Diamond-shaped openings occur when the cuts are made at an angle.

3-162. Two ways to prepare stock for diamond cutting. Experimenting can lead to infinite variety.

3-161. Diamond-cut pieces can be assembled to make effective decorations. Proceed carefully with the cutting as explained in the text. It's best to do this kind of work with a smooth-cutting blade.

3-163. Variations are possible. These pieces can be used individually as, for example, door or drawer pulls, or they can be arranged as design overlays.

Multi-Blade Ideas

There are advantages in being able to mount two saw blades on the arbor. For example, using two blades in making kerfs for wood bending reduces the cutting time by 50% because you need just half the number of passes (Figure 3-164).

Of course, there are limits because the arbor is just so long. However, for kerfing and some similar operations, the double-blade idea works fine. You can also use blades with different diameters; for example, you could do a cutoff and form a shoulder cut for a rabbet at the same time (Figure 3-165). This technique can be applied when you need a number of similar drawer fronts. You can also work with a dado and a saw blade to do the same thing. In this case, the rabbet would be completely formed during the one cut (Figure 3-166).

Remember that you do want to be careful about what you put on the arbor. There must always be enough thread exposed so the lock nut can be tightened securely, and nothing must interfere with mounting the guard. When you use blades of different diameters or combine a dado assembly with a saw blade, the tool diameters must be suitable for the work to be done (Figure 3-167).

Rotary Planing

The rotary planer is a special accessory which, usually, is threaded for installing on the main arbor of the machine. It's a circular device with two, sometimes three, knives that are secured with locking screws (Figure 3-168). The knives are removable so they can be sharpened when necessary. Be sure to read the instructions that are provided with the accessory, especially as they relate to how the knives must be installed for correct depth of cut.

One of the obvious uses for the tool is smoothing the surface of stock or, even, reducing stock thickness. This is done with the motor locked in vertical position and with the rip lock secured to hold the tool in the position you have determined. The pass is made from right to left as shown in Figure 3-169. How deep the tool can cut is limited, but even so, you don't always want to work at full depth of cut. Roughness and hardness of the wood are important factors to consider. Cuts will be smoothest when you work so the knives cut *with* the grain of the wood.

By setting the machine as shown in Figure 3-170, you can use the rotary planer to do panel raising. A simple fence, with a relief area for the cutter, can be used. The tilt angle can be from 10° to 15°, and the depth of cut should be planned to leave a slight shoulder on the work. If you get a lot of resistance or chatter, do the job by making repeat passes. Of course, you must make the initial cut on all four edges before adjusting the tool for the following cut. As is usual when work must be shaped on all edges, do the crossgrain cuts first.

Figure 3-171 shows one way you can use the tool for decorative cuts. These are just planing cuts that are "stopped." You can cut to a mark on the work or use a stop block on the fence as a gauge.

3-164.   Cut twice as fast by using two blades. Blades are separated by washers that fit the arbor. Never mount so much that you don't leave sufficient thread for the arbor nut.

3-165.   Blades of different diameter can be used this way. Smaller blade forms a shoulder for a rabbet; larger blade separates the pieces.

3-166.   Combine a dado with a saw blade and you form a rabbet while sawing through the work. It's sometimes necessary to elevate the work so the saw blade won't cut too deeply into the table.

3-167.   Diameters of the cutting tools you combine must be suitable for the cuts you need.

3-168.   A typical rotary planer. Knives are removable so they can be sharpened.

3-170.   If you set up like this, the rotary planer can be used to do panel raising. Make the crossgrain cuts first.

3-169.   Using the rotary planer to do a surfacing job. Take light cuts. Be sure to secure the rip lock each time you change the position of the tool.

3-171.   Use the rotary planer for decorative surface cuts. Cut to marks on the work or use a stop block on the fence.

The planer can also be used to do the kind of work shown in Figure 3-172. The tool is still used in vertical position but moved in a crosscut action while the work is held in a fixed position against the fence. There are limitations here due to the tool's limited depth of cut. This may be bothersome with rabbet cuts but not too critical for tenons since the mortise can be sized to suit.

Horizontal Cutting

This type of cutting is peculiar to the radial arm saw because of the many ways you can situate the cutting tool. For example, with a dado assembly in place, raise the unit well above the table, turn it to the in-rip position, and then tilt it parallel to the table surface. With the motor moved back as far as it will go, the cutter will be in the position shown in Figure 3-173. Settings variations are possible because you can tilt the cutter, move the arm, change the position of the motor on the arm, even alter the relationship between cutter and fence. By using a regular fence, which has a clearance area for the cutter, this simple arrangement can be used to do rabbet cutting on ends and edges of stock. If you work the same way, but with the cutter tilted, you can form, among other things, beveled rabbets (Figure 3-174).

You must not rely on a regular fence for all operations of this nature. For one thing, you want to cover as much of the cutter as possible. For another, there are times when the work must be elevated higher than the table in order to achieve correct relationship between cutter and work for the operation being performed. A design for a special table you should make is shown in Figure 3-175. Note that the jig is made so it can be locked into place by using the same locking mechanism that secures a common fence.

Two operations that can be performed more easily and more accurately because of the jig are shown in Figures 3-176 and 3-177. In one, a length of heavy stock is being grooved on both edges. In the other, grooves are formed in the stock's surface by making the pass with the stock on edge.

3-172.   Cuts like this can be made by using the rotary planer in crosscut position. You can cut as wide as you like but depth of cut is limited.

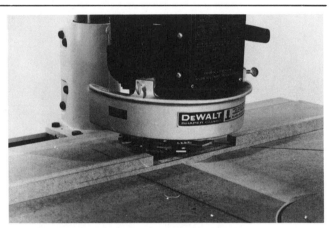

3-173.   Horizontal cutting can be done with a dado assembly if you situate the tool in this fashion. A regular fence, with a clearance area for the cutter, can be used. With this setup you can, for example, make rabbet cuts in long pieces.

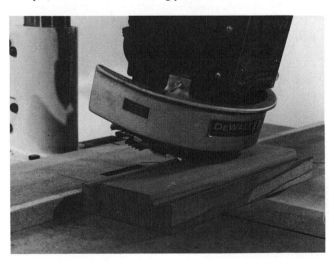

3-174.   Tilt the cutter and you can form beveled rabbets. Be sure to use a guard.

ATTACH W/3/4 SHEET METAL SCREWS

1"

3/16"

1/4 X 1 1/2 X 7 1/2"

5/8 X 1 1/4 X 7 1/2"

3/4 X 5 X 30"

3/4 X 2 1/4 X 30"

1 1/4 X 4"

1 1/4 X 4"

1 X 5"

3/4 X 3/4 X 30"

GROOVE 3/8 X 3/4"

1 1/4"

6"

3/4 X 1 1/4 X 9" (2 PIECES)

3/4 X 8 1/2 X 30"

3-175.   Construction details of a special fence you can make for horizontal dadoing. Top detail shows a guard that should be used with the fence.

3-176.   The cutouts in the fence allow the motor and cutting tool to be brought forward. The amount the cutter projects in front of the fence determines the depth of cut. The two holes visible in the fence are for attaching the guard.

3-177.   You can do some cutting with the stock on edge. Cutter-height is limited unless you widen the slot through which the cutter projects.

The design for another type of table you should make for horizontal cutting is shown in Figure 3-178. This one, also secured by using the same device that locks a regular fence, is positioned at the right end of the table. It can be moved laterally so adjustments between it and the cutting tool can be made. The motor is tilted 90° from crosscut mode so the cutter is parallel to the table and in the position shown in Figure 3-179. With this jig, the work stays put; the motor is moved along the arm so the cutter can do the job you have in mind. **BE EXTREMELY CAREFUL WHEN USING THIS SETUP.**

An example of uses for the table is shown in Figure 3-180. Here, a regular saw blade is used to form a groove in the end of narrow stock. Repeat passes are required with the saw blade lowered a kerf-width for each. Note that a clamped block is used to maintain the work's position. It's not a bad idea either, to clamp the work when you have many repeat cuts to make.

The same setup can be used to form rabbets. If you want the work to go faster or have many similar cuts to make, you can substitute a dadoing tool for the saw blade (Figure 3-181). When you install the 45° angle guide, you can use the same system, with saw blade or dado, to form grooves, rabbets or tenons on the end of miter-cut pieces (Figure 3-182).

An intriguing application for horizontal sawing when done in combination with the special table is the forming of finger lap joints (Figure 3-183). The mating pieces are cut simultaneously by clamping them together and to the back of the jig as shown in Figure 3-184. In this case, the width of

3-178.   Construction details of a table you can make for horizontal sawing. The top detail shows a 45° angle guide that can be used with the table.

3-179.   The table is set up this way at the right side of the tool's table. It is secured by locking its long leg in place as if it were a fence.

3-180.   Work is placed on the table and the blade is pulled through for the cut. Here, repeat passes are used to form a groove in the stock's end. The blade is raised (or lowered) for each cut.

the grooves and the solid stock between them, equals the width of the saw kerf. Each cut is made after the blade has been lowered 2X the width of the kerf. The depth of the grooves, which should equal the thickness of the stock, is controlled by the position in which the work is clamped in place.

For the parts to be even when assembled, one must be higher than the other by the width of the kerf as they are cut. To achieve this, merely rest one of the parts on a strip of wood whose thickness matches the width of a kerf. Accuracy is critical. Be extremely careful when adjusting cutter-height for each pass.

If you want the finger lap joint to have thicker fingers, work with a dado assembly instead of the saw blade. The cutting procedure does not change.

The Radial Arm Saw as a Drilling Tool

At one time, when radial arm saws were produced with a single arbor, any drilling operation that could be performed on them had to be done with special bits which would cut in a direction of rotation that was contrary to conventional tools. Some modern saws, particularly those most suited for home use, are equipped with an auxiliary arbor (or spindle) that pokes from the motor-side opposite the main arbor. The spindle, usually, is threaded to take a three-jaw type chuck (Figure 3-185). Even though the spindle rotates like the main arbor, conventional tools will cut as they should. To see why this is so, hold a bit at the saw end and rotate it toward you. Then do the same thing at the spindle end; the cutting lips of the bit will now be leading as they were designed to do.

3-181.   If you work with a dadoing tool, you can form rabbets or grooves by making a single pass. Don't rush. Hold the work firmly, or clamp it. Pull the tool through very slowly.

3-183.   You can form finger lap joints with the saw blade in horizontal position. In this sample, the fingers and slots match the width of the saw kerf.

3-184.   Both pieces for the joint, one of which is elevated on a shim whose thickness matches the kerf-width, are cut at the same time. Lower the blade 2X the kerf width for each cut. Accuracy is critical. You can also work with a dadoing tool.

3-182.   Miter-cut piece can be positioned by using the 45° guide. The shoulder cuts on this tenon were made in normal fashion. Here, the saw is cutting away the stock that remains. Of course, you can do the whole job this way by making repeat passes.

3-185.   A typical three-jaw chuck. Always use the key to secure the cutting tool.

3-186.   Samples of drilling tools that may be used. Don't work with hole saws or fly cutters or other tools that can't be used safely at saw speed.

While this allows the use of standard drilling tools, there are limitations, the most important of which is the single high speed of the machine. Cutting tools like fly cutters, hole saws, expansive bits, which are efficient and safe to use only at slow speeds, should not be used. Some of the tools you *can* use are shown in Figure 3-186. Spade bits are okay since they cut in good style at speeds higher than you would use with other tools. But even so, make it a rule not to use any cutter that causes vibration or chatter.

Don't leave anything on the main arbor when you use the saw for drilling, but do keep the saw guard in place. This will cover the arbor which, of course, will continue to rotate as you do drilling chores.

Horizontal drilling.   One type of horizontal drilling is done by organizing the machine so the cutting tool points to the rear. This is the same motor position that you would use for out-ripping. You do the drilling by moving the power unit toward the column. Sometimes, when you need holes in the surface of stock, it's possible to secure the work vertically by clamping it in place as if it were a fence. To brace the work, you can use a block of wood between it and

Horizontal Edge-Drilling Platform

THREE PIECES
3/4" x 5" x 34"

3-187.   You can make a basic platform for horizontal drilling simply by putting together three pieces of wood. If necessary, change the dimensions to suit your equipment.

3-188.   The purpose of the platform is to elevate the work. This is necessary so there will be clearance for the bottom of the motor. The bottom edge of the vertical piece is gripped like a fence.

3-189.   Place the work flat on the table and adjust the drill height by raising or lowering the tool's arm. Use a stop or a C-clamp on the arm when you must drill to a specific depth.

3-190.   A simple attachment like this provides a gauge so you can automatically position the work when you are drilling a series of equally spaced holes.

the column. Also, if you are drilling through the stock, back up the work with another piece of wood. This is a general rule for any drilling operation. The backup block will protect anything behind the work and will minimize the splintering and feathering that can occur when the bit breaks through.

Horizontal drilling is the ideal way to go when you need to drill holes in the edges of material; for example, holes for dowels when doing edge-to-edge joints. Because of the motor, you can't situate a drilling tool as close to the table as you might like. The solution is to devise a means of elevating the work high enough above the table so the motor will have clearance. You can accomplish this easily by making the jig shown in Figure 3-187, which provides a platform for the work. The vertical part of the jig provides for backing up the work and also for securing the unit in the table as if it were a regular fence (Figure 3-188). The work is placed on the platform; holes are formed by moving the motor unit forward (Figure 3-189).

Actually, this arrangement is as functional and accurate as any horizontal boring machine. It's a super way to drill holes for edge-to-edge dowel joints because it assures that all the holes will have exactly the same edge distance. If you mark each piece of stock so a similar surface will be kept uppermost, or down on the platform, it won't be critical for the holes to be centered exactly.

To space the holes, you can work to guide lines marked on the work, but the spacing can be controlled automatically if you make the little gadget shown in Figure 3-190. The item is tack-nailed to the platform so the bolt that passes through it can engage a drilled hole and so position the work for the next hole. Bolt and hole diameter can be equal, or you can use the guide with a small bolt and drill pilot holes that you enlarge later. This way, the one guide will be suitable for all work.

When you need blind holes—holes that don't go through the workpiece—you can control how deep the bit will penetrate by using a stop on the arm of the tool to limit how far the motor will travel.

The same horizontal drilling setup can be used to form round-end mortises. It's just a question of drilling a series of overlapping holes to clean out the bulk of the waste (Figure 3-191). What remains will be easy to remove with a sharp chisel.

Other operations that can be done on the elevated platform include, drilling radial holes in round stock, drilling angular holes by slanting the work on a beveled block, and drilling radial holes on a surface. For the latter idea, you need a vertical pivot jig, constructed as shown in Figure 3-192, that can be clamped to the upper, vertical portion of the drilling jig. The work is impaled on the nail-pivot and rotated X-number of degrees for each hole, depending on the spacing you need. The pivot point and the cutting tool must be on the same vertical centerline. The edge distance of the holes—how far in from the perimeter of the workpiece they are—is controlled by the position of the pivot jig on the platform and the height of the cutter, which is controlled by raising or lowering the tool's arm.

Another way to operate for radial holes in stock surfaces is shown in Figure 3-193. Here, while the stock is still pivot-mounted, additional control is established with the clamped-on strips that are cut at a 45° angle on the end that bears against the work. In this situation, the work must be a true circle to begin with. Of course, there is a limit to work size. There is just so much room between the table and the arm when it is at maximum elevation.

3-191.   You can form a round end mortise by drilling a series of overlapping holes and then cleaning out the waste that remains with a sharp chisel.

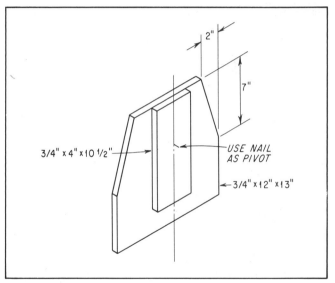

3-192.   The vertical pivot jig is constructed this way. Clamp it securely to the backboard of the horizontal edge-drilling platform. Pivot and drill must be on the same vertical centerline.

3-193.   Another way to drill radial holes in a surface. The clamped boards, which have mitered ends, provide more security. Be sure the disc you are drilling is a true circle.

Holes are often required in the end of workpieces. You can do this on the radial arm saw by applying a variation of the horizontal drilling technique. The differences are these. The drilling tool is situated so it points to the left. This means that the auxiliary spindle end of the motor is swung 180° from the normal crosscut position. The elevating platform, or table, needed to provide clearance for the motor, can be designed as shown in Figure 3-194. Here, the long leg of the jig is gripped like a fence, locked in the position you need in relation to the drilling tool. Be sure that the width of the long leg and that of the outboard support leg are such that the jig's surface will be parallel to the table surface.

When following this procedure, the jig and the drilling tool are in fixed positions; the work, held snugly down on the table and against the fence, is moved forward to engage the bit (Figure 3-195). The distance between fence and bit determines how far from the edge of the stock the hole will be. The position of the hole in relation to the stock's thickness, is determined by the elevation of the bit. To establish how deep a hole will be, clamp a stop block to the table so you can advance the work only to a given point. To space holes, you must readjust the bit by changing the position of the motor.

The same arrangement can be used to drill into the ends of miter-cut work, but you need an angle guide like the one shown in Figure 3-196 to position the work so the holes will be at right angles to the cut edge. The guide and the work, held firmly, are moved forward together for drilling (Figure 3-197). There will be a tendency for the guide or the work to move while you are advancing the pieces, so work carefully. It will help if you face the bearing edge of the guide with sandpaper. Holes drilled in this fashion allow you to reinforce miter joints with dowels (Figure 3-198).

3-194.   Construction details of a table you can make for horizontal end-drilling. The back leg must be long enough so it can be secured like a fence.

3-196.   A 45° angle guide that you can use with the table.

3-195.   This kind of horizontal drilling is done by moving the work into the cutter. Clamp a stop block to the table when you need holes of a specific depth.

3-197.   The work is positioned by the guide. Guide and work are moved together.

You can drill edge holes in the perimeter of circular pieces by working in similar fashion, but since the work can't be guided with a fence, you must make a sliding table so both table and work can be moved together (Figure 3-199). The work is pivot-mounted for turning, and clamped to the table for each hole. This jig can be made like the one for end drilling, with one long leg riding in the "groove" normally used for a fence. The fence locks should be tightened, but not so much that the jig can't be moved laterally.

The Radial Arm Saw as a Router

At one time, there was just one way to do routing operations on the radial arm saw; now there are two. The "old" way, still practical, employs special chucks or adapters that mount on the auxiliary spindle of the machine so conventional router bits can be used for cutting. The special hold- ers are important because router bits have to withstand considerable side thrust and should not be gripped in a conventional three-jaw chuck. The disadvantage of this system is in having to rout at saw speeds. It's all right but not ideal since routing is done most efficiently at high speeds. A way to help compensate is to use a slow feed speed so the cutting tool has more time to do its job.

The "new" system uses the radial arm saw as a carrier for an independent, portable router (Figure 3-200). This is possible because of a unique accessory that is secured to the arbor end of the saw's motor. One type, shown in Figure 3-201, provides a platform to which the portable router can be bolted. Another unit grips the router with an encircling clamp. Either unit can accommodate portable routers of various types and sizes. When working this way, it's a good idea to keep the saw unplugged since its motor is not involved in the routing operations.

3-198.   Being able to drill into the edge of miter cuts allows using dowels to reinforce the joint.

3-200.   Some manufacturers offer equipment that allows the use of a portable router with the radial arm saw. You have true portable router capability plus the flexibility of the tool.

3-199.   Drilling radial holes in the edge of circular pieces calls for moving work *and* table. The work is clamped to the table. Holes are drilled at location points marked on the workpiece.

3-201.   Attachments for mounting portable routers differ. On this Craftsman tool, the accessory provides a base on which the router can be bolted.

A major advantage of the new system is that it combines true portable router capability with the flexibility that is inherent in the radial arm saw. Also, with the portable router you can handle a greater variety of cutters, some of which, together with what they can do, are shown in Figure 3-202.

Router bits can be "pilotless," in which case they resemble the samples shown in Figure 3-203. There are two ways you can work with them. In one, the work remains stationary while the cutter is moved, as shown in Figure 3-204 where, with the machine in crosscut position, the bit is pulled across the stock to form a narrow dado. With the second method, the cutter is in a fixed position. The work, guided and supported by, for example, a fence, is moved against the bit (Figure 3-205). Always feed so that bit's cutting action tends to keep the work against the fence. In this case, the feed is left-to-right; *against* the cutter's direction of rotation.

Router bits are also designed *with* pilots. These can be integral, the pilot being an extension of the bit's shaft, or the pilot end can be fitted with a removable ball bearing (Figure 3-206). The pilot is there so work can bear against it

SHAPE PRODUCED BY BIT	NAME OF BIT	TYPICAL SIZES
	Straight	1/4″ to 3/4″
	Veining	1/16″ to 7/32″
	V-grooving	3/8″ and 7/8″
	Dovetail	1/4″ and 1/2″
	Rabbeting	1/4″ and 3/8″
	Chamfering	5/8″
	Cove	3/16″ to 1/2″
	Beading	1/8″ to 3/8″
	Corner rounds	3/16″ to 1/2″
	Ogee	3/16″ and 9/32″
	Roman ogee	5/32″ and 1/4″

3-202.   A sampling of router bits and the cuts that can be made with them.

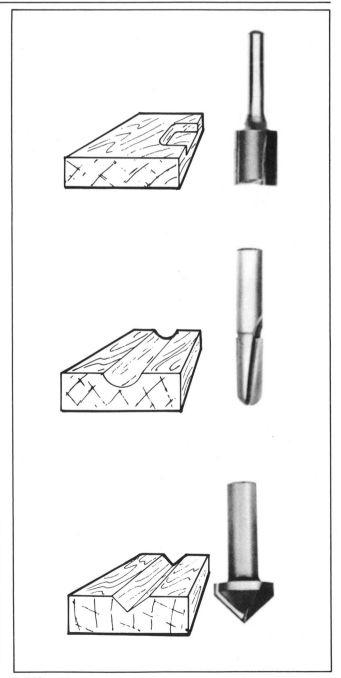

3-203.   These are examples of pilotless router bits.

during the cut. A problem with the integral pilot is that it turns as fast as the bit's cutting edges and this can result in indenting and burn marks. The ball bearing pilot, because it turns independently, does not cause friction and so eliminates the possibility of marring the work.

Bits that have pilots can be used like those that lack them so long as you cut on the edges of stock. An advantage of a pilot is that it allows you to shape curved edges (Figure 3-207). Here, the router is in fixed position. The work, bearing against the pilot, is moved against the cutter's rotation. The maximum width of cut, not its depth (since this is controllable by cutter-height above the table), is from the surface of the pilot to the outmost edge of the bit's profile.

The illustrations in this chapter involve both systems since most operational procedures can be performed either way. Remember the adage about feed-speed. Never try to cut so fast, or so deep in a single pass, that you prevent the cutter from performing as it should; no matter if you are working at saw speed or with a portable machine.

3-206.   Example of router bits that have a pilot. These are ball bearing types. Friction is eliminated because the bearing rotates independently of the cutter.

3-204.   You can use a straight router bit to form dadoes when you work in the crosscut position. Cuts that are wider than the bit's diameter are done by making repeat passes.

3-205.   Form grooves with a router bit by working in the rip position. In this case, the cutter is in a fixed position; the work is moved to make the cut.

3-207.   Shaping an edge with a router bit. The cut is controlled because the work bears against the pilot. To minimize burning and indenting, keep the work moving and don't apply excessive pressure if the pilot is integral.

Straight cuts. Cuts across the grain are done with the machine in crosscut position and the work in fixed position. The cutter is then moved across for the cut. Typical forms produced this way are dadoes and rabbets (Figure 3-208). Since you can make repeat passes, the cut-width doesn't have to be determined by the size of the bit. For stopped dadoes, cut to a line on the work or use a stop on the tool's arm. If the dado is to be blind, that is, the U-shape will not be visible on either edge of the stock, work with two stops. One to set where the cut begins, the other where it ends. You start this procedure, of course, with the cutter above the work, positioned by the first stop. Then you lower it slowly into the work and pull it forward to the position established by the second stop.

The crosscut system can be used for forms other than rabbets and dadoes if you can mount suitable cutters. For example, you can form dovetail slots with a cutter designed for the purpose (Figure 3-209). With cutters like this, the form *has to be* shaped in a single pass so you must be extra cautious with feed-speed.

For grooving operations, work with the cutter set vertically and the machine in rip position. Use a regular fence for support and as a guide and move the work from left to right (Figure 3-210). For stopped or blind grooves, work as described for dadoes. Control the length of the cuts by using stop blocks on the fence.

Work the same way when you need rabbet cuts on long edges (Figure 3-211). The width of the rabbet is not, of course, limited to the diameter of the bit. Repeat passes will widen it.

Horizontal routing. You can do many practical routing operations by working with the height-platform that was suggested for horizontal drilling. The machine is situated so the motor is in horizontal position, with the cutting tool pointing toward the column. Figure 3-212 shows how the arrangement is used to form a groove in a long edge, something difficult to do with other means. The cutter is fixed: the work is moved to form the groove. Note, in this situation, that the feed is from right to left.

You can use the same setup to form a rabbet or a tongue. The rabbet requires one pass. The tongue (Figure 3-213) requires two, the second one made after the stock has been turned over.

Because a straight router bit will form a hole if moved directly into the stock, you can use one to form a round-end mortise. First, "drill" overlapping holes as if you were using a regular drill bit. Then, with the work held firmly on the platform, move it as shown in Figure 3-214, so the router bit will clean out the remaining waste material.

The portable router system can be used in similar fashion but you'll get more from the arrangement if you use it with the special table that is shown in Figures 3-215 and 3-216. The router is set in a horizontal position behind the jig with its business end pointing forward. Figure 3-217, where chamfering is being done with a V-grooving bit, demonstrates a typical operation. Of course, other cuts are possible; it depends on what bit you use. It's like having a horizontal shaping machine.

3-208.   You can form end rabbets by working in the crosscut position. Repeat passes are usually necessary, but work with the largest straight bit you have.

3-209.   Forming a dovetail slot by working in the crosscut position. Cuts like this must be done in a single pass so be sure to keep the work firm and to feed very slowly.

3-210.   A regular fence can be used when routing grooves. For blind or stopped grooves, work as described for the cuts made with a dado. Use stop blocks on the fence to control cut-lengths.

3-211.   Rabbets on long edges are also formed in rip position. You must always feed so the action of the cutter tends to hold the work against the fence.

3-212. The platform designed for horizontal drilling can be used the same way for routing jobs. Here, the cutter is locked in position and the work is moved to form a groove.

3-214. Form a round-end mortise by using the bit to "drill" overlapping holes. To clean out the waste, move the work slowly back and forth while holding it firmly on the platform.

3-213. To form a tongue, just make two passes. It isn't necessary to reposition the cutter. Just flip the stock for the second pass.

3-215. A portable tool can also be used horizontally. A special table is needed so work can be positioned high enough for the cutter.

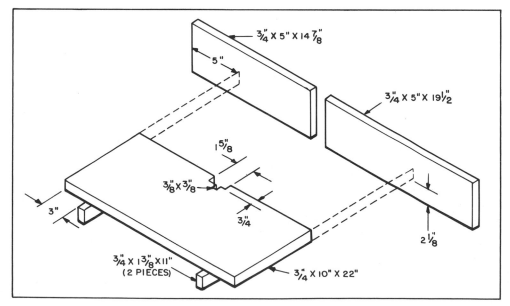

3-216. This is how to make the special table that is needed when a portable router is used in horizontal position.

You can also do horizontal routing by working as shown in Figure 3-218, where a dovetail slot is being formed in the end of a workpiece. To work this way you need to make a table so the stock can be supported and elevated. A simple one, which can be locked in place much like a fence, is shown in Figure 3-219.

You can work the same way to form a dovetail key, or "tongue." Make a cut on one surface of the stock, and then make a similar cut after the stock has been turned over. The dovetail joint is complete (Figure 3-220) when the key is combined with the cut that was demonstrated in Figure 3-209.

Pattern routing.   For pattern routing (sometimes called 'overarm' routing) you need a guide pin that is the same diameter as the bit (Figure 3-221). The best way to set up is to tack-nail a sheet of 1/4″ or 1/2″ plywood to the saw

table and then use the arm-elevating crank for the bit to form a hole in the plywood. Glue a dowel pin in the hole so it projects above the auxiliary table about 3/16″. The pattern, which is the shape of what you wish to cut in the project, is tack-nailed to the underside of the workpiece and then placed over the pin (Figure 3-222). Position the router bit to the depth of cut required and do the cutting with the pattern in constant contact with the guide pin. Since the cutting tool is directly over the guide pin, the pattern design will be duplicated in the work (Figure 3-223).

Pivot cutting.   You can do circular grooves or rabbets on the edge of circular pieces easily if you use a nail as a pivot guide. All you have to do is drive a nail through the center of the work so the point can penetrate the saw table about 1/4″. The distance from the nail to the cutter is the radius of the circle you will route (Figures 3-224 and 3-225).

3-217.   Using a V-grooving bit to do chamfering; a typical operation for horizontal routing.

3-218.   Another position for the portable router when used for horizontal cutting. The work stays put, the tool is pulled forward to make the cut. This same position is used to form a dovetail tenon, or tongue. A cut is made on each side of the stock.

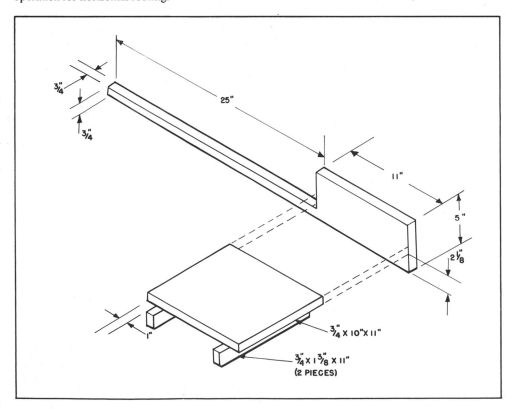

3-219.   This kind of table, locked in place on the right side of the machine, is used for the kind of cut that was shown in the previous illustration.

3-220. Dovetail tongue and slot fit together to form the complete joint.

3-222. The pattern is tack-nailed to the underside of the work. The guide pin and the router bit must have the same vertical centerline.

3-221. This is how to set up for pattern routing. The guide pin must not project more than the thickness of the pattern.

3-223. The pattern is duplicated because the work is guided by the pin. You must be sure to bear constantly against the guide pin throughout the operation.

3-224. You can use the pivot method to form perfect circular grooves. Turn the work slowly in a clockwise direction.

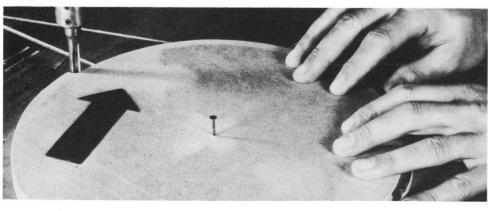

3-225. You can rabbet circular edges by working the same way. Note the direction of feed indicated by the arrow.

Decorative cuts. Router bits offer many opportunities to make surface grooves for purely decorative purposes. A series of equally spaced, stopped grooves on slim stock will produce pieces that can be used as moldings. To limit the length of cut on operations like this, you can feed to a line on the work or use a C-clamp on the arm to limit the travel length of the carriage (Figure 3-226).

If you cut completely across the stock you will have material that can be strip-cut into slim moldings (Figure 3-227).

Curved grooves. You can rout grooves parallel to a curved edge if you use a triangular piece of wood as a guide. This is tack-nailed to the saw table with one point in line with the router bit but spaced away to equal the edge distance of the groove (Figure 3-228). Move the work so its edge bears constantly against the guide. As you make the pass, keep the work positioned so that a tangent to the curve at the point of cut will be perpendicular to the center line of the guide (Figure 3-229).

Freehand routing. Since a router bit will cut in any direction, it's a logical tool to use for cutting intricate de-

signs, house numbers, names and so on (Figure 3-230). Since a freehand operation has feed going in many directions, the results will depend on how well you follow the design. It isn't difficult but does demand careful feed and sharp tools. Success will come faster if you do some practicing in soft wood with minimum grain.

Saber Sawing

You can do curve-cutting on the radial arm saw if a saber-saw attachment like the one shown in Figure 3-231 is available for the tool you own. The accessory, which mounts on the machine's main arbor, converts the rotary motion of the arbor into an up-and-down action. Thus, blank-end saw blades which are similar to but not the same as those used in portable saber saws, can be used for cutting. Note, in Figure 3-232, that the teeth on the blades point down toward the end of the blade, not up as they do on other designs. There is more than enough variety in available blades so you can do a considerable amount of sawing in various materials (Figure 3-233). Don't work with blades that are longer than 3-1/2".

3-226.   You can form decorative moldings by working in the crosscut position to form shallow grooves. You can limit the length of the cuts by using a stop on the tool's arm.

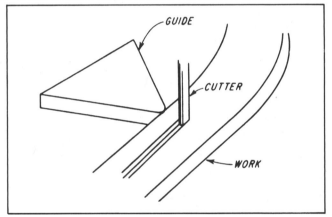

3-228.   View the centerline of the guide as being perpendicular to a line that is tangent to the curve at the cut area. Maintain this relationship throughout the pass.

3-227.   You get slim moldings when you strip-cut pieces that have been surface-routed.

3-229.   This is the way to form a groove parallel to a curved edge. The idea works for inside or outside curves. The edge bearing against the guide must be smooth.

3-230.   Practice before tackling an important job freehand. Work slowly and be sure the bit is sharp. If you have many similar designs to do, it would be wise to set up for pattern routing.

3-231.   You can do saber sawing on the radial arm saw if your machine can take an attachment like this one. The accessory converts the motor's rotary motion into an up-and-down action.

3-232.   Rigid, blank-end blades are used with the saber saw attachment. Note that the teeth point toward the free end of the blade.

SABER SAW BLADES (TYPICAL)

BLADE NAME (OR TYPES)	TEETH PER INCH	CUT FINISH TO EXPECT	CUTTING SPEED	REMARKS
Wood cutting (coarse)	7	Rough	Fast	Use on softwoods 3/4″ and thicker.
Wood cutting (medium)	10	Medium	Medium	Use on softwoods under 3/4″ thick.
Wood cutting (hollow-ground)	7	Smooth	Medium	Good for hardwoods under 3/4″ thick. Also good for softwoods up to 2″ thick when a good cut-finish is required.
	10	Very smooth	Medium	Good for plywood up to 3/4″ thick—may also be used on lumber.
	7	Medium	Fast	Good for plywood up to 1″ thick when fast cutting and a reasonably smooth finish are required.
Double cutting	7	Rough	Fast	Can be used on most wood and fiber materials—blades have teeth on both edges so cutting can be from two directions.
	10	Medium	Medium	
Metal cutting	20	Fine	Slow	Can be used on ferrous metals up to 3/16″ thick—blade should be high speed steel and specially heat treated.
	10	Medium	Medium	Use on nonferrous metals up to 1/4″ thick—blade material should be high speed steel and properly heat treated.
Knife blade	No teeth	Smooth	Fast	May be used on leather, cardboard, rubber, composition tile, and similar materials.

3-233.   Types of blades that can be used for saber sawing and some of the jobs that can be done with them.

An easy way to work with the accessory is to simply drill a hole through the tool's table so the saw blade can pass through (Figure 3-234). Cutting is done pretty much as it would be on a jigsaw. The height of the saber saw is adjusted so the spring hold-down will bear on the work with only enough pressure to keep the work from jiggling. Too much pressure can mar the work and will make it difficult to keep the work moving. Feeding is done with hands placed to accommodate the stock, and to keep it moving so the blade will always saw on the cutline (Figure 3-235).

Because the blades are only gripped at one end, they must be heavy and stiff enough to work without bending or twisting. Thus you can't do the extremely fine cutting that is possible on a jigsaw; a tool that can handle blades so fine you can hardly see the kerf.

A good jig to make for saber sawing on the radial arm is shown in Figure 3-236. The jig, detailed in Figure 3-237, is basically an elevated table that allows the saber saw to be used in various positions; not just the one spot that would be dictated by a blade-hole through the tool's table. Thus, the accessory can be used in a crosscut position or swung around to a rip position. The latter arrangement works fine when you need to make a cut on extra-long material.

The table includes a sliding pivot guide which can be used to automatically guide work for circular cutting. In use, the points of the blade's teeth must be directly on line with the pivot pin in the guide. The best way to start is to cut freehand to the line, then impale the work on the pin and finish the cut by rotating the work in a clockwise direction.

When you need to do piercing, that is, make internal cuts without a lead-in cut from any edge, put the work in place first and then lower the blade so it penetrates a hole that you have drilled in a waste area of the workpiece (Figure 3-238).

Much radial arm saber sawing is done following systems used when working with a portable saber saw. The difference, of course, is that with the portable tool, the work is usually in a fixed position; the tool is moved to do the cutting. However, cutting techniques, like how to get around a sharp corner, and so on, are similar.

Sanding Operations

You can do both disc sanding and drum sanding on the radial arm saw but you must be certain that the necessary accessories (Figures 3-239 and 3-240), are right for the tool you own. This has to do with mounting methods and speed. For example, the disc must be rated safe to use at the saw's rpm. Be sure to read the manufacturer's instructions which will be specific for the accessory they supply.

In this section, we'll cover briefly some of the applications that apply to disc sanding and drum sanding. Many of the ideas that will be demonstrated in the chapters that deal specifically with the sanding tools are usable. It's just a question of applying them to the radial arm saw.

Disc sanding. To utilize the disc sander fully, you must make a special table that imitates a conventional disc sander arrangement. The one shown in Figure 3-241

3-234.   A basic way to use the saber saw is to drill a hole in the table so the blade can poke through.

3-235.   The spring hold-down bears on the work to keep it from jiggling. Don't use so much pressure that it will be difficult to move the workpiece.

3-236.   If you make this special table you'll be able to use the saber saw in crosscut or rip position. The jig includes a pivot guide for circular cuts.

3-237. Construction details of the special table for saber sawing.

3-238. To do "piercing" (inside cuts), put the work in place before lowering the blade through a hole that you have drilled in waste areas.

3-239. What you need for disc sanding. The abrasive paper is self-adhesive. You merely press it against the disc after peeling away backing paper.

3-240. You can also use sanding drums on the radial arm saw. Some manufacturers supply drums of different diameters.

3-241. You need this kind of auxiliary table, that you make, to do disc sanding. The gauge is used on the table to position pieces that have been miter-cut.

incorporates a groove for a "miter gauge" and has a long leg so the unit can be secured using the same locking devices that hold a regular fence. Check to be sure that the height of the jig will allow its surface to be on or slightly above the horizontal centerline of the disc when it is mounted on the machine.

Always try to function so contact between work and abrasive is on the "down" side of the disc. Since the disc, when mounted on the main arbor, rotates in a clockwise direction, the down side of the disc is at the right-hand area of the table (Figure 3-242). When you can't work this way, you may be sweeping a long piece across the disc; remem-ber that the "up" side tends to lift the work and that waste will be thrown upward. Safety goggles are a must, but wear-ing them should be routine procedure anyway.

To smooth a curved edge, move it along the disc but maintain its position so the plane of the disc will always be tangent to the arc. You can work as shown in Figure 3-243, when you need to sand curved pieces to a specific width. The distance between the end of the guide and the disc is the width of the workpiece. This idea works only if the inside edge of the work is smooth to begin with; something you accomplish by drum sanding. As stated above, be sure the disc is tangent to the arc throughout the pass.

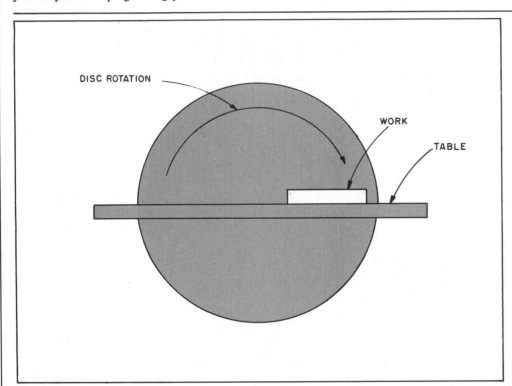

3-242.   Standard practice is to apply work against the "down" side of the disc.

3-243.   How to sand curved pieces to a specific width. The edge that bears against the guide must be smooth and even; something to accomplish by drum sanding.

3-244.   You can smooth long, straight edges by sweeping them across the disc, or you can angle the work just a bit so sanding will be done on the down side. Keep the work moving.

You can do a nice job of smoothing long, straight edges by working as shown in Figure 3-244. Hold the work at a very slight angle, barely enough to clear the up side, and move it from left to right. Keep the pass at a constant speed and apply very little pressure. Remember what was said about the up side if you choose to make contact with the entire diameter of the disc.

Work with the miter gauge to position work that has been miter-cut (Figure 3-245). Keep the gauge in one position if the work is flat and can simply be turned end-for-end for sanding opposite cuts. If the work is shaped so it can't be turned over, sand one end, and then turn the *gauge* around so the work can be positioned for sanding the second end.

To sand cross miters, work with a disc-tilt that matches the angle of the cut (Figure 3-246). Move the work directly forward; use very light feed pressure.

Figure 3-247 shows how the radial arm saw can be set up to do disc surface-sanding. The disc is positioned parallel to the table and its height is adjusted to take an extremely light 'cut'. Feed the work from right to left, slowly and smoothly. This method will work only if you check alignment factors to be sure the disc and the table are parallel.

3-245. The miter gauge is used to position work that has been miter-cut. Both bearing-edges of the gauge are useable.

3-246. You can sand cross-miters this way. When the work is wide, you can keep it fixed and move the disc across, but work carefully.

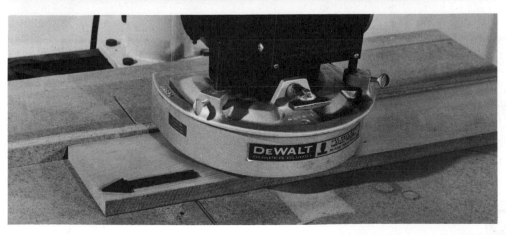

3-247. Using the disc for surface sanding. On wide work make repeat passes, repositioning the disc for each. Take very light cuts.

Drum sanding. The saw's table has an opening, usually in one of the boards that is normally behind the fence, so a drum sander, after being mounted and tilted to vertical position, can be situated as shown in Figure 3-248. The drum can be raised or lowered so a good deal of the abrasive surface can be utilized. Be careful not to lower it so far that it will contact whatever structure is under the table.

You can sand inside or outside curved edges, even straight ones, by working as demonstrated in Figure 3-249. Since the angle between drum and table is 90°, sanded edges will be square to surfaces. Move the work against the drum's rotation. Use very little pressure and keep the work moving steadily. It's likely that the drum will indent the work should you pause at any time. To sand inside edges, put the work in place before you lower the drum (Figure 3-250). If the work is so large that you get interference from the column, situate the drum in a forward position and work with an auxiliary table in which you have formed a hole for the drum.

The drum can be used for some surface sanding operations. Set the machine so the drum will be in horizontal position and pointing toward the column. Set the drum's elevation for a very light cut and then move the work against the drum's rotation (Figure 3-251). Put the work on a height block when the work's thickness is such that the motor interferes with establishing correct elevation for the drum.

A handy drum-sanding jig you can make is shown in Figure 3-252. It locks in place like a fence with the vertical part behind the drum. One job the jig is especially good for is surface-sanding thin material (Figure 3-253). Since the drum's rotation is counterclockwise, work moved behind it is passed from left to right.

If you organize the machine so the drum will be horizontal and pointing away from the column, you create a setup that is quite handy for sanding edges (Figure 3-254). The best way to work is to set the drum so it barely touches the work. Make a pass, and then repeat it without changing the drum's elevation. If the edge isn't smooth enough, lower the drum just a fraction and pass the work again.

Work the same way if you wish to smooth a beveled edge. Use the same pass procedure, but with the drum tilted to match the angle of the work (Figure 3-255).

3-248.   Simple way to do drum sanding is to position the tool so it passes through the opening that is already in the table boards.

3-250.   To smooth inside edges, put the work in place before lowering the drum.

3-249.   Pass the work against the drum's direction of rotation. Use light pressure and keep the work moving constantly. Any pass will cause the drum to indent the work's edge.

3-251.   You can work with the drum to do some surface sanding but there is a limit to how wide the stock can be. Twice the length of the drum is maximum.

3/4" X 4 1/2" X 22"

GROOVE
3/4" X 3/4"

5"

1 1/2 RAD

3/4" X 10" X 16"

3/4

3-252.   A jig like this, with its own fence, can be handy for some drum sanding operations.

3-253.   With the jig, you can pass work between the drum and the fence. This is a good way to surface-sand thin pieces. The cut must be light and the work must be kept moving.

3-254.   How to set up to sand edges. Note that the work is passed between blocks that are clamped to the table.

3-255.   Work the same way when you need to sand a bevel. Take very light cuts. Make two passes, but *don't* change the height of the drum for the second one.

"Lathe" Work

Applying the term "lathe" work to this very special procedure *is* taking some liberties, yet the idea does allow using the radial arm saw to perform some operations that normally are done on a wood-turning lathe.

You can utilize this technique if you make a carrier-type jig like the one shown in Figure 3-256. The jig, which is designed to be secured like a fence, allows work to be mounted between "centers" as it would be in a lathe. The jig allows some latitude in work-length since the end pieces in which the centers are mounted are movable. Each of the end pieces can be locked in the position you select.

The centers are made from ordinary 3/8" x 4" bolts that are cone-shaped at the thread-end by grinding, or even by working with a file. In use, they are locked in place with opposing nuts after they have been situated so the workpiece will hold firmly between them (Figure 3-257). It's a good idea to check frequently as you work to assure that the work doesn't loosen.

The jig, situated as shown in Figure 3-258, is best used with a good, sharp dado assembly, even though a saw blade can be used for narrow grooving. Start with the cutting tool elevated above the work. The cutter can be over the work or behind it, these factors being affected by the diameter of the workpiece. Hold the work very firmly with your hand well away from the cut area. It's a good idea to wear a glove for this procedure. Lower the cutter slowly to make contact and then turn the work against the cutter's direction of rotation.

I hope it's needless to say that this kind of work calls for cautious work-handling. Don't make deep cuts in a single pass. It's better to repeat passes, lowering the cutter a bit for each one. There will be a tendency for the cutter to rotate the work, so keep a firm grip even on minimum-depth cuts. Adjust the guard for maximum cutting-tool coverage on your side of the work.

You can use the technique to turn square stock to round along its entire length or in a limited area or to form wide or narrow grooves. V-grooving can be done by working with the cutter tilted.

You can form integral tenons by working at one end of the stock. Tenons are usually located concentrically, but there are times when the location should be elsewhere. This is accomplished by situating the work on "off" centers instead of true centers (Figure 3-259).

Always check twice before starting to work to be sure that the stock is secure between centers and that the jig is firmly in place. If you wish, you can lock the jig at the front of the saw's table by using a C-clamp.

Other Uses

You can use the radial arm saw for jobs like grinding, wire brushing, and buffing, all work that can be accomplished by mounting particular accessories on the tool's main arbor. It is critical though, to be sure that what you plan to use can be mounted for safe use and can operate at the tool's speed. You can determine this only by checking the manufacturer's literature. Taking chances can result in unhappy times.

Grinding. Having a grinding wheel can be a big help in many areas. With one, you can sharpen drill bits (Figure 3-260), re-shape screwdrivers, re-edge chisels, and so on. So

3-256. This is the jig to make if you wish to use the radial arm saw for "lathe" work. The top detail shows how regular bolts are used as "centers."

3-257.   The double-nut system lets you secure the bolt. Check frequently as you work to be sure the work doesn't loosen.

3-258.   Operations are performed by turning the work very slowly against the cutter's direction of rotation. Make light cuts, use the guard, and always position hands so they are no way near the cutting tool. This is not the kind of work that can be rushed.

3-259.   You can form integral tenons that are concentric or offset. It all depends on how you mount the work between the centers.

3-260.   Mount the grinding wheel and you can do different types of sharpening and re-edging chores. The guard can be set lower than it is shown here. Always wear safety goggles.

that you can hold tools in correct relationship to the grinding wheel, you must make a tool support like the one detailed in Figure 3-261. Use clamps to secure the support to the tool's table; adjust the height of the grinding wheel so its horizontal centerline is on or a bit above the surface of the tool support. Use the regular saw guard, adjusting it so as little as possible of the wheel will be exposed.

Stand to one side and let the grinding wheel run free for a minute or so before working, especially if the wheel is a new one. Some grinding operations throw off sparks so be sure adjacent areas are free of sawdust, or any material that is inflammable.

Wire brushing. Wire brushes, which are available in various grades, can be used for, among other things, removing scale or other unwanted materials from metals (Figure 3-262). Before using one, stand to one side while the wheel runs free. If there are loose wires, you don't want them to fly at you.

With a wire brush, you can do some unique texturing on wood (Figure 3-263). In this particular application, the tool is set in crosscut position and the brush is pulled across the work. The amount and the kind of texturing is affected by whether you work with a fine or a coarse wheel. It isn't necessary to cut very deeply, especially if you work with a coarse wheel. A regular saw guard can be used with the wheels, but since the wires on the wheel can spread quite a bit when they are working and might damage the guard, it might be wise to make and use a special cover like the one shown in Figure 3-264.

Buffing. Buffing wheels (Figure 3-265), are no more than flexible carriers for abrasive compounds that are applied to their edges. To break in a new wheel, which means bringing it to the point where it doesn't have loose threads, hold a piece of wood against it while it is turning. Threads that project but don't separate from the wheel can be removed with scissors while the wheel is still.

When applying the compound, hold it against the turning wheel until the perimeter of the wheel is completely coated.

Always keep a firm grip on the work. Keep it moving but don't force it against the wheel. Gentle pressure should be sufficient for any buffing or polishing operation. Don't neglect to wear safety goggles when buffing, wire-brushing, or grinding.

Trouble Shooting

Figure 3-266 lists possible operational problems that can occur when doing radial arm saw work. Don't continue to work when one of the listed problems is evident. Check the chart to see if one of the solutions will provide a cure.

3-262.   Use wire brushes for, among other things, cleaning metals. Wire brushes come in different grades: "coarse", "medium" and "fine", being common.

3-263.   A unique use for a wire brush is texturing stock. This is done in crosscut position, with the work still and the brush pulled across.

3-261.   This is the kind of stand you need for grinding operations.

3-264.   Always use a guard when wire brushing. If the regular saw guard can't be used, then make one like this.

3-265.   Cleaning or polishing metals is one of the uses for a buffing wheel. Various compounds, applied to the rim of the wheel, are available for performing tasks on different materials.

THE PROBLEM	POSSIBLE CAUSES	WHAT TO LOOK FOR OR DO
WHEN CROSSCUTTING Cut edge not square	Misalignment	Is saw blade travel 90° to fence?—check and reset "0" auto-stop
Edge has bevel	Misalignment	Blade must be perpendicular to table—check and reset blade-tilt "0" auto-stop
Cross bevels, miters not accurate	Misalignment	Use care when making settings—make trial cuts—check auto-stops if any
Blade drags Kerfs wider than normal Rough cuts Excessive splintering	"Heeling" (misalignment)	"Back" teeth of blade not cutting on same line as "front" teeth—needs yoke adjustment—follow manufacturer's instructions
Blade tends to "climb"	Poor practice Bad or dull blade	Don't rush cut—let blade saw at its own pace Replace or recondition
Blade binds	Dull blade Excessive work-overhang Poor practice	Replace or sharpen Provide enough support for work to be level Keep work tight against fence

(Continued on next page)

THE PROBLEM	POSSIBLE CAUSES	WHAT TO LOOK FOR OR DO
WHEN RIPPING Blade drags—kerfs wider than normal—rough cuts—excessive splintering	"Heeling" (misalignment)	"Back" teeth of blade not cutting on same line as "front" teeth—needs yoke adjustment—follow manufacturer's instructions
Work moves away from fence	"Heeling" (misalignment)	"Back" teeth of blade not cutting on same line as "front" teeth—needs yoke adjustment—follow manufacturer's instructions
Work binds between fence and blade	"Heeling" (misalignment)	Check and reset auto-stops—arm must be 90° to fence—blade must be parallel to fence
Kickback	Misalignment Poor practice Dull blade	Check alignment factors Be sure anti-kickback fingers are correctly adjusted Use splitter, if any Be sure to move work completely past saw blade Replace or sharpen
Work hard to feed	Misalignment Poor practice Dull blade	Blade must be parallel to fence Work-edge against fence must be true Replace or sharpen
Bevels not accurate	Misalignment	Use care when making settings—make trial cuts—check auto-stops if any
Work too narrow	Measuring from wrong side of blade	Measure from side of blade nearest fence and from tooth set toward fence
Sawdust thrown at you	Poor practice	Adjust guard as explained in text
WHEN DADOING/ MOLDING Dado-depth not uniform	Misalignment	Table must be parallel to arm—check manufacturer's instructions for adjustment
Bottom of dado or groove is rough	Dado chippers uneven—outside blades poorly matched Inconsistent placement on arbor	Chippers and blades should be jointed and sharpened as a set and kept in prime condition Mark blades and chippers—line up marks each time units are mounted
Dado width inaccurate	"Heeling" Poor setup	"Back" teeth of blade not cutting on same line as "front" teeth—needs yoke adjustment—follow manufacturer's instructions Set adjustable dadoes carefully—dado assemblies sometimes require paper shims for exact width settings—make trial cuts
Dado "climbs"	Cutting too deep—cutting too fast	Don't force the cut—make repeat passes for very deep cuts
Chatter—stalling	Dull tools	Be sure dado units, molding knives are sharp
Dado units or molding knives or wood, burn	Feeding too fast or cutting too deep Accumulation of wood residue on cutters Dull cutters	Slow up feed—make repeat passes when necessary Clean—maintain in prime condition Sharpen, and keep sharp
Molded edges not uniform	Poor work-handling	Keep work firmly down on table—or against fence or guide—throughout pass
Rough molding cuts	Cutting cross-grain Cutting against the grain	Feed very slowly—feed *with* the grain whenever possible

3-266.   Trouble-shooting chart for the radial arm saw.

4. The Motorized Miter Box

The motorized miter box is pretty much like a portable circular saw top-mounted on its own stand. A pivot arrangement allows the tool to be swung down to saw the material that is on the stand's table. That's why it is often called a "chop" saw (Figure 4-1). It is generally recognized as being a fine tool to use for miter cutting which, often erroneously, classifies it as a tool designed exclusively for picture-framing work. It is certainly useful in such a capacity, but it's a more rugged machine than the thought suggests. It's not uncommon to find it used in industry and on construction sites to do cutoff and angular sawing on good size material (Figure 4-2). The saw can be set for left- or right-hand cuts and most units have automatic stops for the most commonly used positions. In addition, there is a scale for settings that might be needed between auto-stops.

Common sizes are 9″ and 10″, which is the diameter of the tool's saw blade. As with table saws and radial arm saws, the machine comes equipped with a combination blade that is usable for cutoff or miter cutting. It's a good blade for sizing cuts and when the quality of the cut is not critical. For ready-to-assemble edges though, it's wise to switch to a smooth-cutting blade like a hollow-ground or a planer blade with carbide-tipped teeth. A particular blade that is widely recognized for its superior performance in powered miter boxes is shown in Figure 4-3. It has 80 carbide-tipped teeth on a 10″ blade and gets by with minimum kerf-width because of a unique tooth configuration that provides clearance. The body being coated with a special, baked-on, anti-grip material also helps. Cutoffs and miter cuts made with the blade are glossy smooth.

The machine can be used to saw materials other than wood. With the proper blade, it can be used to cut materials like non-ferrous metals, plastics, composition products. Whatever blade you consider, be sure that its operating speed is compatible with the rpm of the tool.

A good feature to look for is a braking device, something that will stop the blade much quicker than when allowed to run free after a cut. On some units, braking is automatic; the stopping mechanism takes over as soon as the trigger is released. Other units may have a manual control. A special button, nicely situated near your thumb, is pressed to stop the blade in seconds (Figure 4-4).

The upper part of the blade will be covered by a heavy casting. The lower part, the area that engages the work, will be covered by a pivoting, see-through, plastic shield that affords protection before, during, and after the cut. This, of course, must never be removed. And always wear safety goggles.

4-1.   The motorized miter box has an overhead saw that is pivot-mounted at a rear point. The blade can swing through an arc of more than 45° left or right, but it doesn't tilt. The tool should be bolted to a bench top or, for portability, to a sturdy stand.

4-2. The tool is designed for particular applications so its capacities are limited, but it's a useful tool for jobs that range from rough house-framing to delicate picture-framing. Capacities can be increased by following some of the methods explained in this chapter.

Alignment

To work accurately, you must check out the machine when you first set it up and frequently thereafter. All the tools provide for adjustments you can make so components will have the correct relationship, but methods will vary from tool to tool, so it is important to study the owner's manual. The following are the important considerations:

The table must be level. Its surface must be parallel to a plane that is on the blade's horizontal centerline.

The angle between the surface of the table and the blade must be 90°.

The angle between the fence and the blade at zero setting must be 90°.

The auto-stops must be accurate. These are checked best by marking the work with a protractor and then making a trial cut. This should be done frequently as you work, for the crosscut position as well as miter cuts.

Sawing

Basic sawing is done by positioning the work so it will bear snugly against table and fence. Hold the work securely, with your hand placed well away from the blade, and then swing the blade down slowly to make the cut. (Figure 4-5). Sometimes it pays to secure the work by clamping it to either the fence or the table. Never hand-hold a piece that is too small to be safely held or that puts your hand close to the blade.

Allow the blade to come to full speed before you engage the work. When the cut is complete, bring the table to neutral position and allow it to stop before removing workpieces. If the tool has a manual stop-control, release the trigger before pressing the stop button.

Capacities on tools of this nature are limited. They are not designed for crosscutting or mitering extra-wide stock. However, you can do more with them by employing special techniques; even by making special tables.

4-3. Saw blade of this type does a super job when used on the motorized miter box for finish cuts. Unique configuration behind the teeth provides clean cutting and a minimum kerf-width. The blade has a backed-on anti-stick coating.

4-4. A built-in brake that stops the blade in seconds is an excellent feature. On some tools, the braking is automatic. On others, the special button is pushed to activate the braking mechanism. The button should be depressed after the trigger is released.

4-7. Crosscut capacity is always more than miter-cut capacity, but you can increase either one simply by elevating the work with a height block.

4-8. The height block situates the work closer to the center of the block so you get a longer cut-line. The thicker the height block, the longer the cut-line. Even a small increase in capacity often proves helpful.

4-5. The work is held to bear firmly against the table and fence. The saw is pulled down to make the cut. That's why it's often called a "chop" saw. Keep hands away from the cut area, and always use the guard. Safety goggles, of course, are a good idea.

4-6. Facts concerning tool capacities and how they may be increased. The capacities listed are not standard on all tools, but are used here to illustrate some advantages of using height blocks and making special tables.

4-9. You can double crosscut capacity by making two cuts, the second one after the stock has been turned end-for-end or inverted. Being careful with work-to-blade alignment after the first cut will assure a smooth edge.

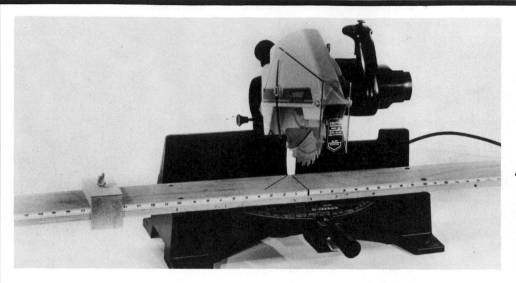

4-10.   A special long table, made to replace the original one, will provide much more support for the work. The table can be as long as you like, but extra-long ones should have outboard supports to keep the unit from rocking.

Limitations are imposed by the diameter of the blade and how high it can be raised (something you *can't* change); by the diameter of the blade-retaining washers (the arbor collars), and by the fence position, which is not adjustable. The maximum depth of cut is controlled by the radius of the blade, less the radius of the collars, less the thickness of the table.

When the saw blade is in its lowest position (and the saw cut has been completed), the surface of the work is a chord of the blade's cutting circle. If, in effect, you can increase the length of the chord, you will increase cutting capacities. The longest chord of a circle is through its center; its diameter. The closer work can be positioned to the center of the blade, the longer the chord and the greater the blade's cutting capacity. Capacities can also be increased by moving the fence farther back from its basic

position. Applicable factors are sketched in Figure 4-6. The capacities that are shown do not apply to all tools, but the ideas are generally workable.

Assume that a tool has a maximum crosscut capacity of 4-1/2″ (Figure 4-7). This can be increased simply by elevating the work on a height block. More of the blade will be working—a longer chord. The idea is helpful on miter cuts (Figure 4-8), as well as crosscuts. Another way to make wider crosscuts than you normally can is shown in Figure 4-9. After the first cut is made, the stock is turned end-for-end, or inverted, and cut again. Careful placement of the stock will assure that the cut will be true.

Special Tables

If you replace the standard table and, sometimes, the fence, on a powered miter box you will be able to increase con-

4-11.   Ideas you can apply when making a long table.

4-12.   The adjustable stop is very handy when you need to cut many pieces of similar length. It's also good for miter work, especially when the stock is flat and can be inverted for consecutive cutting.

4-13.   A wider table is mostly for additional support when working with oversize pieces. The cutout is needed so the table will not interfere with using the miter adjustment handle.

4-14.   The two-pass crosscut is easier to do when a wide table provides overall support for the workpiece.

venience as well as capacity. I've made three tables for my machine, allowing me to do different types of work.

Long table.   For picture-frame work, crosscutting and mitering operations that fall within the tool's basic capacities, or even for various cuts on long stock a longer table whose thickness and width matches the original, will serve nicely (Figure 4-10). Construction ideas for the long table are shown in Figure 4-11.

Cut the stock to overall size, working with material whose thickness matches that of the original table. Some machines have tables 1″ thick. If you don't have this kind of material you can laminate 1/4″-thick plywood or hardboard or 3/4″-thick plywood. Use the standard table as a template or drill the four attachment holes, then counterbore the holes to a depth that will set the screw-head plus washer below the table's surface. If you lack a counterbore,

use a spade bit to form the screw-hold seat, and then drill through for the attachment screw.

If you add the optional length gauge, do it after the new table is in place and the basic crosscut kerf is formed. The tape that was used is self-adhesive, but you can also use a standard case-replacement tape and attach it with contact cement.

Make the stop as shown in the drawing. It should slide smoothly on the table, but clearance should not allow wobbling. The stop is very useful when you need to crosscut many pieces of similar length, and when you are making miter cuts (Figure 4-12).

Extra-wide table.   A table that is wider, also longer, than the original can provide additional support when working with oversize pieces (Figures 4-13 and 4-14). The construction details are shown in Figure 4-15. Proceed as

1″ X 8″ X 46″

4″

12″

CUTOUT FOR RELIEF WHEN MOVING MITER ADJUSTMENT ARM CUT AS SHOWN OR TO SUIT

WIDE TABLE

4-15.   Construction details of a wide table that you can make. Be sure to use the original table as a pattern for drilling the attachment holes.

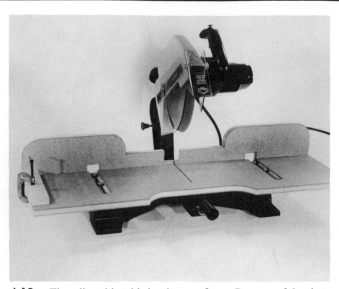

4-16.   The adjustable table has its own fence. Because of the slot arrangement, it can be moved back and forward on the machine's subbase. Be sure the slots allow the heads of the attachment bolts to be below the surface of the table.

4-17.   With the adjustable table moved back, and the work on a height block, you get as much crosscut capacity as it's possible to achieve on this type machine.

for the long table but check against the tool for the amount of clearance you need to permit the miter-adjustment handle to work through its full swing. One way to minimize the size of the relief cutout is to undercut the table at the left and right of the relief so the miter handle can swing under the table.

Adjustable table.   The adjustable table (Figure 4-16), replaces the machine's regular table *and* its fence. It provides additional width and length for more work-support, and since it can be set farther back than the regular table, increases cut-capacity. Use the adjustable table to-gether with a height block and you have as much crosscut capacity as it's possible to get on a powered miter box (Figure 4-17). There is also an increase in depth-of-cut. With the table as far back as it will go, you can saw through six dressed 1x4s (Figure 4-18).

You can make an adjustable table by following the information shown in Figure 4-19. Instead of attachment holes, you form slots so the table can be moved back or forward. The screw slots can be formed on a jigsaw or band-saw, or by making repeat passes on a table saw with a regular saw blade or by working with a dadoing tool. If you work on a table saw, use a stop block to limit the length of the cuts.

The counterbore slot can be formed with a rabbeting bit chucked in either a portable router or drill press. Another way would be to work on a table saw or radial arm saw, making cuts only as deep as required for the wider part of the slot.

Cut the fence to size and make relief notches that are in line with the slots in the table. Shape the relief area by first using the fence as a pattern. Then make any necessary adjustments by custom-fitting the accessory table once it's in place on the powered miter box.

Some Other Uses

The motor unit pivots vertically and swings horizontally, but it doesn't tilt, so you don't cut compound angles as you would with a radial arm saw. Instead, you lean the work at a particular angle against the fence, then make a routine 45° miter cut. This results in a compound-angle cut with the slope determined by the angle between the work and fence.

When the slope of the work must be precise, the angle between the fence and work can be determined with a T-bevel. Many times though, as when making a shadow-box picture frame, the slope angle is not critical and can be decided visually. In any case, for accuracy and safety, a long

4-18.   This illustration shows how the adjustable table helps to increase overall capacity. Here, with the table set back, the saw blade is getting through six dressed 1x4s. The clamp-on stop block assures that all pieces will be the same length.

4-19. How to make an adjustable table. Be sure to check all dimensions against the tool you own.

stop block should be tack-nailed or clamped to the table (Figure 4-20). The distance between the stop and the fence determines the slope angle. Also, the stop provides good bracing for the workpiece.

Kerf-piercing. You may not do this kind of cutting everyday and whether you *can* do it will depend on the size of the workpiece. It's a technique you may be able to utilize merely to decorate a project component or, a more practi-

cal use, make a vent panel; the kind of thing often included in a sink cabinet. The work is centered on the table so you can form equally-spaced, stopped kerfs (Figure 4-21). The kerfs can be centered or not, as the project demands. Work with a stop block when you need similar pieces. Make the first cut in each piece before resetting the stop block for following cuts.

4-20. The saw doesn't tilt, so to cut compound angles, you tilt the work to the slope angle you need and cut as if you were doing a simple miter. Always use a long stop block to maintain the slope angle and to keep the work braced.

4-21. Kerf-piercing, a technique you can use for decorative reasons or to make components like venting panels, is just a method of forming limited-length kerfs that penetrate the work. The kerfs will be longer on the top side of the material.

5. The Jigsaw

Jigsaws, often called scroll saws, work with short, straight blades, that are gripped at each end in chucks. These blades saw in an up-and-down action. How the up-and-down action is accomplished may vary, but generally, an internal mechanism converts the rotary action of a motor into the vertical motion of the blade. Because the jigsaw can work with extremely fine blades, some so slim they can practically turn on their own radii, it is the *only* shop tool that can accomplish the delicate sawing required for projects like inlaid pictures (Figure 5-1). It is also exclusive in its ability to do true piercing, the technique that is used to make internal cuts without a lead-in cut from any edge of the stock.

Because of these unique capabilities, the tool is often thought of only for its craft applications, which is not realistic. The jigsaw can work with fairly heavy blades and average maximum depth-of-cut runs to about 2″. Thus you can work on some heavy stock; even do bandsaw type work like shaping small cabriole legs (Figure 5-2). There is, though, no comparison in cut speed; the bandsaw will win every time when the tools are judged solely on that basis.

With the correct blade and speed, the jigsaw can be used to cut hard and soft metals and other non-wood materials such as plastics, ivory, bone, rubber, leather and paper. Because it is a *relatively* safe and easy tool to use, it is generally viewed as the logical choice when introducing a youngster to the art of power tool woodworking.

There are many types of jigsaws and much variance in size and price, but they all pretty much have the same basic elements (Figure 5-3). The method the Dremel Moto-Shop uses to get a blade to move vertically is a departure from other, more conventional means. The saw blade is gripped between the ends of a U-shaped rocker arm and tension is provided by a cam lock. The pivot-mounted arm gets a rapid up-and-down motion because a link, which is attached to the lower leg of the U, is activated by an eccentric on the motor shaft. As the rocker arm goes up and down, so does the saw blade. The Moto-Shop is small and quiet, but capable and is, in a sense, portable. Its rubber suction-cup feet allow it to be used anywhere. As you can see in Figure 5-4, it has a power takeoff on its motor for accessories that include a specially designed flexible shaft.

On most jigsaws, the mechanism is driven by a V-belt that runs over pulleys on the tool and the motor (Figure 5-5). The pulleys are usually "stepped" so tool speed can be controlled by choosing particular positions for the V-belt.

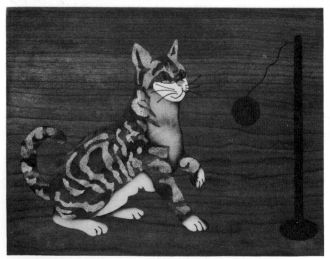

5-1.   The jigsaw is the ideal tool to use when doing artistic projects like inlaid pictures. The work is not difficult although it requires very careful cutting.

5-2.   The jigsaw should not be viewed as a "craft" tool. Most can cut stock up to 2″ thick.

5-3. Jigsaws will have different features but most will have the basic components that are shown here.

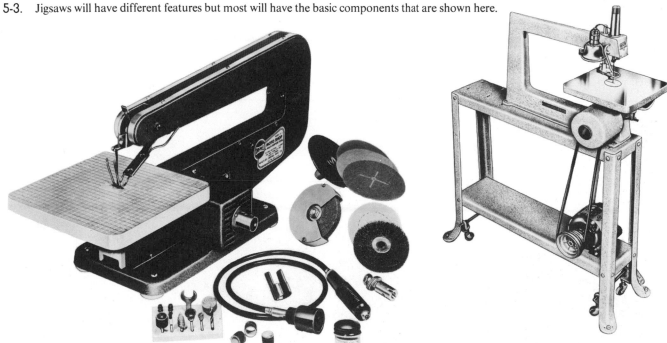

5-4. The Dremel Moto-Shop has a power take-off for running a flex shaft and other accessories. It's a small, lightweight unit, but it's not a toy. Rubber suction-cup feet keep it stable no matter where you use it.

5-5. Many home workshop jigsaws are driven by stepped pulleys that provide various speeds. A light attached to the upper arm is a good idea.

5-6.   A heavier jigsaw has greater capacity and more power. This unit includes a variable speed changer. Turn a handle to get any speed you need between minimum and maximum settings.

Although it isn't shown in the illustration, the belt is covered with a removable shield for safety.

Figure 5-6 shows a model jigsaw that spans the line between home craft and industrial equipment. It has more power and more capacity, at least in throat-depth, than many other units, and can be equipped, like the one shown, with a variable speed mechanism. This is a nice feature since it permits infinite changes between minimum and maximum speeds merely by turning a handle. It also does away with the bother of having to change V-belt position for different jobs.

The Craftsman 18″ "walking beam" saw is a newcomer that has some interesting features (Figure 5-7). It has unusual bevel-cutting versatility because the blade/drive mechanism can be tilted 45° to the left or right. The table, unlike other jigsaws, remains horizontal. The tool is equipped with a miter gauge and a unique clear plastic cutting guard.

Jigsaws that have quickly earned an enviable reputation are the Hegner Polymax Machines (Figure 5-8). The saw operates very quietly with a direct in-line motor and works with minimum vibration. Its major feature lies in its blade attachment and superior system. Each end of the blade is clamped into a special prism. The assembly is then installed between the machine's two reciprocating arms. The prisms are shaped to fit V-grooves in the arms. Tensioning is accomplished by turning a rod at the rear of the saw which, in effect, spreads the arms apart at the blade site. The blade cuts smoothly and never loses tension. The saw has only one speed, which doesn't pose a problem for most work, but this should be remembered when, for example, cutting steel. A very slow feed is essential to avoid blade breakage.

Capacities

The machine's depth of cut is figured in terms of the maximum stock thickness it can handle, which averages about

5-7.   Unique feature of a new Craftsman jigsaw is a blade/drive mechanism that can be tilted 45° to the left or right. Bevel cutting can be done without having to tilt the table.

5-8.   New Hegner Polymax jigsaws have a lot of happy users. Basic machine has a single speed, but an electronic variable speed control is available at extra cost.

2". The second capacity factor is the distance from the blade and the support for the upper structure. This is throat capacity, and the dimension is used to designate the size of the machine. For example, an 18" jigsaw can cut to the center of a 36" circle. Many jigsaws are designed so the upper structure can be removed or swung down. This removes interference posed by above-the-table components and allows cutting of oversize workpieces. In effect, the capacity becomes unlimited. It's a jigsawing technique that is called "saber sawing." More will be said about this use of the machine later, but generally the idea works because it's possible to install a short, heavy-gauge blade by utilizing only the lower chuck. Since the blades must be stiff and fairly heavy, jigsaw saber sawing can't be used for extremely fine cutting.

Another system on some machines, called "indexing," allows turning the chuck positions 90° so the side of the blade will be parallel to the front and rear edges of the table (Figure 5-9). While the basic throat capacity remains unchanged, the new setup allows cutting long stock without interference simply because you are feeding in a different direction.

How Blades Mount

Two chucks are provided. One is in the upper arm, the other below the table (Figure 5-10). Although designs may differ, the purpose of the chucks is to hold the blade taut between them. The amount of adjustment in the chuck and the method for achieving blade alignment can vary from tool to tool. Usually, a set of chuck blocks is provided. A setscrew on one side of the chuck lets you position one of the blocks in a more-or-less permanent position for most normal cutting; a setscrew on the opposite side moves the second chuck block so that the blade can be gripped securely (Figure 5-11). Some designs provide a permanent position for one of the blocks. You can get specific information about your tool from the owner's manual.

The important thing is to install the blade so it will "jig" in a true vertical line throughout the stroke travel (Figure 5-12). It must be vertical when viewed from the side and the front. Many operators make a special guide block that helps to set blades vertically when they are installed. The guide is no more than a squared block of wood (about 3/4" x 4" x 4") with a straight kerf cut carefully along the

5-10.   Jigsaw blades have blank ends and are gripped in both the upper and lower chuck. Correct position of the blade is with the teeth pointing downward.

5-11.   The blade is gripped between blocks in the chucks. Usually, both blocks are movable so the blade can be centered.

5-12.   When the blade is locked in the chucks and viewed from the side, it must not tilt either forward or back. The most efficient setting is shown in the center sketch.

5-9.   When chucks have been "indexed," they can be turned 90° from their original positions. This puts the blade parallel to the working edge of the table so long stock can be cut without interference from the arm.

center of one edge. Situating the blade in the kerf as you tighten the chucks will help assure alignment.

After the blade is correctly installed, check to see if the angle between blade and table is 90°. You can do this with a small square (Figure 5-13), or a block of wood with two adjacent edges you are sure are square to each other. If adjustment is needed, change the table's position, not the blade's. If the machine has a tilt scale and a table-stop screw, adjust them, if necessary, after you are sure of the correct blade-to-table angle. The stop screw, if there is one, assures that the table can be returned correctly to normal position after it has been moved, say, for a bevel cut.

The blade backup is at the bottom of the guide post. Some of these are *universal*, being a slim, steel disc with various blade-size slots cut in the perimeter (Figure 5-14). You choose the slot that is suitable for the blade you are going to cut with and then adjust the device so the steel sleeve (or something similar) bears against the black edge of the blade. The degree of beairng should be a light-touch contact. Another design provides a split sleeve encased in a tube (Figure 5-15). The blade sits in the slot of the sleeve; the tube is used as the backup.

Some manufacturers offer special blade guides that supplement the standard guide and hold-down (Figure 5-16). These are most useful when close following of a line or pattern is critical. They're nice to have on hand for the kind of intricate cutting you must do for marquetry or inlaid work.

Whatever the method, be sure the blade can move easily in the guide and that the backup is not pushing it forward. The backup is there to support the blade *during* the cut.

A spring-type hold-down is situated at the bottom of the guide post to keep the work from moving up and down with the blade. If the machine has a table that can be tilted for bevel cuts, then the hold-down must be adjustable so it will bear evenly on the workpiece (Figure 5-17). Always adjust the hold-down so it barely touches the top surface of

the work. Too much pressure can cause the spring to mar the work and will hinder feeding it. Too little pressure isn't good either, but this will be apparent because the work will chatter excessively.

Blades

Many types and sizes of blades are available, but they all fall into one of two general categories. Those that must be gripped in both the upper and lower chuck are called "jeweler's blades." Others, heavy enough and wide enough so they can function while gripped in the lower chuck only, are called "saber blades."

There is a little bit of overlap here because some of the jeweler's blades are heavy enough to work as saber blades. The general rule is to use the heavier blades as the stock thickness increases. Choose the widest and the fastest cutting blade as long as it does the job for you. Think about saber blades and the heavier jeweler's blades when the stock reaches maximum depth-of-cut thickness and, of course, when you are working on large material that makes it necessary for you to remove the upper arm of the machine.

The chart in Figure 5-18, does not list all the blades that are available, but the selection is an excellent assortment to begin with. If you use the blade chart together with the speed chart that is given, you'll be quite well organized for most of the jigsaw projects you're likely to encounter.

Quite often, it's possible to use discarded band-saw blades and still-sharp sections of used hacksaw blades.

5-14.   A universal guide has a slotted perimeter. You choose a slot that suits the blade. Set the backup roller so it barely touches the back edge of the blade.

5-13.   When the blade is in true vertical position, as it should be, the angle between the blade and the table must be 90° when the table is in normal position.

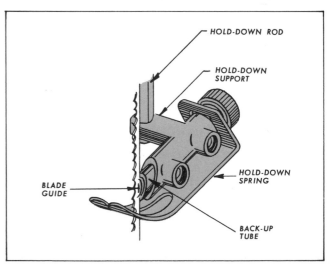

5-15.   Another type of blade guide has a split tube. This is encased in an adjustable sleeve that serves as the backup.

5-16.   A special set of guides, if available for your machine, can supplement the regular guide and hold-down. They help when following a line is critical, as in marquetry and inlay work.

5-17.   The spring hold-down keeps the work from being jiggled by the action of the saw blade, but it should never be forced down on the work. Adjust the hold-down to suit the table angle when you are doing bevel cutting.

BLADE	BLADE DIMENSION			OPERATION				R.P.M.
	Thickness Inches	Width Inches	Teeth per Inch	Stock Thickness (Inches)	Cut Radius	Kerf	Best For	
1	.010	.040	18	1/16-1/8	small	very fine	wood—bone—plastic	1600
2	.020	.110	20	1/16-1/8	medium	medium	aluminum—copper—mild steel	940
3	.020	.110	15	1/8-1/2 in metal, 1/8 and up in other material	medium	medium	metal—wood—bone—felt—paper	1175
4	.028	.250	20	3/32-1/2 (1/4 max. in steel)	large	coarse	aluminum—copper—mild steel	830
5	.028	.250	7	1/4 and up	large	coarse	soft and hard wood—pressed wood	745
6	.012	.023	20	up to 1/8	very small	fine	plastics—bone—fiber—comp. board	1050
7	.020	.070	7	up to 1/4	medium	medium	plastics—bone—hard rubber	1400
8	.010	.070	14	1/8-1/2	medium	very fine	wood—plastics—bone—hard rubber	1525

5-18.   This chart does not list all the blades that are available; just the ones that should be part of a good, starting assortment. Blades are identified by the specifications shown here—thickness, width and number of teeth per inch.

These must be cut off or "snapped" carefully, to a suitable length. When the width of such items doesn't permit mounting in the jigsaw as is, you can always grind down the ends to the chuck size of the machine.

Use wide blades with few teeth at slow speeds for heavy cutting. Use narrow blades with many teeth at high speeds for thin material and for smooth cuts.

5-19. Tensioning device on some jigsaws is a cylinder which may be scaled for different blades. You'll find, after a while, that you will judge blade tensioning for yourself.

5-20. A unit like this will hold a good assortment of blades. Holes in the lower shelf are for machine files, which are also usable in a jigsaw.

Most jigsaws provide a device that permits you to "tension" the blade after it has been secured in the chucks. In most cases, it's merely a matter of pulling or pushing up on a cylinder that is part of the upper chuck assembly arm. It's even possible that the cylinder may be scaled for different blades (Figure 5-19). Whatever the case, more tension is needed on fine blades than on heavy ones; however, producing too much tension will just result in premature blade breakage. Probably the least tension that will do the job is the best to use. The operator's judgment is critical when deciding the degree of tension. You can easily be guided by well-defined indicators of poor tension adjustment. Cuts that are not square, blades breaking quickly, difficulty in following the cut line, and obvious off-vertical movement of the blade when you are cutting clearly indicate the need for tension readjustment.

Since getting maximum use from a jigsaw requires keeping a nice assortment of blades on hand, it's a good idea to provide storage for them by making a unit like the one shown in Figure 5-20. The holes in the lower shelf are

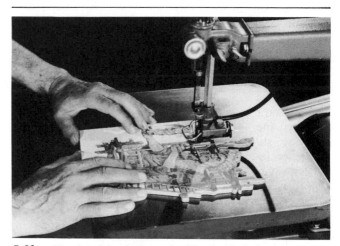

5-21. Hand position is determined by the kind of cutting you are doing. The critical factor is to move the work so the blade will always be on the cutting line. Don't force; always allow the blade to cut at its own pace.

5-22. Heavier blades with coarser teeth will cut more freely because they form a wider kerf. Even so, it never pays to rush. The jigsaw is a relatively "safe" tool but even so, since it cuts wood it can cut you, so work with care.

for a type of machine file that can be used in a jigsaw. These items will be shown later on.

Basic Work Handling

Be relaxed and comfortable. Many jigsaw jobs take a long time to do so a strained position will tire you quickly and will affect the quality of your work. At most times, use the left hand as a guide to keep turning the work so the blade stays on the line; use the right hand to feed. However, there is so much twisting and turning involved with jigsawing that it is difficult to abide by one set rule.

It's not out of line to use both hands in a combination action that provides both guiding and feeding (Figure 5-21). Many times, even during a cut, you'll find it convenient to move from in front of the machine to one side of it. Just be aware that the main job is to keep the blade on the line.

Never crowd the blade but, on the other hand, do not be overly cautious. The teeth on the blade are there to cut, not to burnish. A steady, even feed that constantly produces sawdust is ideal. Don't force a wide blade to turn a corner that is too small for it. You'll end up burning the wood, breaking the blade, and probably running off the line. Keep feed in a from-you-to-the-back-of-the-machine direction. It's the work you must keep turning, not the blade. Most jigsaw blades can be twisted when forced; and they will make cuts you never planned for, especially the finer, more flexible blades.

A good rule is to keep the side of the blade tangent to all curved lines. Worry about the teeth of the blade and the business of staying on the cut line.

If you feel that you are doing everything correctly and are still having difficulty making true cuts, check the relationship of the blade to the guides and the backup, as well as the degree of tension. If problems do occur, it will be mostly when you are doing intricate cutting with small jeweler's blades. The heavier blades will function in pretty good order even with some maladjustment (Figure 5-22).

This is not the case with the others. A good deal of what will be said in the bandsaw chapter about backtracking and in-cutting apply to the jigsaw. However, because the jigsaw can negotiate extremely tight radii, the degree of backtracking and in-cutting possible is not nearly the same.

Patterns and Layout

A "pattern" can be simply an attractive picture that you snip from a magazine and cement to the material you will use in the project; it can even be a photograph. The pattern can be cut in profile to produce a silhouette-type project, or you can cut in intricate, interlocking pieces to make a jigsaw puzzle. Another way to work with an original design or one that you copy is shown in Figure 5-23. The pattern is taped to a hard surface and a sharp knife is used to cut out all or parts of the design. This idea is often used when intarsia work is done.

Various French Curves, which are templates used by draftsmen, can be very helpful when you are forming original patterns (Figure 5-24).

When you work with an original design, you can draw it full-size on the wood or on a piece of paper that you then cement to the stock. The latter method destroys the pattern so if you need duplicates or wish to save the pattern for possible future use, transfer it to the wood by means of carbon paper. In the case of duplicate pieces, the first part you cut can be the template you use for marking other stock.

The transferring-by-squares method is still a fairly effective method when you have a ready-made pattern that you wish to transfer to wood whether you wish to keep the same size of the original pattern, enlarge it, or reduce it. What you do is mark off the pattern in squares of one size and mark off the work with same, larger, or smaller squares. Then you just transfer the design square by square (Figure 5-25). This makes it easy to duplicate any design or pattern. If you make 1″ squares on the original and 2″ squares on the stock, you double the pattern size. And of

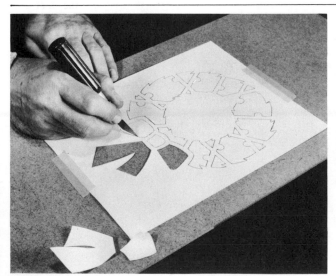

5-23. Be sure a pattern you are cutting is taped to a hard surface. A piece of tempered, hard-surfaced hardboard will do nicely.

5-24. A set of French Curves, normally used in drafting work, can help when laying out designs.

5-25.   The enlarging-by-squares method is an old, but reliable standby. The squares on the workpiece, or paper that will be used as the working pattern, are drawn larger than those on the original. If you work the other way, you can reduce drawings.

5-26.   Spend some time pre-planning how you make cuts. This leads to faster work and better utilization of material.

course it works the opposite way when the work must be smaller than the original.

Many of the methods of work layout that are shown in Figure 5-26 can be used to minimize waste. Sometimes, through planning and good layout, it's possible to cut small pieces from scrap so they may then be joined to form a large part. When you are cutting many parts from a single panel, it's wise to first make all the patterns you need and then lay them out on the panel. Thus, you can minimize waste and, maybe even more importantly, plan for a compatible grain direction on each of the pieces.

Piercing

It's possible to do piercing on a jigsaw because the blade is straight and secured at each end. Therefore, the blade may be passed through a hole in the work before it is secured in the chucks. This is intriguing because you can produce an

internal design without a lead-in cut from an edge of the stock (Figure 5-27). The common procedure is to loosen the blade from the upper chuck, pass it through the blade-insertion hole, and then secure it in the upper chuck. Usual cutting procedures follow, but you do have to repeat the blade-insertion process for each cutout in the design (Figure 5-28).

Figure 5-29 shows good feed direction for various shapes. When the cut is circular, the insertion hole may be drilled anywhere in the waste, but it does make sense to locate the insertion hole near the line simply because it reduces cutting time. Quite often, the insertion hole can be planned as part of the design; one example would be when

5-27. Piercing allows you to make internal cuts without having to cut in from an edge of the stock. Each cutout area requires a blade insertion hole.

5-28. The work is placed over the blade which is locked in the lower chuck. Then the top end of the blade is secured. Quite often, blade insertion holes can be formed as part of the pattern.

Typical feed direction on an example jigsaw job. Note that when the corner is acute, you clean it out by approaching from two directions. Follow the arrows.

5-29. Careful cutting is required especially when you must backtrack to approach a point from another angle. Cutting techniques will vary, depending mostly on whether the corner is square or round.

you need a round corner. Choose a bit that will produce the radius you require and be accurate when you form the hole.

To cut a square corner, start from the insertion hole and approach the corner from one direction. Then backtrack to the hole and approach the corner from the second direction. Often, when you are using a fine blade, it's possible just to turn the corner. It will not be square; but when a tiny radius is not critical, this does not really matter. Wise jigsaw use calls for visualizing the shape and the cut before you start, if only to minimize the amount of cutting you must do to achieve a particular shape.

Choose blade sizes as you would for normal cutting: heavy blades for thick stock, smaller blades for thin material.

5-30.   The "jig" shown here is just a clamped-on, straight piece of wood that serves as a fence. Use a square block of wood to move the work forward.

5-31.   A fence can also be used when you need to cut slots. The terminal holes of the slots, which are drilled on a common centerline, serve as blade insertion holes. You can form square ends for slots by working with a mortising bit on the drill press.

Straight Cuts

For most straight cuts, you will be working freehand, but there are occasions when setting up a guide can be useful. For example, when cutting squares for a checkerboard, doing slots, or even cutting dowels to length, using a guide is most helpful.

The guide you use can be an improvised rip fence, simply a straight piece of wood that you clamp to the jigsaw table. In the case of cutting similar pieces, it's a good idea to use a squared block of wood to feed with (Figure 5-30). The fence will gauge the length of the cut, and the feed block will assure squareness.

Unlike the table saw, you can use a fence on the jigsaw as a stop for gauging duplicate cutoffs. Since the blade moves up and down, there is no kickback and no dangerous binding.

A fence is good to use when cutting slots, especially if you must do them in many pieces (Figure 5-31). When the slot has round ends, drill holes at each end of a common centerline with the hole diameter matching the width of the slot. Insert the blade through one of the holes (as in piercing) and clamp the fence in place to guide the cut. After you have cut the first side, adjust the fence so you can cut the second side. If you require the same slot in many pieces, do the first-side cut in all of them before you adjust the fence.

If the slot has square ends, then you must do some freehand guiding after the slot sides are cut. Many craftsmen, when they require a lot of square-end slots, work as has been described for round-end slots; but they use a mortising chisel instead of a bit.

The same setup, that is, a fence to gauge work-length and a feed block to keep the work square, can be used to cut dowels to length (Figure 5-32).

Remember that the jigsaw is not a speed tool. Feed slowly when using a fence and choose the heaviest blade

5-32.   You can cut dowel and other rounds. Use a fence when you need many similar pieces. Be sure to use a squared feed block.

that will produce the job you want. Guided cuts are tougher to do with the finer blades because they can twist so easily. When that happens, the blade simply moves off the line. Also, the work can move away from the guide. The answer is to use a good blade and a feed that permits the blade to cut without choking.

Pivot Cutting

You can cut accurate circles by using an auxiliary table that you clamp to the regular table. A nail that you drive through the auxiliary table acts as the pivot (Figure 5-33). It is very important for the pivot to be in line with the blade. The blades, because they are somewhat flexible, will tend to drift if you don't do a good job of locating the pivot point.

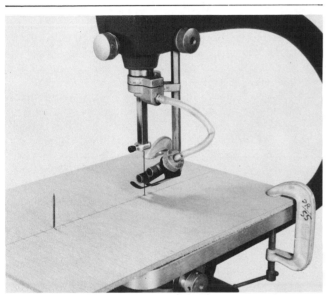

5-33.   How to set up for pivot cutting. The pivot point, which can be a nail, must be directly on line with the points on the teeth of the blade.

5-34.   After the cut has been started, either by making a lead-in cut or by providing a blade insertion hole, the work is placed over the pivot and rotated very slowly. Don't rush or the blade will surely move off the line.

The extra table doesn't have to be more than a sheet of 1/4″ plywood or hardboard. Drill a hole through it so you can insert the jigsaw blade and, if you wish to use the same one for various size circles, drill a series of holes about 1/4″ apart on a common centerline. Then you can insert the pivot through the hole that will give you the correct radius distance from the pivot to the blade.

A long nail as a pivot means you must drill a center hole through the work. If you wish to avoid this, just use a very short nail instead. Then you can simply press the work on it.

Thin blades, when used for pivot cutting, have more

5-35.   An internal piece cut in normal fashion will simply fall through the part it was cut from. If the same cut is made with the table tilted about 5°, the cutout will jam. This is the theory of bevel cutting, and what makes it possible to get deep shapes from a flat board.

tendency to drift than heavy ones. If you must work with a thin blade, apply a bit more tension than you might normally do. In all cases, rotate the work slowly (Figure 5-34).

There are two ways to start the cut. Drill a blade insertion hole so you can start the operation as if you were doing piercing, or make a lead-in cut to the starting point before placing the work over the pivot. For this technique to be successful, you must be sure that the pivot point is exactly on line with the points of the teeth on the blade.

Bevel Cutting

Bevel cutting with a jigsaw enables you to form, among other things, a deep bowl from a flat board.

If you jigsaw a disc in the center of a board, the disc will fall through. If you do the same thing but with the table tilted about 5°, the beveled disc will fall only part way through the beveled opening. The disc will jam like a stopper in a barrel (Figure 5-35).

If, instead of a single disc, you cut a series of concentric beveled rings, each would sink part way through the opening it was cut from; and you would end up with a cone shape. The more rings you cut, the deeper the cone will be (Figure 5-36). When can this technique be used? Well, some of the things you can make or do are shown in Figures 5-37 through 5-45.

These include planters, raised bases, hollow hulls for boat models, trays with raised lips, signs with raised letters, panels with raised sections, drawer pulls cut directly from the drawer front, and blanks for lathe-turning bowls, plates and trays. There are many possibilities to discover after you have tried the technique.

The shape you get depends on the contour of the sections, the wall thickness of the rings, the number you cut, and the projection of each. For example, if you cut six concentric rings in a 3/4″ board that is 6″ square, and each ring projects 1/2″, you get a bowl shape that's 6″ across and 3-1/4″ high. There is little point in trying to figure out beforehand just how much projection you'll get; it depends on

5-36.   A blade insertion hole is required for each cut. It should be drilled at the same bevel angle you use for the sawing, and barely large enough for the blade to get through.

5-38.   Trays and plates with raised lips can be made from a flat board when you use the bevel-cutting technique. The project can be sanded and used as is, or lathe-mounted for additional shaping.

5-37.   After the concentric rings have been glued in their projection position, the assembly can be turned in a lathe. One way to get a bowl using minimum material!

5-39.   Bevel cutting can also be used to form pockets for tools. Trace the outline of the tool as shown here and then bevel-cut.

5-40.   Assemble the pieces with glue and after they are dry, you can sand off the part of the cutout that projects (or leave it). This is a good way to make sliding shelves with customized tool pockets.

5-43.   Model builders will find the technique very useful when making hollow boat hulls.

5-41.   Bevel cutting many concentric rings takes time, patience and careful cutting. You can't sand the cut edges since that would reduce sizes and the parts won't jam as they should.

5-44.   After the "planks" are assembled, the outside contours are finished with cutting tools and sandpaper.

5-42.   How deep a project you can create will depend mainly on the thickness of the stock and the angle of the bevel. The smaller the angle, the more each cutout will project.

5-45.   You can do raised lettering by using the bevel-cutting idea. On jobs like this *always* be sure the cutout is on the same side of the blade. The parts won't fit if you change the direction of the bevel.

the stock thickness, the table tilt, and the kerf width. It's easier to make a trial cut in some scrap and then measure it.

The less table tilt you use, the greater the projection of each individual piece; the more pieces you cut, the greater the total projection. Using too little table tilt can add up to a difficult glue job when you assemble the rings. Try a table tilt of 2° to 5° in materials from 1/4″ to 3/4″ thick but don't use a blade that makes a heavy kerf. A blade that is .020″ thick by .110″ wide by 15 teeth to the inch works fairly well on the jigsaw.

These recommendations are just to get you started since there is no law that says you can't use heavier blades or lighter blades should they be compatible with the stock thickness.

When you cut, be sure to *always* keep the inside piece (the part that will project) on the same side of the blade. If you don't, you will change the bevel direction, and the parts will not fit.

Saber Sawing

To do saber sawing, grip a special saber-saw blade or a very heavy jeweler's blade in the lower chuck only (Figure 5-46). You might wish to do this in the following two examples: when the work is heavy and tough and you feel a saber blade will do the job best and when work size requires that you remove the upper arm of the machine. In the latter situation, you have no choice since there is but one chuck to work with (Figure 5-47).

How you set up for saber sawing depends on the machine you have. The chuck grip should be normal, but some tools have a special backup device for saber-blade use. Check your owner's manual.

When doing pierced work in heavy stock where the use of a fine blade would be out of line, using a saber blade can speed up the job because you don't have to go through the business of releasing from the upper chuck, inserting through the hole, re-securing in the upper chuck, etc. With the saber blade you merely jump from one opening to another. The insertion holes, of course, are still required (Figure 5-48).

Don't force the work. Although the blades you use for this application are stiffer and heavier, they can still bend or twist. Feed so that the blade is doing the cutting at a speed it was designed for.

Inlay Work

The most common type of inlay work on the jigsaw is a kind of pad sawing. It calls for a selection of wood veneers that are fastened together between top and bottom boards with nails driven through the waste areas (Figure 5-49). The design you wish to inlay is drawn on the top board. Since all the veneers are cut at the same time by pad sawing, any

5-46. Only the lower chuck is used to grip saber saw blades. Some machines provide a special, under-the-table backup. This helps to keep the blade stable while cutting is done.

5-47. With a saber blade mounted, and the upper arm of the machine removed, or swung down, you can handle any size workpiece on the jigsaw. Extra-large pieces should have outboard support. Don't force the cut. Feeding just fast enough to keep the blade cutting is the efficient way to work.

5-48. Sometimes, piercing on heavy stock is best done by saber sawing. It eliminates the chore of frequent rechucking at the upper end. You can leave the upper structure in place when work size permits.

piece cut out of one layer will fit the corresponding piece in another layer. The veneers, of course, must be selected for contrast both in color and in grain (Figure 5-50).

As the cutting proceeds, situate each separate piece on a flat board in the same position it occupied in the pad. This will eliminate having to search for and fit the pieces.

When the cutting is finished, the pieces are joined together by placing them on a sheet of gummed paper or something similar. The fully assembled picture is glued, paper side up, to a backup board. After the glue has dried, the paper is dampened with water and rubbed off. Then the exposed, inlaid picture is sanded and finished as desired. In most cases, a smooth, clear coating is used so the beauty of the veneers will not be hidden.

You can see that if the pad is made up of ten different sheets of veneer, you can actually get ten pictures. This is fine for wide-scale production, but a single-version selection of cut pieces should be made for the most promising results. Yes, this produces waste, but it is done for art's sake.

Another possibility is to work without making a pad. Then you cut each part of the picture from separate sheets of veneer. It can be done, but it calls for a lot more accuracy than you need when pad sawing. For all inlay work of this type, use a very fine blade. The kerf width must be minimal.

Intarsia is another kind of inlay work. A recess, usually formed with a router, is filled with a contrasting material that has been sawed to shape on the jigsaw (Figure 5-51). As you can imagine, very careful attention is required when doing the recess and the filler. It's probably best to do the jigsawing first, and then use the piece as a pattern for the recess.

Cutting Sheet Metal

Metal cutting on the jigsaw is similar to cutting wood ex-

cept you select a blade that is best for the material. Metal cutting blades are available in both jeweler's and saber-blade types. It doesn't hurt to lubricate them with something like beeswax since this will help to make tight turns and reduce the possibility of breakage.

If you work directly on the regular table, you will find that burrs will accumulate as the blade cuts. This means a jagged edge and possible feed interference. Very thin material may actually bend because of the up-and-down blade action.

5-50.   Much pre-planning is required to produce a good inlaid picture. The selection of veneers, grain direction on each piece, and so on, are all important. It's possible to buy veneers in kit form for particular pictures.

5-49.   Pad-sawing veneers provides the parts you need to do intricate and fascinating inlaid pictures. Any piece cut from one veneer will fit the corresponding opening in another.

5-51.   This is a sample of the type of inlay work called "intarsia." A recess that is routed or carved is filled with a matching part cut on the jigsaw. It's best to use the jigsawed design as a pattern for the recessing.

A simple way to get around all of this is to sandwich the sheet metal between pieces of scrap plywood (Figure 5-52).

Another way is to make a special insert, one with a hole through it that barely allows the blade to come through (Figure 5-53). This idea is to supply work support as close to the blade as possible. This tends to minimize, if not eliminate, the possibility of getting jagged edges.

Plastics

Certain plastics (phenolics) can be sawed easily with results about what you might expect from a hardwood.

When working with materials like Plexiglas® or Lucite®, use a coarser blade than you would normally and work at a slower speed. Speed and narrow kerfs combine to create enough heat to melt the plastic.

Although woodworking blades may be used, it's wiser to use a skiptooth design. The spaces between the teeth help clear away the chips, and this helps to avoid overheating the work. Some plastics are soft enough so they actually weld directly behind the blade and cause it to bind.

Since most plastic you will use comes with a protective layer of paper, you have a ready-made surface for marking lines and designs. It's wise not to remove the paper until all the cutting has been done (Figure 5-54).

Pad-Sawing Paper

You can saw paper cutouts easily if you sandwich the sheets of paper tightly between pieces of 1/8″ or 1/4″ plywood (Figure 5-55). The idea is to end up for cutting with what is

5-54.   When sawing plastics, leave the protective paper on until the job is done. Regular woodcutting blades can be used but a skip-tooth type is better.

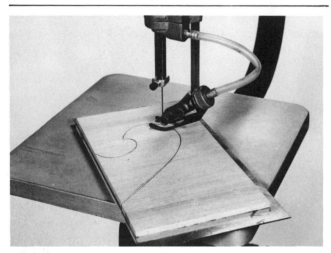

5-52.   A good way to saw sheet metal so you don't get jagged edges is to sandwich the work between pieces of scrap plywood. The pad can be held together with tape.

5-53.   A special insert with a hole through it that is barely large enough for the blade to pass through is another useful idea for sheet-metal sawing. The point is to minimize the opening around the blade.

5-55.   To jigsaw paper, sandwich the sheets between scrap wood. A hundred sheets or more of 20 lb. bond is an example of how thick the pad can be. Experiment with various blades. The right one will leave remarkably smooth edges.

the equivalent of a single, solid block. The tighter the pad, the better the results will be.

Use a blade that will take the turns you must do but try to work with one that is not too coarse. The other extreme is a blade so fine that the paper particles clog it quickly. This can result in burning the work. Properly done, paper cut in this fashion will have remarkably smooth edges.

Filing and Sanding

Special accessories are available for both filing and sanding. The standard sanding attachment has a semicircular shape like a piece of half-round molding. Thus, it may be used for both flat and curved edges. The abrasive is the same as a sleeve you would use on a normal drum sander.

The machine files come in a variety of shapes and with either a 1/8″ or a 1/4″ shank (Figure 5-56). Both the files and the sander are held in the lower chuck only. Most jigsaws provide a block in the lower chuck that has a V-cut in it. The shanks of files and sanders should be gripped in the "V."

Do these abrasive operations at slow speeds. Fast speeds will glaze the paper very quickly; files will simply scrape, which is not the way they should work (Figure 5-57). Remember, they are cutting tools. In general, you can use a higher speed as the abrasive gets coarser. In most cases, it's wise to make a special insert for the tool you are using to minimize the opening around the cutter (Figure 5-58). This is especially important when you are filing or sanding very small pieces.

Don't jam the work against the abrasive. Since you work without a hold-down, it's easy for the tool to lift the work from the table. Besides, trying to speed up the operation by forcing will gain you nothing. A gentle feed with fingers holding the work down on the table is best. The feed should be just strong enough to keep the abrasive cutting.

There are various ways you can improvise filing and sanding attachments. Some craftsmen make use of broken files by grinding a shank on one end. It's even possible to

5-56.   Machine files come in various shapes. Like saber saws, they are gripped in the lower chuck of the jigsaw.

5-57.   Files and sandpaper are cutting tools. It is not efficient to force the work against them. Only enough pressure to keep the tool cutting is the right way to go.

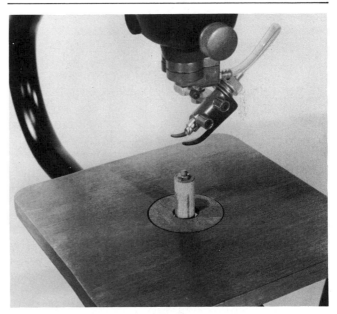

5-58.   Make special inserts for files and sanding sticks. This is a homemade sander; a dowel mounted on a 1/4″ bolt from which the head has been removed. The abrasive paper is attached with rubber cement.

5-59.   There are many ways you can make sanding "drums" to use on the jigsaw. A way not shown here is to mount a round in the lathe and turn down one end to 1/4″ diameter so it can be gripped in the jigsaw's chuck.

use "needle" files. But do be careful since these can snap easily, and most of them have sharp points. A sanding attachment can be just a length of dowel with abrasive paper glued on it (Figure 5-59). One handy gadget is made from an emery stick. This item and a backup piece of stiff sheet metal are cut to jigsaw-blade length and shape at each end to fit the chucks. The unit is then gripped like a jigsaw blade (Figure 5-60).

If you check the standard, small drum sanders, you will find that many of them can be used in the jigsaw even though they are intended for use in a drill press or portable drill. Remember, however—and this is true of filing and sanding generally—production speed on the jigsaw will be slower.

Trouble-Shooting Chart

Common operation problems that can occur when doing jigsaw work, together with their possible causes and cures, are shown in Figure 5-61.

5-60. This flat sanding stick was made by mounting an emery board on a stiff metal backing. The backing must be shaped at each end so it can be gripped in the chucks.

THE PROBLEM	POSSIBLE CAUSES	WHAT TO LOOK FOR OR DO
IN GENERAL		
Blade breakage	Poor procedure	Select correct blade for the operation, material, and material thickness
	Wrong speed	Use correct speed or stay as close to it as you can
	Incorrect blade tension	Adjust to correct tension for the blade and the operation
	Forcing the cut	Let the blade saw only as fast as it can
	Blade twist	Don't try to turn corners that are too tight for the blade's width
Edge of work is bowed	Wrong tension	More tension is usually the solution
	Wrong blade	Don't use very fine blades to saw thick stock
Hard to keep blade on line	Misalignment	Be sure blade guide and backup are correctly adjusted
	Blade guide is not in line with chucks	Check owner's manual for correct adjustment procedure
	Poor practice	Don't force the cut—feed slowly—accuracy is more important than speed
	Incorrect blade tension	Adjust tension for the blade and operation
Very slow cutting action	Blade teeth are too fine for the work	Change to the right blade for the material, and material thickness
	Worn blade	Discard
	Spring hold-down is too tight	Adjust to suit thickness of work
	Wrong speed (usually too slow)	Increase speed until cutting is right
Cut edge isn't square	Misalignment	Angle between table and blade must be 90°
Work lifts from table	Hold-down spring not set correctly	Adjust so there is very light pressure down on the work
Vibration—chatter	Excessive speed	Reduce speed to correct rpm
	Hold-down spring not bearing on work	Check and adjust
Sawdust not blown away from cutting line	Air tube clogged	Remove and clean
	Air tube kinked	Repair or replace

(Continued on next page)

THE PROBLEM	POSSIBLE CAUSES	WHAT TO LOOK FOR OR DO
	Blower mechanism not working	Consult owner's manual for repair procedure
CUTTING METAL Sheet metal edges bend—excessive burring	Inadequate support at cutting area	Make a special insert or back up work with scrap wood
Blade teeth break or wear too quickly	Wrong blade or speed	Use best blade—change to correct speed
Very rough edges	Blade too coarse	Change to finer, suitable blade
CUTTING PLASTIC Kerf closes and binds blade (can be caused by heat)	Bad procedure	Use the right blade and speed
Plastic is marred		Keep protective paper on plastic when cutting
BEVEL CUTTING Pieces do not mesh	Wrong table-tilt	Best table-tilt is 4° to 6°
SABER SAWING Hard to keep blade on line	Wrong blade Forcing the cut No blade support	Use special saber saw blade or heaviest jigsaw blade Feed slowly—guide very carefully Use lower blade backup for support—use special backup if supplied
FILING SANDING File or sandpaper clog too quickly	Wrong speed (usually too fast) Forcing	Slow down to more suitable rpm Don't rush—allow file or sandpaper to cut at own pace

5-61.   Trouble-shooting chart for the jigsaw.

6. The Bandsaw

In depth-of-cut capacity and in cutting speed, the bandsaw is unequaled by any other home-shop woodworking machine (Figure 6-1). While you probably think of it mostly to be used for sawing curved lines, you'll discover its importance for straight-line operations and will be impressed by its ease in doing other jobs that are very difficult, if at all possible, to do on other equipment.

The bandsaw is not designed to be competition for a jigsaw even though, when it is equipped with a fine blade, the applications of the two machines can overlap. With a cut either tool can do, the bandsaw will do it faster. On the other hand, the jigsaw is the only stationary tool you can use for piercing (internal cutting without a lead-in cut from an edge). Actually, piercing can be done on a bandsaw, but it would require breaking the endless blade and then welding it together again after it has passed through the stock. While this kind of thing is done in industry, it's really not a home shop technique.

Some of the more impressive capacities of the bandsaw include resawing to make thin boards out of thick ones, compound cutting to make anything like a cabriole leg, and sawing through a stack of pieces to make many duplicate parts (Figure 6-2).

As with most woodworking machines, you may buy a bandsaw because of some job it does especially well, but once you have it in the shop, you'll find dozens of other practical uses for it.

Types

All bandsaws cut with an endless blade that turns over rubber-rimmed wheels. There can be many differences in size and features, and even in the number of wheels for the blade, but all will have the basic parts that are shown in Figure 6-3.

The typical bandsaw for home shop use (Figure 6-4), will be in a size range of 10″ to 14″. This dimension indicates the distance from the blade to the throat; in a sense, the tool's maximum width of cut. The second capacity factor is the maximum distance between the table and the upper blade guides when they are at their highest point. This is the maximum depth of cut which, depending on the tool, can be anywhere from 4″ to 6″.

At one time, when basic bandsaw design called for two wheels, the throat capacity of a machine had to be a bit less than the diameter of the wheels. With some new designs that work with three wheels, this is no longer true. As

6-1.   The bandsaw's depth of cut and its cutting speed are very impressive. Getting through 6″-thick stock, even on a "small" home-type machine, is no problem. Cuts like this can be done for, among other things, preparing stock for lathe turning.

6-2.   Its depth of cut makes it possible to saw through a pad of many pieces as if it were a solid block to produce a quantity of parts that are exactly alike.

6-3. These are the basic parts of the bandsaw. A second assembly of blade guides and blade backup is under the table.

6-5. Today, many bandsaws are made with three wheels. This makes it possible to increase width to cut without substantially increasing the overall size of the tool.

6-4. The sizes of typical home-type bandsaws run from 10″ to 14″. This is the distance from the blade to the throat and, in a sense, tells the tool's maximum width of cut. Depth of cut can range from 4″ to 6″.

6-6. Many modern units are "motorized." This means that the motor is built in; usually, directly connected to the drive wheel. You skip the task of having to provide a motor and belts and pulleys.

6-7. The "benchtop" bandsaw is very compact, yet will be quite capable in a woodworking shop. This one has a built-in motor and its features include a variable speed control. Units like this can be set up for use in minimum time.

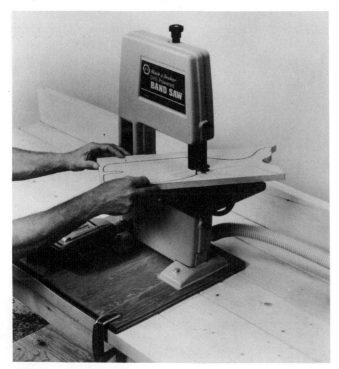

6-8. This Black & Decker bandsaw is designed to be powered by a portable drill. Its power and speeds will depend on the drill you use. Note that it can be attached to a vacuum hose that will draw off the bulk of the sawdust.

shown in Figure 6-5, including a third wheel makes it possible to increase the width of cut even on a small machine.

Quite a few of the units that are available today are "motorized," a term that indicates a built-in power source turns the tool's drive wheel by direct connection, with no belts or pulleys (Figure 6-6). Some of these are the "benchtop" type; very compact and yet with enough capacity to be practical for most woodworking chores. Features may include a variable speed control and a special lever-type switch handle that is removable to prevent unauthorized use of the tool (Figure 6-7).

How about a bandsaw that can be powered with a portable drill? There is one (Figure 6-8). The power and speed of this novel design depends, of course, on the portable drill that is used to run it.

Lastly, there are bandsaws that you can actually make by working with a kit that provides all the parts that can't be made in the average shop—wheels, bearings, castings, and so on. You supply all the wood parts and do the fabricating and assembly work. These kits are available for 12″ and 18″ bandsaws (Figure 6-9).

Generally, the larger the machine, the more powerful it will be and the greater its capacity. A point that might be important to you is the widest blade the tool can handle. If you plan much resawing, the business of cutting thick

6-9. You can buy bandsaws in kit form. All the metal parts and fasteners are supplied. You add the wood and the time needed to put the tool together. The kits are available for 12″ and 18″ bandsaws.

boards to make thinner ones, an extra-wide blade can be an advantage.

Table size is never too great and actually shouldn't be a major factor in the choice of a tool. It is nice though, for the table to have a miter-gauge slot and even provisions for mounting a fence (Figure 6-10).

Adjustments

Blade tensioning and tracking. The blade must be *tensioned*. This means the blade must be taut enough in relation to its size so it won't tend to twist during the cut, or break prematurely. How tensioning is accomplished will depend on the design of the machine. There may be a screw, a crank, a lever, whatever, but the procedure involves moving one of the wheels so the blade will be correctly "stretched" over all of them (Figure 6-11).

6-10. It's a big help if the bandsaw is equipped with a miter-gauge groove and provisions for a fence. Of the two features, the miter-gauge groove is more important. You can always improvise a fence.

6-11. Blade tensioning is done by moving a wheel so the blade will be "stretched" to a particular degree of tautness. On this two-wheel machine, the adjustment is made by turning a screw with a hex wrench.

The correct tension is usually easy to achieve since most machines have built-in tension scales. You simply adjust the movable wheel until the scale pointer indicates the correct setting for the blade you are installing. If there is no tension scale, you can establish tension fairly accurately with the following procedure: First, adjust for maximum tension, and then slowly relax the blade until it can be flexed 1/8″ to 1/4″ with light finger pressure. Make the test on the area of the blade that is above the table and with the upper blade guides raised as high as possible.

A blade that is correctly *tracking* will stay approximately centered on all wheels when it is running. On some machines this is accomplished automatically. The mounted blade will move to, and stay in, the correct position when the machine is turned on. When the tracking procedure is a mutual one, it's usually a question of "tilting" a wheel so the blade will stay on the same plane throughout the path it travels. On a two-wheel bandsaw, tracking is always accomplished by moving the upper wheel (Figure 6-12). Regardless of how tracking is accomplished, never test the setting by turning on the machine. Spin the wheels by hand until you are sure everything is correct.

The information on tensioning and tracking given here is pretty general; there is considerable variance from machine to machine. To be certain that the settings are done correctly, check the instructions that apply specifically to your machine.

Blade mounting, tensioning, and tracking should be done with the upper and lower blade guides, backups, and blade guard out of the way so these items will not interfere with the procedures.

6-12. Tracking is correct when the blade is approximately centered on all wheel rims. In the cut area, the blade must be moving on a true, vertical line. Tracking must be done before the blade guides and the blade backup are adjusted.

Accuracy settings. After the blade is mounted, use a square to check the angle between the blade and the table (Figure 6-13). If it isn't 90°, adjust the table to make it so, and then set the built-in stop, which most bandsaws have, for the normal table setting. Also, at this point, check the bevel scale. With the table in normal position, the pointer on the scale should indicate "zero."

If the table has a miter-gauge slot, it should be checked for parallelism with the saw blade. One way to do this is to clamp a strip of wood to the table so it butts against the side of a wide blade, and then measure from the strip to the miter-gauge slot at each end of the table. If necessary, loosen the bolts that hold the table to the understructure and "rotate" the table one way or the other to make the correction. Another way to check is to use a miter gauge to advance a piece of stock that has been marked for crosscutting with a square. If the blade doesn't stay on the line, you'll know adjustment is needed.

Blade guides and backups. The blade guides and blade supports should be positioned after the blade has been tensioned and is tracking correctly. This must be done carefully if the blade is to run in a true vertical path (Figure 6-14). The guides, usually metal blocks, must be positioned to keep the blade from twisting, but they must not actually contact the blade when it is running free. The best way to achieve this is to use a piece of paper as a spacer when you secure the guide's position (Figure 6-15).

The forward position of the guides is adjusted to suit the width of the blade. They must not be so far forward that they contact the teeth. Setting them so they are close to the gullets between the teeth of the blade is fine (Figure 6-16).

The blade supports, or backups, should be set so they will not contact the blade when it is running free. This will only contribute to blade breakage. It's best to leave a very slight gap between the back edge of the blade and the sup-

6-13.   After the blade is tensioned and tracking is correct, check to see if the angle between the blade and the table is 90°. Adjust if necessary and then set the pointer on the bevel scale to read "zero."

6-15.   There should be a slight clearance between the blade and the guides. A piece of paper can be used as a spacer as you secure the guides. The clearance is required on each side of the blade.

6-14.   Adjust the blade guides after tensioning and tracking procedures. If the guides are not set correctly, the blade can be twisted so it won't follow a true vertical path.

6-16.   The guides should not be so far forward that they will contact the teeth. Position them just behind the gullets on the blade.

port. In this way, the support will work as it should; backing up the blade only when it is cutting (Figure 6-17).

Normal position of the blades and of the blade guard is shown in Figure 6-18. This provides maximum support for the blade and safety for the operator. Use extra care when you can't work this way because of a piece of oddly shaped wood or a particular technique.

Checking as you work.   Normally, when you are making a simple cut, the kerf will be straight and parallel to the side of the table. If you feed straight and the blade runs off the line so that it becomes necessary to compensate by adjusting the feed angle, it's wise to check the blade mounting and all the guides again. If these check out well, then it's reasonable to assure that the problem is caused by something else. This can be incorrect set of the teeth, a condition that can be the result of a poor sharpening job or a saw cut that caused the blade to dull on one side. The blade does not cut in a straight line because the sharp side "leads" off. When this condition is excessive, it can be remedied only by removing the blade and having it resharpened and reset.

When the "lead" is slight, you can do a salvage job by lightly honing the sharp side. This procedure is not a positive approach since you are dulling the sharp side to match the other, but it can save you in a situation where you don't

have a replacement blade or the time to get the mounted one fixed. Of course, you can work with the "lead" problem temporarily by compensating for it as you feed the stock. To do the honing, back up the blade on the dull side with a block of wood and lightly touch the sharp side with a honing stone as the blade is running (Figure 6-19).

Bandsaw Blades

Lumber mills use bandsaws to cut boards from logs. Their machine is sometimes two stories high and will turn blades that are as wide as 12″ or more. Blades for small bandsaws fall into the "narrow blade category" with common widths ranging from 1/8″ wide to 1/2″ wide (Figure 6-20). Some bandsaws can do better. For example, the Inca model 710, a 20″ three-wheel machine, can work with blades that run from 1/16″ wide to 1″ wide. Advantages lie at both ends of cutting extremes. The narrower the blade, the more intricate the cutting you can do. The wider the blade, the more substantial its resawing capability.

6-17.   Set the blade support, or backup, so there will be a slight clearance when the blade is running free. The support should function only when the blade is cutting.

6-18.   Normal position of the upper guides and of the blade guard is about 1/4″ to 1/2″ above the surface of the work. This is best height for blade guidance and safety.

6-19.   Honing, as explained in the text, is an emergency measure that helps to cure a blade of "lead." The sure solution is to resharpen and reset the blade's teeth, or to replace it.

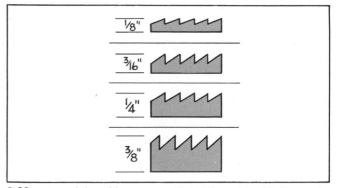

6-20.   Actual size of four commonly used bandsaw blades.

Considering routine bandsaw applications, a 1/4″ wide blade is probably the size you will find most useful.

Two popular blade designs are the "standard" and the "skip-tooth" (Figure 6-21). The latter is so called, logically enough, because every other tooth is skipped. It cuts fast and throws waste out quickly. A third blade to know about is called a "roll-chip." It resembles the skip-tooth and is an excellent all-purpose blade that also does a fairly good job on plastics and metals like aluminum, including the do-it-yourself variety. A very new blade in the field is the toothless blade, but it has an edge that is coated with grits of tungsten carbide. This blade is fine for metals, ceramics, and plastics, it can also be used on wood (Figure 6-22). On wood, however, although the cut is very smooth, cut speed is greatly reduced.

A thin blade with light set will give you the smoothest cuts (Figure 6-23), while a heavy blade with heavy set provides maximum cutting speed and freedom from binding because of the wider kerf that provides more freedom for the blade.

A bandsaw blade will leave its mark in the cut, and this is called "washboarding." It can be slight or so pronounced that it is impractical for some applications. This effect wouldn't bother you, for example, if you were cutting firewood; but it wouldn't be right on the edge of a cornice. Your control over the degree of washboarding rests with choice of blades. For a smooth cut, choose a blade with minimum set. The washboard effect will be there, but minimized.

How tight a radius you can turn with a blade will depend mainly on its width (Figure 6-24). However, there are other factors; the procedure you use to make a particular cut, and the amount of set on the teeth. A blade with much set cuts a wide kerf and this gives the blade more room to make a turn. Therefore such a blade, regardless of its width, can get around a tighter corner than the illustration describes.

Generally, bandsaw blades will cut faster across the grain than with it. In the latter situation, cut speed is reduced, and there will be a tendency for the blade to follow the grain of the wood instead of a marked line. Such things will not affect your productivity, but they are bandsaw facts of life and you should be aware of them.

Storing Bandsaw Blades

The blades can simply be placed full-length over pegs or hooks, but this can make quite a demand on storage facilities. Professional users will "fold" blades in thirds; a seemingly complicated procedure but one that is easy to learn if you follow the steps that are illustrated in Figures 6-25 through 6-28.

6-23.   Blades that have a lot of teeth and minimum set produce the smoothest cuts. When smoothness is not critical, you are better off working with a coarse blade that has more set.

6-21.   The usual tooth pattern on bandsaw blades is shown on the left. The other is the skip-tooth or "buttress" design.

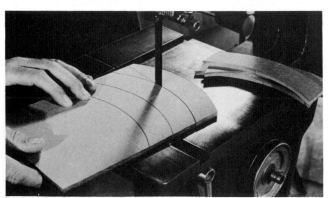

6-22.   Toothless blades have hundreds of particles of tungsten carbide bonded to the cutting edge. They are good to use on plastics and other non-wood materials.

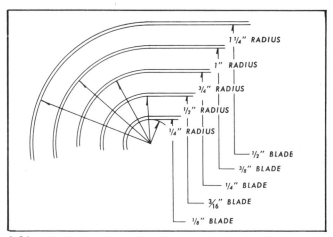

6-24.   Typical turning radius of various size blades. These are not invariable since the type of blade and the amount of set are factors that affect how tight a turn a blade can make.

How to "Fold" a Bandsaw Blade

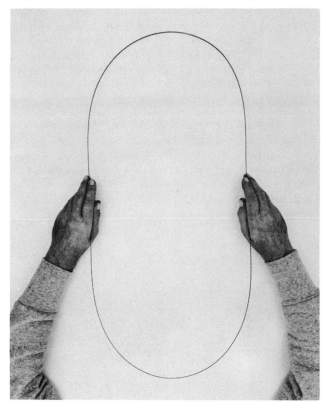

6-25. To start folding a blade, hold it like this with its teeth pointing away from you.

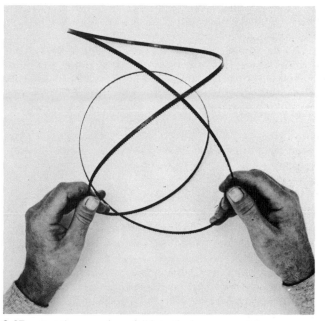

6-27. Let the upper loop fall into the lower one. Bring your hands together so you can trade the loop in one hand for the loop in the other.

6-26. Use your thumbs to fold the upper half of the blade down toward the floor while your fingers twist the blade a bit to turn the teeth outward. You don't have to use much force to accomplish this.

6-28. Bring the blade toward you as it is coiling and it will fall into three uniform loops. Tie with soft wire or tape. Be careful not to kink the blade. Blades have some spring so work carefully, and be sure to wear safety goggles.

After the blade is folded, tie it with a piece of string or soft wire. If you think it's going to hang unused for a long time, coat it with a light oil. Bandsaw blades are expensive so using them and storing them correctly can save you money.

The blades are flexible and do have considerable spring, which you will discover when you unfold them. Therefore, unfold them carefully, especially wide blades. Hold them away from your body and turn your face away. Wear safety goggles!

Also, when you fold and unfold them and when you place them on the machine, be very careful not to bend them. Kinks in a blade are not easy to work with.

Basics of Cutting

It's difficult to establish a "standard" operator's position for the bandsaw. You'll notice in many of the illustrations —and you will discover it in your own work—that there is no invariable rule. The size of the work, the kind of cut, and the direction of feed required will all affect how you stand and where you place your hands.

You will always, of course, be in front of the table, but your position can vary somewhat to the left or right side. Usually, your left hand will do the guiding while your right hand provides the feed pressure. Often, both hands will be used to support the work and to guide it. This is especially true on over-size material. The maximum-support rule applies to the bandsaw as well as other power tools. When the work is so large that you're likely to pay more attention to supporting it than to the cutting, work with an "extra hand," like an extension stand (Figure 6-29).

Another important rule is to keep your hands away from the blade as you maneuver the workpiece. A sharp blade and a steady feed are good safety factors. Try to keep

fingers of the feed hand hooked against an edge of the work. This will guard against slippage that could move your hand to a dangerous area. The sharper the blade, the less feed pressure you need; this reduces the possibility of hand slippage.

The bandsaw looks benign enough, but make no mistake about it. It can do a lot of damage, and very quickly. There are times when it will be better to use a push stick instead of your fingers. Try to work so that fingers are never directly on the cut line.

Bandsaw cutting is basically straightforward, but you can easily box yourself in on some cuts so that you must saw your way out or do considerable backtracking in order to get back to the cut you want. This can happen because you get into a spot that the blade can't handle or because the throat of the machine interferes with feed direction (Figures 6-30 and 6-31).

A partial solution is to visualize the cut and plan how you will accomplish it before you do any sawing. Often, you will find that the cutting is simplified if you do the layout either totally or partially on both sides of the stock; flipping

6-30.   Visualizing the cut beforehand will often eliminate the throat interference that is occurring here. Now the work must be backtracked and the cut finished by making another approach.

6-31.   If the cut shown in the previous illustration had been started this way, it could have been completed in a single pass.

6-29.   Supplying adequate support for large workpieces applies to *all* power tools. Don't get into situations where you must concentrate more on supporting the work than on guiding for the cut.

the stock can occasionally make an "impossible" cut possible.

On complicated jobs, it's more difficult to eliminate backtracking entirely than when the cuts are short. In-cutting (Figure 6-32) can solve some problems. This means making one or several straight cuts to a particular point. When the blade gets there, the waste falls away and there is more room for the blade to turn.

Frequently, it's better to saw out of a situation than it is to backtrack. This simply means leaving the cut line at a point and exiting at an edge of the stock. Then you re-enter close to the problem point and continue the job.

Corner cuts and turning holes can be done in advance with other tools in order to save time and, occasionally, material. You can form square corners with a mortising chisel or just drill holes. Drilling holes isn't a bad idea when you have many to do, especially when the turning radius is tight. This can reduce the bandsaw chore to simple cutting while giving you accurate radii and smooth, drill-produced corners. In either case, whether you use square openings or holes, they must be located accurately to fit in with the design.

Radial and tangent cuts can make it possible for a blade to get around a turn it couldn't do otherwise (Figure 6-33). Radial cuts are simply cuts made from the edge of the stock to the line you have to follow. What they do is permit waste stock to fall away as you are cutting and so provide more room for the blade to turn. Tangential cuts are run-offs. You follow the line until you feel the blade is binding, move off to the edge of the stock, and then come back to where you had left the line and continue to cut in similar fashion.

Freehand Cutting

When cutting freehand, you guide the bandsaw by hand and by sight. The bulk of what has been said so far applies to operator control over the work-to-blade relationship. The basic cutting rule is to keep the blade on the line that you have drawn. The mechanics of the machine are involved in achieving this: correct blade tension and tracking, good blade-guide settings, and sharpness of the blade. Beyond this, making an accurate cut depends on providing good feed direction. It's almost like driving a car. Don't overshoot the curves. Lead into them as they come up. Slacking on feed pressure in such situations will make it easier to be accurate simply because it will provide more time to do the maneuvering (Figure 6-34).

When you approach a curve from a straight line—this applies mostly to rounding off of corners on sized stock—follow the straight edge for an inch or two before you enter the curve cut. When you do start to turn, ease up on feed so the blade can do its job.

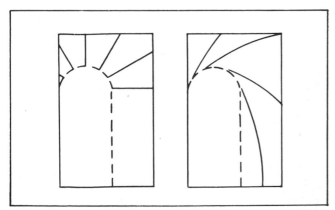

6-32.   You can eliminate much backtracking by starting the job with in-cuts. Waste pieces will fall away as you cut and this gives the blade more room to maneuver.

6-33.   Radial cuts (left), like in-cuts, allow waste material to fall away so the blade can turn more easily. Tangential cutting means moving off the line and out of the work whenever the blade starts to bind. For smoothest results, start each new cut as carefully as possible.

6-34.   Feeding only as fast as the blade can cut and careful work guidance are essential for successful sawing. This is especially important when the wood has a strong grain pattern.

On thick cuts the blade works harder. In such situations you should ease up on feed. When you can, use a wide blade with much set to do the job. If the cut is being done, for example, to prepare a piece of stock for lathe turning or for a part that you know will require much sanding, then the rough results of the heavy blade won't matter. When smoothness of cut of the bandsaw job is critical and you choose to work with a narrow blade, be aware that the blade can "bow" in the cut, especially on wood that has a strong grain pattern. The only way to protect against this, other than changing to a heavy-gauge blade, is feed the work extremely slowly. The smoothness of cut on such operations, especially when you are turning a circle, will not be consistent regardless of how you feed. You'll find differences, and the roughest areas will be where the blade quarters the grain.

Basic Guided Cuts

You can use a miter gauge or a rip fence as guides on the bandsaw (Figures 6-35 and 6-36), but remember that when

6-35. Guided cuts are standard procedure but will be most successful when the blade is in prime condition and you don't apply excessive feed pressure. Marking the cut line lets you check alignment as you saw.

6-36. Rip cuts can be done by using a fence. There will be a tendency for the blade to follow the grain of the wood, so keep the work snug against the fence and feed slowly. When necessary, use a push stick to get the work past the blade.

the work is so guided, you can't compensate for lead. So the blade must be in good shape in order to work without problems.

If the bandsaw does not provide for a miter gauge, you can get by with clamping a straight piece of wood to the table to act as a fence and then moving a backup piece of wood along it to feed the work for the cut. And, of course, you can make the special table shown at the end of this chapter. This table provides a groove for miter-gauge use.

Bandsaw crosscuts are limited by throat interference. In a normal setup, crosscut length can't be greater than the distance from the blade to the throat. To get around this, make an angle cut as close to the line as you can get. Then make a second cut on the line. This process does waste some wood, but it is a solution. When work width permits, you can use this technique with the stock on edge. The end result is the same, but wood waste is kept to a minimum.

Another way is to offset the blade so you can feed the stock at an angle and get a straight cut without throat interference. This can be accomplished simply by making a twist-board. Cut into a piece of 3/4" stock until the kerf is about 9" or 10" long and then turn off the machine while the blade is still in the cut. Back off the guides, turn the board about 20° or 30° and clamp it to the table. Of course, the blade twists with the board, and this permits an oblique feed so you can handle longer stock. Don't use the blade guides for this operation but do use the blade supports.

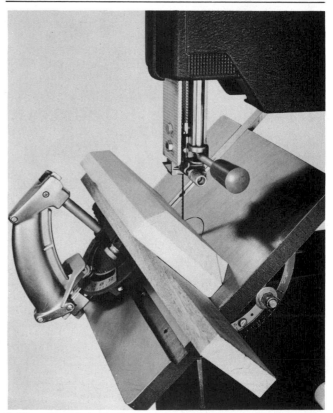

6-37. Chamfering is done with the table set at an angle. The difference between a chamfer and a bevel is that the chamfer cut removes only a corner of the edge.

Such a setup is good for a limited number of cuts since the blade will tend to return to its normal position by cutting through the twist board.

A more permanent answer is to make special guides that will hold the blade in the twist position.

If the bandsaw is equipped with a rip fence, lock it in place to obtain the cut width you need and then pass the work between it and the blade. This will be difficult to do if the blade has "lead." Actually, the heavier the blade and the more set it has, the easier it will be to do guided rip cuts.

Crosscutting to Length

On the bandsaw you can use the rip fence as a stop when cutting pieces to length. When the work is wide enough, simply place one end against the fence and move forward as if you were making a rip cut. On narrow work that could rock during the pass, use a backup block behind the work to do the feeding.

Angle Cuts

Beveling and similar operations. Most bandsaws have tables that can be tilted in a range of 45°. To saw bevels, you simply tilt the table to the angle you need and then feed the stock as if you were making a rip cut. You'll work more accurately if you use a fence as a guide. Always set the fence, whether it is a regular unit or just a clamped-on strip

of wood, on the right-hand side of the table so that both the fence and the work will be "below" the blade. Use the same setup to saw chamfers. The only difference is that a chamfer cut removes only a corner of the work's edge (Figure 6-37).

The fence-table combination creates a V-block setup that is very useful for many jobs. You can cut square stock to form triangular pieces that can be used, among other things, as shelf-support cleats, or, when cut into short segments, as glue blocks. Work the same way to form shallow, opposing kerfs when you are preparing stock for mounting between centers in a lathe (Figure 6-38).

The V-block arrangement is also useful when you need to halve a cylinder (Figure 6-39). This is one way to make half round molding. Stopping the cut forms a slot. This is often done so a wedge can be used to reinforce a joint. When working on rounds, be very careful to feed the stock so it won't turn as you cut.

Bevel cutting can also be done freehand. An example application is shown in Figure 6-40 where stock is being

6-39. Using the "V-block" to halve a round. It's also a good way to slot the end of a cylinder. Feed carefully so the work won't turn as you cut.

6-38. The combination of fence and tilted table makes a very practical V-block arrangement. Here, and in other photos, the blade guides and guard are set too high, but only for the sake of clarity. They should be positioned as close to the work as possible.

6-40. Circular cuts, with the table tilted, produce cone-shaped pieces. This is a good way to prepare stock for lathe turning. Cutting must be done very slowly and very carefully.

pre-shaped for lathe-mounting. This removes a lot of stock you would otherwise have to cut away with lathe chisels. Work like this must be done very carefully and very slowly.

Taper cuts.   A taper cut, whether it is done across the grain or with the grain, is simply a saw cut made at an oblique angle rather than one that is square to adjacent edges. This kind of sawing can be done freehand or by using jigs, the latter idea being most applicable when you need to produce many similar pieces.

The variable taper jigs that were described in Chapters 2 and 3 can be used on bandsaws, although you may have to change overall size to suit your equipment. Step jigs, such as the one shown in use in Figure 6-41, are also suitable. This is the idea to use if you are producing a number of projects, all of which require similarly tapered components.

Notched jigs are especially useful for taper-cutting small pieces; wedges and such. The edge of a strip of wood (or plywood) is shaped as the part you need or what you wish to remove from the workpiece. The jig and the work, guided by a fence, are moved together to make the cut (Figure 6-42).

Working with Dowels

Cutting to length.   Dowels, or rounds, can be cut to length by using a rip fence as a stop. It's a good idea to work with a stop block on the fence so the sawed pieces won't jam between the blade and the fence (Figure 6-43). Hold the dowel very firmly to counteract the tendency of the blade to rotate it.

Spiraling.   Dowels so treated have superior holding power in joints since the spiral provides a path for the glue to spread. To do the job, tilt the bandsaw table anywhere from 10° to 20° and lock the miter gauge in position as shown in Figure 6-44. Its distance from the bandsaw blade is what controls the depth of the groove. When you hold the work firmly against the miter gauge and make contact with the blade, the work will immediately begin to feed into a perfect spiral. However, don't give up hand control; the work can be twisted along the gauge faster than the blade can do the cutting. The idea is to let the work be guided

6-42.   Notched jigs come in handy when you are forming small tapers or cutting wedges. The shape cut into the jig is for the part you want or what you wish to remove from the workpiece.

6-41.   Using a step jig to form a taper. Jig and work are moved together. Be sure to keep the jig snug against the fence and the workpiece tightly in place throughout the pass.

6-43.   You can use the fence as a stop when doing cutoff work, but it's still a good idea to use a clamped-on block as a gauge so there will be room between the fence and the blade for the cutoffs.

automatically while you control the speed.

The same idea can be used as the first step when you wish to form the kind of spirals shown in the lathe chapter. The bandsaw job can mark the line of the spiral and also cut the depth of the groove.

Resawing

Resawing is ripping a heavy board into thinner pieces. The best blade for the job is wide, has coarse teeth, and plenty of set. Such a blade has enough "tail" to help keep it on a straight line and a nice wide kerf for blade room. A skip-tooth blade, the widest your machine can handle, is recommended. This blade will not produce smooth cuts, but that is not the purpose of resawing.

6-44.   You can form spirals in rounds if you work with a fence and tilted table. The pitch of the spiral will be uniform if you hold the work firmly as you rotate it. The blade guard does not have to be this high.

6-45.   Resawing can be done freehand, but so long as the blade is in good condition, it's not a bad idea to use a fence as a guide. A wide blade and a slow feed produce the most uniform results.

On the other hand, you will often use a smaller blade because you want the smoothest cut possible or because the blade happens to be on the machine and the resaw job required doesn't justify a change. This will work but do be aware that there will be more tendency for the blade to bind and to bow in the cut. A sharp blade and a slow feed are essential. Naturally, the less depth of cut involved in the job, the less critical is the blade-width factor. After all, if you are resawing 1″ square stock, it would be no different than a routine cut.

Resaw jobs can be done freehand, and that is probably the method to use if the blade is not in ideal condition. Guiding the saw freehand, you can compensate to some extent for lead. After you have entered the cut and discovered that the blade is cutting fine and free, you can speed up feed as long as you keep within the blade's cutting capacity.

You can also do resaw jobs against a fence, or a guide (Figures 6-45 and 6-46), which is a wise method when you have many pieces of equal thickness to produce. In this situation there isn't much opportunity to compensate for lead, so the blade should be a good one.

If you discover that the resaw job is putting a lot of strain on the motor, you might still be able to accomplish it if you first cut guide kerfs on the table saw (Figure 6-47). These kerfs are saw cuts on the resaw line, and they reduce the amount of material the bandsaw blade must cut.

6-46.   Resawing can also be done with this type of guide. Sometimes it's better than a fence since you can do some compensating as you feed if the blade is in less than perfect condition.

TABLE SAW
KERFS

6-47.   Preparing the stock like this for tough resaw jobs makes cutting easier. The saw kerfs serve as guides and reduce the amount of material the blade must saw through.

6-48.   A pre-shaped workpiece can be resawed to produce a number of duplicate pieces.

6-49.   Many similar pieces can also be produced by pad sawing. The pad, composed of plies that are tack-nailed or taped together, is cut as if it were a solid block.

6-50.   After cutting, all the pieces in the pad will be exactly alike.

Multiple Pieces

To produce multiple pieces quickly, you can pre-shape a thick piece of stock and then resaw it into thinner, duplicate pieces. Or you can make a pad of several layers of wood and saw as if the assembly was a solid block.

The resaw method involves simply drawing the shape of the part you need on the stock and then cutting it out. The shaped piece is then resawed against a fence (Figure 6-48). After the fence is adjusted to maintain the thickness of the cut, you run the pre-shaped part through as many times as possible or until you have produced the number of pieces you want.

The pad method involves putting pieces of wood together in a stack and then sawing them as if they were a solid piece (Figures 6-49 and 6-50). The easiest way to accomplish this is to drive nails through waste areas. On a common, home shop bandsaw, you can stack as many as 24 pieces of 1/4″ plywood and produce 24 duplicate parts in the one cutting operation.

In some situations you can use clamps to hold the pieces together as long as they don't interfere with the cutting. A little trick that can be used is to place double-faced tape between the pieces. The tape will usually hold the parts together well enough for the cutting.

Compound Cuts

Shapes that result from cuts that are made on two or more sides are classified as "compound cuts." The most common example is the cabriole leg and its variations (Figure 6-51),

6-51.   The bandsaw is noted for its ability to make compound cuts in heavy material. A practical application for compound cutting is forming cabriole legs.

but the techniques may be employed to do unsymmetrical shapes and ornamental work as well as to prepare stock for lathe turning.

The basic procedure involves making a pattern of the shape you want and using it to mark two adjacent sides of the stock (Figure 6-52). Cut the work on one side, but do it to produce a minimum number of waste pieces. These are then tack-nailed or taped back in their original positions, and the stock is cut on the second side. The waste pieces from the first cut must be replaced in order for the work to have a base and to reproduce all the original pattern markings for the second cut. If you replace them with nails, drive the nails so the part you are cutting out will not be marred. After the second cut, discard all the waste pieces. Some of the facts on post blocking contained in the lathe chapter can be employed on bandsaw compound cutting, especially when you are doing cabriole legs and similar jobs.

How you can apply this technique when preparing stock for lathe-turning jobs is demonstrated in Figure 6-53. As with any compound cutting, the profile you want is laid out on two adjacent sides. You want to be careful with the layout so centerlines will match. In this case, be sure to leave sufficient stock at each end of the piece so you can mount it in the lathe after you have accomplished the bandsaw cuts.

Pattern Sawing

Pattern sawing is required when the curves on the parts you need are not extreme. The technique to be used lets you cut duplicate pieces without having to do a layout on each and should probably be considered when the job can't be handled by either resawing a shaped piece or by pad sawing.

The idea is to set up a guide block that is undercut at one end to permit passage of the work (Figure 6-54). The end of the guide on the undercut side is notched just enough to snug the blade and is shaped in concave or convex fashion to suit the job being done. It is important for the center of the curve to be in line with the teeth of the blade.

6-52.   For compound cutting, the pattern must be drawn on two adjacent sides of the stock. After the first cut, the waste is tack-nailed or taped back on. Thus, the "second" pattern is preserved and the stock will have a flat base for the second phase of sawing.

6-53.   Compound cutting can also be done to prepare stock for lathe turning. It's a good way to get rid of a lot of material you would otherwise have to shave away with lathe chisels.

NOTCHES FOR BLADE

PATTERN

WORK

6-54.   The pattern sawing technique lets you saw multiple pieces without having to do a layout on each one. The pattern is guided by the clamped-on guide which is notched for the saw blade.

6-55.   Many times, parts with duplicate curves can be sawed this way. It's important to keep the arc of the work tangent to the fence throughout the pass.

6-57.   A circle cutting jig is a platform with a pivot on which the work can rotate. The distance from the pivot to the blade is the radius of the circle. It's critical for the pivot to be in line with the points of the teeth on the blade.

6-56.   Parts with irregular curves can be done in similar fashion. In this case, the guide has a point against which the work bears. Work with the guard much lower than it is shown here.

6-58.   Some manufacturers sell an accessory that is used for pivot cutting circles. Follow the instructions that are supplied with the unit.

6-59.   You can pivot-saw oversize work by supplying an outboard support. Here, the pivot is a pointed rod that is clamped to a sawhorse. Be sure the work is level with the table—saw slowly.

Parts to be shaped are roughly cut to size and then tack-nailed to the pattern. When you are doing the cutting, concentrate on keeping the pattern in constant contact with the guide. Be sure on your first test cut that the blade does not cut into the pattern. If it does, make the notch in the guide arm just a bit deeper. The blade should just barely clear the pattern.

Parallel Curves

Cutting parallel curves can be as simple as following the lines that are marked on the work; and if only a few cuts are involved, that's probably the best procedure to use. However, when you have to make many of these cuts, you can set up a guide system so you can come up with as many duplicate pieces as you want without having to do a layout for each.

When the curves are slight, you can use a fence to gauge the width of the cut (Figure 6-55). Make the first cut in the work freehand; make the others by passing the stock between the fence and the blade. The one important rule is to keep the arc tangent to the fence throughout the pass.

You can't use a fence as a guide when the job involves reverse curves, but a pointed guide block that you clamp to the table in line with the teeth on the blade can be used in its place (Figure 6-56). The distance between the point on the guide and the blade controls the width of the cut. It's essential to do the feeding so that contact between the guide and the side of the work is constant. With this setup, it's not likely that the cut could be oversize; but unless you handle the job carefully and feed easily, you can move off the guide. This would result in the cut being narrower than you want.

Cutting Circles

A pivot jig can be advantageous when you have many circular pieces to do; it can also be handy when you have a single oversize circular piece that might be difficult to do freehand. Any circle-cutting jig is nothing more than a pivot point around which you rotate the work to make the pass (Figure 6-57). In order for the cut to be right, the pivot must be on a line that is at right angles to the blade, and it must be aligned with the teeth. If these rules are not followed, the blade will track to the inside or the outside of the line, depending on the kind of misalignment you have. It's also important for the blade to be in good condition.

There are two ways to start the job. Make a freehand lead-in cut to the line and then set the pivot or cut the work square to begin with (the sides of the square must match the diameter of the circle) and rest one edge of the work against the side of the blade to start the procedure. There should be some pressure against the blade to begin with, and this can cause the blade to crowd a bit until it enters the cut and becomes "positioned." After that, it's just a question of turning the work.

Some manufacturers offer a special accessory for pivot-cutting circles. An example is shown in Figure 6-58. As always, with special add-on equipment, the item should be installed and used by following the instructions that come with it.

Figure 6-59 shows a technique to use when you wish to pivot-cut oversize workpieces. In this case, the pivot is a length of round bar stock that was ground at one end to a point and then clamped to a sawhorse. There are other ways to establish an off-the-table pivot. The important factors are: The pivot must be in line with the points of the teeth on the blade, and the work must be supported so it is level with the table.

Wood Bending

On the bandsaw, you can do wood bending by "kerfing" or by "thinning out." The kerfing idea is the same one that is described in the table saw chapter even though the method of cutting the kerfs differs (Figure 6-60). On the bandsaw, you do the job with the stock on edge and angled to clear the throat. This means the kerfs will be at a slight angle, but the angled kerfs will not interfere with how they allow you to bend the wood. You can feed the work freehand, or you can use a miter gauge that is set at the angle you need to clear the throat (Figure 6-61).

Thinning out is really a resaw job that you limit to the

6-60.   You can use the bandsaw for the kerfing technique that allows you to bend wood without having to steam it.

6-61.   To kerf long pieces on the bandsaw, you must feed the work at an angle in order to avoid throat interference. This won't affect how the wood will bend.

area of the work you wish to bend. What you are doing is reducing the stock thickness at that point to make it flexible (Figure 6-62). Such areas are seldom used as they are since they lack strength. Instead, they are backed up with blocks. The thinned section is a "veneer" that carries the appearance, and the blocks provide the strength. For example, you would use this method for the rails of a table that has straight sides but semi-circular ends.

Sanding

To set up for sanding, a special accessory kit is required that, in most cases, is used in place of the regular guides.

6-62.   The thinning out method for wood bending goes quickly on the bandsaw. The material that is removed leaves a "veneer" that is flexible enough for bending. The area, after bending, is usually reinforced with glue blocks.

6-63.   A typical arrangement for sanding on the bandsaw. The endless sanding belt is tracked like a saw blade. The pattern that backs up the belt is removable so compound curves can be sanded.

The abrasive is an endless belt just like a bandsaw blade, and it is fitted over the wheels with just enough tension to keep it tight.

The accessory kit will contain a backup plate which serves to support the belt when you move work against it. For some jobs, like contour sanding, it's possible to work without the backup plate; but you must be careful to apply the work so that you don't cause the belt to move off the wheels.

An example arrangement is shown in Figure 6-63, but if a sanding accessory is available for your machine, it will be special for the unit. Therefore, follow the manufacturer's instructions to mount and use the materials correctly.

A Special Table

The unit shown in Figures 6-64 and 6-65 was designed for the average homeshop machine. If your unit has an 11″ to 12″ throat and a table that measures in the 12″ x 12″ area, you should be able to make one exactly as shown. The depth of cut on your machine is not a factor.

Before you start construction, follow all the recommended procedures for setting the blade-to-table angle to 90°. It's also important to be sure the angle between the blade and the miter-gauge slot is 90°. If your table does not have such a slot, then make certain that the outer edge of the table is 90° to the blade.

Make the table halves of 3/4″ hardboard-surfaced plywood or something similar. After you slot the adjoining edges and fit the spline, assemble the parts without securing them as a unit and locate the center of the table opening so you can scribe a 3″ circle at that point. You can use a saber saw to cut the half circles but do stay inside the line and finish up with a drum sander. Use glue to assemble the parts permanently but keep the spline in that part of the slot that runs from the hole to what will be the inboard table edge.

6-64.   The special bandsaw jig is an all-in-one unit that can be used for many jobs. Its main component is a large table that is grooved for a miter gauge and for a slide that is used for pivot sawing.

Make the circle insert as shown in the drawing. The seat for it in the table can be done with a router or on a shaper.

The next step is to work on the table saw and make the 1″ opening down the centerline on the outboard side. Then, lower the saw blade to 1/2″ projection and form the rabbets on each side of the opening. Cut the blade slot directly on the centerline of the table hole and make the L-shaped cut on the inboard edge.

To fit this table to the machine table, shape the table guide from a strip of hardwood. This strip should fit in the machine's table slot just snugly enough to avoid lateral movement but still be able to slide smoothly. Put the guide in the slot and position the new table so the saw blade is approximately in the center of the hole. Be sure the outboard edge is perfectly parallel with the kerf line. Clamp the table to the guide and then attach the guide with glue and screws.

Make the two table clamps and attach them so the table can be moved one way or the other about 1″. The table cannot have a fixed position because some of the pivot-guided work you will do with it will require good alignment between the blade teeth and the pivot point. Being able to adjust the table position will let you provide for this.

Shape up the stiffener and drill holes for the attachment screws. Drill for and install the T-nut for the pivot-slide lock. If your machine table lacks a miter-gauge slot so that you can't use the table guide, adjust the width of the stiffener to ride against the edge of the machine table.

Make the table tie from hardwood and install it about 1-1/2″ in from the forward edge of the table to straddle the blade slot.

Now that the table is solid, you can work on the table saw to form the miter-gauge groove. Size this for a gauge you already have on hand or one that you buy for the purpose.

Before you replace the unit on the bandsaw, drill for and install the two, 10-32 T-nuts that are located on the centerline on the inboard side. These should fit flush on the underside.

Critical factors concerning the fence are its overall length and the angle between the fence and the base. The length of the fence, including the base, must miss the front

6-65.   Construction details of the special bandsaw jig. The dimensions that are shown should work okay for any bandsaw with a table in the 12″ x 12″ range, but check before working to see if some modifying is in order.

edge alignment by 1/16″, and the fence-to-base angle must be 90°.

Use hardwood to make the parallel-curve guide and the pattern-cutting guide. Actually, these designs are merely samples. Once you've started using them, you'll come up with designs that will be more suitable for particular applications.

The construction details that are shown in Figures 6-66 through 6-69 are for accessories that can be used with the special table.

Trouble-Shooting Chart

The chart in Figure 6-70 lists possible operational problems that can occur while using a bandsaw. If the solutions that are suggested don't work, then it's a good idea to check the mechanical features of the machine by reading the owner's manual.

6-66.   How to construct a fence for the table. Assembly is pretty straightforward. There should be a space of about 1/16″ between the end of the fence and the T-shaped lock. Use a washer between the components on the top screw. To lock the fence, turn the top screw first, then the bottom one. Don't overtighten.

6-68.   How to make the pivot slide. The base is 3/4″ hardwood, thinned just enough to take the aluminum strip. Attach the aluminum after you have installed the T-nut. The pivot is a headless 10-32 screw that has been pointed at one end.

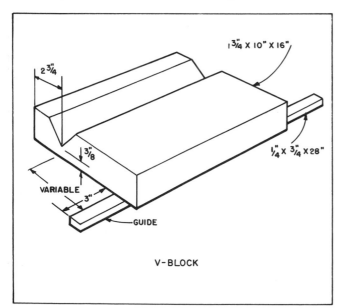

6-67.   Before you glue and screw the guide strip to the underside of the V-block, check on the table to be sure that the base of the V will be in line with the saw blade. With the V-block secured, you can feed rounds and squares for halving or slotting.

6-69.   These are guides you can make for use with the jig. One is for pattern-cutting, the other for parallel-curve cutting. The information that has been supplied for these techniques applies when these guides are used on the special table.

THE PROBLEM	POSSIBLE CAUSES	WHAT TO LOOK FOR OR DO
IN GENERAL Blade veers from cutting line	Excessive "lead"	Replace or recondition blade, or hone the "lead" side
	Poor blade-guide adjustment	Reset the guides to accommodate the blade being used
	Poor work-handling	Use one hand to guide, the other to feed the stock—work more slowly
	Knotty wood—wood with uneven grain structure	Use a very slow feed and a heavy blade—careful handling will minimize problem
	Bad blade	Recondition or replace
Cut isn't square to surface	Misalignment	Angle between table and blade must be 90°—check—reset auto-stop
Blade binds	Turning too sharply	Don't try to turn corners that are too small for the blade in use
Blade breakage	Forcing the cut	Take it easy—let the blade cut only as fast as it was designed for
	Turning too sharply	Don't cut radii too small for the blade in use
	Blade dull—worn—damaged	Sharpen blade or replace
	Misalignment	Check blade guides and backup
Can't backtrack	Kerf clogged with sawdust	Cut more slowly, especially with fine blades—stop machine and clear kerf with small knife
	Poor work-handling	Be careful to keep blade in the kerf when backtracking
Rough cut	May be characteristic of blade being used	If important, change to finer blade but cut more slowly
Blade scrapes when running free	Misalignment	Check for proper clearance between blade and guides—also check backup
Blade makes knocking sound when cutting or running free Cut-quality not consistent	Blade is kinked, bent, or twisted in a local area	Remove from machine and straighten if possible, or discard
Throat of machine interferes with cut	Machine has limited width-of-cut	No cure on some jobs
	Poor planning	Visualize the cut—plan the cutting procedure before starting
Bevel cuts not accurate	Misalignment—poor setup	Recheck bevel scale—reset auto-stops if any—carefully make setups
RESAWING Side of cut is bowed	Blade is too small	Generally, use widest blade available
	Wrong tension	Adjust tension to the blade being used
Blade moves off line when fence is used	Blade has "lead"	Recondition, or hone "lead" side
	Bad or dull blade	Replace—sharpen
	Tough, grainy wood	May be better to do job freehand
Rough cut	Characteristic of wide blades with heavy set	No cure

6-70. Trouble-shooting chart for the bandsaw.

7. The Jointer

One of the first procedures taught in a woodworking class is how to produce a straight edge on the workpiece. Since this is the edge from which all other dimensions are made, it must be smooth and even and square to adjacent surfaces. In a basic woodworking class the job would be done with a hand plane. In a power tool class, it's likely that it would be done on a jointer. This shows the basic correlation between the hand plane and the jointer. Differences have to do with speed (hand planing takes a lot more time)—energy (the jointer does the job under power)—and the minimizing the human error (if the jointer is set up correctly, there is better chance of getting a smooth square edge).

Many professionals routinely make a cut on the jointer before they do a rip cut on the table saw to assure that the edge placed against the rip fence will be true. That's one reason why it's not rare to find a jointer and a table saw set up for simultaneous operation (Figure 7-1). Many times, the two tools are powered by a single motor. The argument against such an arrangement has to do with safety; both tools are running regardless of which one you are using.

A jointer can be used for surfacing operations but this technique doesn't pose much competition for a "thickness planer." For one thing, when using a thickness planer, you will be sure that the planed surface will be parallel to the opposite surface. Also, the machine, even in a "small" size, can do surfacing on workpieces as large as 6″ x 12″. At any rate, the functions of the two machines are quite different. The average home worker will find the jointer the more useful of the two tools.

To use the jointer only for edge-planing and light surfacing would be like limiting table-saw operations to cross-cutting and ripping. Once you become familiar with the machine, you'll be able to do all the operations shown in Figure 7-2, and more.

Types and Sizes

All jointers operate in similar fashion. A cutterhead, usually holding three knives, is situated beneath and between "infeed" and "outfeed" tables. The size of the jointer, as listed, tells the length of the knives. This is a factor that bears mostly on the maximum width of stock that can be surfaced. For example, the machine shown in Figure 7-3 can

surface stock up to 4-1/8″ wide and so is called out as a 4-1/8″ jointer.

The second capacity factor is the tool's maximum depth of cut. This can range from 1/8″ to 1/2″. An increase in overall tool size and in its cut-width doesn't necessarily mean an increase in depth of cut. The 4-1/8″ machine and the 6-1/8″ machine in Figure 7-4 both have a maximum cut-depth of 1/8″. Incidentally, both of the tools are "motorized." That is, power sources are built in; a direct-drive arrangement that does away with pulleys and V-belts. Tools of this nature are close to being ready to plug in as soon as you get them home.

An example of a jointer that spans the line between amateur and professional use is the 6″ unit shown in Figure 7-5. It's heavier and larger overall—its total table length is almost 43″—and it has individually adjustable tables and a 1/2″ depth of cut. Depth of cut is not critical in relation to

7-1.   The jointer is often viewed as a companion tool for the table saw. That's why it's not uncommon to find the two machines set up like this.

WIDE RABBET

CHAMFER

STUD TENON

PERIMETER RABBETS
(RAISING)

END
RABBET

SURFACING
(PLANING)

EDGE RABBET

BEVEL

TAPER

RECESS

LEG SHAPES

7-2. The jointer is the ideal power tool for creating clean, smooth edges on workpieces, but it can do a lot more. Once you become familiar with the tool, you'll be doing work like this—and more.

7-3. The size of a jointer is identified, essentially, by the length of its knives. This tells the maximum stock-width the tool can handle; in this case, 4-1/8″. The second capacity factor is the maximum depth of cut. You can't see the motor on this tool because it's built in.

7-4. An increase in width of cut doesn't necessarily mean an increase in depth of cut. This 6-1/8″, motorized machine has a 1/8″ cut-depth which is the same as that of the smaller tool shown in the previous photo. Depth of cut is not critical for basic jointer functions—edging and surfacing.

7-5. Jointer which is found as often in home shops as in commercial places has capacities of 6″ for width and 1/2″ for depth. The extra cut-depth is very handy when the tool is used for jobs like rabbeting and tenoning.

basic functions such as edge-jointing and surfacing, operations where the cut-depth should be held to a minimum anyway, but for jobs like rabbeting and tenoning, a greater cut-depth can be an asset.

A 4″ jointer is available for multi-purpose tools like the Shopsmith®. It's actually an individual tool, quite suitable for mounting on its own stand, with its own motor, but when mounted on one end of the machine as shown in Figure 7-6, it is driven by the basic power source. A special coupling makes the connection between the headstock and the jointer.

7-6. A 4″ jointer with a 3/8″ depth of cut is available for multi-purpose tools like the Shopsmith®. It's actually an individual tool that is quite suitable for mounting on its own stand and with its own motor.

Parts of a Jointer

Jointers, regardless of how they look, and whether features vary, will have the basic components illustrated in Figure 7-7. The infeed table is where you place the work to start the cut. The outfeed table, whose horizontal plane must be level with the topmost point of the circle described by the cutterhead, is where the work is supported *after* the cut. The infeed table is adjustable since its height, in relation to the cutter, is what determines the amount of material that will be shaved off. The outfeed table may or may not have a fixed position. This can have a bearing on how alignment between knives and outfeed table is adjusted. If the table is adjustable, the knives can have a fixed position in the cutterhead; the table's height is raised or lowered to suit. If the table is stationary, then the height of the knives in the cutterhead must be aligned correctly. Other than that, an adjustable outfeed table doesn't have too much effect on the range of work you can do with this tool. As you will see, it does come into play when doing "recessing," but that is a rather limited application.

It's more important for the infeed table to have a healthy rabbeting ledge, a positive depth-of-cut adjustment, and a locking device that will keep the setting secure.

The fence is a critical component and the longer it is the better, so long as its mounted arrangement will keep it rigid. The fence, set vertically for normal operations, should be tiltable forward and back since the tool is useable for angular cuts; among them, bevels and chamfers. Most jointers will have automatic fence stops for the vertical position and for most-used angular settings.

The cutterhead, a heavy, steel cylinder, is slotted and otherwise designed to receive the knives that do the cutting (Figure 7-8). This is an area where there can be much difference among tools. Since knife installation has to do with operational accuracy and with safety, it is critical that you

7-7. Basic nomenclature of a jointer. All have spring-loaded guards that move aside as the work passes the cutterhead and then swing back. You can't use the guard when doing, for example, rabbeting so you want to be super careful at such times.

read and understand the instructions that are supplied with the machine.

The jointer will have a guard that is spring-loaded in some way so it will move aside as you make the pass and come back quickly to cover the cutterhead after the cut. Some jointers are designed so the guard can be used in front of the fence (normal position), or behind it. The latter position is applicable on such jobs as rabbeting where normal guard position isn't possible. On this kind of work and on other, special techniques, be aware of the situation and work accordingly. It is foolish, of course, to work without a guard when it *can* be used. Feeling that it is a nuisance on some jobs, or for whatever reason, is a poor excuse for taking big chances. Some of the illustrations show operations being done without the guard in place, even when there's no problem in keeping the guard where it should be, but this is only so you can see what is going on. In no way is this meant to indicate good shop practice.

Adjustment Factors

The horizontal plane of the outfeed table must be tangent to the cutting circles of the knives. All jointers provide for accomplishing this critical relationship either by adjusting the height of the knives in the cutterhead even with the outfeed table or by doing the reverse. To check, set a straightedge, which can be the blade of a square, on the outfeed table so it juts out over the cutterhead and then rotate the cutterhead carefully by hand (Figure 7-9). Each knife should barely touch the straightedge. If the straightedge is lifted or if the knife doesn't touch at all, adjustment is required. Make this test at the center and at the ends of each knife.

Signals that can tell of misalignment while you are working are shown in Figure 7-10. The work must pass smoothly from front to rear table regardless of the depth of

7-9. The horizontal plane of the outfeed table must be tangent to the cutting circle of the knives. Depending on the design of the machine, you adjust the table to the knives or the knives to the table.

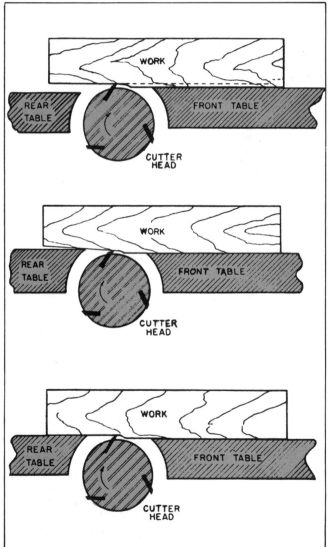

7-10. When alignment is correct (lower sketch), work will pass smoothly over the cutterhead and onto the rear table. The other sketches show what will happen when the outfeed table is too high or too low in relation to the cutting circle of the knives.

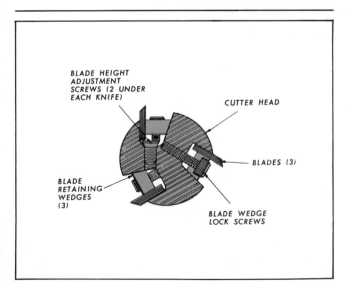

7-8. The jointer's cutterhead is slotted and otherwise designed to receive the cutting knives—usually three. The method of installing and adjusting the knives differs from tool to tool, so check the owner's manual carefully.

cut. If the edge of the work hits the front edge of the outfeed table so you must force it across, the table is too high. If the work should drop at anytime during the pass so that it is gouged by the cutterhead, the table is too low.

Also check the lateral position of the knives. They should project beyond the side edge of the outfeed table 1/32″ to 1/16″. This clearance is necessary so that, for example, work being rabbeted won't be hindered by the rear table.

The next step is to adjust the infeed table so its surface and that of the outfeed table will be on the same plane. When this is correct, set the pointer on the depth scale to read "0". To check out the accuracy of the scale itself, make the test shown in Figure 7-11. Carefully mark the work for an arbitrary depth of cut, say 1/16″ or 1/8″. Set the infeed table until the cut is perfect and then read the scale. This will reveal how much faith you can have on the calibrations stamped on the scale.

The fence. The angle between the tables and the fence when it is in normal vertical position must be 90°. If this isn't exact, jointed edges will not be square to adjacent surfaces. Make the check with a square as shown in Figure 7-12 and, if necessary, adjust the quadrant to read "0". Now, set the auto-stop for the "0" setting. If the machine has other auto-stops—most tools will provide them for left and right 45° settings—fix them now by reading from the quadrant. Later, when you do some beveling work, you can re-set the stops, if necessary, after checking cuts with a protractor.

The mechanism for locking the fence is usually a two-way wrench of some sort. One part of the wrench secures the table's position *across* the tables, the other locks tilt adjustments (Figure 7-13).

Edge Jointing

The general rule is to make all jointing cuts so the knives are cutting with the grain of the wood. It isn't always possible to follow this rule, but it does produce the most satisfactory results and also reduces the danger of kickback and splintering. When you do work against the grain or across it, reduce feed speed to a minimum and keep cuts very light.

On normal work, depth-of-cut settings should not exceed 1/8″. A 1/16″, even a 1/32″, setting is better if it gets the job done since it requires less power and wastes less wood. Often, on hardwoods or on large pieces, the job is done best by making a couple of light passes as opposed to a single heavy one. This is especially true with against-the-grain cuts and surfacing operations.

The jointing pass should be a smooth action from start to finish (Figures 7-14 and 7-15). Place the work edge firmly down on the infeed table with the adjacent surface snug against the fence. Use your left hand to maintain this work position and your right hand to feed. Move the work at reasonable speed and don't stop until you are well clear of the cutterhead. Such advice is sound only because it establishes a jump-off point. Work size, hardness of the wood, and the operation itself will also bear on how you hold the work and how fast you should feed.

Some operators feel the hands should never pass over the cutterhead, but this can interfere with smooth working and can place the operator in some pretty awkward positions. More important is to use the guard and to keep alert. Also, don't joint short or very narrow pieces, or attempt to surface thin material. Be aware of the gap that exists between the infeed and outfeed tables; you don't want work OR ANYTHING ELSE to jam in there!

Jointing End Grain

If you do such jobs in one continuous pass, it's inevitable that the knives will split off a portion of wood at the very end of the pass. To avoid this problem, use a double-pass technique. Advance the work over the cutterhead only enough to joint an inch or two (Figure 7-16). Then lift the work, reverse its position and complete the job with a second pass (Figure 7-17). With plywood, judge the grain direction of the surface veneer as if you were working with solid stock.

When jointing four edges on a piece of work, do the end-grain cuts first in single passes. The third and fourth passes, made with the grain, will remove the imperfections left by the first two cuts (Figure 7-18). This method does not apply to plywood. On such material always use the double-pass method.

7-11.   A good way to check the depth scale is to make a perfect cut of arbitrary depth and then check to see if the pointer shows the same dimension. Make this test when you are sure that the tables are level and you have set the pointer on "0".

7-12.   Use a square to be sure the angle between fence and tables is 90°. When this is correct, be sure the fence is at "0" on the quadrant and then set the auto-stop.

7-13.   Most jointers will have auto-stops at frequently-used angular fence settings. It's best to set these after checking trial cuts with a protractor. Fence tilt and position on the tables are controlled with a type of two-way wrench or lock-knob.

7-16.   Start an end-grain jointing cut by advancing the work just a bit as shown here. Don't do work like this on narrow pieces. Keep the guard in place.

7-14.   Edge-jointing starts with the work positioned on the in-feed table. The only way to be sure the jointed edge will be square to adjacent surfaces is to keep the work snugly against the fence throughout the pass.

7-17.   To finish the end-grain cut, reverse the stock. This method eliminates the splintering that can occur at the end of the cut when the job is done with a single pass. Note the auxiliary, high fence. It can provide extra support on many operations.

7-15.   Move the work smoothly and at a consistent feed-speed until it is past the cutterhead. The guard moves aside and automatically returns to cover the cutterhead when the pass is complete.

7-18.   When using just a single pass, end grain cuts usually result in a splintered edge. It's wise to follow this pass sequence when you must joint all four edges of a workpiece.

Surfacing

Surfacing is usually done to smooth a piece of stock or to reduce its thickness. Occasionally, you might do surfacing to make a distorted piece of wood useable. A surfacing pass is almost the same as a jointing pass except that, of course, the work is flat on the table rather than on edge, and you will be removing a lot more material. Keep the depth of cut to a minimum—just a shaving cut will often get the job done—and use a slow, consistent feed.

It's very important to maintain uniform contact with the tables throughout the pass to avoid tapered cuts, gouges, and generally unsatisfactory results. A sure sign that you are not working efficiently or that you are asking too much of the tool you have, is excessive work-chatter or an obvious decrease in cutterhead rpm. When these factors are present, be aware that you may be cutting too deep or too fast.

Most surfacing operations should be done with a tool that combines a pusher with a hold-down (Figure 7-19).

7-19. To do surfacing successfully, you must be sure the stock is held firmly on the table. A hold-down/pusher helps to accomplish this and also increases safety. *The guard is deliberately held aside in this photo for clarity only.*

7-20.   Ideas for hold-down/pushers. 4″ wide by 12″ long is a reasonable size. Use a cleat that is 1/4″ thick.

Such an accessory, which you can easily make for yourself, does more than help do a good job. It provides an extra degree of safety because it automatically keeps your hands away from the cut area.

Actually, it makes sense to have several pusher hold-downs on hand; the major difference between them is the length and the grip (Figure 7-20). An extra-long one is a good idea since it enables you to use both hands to keep the work in good contact with the jointer tables throughout the pass. An example, together with construction details for making it, is shown in Figures 7-21 and 7-22.

All of them will have a cleat, glued and nailed or screwed in place at one end. The cleat bears against the work's edge. Make the cleat 1/4″ thick. This means that the accessories can't be used on stock that isn't more than a 1/4″ thick to begin with; a good precaution since it isn't wise to joint such thin material.

Salvaging Distorted Stock

There are times when a piece of stock that is not in prime condition can be made useable by joining it. An example is the "dished" piece shown in Figure 7-23. The best procedure is to joint the concave edge first, making as many passes as you need to create a straight edge. Now that you have one straight edge, make a rip cut on the table saw to remove the convex edge. Then, to smooth the rip cut, make an additional pass on the jointer. Extra care is required when you joint a curved edge since there will be little bearing surface for the first cut or two. After these are accomplished, the work becomes easier to handle.

There is little point in starting with a jointer operation if the stock is distorted only on one edge (Figure 7-24). It would be more efficient to joint the good edge and then make a rip cut to remove the bad one.

7-21.   Make an extra-long unit to use on long work. Being able to use both hands to bear down provides additional assurance that the work will maintain contact with the tables.

7-23.   Stock that is distorted like this should be jointed on the concave edge first. Remove the convex edge by ripping on the table saw.

7-22.   Construction details of the extra-long pusher hold-down. It can even be longer than this depending on the overall length of the jointer's tables.

7-24.   When the stock has only one bad edge, it's best to remove by making a saw cut. The sawed edge can then be smoothed on the jointer.

7-25. This kind of distortion can be cured on the jointer but only if the width of the stock is not more than the tool's cut-width capacity.

Warped boards also have concave and convex distortions but they occur across the width of the stock. If the width of the stock is not beyond the capacity of the jointer, the board can be flattened as shown in Figure 7-25. There will be reasonably good bearing points if you make initial passes with the concave side down. The convex side is more difficult to do since you will have to keep the work from rocking and will have to be careful enough so the surfaces of the workpiece will be parallel. In fact, it's probably wiser to work on a table saw to remove the convex side after you have jointed away the concave side (Figure 7-26). These techniques apply only when the size of the stock is in line with the capacities of the tools. Often, it's better to remove stock distortions by straight sawing, or resawing, on the bandsaw.

Boards in "wind," which is a full-length twist, are a different case (Figure 7-27). A very small amount of such material can be handled successfully if you work as you do with a simple warp. In extreme cases, don't even attempt it. Or, if you want to salvage as much as you can, cut the board into shorter lengths and see what you can then accomplish.

Rough stock that must be squared can be handled as shown in Figure 7-28. The idea is to joint two adjacent sides so they will be square to each other, and then to work on a saw to finish the remaining sides.

7-26. Narrow, warped stock can be surfaced by using the jointer to flatten the concave side and saw to rip off the convex surface. The second step can also be accomplished by resawing on the bandsaw.

Rabbets and Tenons

The jointer is an excellent rabbeting machine as long as its maximum depth of cut is sufficient for your needs. Since most home workshop jointers will cut 1/2″ deep and the thicknesses of the wood you will be working with most often are 1″ or under, there really isn't much of a restriction here.

To organize for a rabbet, lock the fence from the front edge of the knives a distance equal to the rabbet-cut width. Set the infeed table to the rabbet depth. Place the work on the infeed table, snug against the fence, and advance over the knives as you would for any other job. When you need a deep cut on tough wood, it's wiser to make a couple of passes, adjusting for more depth of cut after each pass.

Rabbeting can also be done with the stock on edge (Figure 7-29). The method to choose will depend mostly on the size of the rabbet you need, and the thickness of the stock.

To create a tenon or a tongue, flip the stock and repeat the procedure (Figure 7-30).

Such cuts on the end of stock are a little more difficult because you are working across the grain. It may be necessary to make the cuts more shallow and to reduce the rate of feed, not only to make the cut smoother but to reduce the feathering and splintering that can occur at the end of the cut.

7-29.   Rabbeting can be done with the stock on edge. When the fence is short, be sure to maintain contact between work and fence at the cut area. Providing an extra-long auxiliary fence can help.

7-27.   Boards in "wind," which is a full-length twist, are difficult to salvage. It's probably best to discard them. You might be able to get some useable wood if you cut such a board into shorter sections.

7-28.   How to square rough stock. The first cut smooths a side, the second one is done so sides 1 and 2 will be square to each other. Make cuts 3 and 4 on the saw and then return to the jointer to smooth them.

7-30.   Tongues and tenons are formed by making matching cuts on opposite edges. Don't use this technique to form rabbets or tenons on stock that is too narrow to provide sufficient bearing against the fence. It's also a good idea to work with a pusher hold-down.

It's good practice to work with stock that has an over-width of about 1/16″. Then, after the cross-grain rabbet or tenon cut, you can do a jointer pass to remove any imperfection.

In most situations where rabbets and tenons are cut across stock ends, it's a good idea to use a pusher-hold-down device to do the feeding. Remember, too, on such jobs it's not possible to use the guard so you have an exposed cutterhead until the work itself covers the gap. Keep your hands well away from that area and be extra alert.

A way to provide some extra guarding is shown in Figure 7-31. The hold-down block, which is clamped to the fence, helps you keep your hands away from the cut area and also aids accuracy since the work can't rock as you make the cut.

Bevels and Chamfers

Cuts like bevels and chamfers are done much like routine jointing operations except that the fence is tilted to the angle you need and, most times, the full shape requires more than one pass. The best way to work is with the fence tilted so it forms a closed angle with the tables (Figure 7-32). This provides a tight nook that snugs the work so it can be kept steady during the pass. If you must work with the fence tilted in the opposite direction, be extremely careful to keep the work from sliding out from under you. Actually, the safest way to work when the fence is at an open angle is to clamp a guide block to the table so it won't be possible for the work to slide (Figure 7-33). This will provide safety and will also help you work more accurately.

The same thoughts apply to chamfering (Figure 7-34). A chamfer can often be accomplished in a single pass. A bevel usually needs repeat passes.

7-32.   When beveling, tilt the fence to a closed angle whenever possible. Work with a guide/support block to keep the work snugly in place.

7-33.   It's good practice to use a guide/support block when the fence is set at an open angle. It will help you work more accurately and more safely.

Using a clamped-on hold-down block is a good idea when doing rabbeting or tenoning. When you need the same cut on many narrow pieces, form it on a wide piece that you then saw into individual parts.

7-34.   A chamfer is done like a bevel, the only difference being the amount of material that is removed from the edge of the work.

How to Form an Octagon

Making octagonal shapes with a jointer is a question of making similar bevel cuts on all four edges of a piece of stock that has been accurately squared (Figure 7-35). Set the fence at 45° and make a pass to remove each corner. Be sure to use a clamped-on block to provide support for the work. If you must make more than one pass, be sure to make the first one on all four corners before making additional ones. The support block will have to be repositioned for each of the passes.

Tapering

By employing special techniques, you can use the jointer to form shapes like those shown in Figure 7-36. The procedure is fairly straightforward **but it must be done with great care** for the sake of accuracy and safety. To do a simple taper, set the infeed table for a particular depth of cut and then position the work so the starting point of the taper rests on the forward edge of the outfeed table. For example, for a 12″ x 3/8″ taper, mark the work 12″ in from one end and set the infeed table for a 3/8″ cut. Slowly lower the work on to the knives, pull it toward you, and the result will be a taper (Figure 7-37). Take great care that the jointer doesn't grab the stock out of your hands as you lower the work. It's a good idea to keep a loose grip on the stock so that if the jointer does grab it, the machine doesn't pull your fingers into the knives. Also, use a stop block to brace the work.

A block of wood can be used as shown in Figure 7-38, when doing short end-tapers. The taper will be slightly convex. To eliminate the convex factor, tack-nail the height block to the work, so block and work will move together, instead of securing the block to the table.

7-36.   Examples of parts you can make by using the jointer to do tapering.

7-37.   A taper is formed when you hold the work as shown and then pull it across the knives. Start with the work braced against a stop, and then lower it slowly until it rests on the outfeed table. Use a hold-down; keep the guard in place.

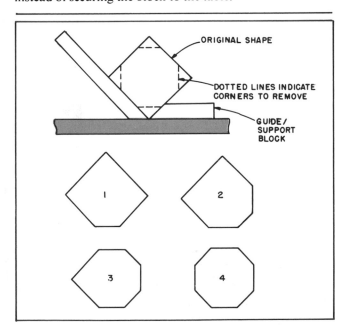

ORIGINAL SHAPE

DOTTED LINES INDICATE CORNERS TO REMOVE

GUIDE/ SUPPORT BLOCK

1   2   3   4

7-35.   Follow this sequence of passes when you wish to change a piece of square stock to octagonal shape. If more than one pass is needed, make the first one on all corners before changing the setting.

TAPER SLIGHTLY CONVEX

BLOCK OF WOOD

7-38.   You can use a height block when doing short end-tapers. The taper will be slightly convex if the block is clamped to the table. If you tack-nail the block to the work so both move together, the taper will be flat.

When the cut must be duplicated on other sides or when you need the same cut on different pieces, it's a good idea to clamp stop blocks to the jointer fence so you will have positive positions for both the start and finish of the pass. Tapers in excess of the machine's maximum depth of cut can be accomplished with repeat passes.

Tapers that are longer than the infeed table must be handled differently. For example, with a 24″ x 3/8″ taper, mark the stock into two 12″ divisions and set the depth of cut for 3/64″. Make the first pass from the first 12″ mark and a second one from the second 12″ mark, and you will have the required taper.

Approximately the same procedures apply when you wish to limit the length of the taper while confining it to some midpoint. The idea is simply to clamp stop blocks to the fence on both infeed and outfeed sides of the cutterhead. These control the start and finish of the cut (Figure 7-39).

For tapering operations, it's a good idea to make a special fence like the one shown in Figure 7-40. The pur-

7-39. Tapers can be "stopped" simply by limiting the length of the cut. Use stop blocks for best control. Ease up at the end of the cut to avoid the splintering that can occur.

7-40. Providing an extra-long auxiliary fence is a good idea for tapering operations. The regular fence will probably have holes through it so the accessory unit is easy to attach with screws. Stop blocks can be clamped in place on this fence.

pose of the auxiliary fence is to provide more longitudinal support for the work than you might be able to get from the regular fence.

The tapering technique, and variations of it, can be utilized extensively to produce legs, rails and other components for chairs, tables and similar projects, or merely to add a design element to a component for any project. Do work carefully. Always use hold-downs to keep the work on the table. Never allow your hands to get close to the cutter.

Recessing

The recessing cut is often referred to as a "stopped chamfer." It's often seen on base members and bottoms of table and stand legs. When you have a jointer with a fixed outfeed table, the cut is made in two passes with stop blocks on the fence to gauge pass length. This still leaves a raised area in the center of the cut since all you've done is form opposite tapers. You can leave it, since it's quite decorative in itself, or remove it by cutting on another tool.

When the outfeed table is adjustable, you can do the cut in one pass merely by lowering both tables an equal amount. Whether you make the cut in one pass or two, you can't cut any deeper than the maximum setting of the jointer.

Figure 7-41 and 7-42 show how recessing is done.

Recessing, like tapering, can be extremely dangerous if not performed correctly. When you lower the stock on to the spinning knives, there is a grave risk that the cutterhead will grab the wood out of your hands and kick it backwards. For this reason, take these precautions: First, use a stop block to keep the wood from kicking back, if practical. Second, lower the wood *very* slowly. Third, keep a loose grip on the wood so that if the cutterhead does grab it, it doesn't take your fingers along with it.

Working with a V-block

For a good amount of routine shop work, a V-block jig provides greater convenience and even more accuracy, especially when you have the same cut to make on many pieces.

The jig, shown in Figures 7-43 and 7-44, is just a V-block with an offset that matches the tool's maximum depth of cut. It has its own fence, but this is just a means of attachment to the regular jointer fence. Attaching this and similar items to the jointer should not be a problem since all jointers usually have holes through the fence for just such purposes.

On maximum cuts, the forward end of the jig rests solidly on the outfeed table, but this changes as you reduce the cut. Therefore, don't bear down too heavily as you pass the knives. It's also possible, when necessary, to use a wooden shim between the jig and the table.

This jig can be used to create a flat on a cylinder, but don't use it for the same purpose on small dowels or on any piece that is too small to be held safely.

Two typical applications for the jig are shown in Figures 7-45 and 7-46.

7-41.   Recessing, when the jointer has a fixed outfeed table, is a two-pass technique with cut-length controlled with stop blocks. Make one pass, and then another after the stock has been reversed.

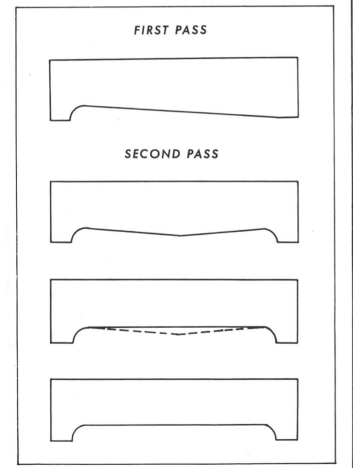

FIRST PASS

SECOND PASS

7-42.   Top sketches show the result when recessing is done on a jointer with a fixed rear table. The raised center area shown by the dotted lines can be removed or left as a decorative detail. When the jointer's rear table can be lowered, recessing is done in one pass and there will be no raised area (bottom sketch).

V-Block Jig

7-43.   A V-jig is a good tool to use when doing chamfering or beveling, especially when you need the same cut on many pieces. Situate the jig so the knives clear the shoulder of the offset. Secure the jig with clamps, or by driving screws through the regular fence.

7-44.   Construction details of a V-jig you can make.

7-45.   To use the jig, hold the work firmly in the "V" and pass it slowly over the knives. The jig was designed for a 6″ machine but it will work as well on a 4″ tool. The width of the V-block should cover the full width of the table.

7-46.   You can do jobs like this but depth of cut will be limited by the size of the "V" in the jig. Don't work on pieces that are too small to be held safely.

Forming Integral Tenons on Rounds

By using a special technique, you can work on the jointer to form integral tenons on cylinders (Figure 7-47), but the operation requires great care both in setup and execution. The idea is to support the work in a horizontal position so it can be rotated against the direction of rotation of the cutterhead. The joiner fence may be used as a stop to gauge the length of the tenon, or you can use an L-shaped guide/support to do the job (Figure 7-48).

Two methods can be used. In one, a block of wood with a hole through it that matches the diameter of the cylinder (or you can make a V-cut to do the same job) is clamped to the jointer as shown in Figure 7-49. The fence is locked in place to gauge the length of the tenon. With the cutterhead rotating, the stock is fed **slowly** through the hole until it contacts the fence, and then it is carefully rotated in a clockwise direction.

The second method employs a heavy block of wood, shaped so it can be firmly clamped to the jointer (Figure 7-50). It's a good idea to bevel the edge of the block against which the cylinder will bear so the cylinder will receive maximum support. **Don't use this technique to form tenons on short pieces.** As usual, getting your hands close to the cutter is taboo. If you should need a short piece, work on stock you can handle safely, and then saw off the part you need. Also, it's not advisable to do this kind of work on small dowels.

Trouble-Shooting Chart

Some problems that can occur when doing jointer work and their possible causes and cures are shown in Figure 7-51.

7-48. The jig can be a heavy block of wood that is cut out to suit the work. The length of the tenon will be controlled by the length of the cutout and how the jig is clamped to the table. Start the operation with the work firmly on the rabbeting ledge and against the jig. Advance the work slowly to make contact and then rotate it slowly against the cutter's direction of rotation. Don't work with short pieces or small diameter dowels.

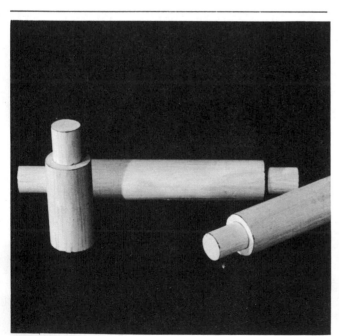

7-47. A very special jointer technique will allow you to form intergral tenons on round stock. Special jigs, designed to suit the work, are required.

7-49. Another tenoning system employs a block that has been drilled or V-cut to accommodate the work. The jointer's fence is set to gauge the length of the tenon.

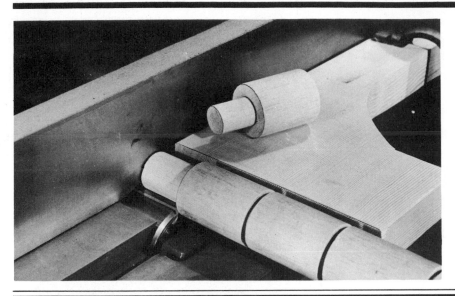

7-50. The position of the jig and the jointer's depth-of-cut setting will determine the diameter of the tenon. This jig is a simple L-shaped affair with its bearing edge beveled to form a nook for the work-piece. When you need short, tenoned pieces, form them on long stock and then cut off the part you need. Always keep a firm grip on the workpiece—and don't rush.

THE PROBLEM	POSSIBLE CAUSES	WHAT TO LOOK FOR OR DO
WHEN JOINTING/ SURFACING		
Jointed edges are not square	Misalignment Poor work-handling	Fence must be 90° to table—check and reset auto-stop Keep work on table and against fence throughout pass
Work hits edge of outfeed table Work drops and is gouged at end of cut	Misalignment	Knives are too low—reset for alignment with outfeed table Knives are too high—reset
Inaccurate depth of cut	Misalignment	Recheck depth-of-cut scale and its indicator
Raised line runs along length of cut	Nick in edge of knives	Regrind and sharpen knives
Rough or chipped cut	Cutting against the grain	Cuts always smoothest when cutting with the grain
Rippled cut	Feeding too fast Poor work-handling Misalignment Work vibrating	Slow feeds produce smoothest cuts Keep work firmly on table Just one knife cutting—reset knives Keep firm grip on work
Cutter stalls	Cutting too deep	Reduce depth of cut—make repeat passes when necessary
WHEN BEVELING Inaccurate cuts	Misalignment Poor work-handling	Check fence setting—reset auto-stops Hold work firmly against fence throughout pass—avoid tilting—use hold-down blocks or guides
Cut is tapered	Poor work-handling	Keep down pressure uniform throughout pass
WHEN RABBETING Work hits outfeed table	Misalignment	Adjust lateral position of knives so cut will clear outfeed table
Cut is wider at one end	Excessive pressure against fence during pass	Use the fence only as a guide
Uneven depth of cut	Poor work-handling	Keep uniform pressure on work throughout the pass
Wrong cut-width	Inaccurate setting	Be sure to measure from fence to end of knives

7-51. Trouble-shooting chart for the jointer.

8. The Thickness Planer

The basic function of a thickness planer is to smooth rough stock or to reduce the thickness of any piece of wood, and to do it while maintaining the parallelism of opposite surfaces. Surfacing can be done on a jointer so long as the width of the stock is not more than the tool's capacity, but producing work that will be of uniform thickness and with parallel surfaces depends on the operator's finesse. The thickness planer does it all, automatically. Place the work on the tool's infeed table and move it forward to engage a feed roller, which turns on its own to move the stock if the machine has automatic feed. The work is fed past the cutterhead, which cuts to a depth that you determine, and emerges in uniform condition and with a ready-to-use surface (Figure 8-1).

There was a time when the thickness planer was strictly an industrial machine. Today, even manufacturers who are noted for heavy-duty equipment are producing thickness planers that are as much at home in a home shop or a cabinet shop as they are in large industrial establishments (Figures 8-2 and 8-3).

Also, there are planers available that have been designed specifically with the "small" user in mind; tools that don't compare with the big brothers as far as capacity is concerned but which are just as husky and efficient and often can be equipped to do more than plane wood. The Foley-Belsaw machine shown in Figure 8-4, is called a Jointer/Planer/Molder and the description is justified because the tool, when correctly organized, can function all three ways. As a jointer (Figure 8-5), it can handle stock up to 6″ wide and has a tiltable fence for doing bevels and chamfers. To change it to the thickness planer mode, you swing away the two tables to reveal a height-adjustable bed which is the bearing surface for planing operations (Figure 8-6). The planer feeds stock past the cutterhead automatically, and has a maximum cut-width of 8″.

Molding operations, or "sticking" as it's called in industry, are done with the tool in planer mode but with specially shaped knives used in the cutterhead in place of the straight knives used for planing (Figure 8-7). Many standard patterns, like the casing designs shown in Figure 8-8, are available. In addition, the company will grind custom knives to your specifications.

A second Belsaw product looks more like a conventional thickness planer, but it too has multiple functions. In Figure 8-9, where the tool is shown without a hood so its mechanisms can be seen, it is set up so it can saw and surface plane in one operation. This is accomplished automatically because the machine is equipped with a power feed that moves the work through the entire pass.

A neat, compact planer-molder, one that requires little space but functions in admirable fashion, is the Williams & Hussey machine shown in Figure 8-10. It's different from others of its type in that it has an open-side design. This allows surfacing stock that is wider than the tool's 7″ capacity by reversing the board and passing it through a second time. This means that one pass will be made against the grain, but you live with it when necessary.

8-1.   Basic function of the thickness planer is to smooth stock, or to reduce its thickness, while maintaining parallelism of opposite surfaces. When the tool has a power feed, the material is automatically fed through at the feed rate that produces the smoothest cuts.

8-2. Many manufacturers of heavy-duty equipment are now producing "small" thickness planers that are quite suitable for small-shop use. This Rockwell unit can handle stock almost 6″ thick and 13″ wide. A 2 hp, 230 V motor is recommended.

8-5. As a jointer, the tool is good size, having a total bed length of 36-1/2″. The maximum width of cut is 6-1/2″; the depth of cut, 1/8″. Fence and guard actions are similar to what is found on conventional jointers.

8-3. The Parks 4″ x 12″ thickness planer is another compact unit that has small shop versatility. It moves work at 16 feet per minute and has a minimum work thickness of 1/16″. Pieces as short as 6″ can be planed. One to 3 hp is recommended. Bench type planers like this must be mounted on sturdy stands.

8-6. Changing from jointer to thickness planer takes an insignificant amount of time, and no tools are needed to accomplish it. As a planer, the tool can handle stock up to 4-1/2″ thick x 8″ wide. Maximum depth of cut when planing is 5/32″. The shortest piece it can handle is 7-1/2″, and minimum thickness is 1/4″.

8-4. New Foley-Belsaw machine is a combination jointer/planer/molder. The tool has a power feed (for thickness planing and molding) and can operate efficiently with a 1 hp, 115 V motor.

8-7. The machine becomes a "sticker" when shaped knives are used in place of the straight planing knives. The machine can turn out different molding designs at the same time. Careful setups are required so the raw material will travel in a straight line.

The tool is small physically, but a tiger functionally. For example, planing the edges of a 2x8 poses no problems (Figure 8-11). The machine is available with either a hand-feed or a power-feed and it has an output capacity of 15 feet per minute. A 1 hp motor provides sufficient power even with the power feed. Another plus is that the tool's cutter-head is designed to take shaped knives as well as straight ones. Thus it can be used to produce moldings of standard or original design (Figure 8-12).

General Use Considerations

All of the thickness planers we have shown, and others, have certain design characteristics and particular capacities that affect how they should be used efficiently and safely. Therefore, reading the owner's manual until you thoroughly understand the tool is a must. For example, you will learn about the shortest piece of stock and the thinnest piece of stock that is permissable to put through the machine. Admonitions of this nature should never be ignored.

For the work to have maximum smoothness, the knives, whether straight or shaped, must be super sharp.

They will be to begin with but you must be sure to keep them that way. Always feed so the knives will cut with the grain of the wood. Take minimum cuts even though the tool's depth-of-cut capacity might be greater. Usually, two light cuts will do a better job than a single deep one. How deep to cut depends on the nature of the wood. For example, softwoods cut easier than hardwoods. Other factors are whether you just need to shave wood to smooth it, whether you are planing rough stock, and whether you are working to reduce the stock's thickness.

Always check the wood to be sure it is not imbedded at some point with a foreign material. Even dirt can nick the knives and thereafter you will have long, raised ridges on the work. Be especially careful with old lumber that may harbor hidden nails. If you are planing work that has been edge-glued, be sure to remove glue-beads, or any surface glue, before planing.

Planer beds are seldom long enough to provide adequate support for oversize pieces. When planing extra-long stock, keep the work level by using outboard supports (Figure 8-13).

8-8.   Many types of standard pattern knives, like those that produce casing, are available. There are even knives that let you make rounds and dowels. If you ever need a non-standard molding, the company will grind one for you from a sketch.

8-9.   This Belsaw product looks more like a conventional thickness planer but it too can produce moldings, and when fitted with a saw blade, will rip and plane stock at the same time. Protective covers have been removed to show mechanisms.

8-10.   Williams & Hussey compact tool is an open-side design. Its small size shouldn't fool you since it can handle stock up to 8″ thick and 7″ wide. It is available with a hand feed or a power feed. The power feed moves work at 15 feet per minute and it can operate nicely with a 1 hp motor.

Distorted stock, boards that are warped or cupped, can't be flattened and brought to uniform thickness simply by passing them through the planer. The rollers that move the board through also flatten it before it reaches the cutter-head. When the rollers release the board, after the cut, it simply springs back to its original condition. Such work-pieces should first be brought to the condition shown in Figure 8-14, by jointer cuts, simple sawing, resawing or even by sanding. The technique to use will depend on the width of the work as it relates the capacity of the jointer or saw or whatever.

If you are running molding, the raw material should be planed (or jointed) to within 1/16″ of the finished thickness and width. The material must then be fed through in a straight line and in perfect alignment with the knives. The best way to accomplish this is to set up as shown in Figure 8-15. The clamped-on strips provide a true path for the workpiece. When the cuts go through the stock, you must provide a wooden auxiliary surface for the wood to ride on so the knives won't cut into the bed of the machine.

Many times, the interior of a board will contain more moisture than its surfaces. If you plane only one side of the board in such cases, you may end up with the work having different degrees of moisture on opposite surfaces, or one side might be dry while the other is "wet." This can result in warpage as one surface dries faster than the other. To guard against this, remove equal amounts of material from both surfaces.

8-13.   Long work must be supported adequately. If it isn't, it will tip at the end of the cut and be gouged by the cutterhead. In the trade, this negative result is called "sniping."

8-14.   Don't depend on the thickness planer to cure warpage or cupping. It's best on such pieces to use other means to bring them to the shape shown here before running them through the planer.

8-11.   The small unit is pretty impressive when it's working. Here, it is planing the edge of a 2x8. The guide blocks are a good idea to keep the work vertical while the pass is made.

8-12.   Here too, using shaped knives instead of straight planing knives, produces moldings. Many standard molding patterns are available. The tool is belt-driven. The entire unit doesn't require more than 24″ x 24″ of bench space.

8-15.   Material being molded must be perfectly in line with the knives and must move in a straight path. You can assure this by using clamped-on strips to form a path for the workpiece.

9. The Drill Press

Today, more than ever, the drill press deserves a high ranking among stationary power tools—as much for non-drilling chores as for forming holes. You can use it for sanding, mortising, shaping, routing, planing, and a host of other practical jobs. Its multi-purpose characteristics range from drilling precise thread-size holes to mixing paint. The extent of its utility in any shop is wide but much depends on accessories you can buy, special jigs you can make, and techniques you can learn. After all, you can't even drill a hole with the best drill press there is unless you have a bit for its chuck.

Types

There are minor or major differences among various types of drill presses, but all will have the basic components shown in Figure 9-1. Overall size, weight, power, range of speeds and how they are selected, capacity, accessories the tool can handle, even the amount of shop space you have

CONE PULLEY SPEED CHANGER

COLUMN

QUILL FEED

QUILL LOCK

CHUCK

THROAT

TABLE LOCK

WORK TABLE

LOWER TABLE OR BASE

9-1.   The basic parts of a drill press. Tools with a cone-pulley speed changer have several fixed speeds.

available—all are factors to be considered when you make a choice.

Often, the only difference between floor model and bench model drill presses offered by the same manufacturer is in the length of the column (Figures 9-2 and 9-3). The taller tool has the edge on capacity between the chuck and the base. If you wished, for example, to drill holes in the edge of a wide door, you could do it by bringing the table way down, or even by swinging the table out of the way and using the base in its place. Many times, a bench-type tool is situated so that the head can be rotated to allow the chuck to project beyond the edge of the bench. Then, in effect, the capacity is from chuck to floor. The second, and probably more important capacity for general operations is the distance from the column to the center of the chuck. This dimension is used to tell the size of the machine, but it's always doubled for this reason: If the real dimension is 7″, you can drill in the center of a 14″-wide workpiece.

On a radial drill press (Figure 9-4), the head is mounted on an arm that can be moved longitudinally. Its capacity is increased enormously; up to as much as 16″. When the head is at maximum extension you can drill in the center of 32″-wide material. On such a tool, you can tilt the head, and this allows fuss-free angular drilling.

The Toolkraft machine shown in Figure 9-5 is unique in that its mechanism is designed to drive two spindles, each with its own range of speeds. The high-speed spindle, with a range of 4,000 to 18,000 rpm, is brought into play by rotating the head 180°. This kind of speed is nice for jobs like shaping and routing, both of which can be done on a drill press. Being able to tilt the head is also a plus for angular drilling.

The drill press may have a fixed table or one that can be tilted. A fixed table is no problem on a radial design or a tool with a head that can be set at an angle, but, for angular drilling it can be a nuisance if the head is stationary. It doesn't mean that angular drilling can't be done, just that you must employ particular improvisations. It's not unusual for a drill press to have two tables; one that is fixed for routine work, the other adjustable for angular settings (Figure 9-6).

If you have a small shop and don't need maximum drill-press utilization, you might get by very nicely with a compact, bench-top unit (Figure 9-7). These tools are not

9-2.   In terms of power, speeds, throat-to-chuck capacity, and other basic factors, the bench model drill press may not differ from a floor model offered by the same manufacturer.

9-4.   The radial drill press has the greatest column-to-chuck capacity. A nice asset is that the head can be rotated and tilted. This can be a help on many drilling jobs.

9-6.   Most drill presses have a single table that is either fixed or adjustable. Craftsman tool can be equipped with two tables; one for routine work, the other for angular drilling.

9-3.   The major difference between floor model and bench model machines is in the capacity between the chuck and the table. Increase in cost has to do mostly with the extra-long column.

9-5.   Toolkraft machine has two spindles. The upper, high speed one is brought into play by tilting the head 180. Speeds are controlled electronically.

9-7.   Benchtop drill press is compact and portable. It's small, but not a toy. Speeds are infinite between minimum and maximum and are controlled by turning a dial.

designed to replace larger machines but they can add a new dimension to drilling operations by providing more accuracy than hand drilling. The tools do what they are supposed to do in terms of rated capacity, power, and so on, but they can be especially useful because of their portability. For example, do you need a true hole through a fence post or other vertical structure? Attach the base of the drill to the workpiece with a clamp or screws, and form the hole in normal fashion by using the feed lever. You know the hole will be square to adjacent surfaces, something that requires finesse to do when working with a hand-held portable drill.

Understanding the Tool

Its essential mechanism is a spindle that has a gripping device at the free end. In most cases, a key-operated, three-jaw chuck is used, but there are times when a substitution is necessary or wise. Such a substitution can be needed when you are using mortising bits and chisels, which require special holding items, or when you are using router bits, which develop sufficient side thrust to warrant a special kind of chuck.

The *head* of the tool is composed of all the parts attached to the top of the column. The *table* is movable vertically, may be swung aside and, on some units, can be tilted. The *quill* houses the spindle and is moved downward by means of the *feed lever.* The return of the quill to normal position is done automatically through a spring action. There is usually an adjustment procedure so this action can be strengthened or weakened. Normally, the quill should return smoothly and without great shock.

It's possible to lock the quill in any extended position or to limit its extension through the use of the *depth stop,* almost always located on the outside of the quill housing (Figure 9-8). Cone pulleys allow you to select speeds. The more expensive drill press can have a built-in, variable speed mechanism (Figure 9-9). On some drill presses the speed is controlled electronically. You turn a dial for any speed that is between the tool's minimum and maximum rpm.

The *base* of the drill press is the table-like casting on which the unit stands. The length of the *column* determines whether the drill press is a *bench model* or a *floor model.* The capacity of a drill press defines the distance from the column to the spindle center and from the chuck to the base. When the capacity is specified as 15″, the column-to-spindle distance is 7-1/2″, which permits you to drill in the center of a 15″ wide board.

Adjustments on a drill press are mostly operational; the tool has to be accurate to begin with. If the table is adjustable, then you should check to see, when it is in normal position, that the angle between it and the spindle is 90°. One way to do this is to insert a length of 1/2″ drill rod in the chuck and then work with a square to achieve the correct angle.

Some Typical Drill-Press Tools

The most common drill-press tools are those used to form holes. These can range from the smallest twist drill to large

9-8.   You can control quill extension on a drill press with a stop rod, or by other means. This is essential since it establishes a mechanical means of controlling how deep you drill.

9-9.   Mechanical, infinitely variable speed changers look like this. The pulleys are two-piece affairs. Their sides open or close as you turn a dial so, in effect, you get pulleys of different diameter.

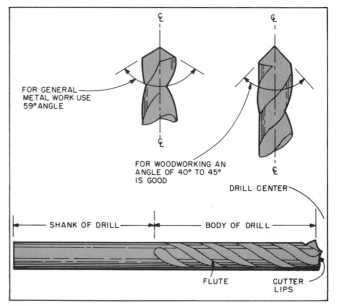

9-10.   Twist drills are really metal-cutting tools. They can be used for wood-drilling but perform best when the cutting angle is as shown in the right-hand sketch.

fly cutters. Although you will use twist drills quite a bit, they really don't do the very best job in wood. They have to be used simply because no other hole-forming tools that cut wood are available in the variety of sizes that you can find a twist drills. The common twist drill works most efficiently in wood when its cutting angle is about 40° as opposed to the 59° to 60° angle that is best for metal drilling (Figure 9-10).

Bits that have spurs and a point (called *brad point bits* or *spur machine bits*) form cleaner holes in wood than twist drills. That's because, while the point locates the center of the hole, the spurs cut through surface fibers cleanly *before* the bit actually starts to remove wood. The result is an exact-size, smooth hole.

Many drilling tools have *flutes,* which are channels up which waste chips can travel to clear the hole. If this didn't happen, waste chips would build up and cause overheating and inaccurate work. That's why it's not good practice to drill the full length of the flutes without retracting the bit frequently as you work. The idea is to have a minimum of waste material in the hole being formed.

Bits with screw points (Figure 9-11) should not be used in a drill press. The screw, being self-feeding, would attempt to control the rate of penetration. This would work if the rpm could be adjusted in relation to the pitch of the screw, but it's feasible only under rigidly controlled conditions. It's better to work with bits that have points. Then, how fast the tool will penetrate is easily controlled by the operator.

Spade bits are excellent drilling tools, especially when you need extra-large holes. They have long, sharp points and slim shanks. The blades are flat and good ones have relieved edges for cleaner, cooler cutting. They may be purchased individually or in sets that include sizes from 1/4″ up to 1-1/2″ (Figure 9-12). Spade bits operate most efficiently at higher-than-average speeds. Even the largest one should be run at about 1,500 rpm.

To drill really large holes, use fly cutters and hole saws. The fly cutter is an adjustable unit that rotates a vertical bit which is at the end of a horizontal arm. Here, a careful set-up and a slow speed are essential (Figure 9-13). Clamp the work securely, and keep your hands well away from the cut area. The cutting bit will be a blur as it turns, so you don't want to "guess" where it might be. Always start such operations at the tool's lowest speed. If a variable speed mechanism is available, you can rev up very slowly until the tool is cutting smoothly and without chatter or vibration. What speed you can work at will depend quite a bit on the diameter of the hole you are forming. If the job doesn't go right, it's possible that the tool doesn't have a speed at which a fly cutter can be used efficiently and safely.

There are various types of hole saws. Some come in sets, each unit designed for a specific diameter. Of course, the saws can be purchased individually but buying in sets usually saves money. Another type of hole saw works with individual blades—three, usually—that can be adjusted to form holes up to 3″ in diameter. The advantage is that one tool can do many jobs. The disadvantage is that the operator, not the tool, will be responsible for accuracy. A third

9-11.   Don't use drilling tools that have screw points. The screw will attempt to control the rate of penetration and this can work only if rpm can be set to match. Work with tools that have simple points.

9-12.   Spade bits are good wood-drilling tools. Sets increase by sixteenths up to 1″ and by eighths from there to 1-1/2″. They work best when used at higher-than-normal speeds.

9-13.   Fly cutters can be used to form very large holes, or to make discs. They must be used at very slow speeds and with the work clamped securely. The cutter can be just a blur, so keep hands in safe positions.

type of hole saw comes with various saw-edged bands that lock in grooves in the head. The bands, each one for a particular size hole, are secured in the head with lock screws (See Figures 9-14, 9-15, and 9-16).

There are other types of drill-press tools that will be shown in sections of this chapter that deal specifically with their use. Some of them can be seen in Figure 9-17.

Speeds and Feed

Excessive speeds on some tools can be dangerous. The general rule is to use slower speeds with larger tools. Sometimes this is not the most efficient way to use a particular tool, but it is done because the safety factor is as important. Be aware that the most efficient setup causes the tool to cut steadily (Figure 9-18). Unless it's designed to work that way, it should not scrape. Chatter, excessive vibration, rough results, and stalling of the motor can all be signs of the wrong speed, the wrong feed, or both.

At the other extreme, a speed that is too slow on some materials and with some tools, together with a hesitant feed, can cause the tool to rub, which won't do anything but dull the cutting edges. A slow speed with heavy feed can make the tool dig in, which can stall the motor or even cause breakage of the cutting edges.

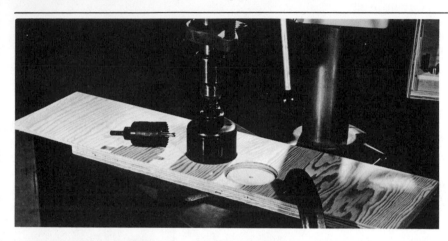

9-14.   Hole saws can be purchased individually or in sets. Each unit forms a hole of specific size. Most sets have a single arbor on which different diameter saws can be mounted.

9-15.   An adjustable hole saw is a single tool that can be used for holes up to about 3″ in diameter. It will probably have two sets of blades, one set to be used for metal cutting.

9-16.   Another type of hole saw comes with saw-edged bands that lock in grooves in the head. Each band is for a hole of particular size. The only large-hole cutter that is variable is the fly cutter.

TWIST DRILL

SPADE BIT

SPUR MACHINE DRILL

MULTI-SPUR MACHINE BIT

PLUG CUTTER

TWIST DRILL W/ADJUSTABLE COUNTERSINK ATTACHMENT

SOLID-CENTER BIT

EXPANSIVE BIT (W/BRAD POINT)

FLY CUTTER

HOLE SAW

ROUTER BIT

DOVETAIL CUTTER

COUNTERSINK

COUNTERBORE (W/PILOT)

MORTISING CHISEL

9-17.   Typical drill-press tools. Router bits must be gripped in special chucks. Mortising chisels work with special bits. How they function will be explained later in this chapter.

There is an ideal speed and feed for any tool and any material, but drill-speed charts, such as the one in Figure 9-19, should be used only as a general guide. Most importantly, the tool should be cutting steadily, smoothly and without excessive vibration, no matter what the material. Increasing or decreasing rpm's can even be justified by differences in boards from the same species.

Feed is the amount of pressure you apply to control penetration. It goes hand in hand with speed, and the best general rule to follow, again, is to keep the tool cutting, taking a bite evenly and without strain.

In any event, when doubt exists, always start at a slow speed. Increase the speed to the point where the situation is as ideal as you can make it.

Supporting the Work

Supporting the work has to do mostly with using a backup under the workpiece, and clamps or a device of some sort to keep the cutting action from twisting the material. These techniques have to do with accuracy and safety. When the appearance of the underside of the piece you are drilling isn't significant, you can rest the work directly on the table and just drill through so long as the opening in the table (usually a hole) is aligned with the spindle (Figure 9-20). However, it's better practice to always use a scrap block under the work no matter what the job. The block will protect the table and will minimize the splintering that can occur when the cutter breaks through the underside of the work (Figure 9-21).

It's sometimes possible to hand-hold the work safely, but only if the size of the work permits it and the hole isn't large. Often, on long work, you can brace one edge of the workpiece against the drill-press column, and this setup will be sufficient to counteract any twist caused by the cutting.

Don't hesitate, however, to use clamps to lock the work to the table (Figure 9-22). Using clamps provides a guarantee that, should the cutter grab in the hole particularly at the breakout point, the work will not be twisted out of your grasp. Such a possibility should be considered if you wish to avoid having your fingers rapped.

9-18.   Correct speed and feed pressure allow the cutting tool to cut smoothly and constantly. Rushing is bad practice but allowing the cutter just to rub isn't good either.

DRILL PRESS SPEEDS		
MATERIAL	OPERATION	SPEED (rpm)
Wood	Drilling—up to 1/4″	3,800
Wood	Drilling—1/4″ to 1/2″	3,100
Wood	Drilling—1/2″ to 3/4″	2,300
Wood	Drilling—3/4″ to 1″	2,000
Wood	Drilling—over 1″	700
Wood	Using expansion or multi-spur bit	700
Wood	Routing	4,000-5,000
Wood	Cutting plugs or short dowels	3,300
Wood	Carving	4,000-5,000
Wood	Using fly-cutter	700
Wood	Using dowel-cutter	1,800
Hardwood	Mortising	2,200
Softwood	Mortising	3,300
Metal	Fine wire-brushing	3,300
Metal	Coarse wire-brushing	1,000
Wood	Coarse wire-brushing	2,200
Soft metals	Buffing (cloth wheel)	3,800
Hard metals	Buffing (cloth wheel)	4,700
Plastics	Buffing (cloth wheel)	2,300
Metal	Using fly-cutter	700
Metal	Grinding—3″-4″ cup wheel	3,100
Glass	Drilling with metal tube	700

9-19.   Stay as close to these suggested speeds as you can. When in doubt, start at a slow speed. Always wear safety goggles when doing drill-press work.

Many times, a fence, in addition to being a guide, acts as a safety mechanism (Figure 9-23). The fence doesn't have to be more than a straight piece of wood clamped to the table in position to gauge the edge distance of the hole. With such an item in place, any twisting force exerted by the drill will be taken by the fence, not your hands.

Drilling to Exact Depth

Drilling exactly to a predetermined depth can be done in one of two ways.

Set the work on the table and extend the drill so that its point contacts the work. Then set the nuts on the stop rod the additional amount needed to achieve the hole depth.

Another possibility is to make a mark on the side of the work to indicate hole depth. Extend the quill so the drill point touches the mark and set the stop-rod nuts accordingly (Figure 9-24).

After you have set up in one of these two ways, you can drill any number of holes knowing that each will be to the same depth.

9-22.   Clamping the work is good practice, especially when you are drilling large holes. It helps you work safely and accurately. This type of clamp is made especially for drill-press work. It locks through the table slots and can be positioned in relation to the size and shape of the workpiece.

9-23.   Working against a fence, which in this case is a type of bar clamp, is a good idea. The fence takes any twisting action caused by the operation—and—it controls edge distance when you need a series of holes on the same line.

9-20.   You can work this way to form through holes, with the bit centered over the hole in the table, but be aware that some splintering and feathering will occur where the bit breaks through.

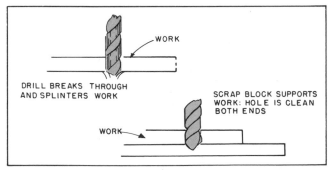

9-21.   It's better, even when the appearance of the underside of the work doesn't matter, to use a scrap between the work and the table.

9-24.   Aligning the drill-point with a mark on the work and then setting the stop rod in a way to set up for drilling to a specific depth. Now you can drill any number of holes knowing that each will be just so deep.

Work Layout

Be careful and accurate when you are measuring and marking lines. The pencil you use should be about 3H and should always be sharp.

The easiest and most accurate method of marking a hole location is to draw intersecting lines that tell you the center of the hole. Puncture this point with an awl and position the point of the drill there. A combination square can be used to draw lines at right angles to an edge and may also be used as an edge-marking gauge. Dividers (or a compass) do a good job when it is necessary to pick up a dimension from one piece (or a drawing) so you can carry it to another. Dividers are also a good tool to use when you wish to divide a line into a number of equal spaces.

There are many ways to proceed with work layout and what you do depends on the job and whether you have one piece to be drilled or a number of pieces to be drilled alike. Templates can be used. You can make these of stiff cardboard, hardboard, plywood or even sheet metal if the long-term use justifies it (Figure 9-25). Some pieces of hardware, such as a hinge, hasp, or drawer pull, provide their own template.

An often-used trick to use when ordinary layout proves impractical or too time consuming is to insert headless nails in appropriate locations in one of the pieces. When this piece is pressed against the mating part, the nails provide drill location points (Figure 9-26).

To mark hole locations on a series of boards that will be joined edge-to-edge by doweling, align the board edges and butt them surface to surface. Mark hole locations on one edge and carry the line across all pieces by using a square (Figure 9-27).

Use a fence as a guide whenever you must drill a series of holes with a common centerline. You will still have to mark the spacing of the holes but the fence will guarantee that all the holes will have the same edge distance. You can easily make such a fence by nailing or screwing together two straight pieces of wood so they form an "L". The base of the "L" is clamped to the drill-press table; the vertical parts acts as a support and guide for the work. Stop blocks, or even C-clamps, can be used with the fence whenever you have similar pieces that require a hole, or several holes, in a particular location (Figure 9-28).

Fixtures, or jigs, can also be used to guarantee accuracy when drilling similar pieces. The procedure is useful mostly for production-type work, and of course the fixture must be designed for the job on hand. Examples are shown in Figure 9-29.

Auxiliary Tables

Such tables can serve dual purposes. They are instantly available setups for, in one case, drum sanding, which is a very good drill-press application; and they are handy tool shelves when work is being done on the regular drill-press table (Figures 9-30 and 9-31). A one-piece table is probably more convenient for a small drill press while a split-table model will go with almost any tool. Actually, either would be easy to scale to suit your equipment.

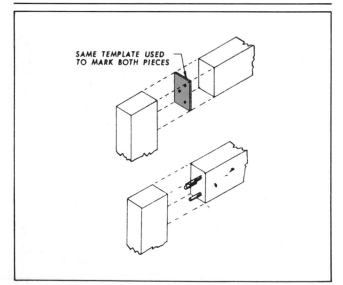

9-25.   Drilling accuracy depends greatly on careful layout. When the same marking is required on many pieces, it pays to make a template. This will eliminate the human error that can occur when layout is done on individual parts.

9-26.   If you tap in brads at location points and then snip off their heads, you can press one part against another to get correct mating locations.

9-27.   Use a square this way when you need the same hole location on a number of pieces.

9-28.   Always try to improvise setups so hole locations can be gauged automatically. Here, C-clamps on a wooden fence act as stops that position the work.

DRILL GUIDE

WORK

OPENING SHAPED TO FIT WORK

DRILL GUIDE HOLES MAY BE BUSHED. (THIS MUST BE DONE WHEN WORKING WITH METAL)

9-29.   When needed, you can make special fixtures so any number of pieces can be drilled exactly alike. It's a technique that is justified only for "production" runs.

9-30.   The easy-to-make hinged table is fine for drum-sander work. You know that the sanded edge will be square to adjacent surfaces.

9-31.   When the hinged table isn't needed, it can be swung aside and used as a holding platform for other operations.

9-32. How the hinged table is made. The hole for the column must be sized to suit your machine.

9-33. Construction details of a similar table that might be more convenient for a smaller drill press. It's also good for drum sanding but since it lacks a hole for the sander, it must be swung aside so the drum can be lowered.

9-34. The case has space for many small tools. Plan the holders for tools you will use most frequently.

In either case, the attachment design is a split-clamp arrangement. A turn of a wing nut enables you to position the accessory anywhere, vertically or horizontally. The clamps must lock tightly on the drill-press column. If you have a hole saw or a fly cutter that will cut the correct size hole, it's a good idea to form the support arms from a single piece of stock. Then you can cut on the hole centerline, and the material removed by the saw cut will be just enough to give you good, split-clamp action.

Construction details for two such tables that you can make are shown in Figures 9-32 and 9-33.

Column Storage Rack

Drill-press work will be easier if you keep frequently used tools close at hand so you don't have to walk, stretch, or stoop every time you need one. That's the objective of a column storage rack (Figure 9-34). It is not a substitute for a large cabinet, but if you analyze your work and outfit the case to suit your needs, you'll find it a big help. The split-clamp lock described for the auxiliary tables also applies to this storage case (Figure 9-35). Actually, you might be able to mount both the case and a table without critically reducing the distance between the spindle and the table proper.

Two Advanced Jigs

A couple of very professional jigs will be described here even before the main material about drill-press work is given. For one thing, it seems a good way to demonstrate immediately how flexible the drill press can be. Also, a good many of the operations shown later in this chapter will be done on these jigs rather than on commercial units you might have to spend a lot of money for. (Assuming that accessories like this *are* available—which isn't likely!)

After you have read the whole chapter, you can return to this section and make a decision on which of the two jigs will be most useful to you. You might base your decision on the accompanying construction details or particular operations. Whatever, jigs like these are what make the drill press flexible. Otherwise, it wouldn't be useful for anything but drilling holes.

Jig #1 is basically a table attached to a base that is secured to the regular drill-press table with two C-clamps (Figure 9-36). The table hole centers under the drill-press spindle and permits the use of drum sanders and three-lip shaper cutters. Individually adjustable fences are used for shaping straight-line work. Fulcrum pins support curved work that must be shaped freehand.

This jig has a drilling fence that can be used in place of the shaping fences for drilling holes at equal distances from the edge of the work. A built-in spacer can be used to automatically gauge the distance between holes. It is organized for a pivot guide for rotational passes against a cutter and has an indexing head. These and other features have prompted it to be called the "Woodworking Champ of any Shop."

Once made, the jig becomes a lifetime tool so it makes sense to construct it accurately to begin with. Start by making the base assembly, checking its dimensions against the size of the table on your drill press. The only change that might be necessary is a reduction or increase in the overall width. Once the base is assembled, you can add components. If you are a beginner, it would be wise to pause after the basic table construction. You can add other items to it after you have become more involved in drill-press work.

Construction details and a few typical applications are shown in Figures 9-37 through 9-40.

Jig #2 contains a drawer that provides for storage of tools that you use with the tool (Figure 9-41). Actually, this design evolved from a simpler version that was made for drum sanding and drum-sander storage. The drill press is a great tool for such work, but the regular table just won't do. For rotary sanding only, you can get by with nothing more than an inverted, U-shaped structure; holes at the top allow the drum to pass through (Figure 9-42).

Since the same general construction serves for other rotary tools, it is logical to provide for different size table inserts.

Critical construction points of this jig follow. Cut the table to size and bisect the long dimension with an accurate centerline. On the centerline at the rear of the table, make an accurate half-circle cutout to fit the column.

With the table in place, use the drill press to form a small hole on the centerline. This hole is the center of the table opening.

Work on a table saw to form the slot and the groove for the slide. The slide should not fit loosely; provide for a good fit even if it means having to exert a little pressure to move the slide to and fro. Shape one end of the slide support to conform to the table opening.

Shape and attach the rails with glue and screws that are driven up through the underside. The rails provide location points for the case sides which you can attach after forming the rabbets along the bottom edge.

Cut the case bottom to size and assemble, without gluing what you have done so far. Put the unit in place on the drill press with the centerline exactly so and scribe mark the location of the front edge of the regular drill-press table so you will know exactly where the dado for the clamp ledge must go. This factor is critical for automatic jig alignment; therefore, take the time needed to do it correctly.

9-35.   How the case is made. You can assemble the case as a single unit and then saw it to get two pieces that are then hinged together.

9-36.   Advanced Jig #1. Here it is set up in the shaping mode. Fences are individually adjustable just as they are on a regular shaper. Other applications will be shown as we go along.

9-37. Construction details of advanced Jig #1. It will take some time to make, but the results will be worth it.

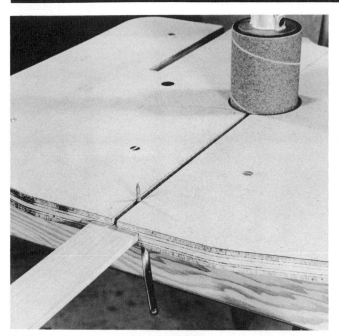

9-38.   The pivot guide must fit precisely in the table's T-slot. A roofing nail, with its point smoothed, makes a good pivot pin. Recess the underside of the pivot guide for the head of the nail.

9-39.   The lock assembly for the pivot guide is attached to the underside of the table with roundhead screws. A 1/4″ bolt is bent up to make the L-shaped lock handle.

9-40.   The indexing head mounts on the pivot pin. Since this pin must go through the indexing head in order to hold the workpiece, keep several lengths of roofing nails on hand for different jobs.

A point about the drawer is its peculiar shape at the back (Figure 9-43). This design prevents the drawer from becoming a receptacle for dust and chips. The U-shape actually collects a good percentage of waste which is easily brushed out or vacuumed away.

Construction details of the advanced Jig #2, together with facts that pertain to it, are shown in Figures 9-44 through 9-49.

9-41.   Design the interior of the drawer to suit the tools you will use most frequently. A 1″-thick board, perforated with various size holes will store many straight shank cutters.

9-42.   A simple table that is fine for drum-sander operations. Being able to move the drum vertically allows full use of its abrasive surface.

9-43.   The drawer back has a peculiar shape because it must clear the cutter and keep waste out. The pocket so created collects a good percentage of waste material; then it's easy to vacuum or brush it away.

9-44.   Construction details of advanced Jig #2.

9-45.   Advanced Jig #2 will align automatically if you make the back cutout very carefully and install the clamp ledge accurately. Important construction factor is for the center of the hole in the table to be in perfect alignment with the spindle's centerline.

9-46.   It's a good idea to have number of inserts, each with a different size center hole. Thus you can minimize the opening around whatever cutting tool you are using.

9-47.   A fly cutter can be used to form the discs that are used as inserts. Various size bits can make the center holes. Make the discs to fit tightly in the table recess so you won't need a special means of holding them down.

9-48.   The pivoting fence can function as well as one that has a parallel motion. The pivot bolt should have a fairly tight fit. Use a C-clamp at the free end to secure settings.

9-49.   The different guides are designed around 10/32 screws which thread into the aluminum slide. Bearing surfaces should be as smooth as possible.

Drilling for Wood Screws

There are two different diameter holes that should be drilled before driving a screw, in order for the fastener to have maximum holding power. One is the *body hole,* which equals the gauge of the screw, the other is the *lead hole,* which allows the screw to penetrate while providing enough material for the screw-threads to grip (Figure 9-50).

If the head of the screw will be above the surface of the work, which is true of screws that have round or oval heads, then just the two holes are required. If the screw has a flat head, so it can be driven flush with the surface of the work, or if you wish to conceal the screw by using a wood plug, then, in addition to the body hole and the lead hole, you need either a countersink or a counterbore (Figure 9-51).

A good procedure is to drill lead holes first and then open up the top portion to body-hole size. Countersinking is done so flat-head screws can be driven flush. Control the countersink depth by using the stop rod. On hardwoods, countersink to the full depth of the screwhead. On softwoods, stay a bit on the minus side. The screw will pull flush as you finish driving.

When you are driving very small screws in softwood, you can often simply make a straight hole with an awl. It's also possible to do this with some hardwoods. Make a judgment after testing with one or two screws.

HOLE SIZES FOR WOOD SCREWS			
SCREW GAUGE	BODY HOLE	LEAD HOLE	SCREW GAUGE IN INCHES
0	53	—	.060
1	49	—	.073
2	44	56*	.086
3	40	52*	.099
4	33	51*	.112
5	1/8	49*	.125
6	28	47	.138
7	24	46	.151
8	19	42	.164
9	15	41	.177
10	10	38	.190
11	5	37	.203
12	7/32	36	.216
14	D	31	.242
16	I	28	.268
18	19/64	23	.294
*In hardwoods only.			

9-50.   These are the hole sizes to use for screws so the fasteners will have maximum holding power. Stay as close as you can when you don't have the exact one, but try to be on the minus side.

A counterbore is required when the fastener head must be set below the surface. The counterbore is no more than a shallow hole sized to suit the head of the screw or bolt or whatever. Special counterboring tools are available, but you can form the counterbore first, using a spade bit or something similar instead, and then do the lead and body holes (Figure 9-52).

Such holes are often sealed with plugs cut from the same type of wood. Special tools for cutting out such plugs are available, and they will be discussed in the section on plug cutters in this chapter.

Special drilling tools are available so you can form starting holes for various sizes and types of screws without the fuss of changing from bit to bit. The one shown in Figure 9-53 forms body hole, lead hole, and countersink in one operation. Others of the same type are designed to include a counterbore. Such cutters should be purchased in sets since no one unit will do for all screw sizes.

BODY HOLE

LEAD HOLE

COUNTERSINK

COUNTERBORE

9-51. Nomenclature for screw holes are illustrated here. A countersink is used when the screwhead must be flush. A counterbore forms a hole so the screw can be concealed with a wooden plug.

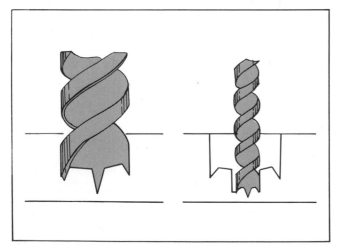

9-52. Often, a bit can be used in place of a counterbore. Do the counterboring first, then the body and lead holes.

9-53. Special tools do multiple operations for screws. This one forms lead and body holes and also countersinks; others will also form a counterbore.

Drilling Equally-Spaced Holes

A basic procedure for drilling equally-spaced holes is simply to pencil-mark the distance between holes and then drill. It works, of course, but accuracy depends on layout and work handling. The least help you should provide is a fence against which you hold the work while you are drilling. The fence doesn't have to be more than a straight piece of wood clamped to the drill-press table. Secure the fence's position so the distance from its front surface to the point on the bit equals the edge distance of the holes. If you are drilling holes for dowels to be used in edge-to-edge joints, the holes do not have to be centered *exactly* in the stock. Just be sure the same surface of each piece will be against, or face away from the fence, as you do the drilling. When assembling, the same surface on each piece must be either up or down.

The pivoting fence, which is one of the components of advanced Jig #2, serves very nicely for this type of application (Figure 9-54).

The fence on advanced Jig #1 serves in similar fashion (Figure 9-55), but this jig design includes an adjustable gauge which can be used to provide correct spacing automatically. After you have drilled the first hole, position the gauge so the distance from its pin to the hole equals the spacing you need. Thereafter, placing the pin in the hole that is already drilled will position the work for the following hole (Figure 9-56). By repeating the procedure, you can drill as many equally-spaced holes as you require without having to go through a layout procedure. The holes will have to be drilled to match the 1/4″ diameter of the pin, but they can be enlarged. The initial holes, drilled to provide accuracy, can serve as pilots.

Using Fences for Drilling Series of Holes

9-54.   Always use a fence when you must drill a series of holes on a common centerline. The pivoting fence on Jig #2 is fine for this purpose.

9-55.   The same idea applies to Jig #1. Be sure to use a scrap block under the work when you are drilling through-holes.

9-56.   The fence accessory provides automatic gauging of equally spaced holes. The pin seats in each hole drilled and so positions the work for the next one.

Angular Drilling

Three kinds of off-vertical holes can be drilled; the position of a chair leg in each type of hole best illustrates each type of angle. At a simple angle, the leg tilts in one direction. The angle is obvious when you view it from one side. The equal compound angle has the leg tilting the same amount in two directions. The angle will be the same whether you view the leg from the front or the side (Figure 9-57). With an unequal compound angle, the leg tilts two ways but a greater amount in one direction. The angle viewed from the front is different than the angle viewed from the side.

When the work size permits, the simple angle is done by tilting the drill-press table. If this is not feasible, then you must leave the table in normal position and use a height block under one edge of the work. Size the height block to give you the angle you want.

The equal compound angle is popular. It has some overall factors that are interesting and that can make many jobs easier to do. If you mark perpendicular diameters on a circular piece of wood and then drill simple angles with the layout lines in line with the spindle, you will have a compound angle position for what you insert in the hole.

What makes many of these jobs difficult is not the operation but the size of the workpiece. However, even considering size, you can facilitate matters through careful designing. Let's assume you have a round or square table on which you wish to splay the legs. Picture the understructure as legs attached to two crosspieces. If you drill simple angles at the end of each crosspiece and then assemble the crosspieces with a centered half-lap joint so that they are at right angles, what you inset in the holes will be equally splayed about the table.

On all angular drilling, be aware that the side of the cutter may contact the work before the point does. The drill will wander unless you make contact with an extremely slow feed until the bit is firmly positioned. This is less of a problem when the cutter has a long point, like a spade bit (Figure 9-58). When angles are extreme, it's good practice to work with a leveling block, situating it as shown in Figure 9-59. The idea is for the hole to be started in the block. Then the bit will be firmly set before it contacts the work.

On multi-purpose tools like the Shopsmith®, where the saw table also serves as the drill-press table, the rip fence can be used to provide support for the work (Figure 9-60). When the miter gauge is used in conjunction with a clamped-on strip of wood, the resulting V-jig provides a good arrangement of angular-drilling circular pieces (Figure 9-61).

9-58. Simple-angle holes can be done this way when the drill-press table can be tilted. Spade bits are good to use because their long points will make firm contact before the bit actually starts cutting. Clamping is essential.

9-57. For equal compound angular drilling, the drilling line is always at 45°.

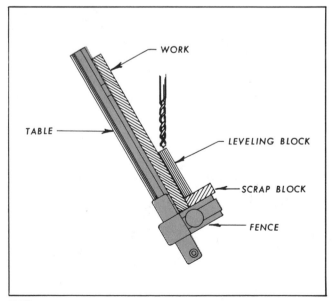

9-59. It's a good idea to use a leveling block when drilling is done at an extreme angle. The block does much to keep the bit from wandering.

Radial Holes

Holes drilled on a circular path through the surface of stock, those drilled into the edge of circular pieces, and those drilled through the diameter of cylinders, are classified as radial holes. Drilling into a surface can simply be a matter of making a layout on the work, marking the hole locations on the circumference of a circle drawn with a compass. For more convenience and greater accuracy, you can work with pivot guides. These are just setups that allow the work to rotate on a central point; the distance from the point to the bit is the radius of the circle. The advanced jigs are designed to permit this kind of work. Because of the built-in slides, the radial distance of the holes is adjustable. Several applications of the technique are shown in Figures 9-62, 9-63 and 9-64.

9-62. Within its limits (the number of slots that you cut), the indexing head on the advanced jig automatically positions the work for various radial hole locations.

9-60. When a fence is available, use it to provide support for the work. This setup is peculiar to multi-purpose tools like the Shopsmith®.

9-63. You can work with just the pivot guide to drill radial holes but this provides for radial distance only. Hole spacing is controlled with layout lines.

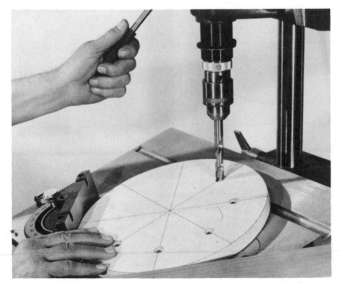

9-61. Also on multi-purpose tools, you can use the miter gauge in conjunction with a clamped-on strip of wood to make a "V" arrangement that will cradle circular pieces. Be sure the center of the "V" is aligned with the center of the spindle.

9-64. The pivot pin can go through the work if a center hole doesn't matter. Otherwise, use a short pin for situating the work.

You can operate in similar fashion without the jigs if you drive a nail through a piece of plywood that you then clamp to the drill-press table. The nail is the pivot on which you center the work. When you wish to avoid a center hole that goes through the wood, cut the nail short and use it as a stud on which you press the work.

Edge holes require a completely different arrangement. The table of the drill press is tilted to a vertical position and a V-block is used to support and position the workpiece (Figure 9-65). Be sure the bottom of the "V" and the center of the drill tool are on the same vertical line.

Radial holes through cylinders can be drilled accurately with the use of a V-block (Figure 9-66). Here too, it's essential for the center of the "V" and the point of the drill to be aligned.

Figure 9-67 shows the construction details of a special type of V-jig you can make. The jig can be used when you need one hole, but its asset is that it can be organized to provide automatic spacing when you need a series of radial holes on a common centerline (Figure 9-68). The nail engages the first hole drilled and so positions the work for the next hole. The nail also keeps the work from turning, so you know all holes will be on the same line.

You can create a V-block setup on the drill press by tilting the table to 45° and adding a clamped-on strip so the result is a "V" that cradles the work (Figure 9-69).

9-65. Edge holes in circular pieces can be drilled this way. The clamped V-block supports and positions the work. The center of the "V" and the point of the bit must be on the same line.

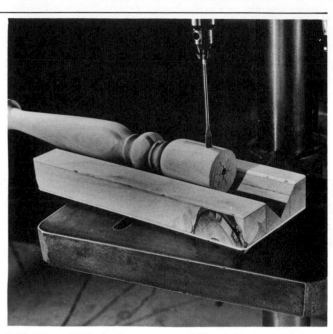

9-66. Use a V-block when you must drill radial holes through a cylinder.

9-67. This special V-block jig is adjustable so it can be used to gauge distance between holes when a series of radial holes are needed in a cylinder.

Large Holes

What is a large hole? Arbitrarily, you might say it's anything above the maximum size you can do with a spade bit, which is 1-1/2″. Going above this measurement is a question of having the tool that will do the job. Fly cutters provide a good solution simply because you can bore any size hole between the minimum and maximum settings (Figures 9-70, 9-71 and 9-72). Fixed hole saws can be used, but being equipped for anything can be expensive; few, if any, of the adjustable types go above approximately 3″. Fly cutters can produce up to a 6″ diameter. Above this, you might regard the job as a piercing assignment for a jigsaw or a saber saw.

9-68. The jig is adjusted so the nail, engaging the first hole, will hold the work and position it for the following hole.

9-69. A tilted drill-press table plus a clamped-on strip of wood form a neat V-block. As always, the point of the bit and the center of the "V" must be on the same line.

Using Fly Cutters

9-70. Some fly cutters can be used for holes up to 6″ in diameter. You must work very carefully, using minimum speed and feed pressure. The work *must* be clamped. Keep hands away from the cutting area.

9-71. Fly cutters can be used on non-wood materials like this "Corian." Steady streams of ribbon-like waste indicate efficient feed pressure and correct rpm.

9-72. Fly cutter is used here for a double cut to create a wooden ring. Be careful at breakthrough for the ring will be free in the hole.

There is a drill-press solution with the appropriate technique and jig (Figure 9-73). However, the chore is really a routing operation. A center hole drilled in the work is placed over the dowel pin in the adjustable jig. The jig is secured to gauge the radius of the hole, and then the work is rotated so the 1/4″ router bit forms a circular groove. On thick work it may be necessary to rotate the work several times, cutting a bit deeper after each pass.

Large hole forming, no matter what the cutter, calls for maximum security for the work and ample clearance for your hands. Position the work and then clamp it solidly to the drill-press table. Use a slow feed and a slow speed. The outboard, cutting end of a fly cutter can be just a blur even at slow speeds, so keep your hands well away.

How to Drill Deep Holes

The maximum depth of a hole you can normally drill is limited by the maximum extension of the quill regardless of the length of the drilling tool (Figure 9-74). If, for example, the drill bit is fluted so it can drill 6″ deep, but the quill extension is limited to 4″, then 4″ is the maximum penetration. However, you can get more from the bit if you work this way: Drill the hole 4″ deep. Then with the machine turned off, raise the table so the bit bottoms in the hole already formed. Now you can drill again to increase the depth of the hole.

You can drill a hole that is two times the maximum penetration by working from both sides of the stock. The idea is to drill opposing holes on the same vertical center-line (Figure 9-75). This can be accomplished by accurate layout but you'll be more sure of hole alignment if you use the technique that is shown in Figure 9-76. The work is positioned accurately for the second hole because it is placed over a guide pin that has been secured for alignment with the drilling tool. The guide pin can be a dowel that is placed in a hole drilled in a platform that is clamped to the drill-press table. The pin can be hole-size, or if you want a setup that can be used for various situations, it can have a minimum diameter. The first holes drilled, with a bit that

9-74. No matter how long the bit you are using, the deepest hole you can drill in one pass is limited by the maximum extension of the quill on your machine.

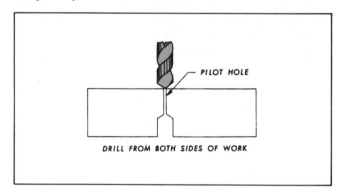

9-75. On thick stock, you can drill a through pilot hole and then open up to full size by drilling from both ends.

9-73. The jig that permits a router bit to be used for cutting extra large holes is shown here. A center hole drilled in the work fits over the dowel pivot. The work is then rotated against the direction-of-rotation of the cutter.

9-76. This is a way to drill accurately from both ends of the work in order to double the hole depth. The guide pin is secured in a board that is clamped to the table after pin and bit have been aligned.

suits the diameter of the pin, can be enlarged later to the hole-size you need.

Extension bits can be used for very deep holes, but they are not too usable on bench model machines because of the limited chuck-to-base capacity. Some operators get around this limitation by swinging the drill-press head so it projects over the edge of the bench. Thus, they get a chuck-to-floor capacity.

Be careful with extension bits because they can whip. Use a slow speed and have the point of the bit embedded in the work before you turn on the tool.

It is good practice when drilling any hole, but especially important when drilling deep holes, to retract the drilling tool frequently so waste material will be ejected from the hole (Figure 9-77). This will result in a smoother job and will minimize heat buildup in the tool and in the work.

Concentric Holes

Picture concentric holes as longitudinal openings through the center of a cylinder. The techniques to use don't differ too much from those described for deep holes. Differences arise, sometimes, in methods for holding the work. A very useful holding device can be made from a screw clamp merely by cutting matching "V's" in the jaws. This permits round work to be gripped securely. If the screw clamp is large enough, one of its handles can be braced against the drill-press column to counteract any twist created by the cutting action. Further security is achieved by using a C-clamp to lock the screw clamp to the drill-press table (Figure 9-78).

Figure 9-79 shows how you can organize to drill concentric holes in cylinders that are too long to be handled in conventional fashion. You work with a V-block that rests on a support that is clamped horizontally, and which is aligned vertically by a second clamped-on block. The setup must be organized so the hole can be located accurately when the work is placed in the "V".

The work being done in Figure 9-80 is not really concentric drilling, but it does show how you can make an

9-78. A screw clamp with matching V's cut in its jaws make a good holder for concentric drilling of round or square stock. Handle of clamp is braced against column to counteract twist of the cutter—or—use a second clamp to secure the first one.

9-79. Concentric drilling can be done this way with the V-block that is cradling the work supported by side and bottom clamped-on strips.

9-77. It is especially important on deep holes to retract the bit frequently so chips won't clog in the hole. This will result in a smoother job and with minimum heat buildup in the tool and the work.

9-80. A way to drill end holes in long stock. When necessary, secure the screw clamp by using a second clamp. Here, the depth of the hole is controlled with a brushing that is on the drill.

arrangement that permits end-drilling in long pieces. The work is secured with a screw clamp that rests on the drill-press table. It may be okay to hand-hold the work if the hole is slight and shallow, but, usually, it's better to secure the screw clamp's position by using a second clamp. This can also aid accuracy if you have many pieces to drill. The amount the screw clamp projects beyond the tool's table can be the "gauge" that positions the workpieces.

Countersinking

Countersinking is usually done for flat-head screws that must be driven flush with the work's surface, but it is also required for screws with an oval head. The countersink for the oval-head screw is not as deep as the one needed for a flat-head screw. The countersink itself is a cutting tool, used something like a drill bit, that forms the inverted cone for the screw-head. They are available with different bevel angles to suit the fastener. Wood screws require one angle, machine screws require another (Figure 9-81). When you need just one countersink you can probably judge by eye how deep to go. When you need to form a number of similar countersinks, then it's best to establish a depth-control by using the drill-press stop rod.

Countersink in hardwoods to the full depth of the screwhead; stop a bit short when working on soft woods, since the screw will settle the final amount when you drive it all the way in.

A countersink is often used to form the seat for the screw and also a counterbore for a plug that will hide the screw (Figure 9-82). The method is theoretically wrong, and shouldn't be overdone, but it's a handy technique to use occasionally. It simply means going deeper with the countersink than you need to go for the screw head alone. Con-

sider two factors. Be sure you have a plug-cutting tool that matches the diameter of the hole formed by the countersink—and—be aware that you are burying the countersink more than is ordinarily required. Therefore, retract frequently to clear waste from the hole and thus avoid the possibility of burning the tool or the work (Figure 9-83).

Another "offbeat" use for a countersink is to use it in limited fashion somewhat like a V-shaped router bit. Used as such, it can form decorative surface-grooves like those in Figure 9-84. It can also be used to chamfer edges so long as you make light cuts and, since the cutter does not have a pilot, provide a guide for the work. One way to do this is to set a guide pin in a piece of plywood and then clamp the plywood to the table so the guide pin is centered under the countersink. The work bears against the pin as you move it against the cutter's direction of rotation.

Countersinking in thin sheet metal calls for a "dimpling" procedure. Using a countersink in normal fashion

9-82. Countersinking deeper than necessary will form a counterbore for a wooden plug. It's really not the way to use a countersink but you can get away with it on occasion.

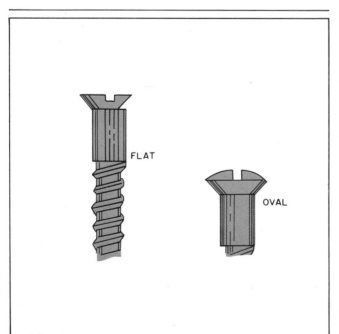

9-81. Countersinks are used to form an inverted cone for screwheads. They are needed for flathead and oval head screws.

9-83. If you use the countersink to form a counterbore, be sure to retract frequently. Also, be sure you can produce plugs that will match the diameter of the hole formed by the countersink.

would simply form a sloppy hole for the screw head. To get around this, shape the end of a hardwood dowel so it matches the angle of the countersink you need. Use the countersink in a backup block. Chuck the dowel and use it, more or less, like a press to form the metal into the countersink shape. Success depends greatly on the gauge and the softness of the metal. It works fine on, for example, do-it-yourself aluminum. Using a slow speed and putting a dab of paste wax on the end of the dowel are also helpful (Figure 9-85).

Using Rotary Rasps

Rotary rasps are generally little tools, but on a drill press you can do big jobs with them—making joints, doing shaping and pattern forming, producing integral tenons, or accomplishing pesky short-run chores quickly, especially when they are required on workpieces that might be diffi-

cult to handle in conventional fashion or on other machines (Figure 9-86).

There are many types of rotary rasps, ranging from the imports that are shown in Figure 9-87, through solid steel units that have rasp-type teeth, and the "cheese grater" designs that are part of Stanley's Surform line. Don't confuse rotary rasps with machine files. The latter are designed for metal working and are not really suitable for shaping wood. For one thing, they will clog very quickly.

The imported rasps differ from the common-rasps in that each of the dozen or so units is meant to do a particular job. This primary purpose usually dictates the shape of the tool but, as usual, imagination can lead beyond the single application. They cut differently, too. On most of the tools the teeth are like raised chisel edges so they shave rather than scrape. This leads to faster, smoother cutting that, under correct feed-speed conditions, produces edges that require little additional work.

9-84. Another off-beat use for a countersink—forming V-shaped grooves. Use a high speed and keep cuts light. Use repeat passes to achieve very deep grooves.

9-86. These are some of the shapes you can form with rotary rasps. The samples shown here were cut from larger pieces. Never try to work on material that is too small for safe handling.

9-85. Countersinking thin sheet metal would result in sloppy holes, so "dimples" are formed instead. The "tool" is a rod, shaped at one end like a countersink. It is used to stamp or to "spin" the metal into countersunk holes that are in the backing block.

9-87. Each of these rotary rasps is designed for a specific job but capabilities overlap. Some of these tools were used to make the cuts shown in the previous photo.

Making a special table. To get the most out of the rotary files, you should make the table and the accessories used with it, shown in Figure 9-88. It's a pretty straightforward project but must be made accurately. Unless the guides and the table are true you won't get professional results from them.

The dimensions of the table should be okay for any drill press. Your best bet is to cut the table to overall size and then form the dado for the fence. Draw a centerline at right angles to the dado and lay out the cutout for the drill-press column. You can accomplish this by forming a large hole and then meeting it with two saw cuts or by working with a saber saw.

Form the table guides and clamp them in place after you have positioned the table on your drill press. These guides should have just enough plus tolerance for the table to slide easily. Attach them permanently with glue and screws; also the two-part fence.

When you make the end-cut, miter, and vertical guides, check out your cuts with a square and be sure the blocks that will be used to position the workpieces are accurately placed.

The main function of the vertical guide is to hold work on end when you're forming integral tenons on stretchers and the like. The height of this guide works out fine for many common jobs, but when the length of the workpiece goes much beyond 12″, it might pay to tilt your regular drill-press table 90° and clamp the work directly to it.

A guide for this application can be just two straight pieces of wood about 5″ wide and 15″ long, nailed together along the long edge to form a right angle. This "jig" is clamped to the drill-press table and the workpiece is clamped in the corner.

Applications and use hints. Figures 9-89 through 9-94 demonstrate some of the jobs you can do with the rotary rasps. The imported tools are made of case-hardened cutting steel and can operate between speeds of 1,500 and 10,000 rpm.

On speed, my own experience prompts me to recommend, in general, 2,000-3,000 rpm. The higher speeds, especially in hardwoods, can cause burning and in soft gummy woods can clog the teeth quickly.

The teeth are keen and stay that way for a long time. Moderate speeds plus light feed pressure keeps them sharp.

When using tools that get buried in the work (for example, the "dowel mills") treat them as you would drills, retracting frequently to remove waste, clear the teeth, and keep the tool cool.

Depth-of-cut should not be excessive. I found that in pine I could cut a groove about 1/4″ wide by about 3/8″ deep without sweating too much. This is an example of how much material the tools can remove in one pass.

How you are cutting—with the grain, across it, down into end grain—must affect speed and feed. When in doubt, start at the slow end and add rpms until the tool is cutting smoothly.

Even under ideal conditions, the teeth will clog, but you can clean them easily with the same kind of brush you use on your files. For real problem clogging, first dry-brush the tool and then soak in a solvent for a minute or two, and brush again.

9-88. This special table (and the guides that are used with it) help you get the most out of rotary rasps.

9-89. These rotary rasps, called "dowel mills," are made so a plug or short dowel cut by one will fit the hole formed by the next size up.

9-90. The heavy-duty mill looks like a stubby dowel mill but has thicker walls and is good for fast stock removal when doing such jobs as rabbeting. Note the use of the guide to feed the stock.

9-93. The dovetail groover can also be used to form matching tongues or tenons; the latter by making back-to-back passes on stock ends or edges.

9-91. Combination cutters are available in different sizes. They can be used to form tongue-and-groove joints and for light surface-planing jobs.

9-92. A 45° angle cutter can form chamfers and do similar work. Feed with such cutters must always be slow and preferably *with* the grain. Do the cross-grain cuts first when shaping is required on four edges.

9-94. The combination cutter can also be used to form integral, short tenons. A very slow feed with frequent retractions is necessary to prevent burning. Be sure to use the vertical guide and to clamp the work.

Special table for the surform drum.   Although it's mainly for use with a Surform drum, the special table shown in Figures 9-95 and 9-96 can also be used with conventional drum sanders. It's designed so that you can lock it in place by using a clamp to press the legs against the drill-press column. Used alone, it gives you a work surface above the bottom edge of the cutter. Thus, you can work on the entire stock-edge.

The guide support should be a pretty accurate fit in the slot and should be attached with the crossbar before you secure the guide. Shape the guide to equal the diameter of the drum and screw-attach it by using the drum itself (locked in the chuck) as a gauge.

Since this technique can be used with different cutters you'd be smart to make yourself several guide supports or one support with screw-attachable guides of different sizes.

One caution—this table is designed, as it should be, for very light finishing cuts. The clamp lock may not be sufficient to keep the guide from moving away from the cutting tool if you are heavy-handed or wish to remove a lot of stock. If so, you can still live with the table as designed but do add the two table guides called for on the shaper table. Attach them permanently before locating the drum guides.

Shaping on a Drill Press

The drill press makes a good shaper as long as you are aware of two limiting factors. The highest speed doesn't match the rpm's you can get from an individual machine; the spindle is above the table instead of being under it. Since you can compensate to a great degree for lack of speed simply by slowing up the feed and since the above-the-table spindle position is not critical for the bulk of shaping work, you can get along quite well.

Special equipment. In order to do shaping operations on the drill press, you must have a special table that is designed specifically for that type of work. The accessory can be a commercial unit that you buy (Figure 9-97), or as some of the illustrations show, it can be an attachment for one of the advanced jigs. Beyond this, you need an adapter that is used in place of the regular 3-jaw chuck. What the adapter will look like depends on the drill press you will use it on, but it will have a threaded shaft and a lock nut for securing cutters. Sometimes, collars are supplied with the adapter, or they may be extra-cost items. Collars are used over or under or between cutters, depending on the job (Figure 9-98). Their main purpose is to control depth of cut. Their use is optional for straight-line shaping done against a fence, but essential when shaping is done freehand.

Cutters. The most practical type of cutter for drill-press use is the one-piece, three-blade unit. Actually, it is one of the most popular types of cutters even for use on an individual shaping machine. Many designs are available; some for full profile cuts to produce a specific, standard shape, others are combination types where only part of the profile is used to achieve a form (Figure 9-99). Actually, there is no reason why you can't use either type in any way you choose if it leads to the end result you want.

Some general rules. Always use the fastest speed you have. Work against a shaper fence whenever possible. Try to keep the cutting tool under the work if at all possible (even though it may be shown in accompanying illustrations over the work for the sake of clarity). One reason is for safety; the other is to guard against gouging the work should you lift it accidentally during the pass. Feed the work into and against the rotation of the cutting tool. Hold hands away from the cutting area and try to feed so fingers

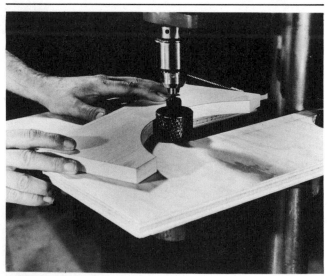

9-95. Stanley's rotary rasp, one of the Surform tools, should be run at between 1,500 and 2,500 rpm depending on the hardness of the wood. If you make the special table that is shown here, you can use the rasp to do pattern forming.

9-96. Construction details of the special table for the Surform rasp. The circular guide must equal the diameter of the drum and be aligned exactly with it.

9-97. A typical setup for shaping on a drill press using commercial accessories. The unit includes an auxiliary table that bolts to the drill-press table and fences that are individually adjustable.

9-98. Drill-press shaping calls for special adapters to hold the cutters. Collars, used in various ways, are more essential for freehand shaping than when shaping against a fence.

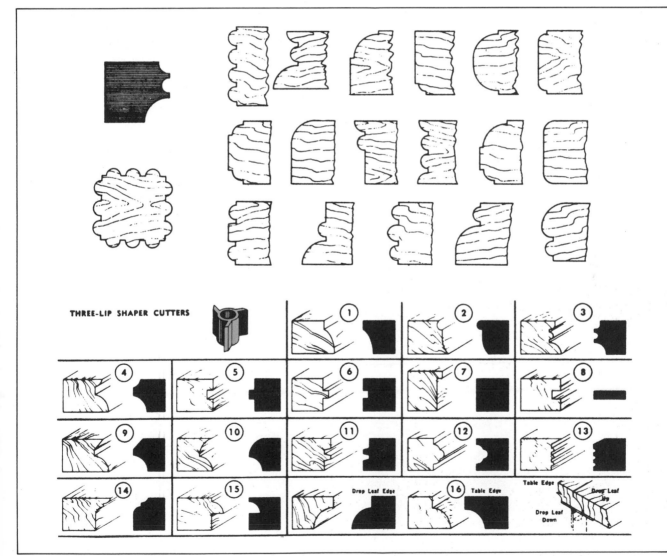

9-99. Many profiles are available in three-lip shaper cutters. Some are combination cutters. All of the profiles shown in the bottom sketch were done with the single cutter that is shown at the left.

ROTATION

DEPTH OF CUT

FEED

WORK

WITH FENCES IN LINE, CUT REMOVES PART OF WORK EDGE

CUT

WRONG

WHEN ENTIRE EDGE OF STOCK IS REMOVED, OUTFEED FENCE IS ADJUSTED TO PROVIDE SUPPORT AFTER WORK HAS PASSED CUTTER

CUT

NO SUPPORT HERE

FEED

WORK SUPPORTED HERE AFTER CUT IS MADE

FENCE MOVED BACK

CUT

TYPICAL SHAPER CUTS INVOLVING PARTIAL EDGE REMOVAL

TYPICAL SHAPER CUTS INVOLVING ENTIRE EDGE REMOVAL

9-100.   These are the important facts regarding fence alignment when doing shaping operations. It is most important for the work to be supported *before* and *after* the cut.

are hooked over work edges to guard against slippage. Don't force the work; make all passes with a slow, steady feed. Don't try to shape pieces that are too small to be held safely.

Shaping straight edges. Straight pieces should be shaped by using a fence to support and guide the work and to establish the depth of the cut. When the cut removes only part of the work's edge, infeed and outfeed fences are adjusted so their bearing surfaces are on the same plane. When the entire edge of the stock is cut away, then the outfeed fence is brought forward an amount that equals the depth of cut (Figure 9-100). These techniques are employed so the work will have full support both before and after the cut. Example operations showing both practices are demonstrated in Figures 9-101 and 9-102.

When straight-shaping, there isn't much of the cutter projecting in front of the fences, and what is there will usually be covered by the work, yet this shouldn't lull you into feeling "safe." In fact, it pays to provide an extra guard like the one shown in Figure 9-103. It can be attached to the infeed fence of any shaper setup and is adjustable longitudinally and vertically so it will suit many sizes of workpieces. It is shown being used with the shaping attachment that is available for a multi-purpose tool, but if you follow the construction details provided in Figure 9-104, it will be usable, perhaps with some modifications, on the equipment you work with.

Freehand shaping. Freehand shaping is necessary when you wish to shape the edges of a workpiece that has inside or outside curves. Since work-support and depth of cut can't be supplied by using a fence, substitute means must be employed. These consist of *collars* which are mounted on the adapter together with the cutter to control depth of cut, and *fulcrum pins* which provide a point against

9-101. This is a shaping cut done with a blank knife. The entire edge of the stock is removed. Therefore, the outfeed fence is brought forward a distance equal to the depth of cut. Note that the work is being done on Jig #1.

9-103. This is a guard you should make for straight-line shaping. It is screw-attached to the infeed table and can be adjusted to and fro and vertically.

9-102. An example cut that requires the fences to be on the same plane; only part of the stock's edge is removed. The stock is moved against the cutter's direction of rotation. On a drill press, this is from left to right. Use a slow feed and the highest speed you have. Work so cutting is done *with* the grain.

9-104. Construction details of the straight-line shaper guard you should make.

which you can brace the work before engaging the cutter (Figure 9-105). Basic freehand shaping is done as shown in Figure 9-106. The work, held firmly against the fulcrum pin, is advanced very slowly until it engages the cutter and seats solidly against the collar. You can still hold against the infeed pin as you continue to make the cut. As you near the end of the pass, swing the work so it will bear against the collar *and* the outfeed pin. Some operators ignore the outfeed pin but I can't see the point in making it standard practice. There are times when the size and shape of the work make it necessary to do without the second pin (Figure 9-107). In such cases, be especially careful at the end of the cut.

9-105. Fulcrum pins are very essential when you do freehand shaping. They provide support for the work but they don't guarantee safety. Never get your hands close to the cutter. Don't try to shape small pieces.

9-106. Work is braced against the infeed fulcrum pin and slowly advanced to contact the cutter and to bear against the collar. At the end of the cut, brace the work against the outfeed pin. Feed direction is left to right.

9-107. Some pretty intricate forms can be shaped when you work freehand. Sometimes it's necessary to remove the outfeed pin—if so, be especially careful at the end of the cut.

Freehand shaping is also used to shape edges of internal cutouts. The work is placed in position before the cutter is lowered (Figure 9-108). After that, the shaping proceeds in pretty normal fashion but with special attention for safety since it's not likely that you'll be able to work with the fulcrum pins.

A guard that you can make for use when freehand shaping is shown in Figure 9-109. It can be attached to the table of a commercial jig, or to the advanced jig, by installing a couple of T-nuts so the threaded rods can be secured. Check the dimensions that are given against your equipment. The idea is for the shield to cover the entire cutting area while still allowing access for the shaper adapter and the cutter.

Remember that the collar, or collars, that you mount with the cutter, determines the depth of the cut. Always be sure that the cut you are making allows for sufficient bearing surface between the work-edge and the collar. The collars turn with the cutter, so keep them clean and smooth to reduce friction.

9-108. For internal cuts, set the work in place before you adjust the cutter. Feed direction must always be the same. Make repeat passes for exceptionally deep forms; just adjust the cutter after each pass.

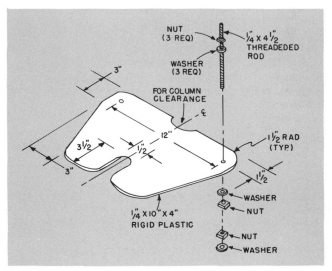

9-109. This is a guard you should make to use when freehand shaping. The text explains how it can be attached to the shaping table.

Routing on the Drill Press

Unlike drill bits, router bits have a special ability to cut sideways. When you lock a bit in the down position and push the work into it, it cuts a groove that matches the shape of its blades. Many varieties of straight and shaped cutters are available (Figure 9-110). Straight-bladed bits are most common because they produce straight-sided grooves, slots, and, by using the repeat-pass technique, rabbets or dadoes of various widths. Shaped cutters are available with various profiles so they can be used, for example, to put a fancy edge on wood (Figure 9-111), or even to make the mating shapes of a dovetail joint.

Because router bits cut in a way that produces considerable side thrust, **they should be gripped in a special router chuck** instead of the conventional 3-jaw chuck. Whenever possible, feed the work against the cutter's direction of rotation. When working against a fence, the work is moved from left to right (Figure 9-112). This way, the cutting action tends to keep the work against the fence instead of pulling it away. Router bits, like shaper cutters, function best at high speeds, so always use the drill press's highest rpm. Generally, this will not be the most efficient speed for the bits, so you'll have to compensate by using a slower-than-normal feed rate and by not making deep cuts in one pass. You'll get best results when the cutter works *with* the grain of the wood. Cross-grain cuts are often needed and are feasible, but you'll have to do them much more slowly.

Straight cuts. Straight routing should be done against a fence that will support the work and act as a guide. For example, if you needed a groove 1″ from an edge, you would set the fence to determine the edge

9-110. Router bits come in various shapes and sizes. All of them should be run at high speeds.

9-113. On a drill press, and when working against a fence, the pass will be from left to right. Wide, deep cuts like this can be made in a single pass IF your machine has the power and speed. Otherwise, rely on repeat passes.

9-111. The only difference between this and a shaping operation is that a router bit is used. Many routing operations can be done more conveniently when a shaper fence is used.

9-112. When doing straight routing, always feed so the cutter's direction of rotation tends to hold the work against the fence.

9-114. This special table, together with its accessory fence, will be very useful for many routing operations.

9-115. The fence, used like a slide, lets you feed work at right angles to the cutter. You'll work more accurately if you clamp the stock to one or both of the fence's guides.

9-116. Make the base for the table from stock 2x4s V-notched at the end to fit the drill-press column. Have the base set in place when you attach the table.

9-117. Like some of the other drill-press jigs we've shown, the router table can be swung aside to serve as a holding platform during other operations.

distance. Commercial shaper tables, which have a fence and are available as drill-press accessories, can be used (Figure 9-113), or you can work with one of the advanced jigs. A special table that serves nicely for routing operations and that you can make yourself is detailed in Figure 9-114. Construction isn't difficult and the table has features not found on ready-made units. The H-shaped fence can be clamped to serve for straight routing, and since it can be used with a sliding action, serves nicely for moving work when routing is done cross-grain (Figure 9-115). Because of the way the table's base is designed, the unit can be swung aside when it is not needed and then it serves as a holding platform during other operations (Figures 9-116 and 9-117).

9-118. This is a guard you should make and use when doing routing operations. It is adjustable vertically so it can be set for various stock thicknesses.

9-119. Construction details of the routing guard.

Make a guard. Router bits look harmless enough but any tool that cuts wood should be treated with caution and respect, and anything you can do or make to help you keep fingers away from danger zones is sensible. It's not likely that you'll find a readymade guard for drill-press router operations, but I made and use the one shown in Figures 9-118 and 9-119, and so should you. The shield's U-shaped bracket is secured with the same bolt that tightens the split casting for the depth stop-rod. The prototype was made for a Rockwell drill press. Be sure to check dimensions of the brackets against your own machine before you cut the parts. When using the shield, adjust its position after the cutting tool is organized for the job.

Curves and circles. You can do circular routing by using a pivot guide or you can guide the work by clamping or tack-nailing a V-block to the table (Figure 9-120). Position the block to obtain the necessary edge distance, and be sure the bottom of the "V" is aligned with the point of the cutter. The cutter is lowered after the work has been placed; the pass is made in a clockwise direction. Only bits that will cut when moved directly downward can be used for such operations.

"Odd"-shaped pieces that must be edge-grooved can be handled as shown in Figure 9-121. The guide board is shaped to suit the workpiece and is clamped so the router bit will cut where it should. Success of such work will depend on how carefully you make the cutout in the guide.

Pattern routing. Pattern routing is a way to do intricate shapes with good guarantee of accuracy. It is also a good method to use when you require many similar pieces.

For this type of routing, secure a router bit-sized post in a board that you attach to the drill-press table so the post is exactly aligned with the cutter. Cut the pattern you wish to reproduce in a piece of plywood or hardboard. The pat-

9-122. This is the "secret" of pattern routing. The pattern rides a pin that is set in the table (or a board) directly in line with the router bit. The pattern is tack-nailed to the underside of the work.

9-120. You can do circular routing by rotating the work against a V-block. A shaped bit is used here, but full depth-of-cut was achieved by making repeat passes.

9-123. As the pattern rides the pin, the shape is duplicated in the work above it. The best way to align the pin is to "drill" the hole for it with the router bit that will be used for the cutting.

9-121. Specially shaped guide boards are used for "odd" shaped pieces. The cutout in the guide board must match the shape of the work.

9-124. A router bit can be used much like a drill to form overlapping holes as the preliminary step when forming a round-end mortise. Clean out the slot by moving the work back and forth very slowly.

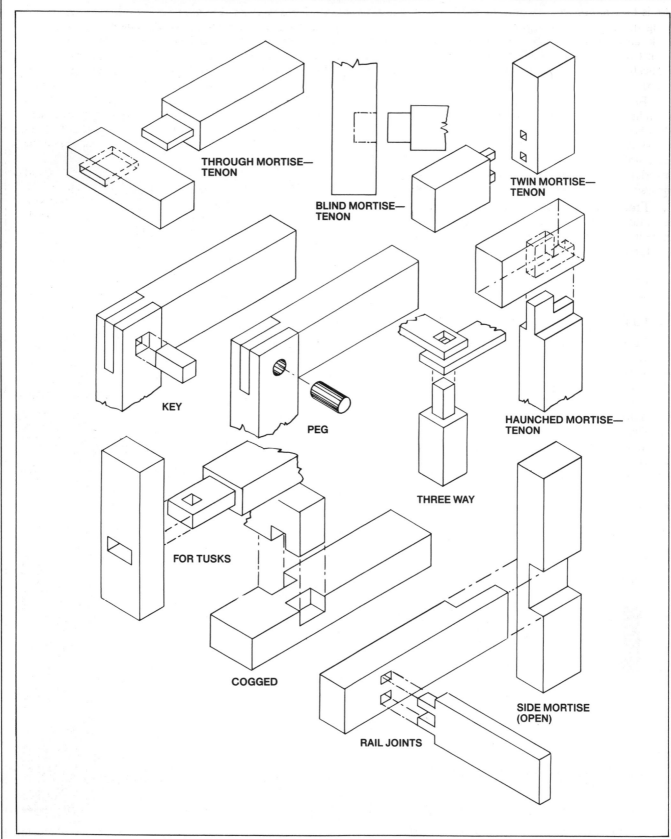

THROUGH MORTISE—
TENON

BLIND MORTISE—
TENON

TWIN MORTISE—
TENON

KEY

PEG

HAUNCHED MORTISE—
TENON

THREE WAY

FOR TUSKS

COGGED

RAIL JOINTS

SIDE MORTISE
(OPEN)

9-125.   Various types of joints you can make by using mortising equipment on the drill press. The "key" and the "peg" are additions that lock the basic joint.

tern is tack-nailed to the work and situated over the post. Bring the cutter down to the depth you want. Move the work and pattern so the pattern is constantly bearing against the post. Since the post and cutter are in line, you duplicate the shape of the pattern (Figures 9-122 and 9-123).

Routing a mortise. A router bit will function much like a drill bit if you move it vertically into the work. Thus you can use one to form overlapping holes (Figure 9-124). After the "drilling" is complete, you can move the work slowly to and fro so the bit will clean out the waste material that remains. Routed mortises will have round ends, so the tenon you use must be shaped to suit.

Freehand routing. When doing freehand routing, you must be very careful to hold the work firmly as you guide it. Cutting action will vary with differences in grain structure, and it's quite easy for the work to move away from the line you are trying to follow. The deeper you try to cut in one pass the more obvious the movement away from the line will be.

Mortising

Mortise-and-tenon combinations account for some of the strongest and most durable joints in woodworking (Figure 9-125). The closest competition is the dowel joint, but only when two dowels are used. Twin dowels are necessary to gain the anti-twist strength that a tenon in a mortise provides automatically.

The tenon is an easy table-saw job, but the mortise sometimes puzzles the beginning craftsman. The mortising bit forms a hole much like a drill bit, but it is encased in a square, steel sleeve that is really a four-sided chisel. The job of the chisel is to clean out the corners left by the bit, and the result is a square hole. Since one side of the chisel is slotted, waste chips can escape (Figure 9-126).

In order to use the chisels, you must have a special casting that locks in some fashion to the end of the quill. Usually this component is part of a kit you buy that includes a special fence and a hold-down (Figure 9-127).

General considerations. Two factors apply no matter what your equipment is. The chisel must be square to the fence so cutting will be done parallel to the work edge. There must be at least 1/32"—but not more than 1/16"—clearance between the spurs on the bit and the cutting edge of the chisel. Keep this clearance to a minimum but not so tight that you create excessive friction between bit and chisel. Not enough clearance will result in overheating and damage to the tools. Too much clearance is needless and can result in large waste chips that may clog inside the chisel.

Generally, the larger the chisel, the slower the speed should be, especially in hardwoods. For chisels up to 1/2" size, use of speed range of 1,700 rpm's to 3,500 rpm's in softwood and a maximum of about 2,000 rpm's in hardwoods. These rules apply best under ideal conditions. There are differences in softwoods and hardwoods, even in boards cut from the same tree. You must also consider whether you are cutting across the grain, with the grain, or into end grain.

Regard these rules as generalizations and break them according to how the cut is going. Stay away from excessive feed pressure; but, on the other hand, a feather touch won't work since the chisel cuts under quill-feed pressure only. The rate of feed and speed are probably correct when the waste chips move smoothly up the flutes of the bit and easily out through the escape slot in the chisels. Retracting can

9-127. Typical mortising setup on a drill press. The special casting attaches to the end of the quill and is used with the standard chuck. The accessory will include a fence and special hold-downs.

9-126. The mortising bit and the chisel work together. The bit forms the round hole to remove the bulk of the waste; the chisel cuts away the remaining corners. The result is a square hole.

also help to keep things going well. Control the depth of blind mortises by using the quill-feed stop rod.

Cutting. Forming a good mortise calls for a particular sequence of cuts. What you must avoid is allowing the chisel to move toward a cavity that is already formed—and—the work must be secure enough so it doesn't move away from the chisel during the cut. The correct cut patterns and negative factors to be aware of are shown in Figure 9-128. Work to guidelines that you mark on the workpiece. After the bulk of the waste has been removed, repeat the procedure to be sure the cavity is as clean as can be (Figure 9-129).

Some splintering will occur when the chisel breaks through on mortises that go through the stock. You can minimize this by using a scrap block under the work; but for a perfect job, work on stock that is slightly thicker than necessary. After mortising, you can do a light shaving cut on the table saw or jointer to remove the imperfections.

When you get to forming the tenon, don't size it so it must be forced into the mortise. It should be a slip fit that allows some room for glue. If it's a blind mortise, cut the tenon about 1/32″ or so shorter than the depth of the mortise. A slight chamfer on the end of the tenon is also a good idea.

A few handy, mortising variations are shown in Figures 9-130 through 9-133.

9-129. Make the end cuts first, then successive overlapping ones to clean out the stock that remains. Ideally, the overlapping cuts should be about three quarters the width of the chisel.

TWO FACTORS THAT MAY SPOIL A MORTISE:
A. Chisel tends to lead off toward the cavity already formed.
B. Work tends to creep away from the chisel as the cut is being made.

Always make end cuts first. Overlap cuts so that chisel always makes a cut that is at least 3/4 size.

Chisel will lead toward cavity and make a tapered cut.

Overlap cuts and use smaller chisel if necessary.

CORRECT CUT PATTERNS

OR

On wide mortises—leaving a narrow shoulder to cut is wrong.

9-128. Facts that pertain to drill-press mortising.

Special Mortising Jig

You don't have to restrict mortising to square stock. If you make a V-jig accessory to replace the conventional fence arrangement, you can form square cavities on round stock or on the corners of square pieces. Operational considerations don't change, and you use all the items that normally attach to the quill (Figure 9-134).

These procedures make it possible, for example, to mortise rails into round legs, to attach corner-to-corner stretchers or rails when square legs are used, and to install shelves on round posts by forming radial mortises.

When you make the jig, be careful of the dimension from the center of the "V" to the back edge of the jig. It should equal the distance from the center of the spindle to the back edge of the table to easily achieve alignment each time the jig is used.

When you use the jig be sure that the spindle and "V" have the same centerline and that the chisel is square (Figure 9-135). Place your work in the "V" and trap it with the hold-down. Similar cuts on multiple pieces can be gauged easily by tack-nailing a stop block across the "V." The same idea applies when you do radial mortising. Alignment of repeat cuts when forming slots is controlled by drawing a longitudinal line on the work after you have formed the first cavity. Thereafter, keep the edge of the chisel on the line.

Concentric mortises are feasible if you devise a means of holding the work in relation to the cutting tool. The same modified screw clamp that was shown for simple concentric drilling can be used. It will work fine on either round or square stock.

Decorative Work

You can do luxurious carving, as well as create such items as drawer fronts and door pulls with a custom look, on your drill press. The accompanying, illustrated samples of such work are simply a place to start; you can go much further by adapting the technique to your own projects and tools.

Mortising Variations

9-130.   A side mortise is used, for example, when rails are set in flush. When the cut is required on matching pieces, you can often do two at once by clamping the pieces face-to-face and making the square cuts on the joint line.

9-131.   To cut a side mortise on one piece, place a scrap strip between the work and the fence. If the side mortise is shallower than your smallest chisel, make the setup so the surplus bite comes out of the back-up strip.

9-132.   The "tusk" is like a key. The square hole you form for it is spaced so placing the tusk forces the rail against the shoulder of the tenon. Joints like this often serve as decorative details.

9-133.   An interesting variation of the basic technique is shown here. The fingers can be shaped as long slots which are then cut apart by sawing so they become tenons, or fingers.

"X" = CENTER OF SPINDLE TO BACK EDGE OF TABLE

HOMEMADE HOLD-DOWN

THUMB SCREW ¼" × 1½"

¾" D.

FORM THREADS BY TURNING IN UNDERSIZE HOLE

OVERALL SIZE = 2¼" × 2¼" × 4½" SOLID OR BY LAMINATING ¾" STOCK

POST BLOCK   POST

¾" D. × 9½"

V BLOCK

BASE

9-134.   You can form mortises in cylinders but you must make this kind of jig to do it.

9-135.   Work with standard mortising equipment and our special jig to form square holes in cylinders. The work is cradled in the "V" and secured with the regular hold-down. Cutting proceeds in normal fashion but you must be careful not to allow the work to turn.

9-136.   This fly cutter, which does not remove a disc, can be used to do some decorative "carving."

Much of what is shown is done with a fly cutter and has a sloping bit rather than a vertical cutter (Figure 9-136). As the tool is fed, its pilot drill makes a center hole and the blade makes a circular recess with a sloping bottom. When a second cut is done close enough to overlap the first, new angles and interesting patterns result (Figure 9-137). The cutter (called Adjust-A-Drill by Jet Tool Company) is available in two sizes. Since both have adjustable bits, a wide range of designs is possible.

This kind of decorative work can be done on almost any wood, but stock such as maple and birch is best to use.

Work with a ruler and compass to plan designs. Mark centers accurately and drill pilot holes first, either by working with a similar size bit or by taking the cutting blade out of the tool and using the pilot drill alone.

Always clamp the work and run the drill press at a slow speed. Do larger circles first and use the quill stop to control depth of cut (Figure 9-138). As with all fly cutters, keep hands away from the cutting area. Use a slow feed; and when the tool is at full depth, hold it there a second or two. A burnishing effect results that helps produce a smooth finish.

You can increase speed as you decrease the hole diameter. If the wood you are using leaves a rough nap, try dampening the wood after the initial cuts. When it dries, make a very light smoothing cut to remove the fuzz raised by the moisture.

The pilot-drill holes can be left open for a lacy effect; or they can be plugged with dowels, discs or buttons. Such pieces can have a contrasting tone. While the finished jobs can be spray painted, natural finishes seem more appropriate especially on hardwoods.

Drilled moldings. Decorative effects can be achieved by drilling on the centerline of two boards that are clamped together (Figure 9-139). When the drilled boards are separated and strip-cut on the table saw, you get individual pieces that are like those shown in Figure 9-140. The pieces can be used as is, maybe mounted on a heavier backing, or they can be joined edge-to-edge to form panels.

9-137. Overlapping cuts produce interesting patterns. For this operation, the pilot bit was removed from the cutter. Be sure the work is very secure, and that you feed very, very slowly. Also, check frequently to be sure the cutter doesn't loosen.

9-139. Clamp two pieces together and bore deep holes on the joint line. When the pieces are separated and strips cut, you have slats that can be used as moldings, or they can be joined edge-to-edge to form open work panels.

9-138. Boring decorative concentric circles is done in succeeding steps with the cut-diameter reduced for each. After boring, the piece can be shaped as a circle, oval, square, whatever.

9-140. The effects you get depend on the drilling pattern.

The results will depend on the layout you use, the size of the holes, whether you drill through holes or blind holes, and so on (Figure 9-141). If you do some experimenting with how you do the strip-cutting, you can create some unusual designs. For example, instead of sawing in normal fashion (with the stock flat so you cut *across* the holes), saw with the stock on edge so the openings will be a section of the holes. This sawing method was used to produce the samples shown in Figure 9-142. The holes, drilled to a specific depth, were formed with a spade bit.

For something different, try doing the "piercing" with a mortising bit and chisel. You can produce square openings or work with the chisel turning 45° from its normal position. The openings, of course, will still be square but they will appear to be diamond-shaped. See Figures 9-143 and 9-144.

Plug Cutters

Concealing a screw or bolt hole with a plug cut from an ordinary dowel that you buy in the local hardware store is not the best method to use. Such items are not always accurate, and you can't find them in all kinds of wood. Furthermore, it would be too much to expect that the grain of the plug would match that of the wood you are using.

Plug cutters are good solutions to this little headache since you can cut plugs from the same material you are working with and match the grain so closely that the plug would be hard to find (Figure 9-145).

The plug cutter used in the drill press can also make dowels. Length is limited to about two inches, but this is long enough for dowel joints. You can use scrap pieces of lumber as stock; and since hardwood dowels are not inexpensive this alone helps justify the cost of the tool (Figure 9-146).

Once the dowels are formed you can make a cut on either the table saw or the bandsaw to separate them from the base stock.

Integral tenons. By using a special technique, you can work with plug cutters to form integral tenons on round or square stock. The idea, illustrated in Figure 9-147, is to first cut kerfs on four sides of the work to a depth that will match the diameter of the tenon. The next step is to situate the work in the drill press so the plug cutter can be used as shown in Figure 9-148. The work must be done carefully. If you are accurate with the kerfing, and locate the plug cutter precisely, the waste will fall away to reveal a neat, integral tenon (Figure 9-149).

9-141. Ideas you can use to form decorative, drilled moldings.

9-142. Variations are possible depending on how you cut the drilled pieces. These pieces were produced by strip cutting with the stock on edge.

9-143. You can do the same kind of work with a mortising chisel.

9-144. The holes formed with the mortising chisel will, of course, be square, but since the chisel was turned 45°, they appear as diamonds.

9-145. There are many advantages to cutting your own plugs; among them, you can choose your own wood species and you can control grain direction.

9-146. Some plug cutters are long enough to produce dowels that can be used in joints. When cut in end grain, the dowel will have a strong cross-section. Adjust the speed according to the work, but start somewhere between 1,200 rpm and 1,800 rpm. Feed slowly and retract frequently. After the dowels are formed, you can separate them from the base block by sawing.

9-147. The first step when forming an integral tenon is to cut kerfs just deep enough to match the diameter of the tenon.

9-148. Then the plug cutter is used to remove the waste.

9-149. If you have worked carefully, the waste will fall away and reveal a nice, smooth tenon.

Another use for these special tools is shown in Figure 9-150. If you have mislocated a hole, or have one that must be enlarged, you can cut a plug to fill the existing hole. Then you can establish a new center for the new hole.

V-Block Work

V-blocks make excellent holders for drilling diametrical holes through cylinders and tubes. The V-shape is formed with saw cuts; the holder is clamped to the drill-press table so the point of the bit is on the V's centerline. The result is that the longitudinal diameter of the work is put on the same plane.

When drilling a series of holes, it's best to draw a line on the work to help keep you from rotating it as you go. When the job calls for a series of equally spaced holes, you can drive a nail through the first hole drilled: the distance from the nail to the bit equals the hole spacing (Figure 9-151).

There are times when a special V-block design can solve a particular problem. The one shown in Figure 9-152 has V-cuts that intersect at a 90° angle. The seat formed by the intersecting "V's" positions a ball-shaped workpiece so

it can be drilled diametrically with great accuracy. How to handle such a piece depends on the work. If the piece being drilled is large, and the hole is small, you can probably hand-hold it. When in doubt, use a screw clamp to secure the work after it has been positioned in the V-jig.

Drum Sanding

A drum sander is a fine tool to use for many edge-smoothing operations, and the drill press is a good tool to use it on. A major consideration is to work so the sanded edge will be square to adjacent surfaces. This can be accomplished without fuss if you work as shown in Figure 9-153. The table is swung aside so work resting on it can be brought to bear against the abrasive surface. It's not a bad way to work, but keeping the work level depends as much on you as it does

9-152. The intersection of two V-cuts makes a good cradle situation for drilling into or through ball-shapes.

9-150. Plugs are often used to fill holes that must be relocated or enlarged. The plug provides a center for the new drilling.

9-151. A V-block setup like this will provide for automatic spacing. Drill the hole for the nail guide in the "V" after drilling the first hole in the work. The nail also keeps the work from turning.

9-153. The drill press is a fine tool for running a drum sander. Easiest setup is to swing the table aside and work this way.

on the table. To supply more work-support surface without reducing the efficiency of the operation, you can make an auxiliary table like the one shown in Figure 9-154. In both cases, since the drum can be moved up and down through quill action, the entire surface of the sandpaper can be brought into play.

Abrasive sleeves for drums are available in various grits, and the texture of the sandpaper has some bearing on

the speed the drum should turn. Generally, a speed of about 1,500 rpm is okay for coarse paper, while about 2,000 rpm is better for finer abrasives. In all cases, you must remember that the abrasive particles are cuttng tools and that you must give them a chance to work. Excessive pressure against the sanding surface does more harm than good; premature wear of the abrasive, burning the sleeve or the work, sanded edges that are irregular—all these can result from trying to work too quickly.

Sanding drums can be used to smooth straight or curved edges and the inside edges of cutouts. With special setups, they can function to smooth parallel curves, circular edges, and, to some extent, can be used for surface-sanding. Such operations are shown being done on one of the advanced jigs in Figures 9-155 through 9-159.

9-154. A special drum-sander table will provide more support for workpieces. The table's bottom ledges are for clamping the unit to the drill-press table.

9-155. When doing inside edges, place the work before you situate the drum. Work with a speed of about 1,500 rpm with coarse paper—about 2,000 rpm with fine paper. Note that this sanding chore is being done with one of the advanced jigs.

9-156. You get perfect circles when you pivot-guide the work. Best method is to advance the work until the drum is cutting. Then lock the slide and rotate the work in the direction of the arrow.

9-157. Inside or outside curved edges can be passed through between the guide on Jig #2 and the drum. Work this way when you have many similar pieces to do. A single piece can be handled freehand.

9-158. You can sand edges in fine style when you run the work between the drum sander and a fence. Remember, this is a *sanding* operation so don't try to take deep cuts. Note the direction of feed.

9-159. This is an excellent way to smooth surfaces on thin materials. Use a slow but constant feed. Pausing at any point will cause the drum to gouge the work.

9-160. The usual method of doing pattern sanding is to use a solid disc under the drum as a guide. It works, but only part of the drum can be used and it can quickly wear or clog. By making a table like this, with a drum-size hole through it and a ring used as a guide, the entire surface of the drum can be brought into play.

9-161. The pattern is tack-nailed to the underside of rough-cut work and rides against the guide ring throughout the operation. The work is sanded to match the pattern. When using this method, the pattern must be smaller by the cross-section width of the ring.

9-162. You can make special drum sanders by cementing sandpaper around a length of dowel. It's also possible to center-drill rounds so they can be mounted on a bolt, which becomes the shaft that is gripped in the chuck.

Pattern sanding. The standard way to do pattern sanding with a drum is to make a guide to match the diameter of the drum, and to attach it concentrically with the drum, to a board that is clamped to the drill-press table. A pattern, which is a duplicate of the shape you need, is tack-nailed or otherwise attached to the bottom of rough-cut workpieces. Since the pattern rides against the guide, workpieces are sanded to match. This is a tried-and-true method, but it does have one problem; only a limited area of the abrasive surface can be used, and it can become clogged or worn very quickly.

An improvement is to make the table that is shown in Figure 9-160. This is like the table that was shown at the beginning of the drum sander section, but with a raised ring added. The ring is the guide that serves for pattern sanding

9-163. Make a flap wheel by inserting strips of sandpaper in a slot cut in a dowel. This type of flexible sander can be used on contours, odd-shaped pieces, and on the inside of small holes.

9-164. Sanding dowels and similar workpieces is done best when the free end of the work is held in a hole drilled in a board that is clamped to the table. This will keep the work from whipping.

(Figure 9-161). The advantage is that the drum can be raised or lowered so its entire surface can be utilized because of the hole in the table. The only difference between this and the standard procedure is that here, the pattern must be reduced to compensate for the cross-section width of the guide ring.

Other sanding techniques. If you think of the drill press as a tool that can turn "things" and always use it safely, you can create special setups to solve particular problems. Some shop-tested ideas are demonstrated in Figures 9-162 through 9-166.

Some Metal Drilling Techniques

There are some similarities between wood-drilling and metal-drilling, but it is the *major* differences you must be aware of. For one thing, while you can drill a good-size hole in wood in one operation, it's not a good idea to do so in metal. The wise practice, for safety and accuracy, is to start with a small hole and then, by changing drills, to gradually increase the size you want. Work must always be firmly supported, preferably on a scrap block. Parallel supports

are often used under the work, but it's an error to separate them by much (Figure 9-167). An idea, often used by professionals, is to employ a V-block as the under-the-work support. The V-block is situated so the drilling will occur as close to the bottom of the "V" as possible (Figure 9-168).

Metal drilling develops considerable twisting action, especially when the drill breaks through. Therefore, the work must be clamped securely or you must provide stops that will keep the work from trying to rotate with the drill. A setup you can use, especially when you have many similar pieces to drill, is shown in Figure 9-169. Nuts and bolts are locked in the table slots and the work is braced between them. If the stops are located an equal distance from the drill's centerline, you'll know the hole will be in the center of the work.

A good gripping device to have is shown in Figure 9-170. This is often called a "drill-press vice" and it's great for metal drilling because it's designed for easy clamping or bolting to the drill-press table. Because its faces are V-cut, it will grip round stock as well as straight pieces.

Drilling speeds. Good operating speeds will vary with the size of the drill and the material being worked. The

9-165.   For special applications, think about designing jigs, like this one which is used to taper dowels used for ship model masts.

9-166.   To do shorter pieces, just grip them in the chuck and apply the sandpaper. You'll get a more even finish if you work with sandpaper that is wrapped around a block of wood.

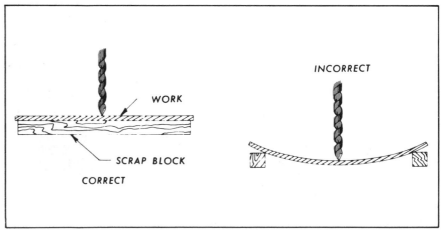

9-167.   Good support is achieved by using a scrap block under the work as you do when drilling wood. Parallel supports should be positioned very close to the drilling area.

chart in Figure 9-171 is a reasonable guide for most types of work you might do. It's possible that the tool you own may not be capable of the ideal speed. When this is so, use the speed that comes closest, preferably, for safety's sake, on low side. Always be aware of the maximum drilling capaci-ty of the tool you have. This kind of information will be found in the owner's manual.

Good speed and correct feed, when done with a sharp cutter, will curl a ribbon of metal out of the hole. The drill must cut constantly or you will merely rub the metal. This

9-168. Many operators like to use a V-block. Both the block and the work are clamped in place.

9-169. A good way to counteract twist when drilling metal is to use a nut-and-bolt arrangement like this. It's an especially good system when you need to drill many similar pieces.

9-170. A drill press vise is a good grip-ping tool for metal drilling. V's cut into its faces grip and position round stock.

DRILL SIZE	MATERIAL			
	SOFT METALS	SOFT CAST IRON	MILD STEEL	PLASTICS AND HARD RUBBER
1/16	6,000-6,500	6,000-6,500	5,000-6,500	6,000-6,500
3/32	6,000-6,500	4,500-5,500	4,000-5,000	6,000-6,500
1/8	6,000-6,500	3,500-4,500	3,000-4,000	5,000-6,000
5/32	5,000-6,000	3,000-3,500	2,500-3,000	4,000-5,000
3/16	5,000-6,000	2,500-3,000	2,000-2,500	3,500-4,000
7/32	4,500-5,000	2,000-2,500	2,000-2,500	3,000-3,500
1/4	4,500-5,000	2,000-2,500	1,500-2,000	3,000-3,500
9/32	4,000-4,500	1,500-2,000	1,500-2,000	2,500-3,000
5/16	3,500-4,000	1,500-2,000	1,000-1,500	2,000-2,500
11/32	3,000-3,500	1,500-2,000	1,000-1,500	2,000-2,500
3/8	3,000-3,500	1,500-2,000	1,000-1,500	1,500-2,000
13/32	2,500-3,000	1,500-2,000	1,000-1,500	1,500-2,000
7/16	2,500-3,000	1,000-1,500	400-1,000	1,500-2,000
15/32	2,000-2,500	1,000-1,500	400-1,000	1,500-2,000
1/2	2,000-2,500	1,000-1,500	400-1,000	1,000-1,500
9/16	1,500-2,000			1,000-1,500
5/8	1,500-2,000			1,000-1,500
11/16	1,500-2,000			1,000-1,500
3/4	1,500-2,000			400-1,000
FEED	Medium	Medium	Heavy	Light
LUBRICANT	Dry or paraffin oil	Dry	Lard oil	Dry

9-171. Speed and lubricant suggestions for various kinds of non-wood drilling. The owner's manual will tell you the maximum size holes the tool can drill in wood and steel.

will accomplish nothing but drilling the tool. So the general rule is, work with sharp drills, don't rush, but feed so the drill will keep cutting.

Twist drills.   Twist drills are available in fractional, letter, or number sizes. Since you probably won't be equipped with complete sets of all three, you can work from the chart of decimal equivalents to select a size that comes close to what is called for (Figure 9-172). If nothing but the exact one will do, then you'll just have to acquire it.

Layout work.   Work with a sharp scribe to do layout work. On some metals a scribed line doesn't show too clearly. In addition, it's often poor practice to incise the line, so surface-coaters are used. By using these and scribing lightly, you can do layout work without cutting into the metal surface (Figure 9-173).

Always use a prick punch to mark hole centers. In addition, a center punch can be used to form a slight well into which you seat the drill point when you start drilling. Without it, especially on round surfaces, the drill point can wander off the mark (Figure 9-174).

You can work with extreme precision if you use the prick-punch mark as the center for scribing the hole size you want. The scribed circle is a guide to tell you if the drill is moving off-center. To get to a 1/2″ hole, it isn't uncommon to start at 1/16″ or 1/8″ and then work up through several other sizes to get to the final 1/2″.

A sure way to locate work so the hole mark is centered exactly with the drill is to work with a centering pin (Figure 9-175). This doesn't have to be any more than a short length of 1/8″ or 1/4″ drill rod sharpened at one end. In practice, you secure the pin in the chuck and lower it so the point engages the center-punch mark. Then you clamp the work and substitute the drill for the pin.

FRACTION	NO.	DECIMAL	FRACTION	NO.	DECIMAL	FRACTION	NO.	DECIMAL	FRACTION	LTR.	DECIMAL
	80	.0135	3/32		.0937		5	.2055	25/64		.3906
	79	.0145		41	.0960		4	.2090		X	.3970
1/64		.0156		40	.0980		3	.2130		Y	.4040
	78	.0160		39	.0995	7/32		.2187	13/32		.4062
	77	.0180		38	.1015		2	.2210		Z	.4130
	76	.0200		37	.1040		1	.2280	27/64		.4219
	75	.0210		36	.1065				7/16		.4375
	74	.0225	7/64		.1094				29/64		.4531
	73	.0240		35	.1100				15/32		.4687
	72	.0250		34	.1110				31/64		.4844
	71	.0260		33	.1130	**FRACTION**	**LTR.**	**DECIMAL**	1/2		.5000
	70	.0280		32	.1160				33/64		.5156
	69	.0292		31	.1200		A	.2340	17/32		.5312
	68	.0310	1/8		.1250	15/64		.2344	35/64		.5469
1/32		.0312		30	.1285		B	.2380	9/16		.5625
	67	.0320		29	.1360		C	.2420	37/64		.5781
	66	.0330		28	.1405		D	.2460	19/32		.5937
	65	.0350	9/64		.1406	1/4	E	.2500	39/64		.6094
	64	.0360		27	.1440		F	.2570	5/8		.6250
	63	.0370		26	.1470		G	.2610	41/64		.6406
	62	.0380		25	.1495	17/64		.2656	21/32		.6562
	61	.0390		24	.1520		H	.2660	43/64		.6719
	60	.0400		23	.1540		I	.2720	11/16		.6875
	59	.0410	5/32		.1562		J	.2770	45/64		.7031
	58	.0420		22	.1570		K	.2810	23/32		.7187
	57	.0430		21	.1590	9/32		.2812	47/64		.7344
	56	.0465		20	.1610		L	.2900	3/4		.7500
3/64		.0469		19	.1660		M	.2950	49/64		.7656
	55	.0520		18	.1695	19/64		.2969	25/32		.7812
	54	.0550	11/64		.1719		N	.3020	51/64		.7969
	53	.0595		17	.1730	5/16		.3125	13/16		.8125
1/16		.0625		16	.1770		O	.3160	53/64		.8281
	52	.0635		15	.1800		P	.3230	27/32		.8437
	51	.0670		14	.1820	21/64		.3281	55/64		.8594
	50	.0700		13	.1850		Q	.3320	7/8		.8750
	49	.0730	3/16		.1875		R	.3390	57/64		.8906
	48	.0760		12	.1890	11/32		.3437	29/32		.9062
5/64		.0781		11	.1910		S	.3480	59/64		.9219
	47	.0785		10	.1935		T	.3580	15/16		.9375
	46	.0810		9	.1960	23/64		.3594	61/64		.9531
	45	.0820		8	.1990		U	.3680	31/32		.9687
	44	.0860		7	.2010	3/8		.3750	63/64		.9844
	43	.0890	13/64		.2031		V	.3770	1		1.0000
	42	.0935		6	.2040		W	.3860			

9-172.   This chart gives decimal equivalents of fractional, letter, and number size twist drills.

Tapping

The drill press may be used to overcome the difficulty of keeping a tap square to the work. Any of the three kinds of taps, when secured in the drill-press chuck, will be square to the work surface throughout the job (Figure 9-176).

However, tapping is never done under power. The drill press merely assures squareness; the tapping is done by turning the chuck by hand as you apply very light feed pressure. To do this, use a short length of metal rod (or a suitable bolt) in the chuck holes normally used by the chuck key (Figure 9-177).

The tap works by cutting metal. To remove waste, turn the chuck to the right about one-fourth turn for every half turn to the left. Use a drop of oil on the tap as you go. Be careful when withdrawing the tap. Keep some feed pressure as you continue to turn the chuck to the right until the tap is clear.

Tapping can't be a haphazard operation, not if the screws or bolts are to hold as they should. Good practice calls for drilling the right size hole before forming the threads, and the hole will differ depending on whether you are forming "National fine" or "National coarse" threads. The chart in Figure 9-178 will tell you what size hole to drill for each tap.

Spot Polishing

Getting an attractive finish on a metal surface by "grinding" overlapping spots is spot polishing (Figure 9-179). The tools can be made as shown in Figure 9-180. The abrasive you use can be judged in relation to the hardness of the metal. The plain rod that is illustrated can be used when a mixture of emery dust and light oil is applied to the work. Abrasive paper or steel wool can be worked dry.

Always do some test work first on scrap stock. Use a fence so you can move the work in a straight line and try to overlap the spots evenly. Feed pressure should be very light; and speed must be judged on the basis of the abrasive, the material being worked, and the results you are getting. Start at a slow speed and increase the speed gradually to what does the job you want.

MATERIAL	DYE
Rough Metals	White or blue chalk, rubbed on surface.
Castings	White (mixture: 50-50 white lead and turpentine).
Smooth Steel	Copper sulfate (2 tablespoons in 1 cup water—crystals available at drugstore or chemical house) or layout compound (purple coating, available at hardware store).
Bright Sheet Metal	Layout compound.
Keep layout dye in discarded shoe polish bottle—one with dauber which may be used to apply the dye. Apply dye evenly and smoothly on the surface of the metal.	

9-173.   Suggested surface-coaters you can use when preparing various types of metal for layout work. Keep scribe marks light—just barely enough to scribe through the coating.

USE PRICK PUNCH FIRST TO MARK CENTER LOCATION

THEN ENLARGE MARK WITH CENTER PUNCH

Ⓐ

SCRIBE HOLE-SIZE CIRCLE AS A GUIDE

Ⓑ   PUNCH MARKS

IF DRILL CREEPS OFF CENTER

Ⓒ

HOLE TO BE DRILLED

MAKE SEVERAL CHISEL MARKS AS SHOWN TO BRING DRILL BACK ON CENTER

9-174.   Hole locations should be marked with a prick punch and then indented further with a center punch. You can sometimes correct an error by using the technique shown in the sketch at the bottom right.

When you make the tools, be sure that the working end will bear flat against the work.

Trouble-Shooting Chart

Check the facts that are listed in Figure 9-181 when you have an operational problem. If the cause and the cure are not listed, then it's best to re-study the owner's manual for a possible mechanical fault.

9-177. A tapping operation in the drill press is done for accuracy —it is never done under power, not in the home workshop anyway unless it is equipped for in-depth metal working. Here, the tapping is done by turning the chuck by hand.

9-175. A centering pin can be used to situate work so drilling will be exact. The wood block is there to keep the work level.

TAPER   **PLUG**   **BOTTOMING**

9-176. When you have a hole that is clear through the material, use the "taper" or "plug" tap. When the hole does not go through, start the job with the "taper," use the "plug" to the bottom of the hole, and finish with the "bottoming" tap.

	TAP		TAP DRILL		
NO. OR FRAC- TION	NC	NF	NC	NF	DRILL FOR CLEARANCE
0		80		3/64	51
1	64	72	53	53	47
2	56	64	50	50	42
3	48	56	47	45	37
4	40	48	43	42	31
5	40	44	38	37	29
6	32	40	36	33	26
8	32	36	29	29	17
10	24	32	25	21	8
12	24	28	16	14	1
1/4	20	28	7	3	Same as tap
5/16	18	24	F	I	Same as tap
3/8	16	24	5/16	Q	Same as tap
7/16	14	20	U	25/64	Same as tap
1/2	13	20	27/64	29/64	Same as tap
9/16	12	18	31/64	33/64	Same as tap
5/8	11	18	17/32	37/64	Same as tap
3/4	10	16	21/32	11/16	Same as tap
7/8	9	14	49/64	13/16	Same as tap
1″	8	14	7/8	15/16	Same as tap

9-178. Drill the correct size holes for each tap you plan to use. This is important for easy working and good threads. The clearance hole will remove threads should this ever be necessary.

9-179. Spot polishing is often called "damaskeening." The results are most effective when the spots overlap and are in line.

SHAFT MAY BE HEADLESS BOLT THREADED INTO METAL BASE. BASE CAN BE MADE FROM ROUND BAR STOCK.

TURNED, HARD MAPLE

LEATHER

SANDPAPER-FINE EMERY

RECESS STUFFED WITH FINE STEEL WOOL

OR USE STRAIGHT METAL (CUT FROM BOLT OR DRILL ROD) ROD OR WOOD ROD (CUT FROM HARD DOWEL)

9-180. Here are suggestions for spot polishers you can make and use in the drill press.

THE PROBLEM	POSSIBLE CAUSES	WHAT TO LOOK FOR OR DO
IN GENERAL		
Bits or other cutting tools overheat—work shows burn marks	Excessive speed	Use correct speed or as close to it as possible—see speed chart
	Not allowing waste chips to clear	Retract cutting tool frequently to remove waste chips from hole
	Dull cutting tool	Sharpen
	Excessive feed-speed	Feed just enough to keep the tool cutting
Bit moves off center	Poor procedure	Use punch to mark center
	Bit "drifts"	Drill pilot hole first, then enlarge to full size—do in steps if necessary
Work splinters when drill breaks through	No backup support	Use a piece of scrap wood under the work
Bit grabs when breaking through	Excessive feed-speed	Slow up at the end of the cut, especially when drilling metal
Work twists or in torn from hands	Poor work-handling	It's usually wise to clamp work to the table or to the fence when one is used
Bit dulls quickly or cutting edges break	Feeding too slow	Too slow is as bad as too fast—feed so tool is continuously cutting

(continued on next page)

THE PROBLEM	POSSIBLE CAUSES	WHAT TO LOOK FOR OR DO
Cutting tool slips in chuck	Tool is not securely gripped	Always use the chuck key—do not rely on hand-tightening
Inaccurate hole-depth	Incorrect setup	Follow instructions for drilling to a specific depth
	Not allowing for bit's point	Allow for brad points, end of twist drill, whatever, when setting up
Bit binds	Work pinching bit	Support the work directly under, or as close to the cutting area as possible
	Excessive feed pressure	Don't try to make the bit cut faster than it can—don't jam the bit into the work
Angular holes move off center	Edge of the bit contacts the work before the center does	Work with a leveling block when necessary—see instructions
WHEN MORTISING Mortise has serrated edge	Misalignment	Be sure the chisel is square to the fence before cutting
Work or cutting tools overheat	Misalignment	There must be a clearance of 1/32″ to 1/16″ between the end of the bit and the chisel
	Insufficient chip removal	Frequently retract cutters to clear waste chips—don't keep the clearance slot in the chisel buried
	Wrong speed	Use correct speed—see instructions
	Dull cutting tools	Sharpen chisel and bit
	Excessive feed pressure	Use only enough feed pressure to keep tools cutting
Walls of mortise are tapered	Chisel moves off toward first cuts	Each cut should be at least 3/4 of the chisel's width
	Work moved	Work must be securely clamped
	No support when forming a side mortise	Always use a backup block
Excessive pressure required to make cut	Dull tools	Sharpen chisels and bits
	Very hard wood	Drill relief holes first when necessary
Work pulls up when chisel is retracted	Wrong procedure	Always use mortising hold-down—add clamps if necessary
WHEN ROUTING Rough cuts—chatter	Speed too slow	High speeds produce smoothest cuts
	Cutting too deep	Make repeat passes when you need very deep cuts
	Vibration during cut	Hold work firmly throughout the pass—use hold-downs when possible
	Wrong pass direction	Feed work against tool's direction-of-rotation

9-181. Trouble-shooting chart for the drill press.

10. The Lathe

The woodturning lathe is often thought of as an "accessory" power tool, something to have around for those occasions when a project called for a cylinder, a round leg, or some such thing. The availability of ready-made spindles pushed the tool even further into the background. Ready-to-use tapered legs and other furniture components, even balustrades and newel posts are just too easy to buy. Modern design didn't help much, causing some to deem the lathe the old-fashioned tool for making old-fashioned parts for old-fashioned projects.

Well, all things come full round, and the creativity and sheer pleasure—akin to sculpturing in the round—that the lathe makes possible are again being recognized. Once you start using the lathe you'll be amazed by its flexibility. Parts that range from long, heavy spindles to postage-stamp size miniatures are all within its capabilities (Figures 10-1 and 10-2). On some machines, those that can be equipped, for example, with a universal chuck, you can do a fair amount of metal turning (Figure 10-3).

One of the fascinations of the lathe is that it is one of the few woodworking machines on which you can turn out a finished project without using another machine. For example, work held between its centers might become a lamp base; a block mounted on a faceplate might become a salad bowl. Shaping, smoothing, and finishing are all done right in the machine.

Reactions to the lathe differ. Some people immediately operate the tool without regard for some basic considerations; others assume that a long period of apprenticeship will be required before they dare try an actual part or project. The latter approach is safer, but it should not be carried to an extreme. The truth is that a beginner can form a good piece of work immediately as long as he uses lathe chisels in a simple fashion. The professional uses a "cutting" action whenever he can whereas the learner should stay with a "scraping" action, a technique that enables him to use any chisel right from the start. In so doing, he can accomplish quality work even though he won't win any speed contests. He can be immediately productive while taking an occasional crack at more advanced chisel usage.

General Characteristics

In concept, all lathes are the same. They differ in features, weight and capacity. The main parts (Figure 10-4) include a *headstock* that is in a fixed position, a *tailstock* that is movable, and a *tool rest* that is adjustable. All parts are mounted on a *bed* or *ways*. The tool rest and the tailstock are

10-1.   The lathe is the only power tool on which you can do this kind of work. The parts you make can be components for other projects or complete projects in themselves—bowls and lamp bases and such.

10-2.   There are no secrets to doing quality lathe work. Once you know the machine and become acquainted with the special chisels that are used, you can turn out projects from newel posts to postage-stamp size miniatures.

movable laterally so they can be situated to suit the size of the work.

Spindle turnings are mounted between the headstock and the tailstock. Bowls, trays and the like are mounted on a *faceplate* that secures only to the headstock. When work can't be mounted between centers and is too small to do on a faceplate, a *screw-center* can be employed (Figure 10-5). This too secures only to the headstock and is designed so small pieces can be worked. In addition, universal chucks, three-jaw chucks and holding devices that you can make yourself can be used with the lathe. Therefore, on a lathe you can fabricate projects or parts for projects that range from corn cob holders to heavy bed posts.

Lathe capacities are figured in terms of maximum spindle length and the maximum diameter of the work that can be swung over the bed (Figure 10-6). Usually, the latter is used to indicate lathe size. On a 12″ lathe, the bed is approximately 6″ from the headstock. Thus, you can swing a 12″ faceplate turning.

The spindle capacity does not limit what you can do in terms of a project. To go beyond the basic work size you can mount, you simply do two turnings and then join them. On many lathes you can do outboard turning. For such work, the workpiece is mounted on the outboard side of the headstock so the work radius is limited by the distance from the center to the floor (Figure 10-7). Therefore, even the lathe-size figure given in catalogs isn't a true picture of maximum work size.

Types

The concept of the lathe hasn't changed from its bow-powered or foot-powered days. Modern ones are still a means whereby mounted workpieces can be shaped symmetrically with special, sharp chisels. The difference between available units has to do with overall size and weight, capacities, and available speeds and how they are achieved. The extremes in sizes, remembering that we are basically discussing tools for homeworkers, can be appre-

10-3.   Some lathes are equipped and have the power and correct speeds so you can work with a universal chuck, something normally used on a metal-turning lathe.

10-4.   The basic parts of a woodworking lathe. The motor is often situated under the bench on which the lathe is bolted. Step pulleys provide several specific speeds.

10-5.   Small work is often done on a screw-center. Here a duplicate of an existing drawer pull has been produced. Often, this is the only way to go when doing restorations.

10-6.   Lathe capacities are listed as the maximum distance between centers and 2X the distance from the headstock spindle to the bed. A "gap bed" lathe, like this one, provides extra capacity for faceplate work.

10-7. Some lathes are organized for outboard faceplate work. You can buy special stands to use in this situation, or you can make your own.

ciated by viewing the examples shown in Figures 10-8 and 10-9. The larger tool is as much at home in industry as it is in a garage workshop. Often it is seen as the "dream" tool by lathe enthusiasts. The smaller one is a true wood lathe but scaled down quite a bit to a compact size. You won't use it to form porch columns but it's nice to have if you are producing parts that are not more than 6″ long or greater than 1-1/2″ in diameter. Within this size area fall such items as parts for miniature furniture and models, candlestick holders, drawer pulls, chess men, and so on.

Within the "maximum" and "minimum" ranges fall a good number of other products, with differences that have to do more with features than capacities, and, of course, with price. An economical unit that has a fairly large capacity is shown in Figure 10-10. It's one of AM&T's "unadorned" tools, designed for function sans niceties. It's light and very basic but capable of efficient turning. Its basic speeds are controlled with step pulleys, which is not uncommon, but you can get more if you add the counter shaft assembly that is shown in Figure 10-11. The conversion range with a 1725 rpm motor is from about 350 rpm to over 3600 rpm. There is no reason why an accessory of this type can't be used with *any* lathe.

Some lathes, not surprisingly, are now being produced with built-in motors and solid-state, variable speed controls

10-8. Heavy-duty lathe is the dream tool of lathe enthusiasts. Features include built-in variable speed changer, indexing head, adjustable safety shield.

10-9. Dremel's Moto Lathe is at the other extreme, but it has all the features you need to produce small parts and projects. Special turning chisels are used.

10-10. The "unadorned" lathe is light and basic but can turn a 36″ spindle or swing a 12″ diameter piece on a faceplate.

(Figure 10-12). On this unit, you just turn a dial to get any speed between 800 and 2800 rpm. Typically, such a motorized unit is ready to go almost as soon as you remove it from its carton. About all you have to do is supply a sturdy stand to mount it on.

When you hear the term "gap bed," look for a machine that has a depressed area directly under the drive spindle (Figure 10-13). This provides more additional turning radius for faceplate mounted work than you would have if the ways were full-length.

Safety

If you judge the safe use of power tools on a scale of ten, the lathe would rank neither at one or ten. As usual, there are no built-in guarantees. The only way to work safely is to know you can be hurt and to behave accordingly. It sounds almost silly to say it, but ties are out as are any kind of jewelry, floppy sleeves and hanging shirttails. Wear safety goggles and, when you are doing sanding chores, a respirator.

Follow the rules concerning handling chisels and hand position on the tool rest. Be very careful with speeds, especially when doing roughing operations.

Work cautiously especially if you are a beginner. Trying to cut too fast or too deeply can throw up splinters and even cause the wood to be thrown from its mounting. Be sure the work is secure before you start cutting, and check frequently AS you work. Always spin the work by hand before you turn the machine on. Look for correct clearance between work and tool rest and, if the work is on a faceplate, between work and ways.

Keep lathe chisels sharp. Dull tools force you to apply excessive feed pressure, and they make no contribution to quality work.

10-11.   Counter shaft assembly is made specifically for the unadorned lathe. It provides a greater range of speeds than you can get from a direct motor-to-headstock pulley arrangement.

10-13.   Gap bed lathe has a depressed area directly under the headstock spindle. It provides more faceplate capacity than is available when the ways, or the bed, is full-length.

10-12.   Motorized lathe has a built-in power source and an infinitely variable solid-state speed control. You turn a dial to get any speed between 80 rpm and 2800 rpm.

10-14.   The points on the spur center (in the headstock) and the cup center (in the tailstock) should be aligned whether they are viewed from the front or from the top.

Adjustment. The one major lathe adjustment is alignment of the *spur center,* which is in the headstock, with the *cup center,* which is in the tailstock. How this is accomplished and maintained may vary from tool to tool, and you'll find instructions for doing it in the owner's manual. The important thing is for the points on the centers to meet when they are viewed from above (vertical alignment) and when they are viewed from the side (horizontal alignment) (Figure 10-14). Since the spur center has a fixed position, any necessary adjustments are made by moving the cup center.

Speeds. The basic rule is to use slow speeds for large work and fast speeds for small work. On all jobs speed changes should be made during the work. You'll notice in the accompanying speed chart (Figure 10-15) that the lowest speeds are suggested for roughing operations and that the rpm's move up as you get into the shaping stages. The high speeds are used for final cuts and for finishing. The exception occurs when you get to maximum-size workpieces. Actually, this restriction is more a safety factor than anything else.

You can get quite close to the suggested speeds if your lathe is equipped with a variable speed changer. In most cases, however, you'll be working with belts and will have to use specific speeds provided by the relationship between pulleys. Stay as close to the suggested speeds as you can. If you must (at least until you require good skills on the lathe), use a lower speed rather than a higher one.

At all times, let the action of the lathe and of the work be your best guide. If it's difficult to hold the chisel or if the work or the lathe vibrates excessively, it's a good sign that you are going too fast.

Centers. The drive center in the headstock has a point for centering the work plus spurs that dig into the wood. The spurs must always seat firmly in order for the wood to turn. It's a good idea to work on one of the spurs with a file, making a very small half-round shape or forming a bevel at one end. In doing this, if you ever have to remove a spindle turning from the lathe before it is complete, you'll be able to re-mate it with the spur center, placing it back in the original position.

The center in the tailstock can be plain or cupped. The cupped design is better simply because it provides more bearing surface and thus less chance for the mounting to loosen. With either one, you should check occasionally, especially on softwoods, and tighten the fit if necessary. Many craftsmen use a tiny drop of oil on the dead center as a lubricant. However, don't overdo it since the oil can stain the wood. Paste wax works fine but don't use too much of it; just polish the point on the center.

The best method is to use a ball-bearing live center in the tailstock. The point on this turns with the work and, therefore, eliminates the loosening and burning problems you can encounter with a dead center.

The various types of lathe centers are shown in Figure 10-16.

Faceplates. Faceplates come in different sizes, ranging from about 3″ up to 10″. They are always mounted in the headstock and make it possible to turn work that can't be mounted between centers. In this way you can do such work as bowls (Figure 10-17), trays, round boxes, and bases for spindles.

Screws are used to attach the work to the plate. The important consideration is to use screws that are heavy

MATERIAL AND DIAMETER	ROUGHING CUT Revolutions Per Minute	SHAPING CUT Revolutions Per Minute	FINISHING CUT Revolutions Per Minute
Wood up to 2″	910	2,590	4,250
Wood 2″ to 4″	810	2,375	3,380
Wood 4″ to 6″	650	1,825	2,375
Wood 6″ to 8″	650	1,200	1,825
Wood 8″ to 10″	650	910	1,025
Wood over 10″	650	650	650
Plastics up to 3″	2,200	3,125	3,875
Plastics over 3″	1,025	1,200	1,680
Non-ferrous metals up to 3″ (with carbide-tipped tools)	650	1,300	3,125

10-15. Use the speeds listed here as guides. The best rule is to judge on the basis of how the work is going. Excessive chatter and vibration usually indicate a speed that is too much for the job.

10-16. Various types of lathe centers. The top one, used in the tailstock, is a "live" center. Its point turns with the work and eliminates the friction that occurs with a "dead" center.

enough to provide security but not so long that they may cut into them when shaping the project.

The tool rest. The tool rest is an adjustable ledge on which you rest the chisel when you apply it to the work. It can be moved either laterally or vertically and will pivot so you have complete freedom of adjustment in relation to the work whether it is a spindle turning or a faceplate job.

The ideal position for the tool rest is about 1/8″ away from the work and about 1/8″ above the work centerline (Figure 10-18). It's a difficult position to maintain constantly unless you are doing work such as straight cylinders or tapers. Still, it's generally a good rule and should be remembered at least as a guide post.

Lathe chisels. A good set of chisels should include a *gouge,* a *skew,* a *squarenose,* a *parting tool,* a *spear point* and a *roundnose* (Figure 10-19). Perhaps the least important of these are the squarenose and the spear point. An ordinary butt chisel can be used in place of the squarenose; the skew, when placed on its side and used in a scraping action, will do many of the jobs performed by the spear point.

If you don't maintain a keen edge on the chisels, you'll be working under a handicap. Your best bet is to study the shape of the tool before you start using it. Keep a stone handy and, as you work, touch up the cutting edge occasionally. You'll find, if you do this, that *re-grinding* jobs, necessary when the chisel must be re-shaped, will be required very infrequently (Figures 10-20 and 10-21).

Carbide-tipped tools are available in various sizes but mostly in roundnose or squarenose shapes. The cutting edges are made of an extremely hard material that will hold sharpness much longer than steel. They can be used on

10-17.   Work that can't be mounted between centers is screw-attached to a faceplate. Always use screws that are heavy enough to hold the work securely. Check them occasionally as you work to be sure they don't loosen.

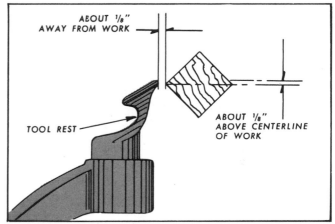

10-18.   This shows the ideal relationship between the tool rest and the work. You can't always work this way, but you should attempt to stay as close to it as possible.

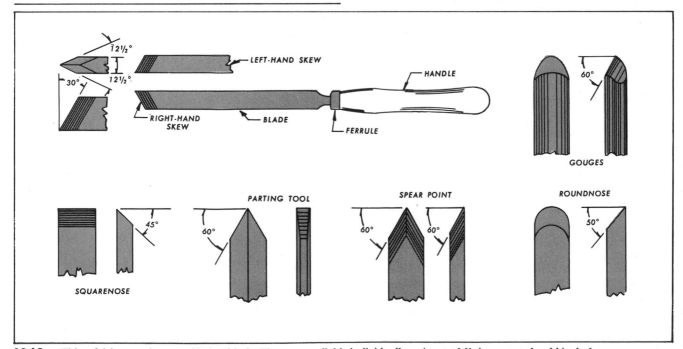

10-19.   This a fairly complete set of lathe chisels. They are available individually or in sets. Minimum set should include a gouge, a roundnose, a parting tool, and a skew.

10-20.   Maintaining a keen edge on the tools as you work is good practice. You'll do better work, faster, when chisels are sharp.

10-21.   Special stones are available for keeping a keen edge on a gouge.

metals have tips of tungsten-carbide. They hold a keen edge for a long time, but tips are brittle so they must be used and stored very carefully.

wood but, more importantly, they make it possible to do freehand turning on metals and plastics at woodworking speeds (Figure 10-22).

Hand positioning.   The basic rule is to hold the forward end of the chisel in your left hand, the handle in your right hand. Don't use your left hand like a fist. Instead, rest the tool toward the tips of the fingers with your thumb gripping against the side or on the top of the blade. Your index finger should rest comfortably on the tool-rest ledge (Figure 10-23).

When you are making a cut that is parallel to the work, the index finger acts as a depth gauge. Both hands and the chisel move as a unit. For many types of shaping cuts, view the contact point between the chisel and the tool rest as a pivot. This point is just about maintained as the right hand provides the cutting action. On many types of scraping cuts, the tool is held at right angles to the work and simply moved forward.

Always feed the chisel slowly and steadily; you don't want to force it and you don't want to jab it into the work. Make the initial contact cautiously; then get a little bolder as you cut. You don't want to overdo it, but on the other hand, just rubbing the tool against the wood won't get you anywhere.

It's a good idea to keep tools so they are behind you or to one side to avoid reaching over the lathe. Don't check work for roundness with your fingers, especially on roughing jobs. Stop the lathe to check or rest the blade of the tool lightly on the turning wood. You can tell by vibration of the tool whether the work is approaching roundness.

Three actions of lathe chisels.   Lathe chisels scrape, cut, or shear.

Scraping is the easiest and safest of the three and the best for the beginner to use. All the tools can be used in such fashion but the technique, even by professionals, is most applicable to the roundnose, the parting tool, the squarenose and the spear point.

The action gives good results and minimizes the chances of gouging. The idea is to place the tool on a horizontal plane and to advance it slowly into the work. The cut

10-23.   This is a good way to hold lathe chisels. The index finger of the left hand bears against the ledge on the tool rest. Grip the chisel firmly, but don't try to "muscle" it.

that is made is the reverse of the chisel shape. For example, a roundnose tool will produce a cove. The cove size is not limited to the chisel size. You can, as you penetrate, pivot the cutting edge in a uniform arc. This has to produce a cove that is broader in its radius than a straight feed would produce.

The scraping action is not limited to shaping. The gouge for roughing (bringing square work to round) can be used in similar fashion. What you do is advance the gouge until it is making a slight cut (from 1/16" to 1/8"); then, while maintaining the penetration, move the cutting edge parallel to the work. Repeat this until the work has come to full round.

When you do a straight scraping action with a spear point, you get a V-shape; with the parting tool, you get a groove. A squarenose, depending on the number of cuts you do, will produce a fillet or a band.

You can work a bit faster if you start the scraping action of the tool with a point just a bit below the work centerline and move it upward as you move it forward.

You will never get as smooth a finish with a scraping action as you will with a shearing action, but all you need do to bring the work to par is apply sandpaper.

As you can see in Figure 10-24, the cutting action calls for bringing the tool edge up by lowering the handle of the chisel. The edge of the tool will remove material in much the same way that a hand plane cuts the edge of a board. This is a situation where it's easy to "dig" the tool so, more than elsewhere, keep the feed light and make the cut slowly. Jabbing the chisel in suddenly or too deeply can wrench it from your hands. It's also possible to ruin the work by lifting large chunks of it.

The cutting action is something you should try after you have done enough with the scraping action to be really familiar with each of the tools. When you first try it, be cautious. Don't become bold until after you have done enough practicing to build up your confidence. A good cutting action should produce a finish that requires little touchup. This can vary from wood to wood. A grainy species will not impress so much and will require sanding even after a professional cutting action.

The shearing action can separate the expert from the amateur, not in terms of ultimate quality but in production speed. It's done best with the gouge and the skew.

It's an action that requires the tool edge to be moved laterally. It takes a consistent bite, removing a layer of

SCRAPING ACTION

CHISEL

TOOL REST

WORK

CUTTING ACTION

SHEARING ACTION

10-24.   The three chisel actions. The scraping action is best to start with but you should progress to the more advanced techniques as you go along.

ARROWS INDICATE TOOL MOVEMENT

A. SHAPING A COVE (SCRAPING ACTION)
B. SHAPING COVE (CUTTING ACTION)
C. SMOOTHING A CYLINDER
D. CUTTING AWAY STOCK BETWEEN
    SHOULDERS

E   ROUGHING
F. FORMING
G. SMALL COVES (DETERMINED
    BY SIZE OF TOOL—SCRAPING)

10-25.   Typical applications of the gouge. It's the best tool to use for roughing cuts; for example, bringing square stock to round.

wood from the surface of the stock. This varies, of course, since manipulation of the chisel in a shearing action is relative to the shape you must produce.

When first trying this technique, do it with a gouge on a roughing operation. Here, the tool is held almost on edge with your thumb behind it to keep it steady and to feed.

While each lathe chisel will do a category of jobs best, the overlap is so great that it's foolish to try to establish hard-and-fast rules. The tools work differently but the action you use, the feed angle, the cut direction, etc. are what influence the shape you get. A squarenose chisel or a spear point can produce a quality bead even though the skew might be the best tool to use for the job. The parting tool is basically for dimensional cuts, yet it is also very fine for shoulders, cleaning out corners and the like.

Practice a bit with each chisel trying to duplicate the shapes that will be described. Get the "feel" of each tool. Don't be surprised if you develop handling techniques that are "you," a kind of trademark.

Applications

The gouge.   This is a very versatile tool and may be used in any one of the three positions (Figure 10-25). Actually, in some applications, all three of the cutting actions come into play. It's the best tool to use for roughing operations. The scraping action works well enough, but you should try to graduate to the shearing action quickly. Here, the tool is held almost on its side and moved parallel to the work. The depth of cut is maintained by the index finger of the left hand as it rests on the ledge of the tool rest (Figure 10-26).

Start roughing cuts somewhere along the length of the stock and direct feed toward an end. Move the tool rest laterally until you've done the same cut along the full length

of the stock. Then readjust it to bring it closer to the work and repeat the procedure until you have the diameter you need.

This is approximately the routine to follow when you wish to reduce stock in a limited area. Just use the gouge between sizing cuts made with the parting tool.

Overall, the gouge is probably the best tool to use when you need to remove a lot of material. It is not a good tool to use on faceplate work.

The skew.   The skew can be used in any one of the three actions (Figure 10-27). Typically, to scrape, place the tool on a side while you hold it at right angles to the work and then move it directly forward. The result will be a half-V. Flip the chisel and repeat, and you will get a full-V.

10-26.   The gouge is placed almost on edge when it is used to shear. Be reasonably cautious when you work. It's better to go over the work several times instead of trying to remove a lot of material with a single cut.

ARROWS INDICATE TOOL MOVEMENT

A. FORMING AND SMOOTHING A TAPER   E. SQUARING ENDS OF STOCK
B. TRIMMING ENDS   F. CUTTING TO LENGTH
C. SQUARING A SHOULDER   G. FORMING BEADS
D. V CUTS (ALSO WITH HEEL OF TOOL) H. SMOOTHING A CYLINDER

10-27.   Typical applications of the skew. It can produce surfaces that require little sanding, but it takes a little practice to master skew-technique.

You can demonstrate a typical cutting action by holding the tool on its edge and then moving it forward. In this position the tool presents a sharp point to the work. It cuts fast and will leave a smooth finish. When you do this on the end of a cylinder or to square a shoulder, it's best to hold the chisel at a slight angle so that one of the bevels on the cutting edge will be flush against the work. When you work in this manner, you'll be using more than the point of the cutting edge.

Probably the smoothest cut you can make in lathe work is with the skew in a shearing action, but it's one of the toughest to master (Figure 10-28). Overall, you should picture the cutting point as being near the center of the edge of the chisel and high on the work. You can start by placing a bevel of the cutting edge flat on the work so no cutting occurs; tilt slightly until the edge begins to penetrate. Then move the tool in parallel fashion. Don't try to cut too deeply or to feed too fast.

The skew is often used to do ball shapes and beads. This advanced technique is best started by resting the heel of the cutting edge on the centerline of the form and then rotating the chisel in a 45° arc. Since you won't be able to

10-28.   Best results with the skew are obtained with a shearing cut. You'll become professional with it in faster times if you keep its edge keen enough to shave with.

THE ROUND NOSE TOOL IS ALWAYS USED IN A SCRAPING ACTION AND IS USED ON ANY CONCAVE SHAPE

ARROWS INDICATE DIRECTION OF TOOL MOVEMENT,

A. FORMING   B. SMALL COVES   C. LARGE COVES   D. HOLLOWING

10-29.   Typical applications of the roundnose chisel.

10-30.   The roundnose chisel is always used in a scraping action. When you move it directly forward, you form a cove. For a cove that is greater than the width of the chisel, use a pivoting action.

10-31.   The bulk of faceplate turning is done with a roundnose chisel. When doing inside contours, situate the tool rest to provide maximum support for the chisel close to the cutting area.

achieve the full shape in one pass, you must imagine the final shape and direct the chisel along lines that, when repeated enough times, will result in the form you want.

The skew is not the tool to use on faceplate work until you limit it to a scraping action.

The roundnose. This is a very easy chisel to use simply because it is always used in a scraping action (Figure 10-29). To do a cove, just move the chisel directly forward (Figure 10-30). To enlarge the cove, combine a pivoting action with the forward feed. The sharper the tool, the faster you will cut and the smoother the results will be.

The roundnose is a very fine tool for faceplate work, especially when you are doing a hollowing operation. This occurs when you are forming a bowl or doing a round box. The point to remember is to situate the tool rest to provide maximum support for the chisel near the cutting edge even if it means the rest has to be situated inside the hollow being formed (Figure 10-31).

The parting tool. The parting tool is always used in a scraping action with the blade resting on an edge and with the feed action directly forward (Figure 10-32). The operation will go faster if you start with the handle a bit below the

tool rest and raise it gradually as the cutting edge penetrates. You can also do it the other way: start with the handle on the high side and lower it as you go.

Quite often, the parting tool is held in one hand while the other hand grips outside calipers that ride the groove being formed. In this way, you'll know when you have reached the penetration you want on dimensional cuts.

When the cut is very deep, make slight clearance cuts on each side of the main groove to provide room for the body of the blade and thus prevent burning (Figures 10-33 and 10-34).

The squarenose. Beginners will find the squarenose a very easy tool to handle. Keep it sharp, use it in a scraping action and feed it slowly, but steadily (Figure 10-35). When you move it directly forward, you form a fillet that matches the width of the chisel. Move it parallel to the work and you get a smoothing action. Feed it at an angle and you can form V's. Also, it's a very practical touchup tool for such operations as cleaning shoulders and smoothing convex forms.

Ordinary butt chisels can be used in place of the squarenose (Figure 10-36). If you are equipped with a set,

SIZING CUTS AND GROOVES

SHOULDERS

ARROWS INDICATE DIRECTION OF MOVEMENT

CUTTING V'S

CUTTING V ON TAPER WHERE OTHER TOOLS MAY NOT FIT

CLEANING ENDS

10-32.   Typical applications of a parting tool.

DIAMETER OF SHAPE BEING TURNED IS DETERMINED BY DEPTH OF SIZING CUTS

10-33.   One way to do sizing cuts with the parting tool. The cut will be smoother if you start with the tool handle below the tool rest and swing it up slowly as you cut. It's mostly a scraping action.

10-34.   Cutting with the parting tool to a depth that is gauged with outside calipers. Be sure there is enough room in the groove for the calipers. Don't force either the cut or the measuring tool.

ARROWS INDICATE TOOL MOVEMENT

A. SMOOTHING   E. FORMING V
B. SQUARING A SHOULDER   F. FORMING RECESSES—BANDS
C. FORMING A SHORT TAPER   G. FORMING SMALL SHOULDER ON COVE
D. SMOOTHING CONVEX SURFACE (BEADS)

10-35.   Typical applications of a squarenose tool.

you'll be well organized for this aspect of lathe work. You can choose a chisel width that is best for the job on hand. Use the widest chisel for smoothing jobs; use the narrowest one for touchup work such as cleaning shoulders.

The spear point.   Often called a "diamond" point, the spear point is handy because its sharp point can produce clean lines, edges and corners. While it can be used to form V's and chamfers, mark dimensional lines, even do smoothing, it is most valuable for touchup applications. Your best bet is to limit its action strictly to scraping (Figures 10-37 and 10-38).

10-36.   Ordinary butt chisels can be used like a squarenose lathe tool. Keep the bevel side down and use a scraping action.

ARROWS INDICATE DIRECTION OF TOOL MOVEMENT

A. SQUARING (TRIM CUTS ONLY)   D. CLEANING CORNERS
B. SMOOTHING   E. SLIGHT CHAMFERING
C. FORMING V's   F. MARKING DIMENSION POINTS

10-37.   Typical applications of the spear point.

10-38.   The spear point is a good tool for touch-up work—cleaning out corners and such. Work with the bevel side of the chisel pointing down.

10-39.   With carbide-tipped tools, you can shape metals and plastics at woodworking-lathe speeds. They are nice to use on small jobs, even in wood.

The carbides.   Carbide-tipped chisels, while they can be used on wood, are nice to have mostly because they allow you to work on materials like metal and plastics at woodworking-lathe speeds (Figure 10-39). Most times, slow speeds are best, especially on hard materials. Waste should come off cleanly. Should the work begin to chatter or if you find you are getting a ridged surface instead of a smooth cut, it's a pretty good indication that the work is turning too fast, that you are feeding the tool too fast, or that you are trying to remove too much material in one bite.

The angle of the tool can help you do a better job with carbides. For wood and plastics, the tool handle should be slightly below the tool rest. For steel, keep it about level; for non ferrous metals, raise it (Figure 10-40).

Tungsten carbide is very hard and will hold a keen edge for a long time, but it is quite brittle. Be sure that the cutting edges are protected; avoid banging them against hard surfaces.

Molding Knives as Chisels

If you own a molding head (used on a table saw or radial arm saw) and an assortment of knives, you can have a lot of practical fun and do some fine work simply by making a handle for the knives so they can be used like lathe chisels. In fact, this technique is so intriguing that it pays to buy a few molding knives for the purpose even if you don't have the machines they are ordinarily used on.

There are various ways you can work to supply a handle. The design shown in Figures 10-41 and 10-42 works fine and isn't difficult to assemble. Other methods include riveting or bolting together two strips of 1/8″ thick (or heavier) aluminum or steel, or welding a short length of flat steel to a "handle" of steel tubing. In all cases, the design must provide for a flat area at one end to which the molding knife can be bolted securely.

The knives are always applied with a scraping action and with minimum feed pressure (Figure 10-43). In some cases, where the shape you want is large and there is much material to remove from adjacent areas, it pays to remove

TURNING WOOD AND PLASTIC   TURNING STEEL   TURNING NON-FERROUS METALS   FACE PLATE TURNING

10-40.   How to hold carbide-tipped tools in relation to the kind of material you are cutting. These are good suggestions to start with, but the best guide is how the tool is cutting. Start at slow speeds, especially on hard materials.

the bulk of the waste with conventional chisels and then do the detailing with a molding knife (Figure 10-44).

The idea will work on softwoods or hardwoods, but be especially careful on soft species. You will not get good results by forcing the cuts. The wood should scrape away in a fine dust. Working so fast that you lift chips is not good practice; in fact, you will ruin fine detail.

It's a good idea to practice a bit on a scrap turning. Use a slow speed to start and move the knife directly forward. As it begins to cut, add a slight up-and-down action to the handle as you continue to penetrate. As you can see in Figure 10-45, you can accomplish some fairly professional detail work in this fashion.

Designing ideas.   The worst thing you can do, unless you are just experimenting with chisels, is to start

10-43.   You can do some very detailed work with molding knives if you use a scraping action and don't try to rush. This handle is two pieces of aluminum bar stock, riveted together.

10-41.   One way to make a handle so you can use molding knives as lathe chisels.

10-44.   The larger the knife you are using, or the larger the shape you are forming, the slower the feed. You can help the scraping action by combining it with a slight up-and-down motion.

10-42.   How the handle for molding knives is assembled. The wooden parts are held together with woodscrews that pass through holes in the metal bar stock.

10-45.   The shape you get will, of course, depend on the knife you use. Hold the handle very firmly to reduce vibration. Molding knives come in sets of three, so change frequently to avoid wearing one knife more than the others.

work on a lathe turning without any idea of what the result will be. Like the sculptor and his stone, you must visualize what is in the wood (Figure 10-46). Your best bet is to do this on paper by first drawing a centerline and then combining classic forms to produce a good design.

Those same molding knives previously suggested for cutting are ready-made patterns for layout work. All you have to do is trace around them (Figure 10-47). If you don't

10-46. You must have a good idea of what the finished part will be before you start cutting. Think like a sculptor.

10-47. Molding knives are excellent, ready-made patterns for planning the shape of turnings.

own molding knives, you can probably find full-size profiles in tool manufacturers' catalogs. You can cut these out and mount them on cardboard. Study the classic forms shown in Figure 10-48. No matter what turning you study, you'll find that these forms supply the bulk of the design.

Another good idea is to study the profiles of standard moldings. These too are based on classic forms. It's not a bad idea to amass an assortment of slim cross-sections cut from moldings you can buy in any lumberyard. The catalog of a picture frame supply house will include such profiles in sketch form. So equipped, you will have no problem designing the project before you mount the stock in the machine. If the design looks good on paper, so will the final product. Remember that just covering the full length of a turning with detail after detail seldom results in an item you will want to live with.

You don't have to do the drawings "in the round." If you work on a centerline and do a half profile, you'll know what the turning will look like (Figure 10-49). Also, the drawings can be transferred to cardboard, or drawn directly

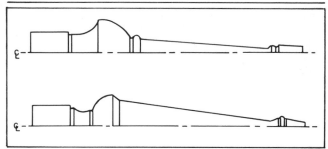

10-49. Patterns do not have to be drawn full-round. Doing a half-profile on a centerline is a good way to operate. When patterns like this are cut out, they can be used as checking templates.

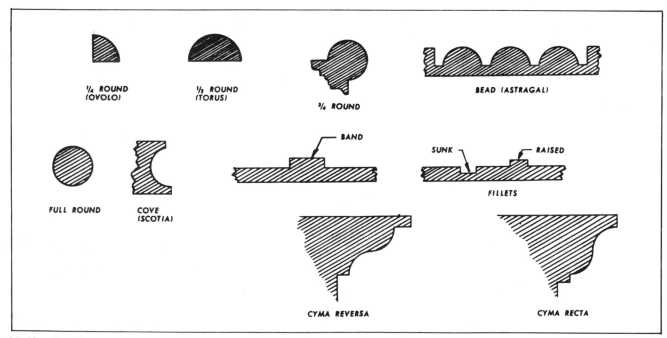

10-48. Examine any project that has been turned in a lathe and you'll find many of these classic forms.

on cardboard so that when cut out, they can be used as templates for checking the work as you go. Templates make much sense when you have duplicates to make.

Spindle Turning

Spindle turning is done with the work mounted accurately and firmly between the lathe's centers. On most lathes, the adjustment to accommodate the length of the stock is made by moving the tailstock. Being careful with this first step, mount the stock properly to minimize the vibration that can occur when raw stock starts to spin (Figure 10-50).

Mounting the work. Before you mount the work

10-50. Spindle turning will go smoother if you are careful about locating the centers at each end of the stock. Accurate placement at each end will reduce vibration during initial roughing cuts.

10-51. Various methods that can be used to locate center points on materials of different shapes.

10-52. This is how you can make a center-finder. The tool can be used on square stock as well as round pieces.

10-53. Another type of center-finder you can make. The work is placed within the closest matching circle and marked by using an awl through the tool's center-hole.

in the lathe, you must find the center of the stock at each end. If the stock is square, all you have to do is draw intersecting diagonals at each end. The point at which they cross gives you the center. When the work is not square, use the following trick. With a pair of dividers or a compass, draw lines parallel to each edge of the material. Then, the center will be confined to an area small enough so that you can judge its location with reasonable accuracy (Figure 10-51).

A center-finder does an accurate job of locating the centers on round stock. It's possible you may already have on hand a V-shaped attachment that fits the blade of a combination square. If not, make a special tool like the one shown in the accompanying sketch and make it accurately. To use it, place the stock in the V and draw a line along the edge of the guide. Turn the stock about 45° and draw a second line. The center is where the lines intersect. Note that the center-finder is usable on square stock as well as round (Figure 10-52).

Another type of center-finder you can make is shown in Figure 10-53. This is a disc of rigid plastic with concentric circles scribed into its surface. After the disc is placed so the work is in the closest matching circle, an awl is used to mark through the tool's center-hole.

When the wood is soft, you can use an awl to indent points for the centers. This is all you need at the tailstock end. The spur center in the headstock must be seated firmly. You can accomplish this by removing the spur center from

the lathe and tapping it in place in the work with a mallet (Figure 10-54). Don't use a steel hammer. If the wood is quite hard, take the time to make shallow saw kerfs on the lines you have drawn to find the center.

To situate the work in the lathe, place it firmly against the spur center and lock the tailstock in place about 1″ away from the opposite end. Then use the tailstock ram to bring the cup center into position. This should be done with some firmness while you rotate the work *by hand*. Both the point and the perimeter of the cup must be in contact with the work. Often, this setting will loosen during prolonged periods of turning and when the wood is soft, so it should be checked frequently. A spot of wax, if you are using a dead center, will help reduce friction. If you use a live center, which has a point and cup mounted on a bearing so that it turns with the work, you'll minimize if not eliminate any problems that might occur (Figure 10-55).

Some turners, when working with very soft wood, use the trick that is shown in Figure 10-56. A furniture glide,

10-55. A live center may have just a point or, like this one, may also have a cup. Both the point and the cup should be in contact with the work.

10-56. A lathe-worker's trick—using an indented furniture glide at the tailstock end. Another idea is to nail on a small hardwood block. This kind of thing is not necessary when you work with a live center.

10-54. The spur center must be seated firmly. Use a soft-faced mallet to tap it in place. On hardwoods, saw shallow grooves that intersect at the center of the work.

with its center indented with a punch, is used for the center-to-work contact. The glide can bear up under a lot of turning, but since you now have a metal-to-metal contact, you should keep the area lubricated with either oil or wax. Another idea is to nail a small block of hardwood to that end of the work.

Whenever possible, reduce the size of the work before you mount it in the lathe. For example, if you are to turn a square to round, remove the corners of the workpiece by sawing. This will reduce considerably the amount of preliminary cutting you must do with lathe chisels.

Layout.   After the stock has been turned down to the point where you are ready for actual forming, it should be marked to define particular areas. A simple way to do this is to use a ruler on the tool rest with the work turning at slow speed. Mark the dimension points with a pencil (Figure 10-57).

You can work in similar fashion with a flexible tape but with the work stationary. Make your dimension points about 1/2″ long. When you turn on the machine, the marks will be visible enough so you can hold a pencil against the turning stock to complete the line.

When you have duplicate pieces to form, it pays to make a marking gauge like the one shown in Figure 10-58.

This gauge is a piece of wood with brads driven into one edge. You hold it against the turning stock and the brads mark the dimension points. This method is good to use for simple turnings.

For more complex turnings, you should make a full-size cardboard template of the project. The template (Figure 10-59) provides a profile for checking the shape of the work as you go. The centerline, straight edge can be used for marking dimension points.

A trick you can use to make a turning to replace a broken part is to use the part itself as a template. Slice the part down the center on a bandsaw or with a handsaw to give you an accurate profile of the part you must shape. Place this on the stock and trace around it. Then, as shown in Figure 10-60, use a saw to cut into an adjacent side for dimension lines that match the profile. Cut to the full depth of each design feature; make kerfs on outer sides of all beads and other raised elements. You can then proceed with the turning, working first to clean out stock between designs and then to shape the details.

10-57. Using a ruler and a pencil to mark dimension lines on a spindle.

10-59. A profile template serves two purposes.

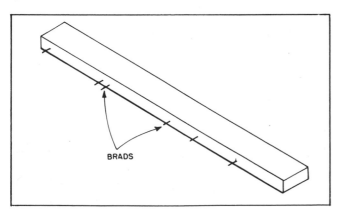

10-58. A marking gauge is a good idea when you have many similar pieces to produce. The brads mark the dimension points when the tool is held against the stock.

10-60. With the profile marked on the work, you can use a saw to establish dimension lines that can be used as guides for depth of cut.

Slender work. Long, slender spindles require the support of a steady rest to keep the work from whipping and to avoid deflection under cutting pressure. Accessories to provide this support are available, but you can make a suitable one for yourself. This support is a V-block mounted on a platform that you can clamp to the lathe bed. Size the vertical block so the center of the V is on the work centerline. Situate it as you go so the work is supported near the area where you are cutting.

Long work. No matter what the capacity of your machine, there is a limit to spindle lengths you can mount. For pieces longer than this limit, you simply turn separate parts and then join them. You can do this by drilling holes in the mating ends and then using a dowel between them. Or you can form a tenon right in the lathe on the end of one of the pieces and drill a hole in the other. More about how to drill the holes will be given later.

Sanding. Final finishing is done by using sandpaper while the part is turning in the lathe. The normal sanding procedure which calls for a progression through finer grits should not be regarded as a hard-and-fast rule. There is no point starting with a very coarse paper if the turning is quite smooth to begin with. In most cases, the medium-grit paper will do, and even this should be used cautiously around small details.

For straight cylinders, long tapers and similar areas, the sandpaper can be wrapped around a smooth piece of wood. Another way is to hold a strip of sandpaper between your hands and to use it like a shoe-polishing cloth.

A sanding disc is a good tool for smoothing cylinders and tapers (Figure 10-61). Keep a firm grip on it and don't force the cutting action. Keep the disc moving smoothly along the full length of the project.

A good way to get an extremely fine finish is to work with sandpaper until the wood is as smooth as possible. Then dampen the work with a line-free cloth; but don't soak it. After it has dried, use fine steel wool to do the final smoothing. You can get a burnished finish if you use a slim, almost flexible strip of wood as if it were sandpaper. The wood-to-wood contact produces a smoothness and a gloss that is difficult to duplicate with other methods.

Using non-lathe tools. We suggested using mold-

10-61. A sanding disc is a good tool to use for smoothing cylinders and tapers. Apply light pressure, and keep the disc moving. If you get a lot of chatter when you do this, you'll know the work is not full-round.

10-63. A round file can be used for detail work but use those with a heavy cut. Keep the file moving, and clean it frequently with a wire brush.

10-62. A Stanley Surform rasp can cut away material pretty quickly, but don't consider it a "smoothing" tool. Move the rasp against the work's direction of rotation. Keep a firm grip, but don't apply a lot of pressure.

10-64. A hand plane can be used to remove stock when the work is cylindrical. Hold the plane at an angle and keep it moving longitudinally. A very light cut is essential.

ing knives as "shapers" for lathe work. We further suggest that it's possible to use other types of shop tools to speed up or to make easier, some particular lathe applications. The point is, no law says you must do everything with lathe chisels. Some of the ideas we've tested were done with items like wood rasps or files, rotary rasps in a portable drill, hand planes, Surform tools, and so on. Figures 10-62 through 10-64 are demonstrations of some of the "off-beat" methods we've used. Don't be a purist and shy away from this aspect of lathe work. In the final analysis, it's what you produce that counts—not how you got there.

Duplicating

One of the aspects of lathe work is that you often need many similar pieces. If you are making a table that has turned legs, you need four pieces that are alike. On the other extreme, if you are making a crib or a cradle with spindle sides, you may need several dozen duplicates. You can, of course, work in routine fashion and rely on your own expertise to produce the pieces, but there is another way to go. Many manufacturers of lathes supply, as accessories, special pieces of equipment that allow you to produce duplicates with a minimum of fuss.

Basically, such an attachment supplies a cutting tool that can be organized to follow a profile template that is clamped, or otherwise attached to a platform. A guide on the handle of the cutting tool follows the outline of the template, and the cutter shapes the work to match. Figures 10-65 and 10-66 show how such a system works. Since there are considerable differences among duplicators, you must follow the supplier's instructions implicitly in order to work professionally.

Faceplate Work

Not all lathe projects can be accomplished by mounting the work between centers. Items like bases, round trays, short candlesticks, wheels, bowls, and so on are produced while they are mounted on a faceplate. The faceplate, which may be attached in a way that is peculiar to the machine you have, is secured to the headstock end of the tool (Figure 10-67).

10-65. There are various types of lathe duplicators available. They work in various ways, but essentially, a special cutter is guided by a template. Accessories like this are handy when you must shape duplicate pieces.

10-67. Faceplate turning is the way to go when you need trays, bowls, bases, and the like. Use a roundnose tool for the bulk of the shaping, other chisels for details. Here, a parting tool is used to form a groove.

10-66. For straight cuts, the guide is just a straight strip of wood. It's a good idea to remove the bulk of the waste material in normal fashion before you use the duplicator.

10-68. Scribe a circle that is a bit larger than the diameter of the faceplate. This makes it easier to center the faceplate on the work.

10-69. Use heavy screws to attach the faceplate. Be sure they are not so long that you will cut into them when doing the turning. There are special mounting methods to use when the work is too thin for screw-attachment. Always saw off as much waste stock as you can before you do the turning.

10-70. An ordinary marking gauge may be used to mark lines on a perimeter. Turn the work by hand.

Mounting the work. Draw lines from corner to corner on the square stock and from the intersection scribe a circle that is just a fraction larger than the diameter of the faceplate (Figure 10-68). After that, draw a second circle as a guide for rough cutting the blank stock to round on the bandsaw or jigsaw. The least you should do is remove as much of the waste as possible with straight saw cuts.

Use screws to fasten the faceplate to the turning block, but be sure to choose a size that will not interfere with chisel work (Figure 10-69). The general rule is to use the longest, heaviest screw. This you must do in line with the base thickness of the finished project.

After you have mounted the work in the machine, spin it by hand to be sure you have clearance between the blank and the lathe bed.

Templates and marking. To find the center, turn the work slowly with a pencil resting on the tool rest. Touch the work lightly with the point and then move slowly toward the center. This will quickly reveal the midpoint of the mounted work.

To scribe a circular dimension line, you can use dividers or a compass. Don't dig the dividers in either the center point or where you are scribing; a light touch is sufficient. To mark the perimeter after you have turned the work to full-round, you can use an ordinary marking gauge; or you can do the job simply with your fingers holding a pencil. In this case, your fingers would act as an edge gauge. This kind of marking can be done while you are turning the work by hand (Figure 10-70).

Templates, like those described for spindle turning, are just as useful on faceplate work, especially if you must turn out more than one piece of the same design. Make the template so it has a profile side and a straight edge. Carry the main detail points of the design across to the straight edge, and you will have a single template that will serve for marking dimension lines and for checking the shape as you work (Figure 10-71).

ONE SIDE FOR MARKING DIMENSIONS

OTHER SIDE FOR CHECKING PROFILE

WORK

TEMPLATE

10-71. A profile template can do double duty on faceplate work as well as on spindle turnings.

Depth gauge. You can easily make the depth gauge shown in Figure 10-72. It's nothing but a hardwood block through which you pass a dowel. The lockscrew will work if you just drill an undersize hole for the screw to be used. Put a drop of oil on the screw and drive it home so it will form its own threads. This gauge is useful for checking the depth of items such as bowls and round boxes.

Chisel technique. This technique doesn't differ too much from spindle turning, but you should use a scraping action exclusively. The tool rest may be situated in front of the work, at the edge, behind it, even inside it. Be sure at all times that the tool-rest-to-work relationship provides maximum support for the chisel close to where you are cutting (Figure 10-73).

You'll find the roundnose a very useful tool, especially for the bulk of the waste-removal chore. Work will go faster if you set the tool rest for the point of the chisel that is on the work centerline and if you drop the handle a little below the tool rest. Don't use the gouge or the skew, although it is not out of line to work with the latter if you limit the application, for example, to cutting lines with the point or cleaning out shoulders.

A faceplate-mounted, heavy block of wood can cause considerable vibration so start at lowest speeds. Speed up only as you lighten the load by removing waste and only as long as you don't cause excessive vibration. Typical faceplate turnings require more time than spindle work simply because a lot of material must be removed before you get to the actual shaping. Therefore, patience is in order. Rushing the job can cause you to jab in the chisels, which can only do more harm than good.

Joining work. Quite often, it's necessa. · to join a spindle turning to a base that you form on the .aceplate. Your best bet here is to plan on drilling a center hole in the base and form an integral tenon on the spindle. Actually, you can drill a hole in each part and join them with a dowel. More about drilling will be given later (See Figures 10-74 and 10-75).

Thin work. When work is too thin to mount on a faceplate, you can often get the job done by putting the blank on a nut and bolt that you then grip in a lathe-

10-73. You'll find a scraping action with a roundnose tool the handiest technique for faceplate work. Always situate the tool rest to supply maximum support for the chisel where it is working.

10-74. When shaping parts that must be joined, you can form an integral tenon as part of the joint. Size it for a slip fit. Having to bang it into place is not good practice.

10-72. An easy-to-make gauge will let you judge the depth of faceplate turnings. It's especially useful on jobs that require deep cutting; for example, a round box.

10-75. The tenon idea is good when you must join a spindle turning with a part made on the faceplate. The wedge is optional but provides a lot of additional strength.

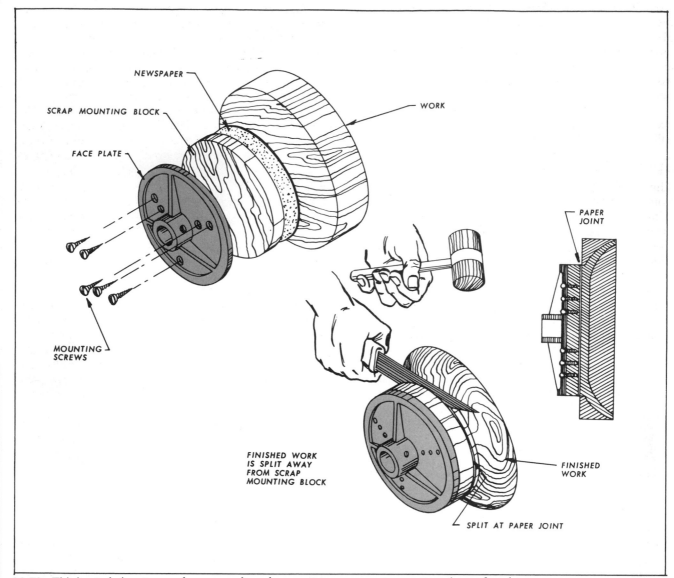

NEWSPAPER

SCRAP MOUNTING BLOCK

FACE PLATE

WORK

MOUNTING SCREWS

PAPER JOINT

FINISHED WORK IS SPLIT AWAY FROM SCRAP MOUNTING BLOCK

FINISHED WORK

SPLIT AT PAPER JOINT

10-76. This is a technique to use when you can't or choose not to use screws to mount work on a faceplate.

10-77. A deep bowl from a flat board is the result when bevel-cut rings are joined together. It's a practical idea for lathe work but it starts with a jigsaw operation. The chapter on the jigsaw explains how bevel-cutting is done.

10-78. A screw-center is used to mount work that is too small for spindle turning or to put on a faceplate. Be sure that the screw fits tightly and that the bottom of the workpiece is flat.

mounted chuck. When this procedure is not practical, glue the work to a piece of scrap that is thick enough to be face-plate-mounted. If you use ordinary newspaper between the pieces, you'll find they are not too difficult to split apart after you have done the forming. This method will also work when you don't want screw holes to show in the bottom of the project. (Figure 10-76).

Another idea, if a couple of screw holes in the part you need are acceptable, is to simply screw-attach the piece you will work on to a faceplate-mounted piece of scrap.

Special Techniques

The drinking cup trick.   You can make a deep bowl from a thin board by using the old idea of the collapsible drinking cup. If you jigsaw a disc in the center of a board, the disc will drop through when you have finished cutting. However, if you do the same thing but with the machine table tilted about five degrees, the cut will be a bevel and the disc will fall only part way. If you do this with a series of concentric cuts, each ring will jam into the next one and the end result will be a cone shape. The more rings, the deeper the cone will be. When these are glued together, you mount them like any piece of faceplate work and then do the turning (Figure 10-77). The turning, of course, is lathe work; check the jigsaw chapter for a detailed explanation of how the beveling is done.

10-79. Lathe-chisel handling techniques don't differ too much just because the work is small and mounted on a screw-center. However, a more delicate touch does help.

The screw-center.   Jobs that are too small for spindle turning and not practical for mounting on a face-plate can often be done on a screw-center. This is the method to use for finials, round drawer pulls, and the like.

The screw-center is a special accessory that mounts on the spindle like any other attachment. Find the center of the work as you would for any other job. Use an awl in soft-wood or drill in hardwood so you can seat the screw. The screw should fit tightly, especially if the part will require considerable turning. One trick is to cement a piece of sand-paper to the face of the screw-center to increase the grip (Figures 10-78 and 10-79).

Built-up sections.   There are many lathe jobs that require a large diameter in a limited area of the work. Aside from using a large enough blank to begin with, which really produces a lot of waste, there are two methods you can use to facilitate such work. In one, you can use another wood-working tool such as the bandsaw or the jointer to reduce the stock in particular areas. In the other, you can add wood by gluing in those areas that require it.

The glue-on chore must be done with some precision. The joint should be invisible after the turning is complete. Unless you deliberately plan otherwise, the grain pattern and direction should be compatible. Getting these results calls for discernment, as well as a good glue job. Be sure that mating surfaces are flat and true before you apply the glue and the clamps. Don't rush; let the glue dry thoroughly before you mount the work in the machine.

This kind of thinking applies to faceplate work as well as spindles. To build up a thick blank, you can glue thin pieces together. To facilitate the removal of waste in the lathe, the glued-on pieces can be rings that you precut on a jigsaw or even with a saber saw. If the project is to have sloping sides, play along with it by cutting rings of increasingly smaller diameter.

An interesting lathe procedure is to glue together blanks of contrasting woods. These can be simple or complex. They don't look like much in the rough form following the glue job, but after the turning they become intriguing inlaid projects (Figures 10-80 and 10-81).

Select wood for this technique to produce good contrast and, less importantly, similarity in degree of hardness. To experiment, try combining rosewood and maple, redwood and pine, birch and cherry, holly and walnut. Once

10-80. You can achieve fascinating results when you combine contrasting woods to build up lathe blanks. The gluing job usually takes more time than the turning.

10-81. Constructing lathe blanks by combining contrasting woods applies to faceplate work as well as spindle turning. A bowl has a lovely character when the technique is used. You must do a perfect job of gluing the pieces together.

10-82. Identical half-rounds are produced by halving a turned piece or by joining two separate pieces to begin with.

10-83. Two pieces for a split turning can be joined by using nails at end, waste areas or by using paper in a glue joint, or even with corrugated fasteners as shown here. Drive the fasteners flush— even though we've allowed them to project here. The mating surfaces of the two pieces must be *flat*.

you've tried it, you'll realize the technique's potential. Often, the preliminary gluing job to build up the blank can take up more time than the actual turning.

Split turnings.   A common split turning is one that is halved after the piece is shaped to produce two identical half-columns (Figure 10-82). This can be accomplished with solid stock by cutting on the bandsaw after the turning is complete, or you can work with the paper-glue joint that has already been described.

Another way is to make the blank by joining two similar pieces without using glue. This you can do by nailing the parts together at the extreme ends in areas that you know will be waste, even by using corrugated fasteners at each end of the pieces (Figure 10-83).

Needless to say, the mating surfaces of the joint, whether you use glue or not, must be flat and true. If you check over the sketches in Figure 10-84, you'll discover that the idea can be used not only for quarter-round molding, but also for half-moldings.

This is not the method to use every time you need a short piece of molding, but it's a fine procedure when you need something special.

Drilling.   There are several ways to do drilling in the lathe. In one, the chuck and bit are mounted in the tailstock. The bit is still and the work turns. Feed is accomplished by moving the tailstock forward or by using the tailstock ram. Such jobs are easier to do when the work is on a faceplate (Figure 10-85). In the second method, the drilling tool is in the headstock; the work is held against the center in the tailstock. Here, of course, the bit is turning and the work is still. The first method is preferred for faceplate work, the second method for spindles. Whatever way you work, standard drilling rules apply. Use slow speeds for large holes; increase speed only for small holes.

Quite often when you need a center hole all the way through a project for an item such as a lampbase, it's better to prepare for it before you turn the work. For this, you can use a kind of split-turning technique, running small center dadoes in each piece before you bond them with glue. Fill the hole at each end with a "key" so you'll have a solid area for the centers (Figure 10-86). After turning, you can hand drill through the keys to reach the square hole you have formed with the dadoes. If you do a good gluing job, it will be difficult to discover that the project is not a solid piece.

When the project length permits, you can lathe-drill through center holes by working from both ends of the stock.

Drilling can also be done on the perimeter of pieces; and if your lathe is equipped with an indexing device, you have a means for automatically gauging the spacing of such holes (Figure 10-87).

Your best bet is to make a drill guide that you use in place of the tool rest (Figure 10-88). Be sure that the guide hole is on the work centerline. It isn't necessary to make provision for drilling different size holes. If you provide, for example, a 1/8″ or a 1/4″ hole through the guide, you can accept it to use as is if that hole size is what you want or as a pilot hole that you can then enlarge to the size you require.

STOCK GLUED
WITH PAPER
JOINT

THEN TURNED

THEN SPLIT APART
ON JOINT WITH
SHARP KNIFE AND
MALLET AND YOU
HAVE SPECIAL 1/2"
ROUND MOLDING

OR GLUE LIKE
THIS

AND SPLIT TO
GET 4 PIECES
OF FLAT MOLDING
LIKE THIS

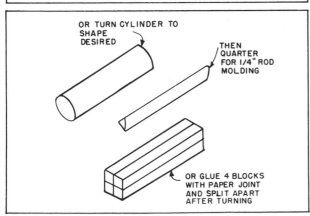

OR TURN CYLINDER TO
SHAPE DESIRED

THEN QUARTER
FOR 1/4" ROD
MOLDING

OR GLUE 4 BLOCKS
WITH PAPER JOINT
AND SPLIT APART
AFTER TURNING

10-84.   Here are some ideas you can experiment with to produce flat, half-round, or quarter-round moldings.

10-85.   You can do concentric drilling by mounting a chuck in the tailstock. Cutting is done by advancing the tailstock ram. Turn the work at slow speeds; take it easy as you advance the bit.

2 PIECES GLUED

KEY GLUED

GROOVES CUT ON
TABLE SAW

OR USE BLIND GROOVES WHICH
MAY BE REACHED BY DRILLING
WHEN TURNING IS COMPLETE

10-86.   Holes through long work can be "pre-formed" by gluing together pieces that have matching grooves. A good way to go when you are shaping a tall lamp base.

10-87. Indexing device can be as simple as equally-spaced holes in one of the driven pulleys. A pin, engaging one of the holes, keeps the spindle in a fixed position. This is the way to work when you need to mark lines or to drill holes on the perimeter or face of lathe-mounted work.

10-88. When you make a block like this and mount it in place of the tool rest, you have a means of guiding drills for holes in the edge or the surface of faceplate-mounted work. The guide hole must be on the horizontal centerline of the spindle.

10-89. Methods you can use to lay out spirals. This application is listed as a lathe job but it's really mostly hand work. The lathe is a convenient way to hold the stock.

Spiral work. The forming of spirals is usually classified as lathe work, but truthfully it's mostly a hand job with the lathe used as a holding device after the stock has been turned to full-round.

The layout can be done precisely by dividing the total length of the spiral into equal spaces, each one about the diameter of the stock. The next step is to draw four lines along the length of the stock. These should run from common perpendicular diameters at each end. What these lines do is divide the cylinder into four equal 1/4 rounds. Next divide each of the spaces into four equal parts and, using a heavy piece of paper as a guide, mark diagonals across each of the small spaces (Figure 10-89).

You can also work in fairly good fashion without all the layout by using a long strip of paper immediately. The paper can have parallel sides or be tapered. This paper is wrapped around the cylinder in spiral fashion, and the spiral line is marked by following the edge of the paper with a pencil (Figure 10-90).

Actual work is started by using a handsaw to cut the spiral line to the depth you want. As a depth gauge, you can make a mark on the saw or clamp a wood block to it. Work on the cut line with a round or square file, depending on how you visualize the final product (Figure 10-91). In essence, the initial file work opens up the groove you cut with the saw.

Then you can work with a flat file to shape the sections between the grooves (Figure 10-92). A rasp will speed up the job, but it's best followed by a smoother cut file before you get to the sandpaper chore, which is the final step. It's possible to have the work turning as you do the sanding, but you must be very careful to follow the spiral as you hold the sandpaper in shoe-polishing-cloth fashion. Start the spiral at slow speeds; increase the speed as you become confident.

Working with chucks. Sometimes it's not possible to hold work between centers, mount it on a faceplate, or secure it to a screw-center. At such times, it's good to know the technique of making wooden chucks.

A chuck doesn't have to be more than a tenon affair that you put on a screw-center (Figure 10-93). The tenon is

10-91. After the saw cut, which determines how deep the cuts will be, you can start the shaping with a square or a round file. Keep the file working as you rotate the work by hand.

10-92. After the initial forming, switch to a file with a flat surface to round off edges. A rasp removes material quickly, but you should follow this phase of the job by working with a finer-cut file and then with sandpaper.

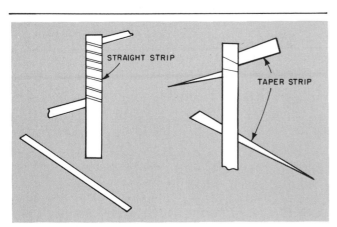

10-90. This is a simple way to make the layout for spirals. The "pitch" of the spiral will be determined by how you start wrapping the guide strip around the work.

10-93. A special chuck can be a screw-center mounted piece with a tenon on which the work can be pressed.

10-94. This is a typical split chuck. The tenon on the work is gripped by the jaws of the chuck because of the ring that forces them together. Don't apply too much pressure when you are using the lathe chisels.

designed to be a snug fit in a center hole that is in the work. This makes sense simply because, many times, it's better to drill a needed hole in the work before it is turned. Then it can't be mounted on a screw-center unless you provide the tenon-chuck.

Another way to proceed is to make a split chuck. A tenon on the work is gripped by the "jaws" of the chuck because of the ring that forces them together (Figures 10-94 and 10-95).

The whole chuck area should be viewed as a means of getting a job done when it can't be accomplished in the usual fashion. There is no point in trying to be prepared for such eventualities except to know the techniques to use. Wait for them to occur before you make tools.

Turn a box with a fitted cover.   This kind of lathe project also uses a type of chuck technique. The procedure starts with mounting the wood for the body of the box on a faceplate and turning it to the shape you want on both the inside and the outside. Mount the stock for the lid on a second faceplate and form a recess in it that will fit the opening of the box's body. The body, still on its own

DRILL TWO
1/4" HOLES THROUGH BLOCK

LENGTH OF TAPER

TURN TO CYLINDER
AND TAPER TO HERE

DRILL HOLE LENGTH
OF TAPER

MAKE TWO SAW CUTS THROUGH
STOCK TO HOLES

SETSCREW

THIS END DRILLED
FOR SPINDLE

METAL RING FITS OVER
TAPER AND IS USED TO
CLAMP WORK IN CHUCK

10-95. The procedure to follow when you are designing a split chuck. It's a good idea to use a dense hardwood like maple or birch. Chucks like this are made only when the job can't be done in more routine fashion.

faceplate, is returned to the lathe and used as a chuck to hold the lid for finishing.

Since the body of the box is used as a chuck, the fit between it and the lid should be fairly tight. After the lid is formed and the sanding has been done, separate the parts and touch up by hand the lip on either the body or the lid so the two pieces can mate with a slip fit. The procedure, step-by-step, is demonstrated in Figure 10-96.

How to shape a ball. You might not do this kind of lathe work everyday, but it's an interesting technique and can come in handy. The first step (Figure 10-97), is to mount the stock between centers and to remove most of the waste material. What you end up with is a square with a tenon at each end. The square becomes the ball; the tenons

are simply holding sections. A template, which is half the ball shape, is used as a guide for the shaping and as a smoothing device.

The next step is to mount the work on only one tenon, either by using a conventional three-jaw chuck or a special wooden chuck that you design for the purpose. Now you can cut off the outboard tenon and work to achieve the final shape of the ball. The final step is to use the template as a touch-up device by placing fine sandpaper between it and the ball shape. Use a light touch; do the final finishing by hand-holding the sandpaper.

After the ball is finished to your satisfaction, you can separate it from the remaining tenon by using a skew or a parting tool. The connection area is then touched up by

10-96. This is the step-by-step procedure to follow when you wish to form a box with a fitted cover. This kind of work is done more accurately when you work with two faceplates.

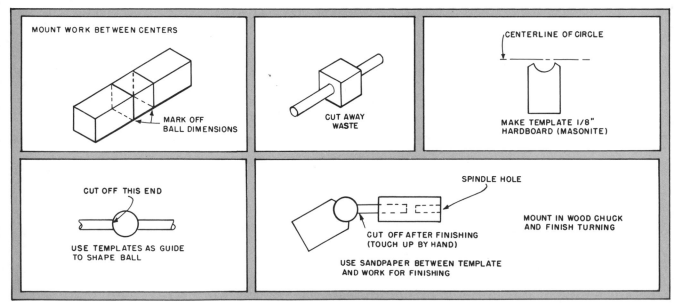

10-97. This is the correct procedure to follow when turning a ball shape. Leave the second tenon in place if the ball is to be attached to another component.

hand. If the project is going to be attached to another component, say, a column or a newel post, leave the last tenon in place so it can be used in the joint.

How to turn a ring.   There are a variety of techniques you can use to do ring work, and the choice will usually depend on the cross-section profile you want. For example, to produce a ring with a square cross-section, mount a blank on a faceplate and turn it to full-round, with the diameter to match the outside diameter of the ring. Make one cut with a parting tool on the perimeter of the work, cutting a bit deeper than what you want the cross-

section of the ring to be when viewed from its front. Make a second cut on the face of the stock, again with the parting tool. The second cut is done to meet the first one. When the two cuts meet, the ring will fall off onto the shaft of the chisel. The rim of the ring can be shaped before you separate it from the body of the faceplate-mounted stock. (See Figures 10-98 and 10-99).

The procedure differs if the cross-section of the ring is to be, say, circular or an oval shape. In this case you combine faceplate turning with chuck turning (Figures 10-100 and 10-101). Start the job with faceplate-mounted stock and

10-98. Forming a simple ring is a two-step procedure. The second cut separates the ring from the base stock. As shown in "B", the perimeter of the ring can be shaped before the ring is separated.

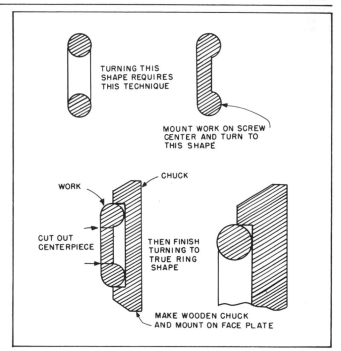

10-100. You must use this procedure if the ring has an oval or circular cross-section. The second part of the job requires a chuck that is just right for the work.

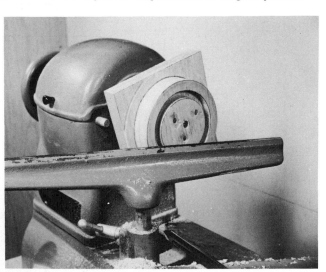

10-99. The stock for simple ring-making can be attached to a faceplate-mounted block with either screws or nails. The sequence of the two cuts really doesn't matter unless you are shaping the perimeter. Then the surface cut should come last.

10-101. After the "face" of the ring has been formed, the work is mounted in the special chuck so the center area can be cut away and the opposite side of the ring can be formed.

turn half of the ring's shape. Next, make a chuck with a recess that will provide a snug fit for the part you have semi-shaped. This is then pressed into the chuck and the final shaping of the ring is done.

All chuck work of this type requires an accurate dimension in the cavity that holds the work. If you make a mistake, it's often possible to compensate by wrapping a strip of masking tape around the ring to make it fit snugly.

A project like a circular picture frame or a one-piece circular molding that may be used to edge a flat tray can be done in this fashion (Figure 10-102). Mount the work on a

faceplate and recess it to form a rabbet. Shape the perimeter as you wish. Then make a chuck to fit the rabbet diameter and shape the work on the opposite side. View the original rabbet cut, in the case of a picture frame, as the recess that holds the glass. If you are making a tray, simply cut a disc that fits inside the turning.

Ovals. The major factor in this process is a layout that you do on the ends of the stock after you have turned it to true round. Your best approach is to make a template that locates the true center plus two "off centers" that are on a common diameter. Note in Figure 10-103, that it's a good idea to draw a "ridge" line on the work. Once you have this line, it's easy to position the template to mark the common off centers.

Mount the work on one of the off centers and turn it as you would normally until the cut nears the ridge line (Figure 10-104). Be careful when positioning the tool rest.

10-102. This is the way to work if you wish to make a circular picture frame that includes a rabbet for glass. Use the same procedure to produce circular trays and similar projects.

10-104. The work is turned on each "side" to the ridge line. This puts the work off balance for a good amount of cutting, so work carefully and be sure to position the tool rest for tool support and for clearance.

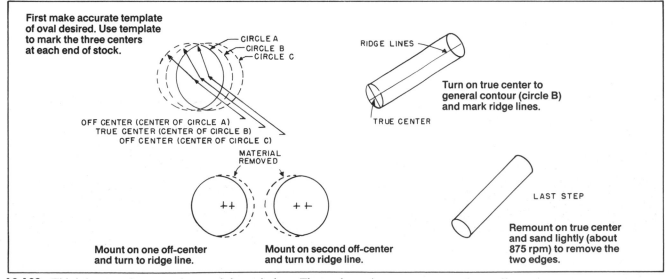

10-103. This is how turning to produce oval shapes is done. The work requires a true center and two off-centers.

10-105. After the lathe-chisel work is done, the job is finished with sandpaper with the work mounted on the true center.

10-106. A typical part that calls for offset turning. Note that the centers for lathe mounting ignore the projection on the work.

10-107. Turning is done in usual fashion but be very aware of the projection on the work. It's probably best to work at a less-than-normal speed. Keep your hands well away from the offset.

One side of the work will come closer to you than the other; the off center makes it possible to cut on just one side of the diameter. You'll find after this operation that one side of the stock is oval while the other side remains round. Shift to the second off center and repeat the operation. The final step is to use sandpaper to remove the ridge line (Figure 10-105).

Offset work. In this type of work, parts have a projection that is not uniform about a centerline. You can find this on leg designs that end in a right angle departure from the "spindle." The cabriole leg is another good example. The idea here is that lathe turning can be applied to part of the project either before or after the overall shape is established. As you can see in Figures 10-106 through 10-108, the turning is done on the true-center portion of the work—either in an overall or limited area. In the case of the cabriole leg, you can turn a round foot after the part has been bandsawed to shape.

This is not a difficult chore, but you must be aware that the off-center portion of the project can be a hazard. Always be sure, after you have set the tool rest, that you hand turn the work to check clearance. When you start cutting, keep your hand clear of the projection area. As far as lathe mounting is concerned, the work is unbalanced, so you are bound to get more vibration than you would from a symmetrical piece. Start at very low speeds. Increase the speed only if results indicate that you can do so without danger to yourself or to the work.

Finishing. To get to a final smoothness, work through progressively finer grits of sandpaper. The grit you start with must be judged on how smooth the project is to begin with. A very coarse paper may be completely out of line since all you will be doing is creating scratches you will have to remove with other paper. On lathe work, it's often possible to start immediately with a fine paper. Whatever you do, be careful around fine details since excessive sandpapering can destroy them (Figure 10-109).

10-108. You can use the offset turning technique if you wish to turn one or both ends of a cabriole leg. Slow speeds and cautious chisel handling are a must. Keep the tool rest as close as possible but turn the work by hand before turning on the machine to be sure that you have clearance.

When you are satisfied that the wood is smooth enough, dampen it slightly with water. Don't soak it. Let it dry and then do a final smoothing with fine steel wool. Some craftsmen use a handful of fine shavings to do this. It does bring out a degree of shine; but whether you use chips or steel wool, this is just a step before application of color or clear finish.

A simple finish can consist of plain wax. You pick up some wax on a cloth pad and apply it to the turning work. A slow speed is best, and you can apply as many coats as you wish as long as you allow sufficient drying time between the applications. After you are sure the part is evenly coated, do the final polishing with a clean, lint-free cloth.

Apply stain in similar fashion (Figure 10-110). Just be sure you don't saturate the cloth, or you will be spraying yourself as you color the wood. Remember when you do this kind of thing in the lathe that finishing materials require just as much drying time as they do when they are applied with a brush. Rushing the procedure will do more harm than good. Overall, it's best to apply any finish in a diluted state; the heavier the material you are using, the slower the speed should be.

A sanding table. Since it is possible to mount a disc in the lathe, the little table shown in Figure 10-111 lets you use the tool as a fairly efficient disc sander. The table can be as small or as large as you wish; however, even for the biggest machines, it shouldn't be much over about 14″ square. The table understructure sits on the lathe bed and is located with a block that fits between the ways. Organize the table height so it is a bit above the horizontal centerline of the disc.

Be sure that you use a safe speed for the disc you will mount. Note that the table has a miter-gauge groove so you can do end sanding accurately. For the techniques of disc sanding, see the chapter that deals with that particular tool.

A table for routing. With a spindle on which you can mount a router chuck, plus a special table that you can make, you can use the lathe for quite a few routing operations. You must, of course, suit the operation to the horizontal mode the router bit will be in.

The type of spindle you use will depend on the lathe. If it has a solid, unthreaded spindle, you can probably mount a router chuck directly on it. If the lathe has a tapered hole that takes attachments with a Morse Taper, then you can use a spindle adapter like the one shown in Figure 10-112.

10-110. Apply stain, or whatever, with a soft, lint-free cloth. Use a slow speed and don't saturate the cloth. If you are applying several coats of finish, do a light sanding between them. Be sure to allow each coat to dry thoroughly.

10-111. A table like this turns the lathe into a pretty efficient disc sander. Be sure to use a lathe speed that is safe for the sanding disc you are using.

10-112. A spindle adapter of this type can be used for mounting router chucks.

10-109. Working through progressively finer grits of sandpaper is good practice but it doesn't mean that you have to start with the coarsest grit you have.

Most lathes will provide a high speed of about 5,000 rpm which is not ideal, but adequate for routing. Don't use special pulleys to provide higher speeds unless you are sure the lathe is built for it. To compensate for less-than-ideal speeds, you can slow up on feed rates and take small cuts.

The jig shown in Figure 10-113 was made for a 12″ lathe. Unless you have something similar, check the dimensions against your own equipment. Be very careful when making the sliding base; the more rigidity here, the better. If dimension changes are required to suit your tool, work from intersecting lines that represent the vertical and horizontal centerlines of the lathe's spindle.

The applications that are shown in Figures 10-114 and 10-115 are samples of routing chores that can be accomplished. Actually, there is no reason why you can't use a conventional three-jaw chuck for horizontal drilling. The operational change would be that you move the work into the bit rather than the bit into the work. To drill edge holes (for dowel joints) you can use the fence to advance the work; a stop block clamped to the table will control hole-depth. The miter gauge can be used as a guide when you need to drill holes into stock ends. Many of the ideas that were described for drilling on the radial arm saw are applicable here.

Trouble-Shooting Chart

Figure 10-116 describes the possible causes and solutions of some problems you might encounter when doing lathe work.

10-113. This is how you can make a table that allows some router work to be done on the lathe. Check the dimensions against the tool you will be working with.

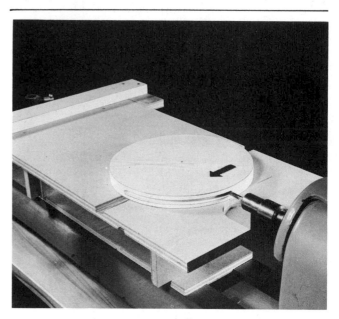

10-115. Use the pivot method if you need to rout a groove into a circular edge. The pivot, situated on line with the spindle, is a nail that passes through the center of the work and into the table. If you don't care to mar the table, drive the nail through a scrap block that you clamp in place.

10-114. Edge grooving is one of the jobs you can do. The work, guided by the clamped fence, is moved in the direction indicated by the arrow. This is a view from the back of the machine. Take it easy with feed-speed, and don't try to cut too deep in a single pass.

THE PROBLEM	POSSIBLE CAUSES	WHAT TO LOOK FOR OR DO
IN GENERAL Work burns at cup center	Excessive friction	Slack off pressure between centers Place wax or soap on cup center
Excessive vibration	Speed too fast for large work Work is not on true center	Use lower speed Use a live cup center Relocate centers if vibration is extreme; slight vibrations not critical, will disappear as work becomes true round
Chatter	Excessive speed	Use lower speed especially when starting job
Lathe chisels hard to hold	Dull tool Cutting too deep or feeding too fast Work loose between centers Work loose on faceplate Poor support for chisel	Sharpen and hone Good shop practice calls for slow feed and moderate bite —also produces smoothest cuts Adjust pressure between centers Retighten or replace screws Stay as close as possible to ideal tool rest position
Work stops turning or slips	Spur center loose or not seated correctly Spurs erode the wood	Adjust pressure between centers—saw diagonals on work, especially on hardwoods Sand damaged end of work and reseat spur center
Scored lines left by sanding	Wrong abrasive grit Sanding too long in one place	Best to work through progressively finer grits until work is satin-smooth Keep sandpaper moving
Hard to achieve super-smooth finish	Stubborn "nap" on wood	Try reversing work between centers—use slightly dampened cloth on work before final sanding (other hints in text)
Spindle turning whips	Work is too long and thin	Use a backup or a steady rest
Excessive vibration— chatter—on faceplate work	Too much speed Work not prepared before mounting Faceplate not centered Mounting screws loosened	Slow down, especially when work is first mounted Cut round before mounting—remove corners with miter cuts Follow instructions for mounting faceplate—slight misalignment not critical Retighten screws—replace with heavier screws if necessary
Wood splinters when rough-turning square to round	Starting cut at ends of stock Cutting too deep Wood not prepared	Work from the center toward the ends Don't rush the job Remove as much waste as possible by sawing before mounting stock
Tool labors when switched on	Spindle turning gripped too tightly	Ease off pressure between centers
Sanding burns work	Too much pressure Too much speed	Sanding builds up heat quickly—apply lightly—keep sandpaper moving Change to lower speed
Work loosens on screw center	Possible on very soft wood Incorrect mounting or application	Use a heavier screw when necessary—check frequently— do not use chisels aggressively Be sure work is tight before starting to cut—use a screw center only when necessary

10-116.   Trouble-shooting chart for lathe work. If the solution to a problem isn't here, then it's best to re-check the owner's manual.

11. The Shaper

We've talked some about shaping operations and demonstrated how they can be accomplished on the table saw, the radial arm saw, and the drill press. These techniques are fine and practical, and you may never need to go beyond them. But you can accomplish much more with a tool specifically designed for shaping operations.

There are several misconceptions about the individual shaper. Among them are the misconceptions that it's difficult to use and that its applications are limited to decorative cutting. Well, if you're into power tool work, you can use the shaper as efficiently as anyone—and once you've become acquainted with its repertoire, you'll appreciate that its use for quickly producing smooth, contoured edges is almost a minor consideration. This is not to discount its finesse in such areas. Forming structural and decorative wall moldings, adding decorative edges on table tops, chair backs, and cornices, and so on, are routine shaper chores. What is often overlooked is, for example, the help it can provide in joinery. Look around your home, and you'll discover myriad professional joints that can be duplicated on a spindle shaper; cabinet door lips, rail and stile joints on doors and windows, drop-leaf table joints, frames for inset panels, and so on. The joints shown in Figure 11-1 were done on a shaper, using a single 1/4″ wide three-lip cutter, but such samples hardly begin to tell the story.

In General

There are considerable differences among shapers, but they must all have the essential components that are shown in Figure 11-2. The variables are caused mostly by whether the unit is a light-duty or a heavy-duty machine, and, of course, this has a bearing on price. The machines work with a vertical spindle, but they differ from the drill press, for example, in that it is mounted under the table and is designed to withstand considerable side thrust and speed. Since the drive mechanism is below, there are no top-side obstructions to interfere with work size and work handling.

Many small shapers have solid spindles, usually 1/2″ in diameter, so cutter selection is limited to those that have a 1/2″ mounting hole. This goes along with the common 1/2″ hole size of popular three-lip shaper cutters, so you have dozens of profiles to choose from. The single, solid spindle, does impose limitations on *types* of cutters you can use, and on some applications, but these factors must be considered on the basis of just how deeply you wish to be involved with individual-shaper work.

11-1.   The shaper is used for much more than decorative cuts. These joints, all made with a 1/4″-wide blank cutter, barely begin to tell the story of its practical applications in a woodworking shop.

11-2.   All shapers will have these basic components. Differences are in overall size, speed, power, and whether the machine has interchangeable spindles.

Some shapers, especially heavy-duty ones, have a hollow drive mechanism (also called a spindle), so they have an interchangeable-spindle capability. The spindle that takes the cutter is secured as shown in Figure 11-3. Being able to change spindles allows you to work with a greater variety of cutters and, maybe more importantly, you can mount a "stub" spindle for doing cope-type cuts which are needed when doing framing for projects like windows and doors. In essence, interchangeable spindles increase your work scope by allowing a greater choice in types of cutters and by facilitating some advanced techniques.

Other characteristics to look for are speed, which can start in the area of 10,000 rpm but might go higher; power, with 1/2 hp to 3/4 hp being a minimum but which, depending on the tool can go up to 2 hp and more; and (probably more important in terms of application) a reversible motor so the cutter can spin either clockwise or counterclockwise. The latter factor lets you decide in which direction you wish to make the pass, but its primary asset is that you can get more from any cutter when you can, by choice, invert its position on the spindle. The change in direction of rotation is always accomplished by means of a switch. The switch might be part of the on-off unit, or it might be a separate control that is located on the motor housing.

The shaper fence is basically a two-part deal that locks securely to the shaper table. Either half of the fence is adjustable, and the entire unit is removable for freehand shaping against fulcrum pins and collars. Fence adjustment is exactly the same as for shaping operations on other tools. When the cut removes part of the work edge, the fences are set in line (Figure 11-4). When the cut removes the entire work edge, then the outfeed fence is brought forward an amount that equals the depth of the cut so the work will have support after it has passed the cutter.

Representative Types

Individual shapers can be "big" or "small," factors that relate to physical size—how much room you must allow for them in your shop—and the power and the flexibility they have in relation to work-scope. Even a compact unit, like the one shown in Figure 11-5, is functional for making joints and for shaping moldings for cabinets and trim work. It works, mostly, with standard, three-lip shaper cutters, and drives them with a built-in motor, at 18,000 rpm, a pretty impressive speed. It's small, but doesn't lack the basic shaper necessities such as adjustable fences, vertically adjustable spindle, and a groove for a miter gauge. The topside cup guard can be set for all operations but is especially useful when doing freehand shaping.

The motorized unit in Figure 11-6 works with a 1 hp motor that drives the spindle directly, so there can be no power loss due to belt slippage. Its free-running speed is 18,000 rpm, and tests indicate that it doesn't slow to less than 14,000 rpm even when shaping hardwood, which isn't bad. Its table, 18″ x 15-1/4″, is a nice size and incorporates a groove for a miter gauge. Like many units of its type, it has a single-diameter, solid spindle, so it is used with cutters that have a matching mounting-hole.

The wood shaper shown in Figure 11-7 is a light-duty machine that has big-tool features, namely, interchangeable spindles and a toggle switch on the motor that is used to

11-3.   This arrangement, on some shapers, allows the use of spindles of different designs and diameters. The drive spindle is hollow. Spindles that hold the cutter are secured with a tapered nut that threads on the end of a stud.

11-4.   Both shaper fences are adjustable. When the cut removes only part of the work-edge, the bearing surfaces of the fences are set on the same plane. The "infeed" fence is where the cut starts. It can be the left or the right fence, depending on the cutter's direction of rotation.

11-5. This compact shaper has a self-contained 1 hp motor that direct-drives a 1/2″ diameter spindle at about 18,000 rpm. It can be used with all three-lip shaper cutters that have a 1/2″ mounting hole and which do not have a cutting circle that exceeds 2-1/2″.

change the cutter's direction of rotation. These are features that extend the scope of work you can accomplish. The drive is a conventional motor that spins the spindle by means of a V-belt; the recommended speed is 9,000 rpm.

A machine that can cause the shaper enthusiast to yearn is shown in Figure 11-8. This is the kind of machine that can be used as comfortably in a home workshop as in an industrial establishment or a school shop. It's big, it's husky, and its interchangeable spindle design allows the use of 1/2″, 3/4″, and 1″ spindles, so there is great latitude in choice of cutters. The basic table size is 20″ x 27″, but this increases to 27″ x 36″ when you add extensions. This is a "serious" tool to consider when you want to get as much as possible from shaper operations. A 1 hp motor is a minimum; a 2 hp to 3 hp, 220 V power source is more in line with the tool's potential.

Cutters

Three-lip shaper cutters, which are usually designed with a 1/2″ mounting hole, can be used on almost any shaper re-

11-6. This motorized high speed shaper is one of those units that is ready for use almost as soon as you remove it from the shipping carton. Often, the price for the tool includes the stand on which you mount it. The direct-drive motor is 1 hp and provides a no-load speed of 18,000 rpm.

11-7. This "light-duty" shaper has features you usually accept as standard on big machines. Among the features are interchangeable spindles and a motor-mounted toggle switch that allows you to change the cutter's direction of rotation. Such features contribute to what you can do with a shaper.

gardless of its size. Some are for a specific job, like the *glue joint* shown in Figure 11-9. Others are combination types, designed so that using only part of the profile produces a particular form. In this category, you find such knives as the *bead and cove* and the *bead and quarter round*. Actually, any cutter can be used for a full or partial cut if the result suits the job. You can be creative by combining cuts made with different cutters, but be sure to sketch what you think the result will be before cutting into good stock, or make a test cut in scrap material first. The three-lip shaper cutters that are shown in Figure 11-10 are just a sampling of what is available.

The two types of cutters shown in Figure 11-11 are a departure from the usual three-lip design. The three-knife unit is like a small-size molding head and can actually work with the same knives that are used in the molding head for a table saw. You must be sure, of course, that the heads are designed in similar fashion to suit how the knives are installed. The cutterhead has a 3/4″ center hole, so it's pretty much a heavy-duty tool. However, it comes supplied with a

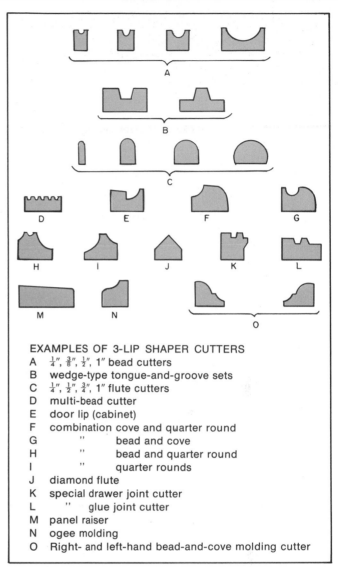

EXAMPLES OF 3-LIP SHAPER CUTTERS

A	$\frac{1}{4}″$, $\frac{3}{8}″$, $\frac{1}{2}″$, 1″ bead cutters
B	wedge-type tongue-and-groove sets
C	$\frac{1}{4}″$, $\frac{1}{2}″$, $\frac{3}{4}″$, 1″ flute cutters
D	multi-bead cutter
E	door lip (cabinet)
F	combination cove and quarter round
G	" bead and cove
H	" bead and quarter round
I	" quarter rounds
J	diamond flute
K	special drawer joint cutter
L	" glue joint cutter
M	panel raiser
N	ogee molding
O	Right- and left-hand bead-and-cove molding cutter

11-10. Examples of three-lip shaper cutters. Many other shapes are available.

11-8. An example of the shaper enthusiast's dream tool. You'll find this kind of equipment in industry, in school shops, and in many home shops. Its interchangeable spindle capability allows the use of spindles up to 1″ in diameter. Thus, you can use cutters that would be out of line on a small machine.

11-9. The glue-joint, three-lip shaper cutter is an example of a unit designed for a particular job. The one cutter is used to shape both mating surfaces. The interlocking projections are a perfect match.

11-11. Special types of cutters that can be used on some shapers. The left one can be used with the same knives that are used with a table saw molding head. Blank knives, that are available for the right one, can be ground to suit a particular application. You must be extremely careful when you secure the knives between the collars.

bushing so it can be mounted on a shaper with a 1/2″ spindle.

The other cutter works with knives that are gripped between slotted collars. The advantage is that you can buy blank knives and grind them to any shape you wish, a job that must be done in a very professional manner. Actually, it's possible to grind a different shape at each end of the knife. You must be extremely careful when installing such knives. If the collars do not bear equally and tightly on both knives, the less secure one could become a projectile when you flick the switch. This can happen because you have done a poor job of securing the knives to begin with, or because you have installed knives of different widths. This would cause one knife to be gripped more securely than the other. Be sure to read the manufacturer's instructions very carefully should you use this type of cutter.

There are cutters that are especially ideal for particular woodworking operations. The matched set shown in Figure 11-12, called a *complete cabinet set,* makes the *stile* cuts and the *cope* cuts that are needed for professional assembly of doors and windows and the like. When they are used correctly, the parts they form go together with superb precision (Figure 11-13). They work with carbide-tipped blades, so the cuts they make are as smooth as can be, even when done across the grain.

Some manufacturers carry the design of combination cutters to intriguing extremes. It's not a matter of a single unit that is usable for partial cuts, but of a set of cutters that can be combined in various ways to produce any number of standard or original molding forms. Freud's *Woodworking Box* (Figure 11-14) consists of four carbide-tipped cutters that can be assembled to shape half-rounds, ogees, corner-rounds, coves, and so on, and probably more important—they can produce complete shapes needed for panel doors and a variety of interlocking joints.

Cutters of this type can't be used on *every* shaper. For one thing, the standard bore is 3/4″, although it can be bushed down to 1/2″. Equally important is the cutting circle of the tools. One set has a diameter of 4-1/8″; a larger set has a 5-1/2″ diameter. These factors should be checked out against the equipment you plan to use them on.

11-12.   This matched set is used to shape the *stile* and *cope* cuts that are needed for professional assembly of doors, windows, and so on.

11-13.   Matched sets are a joy to use. The *cabinet set* forms shapes that mate with superb precision. Shapes include the decorative edges as well as the groove in which a wooden panel or a sheet of glass can be installed.

TWO PASSES   TWO PASSES

FOUR PASSES   TWO PASSES

11-14.   The unlimited variety of shapes and joints that can be produced with Freud's *Woodworking Box* is due to four separate cutters that can be combined in various ways. Results can be varied by whether you make one, two, or more passes. The four samples shown here barely begin to tell what can be accomplished with this set of cutters.

Mounting cutters. Cutters mount on the spindle as they do on a shaper adapter used in the drill press. Again, the difference here is that the spindle is under the table instead of over it (Figure 11-15). Collars are used in freehand work to control the depth of the cut, but they are also used when working with a fence to take up spindle length that is not occupied by the cutter.

Collars made for the shaper are available in various thicknesses and diameters. Many shaper craftsmen will make up special collars to suit a particular application. You can even buy ball-bearing collars. The advantage of this feature is that the collar will not turn with the spindle, thus eliminating scoring and burning that can occur with solid collars. The most you can do with solid collars is to keep them clean and polished.

Some Safety Considerations

Never allow your hands to come close to the cutting tool—a pretty obvious consideration, but the point must be made. Never try to shape pieces that are too small or too narrow for safe hand positioning. It's standard practice to do such work on large pieces and then to remove the part you need by sawing. This applies to straight pieces and to curved work as well (Figure 11-16). When moving stock, try to work so fingers are hooked against edges. This will help to guard against your hands slipping to where they should not be.

When working against collars, be sure the workpiece has sufficient bearing surfaces against the collar. As stated before, keep the collars clean and polished. Soiled or scarred collars will not only mar the work, they will make it harder to feed. Be sure to work with fulcrum pins when doing freehand shaping. One pin is usually supplied, and the table is drilled so the pin can be used on either side of the cutter. I think it's a good idea to buy an extra pin and to use both. Thus, you can have work support before, during, and at the end of the cut.

Whenever possible, arrange the setup so the cutter will be under the work. This positioning will put the work between you and the cutter and will eliminate the possibility of the work being damaged should you accidentally lift it during the pass.

11-16. It's wise to produce slim moldings by working on stock that is safe to handle and then sawing off the part you need. This applies to straight moldings as well as curved pieces like the one shown here.

11-15. Cutters, and collars, lock on the spindle by means of "double nutting" or by a keyed washer that is positioned under a single lock nut. The key on the washer fits a groove that is in the spindle. Whatever the system, its motive is to keep the cutter from working loose.

11-17. This new type of guard, available on some shapers, is a heavy piece of tough plastic that is mounted on a bearing and which is secured on the spindle together with the cutter. It's a good item to use when doing freehand shaping and, on many jobs, can be left in place when doing shaping against fences.

11-18.   Often, an adjustable ring or cup is provided. Its main purpose is to provide protection when working against fulcrum pins, but it can also be situated over the spindle when fence-work is being done.

11-19.   Many manufacturers offer spring-type hold-downs as accessories. When correctly situated, they help to keep work flat on the table and snug against the fence. Always situate the hold-downs so they can't snap into the cutter after the work has gone by.

Always work with the guards supplied with the tool and, when necessary, buy those that are listed as accessories. The spindle guard shown in Figure 11-17, is a newcomer and makes a lot of sense. It's a heavy piece of Lexan® mounted on a bearing that locks on the spindle together with the cutters. It provides a good deal of hand protection and does not interfere with vision. Speaking of vision, don't neglect to wear safety goggles.

Other accessories that can help you work more safely, and even more accurately, are shown in Figures 11-18 and 11-19.

There is always an operation that doesn't allow the use of guards for the complete protection we like to have. In such cases, work with extreme caution. Go through a "dry" run—that is, go through the motions with the tool turned

11-20.   The fence-mounted guard is adjustable so it can be set to accommodate various stock thicknesses. It puts a rigid, plastic shield between you and the cutter.

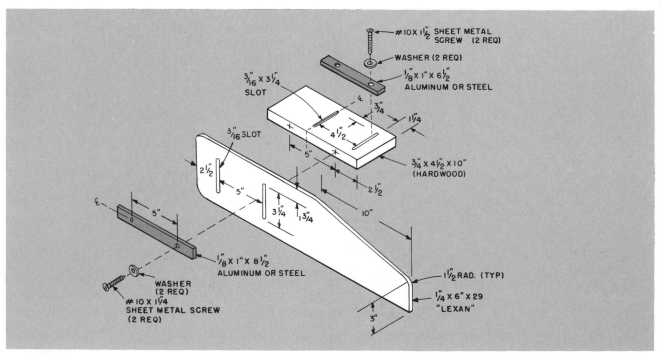

11-21.   Construction details of the fence-mounted guard.

off so you can preview the procedure and judge how best to place yourself and your hands.

Guards you can make. Staying whole while working on power tools has much to do with mistrusting the tools and avoiding tool reliance on basic guards. Manufacturers *are* concerned with safety. It's foolish to think they are not interested in the well-being of customers. When they supply a guard, I use it, but beyond this, I design special fixtures when I feel one is needed, and, often, I will use something that provides extra protection even on routine operations. Frequently, there is a double benefit in doing this; a safety jig can also help me work more accurately.

There are two such devices that I use routinely when doing shaper operations. One of them is used for all operations that are done with shaper fences (Figures 11-20 and 11-21). The safety shield is adjustable to-and-fro and vertically, so it can be situated close to the cutter regardless of the type of cut or the thickness of the stock. It attaches with screws to the top edge of the shaper fence and can be used regardless of the cutter's rotation. It is mounted as shown in Figure 11-20 when the feed direction is left-to-right. When feed direction is right-to-left, then the mounted bracket is inverted and set on the opposite fence. The shield is turned end-for-end.

The second guard is a large, clear plastic shield that provides extra protection when doing freehand shaping against collars (Figure 11-22 and 11-23). The whole unit, which you may have to size to suit your equipment, is adjustable so it can cover the cutting area and a good part of the workpiece. The shorter slots provide access to the spindle and to the fulcrum pins. Adjust the height of the shield so it will be as close to the work as possible; bring it as far forward as you can.

Operational Techniques

Regardless of which way the cutter turns, the work must always be fed against the direction of rotation. When the cutter is turning counterclockwise, the work is fed from right to left. When the cutter is turning clockwise, the work is fed from left to right (Figure 11-24). This system applies whether you are working with the fences or doing freehand work against collars.

Work may be placed flat on the table or on edge. Since there is nothing above the cutter (like a drill-press spindle) you can handle any work of reasonable width when doing an on-edge pass. What can help though, is an extra-high auxiliary fence that you use in place of standard equipment (Figure 11-25). The extra fence-height helps to keep wide pieces in true vertical position as you make the pass. An additional aid is the "third hand" that is shown set up for use in Figure 11-26. The work support assures that the work won't tilt as you are making the cut. Since it is adjustable, it

11-23. Construction details of the guard for freehand shaping. Check the dimensions against the size of your own equipment.

11-22. This plastic shield is designed for use when doing freehand shaping. It can be set to cover a good part of the work as well as the cutter.

11-24. Feed direction is always against the cutter's direction of rotation. Feed is from left to right when the cutter is turning clockwise. Best results are obtained when the feed is slow and steady and made with the grain of the wood.

is usable with various stock widths. Construction details for the auxiliary fence and the adjustable work support are given in Figures 11-27 and 11-28.

Incidentally, if the high-rise fence is in place, you can continue to work with it if the next phase of the operation calls for a partial edge-cut (Figure 11-29).

Try to feed so that you are cutting with the grain, which will always produce the smoothest cuts. When conditions demand otherwise, slow up on the pass. Many times in such circumstances, it's wise to do the job in repeat passes; simply increase depth of cut after each pass until you have the shape you want.

Cross-grain cuts will usually result in some slight imperfections at the end of the pass. You can minimize these by being very cautious at the end and finishing with minimum feed speed. You can eliminate them by shaping a piece that is a bit oversize and then doing a jointer cut or a slight rip cut with a hollow-ground blade on the edges after the shaping operation. The idea is to remove any imperfections by making a second cut.

When you must shape all edges or adjacent edges of a workpiece, do the cross-grain cuts first. The final with-the-grain cuts will remove the imperfections left by the previous passes (Figure 11-30).

Miter gauge work.   Most shapers provide for the use of a miter gauge. It's a good idea to use one on all cross-grain work if work-size permits, but its use is critical when

you must shape the end of narrow stock. It's not likely that you'll work accurately when hand-holding such pieces, but, more importantly—the procedure isn't safe. Some miter gauges can be equipped with accessory hold-downs that keep the work in firm position as you make the pass (Figure 11-31). The least you should do, lacking a miter gauge, is to make a right-angle backup block to use in its place. Even this minimum attention will help to keep the work square to the cutter and to prevent it from rocking.

A more professional way to go is to take the time to make the sliding jig that is shown in Figure 11-32. The work, resting on the platform, is secured with as many of the four eye bolts as you need to use. Thus, you can work accurately and safely, since your hands don't have to come anywhere near the cutter (Figure 11-33). Adding the angle guide makes it possible to do work on miter-cut edges. Figure 11-34 shows a setup you can use to form grooves for a spline-reinforced miter joint. On jobs like this, the jig can be organized to handle wider work by removing its forward, left-hand post. On jobs done with the jig, allow for the thickness of the jig's platform when you set the height of

11-25.   An extra-high fence, that you can simply clamp in place, provides good support when shaping pieces that are held on edge.

11-26.   A "third hand" is provided by a work-support that is adjustable in relation to the thickness of the stock. It helps to keep the work in true vertical position while you are making the cut.

11-27.   Construction details of an auxiliary high fence that you can make. The fence is secured to the shaper's table with clamps.

11-28.   How to make an adjustable work support.

11-29.   You can continue to work with the high fence if the next shaping phase does not require removing the entire edge of the stock.

11-30.   Crossgrain cuts should always be done with minimum feed-speed. When stock must be shaped on all edges, do the crossgrain cuts first.

11-31.   Work with a miter gauge when doing end cuts, especially if the stock is narrow. Trying to hand-hold such pieces can be dangerous and certainly won't contribute to accurate work. Note the hold-downs, an accessory for the miter gauge.

11-32.   The sliding jig, that you can make, provides accuracy and safety when doing end cuts. The small pieces on the right are pads that are used under the eye bolts.

11-33.   Work, resting on the jig's platform, is secured with as many of the eye bolts as are needed. The work will be secure, and your hands will be in a safe position, as you move the jig forward to make the cut.

11-34.   The angle guide lets you position miter-cut pieces. Here, grooves are being formed for a spline that will reinforce the joint.

the cutter. Construction details for the sliding jig are given in Figure 11-35.

Fence position.   When you are doing a full cut, the outfeed fence must be advanced to support the work after it has passed the cutter. The best way to do this is to start with the outfeed fence retracted. Then adjust the infeed fence for the depth of cut you wish. Make a partial pass—that is, hold the work against the infeed fence and feed until an inch or so of the work edge has passed the cutter. Turn off the machine and then adjust the outfeed fence until it bears lightly against the shaped edge (Figure 11-36).

Feed speed.   Feed speed, regardless of the power and rpm's of your machine, should always be slow and steady. Make wise judgments in relation to the results you are getting and in tune with how the machine is reacting. It's never wise to cut so deep or so fast that there is an obvious decrease in rpm's or a noticeable objection in terms of motor sound. The harder the wood, the deeper the bite, the more cautious you must be. You will find when you force the cut that you will get obvious burn marks. Some of these will be difficult to remove, so it makes sense not to create them at all by working with sharp tools, sensible feed, and reasonable depth-of-cut settings.

Freehand Shaping

Work that has a curved edge, whether it is uniform or irregular, can't be shaped against a fence, which is the only reason the process is called "freehand shaping"; controls are

11-36.   Fences are set in line for partial cuts; the outfeed fence is brought forward for full cuts. The idea is to supply full support for the work throughout the pass.

11-35.   Construction details of the sliding jig. When you use it, be sure to allow for the jig's base when you set the height of the cutter.

11-37.   Fulcrum pins provide support for the work at the start and the end of the cut. This setup is actually a portable router that is mounted to the underside of a special table.

11-38.   Unobstructed table surface of the individual shaper is an asset when doing freehand work. You can work on any side of the table that is convenient in relation to the size and shape of the workpiece.

still definitely in order, and they are supplied by fulcrum pins and collars on the spindle. The pass is started with the work firmly braced against the infeed pin. Then, the work is moved slowly to contact the cutter and to edge it forward until it bears snugly against the collar that is on the spindle along with the cutter. This is the trickiest part of the operation, so make the initial contact with caution. If you rush, the cutter can splinter the work, even jerk it from your hands. Once the work is firmly seated and enough of its edge has been shaped, you can swing it free of the first pin and use the outfeed pin for support (Figure 11-37). One of the most important safety factors is for the work to have adequate bearing surface against the collar.

An advantage of the individual shaper is its unobstructed table surface. You can actually position yourself on any side of the table that is convenient in relation to the size and shape of the workpiece (Figure 11-38). Because of this freedom, you can often do shaping operations on assembled components, even when the cuts are required on an inside area (Figure 11-39). Do be sure on such operations that you are always feeding the work against the cutter's direction of rotation. This is a hard-and-fast rule of all shaper operations.

Strip Molding

When you need a piece or two of slim molding, it's okay to shape the form on a wide workpiece and then remove when you need by sawing. When you need slim molding in quantity, then it's best to create a special setup so the work can be done on pre-cut pieces, conveniently and accurately. A system you can use is shown in Figure 11-40. Workpieces are fed in one end of the jig and pulled out the other.

The jig has two hold-downs. The inner one is set to bear down on the work; the outer one keeps the work against the shaper fences. Since both parts are adjustable, you can organize to accommodate pieces of various widths and thicknesses. The jig is easy to set correctly, if you do it

11-39.   To do inside work, you merely situate the work so the cutter is inside the opening. Thus, you can work on assembled components. Remember always, that feed direction must be against the cutter's rotation.

11-40.   It's best to work with a special jig when you need to shape a quantity of slim moldings. The pre-cut pieces are pushed into the infeed end of the jig and pulled out the other.

with a sample workpiece in place. Adjust both hold-downs to keep the work snug, but don't bear down so much that you must force the work through. Construction details are shown in Figure 11-41. Note that there is a mounting bracket for both the infeed and outfeed fences of the machine.

Bevels and Chamfers

If you use blank knives and work with the jig shown in

Figure 11-42, you can form smooth bevels or chamfers on stock of just about any size. The jig, which is made for a 45° cut, holds the work at the correct angle and provides support throughout the pass (Figure 11-43). Since the cutter is exposed, be sure that you always stand behind the jig and with your hands on the uppermost edge of the workpiece. Don't use this idea on narrow stock. If you work with a 1″-wide blank knife and make the setup carefully, you can do a full bevel on 3/4″ stock in a single pass.

11-41.   Construction details of the strip-molding jig. The hold-downs are adjustable to accommodate stock of various widths and thicknesses.

11-42.   How to make a 45° bevel and chamfer guide.

V-Block

Circular pieces can be edge-shaped by working against fulcrum pins, but you'll get more work-support and will have better control if you employ a V-block (Figure 11-44). Design the jig so that it can be secured to the table with nuts that thread into holes that are there for shaper-fence attachment. If you form slots in the jig (Figure 11-45), then it can be adjusted for the width of the cut and to accommodate workpieces of various diameters. Make the jig carefully; its

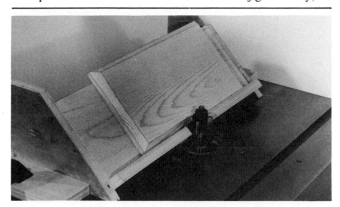

11-43. Here, the guide is being used to form a chamfer. The jig is not meant to be used with narrow pieces. Always stand behind it, and keep hands on the top edge of the workpiece.

11-44. A V-block is a good jig to use when you need to shape circular work, especially when you require a few similar pieces.

11-45. This is one way to design a V-block. The slots in the jig allow for adjusting cut-width and for positioning to accommodate various-diameter workpieces.

guide-edges must be straight and smooth. Also, the workpiece must be a true circle and with a smooth perimeter. Imperfections will be very obvious when the shaping is complete.

Scalloped Edges

You can form decorative scallops on work-edges if you make a special fence like the one shown in Figure 11-46. The setup allows you to brace work against a stop so you can use a pivot action to make contact with the cutter, and then reverse the action to break the contact. The result is shaped arcs which can be equally spaced along the edge of the board (Figure 11-47). The fence is a straight board with a series of equally spaced holes drilled along the bottom edge. A pin in the holes acts as a stop for the work. To do the job, you brace one edge of the work against the pin and then move directly forward to make the cut. Pull the work back, set the pin in the next hole, and then make the next cut. Just keep repeating the same procedure. Spacing of the cuts will depend on how you place the stop pin. Be sure to use at least 3/4″ stock for the fence. Quarter-inch holes, spaced one inch apart, will do to start. You can always add more holes if you wish. Use a short length of 1/4″ drill rod as the stop pin.

Trouble Shooting

Check the chart in Figure 11-48 for possible solutions to operational problems that might occur when using a shaper.

11-46. The fence you need for doing scalloping is just a flat board with a series of holes drilled along its bottom edge. It can be attached to the regular shaper fences with clamps or screws.

11-47. To do scalloping, brace the work against the pin, then make contact with the cutter by pivoting the work. Then, pull the work back, re-situate the pin, and cut again. The pin, used in the drilled holes, assures that the cuts will be spaced equally.

THE PROBLEM	POSSIBLE CAUSES	WHAT TO LOOK FOR OR DO
IN GENERAL Burn marks on work or cutters	Cutting too deep	Light cuts, especially on hardwoods, are best—make repeat passes when necessary
	Forcing	Feed the work slowly and steadily—slow passes produce smoothest cuts
	Dull cutter	Hone on flat side, or follow manufacturer's instructions
No support after the work passes cutter	Misalignment	Adjust the outfeed fence to compensate when the entire edge of stock is removed
Work hits outfeed fence	Misalignment	Infeed and outfeed fences must be aligned when only part of the workedge is removed
Work gouged at end of cut	Misalignment	Check fence alignment whether removing part or entire edge of stock
End splinters on cross-grain cuts	Characteristic of procedure	End cut very, very slowly Make cross-grain cuts first—following with-the-grain cuts will remove blemishes Use back-up block Shape oversize piece—remove blemish by sawing or sanding
Depth of cut not uniform	Misalignment Human error	Check position of fences Use hold-downs when possible—maintain consistent pressure against fences (or collars)
Work knocked back	Wrong feed direction	Always feed *against* the cutter's direction of rotation
Cuts not smooth	Wrong rpm Cutting against the grain Dull cutter Cutting too deep Rushing the cut	Use high speed if machine has variable or different speeds Cut *with* the grain whenever possible Hone on flat side, or follow manufacturer's instructions Make repeat passes to achieve full depth of cut Feed slowly for smoothest cuts
Irregular edge	Inconsistent pressure Lifting work	Hold work firmly against fence (or collars) throughout pass Keep work flat on table, especially important when cutter is over work—use hold-downs whenever possible
Inaccurate cuts	Poor work handling	Check profile of cutter against work edge as height adjustment is made—with motor off!
FREEHAND SHAPING Work edge marred	Collars dirty or gummed up	Clean the collars—keep them smooth—store them carefully
Work difficult to hold	Not enough bearing surface	Be sure work has enough bearing surface on collars—very important safety factor!
Work kicks back	Biting too deep at start of cut No fulcrum pin	Easy does it—move the work very slowly into the cutter until it bears enough against the collars Brace against fulcrum pin before contacting cutter—a fulcrum pin on each side of the cutter is a good idea
Variation in height of cut	Poor work handling	Keep work down on table throughout the pass
Gouges	Cutter position	Work with cutter under the stock whenever possible
Rough cuts	Feed direction	Move work so cutting is done *with* the grain whenever possible

11-48.   Trouble-shooting chart for problems that can occur when doing shaper operations.

12. The Belt and Disc Sanders

Belt sanders and disc sanders have become standard finishing tools in woodworking shops. They are available as individual tools or as a machine that offers both functions. In concept, the disc sander is a fairly simple tool. That's why some workers will rig up their own disc sanders by mounting a suitable plate directly to the shaft of a motor that provides adequate power and correct speed and then adding a table for work support. Disc sanding can also be an auxiliary function of other tools. We've already demonstrated how the radial arm saw and the lathe can be used for fairly efficient disc sanding.

When considering individual tools, most woodworkers lean toward the combination machine. It provides both items mounted on a single stand and powered by one motor. The mounting arrangement doesn't impose serious operational restrictions. Anything you can do on either as individual tools may be accomplished when they are combined.

No matter which way you go, you'll find that these abrasive tools rank among the best finishing tools you can have in your shop. They do not replace portable versions, but they will substantially reduce the amount of postconstruction finishing that remains to be done. You can finish project components as you go so they are fairly well organized for final coats before you even assemble them. Also, many sanding jobs are much easier to do when you can apply the work to the tool, such as a final touch on the end of a 2x4 or the precise finished sanding of a picture-frame miter.

Sizes

Discs can range up to 12"—a lot more in industry—but in any case, the dimension indicates the diameter of the disc. The larger the disc, the more power you will need to run it efficiently.

Belt widths, for our purposes, range from 3" to 6". Two common belt sizes for tools normally found in small shops are 4" x 36" and 6" x 48". The latter dimension indi-

cates in each case (36" and 48") the length of the belt. The larger the disc, the wider and longer the belt, the more abrasive surface you have to work with.

Some Examples

Like all power tools, sanding machines can be small or large, built for continuous heavy-duty use or for the routine finishing chores that are common in all woodworking shops. There are always the "dream" tools for those of us

12-1.   This heavy-duty belt-disc combination sander is driven by a 1 hp (or better) motor and sits on a totally enclosed stand. The belt size is 6" x 48", and the disc is 12". Each unit has its own tilting table.

who are not involved with industrial applications, and, in this category, one of them is shown in Figure 12-1. It is guarded as much as any machine of this type can be, has two tilting tables with miter-gauge grooves, and runs a 12″ disc and a 6″ x 48″ belt. The total abrasive surface is impressive. Machines like this should be powered with a 1-1/2 hp, 220 V motor so they can be used with maximum efficiency.

A generally more practical concept for home use, in terms of cost anyway, is shown in Figure 12-2. This machine turns a 9″ disc and a 6″ x 48″ belt, so the total abrasive surface isn't anything to snicker at. It has a table, with a miter-gauge groove, for the disc, and a "stop" that is used

12-2.   This smaller combination unit also drives a 6″ x 48″ belt, but the disc is 9″. There is a tilting table for the disc, a "stop" for the belt. It should be operated with a 3/4 hp to 1 hp motor.

12-3.   The "no-frills" belt/disc sander is minimal in cost but high in performance. Belts used are 4″ x 36″; the disc, which together with its table is added at extra cost, is 6″. Like all tools of its type, the belt may be used in either the vertical or horizontal position.

on many belt-sanding operations. Like all combination tools—and also individual belt sanders—the belt sander can be used in either the horizontal or vertical position. A 3/4 hp motor is recommended.

The people who produce the "unadorned" tools offer a no-frills 4″ x 36″ belt sander to which you can add a 6″ disc/table assembly. What you have here are the essentials of a combination sanding machine at minimum cost (Figure 12-3). It's a lightweight tool, but sturdy, and can be operated with a 1 hp motor. As with any power tool, what you get out of it relates to the way you use it. If you make it part of your shop, you won't have to make excuses to anyone.

In the area of low cost belt sanders, consider the unit that is shown in Figure 12-4. You make it, working with a kit that supplies all the metal parts and castings. The extras that are required include your time and effort and whatever wood is needed. It's not a toy. It turns a 6″ x 48″ belt and can be operated efficiently with a 1/2 hp or 3/4 hp motor.

Something new in the way of belt sanders is shown in Figure 12-5. It drives a 2-1/2″ x 16″ belt, so it's not a big machine, but it should not be judged in relation to conventional, stationary tools. Its asset is that it can be bench-mounted (as shown), and it can also be used as a portable sander. It falls within the category of that new breed of power tools called "compacts." It's light, it's basic, and it's very practical in the area of the chores it was designed to accomplish.

12-4.   You can make your own 6″ x 48″ belt sander by working from a kit that includes all the metal parts. You supply the wood and the motor. The finished machine has all the necessary adjustment features.

The individual, small disc sander will resemble the unit shown in Figure 12-6. It can be mounted on a bench or on its own stand. Preferably, the table should be adjustable to various angles, and it should have a groove for a miter gauge. Tools like this will be driven by a V-belt that runs between the motor pulley and the tool pulley. The best place for the motor is *under* the surface on which the sander is bolted. Always be sure to follow the manufacturer's instructions regarding the power of the motor and the maximum speed at which the disc can be operated.

Sanding Safely

We're inclined to forget that abrasives are cutting tools. They bring wood to smoothness by removing material. If you can do that to wood, they can do that to you. Therefore, obviously, you must work so that your fingers, or any part of your body, cannot come in contact with the abrasive surfaces.

Sanding produces a lot of dust, and no matter how the machine is designed, some of it will be airborne. Therefore, wear a dust mask; even a respirator is not out of line. Also, wear safety goggles; it's an extra precaution that makes sense, especially if you are doing an operation that requires the work to bear against the "up" side of a sanding disc. In such a case, waste particles will be thrown up toward you.

Situate the tables so that there will be a minimum gap between the table's ledge and the abrasive. This provides maximum support for the work and guards against work or fingers being drawn down to where they should not be. Don't hand-hold small pieces. When necessary, grip the work with a clamp or even a pair of pliers.

When sanding metals, remember that sparks can result and cause fires should they contact wood dust. So, when you change from wood to metal sanding, be sure that you first clean the tool. Actually, this should be a routine procedure anyway. Never allow wood dust to accumulate around any tool.

Other safety factors will be mentioned as we get into using the tools.

The Belt Sander

This tool uses an endless abrasive belt that rotates over two drums. The bottom drum is powered; the other drum is an idler. Since the abrasive moves in a straight line, the belt sander is an especially good tool for doing sanding that is parallel to the wood grain.

The width of the belt does not indicate a limit on the width of the stock you can sand. By making repeat passes and adjusting the work position after each pass, you can sand boards that are wider than the belt itself.

Cross-grain work is also permissible but done mostly when you wish to remove a lot of material quickly. It should always be followed by with-the-grain sanding to remove scratches that remain after the cross-grain work.

All belt sanders can be used in either a vertical or horizontal position. This is possible because they tilt back from the bottom end. In general, use the vertical position for any kind of end sanding; use the horizontal position for surfacing and sanding of edges on long pieces.

Adjustments.   The back of the belt is marked with an arrow to indicate the correct direction of rotation. When you view the drums, you'll note that they turn "down" or in a clockwise direction. Point the arrow on the belt so it will follow the same route.

To mount a belt, lower the upper drum. This decreases the distance between the drums and permits the belt to slide

12-5.   A novel concept is this compact belt sander which can be removed from its mounting as a stationary tool and used as a portable unit. It drives a 2-1/2″ x 16″ belt and is equipped with a dust collecting bag.

12-6.   This basic disc sander has a minimum of parts—a base, an adjustable table, and the disc. The tool can be bench-mounted or set on its own stand. Motor mounting, preferably, should be under whatever the tool is mounted on.

12-7.   Tracking adjustment keeps the belt centered over the drums. This should be done carefully when a new belt is installed and readjusted any time the belt tends to move to the left or the right. Be sure to mount the belt so that it will run in the direction indicated by the arrow that is printed on the back of the belt.

into place easily. Then, raise the drum until there is no visible slackness in the belt. Don't overdo this *tensioning* adjustment. The second adjustment is *tracking,* which is centering the belt over the drums and keeping it moving in the same line (Figure 12-7). Tracking is accomplished with a tilt action in the upper drum. Tilt one way and the belt will move to the left; tilt the other way and the belt will move to the right. The idea is to adjust so the belt does neither. Your best bet is to sight the upper drum and make an as-close-as-possible arbitrary adjustment. Then turn the motor switch quickly on and off. If the belt moves one way or the other, make an adjustment to compensate.

When the belt is tracking correctly, you may use the machine. After a short period of work, increase the tension a slight amount. You may find that slight tracking readjustments may become necessary as you work. At such times, you may work the adjustment knob as the belt is turning.

The methods of accomplishing tensioning and tracking may vary from machine to machine, so read your owner's manual carefully for specifics in relation to the tool you own.

Regardless of whether the machine is in vertical or horizontal position, the table, when set in normal position, should be square to the abrasive surface. Check this with a square as shown in Figure 12-8, and then, if the machine is so equipped, adjust the bevel scale and auto-stops.

Edge sanding.   Use the machine in the vertical position with the table adjusted to form a right angle with the abrasive surface. Rest the work solidly on the table and advance it slowly to make contact. When the work is curved, make the pass in a sweeping motion; remember that the belt cuts quickly, so allowing the work to sit too long in one position will produce too flat a surface (Figure 12-9).

If you are going from a flat edge to a round edge, approach the job with a flat edge parallel to the belt and swing gently into the curve. In essence, the surface of the belt should be tangent to the curve at point of contact at all

12-8.   The normal position of the table on the belt sander is 90° to the abrasive surface. Check this with a square, and then, if the tool has them, adjust the bevel scale and auto-stops.

12-9.   It's important to keep the work moving. Hesitating, especially on curves, will result in a "flat." Gentle pressure and several passes to get a job done are better than a heavy-handed, quick job.

times. Usually, you should do preliminary cutting with other tools so the amount of material to be removed by sanding will be minimal. In any case, excessive pressure against the abrasive is poor practice. It is better to make two or three light-pressure passes than a single heavy one.

Try to work so you will be using the entire width of the belt. Keeping the work still will clog the belt in one area and may very well stretch it out of shape.

For square ends, move the work directly forward into the belt. When possible, use a miter gauge to assure squareness (Figure 12-10). Here too, it's a good idea to move the work across the belt as you move it forward. This can be done whether you are working freehand or with a miter gauge. Another reason to keep the work moving is to avoid obvious striations that can result when you do nothing but feed directly ahead. This factor is more critical with coarse papers than with fine papers.

How you do inside corners will depend on the design of the machine. If there is an outboard guard, it must be removed. You must adjust tracking so the edge of the belt moves right on line with the outboard edge of the backup plate. Then the job becomes pretty straightforward end sanding. Do one side of the corner, then flip the stock and do the other (Figure 12-11).

Angles. Simple bevels are done by tilting the table; the job is fairly much an end-sanding chore. You will be more accurate if you work with a guide. The guide can be the miter gauge or, lacking one, a piece of wood that you clamp in place after checking its position with a square. If the edge is compound, then you must set both the table and the miter gauge (Figure 12-12). The angles you use must be compatible with the miter-gauge and saw-blade settings you organized for the original cut. Remember that sanding removes material, so original cuts should be made a fraction oversize.

To do chamfering or to "break" edges (which simply means to destroy a sharp corner), adjust the table to the

TABLE

12-11.   You can do a fair job of sanding inside corners by working this way. On some tools, it may be necessary to remove an outboard guard. Be sure to track the belt so that its edge is in line with the outboard edge of the back-up plate. Be careful with hand positions—abrasives are cutting tools!

12-12.   To sand bevels, tilt the table to the angle you require. Here, both the miter gauge and the table are adjusted to match the original sawing angles of a compound cut.

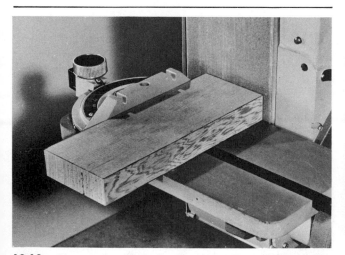

12-10.   You can do end sanding by moving the work directly forward, but, if work size permits, it helps to move the work laterally as well. Use all areas of the belt so that it won't stretch unevenly or try to move off the drums.

12-13.   You can work freehand to do small chamfers or to "break" edges. If accuracy is critical, or if you have many similar pieces to do, work with a miter gauge or clamp a strip of wood to the table to use as a guide.

angle you want, then move the stock directly forward (Figure 12-13). If you have chamfering to do on many similar pieces, it pays to make a trough jig like the one shown in Figure 12-14. The jig is adjustable so it can be set to control the angle *and* the amount of chamfer. When setting up the jig, use the top brace to lock the angle of the uprights and the opening between them. Then, attach the jig to the sander's table with a pair of C-clamps. Place the work on the sander's table and against one of the jig's upright. Then, move the work forward to contact the abrasive. The opposite upright acts as a stop to control how much material is sanded away.

Workpieces can be held flat or on edge, so it's easy, for example, to uniformly chamfer all edges of a piece. Slight chamfers can be done by sanding only; heavy chamfers should be formed first by sawing. When you have a lot of work to do, shift the jig occasionally so that you don't work on one slim section of the belt.

When the bevel you are doing is on stock that is not longer than the belt is wide, then, as previously mentioned, the operation is pretty much an end-sanding chore. For longer work, you will have to sweep across the belt and the results will depend on how skillfully you do it. Start close to an end, apply very light pressure and maintain it as constantly as possible as you feed across. Excessive pressure can cause the belt to dig in at one edge or the other.

12-14. This trough jig is used to chamfer edges accurately. It's especially useful when you have many similar pieces to do. The jig is adjustable, so you can control both the angle and the amount of material you wish to remove.

12-16. Surface-sanding is done best by bracing the work against the table, or, as shown here, against a stop. When work-size doesn't permit this setup, remember that the action of the belt will tend to pull the work from your hands and throw it in the direction of belt-travel.

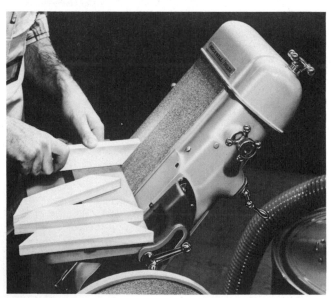

12-15. On some angle-sanding jobs, you can work more conveniently by tilting both the table and the sander. Be sure the components are locked securely before you start work. Check the first sanded piece with a protractor to be sure your settings are correct.

12-17. An L-shaped jig that you can make serves as a stop and keeps the work on line. Make the jig longer than shown and use slots instead of holes for attachment, and the jig will be adjustable for various work-lengths.

You can, if you wish, clamp a straight piece of wood to the table parallel to the belt. Then, you can pass the work between the guide and the abrasive. This procedure must be a light-touch operation.

On some angle-sanding jobs, you'll be able to work more conveniently if you tilt both the table and the sander (Figure 12-15).

Surface sanding. The most practical way to do surface sanding is with the machine in the horizontal position and with a stop or table in place against which you can butt the work (Figure 12-16). On large work, where a stop can't be used and you must work freehand, be aware that the action of the belt will tend to pull the work from your grasp and throw it in the direction of belt-travel. So, when you must work without a control, keep a firm grip, don't force the work down on the abrasive, move the work against the belt's direction of rotation, and don't stand where the work might be thrown your way.

When the machine you are using doesn't provide a stop of some sort, you can make an L-shaped one yourself and use it as shown in Figure 12-17. The stop can be at-tached with clamps or, preferably, by using bolts in thread-ed holes that might be in the machine for attachment of normal accessories. If you make the L-stop longer than it is shown in the photograph and cut slots in the attachment holes, you'll be able to adjust it for various work-lengths.

Another useful fence that you can make is shown in Figure 12-18. This is simply two pieces of wood assembled at right angles. The vertical member serves as a fence; the base is a means of securing the jig to the machine. It is useful when you wish to surface-sand pieces that are exceptionally long. The work, braced against the fence, is moved against the belt's rotation. The success of jobs like this depends as much on how you handle the work as it does on how you set up for it. The pass must be smooth and steady and without excessive pressure against the belt. You can always make another pass when necessary.

Diagonal sanding can be done when you wish to remove a lot of material quickly. This is done by using the fence just described, but the fence is situated so that the work can be passed across the belt as shown in Figure 12-19. Sanding this way will, of course, leave cross-grain

12-18.   A fence is a good accessory when the tool is used in the horizontal position. It can be used as a guide when sanding edges as well as surfaces. This simple L-shaped fence is bolted in place using holes that are provided for other accessories.

12-20.   The top drum is used like a drum sander. Some work, like smoothing a cabriole leg, must be done freehand, so control is your responsibility.

12-19.   You can remove material quickly if you make diagonal passes across the belt. This doesn't leave a smooth surface, so it must be followed by with-the-grain sanding. Don't force when making the pass, or you'll move the belt off the drums.

12-21.   When you are sanding edges and want them to be square to adjacent surfaces, it's best to work with a fence that will keep the work correctly positioned. Keep the work moving to avoid indents.

scratches, so you must do additional with-the-grain passes in routine fashion in order to bring the work to acceptable smoothness.

Incidentally, the same fence, when set up in line with the belt, can be used to work stock that requires edge-sanding.

Inside curves.   All belt sanders permit the use of the top drum as a "drum sander." If there is a guard, it must, of course, be removed. Such work can be done freehand; in fact, it must be done so if you are smoothing a component like a cabriole leg (Figure 12-20), or doing irregular edge scalloping to achieve an antique effect. But, when you want the sanded edge to be square to adjacent surfaces, then it makes sense to provide a guide that will allow you to support the work in correct position (see Figures 12-21 and 12-22).

Sanding knobs and such.   Since the rear of the sander does not have a back-up plate, the slack area of the belt can be used to sand round knobs, ends, and similar shapes (Figure 12-23). When you use the soft side of the belt, confine the activity to the belt's center three inches. Working on the edges of the belt may cause it to creep off the drums. Use a light pressure, and be aware that waste will be thrown in an upward direction. Here, as elsewhere, take precautions to protect your eyes and your lungs.

The Disc Sander

How to mount paper.   There are many ways to mount paper on a disc sander, and everyone usually ends up with one method that he finds preferable. One older method is the use of a disc stick that is almost like a stick shellac wrapped in a cardboard tube. You peel back the paper and apply the exposed sticky material to the revolving disc until the disc is fairly evenly coated. Then you press the abrasive sheet against the disc. This method works best when you "warm" the disc by holding a block of wood against it while it is turning.

Another method involves the use of a special rubber cement that is applied with a brush to both the disc and the paper. When the cement dries enough to be tacky to the touch, you press the sheet and disc together.

You can also buy abrasive discs which are self-adhesive. Using them is just a matter of peeling off a backing paper and then applying the abrasive to the metal plate. Be careful when you make contact that sandpaper and the disc will mate correctly.

Whatever method you use, always be sure to clean the old adhesive from the disc before applying a new coating. If there are sticky areas, use a solvent to soften the adhesive and then rub off with fine steel wool. Always be sure to apply the adhesive evenly in order to get the sandpaper flat on the disc; any bumps will result in imperfections on the sanded surface.

Incidentally, when you are doing a job that can be accomplished best by working through two grits of paper, you can organize a "double-sanding" disc. This is simply a matter of cutting a circle from the center of the coarser paper and then cutting a disc from the finer paper to fit it.

Both pieces of paper are mounted on the sanding disc so you can work on the outer portion of one grit and the inner portion of the second grit.

After mounting a new disc, run the machine freely for a minute or so and stand away from the edge. This procedure tests whether the bond between the disc and sheet of abrasive is good enough to be safe.

Direction of rotation.   Most discs will turn in a counterclockwise direction, which means you should place the work on the table on the left so you will be using the "down" side (Figure 12-24). Using the "up" side will cause the disc to lift the work and will throw grit into your face. Even so, sometimes it's necessary to use the "up" side, such as in sanding a long edge freehand and sweeping across the full diameter of the disc. When you have to use the "up" side, keep a firm grip on the work, hold it snug to the table and wear goggles.

To some extent, you can choose the abrasive-surface speed at which you wish to work. The slowest speed is at

12-22.   This all-purpose fence can provide support for sanding long pieces and can serve as a guide when you are using the machine as a drum sander. Check the dimensions against the machine you are using.

12-23.   Use the "soft" side of the belt to sand knobs, round ends and so on. Confine sanding to the belt's center area. Use light pressure, and be aware that waste will be thrown upward.

the center of the disc; it increases as you approach the outer edge. Remember this is surface speed, not rpm's. Also, if you held a piece of wood directly against the midpoint of the disc, you would create circular marks but do no sanding.

General operational procedures. Remember that the disc rotates. Therefore, it can't be used to do with-the-grain sanding. It is possible to surface cut by feeding with the stock on edge and its surface against the disc, but you will have arc marks that will have to be removed later by sanding with the grain. The depth of the arc marks will, of course, depend on the grit of the paper you are using.

It is always best to work with a light, smooth feed. Pressure should never be excessive even when you must remove a lot of material. A few light touches do a better job than a single heavy push. This approach is better for the work, and it will help prevent clogging the paper quickly. The no-force rule is especially true when you are working on material that is longer than the disc diameter (Figure 12-25). Forcing against the edge of the disc can cause gouging. Also, since disc speed is high, too much pressure can cause excessive heat which can burn the wood and the paper.

Keep the work moving. If you hesitate in one spot when sanding a curve, you will create a flat surface in that area. If you are doing end sanding, move the work directly forward into the disc but add a lateral feed after you make contact. The length of the lateral stroke can be from the outer edge of the disc to somewhere close to the center.

Although the disc can't get completely inside the corner of the right-angle cut, you can get close enough so that only a little extra hand work will be required to complete the job. It is best to sand one leg of the work by moving it across the abrasive until the edge of the disc almost touches the adjacent side. Then, flip the stock and sand the second edge by moving directly forward. When both legs of the cut are long, then it might be best to do each by moving across the face of the disc. In either case, don't force when you approach the inside corner. The exposed edge of the disc can mar the work.

Round off corners by using a gentle, sweeping motion. Start by holding the flat of the work parallel to the disc and then moving in to make light contact. Once you touch, start the sweeping motion. The plane of the disc must be tangent to the arc at all times.

Square ends and miters can be guided with a miter gauge (Figure 12-26). In either case, the work and the miter gauge may be moved laterally after the initial contact is made. When you have many similar jobs to do and the material to be moved by sanding is minimal, it's a good idea to clamp the miter gauge in position so all you have to do is move the stock directly forward. If you don't have a miter gauge, simply substitute a straight piece of wood for the gauge. The angle between the wood guide and the disc can be established with a protractor.

12-24. Always use the "down" side of the disc (arrow). Working on the "up" side will lift the work from the table and throw grit at you. Remember these factors when a job calls for sweeping the work across the disc.

DO NOT FORCE THE WORK

12-25. Be very careful when sanding material that is longer than the disc's diameter. For one thing, you'll be contacting the "up" side of the disc. For another, it's easy for the edge of the disc to dig into the work and cause gouging.

12-26. It's always best to work with a miter gauge when sanding ends or miter cuts. Remember that sanding is a finishing chore, so make initial sawing cuts as accurately as possible so there will be a minimum of material to be removed by sanding.

Chamfer jig. Chamfering can be done freehand, but when required on more than one edge of the stock or when it must be repeated on similar pieces, it's wise to make a simple jig as a guide. A chamfering jig is no more than a notched board that is clamped to the disc sander table. The long leg of the notch holds the work in position for the correct chamfer angle; the short leg limits the amount of material that can be removed. Thus, whether you are doing two pieces or a hundred pieces, you'll know that all the chamfers will be uniform (see Figures 12-27 and 12-28).

12-27.   A simple jig that lets you do accurate chamfering work. The short leg of the jig assures that exactly the right amount of material will be removed from the work.

12-28.   The work is held against the long leg of the jig, then moved directly forward. This is an excellent control when you have many similar pieces to do. Change the jig's position when necessary so that you don't wear the paper in one area.

Pivot sanding. This type of sanding is a fine way to sand perfect circles or arcs. The setup for the work doesn't have to be much more than a piece of plywood through which you have driven a nail for use as a pivot. When you clamp the plywood to the table, the nail should be about center on the down side of the disc, and the distance from the nail to the abrasive should equal the radius of the work.

An adjustable jig for pivot sanding is another possibility. The platform is a piece of 3/4″ plywood that is dadoed to receive a sliding, hardwood bar (Figure 12-29). If you make the sliding bar to fit tightly in the dado, you won't have to worry about clamping it in place for various radii settings. Drive a small roofing nail through one end of the bar. Make another bar to match the groove in the sander

12-29.   This is a simple jig you can make for pivot sanding. The arrow indicates the pivot point, which is just a short nail driven through the end of the sliding bar. The center of the work is pressed down over the pivot point.

12-30.   Then the work is rotated in a full circle. When you have much of this to do, reposition the platform frequently to avoid excessive wear on one area of the disc.

table and assemble the platform and the bar so there is about a 1/8″ gap between the front edge of the platform and the disc. Clamp the platform to the table so the sliding bar is about centered on the down side of the disc. This position is variable. When you have many pieces to do, it makes sense to shift occasionally so you will be using the full width of the down side.

To use the jig, set the pivot point away from the disc a bit more than you actually need for the work. Place the work in position on the point and tap the sliding bar forward until the disc contacts the work line. Then, slowly rotate the disc to sand the full circle. It doesn't matter whether you turn the work left or right (Figure 12-30).

The pivot technique, as shown in Figure 12-31, can

also be used to round off ends.

Figures 12-32 and 12-33 show a more sophisticated version of a pivot jig. The slide bar fits a 45° dovetail cut that is formed by beveling the inside edges of the jig's top pieces. The T-nut that is in the slide allows the use of various types of pivots. Thus, you can do pivot sanding even when the work should not have a center hole. The L-shaped lock rod, which threads into a second T-nut that is centered in the dovetail, lets you secure the slide in any position. Lock the slide after you have made contact with the disc.

In pivot cutting, it's assumed that you have bandsawed, jigsawed or somehow prepared the work so that the bulk of the waste has been removed before you go to the final sanding.

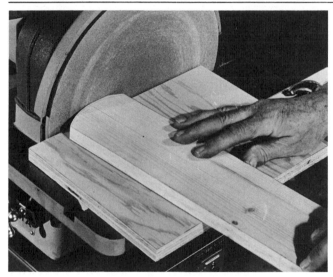

12-31.   The pivot jig may also be used to sand rounded ends. Be sure the pivot point is on the centerline of the work.

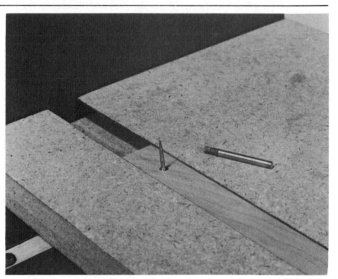

12-32.   A more sophisticated pivot jig provides for mounting different types of pivots and includes a lock for the sliding bar.

12-33.   Construction details of the advanced pivot jig. The dovetail slot is the result of bevel cuts made on the edges of the two top pieces. Installing a T-nut at each end of the slide increases the jig's versatility.

12-34.   You can sand pieces to exact width by using a straight piece of wood as a guide. The guide is offset to barely clear the "up" side of the disc. Here, the angle is exaggerated so it can be seen. The idea is to use as much of the disc from the outboard end to its center as possible. Keep the work against the guide as you make the pass.

12-35.   This simple jig can be used for sanding curved pieces to exact width. The work, turned constantly to maintain the point of tangency, is passed between the disc and the dowel. The work-edge that bears against the dowel must be smooth and uniform.

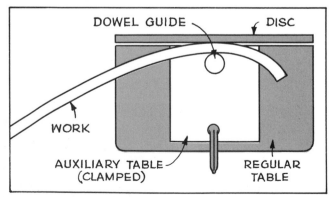

12-36.   Here's another way to work when you need to sand curves so they will be a particular width. The guide is simply a pointed piece of wood that is clamped to the tool's table.

Sanding to width.   You can sand straight or curved edges to exact width if you clamp a guide to the sander table so you can pass the work between the guide and the abrasive.

For straight edges, use an offset fence as a guide. This fence can be a straight piece of wood clamped to the sander table so the distance from its inside edge to the down side of the disc is a bit less than the width of the workpiece. The guide is angled just a bit so that when the pass is made, the work will contact the disc on the down side only (Figure 12-34).

To do the sanding, place the forward edge of the work on the up side of the table. Then move it forward in a steady, smooth manner. Don't take too deep a bite, and remember that since the abrasive does remove material, the original saw cut on the stock should be a bit oversize.

Both this idea and the pivot circle-cutting technique can be used to do beveling simply by tilting the sander table.

There are two ways to sand curves to width. With one, you install a dowel guide in the platform that you clamp to the sander table. The distance between the dowel and the disc equals the thickness of the work. You pass the work between the dowel and the disc, turning the work as you go to maintain the point of tangency (Figure 12-35).

Another way is simply to clamp a pointed stick to the sander table. The work is passed between the point on the stick and the disc (Figure 12-36).

In either case, it's assumed that the stock has been bandsawed or jigsawed so that a minimum of material remains to be removed. Also, the inside edge (the one that will ride the dowel guide or the point on the stick) must be sanded smooth before you do the outside edge. The inside surface can be done on a drum sander or by using the top drum of the belt sander.

Pattern sanding.   Pattern sanding calls for an auxiliary table that is clamped to the regular table (Figure 12-37). A rigid, metal guide strip is attached with screws to the front edge of the auxiliary table. Size the guide strip so its length is a bit less than the radius of the disc and its width is 1/4″ or so more than the platform's thickness. The pattern, which is the shape of the work you want but undersized to compensate for the guide thickness and some clearance between the guide and the disc, rides the guide. The work, cut slightly oversize to begin with, is tack-nailed to the pattern. As you move the pattern while keeping it in contact with the guide, the work is sanded and matches the shape of the pattern. A simple way to secure work to the pattern instead of tack-nailing is to drive nails through the pattern so the points project on the top side. Then the work is simply pressed down on the points.

This method is not efficient when you need only one piece, but it is a very fine technique to use when you require many similar pieces.

Pointing dowels or other round stock.   This process may be done freehand, but it's better to work with a guide. Simply drill a hole through a piece of wood with the size of the hole to match the size of the work (Figure 12-38). Clamp the guide block to the sander table at the required

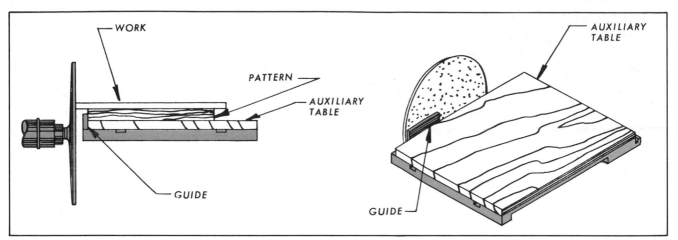

12-37.   The setup for pattern sanding. The pattern is kept in contact with the guide strip. The work, tack-nailed to the pattern, is sanded as the pass is made. The pattern must be smaller than the part you want by the thickness of the guide strip *plus* the clearance between the guide strip and the disc.

angle and then pass the work through the hole to make contact with the disc. Rotate the work to do either pointing or chamfering. To get a flat surface, move the work directly forward; don't allow it to rotate at all.

Metal work.   Sanding metals (or plastics) doesn't differ too much from sanding wood materials on either the belt sander or the disc sander. Use the correct abrasive and when working with hard materials, use less feed pressure. It's important to wear goggles on all abrasive operations but especially critical when abrading metals. Remember what was said about the possibility of fire when changing from wood sanding to metal sanding.

You'll find that many of the ideas described for woodworking will do for metal. For example, if you need a perfect circle in sheet metal, you could use the pivot sanding technique on the disc sander exactly as described for wood. When the metal is very thin and you have done the original cutting by supporting the sheet metal still on the scrap wood, do the pivot sanding with the sheet metal still on the scrap backup.

Metals do get hot. When doing work on small pieces, it's better to grip them with pliers instead of your fingers.

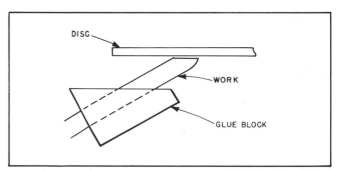

12-38.   The guide used for pivoting dowels and doing similar work is a block of wood with a work-size hole through it. Rotate the work to form a point or a chamfer; move it directly forward if you need a flat.

Trouble Shooting

Some of the problems you might encounter when doing belt sanding, drum sanding as done on a drill press, or disc sanding, are listed in Figures 12-39 and 12-40. If the suggested curves don't help, then it is best to check for possible mechanical faults.

DRUM SANDING		
THE PROBLEM	POSSIBLE CAUSES	WHAT TO LOOK FOR OR DO
IN GENERAL		
Sleeve slips—moves off drum	Sleeve too loose	Tighten drum-expansion nut—or follow manufacturer's instructions
Sanded edge isn't square	Human error	Freehand sanding is hard to control—work with a table, or a jig
	Misalignment	Be sure angle between table or jig and drum is 90°
Indentations in work	Work held still in one spot	Keep work moving, or drum will sand concave form
Sanding drum distorts	Excessive bite or feed pressure	Allow abrasive to cut freely—don't force

(Continued on next page)

DRUM SANDING (Cont'd.)		
THE PROBLEM	POSSIBLE CAUSES	WHAT TO LOOK FOR OR DO
Abrasive sleeve or work shows burn marks when thickness sanding	Biting too deep	Slight abrasive action is critical—make repeat passes when necessary
NOTE—Some of the factors covered in the disc sanding chart such as, SANDING MARKS, BURN MARKS, CLOGGED SANDPAPER, also apply to drum sanding.		

BELT SANDING		
THE PROBLEM	POSSIBLE CAUSES	WHAT TO LOOK FOR OR DO
IN GENERAL Belt moves to left or right	Misalignment	Adjust tracking to keep belt centered
Belt slippage	Excessive feed pressure Belt tension	Don't force work against the belt Follow manufacturer's instructions for correct belt tension
Inside curve not square to work surfaces	Poor work-handling	Use an extension fence to keep work square to drum
Belt becomes "floppy"	Too much sanding in one area	Work so that entire belt area is used
NOTE—Some of the factors covered in the disc sanding chart such as, SANDING MARKS, INACCURATE MITERS OR BEVELS, BURN MARKS, CLOGGED SANDPAPER, and others, also apply to belt sanding.		

12-39.   Trouble-shooting chart for belt sander and drum sander operations. Most of the drum-sander thoughts apply to work done on the drill press.

DISC SANDING		
THE PROBLEM	POSSIBLE CAUSES	WHAT TO LOOK FOR OR DO
IN GENERAL		
Work lifts from table	Using wrong side of disc	Work on the "down" side of the disc
Miters not accurate	Misalignment Human error	Check miter gauge—reset auto-stops Work carefully—mark miter-line with combination square—use a jig
Sanded edges are beveled	Misalignment	Angle between table and disc must be 90°—check auto-stop
Bevels not accurate	Misalignment	Make settings carefully—check auto-stops if any
Burn marks on work	Excessive feed pressure Work held in one spot Excessive use of center of disc Worn sandpaper—wrong grit	Don't force the work against the disc Keep the work moving Outer edge of disc sands more freely than center Replace sandpaper—don't use fine grits for heavy stock removal
Work jams between disc and table	Misalignment	Keep table close to disc—not more than 1/8" away
Sandpaper tends to loosen or has bubbles	Bad application Distorted sandpaper Dirty disc	Follow manufacturer's application suggestions Discard if very bad—store abrasive on flat surface Be sure disc is clean and dry before attaching sandpaper
Sanding marks on work	Work held motionless Sandpaper too coarse Work sanded across the grain	Keep work moving Work with correct sandpaper grit for the job being done Use fine grit when surface-sanding—finish by hand or with portable sander
Inadequate job on metal	Wrong abrasive	Use sandpaper designed for metal working
Sandpaper clogs too quickly	Excessive feed pressure Sanding painted surface Wood is wet or gummy	Allow sandpaper to cut at its own pace Use open-grain sandpaper—better to remove paint with proper solvent No cure
Chatter	Inadequate support	Provide support for the work as close to the disc as possible

12-40.   Trouble-shooting chart for the disc sander.

13. The Belt Sander/Grinder

The belt sander/grinder, simple in concept but broad in application, can occupy its own special niche in any woodworking shop. The closest you can come to organizing another power tool so that it will function somewhat like a sander/grinder is to put a narrow, abrasive belt on a bandsaw. But the setup can't challenge the versatility of this relatively new woodworking-metalworking tool. Because of the variety of belts that can be used on the tool—they range from basic abrasives to cloth and felt—it is practical for functions that include sanding, grinding, sharpening, finishing, and polishing.

The machine works with an endless belt that is powered by one motor-driven wheel and tracks over a series of idler wheels (Figure 13-1). The belts travel at speeds of up to 5,000 surface feet per minute. Because of this exceptional speed, you can sand wood or grind metal with very little heat build-up at the point of contact. You can overheat a cutting edge you wish to hone, but it will be more your fault than the tool's.

A major feature of the sander/grinder is that two of its idler pulleys can be positioned to change the route of the belt. Thus, you can arrange belt travel, when necessary, to suit the size and shape of the work. But more importantly, you can thread the belt through an opening in the work before you set it over the pulleys. Thus, you can do internal sanding or grinding (Figure 13-2).

13-1.   The parts of the belt sander/grinder. The spring-loaded upper arm provides belt tension automatically.

13-2.   A fine feature of the machine is that it can be organized for internal sanding or grinding.

Examples

Sander/grinders can be "big" or "small," but they all function the same way. Differences occur in overall size, power requirements, and belt widths and lengths. With some units, you can drive a disc sander along with the belt. Such a unit is shown in Figures 13-3 and 13-4. It drives a 1″ x 42″ belt at about 3,000 surface feet per minute; the disc diameter is 8″. Part of the disc sander setup is an adjustable table that is grooved to receive a miter gauge. The minimum power requirement is 1/3 hp.

Somewhere between the big and the small—referring to physical size, not capacity or function—falls the motorized unit shown in Figure 13-5. Its built-in 9.0 AMP motor moves the belt at 5,000 square feet per minute, which is as fast, or faster, than any machine of its type. Included in the broad range of accessory belts that are available for it are: fine, medium, and coarse grits for sanding wood or grinding metal, special abrasive belts for cleaning and polishing metals or plastics, a brushing belt that is specifically for rust removal, a felt belt that is used with jeweler's rouge for buffing and polishing metals like brass or silver. Thus, with the one tool, you do jobs that range from wood sanding, through tool sharpening, through maintaining heirloom candlesticks.

Dremel's version (Figure 13-6) requires only about one square foot of space and is as much at home in an apartment as it is in a workshop. Its built-in motor drives a 1″ x 30″ belt at 2,700 surface feet per minute, and a 5″ diameter sanding disc at 4,400 rpm. It has all the features that are characteristic of belt sander/grinders—adjustable table, removable platen, internal sanding capability, and so on.

13-4.   Some machines can be equipped with a disc sander. It may be a basic part of the tool or available as an accessory. An adjustable table that has a miter-gauge groove can be a big help on many sanding jobs. Standard disc-sanding techniques are used.

13-3.   This "large" machine requires a minimum of 1/3 hp. It may be mounted on a bench or on its own stand. A machine like this requires operating room at the front and on the left side.

13-5.   This "medium" tool has a built-in motor that turns the belt at a very fast 5,000 surface feet per minute. The manufacturer offers a wide range of belts, so the tool can be used for jobs that range from sanding and grinding to polishing metals. The latter application should be limited to non-precious metals.

Adjustments

There are three basic adjustments on any belt sander/grinder. The belt must be *tensioned*. The belt must *track* correctly. The table, when in normal-use position, must be 90° to the platen. Of the three, the tracking adjustment will require the most attention on your part. To set the table correctly for routine use, use a square as shown in Figure 13-7. When

13-6. The compact Dremel tool is only 15″ high and uses only about one square foot of bench space. However, its small size does not limit its functions. The 5″-diameter sanding disc is a basic part of the unit.

13-7. For normal operations, the angle between the table and the belt should be 90°. Tables may be tilted but do not have bevel scales or auto-stops. Critical table angular-settings should be checked with a protractor.

the setting is correct, lock the table's position by using whatever means is provided in the tool's design. Usually, it's a matter of tightening a bolt or a nut. Be sure the table is situated so that there is a minimum gap between its forward edge and the belt. There must also be clearance on each side of the belt. This adjustment is possible because the platen, a steel strip that backs up the belt, can be moved horizontally one way or the other. It's also important for the belt to be vertically aligned with the platen. But this, assuming the platen is in true vertical position, mostly has to do with tracking.

Belt tensioning will be provided automatically because the top idler pulley is attached to a spring-loaded arm. To mount a belt, or to remove one, press the arm downward, then release it, after the belt has been placed over the pulley. The spring pushes the arm upward, which pulls the belt taut. Some machines go a bit further, allowing you, by one means or another, to increase belt tension beyond the automatic setting.

A good tracking arrangement allows the belt to move smoothly over the pulleys and in a true vertical line over the platen. Adjustments for this can vary and have to do with the design of the machine. Sometimes, it's just a matter of tilting the upper idler pulley; sometimes the procedure involves more attention. The only way to accomplish it efficiently is to follow the instructions that are provided with the tool. In any event, check first by hand-turning the belt

BELT ON BOTH SIDES OF PLATEN

WORKPIECE

BELT BETWEEN IDLER AND PLATEN

13-8. The system to use for changing to internal sanding or grinding can vary from machine to machine, but basically, it's a matter of passing the belt through the work before it is placed over the top pulley. The belt straddles the platen.

through several revolutions. Make adjustments, if necessary, then turn the tool on and off quickly just to be sure.

Setting the machine for internal sanding can also vary from tool to tool. In any case, the tracking of the belt is changed so that it can be passed through the work before it is placed over the upper pulley (Figure 13-8). In some cases, the rear idler pulley is relocated to a place under the table where it can supply back-up support for the belt. When the re-tracking is finished (it takes more time to tell about it than to do it), the belt will be straddling the platen. The abrasive side against which you apply the work will, of course, be facing forward.

Platens

The standard platen is flat and long enough to back up the belt for a good part of its working surface (Figure 13-9). When working on corners or small edges, use the full width of the belt so it won't stretch in a limited area, a situation that can cause the belt to track incorrectly. Some machines offer special platens, either as standard equipment or as accessories, that are shaped for particular applications. The one shown in use in Figure 13-10, has a convex radius, which makes it particularly suitable for sanding tight, internal or external curves. Many workers make their own platens. I've seen them V-shaped and as various diameter rods. It's also possible to work with platens of lesser widths than standard equipment. Thus, you can work with belts that are 1/4″ wide, 1/2″ wide, or whatever. Some manufacturers offer belts that are narrower than the standard 1″. Or, you can make your own by slitting standard ones to the width you require.

13-9. The standard platen is flat and as wide as the belt. Avoid working on a limited area of the belt when doing deburring jobs like this. The extra pulley at the top comes into play when the machine is organized for internal work.

In General

Most belt sander/grinders are pretty well guarded, but, if not, be sure to operate so that your hands or the work can't be snagged by the belt. Adjust the table or any work surface that you may improvise, so that there will be minimum clearance between the work area and the belt. Always wear safety goggles. Use your hands so that they can't make contact with the abrasive surfaces—the tool is not for trimming fingernails.

Excessive pressure is never necessary when you are feeding work. The abrasives will cut fast enough without forcing the contact. Keep the tool clean. Be an especially good housekeeper when changing from wood sanding to metal grinding. If the tool runs as a disc as well as a belt, be aware that both items are turning at the same time.

13-10. Special half-round platens are available and very useful for sanding inside or outside concave forms. The belt conforms to the shape of the platen when the work is pressed against it. Many operators make special platens to suit particular work forms.

13-11. When used with the correct abrasive belt, the sander/grinder becomes a fine tool for deburring cold chisels and similar tools that become deformed even when used correctly. Slow and easy does it; the abrasive removes material fast enough. Always wear safety goggles.

Applications

There are many practical, routine chores that can be done on the sander/grinder. Among them are sharpening tools like drills, chisels, knives and scissors, refinishing screwdrivers and hammer heads, deburring metals, smoothing wood, plastics, and metals, refinishing and polishing metals, and more. Some of the applications are demonstrated in Figure 13-11 through Figure 13-17.

13-12.   The sander/grinder is a good sharpening tool. The table is tilted to conform to the bevel angle of the cutting edge. Move the tool being sharpened smoothly across the abrasive. Very fine belts are available for this kind of work.

13-13.   On some tools, it's necessary to use a height block in order to position the work at the correct angle. You don't have to worry too much about overheating cutting edges, but don't force the action.

13-14.   When sanding tight, internal areas, avoid letting the edges of the platen and the belt mar adjacent surfaces. A narrower platen and bolt can help. Some manufacturers offer such items. If not, it isn't difficult to supply your own.

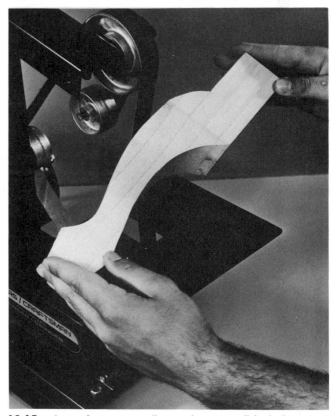

13-15.   Lots of contour sanding can be accomplished when you remove the platen. Be extra careful with work-handling so that you don't cause the belt to track off the pulleys. You can remove the table if this will help you manipulate the workpiece.

13-17. Work with special belts for polishing and buffing. Felt belts can be used with jeweler's rouge to bring out the luster of metals like brass. Very little pressure is required for efficient operation. Keep the work moving.

13-16.   The "free-belt" sanding technique can also be used for grinding operations like this, which is a good way to renew hammer heads. Belts are easy to change, so work with the abrasive most suitable for the job.

14. The Bench Grinder

W hile the bench grinder can be a very versatile tool, its main function in a woodworking shop is to renew the worn edges and maintain the sharp edges of cutting tools. These cutting tools may be hand tools, such as butt wood chisels, or power-driven cutters, such as jointer knives and twist drills (Figure 14-1).

The function of the grinder as a safety tool is often overlooked. With a grinder, you are more likely to keep tools sharp, and sharp tools mean better and safer work. In addition, you are more likely to remove, for example, burrs from the head of a cold chisel or even a nail hammer before they can become dangerous projectiles.

It's true that you can drive grinding wheels on other tools such as the drill press, the radial arm saw, the lathe, or even the table saw. With proper precautions, these temporary setups can be used efficiently. But, a good grinder is the one tool that is specifically designed for the job, and for optimum results, there really is no substitute.

General Characteristics

The most popular grinder is a self-contained unit that resembles a double-shaft motor quite a bit. However, it is so encased with covers, guards and shields that the only areas exposed are those parts of the grinding wheels that you need to see in order to work.

The bench grinder is a plug-in-and-use unit that you bolt down to an existing bench or mount on a special bench that you make or buy as an accessory. The word "pedestal" in the name of the tool merely indicates a particular design of floor stand (usually heavy-duty) on which the grinder rests.

Some grinders are belt-driven. A pulley is mounted on the shaft that drives the wheels. This pulley, by means of a

14-1.   One of the prime functions of the bench grinder in the woodworking shop is to maintain the keen edges on cutting tools. These can range from hand tools to blades used in jointers. Accessories are available that can help you do grinding jobs more accurately. Also, there are jigs and fixtures you can make.

14-2.   The typical bench grinder is like a double-shaft motor that turns two wheels. Thus, you work with, for example, a "coarse" wheel and a "fine" wheel. Tool rests, face shields, and spark arrestors are standard equipment. A lamp, which is usually an accessory, is a big help. A water trough is handy to keep tools from overheating as you grind them.

V-belt, connects to another pulley that is on a separate motor shaft. Such units are cheaper than the self-contained ones, but they require more mounting room. In addition, by the time you add a motor, extra pulley and V-belt, you're really not much ahead financially.

A grinder is often thought of in relation to a polishing head. This polishing head unit does have a horizontal shaft, and you can mount grinding wheels on it, but it does not approach being a safe grinder. Many manufacturers will tell you specifically that the polishing head they show in a catalog is not for grinding.

The size of a grinder is listed in terms of wheel diameter. For example, if it's called a 7″ grinder, you know it is designed to turn 7″ grinding wheels. Home shop sizes run from 5″ to 7″ with motor horsepower ranging from 1/4 to 1/2. When you get into 8″ wheels and motor horsepower 3/4 or more, you are entering the heavy-duty area where the tool is designed for continuous production work in places such as machine shops and garages.

Regardless of the size of the tool, it should be equipped with strong wheel covers, eye shields (preferably adjustable) and adjustable tool rests. If it has a water tray and a flexible

gooseneck lamp, so much the better (Figure 14-2). Such extras as spark arresters, exhaust outlets, and adjustable spark deflectors are good to have and will be found on the higher-priced units.

Grinders can be mounted on a bench top or on their own stands. Many manufacturers offer special stands that go along with the tools they offer. Figure 14-3 shows the construction details of a cabinet-type stand that you can

14-3.   This work stand that you can make provides a good base for a grinder and plenty of storage space for goggles, grinding guides, extra wheels, and so on. The door installs with offset hinges and magnetic catch ala kitchen cabinets. The insides of the drawers can be detailed to suit your own equipment.

make. Its advantage is the storage area it provides for accessory materials. The cabinet may be mounted on casters, but if you add them, be sure they are the type that can be raised or lowered. The cabinet should sit solidly on the floor when the grinder is used.

Wheels

A grinding wheel is made of abrasive grains that are bonded together by means of a special material. Each of the grains is a cutting tool that becomes dull as it does its job and finally tears loose so another sharp grain can take over. The makeup of any wheel involves five factors: the abrasive, the grain, the grade, the structure, and the bond.

The abrasive is the material that does the cutting. Most of the wheels supplied with home-type grinders are of aluminum oxide. This is good for grinding all materials that have a high tensile strength, such as high speed steel and carbon steels. Silicon carbide is good for working on low tensile strength materials like brass, bronze, gray iron, aluminum, and copper.

The grain has to do with abrasive grit size, and there are as many categories here as you will find in common sandpaper. "Coarse" grits run from #12 to #24. "Medium" grits run from #30 to #60. "Fine" grits run from #70 to #120. Even finer grits in the "very fine" and "flour size" categories can run from #150 to #600.

Wheels supplied as standard equipment with the grinder you buy usually fall into the general medium category, even when they are listed as "coarse." The coarse (sometimes called out as a "medium coarse") will be about a #36, and the medium (sometimes called out as a "medium fine") will be about a #60. These grit sizes in aluminum oxide are very good for all-purpose wood-shop work.

The grade of a wheel has to do with the bond, which can run from "very soft" to "very hard." Hard wheels hold abrasives together even under extreme pressure, while soft wheels permit them to loosen easily. In general, hard wheels are used for grinding soft materials while the soft wheels are used for grinding hard materials. Between the two extremes, a medium-hard grade, is best for average work.

In essence, structure refers to the spacing of the grains throughout the wheel. Hard, brittle materials are handled best on wheels with abrasive grains that are closely spaced. Wheels with widely spaced grains do better with soft materials that tend to clog the abrasive.

The bond refers to the material that is used to hold the abrasive grains together. For our purposes, we are concerned with a vitrified bond which consists of special clays and other ceramic materials. The bond material and the abrasive grains are fused at high temperatures to form a glass-like mass. The result is a high-strength, porous wheel with a cool cutting action. The vitrified bond is excellent for general-purpose grinding.

Grinding wheels may be shaped or purchased preshaped to do special jobs. The one shown in Figure 14-4 can be used for, among other things, renewing the serrations in pliers' jaws. The most common wheels are square-edged and round-edged. Cup wheels are good for sharpening tools like gouges and roundnose lathe chisels, but be certain the grinder you are using is equipped to handle them.

Safety and Care of Wheels

Never run a grinding wheel faster than the speed that is listed on the flange. Excessive speed will generate destructive heat and will also subject the wheel to centrifugal force that it may not be able to withstand. Both conditions can result in wheel breakage.

Test a wheel for cracks before you mount it. Do a visual check for chipped edges and cracks that you can see. Then mount the wheel on a rod that you pass through the arbor hole, and tap the wheel gently on the side with a piece of wood. The wheel will ring clear if it is in good condition. A dull thud may indicate the presence of a crack that can't be seen with the eye. If this happens, don't take any chances; discard the wheel.

Good grinding wheels have metal bushings and are fit tightly on the spindle. However, they must not be so tight that you have to hammer them on or so loose that they will not run true. Washers made of blotting paper should be placed on each side between the wheel and the flanges. Be sure the diameter of the paper washers is not less than the diameter of the flanges. The purpose of the paper washers is to equalize the pressure on the sides of the wheel.

Tighten the lock nuts only as tight as they have to be to secure the wheel. Excessive pressure can cause the wheel to break. After the wheel is mounted and all guards replaced, let the wheel run idle for a minute or so as you stand to one side.

Always adjust the tool rests so that they are within 1/8″ of the wheel. This will reduce the possibility of getting the work wedged between the rest and the wheel. Whenever possible, work on the face of the wheel. Chores on a grinder are often done against the side of the wheel, so some words

14-4. This type of grinding wheel, which can be used to renew serrations in pliers' jaws, is just one design that is available preshaped. There are many other wheel designs available, but be sure that they can be used on the machine you own.

GRINDING WHEEL

30°

of caution are in order. Quoting the Grinding Wheel Institute: "Side grinding shall only be performed with wheels designed for this purpose. Grinding on the flat side of straight wheels is often hazardous, and should not be allowed . . . when the sides of the wheel are appreciably worn thereby, or when considerable or sudden pressure is brought to bear against the sides."

This indicates a degree of tolerance for *very light-duty* side-grinding, such as touching up a screwdriver blade or a skew. It *does not abide* heavy-duty applications, such as renewing the edge of a cold chisel or axe or mattock. For these jobs, and similar ones, you must use a wheel mounted with a flat side that is backed up by a plate to withstand side pressure. Even light-duty work should not be overdone, certainly not to the point where the thickness of the wheel is reduced.

Wear safety goggles or a good face mask on all grinding operations, even if the job is as simple as touching up a screwdriver tip. Metal grinding creates sparks, so keep the area around the grinder clean. Always allow the wheel to come up to full speed before you apply the work. Be aware that since grinders do not have brakes, the wheels will continue to spin for quite a while after you turn off the switch.

To Dress a Wheel

"Dressing" a wheel can be done to renew sharpness or to true up the face of the wheel. The most common type of dresser is a mechanical one with star wheels that revolve as the tool is pressed against the wheel. To use it, set the tool rest so the gap between it and the face of the grinding wheel is just enough so the heel of the dresser can brace against the forward edge of the tool rest (Figure 14-5). Tilt the handle of the dresser up at a slight angle but do not make contact with the grinding wheel until after you have turned on the motor. Press the dresser easily against the turning wheel until you get a bite; then move slowly from side to side across the wheel. A small bite and many passes is better than a big bite and one pass.

It takes a little experience to do this job. Work cautiously, hold the dresser with force on the tool rest, do not use excessive pressure against the grinding wheel, and you'll soon master the technique.

Job Possibilities

If you have to remove metal from metal, the job can probably be done on the grinder as long as it's feasible to apply the work to the tool. Welded joints can be smoothed; round or square bar stock can be scored on an edge of the wheel as a preliminary step to hacksawing or cutting with a chisel (Figure 14-6). Burrs that form on the hammer end of cold

14-6.   An "off-beat" job for a grinder—reducing the diameter of a rod so it will be easier to cut with a hacksaw. The face shield has been removed, but only so the operation can be seen more clearly. The metal attachment at the top of the wheel cover is the spark arrestor.

14-5.   Faces of grinding wheels are renewed by using a wheel dresser. The tool creates a lot of dust, grit, and sparks, so use it carefully. Adjust the rest away from the wheel so the ledge on the dresser can butt against the front edge of the rest.

14-7.   You can use this technique to form a square or rectangular hole in sheet metal. Don't make the fold too sharp, or the sheet metal may crack when you unfold it after grinding.

chisels can be ground away. You can even do such jobs as forming a square opening in metal tubing simply by moving the tube directly into the face of the wheel. A similar job can be done on sheet metals if you fold the metal as shown in Figure 14-7 and then, with the fold line forward, move the work straight into the wheel. When you unfold the metal, you have a square opening. Of course the thickness of the wheel dictates the minimum cut. You can do wider cuts by making more than one pass, but you can't make narrower ones.

Working with a portable drill facilitates pointing rods and even reducing end diameters. Chuck the rod in the drill and let it spin as you apply it to the turning wheel. It isn't necessary to apply a lot of pressure, but it is a good idea to avoid using just one spot on the wheel. Working in this manner will usually produce more accurate results than if you try to do it freehand.

Hollow-Ground Edges

Creating a hollow-ground edge is easy to do on the face of the wheel simply because the wheel shape produces the hollow-ground form automatically (Figure 14-8). The tool

must be held at an angle with the work edge against the upper part of the wheel. The more acute the angle, the longer the cutting edge will be. Many times, it's possible to rest the blade of whatever you are sharpening against the rear edge of the tool rest and use this contact as a pivot to bring the cutting edge of the tool forward. Take light touches until the grinding is complete.

Keep the metal cool. Have water on hand so you can quench the item frequently. Allowing the metal to get too hot can destroy the temper of the tool.

14-10.   This special grinder table that you can make has a slot for a miter gauge. If you can't attach it directly to the grinder's tool rests, you'll have to make special supports so the jig can be used in place of the regular rests. Be sure the miter-gauge slot is parallel with the faces of the wheels.

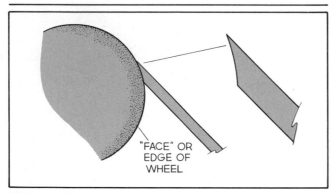

14-8.   Hollow-grinding is done on the face of the wheel. The more acute the angle between the tool and the wheel, the longer the bevel will be. You must, of course, always work with the tool rest. Many times, it helps to clamp a beveled block to the rest to serve as a support and a guide for the tool being sharpened.

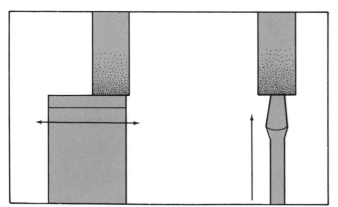

14-9.   To square an edge, move the blade parallel to the face of the wheel. When the edge is narrow, you can move directly forward. Always remove the least amount of material that will do the job.

14-11.   How to make the platform for the special table. Note the notches for the wheels. Be sure the head of the "miter gauge" is square to the bar. You may have to change dimensions to suit your machine, but do make the platform long enough to span across both wheels.

Working Across the Wheel Face

To renew a straight edge, work on the face of the wheel. If the work is wider than the wheel thickness, then you must pass laterally while keeping the work edge parallel to the face of the wheel. If the work edge is narrow, you can move the work directly forward (Figure 14-9).

To do this kind of work with more accuracy than you might be able to achieve freehand, make the miter-gauge jig shown in Figures 14-10 and 14-11. This jig is no more than a platform with a groove cut to receive the bar of a right-angle guide. You can make it for one wheel or long enough to span across both tool rests. Attach it with clamps or drill a few holes through the tool rests so you can secure this jig and others like it with wood screws driven up through the bottom.

Using jigs with the grinder is very important. Anything that can be sharpened can be sharpened freehand, but it takes a considerable amount of experience to do the job professionally. Creating holders for tools will help eliminate human error. Quite a few jigs are sold as accessories for the grinder. Some are simple and hold only a few tools; some are complex and make it possible to hold objects that range from plane blades to scissors. Special ones are sold for sharpening twist drills (Figure 14-12). Anytime you can make a job easier or better by buying or making a jig, do so.

Tips on Sharpening

Twist drills.   Twist drills can be sharpened freehand, but it's a tricky job that even some experienced mechanics never master. To get some idea of the proper technique, choose a new, 1/2″ twist drill and go through the following procedure with the grinding wheel still.

Hold the drill near the cutting edge between the thumb and index finger of your left hand. Hold the shank end of the drill between the thumb and index finger of your right hand. Place the drill on the tool rest so its centerline makes the required angle with the face of the wheel, then slightly lower the shank end. Since you are working with a new drill, it will be easy to gauge the angle simply by placing the cutting edge of the drill flat against the face of the wheel.

14-12.   Special twist drill holders are available as accessories. These are adjustable for many sizes and styles of drills and come with specific instructions for their use.

14-13.   This simple jig, which can be used on the platform already described, can provide a lot of help when you must sharpen twist drills. Position the drill as shown on the right, and make a small clockwise turn as you move the drill away from the guide block and bring it parallel to the pencil mark. Try this with a new drill and the wheel still a few times to get the feel of it.

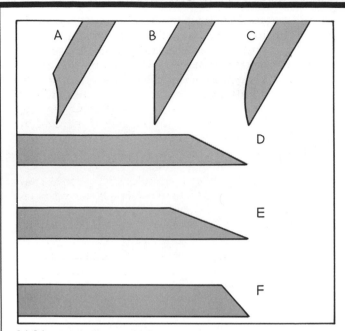

14-14. Hollow ground (A) and flat ground (B) show good ways to shape a cutting edge. It must never be rounded as in (C). This can result from poor grinding. The bevel length should be about 2x the chisel thickness (D). A longer bevel (E) might work better on softwoods, but it will knick and dull easily. The edge should never be blunt as in (F).

14-15. After the grinding chore, wood chisels should be honed as shown here. Be sure to maintain the slight clearance between the heel of the cutting edge and the stone when you are honing the bevel.

14-16. A flat-ground edge is honed in a similar fashion. The clearance provides a slight, secondary bevel that contributes to the keenness of the cutting edge.

Advance the drill to place its heel against the grinding wheel and then, in a combination action, slowly raise the shank end of the drill while you use your left-hand fingers to twist the drill in a counterclockwise direction until the grinding approaches the cutting edge. Don't exert a lot of pressure; don't try to work too fast. After you have gone through this procedure a dozen times or so with a new drill, test your skill by sharpening an old one.

Another possibility is to make the jig shown in Figure 14-13 and work against the side of the wheel. To use the jig, place the drill so the cutting lip is against the side of the wheel and the body of the drill is against the guide block. To do the sharpening, the drill is rotated as it is swung to a position that is parallel to the pencil line. Here too, in order to do a good job, it's wise to go through the procedure with a brand new, large size drill and with the wheel stationary. Doing this a few times will give you the feel of what is involved. Naturally, the angle of the guide must be changed if the point angle of the drill is not 59°.

Wood chisels. Some of the facts that apply to the cutting edges of wood chisels and similar tools are shown in Figure 14-14. These tools cut best when they are square across the cutting edge and have a hollow-ground bevel. Squaring the edge is necessary only after the chisel has seen considerable use and knicks appear. It is done by placing the chisel flat on the tool rest and moving it parallel to the face of the grinding wheel. This can be done freehand or by using the miter-gauge jig described previously. Remove only as much material as you have to.

To do the bevel, tilt the tool rest to the required angle and again move the chisel across the face of the wheel. If the chisel is narrow enough, the lateral motion may not be necessary. Another method is to make a special guide block that provides the necessary bevel angle. The length of the bevel should be about twice the thickness of the chisel; this usually produces about a 30° angle.

Some amount of burr will be left on the cutting edge, so the grinding operation should be followed by honing the chisel by hand on a flat stone (Figure 14-15 and 14-16). This

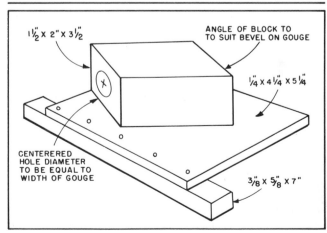

14-17. This gouge guide helps when touching up or reshaping a gouge. The diameter of the hole in the block is equal to the overall width of the tool's blade.

should be done with the chisel tilted on its bevel but with a little extra tilt to get some clearance between the heel of the cutting edge and the stone. The chisel should also be level but resting on the back surface of the blade. Alternate between the two positions until all the burrs are gone and the edge is keen enough to cut a hair.

The honing operation actually produces a secondary bevel that does a beautiful cutting job. When you use chisels with care, the honing can be repeated quite a few times before it becomes necessary to go through the grinding procedure again.

All of the information in this section applies to hand-plane blades and similar items, as well as to wood butt chisels.

Guide for a gouge.   A guide you can use, together with the platform jig already described, to help you do an accurate job when reshaping or touching up a gouge or a similar tool is shown in Figure 14-17. The diameter of the hole in the block is equal to the overall width of the tool's blade; the block's angle must suit the bevel angle of the cutting edge. The guide is clamped or otherwise secured to the platform so the chisel can be passed through it to contact the grinding wheel, as shown in Figure 14-18. Once the contact is made, the tool is rotated slowly until the entire bevel area has been ground down. You will have better control over the procedure if the hole in the guide is a tight fit for the blade of the tool.

Jointer knives.   Jointer knives are done much like chisels, but it's not recommended that you try to do them freehand. Instead, work with one of the two jigs shown in Figures 14-19 and 14-20. One jig spans across both wheels of the grinder and offers the advantage of being able to go from coarse grinding to fine grinding without a jig change.

Of course, if the knife is in fairly good shape to begin with, you can confine the grinding to the less coarse wheel.

The second jig employs a sliding block that has been kerfed at the correct knife angle. The knife must fit snugly in the kerf before you do the grinding. This is especially important because three knives are involved. If you don't grind them carefully, the knives will be of different width and, because of the knife-adjustment method employed by some jointers, you will end up cutting with just one or two of the knives.

When you use the jigs, be sure that you go through each grinding procedure on each knife before you make any jig change. This assumes that more than one pass will be required to create a new edge. No matter what, keep the cuts extremely light, and do not permit the knives to become overheated. You can do honing on the knives after grinding or between grindings as described for wood chisels, but

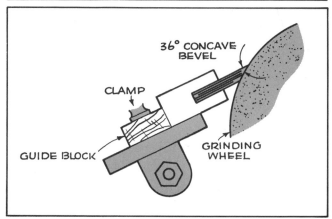

14-19.   This jointer-knife jig employs a sliding hardwood holder that grips the knife securely. It moves across a guide block that is clamped to the grinder's tool rests. If you must make a second pass, don't change the position of the guide block. Instead, place a piece of paper between the guide block and the knife holder.

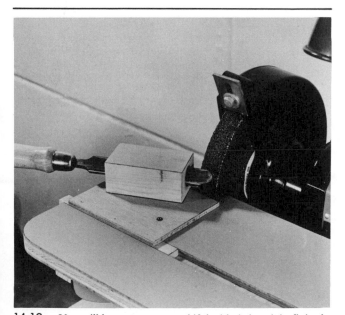

14-18.   You will have more control if the blade is a tight fit in the guide's hole. The guide can't do everything—be careful when making initial contact and as you rotate the blade. Note that the guide is used on the specially-made grinder jig.

14-20.   This holder for jointer knives is used with the grinder platform. It is adjustable so it can be used with knives of different widths. The kerf for the blades must provide a tight fit.

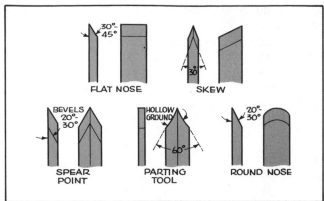

14-23. Typical cutting edges that are used on wood-turning chisels. Always follow up the grinding chore with a honing operation. It's also wise to keep honing the tools as you work. Grinding should be more for reshaping.

14-21. Remove knicks from a screwdriver tip by moving it directly forward into the face of the wheel. It may be flat-ground on the side of the wheel, but a small amount of hollow-grinding may be better. Don't overdo the slimness of the tip. It must be sturdy enough to withstand the torque when driving a screw. It's important for the sides of the tip to be parallel.

14-24. Do scissors and shears on a fine grit wheel that is square across the face. Make very light passes and keep the motion uniform to guarantee a straight cutting edge. The final keenness is obtained by honing on a flat stone.

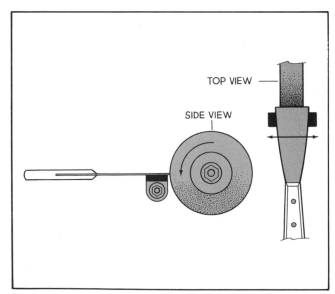

14-22. All you want to do with a putty knife is square off the edge—then remove the burrs and smooth the end by working on an oilstone. How "sharp" the edge must be will depend on the material you wish to remove. Thin materials like this overheat quickly, so use a light touch and dip the tip in water frequently.

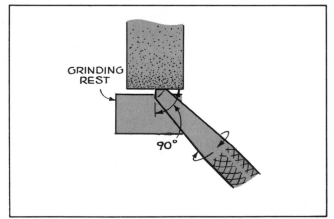

14-25. To re-do a punch, adjust the tool rest to the correct angle (the *original* angle on the punch), then simply rotate it against the turning wheel to make the end symmetrical. As usual, grind away only as much material as necessary.

don't overdo the secondary bevel since this will weaken the cutting edge.

Miscellaneous sharpening chores. Some other tools and methods to use to keep them in good working order are shown in Figures 14-21 through 14-26. In these illustrations and others that were used in this chapter, guards were not situated as they should be for safe operation. This is not a recommendation that you work the same way. These no-guard situations were created for photography purposes only. Always *use* the guards, and always *wear* safety goggles.

14-26.   A draw knife can be ground with a single or a double bevel. It will be easy to maintain the original bevel since there are sure to be unworn portions at each end of the blade. Use light pressure and be sure to move the knife parallel to the face of the wheel.

15. A Workbench That's A Total Power Shop

Most workshops begin with a workbench and evolve around it. Because of the growing need to save space, and the introduction of benchtop power tools, I decided to design a workbench that would be a complete woodworking station. The workbench *is* the shop. The top of the unit has hinged, cut-out panels with compact tools attached, sewing-machine fashion, to the underside. You flip each tool as needed, then fold it away when the job is done. Shelves below, and a built-in cabinet, hold additional tools which can be secured to the top through T-nuts to steady them for use.

This workbench is larger than conventional benches for two reasons: to allow the space required for the tools, and to provide a generous area for fabrication and assembly work. (See Figures 15-1 through 15-4.)

Building the workbench is not a weekend project, but, you can use it before it's complete. Once the top is made and the substructure assembled, it is functional and, in fact, can be used for subsequent steps in its own production.

15-1.   A new concept in workbenches. This workbench has a built-in table saw, two Record woodworking vises and a lot more.

15-2.   The bench is larger than conventional units, to accommodate built-in tools and to provide a generous work surface, ample for assembly and finishing of large projects. I cover the bench with a piece of indoor-outdoor carpet when doing such tasks.

15-3.   Lo! In addition to the table saw, there is a lift-up band-saw, and a tilt-up drill press, grinder/disc sander, belt sander/grinder, and something not shown here, a lathe on a lift-up shelf. Other tools, stored on shelves or in the cabinet, are secured for use with screws that thread into T-nuts installed in the benchtop.

15-4.   The bench has a built-in cabinet, shelves, and drawers—plenty of storage area for additional tools and accessories, as well as expendable materials. The cabinet doors are sliders, but they can be removed when necessary.

Bench Top (Figure 15-5)

The easiest method to make this top is to buy two 25″ x 96″ maple countertops and glue them together. The 9″ strip that you remove, preferably with a cutoff saw, to arrive at the required width of 41″, can be used for other purposes.

An economical and practical method is to assemble eight pieces of 2″ x 6″ x 96″ vertical grain fir, as shown in the drawing. Seven of the pieces must be rip-cut to remove 1/16″ of one edge so the parts will have square mating edges. The opposite edges will have square shoulders because of the tongue-forming cut. If you follow this procedure, the total width of the assembly will be 40-15/16″, a scant less than the 41″, but not critical.

The work is easy to do on a table saw, with the pieces passed vertically to form the groove, and a two-pass procedure, with the work flat, to form the tongue. It's a good idea to shape the groove about 1/32″ deeper than necessary to be sure that the edges will really butt and that there will be room for excess glue. Don't be *too* precise when forming the tongues and the grooves. Having to force them together with gluing and clamping will cause problems. An easy, slip fit is the correct way to go. Improvise a work surface by spanning a couple of sawhorses with a sheet of 3/4″ plywood, a material you'll need later anyway.

Hint—assemble four of the pieces, then the remaining four, and finally, the two halves. Working this way will minimize the possibility of the assembly bowing under clamp pressure. Be sure to remove all excess glue before it has a chance to dry.

15-5.   These are the techniques to use should you decide to make the bench top by working with raw material. I used vertical grain fir, but nothing changes should you decide to use a material like maple or birch.

Sub-Structure
(Figures 15-6, 15-7, and 15-8)

Cut the main rails, cross rails, end rails, and legs to length. The detail sketches in Figure 15-7 show how these components are assembled. The cross rails are let into dadoes formed in the main rails; corner legs and main rails are connected with a half-lap joint (Figure 15-9). The end laps will be easy to form if a radial arm saw is available, but the cuts are hefty enough so working with a handsaw won't be a problem. Form the shoulder first, then make a second cut to remove the waste piece. The center leg is notched for the radial and the lower frame pieces. Assemble these parts with the fasteners that are called for, then add the end rail and the leg returns.

Make subassemblies of the frames, dividers, and connectors, and add them to the sub-structure. Attach the connectors to the frames and the legs with glue and #12 x 2-1/2″ FH wood screws. Be sure to allow for the stretchers when installing the connectors.

Shape the eight drawer guides and put them in place with glue and a single 4d finishing nail at each end.

Cut the shelves to overall size, then carefully lay out and form the notches that are needed at the leg areas. The left-hand shelf is shaped as shown in Figure 15-8. The cut-out will be used as the mounting plate for the bandsaw. Attach the shelves with 4d box nails spaced about 10″ apart. Don't neglect to include the shelf cleat that supplies support for the shelves where they join.

KEY TO CUTOUTS

A . . . 18-1/2″ x 28″—B&D 8″ table saw (saw bolted in place—saw and bench surfaces are flush)

B . . . 16″ x 25″—Skil 10″ bandsaw (lift-out panel)

C . . . 12″ x 25″—Shop-craft 1/2″ or 3/8″ drill press (two-piece hinged panel)

D . . . 12″ x 24″—Rock-well belt sander/grinder (hinged panel)

E . . . 12-1/2″ x 16″—B&D bench grinder/disc sander (hinged panel)

15-6. This is how the bench sub-structure goes together. Key numbers relate to the materials list (Figure 15-17).

15-7. These details show the joints that are used in the substructure.

15-8. The cutout in the left-hand shelf is used as the mounting plate for the bandsaw. Check the size of the tool you plan to use before doing the cutting.

15-9. Main rails and corner legs are joined in a half-lap. Use glue and four 1/4″ x 2″ FH machine screws. Note hardware required for other areas.

15-10. You can do the cutting out with a saber saw, but I prefer the smooth edges that result from using a router equipped with a template guide. Guide strips are tack-nailed to the bench top. Get through the top by making repeat passes.

8 1/8″ OR TO SUIT
(BE SURE TO ALLOW FOR
1 1/2 THICKNESS OF BENCH TOP

#12 X 2″
FH SCREW
C'T BORE &
PLUG

OPENING FOR
SAWDUST—CUT
TO SUIT

- **ASSEMBLE FRAME WITH GLUE AND CORRUGATED NAILS**
- **SECURE BACK BY NAILING THROUGH CROSS RAIL AT TOP AND INTO CLEAT AT BOTTOM**
- **GLUE AND NAIL SAW PLATE TO FRAME**
- **SECURE FRAME WITH SCREWS AT FRONT AND WITH NAILS THROUGH BACK**

SAW IS BOLTED
TO SAW PLATE

15-11. This is the design of the area required for the built-in table saw. Be sure the surface of the saw will be flush with the top of the bench.

Install the Top

The next step is to attach the top. Place it so that it will overlap the sub-structure 3″ on all four sides, and anchor it with #12 x 2″ screws that you drive into the main rails and cross rails. Space the screws about 12″ to 14″ apart, and drive them through holes counterbored about 3/4″ deep. The counterbored holes are filled with wood plugs.

Figure 15-6 also shows the cutouts for the tools that I installed and identifies the brands. It's a selection I made because I feel that they are a pretty fair picture of available benchtop power tools. Although a check reveals that all compact tools come pretty close in size, it's wise to examine those you have, or plan to buy, to be sure the sizes suggested for the cutouts will be usable.

The opening can be formed with a saber saw, but I prefer working with a router because of the resulting smooth edges (Figure 15-10). Guide strips, tack-nailed to the bench top, are followed by the router, equipped with a template guide. Make repeat passes, deepening the groove about 1/4″ each time. Work with a 1/4″ router bit. This reduces the size of the pieces that are cut out, so you must compensate by gluing on 1/4″-thick strips of wood.

The piece cut out for the table saw is discarded. The bandsaw piece rests on cleats. The remaining three are hinged so they can pivot to use position. These openings require cleats so the panels can be supported when they are in neutral position. The cleats don't have to extend into the

opening more than 1/2″ or so and should be situated opposite the hinge end—except for the two-piece drill-press panel. Here, the cleats should run the long dimension of the opening.

Table Saw Compartment (Figure 15-11)

Make the back and attach it by nailing into the cross rail and the bottom cleat which is secured to the shelf. Make the frame as a subassembly, using glue and corrugated nails at the joints, and put it in place by driving screws through the leg returns and through the back. Attach the saw plate, after mixing the opening for sawdust, by using glue and driving 5d box nails. Be certain that the assembly is situated so that the surface of the table saw will be flush with the bench top. There is ample room under the saw for a box to catch sawdust (Figure 15-12).

Panels (Figure 15-13)

Cut these to size, then form the rabbets that are detailed in the drawing. Attach them to the sub-structure with glue and 1″ nails. Shape the trim and attach it as shown, with glue and 3/4″ brads.

15-12.   There is plenty of room under the table saw for a box to catch sawdust.

15-13.   The front panels are installed this way. The right end and the back for the bench are left open so the shelves can be used for additional storage.

Cabinet (Figure 15-14)

Make the side and the filler, and attach them by nailing into the cross rail and, at the bottom, into a cleat that is secured to the shelf. The back is anchored by nailing into its edge through the side piece and by adding a cleat behind it at its bottom edge.

Install the shelf cleats and the shelf, then shape the grooved pieces that are required for the sliding doors. The top frame piece is 2″ wide, because I had to provide a notch to get clearance for the Record woodworking vise I installed. Note on the drawing the relationship between the depth of the top and bottom grooves and the height of the door. This is so that you can lift the doors to clear the bottom groove when you wish to remove them.

15-14. Construction details for the built-in compartment. Cut parts oversize, and trim to fit on assembly. Sliding doors are removable.

Drawers (Figure 15-15)

There's nothing fancy here, but if you use glue in all the joints (except the bottom), the drawers will be sturdy enough for the purpose. Anyone desiring fancier joinery is, of course, free to do so.

The bottoms are attached *under* the sides, rather than being let into grooves cut in the sides, so as to get as much drawer-depth as possible. When cutting the sides and the dadoes, allow for a bit of clearance so the drawers will slide easily.

The materials listed are for four drawers, but the bench will accommodate eight. You can add four more at the "back" of the bench.

15-15. The drawers require basic construction—no heirloom procedures here, unless you choose to do more advanced work. The bench can contain a total of eight drawers.

Lathe Shelf (Figure 15-16)

The shelf is attached to the edge of the bench with a length of 1-1/2″ continuous hinge. Thus, it can be lowered when it is not in use. The supports, which pivot about the lag screws, swing out of the way under the 3″ bench-top over-lap. When the supports are used, they are anchored with lag screws. Be sure when the tool is not in use that you remove the sharp-pointed lathe centers.

15-16.   The lathe has its own shelf which is hinged to the back edge of the bench top. The lag screws, which serve as pivots, are tightened or loosened depending on whether the shelf is up or down.

KEY	PART	NO. PCS.	SIZE	MATERIAL
WORKBENCH MATERIAL LIST				
SUB-STRUCTURE (Figure 15-6)				
1	Rail	2	1-1/2″ x 5-1/2″ x 88-1/2″	VG fir
2	Legs	6	1-1/2″ x 5-1/2″ x 36″	VG fir
3	Cross rail	3	1-1/2″ x 5-1/2″ x 33-1/2″	VG fir
4	End rail	1	1-1/2″ x 5-1/2″ x 33-1/2″	VG fir

(Continued on next page)

KEY	PART	NO. PCS.	SIZE	MATERIAL
SUB-STRUCTURE (Figure 15-6) (Cont'd.)				
5	Leg return	2	1-1/2″ x 2″ x 31-1/2″	VG fir
6	Leg return	2	1-1/2″ x 2″ x 36″	VG fir
7	Stretcher	2	1-1/2″ x 2″ x 32″	VG fir
8	Frame	4	1-1/2″ x 2″ x 79″	VG fir
9	Divider	4	1-1/2″ x 2″ x 7-1/2″	VG fir
10	Connector	8	1-1/2″ x 2″ x 12″	VG fir
11	Drawer guides	8	1″ x 1-1/2″ x 34″	VG fir
12	Shelf	2	3/4″ x 35″ x 43-1/2″	Fir plywood
13	Shelf cleat	1	1-1/2″ x 2″ x 24″	VG fir
SAW COMPARTMENT (Figure 15-11)				
14	Back	1	3/4″ x 24-3/4″ x 35″	Fir plywood
15	Cleat	1	3/4″ x 2″ x 30″	VG fir
16	End frame	2	1-1/2″ x 4″ x 16″	VG fir
17	Front frame	1	1-1/2″ x 3″ x 24″	VG fir
18	Back frame	1	1-1/2″ x 2″ x 24″	VG fir
19	Saw plate	1	3/4″ x 16″ x 28″	Fir plywood
PANELS (Figure 15-13)				
29	Right panel	1	5/8″ x 21″ x 40-3/4″	Fir plywood
30	Left panel	1	5/8″ x 12-1/4″ x 21″	Fir plywood
31	Trim (NOTE: Trim pieces listed longer than necessary. Trim to fit on assembly.)	2	1/2″ x 3/4″ x 24″	Fir
		2	1/2″ x 3/4″ x 45″	Fir
		2	1/2″ x 3/4″ x 15″	Fir
CABINET (Figure 15-14)				
20	Back	1	3/4″ x 24-3/4″ x 27-1/2″	Fir plywood
21	Side	1	3/4″ x 13″ x 24-3/4″	Fir plywood
22	Filler	1	3/4″ x 5-1/2″ x 13″	Fir plywood
23	Shelf	1	5/8″ x 16-3/4″ x 27-1/2″	Fir plywood
24	Cleat	2	3/4″ x 1-1/2″ x 16-3/4″	Fir
		1	3/4″ x 1-1/2″ x 26″	Fir
25	Side frame	2	3/4″ x 1-1/2″ x 22″	Fir
26	Bottom frame	1	1-1/4″ x 1-1/2″ x 29″	Fir
27	Top frame (NOTE: Frame pieces listed longer than necessary. Trim to fit on assembly.)	1	1-1/2″ x 2″ x 29″	Fir
28	Door	2	1/4″ x 14″ x 17-7/8″	Hardboard or plywood
DRAWERS (Figure 15-15)				
32	Sides	8	3/4″ x 5-1/4″ x 17″	Fir plywood
33	Front	4	3/4″ x 6-3/4″ x 19-5/8″	Fir plywood
34	Back	4	3/4″ x 5-1/4″ x 17-1/8″	Fir plywood
35	Bottom	4	1/4″ x 17″ x 18-3/8″	Hardboard or plywood
36	Pulls (NOTE: Materials listed for drawers are for four units.)	4	1″ x 1-1/4″ x 10″	Fir
LATHE SHELF (Shopcraft 7″ x 32″) (Figure 15-16)				
37	Lathe shelf	1	1-1/2″ x 7″ x 45-1/2″	VG fir
38	Hinge	1	1-1/2″ x 45-1/2″	Continuous (brass)
39	Support	2	1-1/2″ x 3″ x 10″	VG fir

15-17.   Materials list for the workbench. Some parts are listed longer than necessary so that they can be trimmed to fit on assembly.

Finishing

Do as much smoothing as possible on individual components as you go, bringing them to acceptable smoothness prior to assembly. When the bench is complete, or at stage where you wish to use it before going on, do a final sanding with fine sandpaper.

Apply a liberal coat of sanding sealer to *all* surfaces. Remove any sealer that does not soak in with a lint-free cloth after waiting about ten minutes or so—or follow the directions on the container.

Sand once more when the sealer is thoroughly dry and, after removing the dust with a tack cloth or something similar, apply a second coat of sealer. Wipe off the excess, then wait at least twenty-four hours for the second application to dry. Then sand again. Remove the dust caused by sanding, then go over the bench with a liberal coat of paste wax, rubbed to a polish. Repeat the wax coating occasionally to keep the bench surfaces in prime condition.

The remaining illustrations in this section (Figures 15-17 through 15-31) show additional construction details and some thoughts on tool applications.

15-18.   The cutout for the bandsaw is secured with two 1/4" x 2" FH machine screws that thread into T-nuts installed in the support cleats. These same screws are used to anchor the plate on which the bandsaw is bolted when the tool is used.

15-20.   A simple way to provide for lifting the tool panels— install a 1/4" x 3-1/2" U-bolt. Drill holes for the legs of the bolt, and form a 1/2"-deep groove between them so the bolt will not project above the bench top. Double nut the bolt, or use a single lock nut.

15-19.   The panels that support the tools must lie flat on the bench top when the tools are in use. That's why ordinary hinges won't do. Heavy-duty Soss hinges solve the problem. The hinges come with a template, so you can accurately locate the holes that are needed for hinge installation.

15-21.   The plate for the drill press is two pieces; a single-piece plate would prevent sanding close to the tool when it is in use. The tool-mount plate is 13" long and is attached with Soss hinges. It's okay to attach the second plate with a length of continuous hinge. Just be sure the knuckle of the hinge doesn't project higher than the bench surface.

15-22. Because the table saw is built in, its crosscut support increases to 41″. For ripping support, you have the full 96″ of bench-length. The open areas around the saw are provided for attachment or removal of the rip fence and guard.

15-24. The tool plates can be anchored to the bench with a C-clamp. Whether this is needed will depend on whether the job you are doing creates a lot of vibration. Tools are bolted to the underside of the plates. Position them as close to the hinge-point as possible. Note the plate and the double nuts on the U-bolt.

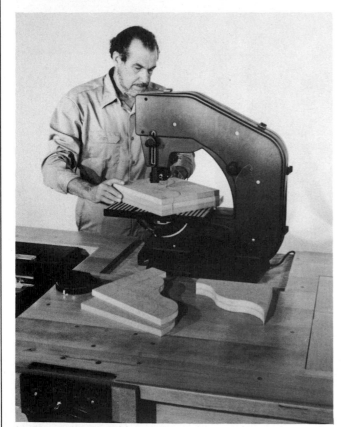

15-23. The 10″ bandsaw is bolted to the piece that is cut out of the left-hand shelf. In use, it rests on the same cleats that support the bench cutout. The bandsaw is stored, on its plate, in the area provided under the bench. Being a benchtop tool, it is light enough that lifting it is no great task.

15-25. The mounting plate for the belt sander/grinder can be full-length since it won't interfere with work position. To store the tool, its table must be adjusted to vertical position, but this takes seconds. Be sure to install the rubber feet that are supplied with some of the tools.

15-26. Surprise! A 7″ x 32″ lathe becomes functional when the shelf to which it is attached swings up level with the bench top. The shelf is hinged to the edge of the bench and is supported by swing-away brackets. Note the installation of a second Record woodworking vise.

15-29. Many benchtop tools come with templates or diagrams that tell you exactly where to locate holes for attachment bolts. These, of course, can be used to locate the T-nuts through which bolts, or screws, that are used to secure the tool can be threaded.

15-27. The lathe is tilted down to its non-use position so that it won't interfere when the grinder/disc sander is brought up for use. If there is water in the grinder's trough, be sure to empty it before swinging the tool to storage mode.

15-30. I installed two quick-release, Record woodworking vises with adjustable "dogs." Holders like this are an important component for any woodworking bench. The fixed jaw can project beyond the edge of the bench, or it can be set flush by notching the bench-edge.

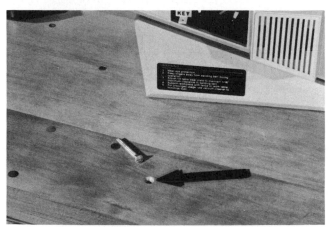

15-28. Provide for extra tools by installing T-nuts in the underside of the bench top. Countersink the holes so they can be "plugged" with fh machine screws when the tools are not in use.

15-31. Because the bench is heavy, and you'll want to move it around for use and for storage, it should be equipped with heavy-duty, adjustable castors. These are a Sears-Roebuck product that are manually adjustable. Other, foot-operated types are available. Always set the bench on its feet when it is being used and when it is in storage. Use the casters only for moving it around.

The Complete Book of
PORTABLE POWER TOOL TECHNIQUES

by R.J. De Cristoforo

to Mary

Introduction

I grew up with R.J. De Cristoforo. No, I didn't go to school with him; we weren't kids together in the same neighborhood. Nonetheless, I feel like I grew up with him. Like so many of today's craftsmen and craftswomen—both professional and amateur—I've worked with his books and articles for much of my life.

When I first began to take a real interest in working with tools in the early 1960's, 'Cris' had already established himself as a workshop expert. Whenever I'd pick up a magazine such as *Popular Science* or other publications with articles aimed at the do-it-yourself crowd, like as not I'd find some advice from R.J. De Cristoforo. If I went to the library to look up a shop technique or method, I'd usually find Cris' name in the card catalogue. It was no wonder. The last time anyone counted, Cris had over thirty books and a thousand magazine articles to his credit.

But quantity doesn't tell the whole story. Cris' innovations with tools are legendary. In his writings, he has expanded the uses and capabilities of common workshop tools far beyond what even the manufacturers have envisioned. The jigs and shop-built accessories that he has invented have enabled many tool owners (such as myself) to do more and better work than we would have otherwise thought possible. Robert Stevenson, the former Home and Shop Editor of *Popular Science*, put it this way: "For me the arrival of a new article from Cris was always a welcome event, and I shoved other work aside to see what new and surprising ideas his manuscript contained. I was rarely disappointed…it was in these articles that his imagination and ingenuity in the use of power tools came into fullest flower. In the *use* of tools, R.J. De Cristoforo has been a true pioneer."

When I became a workshop editor in the early 1980's, our publishing staff decided to try to put together a complete woodworking encyclopedia from existing books. We scoured the publishers' lists for the best and the most complete books on cabinetry, carpentry, finishing, and so on. Eventually, we chose seven books that we felt were a must for any serious do-it-yourselfer. One of those books was *De Cristoforo's Complete Book of Power Tools, Both Portable and Stationary*, first published by Popular Science Books in 1972. After reviewing all the other books on the market, we felt this was *the* classic text of power tool techniques and methods.

As fate would have it, just a few years later I found myself in the midst of a publishing project to outclass the classic. In the dozen years since Cris had written his first 'definitive' book on power tools, he had amassed dozens of new ideas, jigs, and techniques. He had collected so much new information, in fact, that it was decided that there was enough material for *two* new books—one on stationary tools, and the other on portable tools. The first, *The Complete Book of Stationary Power Tool Techniques*, was published in 1985 by Popular Science Books. As for the second—well, here it is.

Though *The Complete Book of Portable Power Tool Techniques* is intended as a companion volume to De Cristoforo's book on stationary power tools, you'll quickly find that it's a wonderfully useful text all by itself. There are few books on the market that provide such complete information on portable power tools, and none that make such ingenious use of them. It has all the makings of another workshop classic: Not only will the present generation of do-it-yourselfers get a lot of use out of this book; it will be something that our kids will grow up with.

Nick Engler
September, 1986

Using Tools Safely

1.

It's an old truism that a tool is only as good as the worker who uses it. The thought also applies to safety; it's as much in the mind as it is in the hands, or in the tool. Being aware that tools are disinterested helpers, lacking the intelligence that can determine whether their cutting edges are directed toward wood or a finger, must be a constant consideration.

If you use a hand as a backup when drilling a through hole, you ask for trouble. If you are sawing a panel with a circular saw and are thinking about the golf game you're anxious to get to, you're in danger. If you don't position a ladder correctly when, for example, sanding a fascia strip, you might get back to the ground too quickly—with a plop!

It isn't enough to take routine precautions like wearing safety goggles and a dust mask when sanding (Figure 1-1). It's also necessary to preview the operation and to plan it to avoid potential problems.

Getting to know a tool, how it functions, what it can do, how to use it, and its limits are important safety factors. However, be aware that expertise is not a shield that keeps you from harm. In fact, too often expertise breeds overconfidence, a dangerous state of mind. Being a bit afraid of a tool, no matter how well you learn to use it, is as logical as being sure your car's braking system is in dependable condition.

It's significant that a worker's regard for safety can vary from tool to tool. A portable saw might be used with more respect than a portable drill or sander, yet the seemingly less dangerous tools can also do harm. The point is that the degree of damage should not cause the operator to overlook that there should never be damage at all.

Generally, the potential hazards when working with power tools are no different than those of everyday living, but there is an important difference. Your safety in an automobile depends on the care of other drivers as much as on yourself. When you use a tool, you alone control the risk factor. Accept that tools can't think. Don't be complacent because the tool has a guard.

Safety rules provided with a tool, printed in books and magazines, are often ignored. It can't happen to us, but it CAN. And that's the crux of the matter—accepting that you are vulnerable.

Tool Guards

Not many portable tools can be equipped with guards that completely cover what the tool drives. You can't shield the entire length of the blade on a saber saw, so you must always be aware of the exposed cutter under the work and keep hands somewhat in the position shown in Figure 1-2. The

1-1.   Many factors are involved in working safely with power tools—among them protection for eyes (even if you must get special prescription glasses) and lungs. It's also critical to accept that safety is as much in the mind as it is in lists of rules.

1-2.   Blades on some tools, like the saber saw, can't be completely shielded. Always be aware that much of the blade is exposed *under* the workpiece.

same thought applies to other tools like portable routers and sanders. Of course, on these items you'll probably have both hands on the tool. Be careful when you start the operation and when you lift the tool at job's end. Some safety factors have to do with how a particular tool should be used; these will be discussed in other chapters.

The portable circular saw (Figure 1-3) has a swiveling guard that retracts into the fixed upper guard as the cut is made. When the cut is complete, the movable guard automatically returns to cover the bottom area of the blade. This means that during the cut, like the saber saw, part of the blade is exposed *under* the work. While a lot of blade projection may be a more efficient way to saw, it's becoming more common, for safety's sake, to keep the projection to a minimum. Always be aware of that under-the-work danger.

It's amazing how often I've seen the lower guard tied back. It's pointless to go into why this is considered more efficient. Let's just say it's a dumb thing to do.

Some portable tools like grinders, polishers, and disc sanders may have partial guards that are often sold as accessories. Either to save a few dollars or because the operator feels they're in the way, the guards are not always in evidence. If you're going to use a tool it's just common sense to protect yourself as much as possible.

Let's make this point now—if there are demonstration illustrations in this book that don't show a guard when the tool has one, IT'S NOT THAT I'M DISOBEYING MY OWN RULES, BUT ONLY SO THE ACTUAL CUT CAN BE SEEN MORE CLEARLY.

Tool Toting

Portable tools are applied to the work and carried to the site. Too often, a tool is kept running between cuts. It's a much

1-3. Portable circular saws have a fixed upper guard and a pivoted lower one that retracts during the cut and then returns to cover the blade when the cut is complete. Tying the lower guard back, as some workers do, is asking for trouble.

better practice, let alone safer, to allow the tool to stop at the end of a cut and then start it again for the next one. Don't set a tool down until the blade or bit, or whatever, has stopped moving. If you're using an extension cord, plug the tool in at the site. Don't make all electrical connections before walking, or climbing a ladder or scaffold, to where the tool will be used.

Extension Cords

Portable power tools are often used with electrical extension cords for on-site work. The right cord allows the tool to work efficiently. A bad choice can harm the tool and set up some potentially hazardous electrical conditions. The cords needed for tools are a bit different than those used inside for lamps and such, but overall it's just a matter of matching the extension cord to the job.

"Ampacity" is a term that applies to current-carrying capacity in terms of amperes (amps). In this area you can base a judgement by reading the specification plate on the tool which will, or should, state the amperage. If you have several tools and a single extension cord, the cord should be suitable for the tool having the highest amperage rating. The point is, don't use a cord with an amperage rating that is lower than the tool to be powered.

Two factors go together—the tool's amperage and the length of the cord. As one or the other or both of them increase, so must the gauge of the cord's wires. Undersize wires (for the job) cause voltage drop. It's something like feeding a gallon of water at one end of a pipe but getting a pint at the opposite end. Double amperage or double same-size wire length equals double voltage drop. This can result in tool-power loss, excessive heat, and even burnout. "Fatter" wires have less resistance than "thin" ones and help to bring voltage-drop to acceptable levels.

A #12 extension cord, which is usually available only in a heavy-duty grade, is generally acceptable for typical portable power tool use. The chart in Figure 1-4 gives more specific information. Sometimes choices are made on the basis of cost and weight; a #12 is three times a #16 in cost and weight, and even more when compared with #18. A factor though, as we mentioned, is that #12 is usually a heavy-duty grade.

Safety with Cords

The important factor is this—if the tool has a three-prong plug, then the extension must be compatible; three wires, with a three-prong plug at one end and a three-hole receptacle at the other end to receive the tool's plug. Of course, these safety factors are nullified if the starting outlet (where you plug in) isn't correctly grounded or if you don't, when necessary, use a proper grounding-adapter procedure. If in doubt, have the electrical system checked by a qualified electrician so you don't operate with false security.

Tool cords or extensions that can be used on less than 150V will have plugs like the one shown in Figure 1-5A. The grounding pin, WHICH MUST NEVER BE REMOVED, engages with the third, specially shaped hole in the outlet.

An adapter, like the one shown in Figure 1-5B and attached as in Figure 1-5C, can be used to accommodate a conventional two-prong plug. The lug on the adapter must be firmly attached to the outlet box. As we said, for systems like this to work, the box itself must be CORRECTLY GROUNDED. Such adapters should be viewed as temporary measures for use only until a correctly grounded outlet box is installed, preferably by a qualified electrician. These adapters are NOT used in Canada.

Most tools designed for operation on 150-250V will have a plug like the one shown in Figure 1-5D. This must be used with a matching, correctly grounded receptacle that is wired to deliver the correct voltage. DON'T use adapters with this plug design.

The grounding precautions do not apply to modern, double-insulated tools that are equipped with a two-prong plug. These tools have a built-in safety factor that is designed to prevent shorting through parts of the tool you handle so a two-wire extension cord can be used safely. More about this in a bit.

Double Insulation

A double-insulated tool has all the electrical components and the basic insulation required for it to work. But, additionally, its components such as motor, controls, brushes, and so on, are surrounded by what you might call secondary insulation

or correctly engineered air space. Should the basic insulation fail, electricity doesn't get to the handle or casing of the tool. You wouldn't be "shocked" even though the failure situation might blow a fuse.

Essentially, this is also true of a three-wire, three-prong setup so long as the system is actually grounded. If, as is often the case, grounding doesn't exist, then the operator becomes the grounding medium and the results, in case of accident or failure, can be unpleasant. But when a three-prong tool is properly installed in a correctly grounded three-hole outlet and correctly used, it's as safe as you can expect any electric tool to be. It's the unknown, or shall we say, "hidden" aspects of the electrical environment that might cause problems. It's also things like removing the grounding prong of a three-prong plug because only a two-hole outlet is available.

The double-insulated tool, among other things, guards against our own mis-deeds. The safety is part of the tool, built into it, and doesn't depend on how the end of the cord is designed.

As good as they are, double-insulated tools are not 100% safe. I don't care to use any electric tool in or around water. Water penetration of uninsulated parts poses a potential hazard. If you touch the metal chuck of a drill while the bit is touching a hidden, hot wire, and if your feet happen to be on a good ground, you might be in for a jolt. A lot of "ifs" but they make a point.

CORD LENGTH	EXTENSION CORDS WIRE SIZE B&S GAUGE					
	AMP RATING OF TOOL (FULL LOAD)					
	0 - 2.0	2.1 - 3.4	3.5 - 5.0	5.1 - 7.0	7.1 - 12.0	12.1 - 16.0
25	18	18	18	18	16	14
50	18	18	18	16	14	12
75	18	18	16	14	12	10
100	18	16	14	12	10	8
150	16	14	12	10	8	8
200	16	14	12	10	8	6
300	14	12	10	8	6	4
400	12	10	8	6	4	4
500	12	10	8	6	4	2
600	10	8	6	4	2	2
800	10	8	6	4	2	1
1000	8	6	4	2	1	0

Note: This table is for 115V tools.

1-4.   Choosing the correct extension cord assures sufficient power where it's needed. It's a good idea to have several on hand and to use the shortest one that will do.

1-5.   Various methods of grounding. You're asking for trouble if you remove the grounding pin from a three-prong grounding plug. These systems work only if the connection is made to a CORRECTLY GROUNDED outlet.

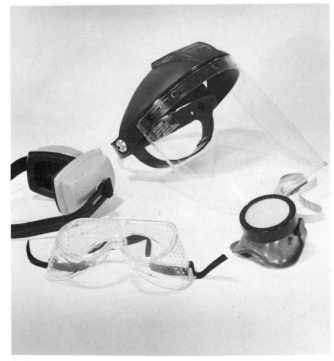

1-6.   All tool users should have a complete set of safety products on hand. These items will protect your eyes, ears, and lungs—BUT ONLY IF YOU USE THEM!

Protecting Eyes, Ears, and Lungs

The safety items displayed in Figure 1-6 should be standard equipment in all shops. The wisdom of using safety goggles and face masks gets a lot of publicity so it isn't difficult to convince most people to use them. However, the harmful effects of dust and noise are often overlooked or ignored.

Headphone-type hearing protectors are as important as any safety device. High frequencies can be generated by high-speed electric motors and even by some woodworking operations. The effects are cumulative; each exposure contributing to possible hearing impairment. Good ear protectors that will screen out high frequencies while still allowing normal conversation, are available and they won't eliminate the woodworking noises you SHOULD hear. They should be used with all powered tools including products like weed cutters, lawn mowers, chain saws, and such.

Don't feel that a dust mask is necessary only when doing sanding chores. Many sawing, routing, and shaping operations can produce particles best kept from your lungs. Be sure to keep the filters in the mask clean and to replace them as often as necessary.

Unauthorized Use

Power tools are intriguing to children. Add to this the desire to imitate dad or mom and you may have a potential disaster.

Unlike many stationary tools, portable tools don't have built-in locks with removable keys so it's best never to leave a tool plugged in when it's not being used. Actually, this is good safety practice anyway. Put tools away when you're through working, preferably in a cabinet with a lock. Put the key in a secret place.

Work Uniform and Shopkeeping

A special uniform to wear when using tools makes sense. Shirt and trousers should fit snugly. Shoes should be heavy, preferably with steel toes and non-slip bottoms. The latter feature is especially important when using a ladder or working on a roof. It's rarely necessary to wear gloves, and a necktie is OUT, period. Avoid any loose clothing that might snag on a tool or shop furniture or on-site objects. Rings, wristwatches, bracelets, and other adornments are hazards. Cover your hair, whether it's long or short, for safety and protection from dust. A hard hat, like those used by construction workers, should also be part of your uniform for use in particular environments.

Treat your shop, or any work area, as if it were a kitchen. Tables, benches, tools, accessories, and so on should be kept in pristine condition. Keep a bench brush and a vacuum cleaner handy, and use them. Don't allow litter, sawdust, and wood scraps to clutter the work area. This creates dangerous hazards that can cause a nasty slip or trip.

Keep tool surfaces like the baseplates on circular saws and saber saws and the surface of a router/shaper table in new-bright condition. Dirty tools aren't nice to work with and rough bearing-surfaces make it more difficult to move the tool and can mar the workpiece. Clean such areas and then apply paste wax rubbed to a polish. Don't use oil; this collects sawdust and dirt, and it doesn't do the workpiece any good.

It's not wise to work in a wet location or to expose tools to rain.

The shop, or any work area, should be well lighted. Extension lights, with the bulb protected in a wire cage, can provide illumination for on-site work.

Good Work Practice

Don't overreach, no matter what the operation or the tool. Don't struggle with workpieces that are too large for you to handle safely. When necessary, ask someone to help but be sure to describe the procedure to the assistant.

Always provide firm support for the workpiece (Figure 1-7). Support stands and small workbenches you can carry about are available commercially. Sawhorses are a great aid, really a must for on-site work. By spacing them correctly you can, for example, support a twenty foot 2x4 or a plywood panel, and when spanned with sturdy lumber they can be used as low scaffolding. Readymade sawhorses like the one shown in Figure 1-8 are available or you can quickly and easily make some with 2x4s and a pair of special brackets (Figure 1-9). Other designs for sawhorses you make from scratch are shown in Figures 1-10 through 1-13.

Don't work with dull tools. You won't get good results. Also, dull tools make it necessary to apply more pressure

1-7. Good support for the workpiece is essential. You may not have a workbench for on-site work but other means are available. This is the "Versa Ladder" organized to serve as a temporary bench.

1-8. Readymade sawhorses are available. This one is all metal and can be folded for storage.

1-9. You can assemble a basic A-frame sawhorse in very little time by using lengths of 2x4 and available sawhorse hardware. Note that no angle-cut is required at the top of the legs. A plywood shelf will increase rigidity.

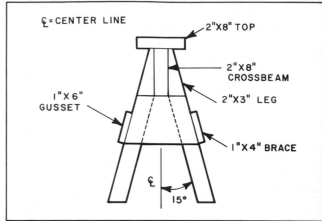

1-10.   This sawhorse design allows assembly without having to cut angles. The width of the 1x4 under the rail and rail support determines the splay of the legs. The 2x6 rail provides more work surface than a 2x4 and allows some room for a screw-on vise.

1-11.   I call this the "toughie" horse. Use lag screws, carriage bolts and nuts, and waterproof glue to assemble all parts. Use straight grain fir and apply several coats of exterior sealer.

1-12.   This version requires angle-cuts on the legs. The legs should splay from 15 to 20 degrees. It's best to attach the legs to the rail before cutting the gusset.

1-13.   This sawhorse does double duty since its top serves as a tool box. Assemble the compartment as a unit before adding other components. You can use a strip of continuous (piano) hinge for the lid instead of conventional ones.

when you move the tool, which establishes a situation where your hands might slip.

Always disconnect the tool when you must change a saw blade or a router bit, or whatever. Don't leave a power tool running when you need to turn to another chore or area of a workpiece regardless of how little time is involved. It's prudent to wait for the cutter to come to a halt before you move away.

Be aware that something is wrong when you must force a cut. Usually, it means that the cutter is dull or that you're trying to cut too deep. Most of the time, extra deep or oversize cuts must be accomplished by making repeat passes.

Don't mix tool-use with socializing. Keeping a conversation going while you're using a tool is not allowed. Politely advise friends and neighbors not to barge into the shop if they hear the noise of a tool. You don't want them to startle you.

Stay alert; keep your mind on the job at hand. Don't use tools when you're tired or upset and, like driving, alcoholic beverages and tool-use don't mix.

Good Tool Practice

It's critical to know the tool, especially if you are using it for the first time. Read and reread the owner's manual that is supplied with the equipment. Learn the tool's applications and, ESPECIALLY, its limitations. Don't use a tool for something it was not designed to do. For example, you don't use

1-14.   Ladders are available in wood or metal. Wood is subject to deterioration. A metal ladder is lighter but must never be used near electrical installations. Choose ladders carefully; your safety depends on them.

drill bits in a router or substitute a grinding wheel for the blade on a circular saw. Make it a habit to check all locking devices before turning on the power.

Mount cutters or accessories by carefully following the installation instructions. Don't use saw blades that are larger in diameter than the saw can take. Check the maximum rpm of the blade; it must not be less than the tool's speed.

Don't work with damaged tools or tools with frayed cords. Be sure to mount blades and cutters so they have the correct direction of rotation.

Don't work on pieces too small to be safely held or, at least, grip them firmly in a vise or with clamps. If you need a shaped, narrow piece (router work), form it on a large workpiece and then cut off the part you need.

Be sure you know what you are going to do before you start an operation. If you preview the chore you can judge how best to support the work, how to move the tool, and the best positions for your hands. Often, and especially with new tools and operations you haven't tried before, it's wise to do a dry run. That is, go through the operation with the tool unplugged. Become "tool wise".

There are some operations in woodworking that are done without standard guards. When involved with these, be extra cautious about how you proceed, or choose another method of getting the same result. Never, regardless of what you are doing, use your hands so they are too close to the cutting area. To put it bluntly, a cutting tool can't distinguish between wood and flesh. As we said, they're great helpers but they function with the belief that you know what you're doing.

Ladders

Because portable power tools are often used on-site, and this frequently involves getting to another level, it's important that what you use to get there is strong and used correctly. Since a ladder is the common means, getting a sturdy one is the first step (Figure 1-14). Today, ladders have stickers and labels of various colors so the consumer knows something about the product before he buys it. For example, an industrial grade wooden ladder will have a yellow label. If the same color is on a metal ladder, it's a heavy-duty type. The ladder should also have some information about how it can be used. This also applies to extension ladders—safe overlap lengths, good angle when setting the ladder against a vertical surface, and so on.

Good ladders can be found in wood or metal. Wood ladders are subject to weather-deterioration; metal ones should never be used near electrical lines.

"Versa Ladders" (Figure 1-15) are uniquely designed with pivoting joints so they can be set to different heights, used as scaffolds, or even as work supports.

You can buy accessories for some ladders like the scaffold support shown in Figure 1-16 or the ridge hooks for roof work shown in Figure 1-17.

Basic Ladder Rules

■ Place a solid footing under each foot of the ladder when working on soft ground.

- Tying the bottom rung of the ladder to a fixed object, especially when it's on a slippery surface, is good procedure.
- Don't stand on the top ledge or the paint shelf, or straddle the top of a step ladder.
- Don't overreach in any direction while on a ladder.
- When climbing, keep your weight centered and use your hands on the rungs, not the sides.
- If you're climbing to a roof, have at least three feet of the ladder projecting above the roof line.
- Never try to make a long ladder by splicing together two short ones.

1-16.   Accessories for ladders include special brackets like this one. Consider renting such equipment since you may not need it too often. Knock-down scaffolding is also available at rental places.

1-15.   The unique "Versa Ladder" can be used conventionally or "folded" to serve in other ways, among them, as a scaffold.

1-17.   Using a ladder on a roof calls for special precautions like these ridge hooks. I would also add a heavy rope tied to an immovable object on the other side of the building. Also, be sure to wear non-slip shoes.

2. The Portable Circular Saw

tretch your imagination a bit and you will see that the portable circular saw is something like a table saw or radial arm saw that you hold in your hand. That's one of the virtues of this and other carry-about tools. You bring the tool to the work instead of bringing the work to the tool. For example, you can use the portable saw to trim-cut roof boards or sheathing or deck boards that are already installed, or reduce the length or width of a plywood panel without having to muscle it over the table of a stationary tool.

The usual alternative to the powered saw is a handsaw which requires effort to use and considerably more time to complete a cut (Figure 2-1). The power tool has built-in accuracy features, and when handled correctly cuts straight and square edges with a minimum possibility of human error. Some apprenticeship is necessary but the amateur can quickly get professional results.

The tool was originally developed as an aid for construction people who must size house-framing boards and timbers right on the job. Today there are dozens of models available that look alike and have similar features (Figure 2-2). Different manufacturers offer units that span a broad range of light-duty and heavy-duty tools with differences in size, power, and price.

It's not uncommon to hear the tool referred to as a "Skilsaw"—probably because the Skil people were originators—but other names such as "cutoff saw", "utility saw", and "builder's saw" are also used. The descriptive titles fit but it's an error to limit the saw's use to the area of woodworking implied by the name.

With some know-how, accessories you can buy, and jigs that you make, you can broaden the tool's workscope to include jobs that are routine on stationary equipment. For example, it can be used to form dadoes and rabbets, cut

2-1. The portable circular saw substitutes electric power for muscle. It took more than 30 seconds to make the handsaw cut, only about 3 or 4 seconds using the power saw. The power tool has built-in accuracy.

2-2. Portable saws vary in appearance, size, and weight, but most will have the features shown here.

bevels and miters, do compound cuts, single-cut multiple and similar pieces, and so on.

Types and Sizes

The size of the saw is indicated by the diameter of the blade. The "average" might be around 7¼" or 7½", but the range is from under 5" to better than 10" (Figures 2-3—2-6). Blade diameter is important but should not be the sole factor when making a choice. Also consider its maximum depth of cut— the thickness of material the blade can get through on both straight cuts and 45° bevels. There's no problem if your woodworking will be limited to ¾" lumber or plywood, but it's more realistic to think in terms of 2" lumber. Even here, consider the difference between dressed lumber and rough lumber. Standard 2" dressed lumber is actually 1½" thick,

whereas lumber in the rough (not planed) is at least a full 2". So, if lumber in the rough will be part of the work picture, you may need more depth of cut than the person who works on dressed stock only.

Since sharpenings reduce the diameter of a blade, getting one that is just enough for a piece of work when the blade is new may not be wise. Also, a blade that is constantly buried in the cut won't function efficiently and will cause burn marks on itself and the wood. All of which seems to indicate that it's better to overestimate when deciding on capacity. Overall, you should be able to make square and 45° bevel cuts through 2" dressed stock.

Generally, the larger the size the more powerful, heavier, and more expensive the tool will be. Getting the biggest size, regardless of cost, isn't being tool-wise. A smaller saw with

Features to Consider in Circular Saws

2-3.   Skil's 7¼" saw has a burnout protected 2 hp motor and a clutch to help prevent kickback should the blade bind in a cut. A special lock-out switch can be used to prevent accidental starts.

2-5.   Makita's 4⅜" saw weighs only a bit more than six pounds yet it is rated at 7.5 amps so has the power to cut wood, paneling, aluminum, and plastic. It's a high-speed unit; the blade turns at 11,000 rpm.

2-4.   This Porter Cable unit is double insulated and has a heavy-duty wrap-around base with a single sight line that serves as a guide on straight, angle, or bevel cuts. Depth of cut at 90° is almost 2½".

2-6.   Weight, and usually power, goes up with size. This 10¼" saw weighs a bit more than 18 lbs. and is powered with a 12 amp motor for heavy-duty work. Electric brake stops the blade when the trigger is released.

adequate horsepower (say a minimum of 1 hp) may be a better buy, so long as it will perform the tasks with the frequency of use you anticipate, because it may be more comfortable to handle. Looking forward isn't difficult. Are you going to build a house and then add decks and fences, or do major remodeling work? Or do you wish to have the tool on hand for those occasional chores? This can make the difference between choosing a light-duty tool or a heavy-duty version. Here, manufacturers offer help since many catalogs state duty-performance, presenting units as "industrial", "homeowners", and so on. Another aid is the length of the guarantee. A two-year guarantee obviously indicates a tool considered longer-lived than one with a one-year backup.

Blade speed is specified in rpm when the blade is running free. Keeping close to this specification when the blade is working has to do with horsepower and, of course, the material being sawed. Some slow-up will occur under almost all conditions. So consider rpm in this light—a fast turning blade that slows down considerably when cutting isn't really going to be faster than a slower tool that does not bog down. Of course, how the tool is handled—how fast YOU try to cut—affects its cut-consistency, but more about that later.

Because the tool is designed for square cuts and beveled ones, it should have scales that help to preset the tool (Figure 2-7). It's rare that these can be accepted prima facie but they do serve as a beginning. It's always best to make a test cut before going further.

A basic accessory is an edge guide like the one shown in Figure 2-8. It's used when you need to make a straight cut parallel to an outside edge. It may be supplied with the saw or offered as an accessory.

If it can be arranged, it's a good idea to actually test the tool you're interested in, or have the salesperson do it for you with a demonstrator model. Be sure to "heft" it yourself. When all other factors are satisfactory, how the tool feels in your hands can logically determine which saw to choose from a variety of units. Weight and ease of handling can also be important safety factors. A tool that is too heavy for you, or one that feels awkward when you grip it, can make you uncomfortable and thus be a hazard.

In General

After purchasing the saw, you should spend more than a few minutes practicing to become familiar with the tool and how it handles. Make test cuts on some ¾" plywood that is clamped securely to a bench, and on a length of 2x4 adequately supported across sawhorses or some similar support. Set the blade projection so it doesn't exceed the thickness of the material by more than ¼". A greater projection is actually more efficient since the cutting arc is less, but for safety's sake it's best to keep it to a minimum. Place your right hand with a finger on the trigger and your left hand on the secondary grip (Figure 2-9). Position yourself so you are not in line with the path of the saw blade. Place the saw so its weight is supported by the bulk of the stock, not the part that will be cut off.

2-8.   An edge guide may be supplied with the tool or offered as an accessory. It's used to guide the saw when making a cut parallel to an edge.

2-7.   Depth of cut and bevel scales don't all look like this. The scales can be used for casual sawing but when accuracy is critical it's best to make a test cut before sawing good stock.

2-9.   It's good practice to grip the saw firmly with both hands. Feed-speed should be just enough to keep the blade cutting. Take a position that keeps your body out of the line of cut.

The upper portion of the saw blade is guarded by a fixed housing. The lower portion is covered by a guard that should automatically telescope into the top housing as you move the tool forward to make the cut. Always be aware that the portion of the saw blade in the cut and the area of the saw blade that extends below the stock are not covered by the guard during the cut. When the cut is complete—the blade has cleared the wood—the lower guard will return and the blade will be completely covered. Move the tool completely off the wood to be sure that this happens. Always let the blade come to a halt before resting the tool.

The teeth on the saw blade will (should) point toward the front of the tool (Figure 2-10). This direction of rotation makes it cut on the "up" stroke and suggests that the good face of the stock should be "down" when you cut since any splintering or feathering will occur where the teeth leave the work. This factor is critical only when the material you are cutting, like a fancy plywood with a single good side, deserves such consideration. Don't let it bother you if, for example, you're cutting wall-framing studs.

Feed Speed

Feed speed (how fast you try to move the tool) should be judged by how the saw is cutting. The thickness and the density of the stock, whether the cut is parallel to or across the grain, the saw blade being used and its condition, are all factors that affect how fast you can go. Actually, you shouldn't be out to set speed records. Usually, the quality of the cut is more important. The rule to obey is to be sure the blade cuts steadily without being forced. Too slow and you won't accomplish much while the blade burnishes and dulls. Too fast and the blade chokes.

Portable circular saws will kick back quickly if you bind the blade by twisting the tool as you make the pass. An answer here, as we'll show, is to use guides that keep the tool moving in a straight line. Binding can also happen on long rip cuts, especially on green wood, because the kerf (the groove formed by the blade) tends to close behind the blade. When your first cut indicates that this is likely to happen on subsequent cuts, it's wise to do something about it. Some operators simply tap a shim into the kerf to keep it open, but a better

idea is to make and use the "kerfer" that is shown in Figures 2-11 and 2-12. An item you can buy, the "KerfKeeper" offered by the Adjustable Clamp Company, is another solution to the problem (Figure 2-13).

Some tools are equipped with a "slip clutch". Its job is to allow the saw blade to slip when the blade is confronted with an adverse situation such as a knot in the wood or mishandling that causes the blade to bind. Even though the motor still turns, the blade does not. The idea works but it's a tricky mechanism simply because its efficiency depends on how the operator adjusts it. Do the job right by carefully following the instructions that come with the tool and by frequently checking the adjustment.

In most cases it's simply a question of tightening the retaining nut on the arbor just so. Tighten the nut too much and the clutch won't work; if it's too loose, slippage can occur to the point where the saw loses efficiency. When the situation is optimum, the slip clutch will protect the motor and help to avoid kickback. The slip clutch can add to safety when operating the saw but remember that the most depend-

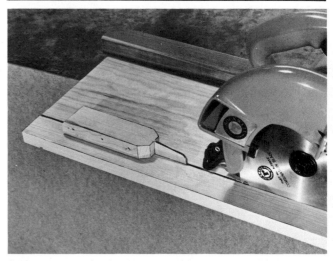

2-11. The kerf tends to close behind the blade especially on long rip cuts and when cutting green wood. You can make a "kerfer" and use it as shown to prevent the binding hazard.

2-10. Saw blades cut on the upstroke, so the face side of the stock should be down since most splintering and feathering will occur when the teeth leave the cut.

2-12. One way to make a kerfer.

able safety device should be you. Always work with a sharp blade and move the tool so the blade can do its job without being forced.

Another safety device found on some portable circular saws is an electronic brake. No extra buttons to push or procedures to go through are required for the brake to operate. When you release the tool's trigger, the brake automatically goes into action—the blade says "whoosh" and stops, just like that!

Saw Blades

Most saws will be supplied with a combination blade, a compromise design that can be used for crosscutting, ripping, and even mitering. It's an adequate blade to start with but not the best blade for optimum results on particular cuts and various materials. Use it on plywood and you'll get a good deal of splintering and feathering so the cut edge will require further attention.

Many other blade designs, some of which are shown in Figure 2-14 are available. It's wise to gradually acquire an assortment and to limit each to the chore it does best. There's little point in using a paneling or hollow-ground blade to saw studs and it won't do the blade much good. On the other hand, a hollow-ground blade will produce respectable miters. Smooth plywood cuts result when they are done with a paneling saw or a similar unit simply called a "plywood blade".

If you have a lot of cutting with-the-grain to do, switch to the rip blade. Its fast cutting action puts minimum strain on the motor and its deep gullets quickly throw off rather large waste-chips. The crosscut blade, with its many, small, sharp-pointed teeth severs wood fibers cleanly so you have smoother results when sawing across the grain.

2-13.   The "Pony" Kerfkeeper is offered by the Adjustable Clamp Company. It keeps the kerf open, but because it has surfaces that bear against both the bottom and top of the workpiece, it also helps to keep material from sagging during the cut.

Rip Cut: A saw cut made with the grain.
Crosscut: A saw cut made across the grain.
Miter Cut: A saw cut made at an angle across the grain.

PANELING…is hollow ground and has many, extra fine teeth. Use on plywood and similar laminates for splinter-free cutting. Cut edge can often be used "as is."

HOLLOW-GROUND…often called a "miter" or "planer". Will not cut as fast as some other blades but leaves a smooth finish, especially on crosscuts and miters.

RIP…has large set teeth with deep gullets for fast cutting *with* the grain. Design provides for good clearance of waste and minimum binding.

FINE-TOOTH…many small, very sharp teeth makes this a good blade for fine cut-off work. Can be used on soft wallboard, Celotex, and very thin plastic materials.

CROSSCUT…designed for getting smoother results when cutting *across* the grain. Good for plywood when a special blade is not available.

PERMA-GRIT (SKIL)… Tungsten carbide grit on edge and ½" down. Provides smooth finish when cutting thin veneers, plywood, and non-wood materials like fiberglass and plastics. Must not be used on metal or stone.

2-14.   Examples of saw blades that are available for portable power saws. It's wise to start a collection so you can select a blade for optimum results on particular jobs. Always work with sharp blades.

Saw blades that have tungsten carbide teeth (Figure 2-15) are as common today as all-steel blades, and as usable on a portable saw as they are on a stationary machine. They're more costly than other types but they cut easier, smoother, and they stay sharp for much longer periods than steel blades. However, there isn't ONE blade that does everything perfectly. The examples in Figure 2-15 include a rip, crosscut, and combination blade.

Tungsten carbide is tough, but has a degree of brittleness so it can't be abused. Don't place the blades on steel surfaces or store them so their keen edges might be nicked.

Abrasive blades can add to the usefulness of a portable saw. Various types are made for cutting non-wood materials like stone (Figure 2-16), non-ferrous metals, plastics, even concrete. Be sure you know what the disc was designed for before buying and using it. These are special cutters and must be used with respect. Don't use them on wood or even think that you can do grinding on their sides. Carefully follow mounting instructions. A good safety procedure is to allow the disc, especially a new one, to run free for a minute or so before applying it to the work. Forcing is a no-no—safety goggles, of course.

Cutting Techniques

Crosscutting (sawing across the grain of the wood) and ripping (sawing parallel to the grain) are basic functions. Although the tool is often used freehand, you'll get better results and will actually be safer if you establish a guide against which to move the saw. This doesn't have to be more than a strip of wood, clamped or tack-nailed to the workpiece (Figure 2-17). If you keep the tool bearing against the guide, there is little chance that you might inadvertently twist the tool and cause the blade to bind. The distance from the edge of the baseplate to the cutting line is easily established by a one-time test cut. Thus, you will always know where to establish the guide strip for accurate cutting. This dimension can vary depending on the style of saw blade you're using, so you must check it each time you change blades and also after you've had a blade sharpened.

An edge guide, sometimes supplied with the tool and other times offered as an accessory, can also be used on rip cuts (Figure 2-18). While it can be used to establish the width of the piece being cut off, it doesn't have enough bearing surface to relieve you of the responsibility of keeping the saw

2-15. Blades with teeth of tungsten carbide are also available for portable saws. When properly made they cut better than all-steel saws and stay sharp for much longer periods of time.

2-17. You'll do a better job of cutting if you use a guide for the saw whenever possible. Keep the edge of the baseplate firmly against the guide throughout the pass.

2-16. Silicon carbide wheel slices smoothly through 1″ marble slab. It can also cut materials like brick, concrete, and plaster. Be sure to read instructions that come with the wheel. Don't abuse it!

2-18. The edge guide is used for making cuts parallel to an edge. It doesn't have much bearing surface so keeping the saw moving in a straight line is the operator's responsibility.

moving in a straight line. Both tool-guide examples have been demonstrated on rip cuts, which we'll talk more about later, but the practice also applies to crosscutting.

Crosscuts are often short cuts, across a 2x4, a 1x12, and so on, so it's often more convenient to use a guide that can be held to the work by hand. For example, you can use a common shop square as a guide, or you can make a special guide with more capacity by nailing two pieces of wood together to form an "L". The short leg should bear against the edge of the work while the long leg performs as the guide for the saw. There are quite a few commercial accessories that serve as guides for crosscut work. Two examples are shown in Figures 2-19 and 2-20.

Of course, this and other portable saw cutting can be done freehand by relying on your own expertise to keep the blade on the cutline. In any case, when starting the operation, place the front edge of the base plate firmly on the work with the guide notch in line with the direction of the cut. Start the saw, and after the blade has arrived at full speed, move the tool slowly forward for the actual cutting. Remember that the saw kerf has width so it must occur on the waste side of the stock.

When you approach the end of the cut, the guide-notch area of the base plate will be off the work, so you'll have to watch the blade itself to be sure it stays on the line. This applies more to freehand cutting than when you're moving the saw against a guide. In the latter case you can just concentrate on keeping the edge of the base plate snug against the guide strip throughout the pass.

Keep both hands on the saw (Figure 2-21) if possible. However, there are times when you may need one hand to secure a guide or to keep the work firm. Never work in a situation where you must use a free hand to brace yourself. Always be sure that both you and the tool are firmly planted. If a situation causes doubt, pause, step back and re-evaluate. The importance of being aware of what might occur, and what it demands of you, can't be emphasized too strongly.

Always try to set up so the weight of the saw will be supported by the bulk of the stock. This isn't always possible, especially on on-site work, but many times you can make a choice. For example, let's assume you must trim off the end of a long 2x4. Whether the saw will rest on the waste portion of the wood or on the body of the piece depends on which side of the 2x4 you stand. The same thinking applies if the piece you're cutting off is the one you need. The extra thinking required is in determining which side of the cut mark you want the kerf to be on. Cutting on the wrong side can shorten the piece you need by the width of the kerf.

Sawing Extra-Thick Stock

Sawing through stock that is thicker than the maximum depth of cut of the blade can be accomplished by making matching cuts from opposite surfaces (Figure 2-22). A cut is made on one side, and then the stock is flipped for the second cut. In such cases, layout and correct positioning of the saw for each cut are of primary importance if the two are to mate exactly. When you have many such cuts to make on similar materials, it will pay to make a U-shaped guide that can be clamped to the work so the two cuts will meet exactly. An

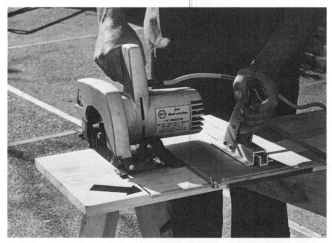

2-19.   This commercial jig is adjustable for various stock widths. Squeezing the trigger handle causes the jig to grip the stock between rear and front flanges. Arrow indicates the cutline guide.

2-20.   Protractor type guide can be used for square or angular cuts. It's usually hand-held but there's no reason why you can't clamp it in place if you wish.

2-21.   Keeping both hands on the saw is good practice but not always possible. Place the front of the baseplate firmly on the work—let the blade come to full speed before you make contact.

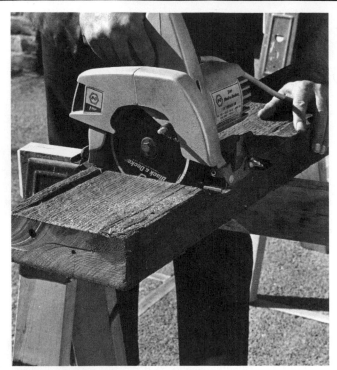

2-22.   Getting through stock that is thicker than the saw's maximum depth of cut requires half-way cuts from opposite surfaces. Align the blade very carefully after flipping the stock for the second cut.

2-23.   One pass trimming of multiple pieces can be done accurately by setting up this way. Clamp or tack-nail the guide strip to the first and last workpieces.

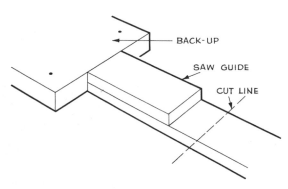

2-24.   A simple setup that lets you cut many pieces of similar length. The saw guide equals the length of the part you want less the distance from the edge of the saw's baseplate to the cutline.

alternative method is to create a setup so the work can be flipped in correct position for the second cut after the first one has been accomplished.

When doing two-pass cutting through thick stock, set the saw-blade projection to the least that will do the job. For example, if you're cutting stock that is 2″ thick, set projection to a bit more than 1″.

Cutting to Length

When it's necessary to cut many pieces to the same length, say studs or deck boards, make a setup like the one shown in Figure 2-23. Many professionals work this way, working freehand and just following a marked line, but accuracy comes easier if you use a stop against which you can butt one end of the pieces and then add a guide for the saw. It isn't necessary to do more than tack-nail or clamp the guide to the first and last piece in the set you are cutting.

Another method you can use to cut pieces of similar length is shown in Figure 2-24. The backup block, or "stop" is secured to a firm surface with nails or clamps. The guide block is the length of the pieces you need less the distance from the baseplate's edge to the saw blade. The guide and the work are butted against the backup and the saw is moved along the guide to make the cut. Some workers hand-hold the guide but it's safer to clamp it in place for each cut you make. The stock from which you're cutting the pieces should be allowed to fall away.

Butt Cuts

The technique that is demonstrated in Figures 2-25 and 2-26 will help when you must trim the ends of boards to make a matching joint. Just overlap the board ends and cut through both of them at the same time. Thus, even a slight error in cutting will not affect how the two ends will join together. The method will work whether the cut is straight, at an angle, long or short, and whether you are ripping or crosscutting. Clamp the pieces together to keep them firm as you saw.

More on Ripping

A good deal of what has been said so far in regard to saw handling applies to rip cuts as well as crosscuts. The primary distinction—whether you are sawing with the grain or across it—often isn't as important as the length of the cut. Choosing the right saw blade is important when you have a lot of ripping to do. If you have one rip cut to make and you already have a combination blade mounted, you won't be faulted for not changing to a rip blade. That's an "out" we all take advantage of. Incidentally, if you are sawing plywood and don't have a special plywood blade, the next best choice is a crosscut blade.

As in crosscutting, and as we have already mentioned, use a clamped or tack-nailed guide strip or an edge guide to help produce straight cuts. A commercial edge guide (Figure 2-27) is okay to use when the width of the cut permits. Remember, however, that it's not as easy to be as accurate with the accessory as you can with a strip of wood. The wood strip will prevent you from being wobbly with the saw.

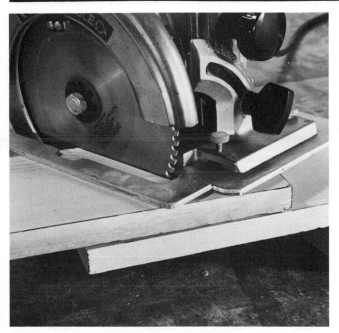

2-25. Overlapping pieces this way lets you produce matching edges in a single pass. Be sure pieces are held together and firmly supported.

2-26. The overlap method can be used regardless of whether you are making straight or angular cuts. The idea assures a perfect joint between the cut edges.

2-27. The position of the edge guide determines the width of the cut. Some edge guides are calibrated but you should check with a rule anyway.

Most saws are designed so the guide can be used on either side of the blade. To choose which side to place the guide, just consider which position involves the least extension of the guide and which provides the most support for the saw. Sometimes a decision has to be based on which end of the work you're going to start from, especially if the board is part of a fixed assembly and you don't have much choice in determining operator position.

With some edge guides you can create a setup by using both a clamped strip and an edge guide. The combination can be useful when it's necessary to cut a number of long pieces of equal width. In this situation the guide rides against the clamped strip and is adjusted after each cut by using calibrations on the guide, if there are any, or by measuring with a rule. Similarity in width of the pieces you saw will depend on how carefully you adjust the guide after each cut.

When material thickness allows it, and you must cut the same amount from a number of pieces, you can do the job by stacking the parts and cutting through them all at the same time. The method is very practical with even the smallest saw when you are working on thin material, say ⅛″ or ¼″ paneling. Of course, the thicker the material, the fewer the number of pieces you can stack. You will work more accurately if you use clamps to hold the parts together.

Angular Sawing

The two basic angular sawing operations are forming bevels or chamfers, which involve working with the blade tilted, and miters, done with the blade in normal position but with the pass made obliquely across the stock. For beveling, the tool is equipped with a tilt scale so the blade can be set to the necessary angle, but when the accuracy of the cut is critical, it's best to use the scale setting only as a guide. Check the test cut with a protractor before you get on with the job. Also, determine if the cutline indicator on the baseplate will work for bevel cuts as well as square ones. Be sure the tilt lock is secure and the leading edge of the baseplate is firmly seated on the wood before the blade makes contact.

The general rules for tool handling and feed-speed apply when making angular cuts. The blade will be working harder simply because it will be going through more wood

2-28. Guiding a saw through a bevel cut is much easier when you establish a guide strip. You can use the bevel scale to set the blade angle but check the cut with a protractor before cutting good stock.

when at an angle than when it is perpendicular. You'll find it easier to work accurately if you guide the tool against a clamped-on guide strip (Figure 2-28), or work with an edge guide. It's good practice to check the real distance from the cut to the side of the baseplate, especially for angle settings you might use frequently. Do this by actually making a short cut in a board and then measuring from the cut to the edge of the plate that will bear against the guide. Make a note of the dimension and thereafter, whether cutting one piece or many, you'll know exactly where the guide strip should be positioned.

Bevels or chamfers on relatively small pieces can be done efficiently if you take the precautions demonstrated in Figure 2-29. The idea is to supply support for the tool and to keep the workpiece secure.

Miter Cuts

You can accomplish a simple miter cut pretty much as you would a crosscut; either by guiding the saw freehand along a marked line or by using a guide (Figure 2-30). Accuracy will

2-31.   The protractor guide may also be used for angular sawing. It can be hand-held or clamped to the work. Always provide good support for workpieces.

2-29.   You can chamfer or bevel shorter workpieces so long as you clamp them firmly and provide support for the saw. Blades work harder when set at an angle so adjust feed speed to suit.

2-30.   Using a guide strip when sawing miters is as practical as its use on straight cuts. Always support the saw on the bulk of the stock—not the cutoff.

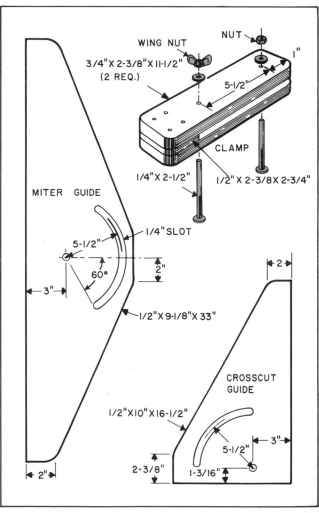

2-32.   Construction details of a guide that can be used for cross-cutting and mitering. Jigs like this should be carefully sanded and then protected with applications of sealer.

depend on how carefully you work when marking the cutline and establishing the guide's position. Since miter cuts are made most often across narrow widths, you can use an adjustable protractor as a guide. Protractors, of various designs, are available as accessories (Figure 2-31) and there are others that you can make yourself.

The construction details of a combination unit that has become standard equipment in my shop are shown in Figure 2-32. Half-inch plywood, a piece of ¾″ lumber, and a couple of bolts are all you need to make the guides. For the half-guide (marked "crosscut guide"), establish the length of the arc to provide 45° and 90° settings. Drill end holes first and then cut away the waste with a saber saw. Do the same for the full guide (marked "miter guide").

Actually, both guides can be used for either miters or plain crosscuts (Figures 2-33 and 2-34). The full guide provides a bearing edge for the saw even before the blade makes contact, a feature many commercial guides don't have. If you wish, you can mark settings for particular angles along the clamp edges of the guides.

Another design for a jig that can be used for either crosscutting or mitering is detailed in Figure 2-35. If you're careful about positioning the lock arm and forming the slot that it requires, the extremes of the slot will be auto-stops for 45° and 90° settings.

Making a Miter Box

To cut narrow components, moldings and such, you can make a kind of miter box that is ordinarily used with a backsaw. The basic design, a U-shaped trough with cuts across it, is the same, but for the portable power saw you must add a saw guide and a ledge that provides support for the saw (Figure 2-36). The special box should also be longer than one designed for a handsaw. Provide for left- and right-hand miter cuts by using a saw guide and have a support ledge for each. The depth of the box can't be greater than the maximum depth of cut of the tool. In use, the box should be nailed or clamped to a solid surface. As always, keep hands well away from the cut area.

2-33.   The full guide will provide a bearing edge for the saw's baseplate even before the blade makes contact.

2-34.   You can switch to the second guide if it is more convenient for the job at hand. If you're careful when forming the slotted curve, its extreme points can act as stops for 90° and 45° settings.

2-35.   Another example of an adjustable guide that you can make. The end points of the slot in the lock bar can be auto-stops for 90° and 45° cuts.

2-36.   You can make a special miter box for use with a portable circular saw. Install guides and saw-support ledges for both left-hand and right-hand miter cuts.

There are many special accessories for doing mitering work with a portable saw that are available commercially. The one shown in Figure 2-37 has a track arrangement to guide the saw. Also, since the track can be tilted, you can do compound angle work. Black & Decker has introduced a "Mitremate" saw guide that can be used with their "Workmate" portable bench and any 7¼" saw (Figure 2-38). It can be used for angular cuts ranging from 30° to 90° and can also be used as a guide for plain crosscutting on work that is not more than 17" wide.

The powered miter box (Figure 2-39) is really a stationary tool but it's designed around the type of portable saw we have been discussing. If you wished to imitate its features, and if your unit has a pivoting action to provide for blade projection, you could improvise by following the construction drawings for a "swing saw table" that are shown in Figure 2-40. This must be made very carefully, with ample provision for full use of the saw's guard, and it must be securely attached to a solid bench when it is used.

Notching

You can form notches, say for mid-point lap joints, or form dadoes and grooves, by setting the blade projection to the depth of cut required and then making a series of cuts as

2-39.   A powered miter box is essentially a portable saw mounted on an arm that allows the saw to pivot downward.

2-37.   Commercial accessory has a track arrangement to guide the saw. Because the track can be tilted and set at an angle, the unit can be set up for compound cuts.

2-38.   The "Mitremate" saw guide is designed for use with Black & Decker's "Workmate" portable bench. Protractor allows settings from 30° to 90° in 5° increments.

1/2" THICK FENCE INSERTED THROUGH SAW BASE

WIDE ENOUGH TO LET GUARD WORK

1/2" HARDBOARD-FACED PLYWOOD

2"X4"X14"

LENGTH OF SHOE

MARKS TO POSITION FENCE AT 90° AND 45° TO BLADE

THICKNESS OF SHOE

WIDTH OF SHOE

SWING SAW TABLE

2-40.   If you would like to try this idea, you can make a swing saw table that imitates a powered miter box. It will work only if your saw provides a pivot action to achieve depth of cut.

shown in Figure 2-41 and 2-42. The cuts can overlap so you completely remove the waste material or they can be spaced so what remains can be removed with a chisel. The only difference between a notch and a groove or a dado is that the latter is likely to be longer. They all are U-shaped.

The best procedure is to make the outline—shoulder—cuts first by guiding the saw with a clamped-on strip of wood. Material between the first cuts can be removed by making repeat passes, either freehand or by relocating the guide strip.

To form the kind of notches that are needed in a stringer for a stairway, you must make two cuts that meet at the base of the angle (Figure 2-43). In order to clean out the waste by using only the saw, each cut must be longer than is needed to form the notch. Extra saw projection minimizes this over-cutting. If this method is not acceptable—for appearance or component strength—then just cut to the line and finish up with a handsaw or saber saw.

Since many similar cuts are required, you can work more accurately by making a template that can be used to guide the saw for each cut. The template (Figure 2-44) situates the saw and also acts as a stop that determines where the cut should end.

The same procedure applies when you must remove a corner from a board or panel (Figure 2-45).

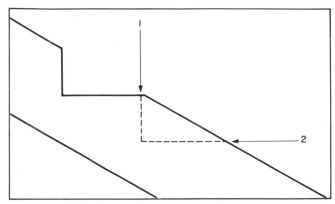

2-43.   This kind of cutout, required, for example, for the treads and risers in stair stringers, needs two cuts that meet at a common point. Overcutting will remove all the waste, or you can saw to the line and finish with a hand saw or saber saw.

2-44.   When many such cuts are needed, as they are in a stair stringer, making a template to guide the saw for each of the cuts will help you work more accurately.

2-41.   You can cut notches for half-lap joints by making a number of passes and then cleaning away the waste with a chisel, or by making cuts that overlap and removing all the waste.

2-42.   You can use the same technique to form dadoes or grooves. Both the notch and the dado are U-shaped; the dado usually being longer.

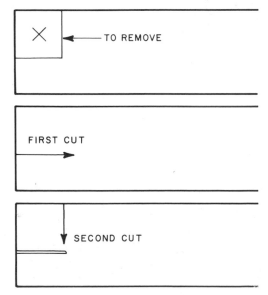

2-45.   The two-pass technique applies when it is necessary to remove a corner from a board or panel.

Making Rabbet Cuts

A rabbet cut is an L-shaped form that is made along the edge of stock or across its end. There are two techniques that you can use with a portable saw. One—set blade projection to the required depth-of-cut and make repeat, overlapping passes to remove the waste. Two—make two cuts that meet at a particular point so the waste is removed as a solid strip.

When you employ the first technique, move the saw along a guide-strip to do the outline—shoulder—cut. Then remove the waste by making repeat passes, either working freehand or by repositioning the guide strip for each of the remaining passes needed to complete the job.

If you use the two-pass technique, which is demonstrated in Figures 2-46 and 2-47, start the job by making the shoulder cut, using a clamped-on strip to guide the saw. The blade projection must be adjusted to conform with the depth of the rabbet. Most times, this is about one half, or maybe a bit more, than the thickness of the stock. The second cut, which must meet the first one, has to be done with the stock placed on edge. This takes a little more organizing since stock-edges are rarely wide enough to supply adequate support for the saw, so a special setup, like the one I use (Figure 2-46), is needed.

The repeat-pass procedure is probably most practical when you need to cut a rabbet on just one piece. If the form is needed on many pieces, then setting up for the two-pass method is better. Actually, when you need many similar pieces, the two-pass idea aids production. For example, assume that you need six or eight components that are an inch or so wide and x-inches long with a rabbet at one or both ends. You can form the rabbet on material—plywood or lumber—that is sufficiently wide and then slice the material into the number of pieces you need.

Making Plunge Cuts

Cuts within a panel, without the need of a lead-in cut from an edge, can be accomplished with a portable circular saw regardless of its design. The basic approach for this operation is to place the saw on the work with the blade situated on the cut-line but with the blade clearing the work surface and with the guard retracted, which it must be in this situation. Then, with blade projection adjusted so it's a bit more than the stock's thickness, pivot the tool downward until it is seated firmly on the base plate (Figure 2-48). This system works if the saw projection on your tool is controlled by a pivoting action. If the tool has an elevator-type depth of cut adjust-

2-46.   This is one way to set up for the second cut when doing a two-pass rabbeting operation. The first cut—the shoulder—was made with the work flat and the saw moved along a guide strip.

2-48.   To start a plunge cut, rest the saw firmly on the front edge of the baseplate and then pivot it slowly downward to penetrate the stock. You can work by lowering the blade with the saw resting on the work. In either case, maintain a firm grip.

2-47.   The arrangement for the second pass of the rabbet cut can be made on the edge of a workbench. The waste piece has been broken off to reveal what the finished rabbet looks like.

2-49.   As with most other sawing operations, you'll work more accurately when plunge cutting if you set up guide strips for the cuts.

ment, line up the retracted blade with the layout mark and then, with power on, slowly lower the blade until its projection is a bit more than the stock's thickness.

This type of operation can be done freehand but, to assure straight cutting and square edges, use a strip to guide the saw (Figure 2-49). In order to clean out corners by using only the power saw, you must saw beyond the point where corners meet. Maximum blade projection will minimize the over-cutting you must do. If you want to, or must avoid the over cutting, saw only to the line from both directions and then complete the cut with a handsaw or saber saw.

It's advisable, after you have accomplished two or three of the cuts, to nail or clamp a support-piece across the pocket (Figure 2-50). This will prevent the part being cut out from binding the blade as it starts to fall, and maybe twists, as it separates from the body of the panel. The piece that falls away should be tack-nailed to the support piece and the support piece should be clamped to the panel. It's a nuisance to work this way but it contributes to safer operation and cleaner cuts.

The plunge-cutting technique can also be used to form slots (Figure 2-51). Work with a guide strip and cut to lines that determine the terminal points of the slots. You can, of course, add other strips of wood that will act as stops for the beginning and end of the cut. Make overlapping, repeat cuts for wide slots, or do outline cuts and then remove the waste by cutting at each end with a coping saw or saber saw.

Cut a Curve—A Circle?

The portable circular saw really isn't designed for such work but you can cut circles by working very carefully with a pivot-guiding system and being very patient about getting through the stock (Figure 2-52). The radius gauge is a thin strip of wood or metal fastened by the same system used to secure an edge-guide and which uses a nail as a pivot point. Actually, the technique is more feasible on thin material. The kerf that is cut is actually a cove, so feed very slowly and don't attempt very small circles.

Sawing must be done in stages with the first pass just deep enough to break the surface of the wood. Thereafter, increase depth of cut no more than $1/16''$ for each pass required. Move the saw slowly and position yourself on the motor side

2-52.   We don't recommend using the circular saw as a substitute for a saber saw but it can be used for limited circular sawing if you follow carefully the procedure described in the text.

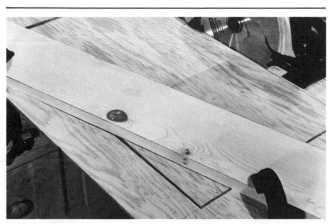

2-50.   Supplying support for the waste piece will keep it from falling away and maybe binding the blade. The support should be attached to both the body of the workpiece and the part being removed.

2-51.   Forming slots can be done by using the plunge cutting technique. Use repeat passes or make outline cuts and then remove the waste by making end cuts with a saber saw.

2-53.   It's also possible to saw a gentle curve if you first make a number of tangent cuts to remove as much of the waste as possible. What remains must be flexible enough so it can be moved away to keep the blade from binding.

Crosscut and Miter Jig

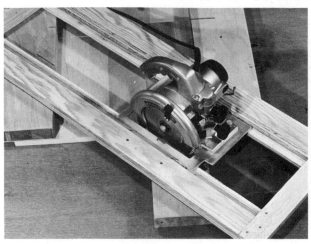

2-54.   A crosscut and miter jig, that you can make, can be used in the shop or for on-site work. Either way, it should rest on a sturdy support.

2-56.   For miter cutting, the track assembly is placed at the angle required. The use of lock pins, set in predrilled holes, lets you set the track at frequently-used angles.

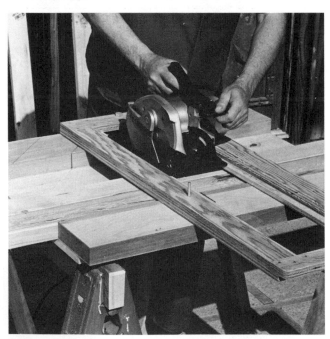

2-57.   By flipping the stock after making the first cut, the jig can be used for jobs like pointing fence pickets. The arrow points to one of the locking pins. These location holes will stand up better if you use steel bushing.

2-55.   Work to be crosscut is placed in the bed of the jig and up against the front fence. The cut is made by moving the saw along the track assembly. Note that you can cut more than one piece at a time.

2-58.   Construction details of a crosscut and miter jig that you can make. Cutting accuracy will depend on how carefully you assemble the unit.

3/4" X 3" X 35-1/2" (2 REQ)
3/4" X 2¼" VARIABLE
1/2" X 3-1/2"
3/4" X 3" x VARIABLE
1/2" X 3-1/4" X 40-1/2" (2 REQ)
1-3/4" X 6" X 38" (2 REQ.)
1/2" HOLES
3/4
45° TO SUIT SAW
1/4"
3/4" X 29" X 38"
CROSSCUT AND MITER JIG

of the tool. Be sure to supply good support for any workpiece in which you're making a circular cut.

Cutting a gentle curve is feasible if you first make a series of tangent cuts so that what is left to remove is flexible enough to avoid binding the blade (Figure 2-53). Techniques like this must be used with great care and are not suggested as substitutes for saber-saw work. The chapter on the saber saw and even the router will show other methods of doing circular cutting.

Special Jigs You Can Make

A crosscut and miter jig (Figure 2-54) can set you up for accurate cutting whether you use it in the shop or secure it to sawhorses for on-site work. The jig is used for crosscutting as shown in Figure 2-55. Workpieces are set on the bed of the jig and up against the front fence. The saw makes the cut as it is guided by the tracks.

Angular cutting is possible when the tracking system is placed as it is in Figure 2-56. The setup can be used for mitering or for jobs like the one shown in Figure 2-57. The work is flipped for the second cut; it isn't necessary to change the position of the track.

You can construct a duplicate by following the details in Figure 2-58. The holes for the pivot pin and the position lock-pins should provide a snug fit. Actually, since holes in wood will wear, you can assure continued accuracy by sizing the holes to receive steel bushings.

The distance between the track bars must suit the saw you own; other dimensions should be right for just about any saw. Check the thickness of the front and rear fences against the maximum projection of the saw blade. If necessary, you can pick up more depth-of-cut by using ¼″ instead of ½″ stock for the track base. If your saw does not have a wrap-around base plate, install a solid platform instead of ledges between the track arms. Cut a slot in the platform for the saw blade, positioned so the edge of the base plate will bear against the left track arm.

To crosscut, keep the saw against the rear fence and then feed it forward after the stock is positioned. The kerf in the back fence becomes a guide for lining up the workpiece. The crosscut position is fine for dado work. Adjust the blade projection for the depth of cut you want and then make repeat passes. If you do the outline cuts first, to marks on the work, you won't have to be so careful with the in-between cuts that clean out the waste. Jigs like this should be carefully made, sanded smooth, and then protected with several applications of a sanding sealer.

Jig Setup For Extra-Long Ripping

The setup that is shown in Figure 2-59 can be used when the width of the cut is beyond the capacity of an edge guide or when the waste, or the piece you need, doesn't provide sufficient support for the saw. Using two guide strips makes it possible to work with an edge guide when a cut is required at some midpoint in a panel.

Guide for Extra-Wide Cuts

The jig shown in Figure 2-60 involves a custom-made T-square with a slotted arm and an accessory base for the saw. In use, the saw and the guide move together; something like having an oversize edge guide. The arm of the square that rides against the work must be straight and smooth. Be sure the workpiece's edge is also straight. Irregularities will interfere with moving the saw in a straight line.

Place a strip of self-adhesive measuring tape on the saw side of the square's arm. It will, at least, allow setting the saw at an approximate position. Lock the saw where it should be by actually measuring from the edge of the workpiece.

GUIDE STRIP PARALLEL TO DESIRED CUT

TRACK

BLOCK TO PROVIDE BLADE CLEARANCE

THIS SETUP WORKS FOR CUTS BEYOND THE CAPACITY OF THE RIP GUIDE, OR WHERE WASTE IS TOO NARROW TO SUPPORT SAW

TEMPORARILY TACKED TO WORK

2-59.   Rip cuts that are wider than can be done with an edge guide can be done this way—using guide strips along with the edge guide. An extra strip raises the tool so its motor can clear the guide strip.

LIP OF SHOE BUTTS AGAINST SLIDE

ADJUSTABLE SLIDE

36″

SCALE FROM EDGE OF GUIDE BLOCK

90°

4″

16″

1/4″ BOLTS COUNTERSINK ALL HEADS

THIS EDGE IN LINE WITH SAW BLADE

SLOT FOR BLADE AND GUIDE

2-60.   This jig is designed so the guide and the saw move together in making extra-wide rip cuts. The saw is locked at a point on the T's arm to establish the width of the cut.

2-61.   A very simple project that lets you use a portable saw like a stationary unit. The saw is inverted and supported on blocks so its baseplate becomes part of the unit's table surface.

2-62.   An important point to be aware of is that the saw blade will not be completely shielded during the cut—the guard pivots downward so the work moves it beneath the table. We show the blade elevated for photo purposes; actually, it should barely poke through the stock.

2-63.   The exposed-blade precaution also applies to crosscutting. Don't try to cut short pieces or rip narrow ones. Hands must always be well away from the cut area.

Make a Table

You can use a portable saw like a stationary tool for simple crosscutting and ripping if you make a table like the one pictured in Figure 2-61. Cut the opening in the top with a saber saw, suiting its dimensions to match the size of the tool's base plate. Attach the support blocks with glue and screws, and then secure the saw, in inverted position, with flathead screws driven through the base plate into the support blocks.

A VERY CRITICAL point to remember, if you make the table, is that the saw blade will not be guarded when you do ripping or crosscutting (Figures 2-62 and 2-63). Because the tool's guard pivots, it will be moved under the work during the pass. Always be aware of this. Don't try to rip narrow pieces or crosscut short pieces. Always keep hands well away from the cut area. We show a higher-than-necessary blade projection in the photos. For safety sake, set the blade so it barely pokes through the work.

Construction details for a very simple unit are shown in Figure 2-64. The design of the rip fence requires that it be clamped in place when it is used.

How to Make a Panel Saw

You have probably seen an apparatus like the one shown in Figure 2-65 being used in a lumberyard so you know how convenient it can be for initial sizing cuts on large panels. Our project, designed around a portable circular saw, is designed to stand vertically so it can be placed against a wall to take up very little floor space. You can, if you wish, add angled braces at the back so the unit can be freestanding. Another thought is to hinge the braces and add locking arms. Then the project can be used as you choose.

The device is basically a frame with the saw in a carriage that is track-mounted to allow vertical movement. The work is placed in the frame and crosscut by moving the saw downward (Figure 2-65). Cables from sliding-door closers (Figure 2-66) connect to the carriage to counterbalance the weight of the saw and carriage. Spring-type sash balances can be substituted for the door closers but they may not be as

2-64.   Construction details of the table project. Remember that it is not intended as a substitute for a stationary tool. The rip fence is secured with clamps at one or both ends.

2-65. A panel saw lets you crosscut standard size panels with minimum fuss. You can make one that allows use of your own portable saw if you follow our instructions.

2-66. The weight of the saw and the carriage it rides in is counterbalanced with sliding door closers. Other methods can be used, but remember that counterbalancing is intended only to help the operator move the saw up and down.

2-67. The carriage, with the saw rotated 90°, can be locked in any position along the tracks. Thus the unit can be used for ripping panels as well as crosscutting them.

readily available. Actually you can accomplish the same result by using a steel weight. The steel weight could be attached by cable to the carriage with the cable running over a pulley at the top of the frame.

No matter how you go about counterbalancing the weight of the saw and carriage, don't design things so the saw will be snapped back at the end of a cut. The whole idea is merely to relieve the weight so you can easily move the carriage up or down.

Since the saw can be rotated 90° and the carriage can be locked at any point on the tracks, the project can be used for ripping as well as crosscutting. When ripping, the saw is in a fixed position; the work is moved to make the cut (Figure 2-67).

One inch OD pipe was used for the tracks. Black-iron pipe (¾″) would work okay, or you can use something with a larger diameter if you wish. Just be sure to have the track material on hand before you start constructing the related parts. The reason for the two-piece, bottom track support is to provide a method of adjustment so the tracks can be set parallel (Figure 2-68).

The carriage holds the portable saw securely and permits its vertical action. The saw is bolted to a plywood plate that fits the cutout in the carrier. Both the plate and the cutout are square. This feature permits the saw to be rotated so it can be used for crosscutting or ripping. Construction accuracy is very critical here (See Figures 2-69 and 2-70). The ends of the top and bottom carriage members are drilled for the tube-tracks and slotted so they serve as split clamps. The lock mechanism consists of a bolt and a knurled nut or wing nut (Figure 2-71).

Study the photographs and the construction details that are shown in Figures 2-72 and 2-73 before you start fabrication. There are choices when choosing material. Construction grade fir is okay so long as you're very selective about choosing good, straight stock. It might pay to spend a little more for something like kiln dried straight grain fir. Inferior material can distort enough to destroy the accuracy you build into the tool.

2-68. The bottom support for the tracking tubes is made in two pieces. This allows adjustment so the tubes can be set parallel to each other.

2-69.   The carriage has a cutout that is sized to fit the plates on which the portable saw is mounted.

2-70.   The saw, mounted on plates, fits in the opening in the carriage and is secured with a simple locking mechanism—small pieces of metal bar stock that bear down on the plate on which the saw is mounted.

2-71.   The ends of the top and bottom members of the carriage assembly are drilled to receive the tube-tracks and then slotted so they act as split clamps.

2-72.   Construction details of the frame for the panel saw.

2-73. This drawing details the construction aspects of the carriage and the saw mounting arrangement.

A Few Practical Commercial Accessories

Portalign's SAW GUIDE is designed for attachment to the base plate of a portable saw (Figure 2-74). When it is used for crosscutting, the saw, in a sense, rides on ball bearings along the arm that serves as a guide (Figure 2-75). Because of the accessory's built-in protractor the saw can be positioned for left or right angle cuts up to 45° (Figure 2-76). The guide capacity of the product is about 15″ on square cuts and across 12″ stock at 45°. The unit can be removed from the saw when it isn't practical for the job on hand.

The SAW MATE is a guide table that uses tracking arms to control the path of the saw (Figure 2-77). It can be used for crosscutting, by keeping the work in place and moving the saw, or for ripping, by securing the saw and moving the work. Miter cuts are possible because the unit's fence can be positioned to hold the workpiece at a particular angle. This type of cut is made as if the saw was being moved for crosscutting. An accessory is shown in Figure 2-78. This can provide a lot of helpful support when working on large panels.

The STRATE-CUT (Figure 2-79) is actually a set of extrusions that can be organized in various ways to provide a guide for a portable saw when crosscutting, ripping, mitering, beveling, and so on. Clamps are provided so the guides can be secured where needed. The guides, because of how they are designed, can extend to more than eight feet, which makes them practical for jobs like ripping a standard panel parallel to its long dimension. Since the STRATE-CUT is basically a guidance system, it can be used with a saber saw or router, or even with a knife for scoring wallboard.

2-74. This saw guide is attached to the baseplate of the portable tool.

2-75. The saw, on its "new" mount, rides along the guide arm. Because of a ball bearing slide arrangement, the saw is easy to move.

2-76. The unit has a built-in protractor so the saw can be guided through angular cuts as well as straight ones.

2-77. A product called "Saw Mate", is a system of tracking arms and a plate on which the portable saw is situated. A pivoting fence lets you position workpieces for angular cuts. The saw still moves in a straight line.

2-78. An accessory for the "Saw Mate" is another table that provides support for large workpieces, like panels. A router was placed in the photo to show that the accessory can also be used for router operations.

2-79. The name for this set of parts is "Strate-Cut". The pieces can be assembled in various ways to provide guidance for a portable saw whether it's being used for straight or angular cuts.

3. The Saber Saw

It wasn't too many years ago that the saber saw was introduced and made as big a splash with portable power tool users as the portable circular saw did when it first appeared. The continuing enthusiasm is justified because of the tool's special, practical features. The only tool that might be more popular, at least as a first-choice, is the portable drill.

With a saber saw you can do on-location chores that might be done on a bandsaw or jigsaw in the shop. But even with stationary tools on hand, the size of the workpiece often makes it more convenient to do a sawing job with a tool that can be applied to the work (Figure 3-1).

Of course, the saber saw doesn't make the stationary tools obsolete. In the case of the bandsaw, the hand-held tool can't compete in cutting speed, nor can it rival the big tool on jobs like resawing, pad cutting, or making compound cuts. The concept of the saber saw demands a stiff, relatively wide blade so it's not about to challenge the jigsaw, which can be used with a hair-thin blade, in terms of extremely fine, tight-radius fretwork. Its advantages are in its small, palm-grip size

and its portability. However, don't misjudge it because of its size or discount its ability to turn a reasonably tight corner. Scroller designs that allow turning the blade as you move the tool can follow some pretty fancy designs, whereas the tools in general have grown up rough and tough and can easily get through 2″ stock or any plywood. With the correct blade, saber saws can be used on plastics, metals, pipe, and even leather or paper.

One of the tool's exclusive features is its ability to make piercing cuts—internal cuts without a lead-in cut from an edge—without the need of a starting hole. Since the blade is chucked at only one end, it's possible to hold the tool at an angle, resting it firmly on the front edge of the baseplate so the blade's teeth begin to cut as you slowly pivot the tool until the baseplate is solidly on the work (Figure 3-2). Thus, you penetrate the work and arrive at the normal operating position to finish the job. More about this technique later.

What makes the tool more flexible, and even more exciting today, is the great variety of blades that are available and the fact that newer models provide different, specific

3-1.   The saber saw makes it easy to work on large panels that might be difficult to muscle over the surface of a stationary tool. Much of the work ordinarily done on a jigsaw or bandsaw can be accomplished with this unique tool.

3-2.   One of the features of the saber saw is its ability to do plunge cutting, which simply means making internal cutouts without the need of a lead-in cut from an edge. The technique will be described later in this chapter.

speeds, or allow an infinitely variable choice through the tool's speed range. Thus, you can choose an efficient combination of speed and blade to saw anything from paper to steel. With the right blade you can do heavy-duty work like notching studs or stair stringers and then, merely by changing to another blade design and possibly another speed, go immediately to more delicate work on cabinets and paneling.

Types and Sizes

The type of saw to consider depends, as always, on the kind of cutting you anticipate and the frequency of use. While the tool design, for some reason or other, bears many names—saber or sabre saw, jigsaw, bayonet saw, scroller saw—the basic function of the mechanism is to convert a rotating action into the up-and-down motion required by the saw blade (Figure 3-3). There is a lot of variation in features like horsepower, weight, blade stroke-length, fixed blade or scroller type, and, of course, price (Figures 3-4—3-10).

Generally, you get what you pay for. A manufacturer isn't going to, or can't, put into a light-duty, single speed, $30 tool what goes into a $100 or better, hefty, heavy-duty, variable speed version. This doesn't discount the less costlier models for light, occasional use. However, they may not cut as fast on all materials and they probably won't stand up as well as the "bigger" saws under continuous, hard use conditions. When the tool has a more powerful motor it will cut faster and more smoothly, run cooler, and have a good, solid feel to it. Its longer life will be due, in part, to huskier construction and better bearings. Sometimes, a more expensive tool will have extra refinements like an auxiliary knob that permits a two-hand grip, and removable base-plate inserts that minimize splintering and feathering when sawing materials like plywood.

Cutting capacity isn't much of a question these days. Getting through 1½″ wood is a basic need and it would be difficult to find a unit that won't do it. The capacity factor is often listed as so many inches in softwood and so many inches in hardwood. Many times, the tool's capacity in aluminum or steel is also rated. These areas, though, are affected as much by horsepower as by blade length. Some tools can be used with special, extra-long blades so you can cut through stock as thick as 4″, but they have the horsepower to do it.

Blade speeds—strokes per minute—are variable. A single speed has limited function; a couple of specific speeds is better, whereas a variable speed control allows near-perfect operating conditions for various materials. High cutting speeds used in combination with a tapered or hollow-ground blade generally result in fine, smooth cuts in wood. Slower speeds are better for getting through metals and some plastics.

Blade Action

Some units provide a consistent up-and-down blade motion, whereas others do sawing with a canted blade (the blade slopes away from the vertical), or one that describes a slight orbit while moving up and down, something like a narrow ellipse standing on its long radius. In essence, the last two blade motions cause the blade to move away from the cut

3-3. Saber saws differ in terms of weight, size, power, and blade strokes per minutes, but all of them convert a rotary motion to the up-and-down action required by the saw blade.

3-4. This Black & Decker unit is rated "professional." Motor fan is designed to clear dust from the cut area. A 4.5 amp motor, and ball and roller bearing construction make it a tool to last for quite a while. The speeds are variable; the blade has a four-position orbital action.

3-5. Makita's double insulated, single speed, 3700 spm saw (they call it a jigsaw) is rated at 2.6 amps and can saw up to 2″ in wood and ¼″ in steel. Lever under the housing is actually the on-off switch. Standard equipment includes six blades, a pivot guide, and an edge guide.

3-6.   Skil's scroller model allows the user to select any of three cutting methods. Set the blade to follow tool direction, or lock it at any 90° interval, or rotate it 360° by controlling it with the front knob. Speeds are variable.

3-9.   If you haven't noticed, this tool is working without a trailing electric cord. It's a cordless saber saw that can cut through 2x4s. The battery powered concept is making its mark in all areas of portable tools.

3-7.   Porter Cable calls this double insulated, heavy-duty unit a "bayonet saw." A unique feature is the roller bearing blade support guide which can increase accuracy and add to blade life. A built-in blower keeps the cut area clear.

3-10.   Top handle unit has an auxiliary side knob, a pretty tough worm gear drive, and an oversize baseplate. Blade action is orbital and moves at 4,500 spm. Tool comes with a special insert that can be used to minimize chipping and splintering.

3-8.   Electronics are also becoming part of the power tool scene. New scroller-type saw has electronic analog feedback that maintains the selected speed under load conditions. Speed dial has 20 incremental settings.

area on the downstroke when it isn't working, and move it forward on the upstroke when the teeth are biting into the wood (Figure 3-11).

The idea behind the alternate actions is to reduce power-wasting drag on the blade's downstroke, when it isn't actually working, and to help it keep the kerf—the groove made by the blade—free of waste material. The purpose is to reduce friction so cutting is easier, and to minimize heat build-up that might burn the wood and shorten the blade's use-life.

Basic Accessories

One feature that should be built into the tool is a baseplate that can be tilted from zero to 45°. The adjustable baseplate allows the saw to be used for beveling, cross-bevels (often called "miters"), and even compound cuts—the shapes achieved by moving the tool at an angle across stock but with the blade tilted. You'll probably find this feature useful, so check for it when you judge various models.

Some units are equipped with, or have available as accessories, special inserts that attach to the baseplate in some way to minimize the open area around the blade. Their purpose is to bear down on surface fibers close to the blade and so eliminate or, at least, minimize the degree of chipping that occurs as the blade teeth leave the work on the upstroke. This is especially useful when sawing plywood.

Edge guides are as available for saber saws as they are for circular saws (Figure 3-12). One will probably be included if you buy a saber saw "kit", but any respectable saw should be designed to accept one even if you must buy it as an accessory. Some edge guides do double-duty. The one shown in Figure 3-13 is designed to accept an adjustable point that

can be used as a pivot to guide the saw through circular cuts. Later, we'll show how this is done and how you can make an accessory that serves the same purpose but which has greater capacity.

A saber saw can be used somewhat like a stationary jigsaw by mounting the tool on the underside of an accessory table (Figure 3-14). Since the blade is chucked only at one end, the smallest blade you use must be stiffer than those that are used in a jigsaw. Actually, the setup emulates a stationary jigsaw when it is used with saber saw blades. In either case, work must be fed very carefully to make sure that the blade stays on the cutline. Because the blade is not held taut between upper and lower chucks, feeding too fast, or twisting the work too abruptly when getting around a turn, will result in ruining a workpiece or, at least, in poor quality.

3-12.   Edge guide, often called a rip guide, is used to guide the saw through cuts that are parallel to an edge. The edge against which it bears must be flat and true.

PIVOT
(CENTER OF CIRCLE)

3-13.   Some edge guides are equipped with a trammel point so the accessory can be used to guide the tool through circular sawing. We'll show how you can make pivot guides with greater capacity.

3-11.   Saber saw blades cut on the "up" stroke. All of them move up and down. Some might be canted, others will describe a slight orbit—it depends on how the tool is designed.

The table that is shown in Figure 3-14 is actually a combination unit, one that can be fitted with a saber saw or a portable router. If you are interested in a table, be sure it will accommodate the portable tools you have or plan to add. Usually, it's best to go for tools and accessories that are produced by the same manufacturer.

The Importance of Saw Blades

A close study of saw blades that are available for the saber saw is almost a course in how the tool is used and a view of its many applications. The blades that are profiled in Figure 3-15 are just a sampling of the many varieties that are available. In most cases, a single blade is packaged with the tool. Like the combination blade usually supplied with a table saw, the free blade will be a general-purpose wood cutter,

good for initial sizing cuts but hardly ideal for all applications. To rely on the one blade for all jobs imposes restrictions and limitations that will reduce the quality of your work, and will even increase your shop chores. It's also a fact of saber saw blade-life that they are subject to breakage. Even if you did choose to work with one blade, you should have a reserve package on hand.

A special blade with many teeth and formed with a tapered or hollow-ground cross-section will cut a kerf with minimum feathering and so reduce if not eliminate the follow-through sanding needed to get a perfect edge. It's a good blade to use on plywood—in fact it may be called a "plywood blade"—and it will also do nicely on lumber (Figure 3-16). As a rule of thumb, blades designed for fine cutting, being narrow and having many teeth, produce a

3-14.   Tables are available that allow you to use the saber saw like a stationary tool. Check before buying to be sure saw and table are compatible. Some tables can also be used with a portable router.

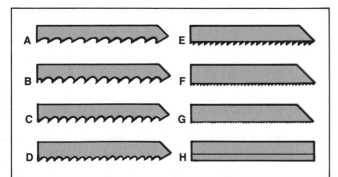

3-15.   This is just a sampling of available saber-saw blades. (A) 7-tooth blade for fast, rough cuts in thick wood and plasterboard. (B) 7-tooth extra long, for sawing logs and timbers up to 4″ thick. Usually 6″ long. (C) 10-tooth, for all-around use on hardwood, softwood, composition board, plastics. (D) 10-tooth taperground, for cuts in plywood, veneer, plastic laminates. (E) 14-tooth, for soft, nonferrous metals (aluminum, copper, brass) up to ¼″ thick. (F) 24-tooth, for fine cuts in thin sheet metal and tubing, either ferrous or nonferrous. (G) 32-tooth, for ferrous metals (iron and steel), pipe, and solid rod and bar stock. (H) Knife blade, for rubber, leather, wallboard, cloth, resilient floor tiles.

3-16.   Taper-ground or hollow-ground blades are best to use when you wish to keep surface chipping and feathering to a minimum. The blades will have many small teeth; are often called plywood blades or scroller blades.

confining kerf and can snap more easily than a wide blade with coarse teeth, so they must be moved carefully and slowly.

Install a blade with wave-set teeth, like those found on common hacksaw blades, and you can use the saber saw almost like a power hacksaw. For jobs on leather, rubber, cardboard, and the like, there is a sharp-edge blade without teeth that installs in the tool like any other blade but cuts like a knife.

If you are involved in remodeling work you can use blades that aren't fazed by an occasional nail, getting through them without damage (Figure 3-17), and others, shaped like the example in Figure 3-18, that allow cutting through moldings and baseboards and other installations that might be flush against a wall (Figure 3-19).

Blades for the saber saw are not expensive enough to prohibit having an all-inclusive assortment that will keep you prepared to cut anything from paper to steel. Actually, being prepared this way can prove to be the most economical arrangement in the long run since you will be less likely to abuse blades by using them on jobs they were never meant to do.

If you plan on using the saw for only occasional wood cutting, then a few dollars will buy the blades you should have. If your work calls for using the tool in depth, then it's wise and economical to purchase assortments. For example, the Sears Craftsman catalog lists an assortment of fifty blades in a storage case for about $26. Buying the blades individually would increase the cost considerably and, as usually happens, you may find yourself without the blade that's best for the job you want to do now.

The blade selection chart in Figure 3-20 doesn't list the blade width or its length or the tooth design, simply because such details would result in repeating blade-use suggestions and would make the chart difficult to use. Actually, the number of teeth per inch is probably the single most important factor except for plywood sawing and similar applications where you want the smoothest cut possible. In such cases, a hollow-ground or taper-back blade design, in addition to many teeth, will produce the best results. The test cuts in Figure 3-21 clearly prove the point.

Normally, you should choose a wide blade (⅜″ or ½″) for straight cutting, especially on heavy stock, and a narrow one (¼″ or less) for forming curves. The thickness of the material should also influence your choice in blade length. Blade lengths can be short (2½″ to 3″) or long (from 4″ to 6″). The lengths can vary according to tool brand, but most manufacturers do supply both long and short blades. The instructions that come with the tool will list available blades that can be used with the tool.

3-17.   Some blades are tough enough to get through an occasional nail without damage or breakage. However, use a blade that's designed for the purpose when you plan on sawing metals.

3-18.   All saber saws can be used with blades that are shaped like this. Called offset blades, they're designed so the teeth will be slightly ahead of or in line with the front edge of the tool's baseplate.

3-19.   Offset blades let you saw right to a surface. A nice feature when, for example, you are removing or repairing sections of molding. Cut just a bit shy to avoid damaging what the material is attached to.

WOOD		
TEETH PER INCH	**MATERIAL**	**RECOMMENDATIONS**
3	Lumber, logs	Fast cuts in heavy lumber (up to 6″ thick) of logs to 5″ diameter.
5	Lumber (nail free)	Fast but rough general cutting; good for ripping stock ½″ to 2″ thick.
6	Lumber	As above, but produces cuts a bit smoother.
7 or 8	Lumber, insulation board	Good general-purpose blade, especially for construction work; medium-smooth cuts.
10	Lumber (especially hardwood) under ½″ wallboard	Smoother cuts, but slower on heavy work; for scrollwork; also good for composition board, plastics. (Some saw makers recommend for general-purpose cutting; others offer special taper-back or hollow-ground versions to reduce chipping of plywood, laminates.)
12 or 14	Plywood	Smoothest cuts in plywood and fine scrollwork; also good for materials such as linoleum or rubber tile, hardboards, nylon, Plexiglas, and fiberglass. Also for plastic laminates, though some makers recommend use of 14 (or even 18) t.p.i. metal-cutting blade.
10 (H.S.S.)	Wood with occasional nail	Special steel will stand up under nail-cutting; also good for materials such as asbestos, laminates, etc.
7 (Flush cut or offset)	Lumber	For cutting flush to a wall, as with baseboards and moldings.
Special-purpose knife edge	Leather, cork, cloth, paper, cardboard, rubber, Styrofoam	Material being cut must be firmly held and supported.
METAL		
6 (H.S.S.)	Aluminum, copper, brass, laminates, compositions	Heavy cutting in plate or tubing; sample maximum cut: ½″ in aluminum plate.
10 (H.S.S.)	Same as above	General cutting with smoother finish than above.
14 (H.S.S.)	Aluminum, brass, bronze, copper, laminates, hardboard, mild steel, pipe	General cutting with smooth finish; maximum in steel: ¼″ - ½″ depending on manufacturers' specifications.
18 (H.S.S.)	Same as above	For lighter materials; maximum cuts about ⅛″.
24 (H.S.S.)	Sheet metal, light-gauge steel, thin-wall tubing, Bakelite, tile, etc.	Finest-tooth blade offered by some makers; wave-set.
32 (H.S.S.)	Thin-gauge sheet metals, thin-wall tubing, metal trim	Wave-set blade cuts fine kerf; maximum in steel: 1/16″. For typical hacksaw jobs.

Note: For information on length and width of blades, see text.

3-20.   Use this chart as a guide when selecting a blade for optimum results on particular materials. Remember that what you can do with a blade is also affected by the power of the saw.

3-21.   Wise choice of blades can make a big difference in the quality of the cut. Cut on the left was made with a coarse, few-teeth-per-inch blade. A small-toothed, taper-back blade produced the superior edge.

3-22.   An interesting factor of blade-use is that a wide, coarse blade can often make as tight a turn as a narrow one. The wider kerf formed by the big blade provides more room for it to turn. The difference will be in the quality of the cut.

3-23.   Cutting edges of toothless blades are fused with particles of tungsten carbide. They're indispensable for sawing many non-wood materials. They can also be used on wood but they are not speed demons.

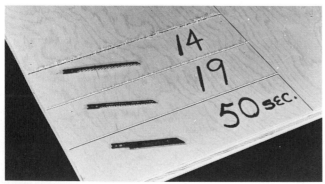

3-24.   Ten-inch-long test cuts show the difference in cut-speed of various blades. From the top—seven-teeth-per-inch blade with set teeth, 10-teeth-per-inch taper-back blade, medium grit tooth-less blade. Notice the difference in cut-quality as well as speed.

It's good practice to choose the shortest blade that will do the job and not tax the tool by using it with blades that are longer and bigger than it can handle. For example, the big 6″ blade varieties are not usually recommended for saws that have less than a full 1″ stroke.

Of two similar blades, the one that has set teeth and is "flat ground" will leave rougher edges than one that is taper-ground or hollow-ground. A very important factor to be aware of is that a blade with few, heavy-set teeth per inch will often turn as tight a radius as a narrow blade with many teeth per inch and little or no set (Figure 3-22). It's even possible that the heavy blade might be able to make a tighter turn than the other because the big blade forms a wider kerf which provides more room for the blade to turn.

Bear in mind that when the chart recommends a particular blade for scrollwork, the narrowest, finest-tooth blade you can use in a saber saw can't begin to match the fretwork designs you can cut on a jigsaw when it is fitted with a fine jeweler's blade. The point is made so you won't try to do work that can only result in blade-breakage.

Some manufacturers offer blades that are intended to fit only their saws. If you are ever in doubt about which blade to buy for the tool you own, take an example blade with you and be sure to match the shank end, the end of the blade that is gripped in the chuck. Although the trend has been toward standardization, there are differences in the combinations of teeth per inch, set, lengths, and widths the makers offer. The owner's manual supplied with the tool will state specifics concerning the tool-blade relationships.

All blades, stiff as they might be, can still bend, twist, or arc in the cut. The main cause of such problems is forcing the cut, asking the teeth to chew out more material than they were designed to handle at a particular feed-speed. You can easily tell when you're guilty of poor practice by sound and feel. If the cut isn't progressing steadily without excessive feed pressure, the blade is being overworked, is dull, or isn't the blade design that's best for the job.

Don't use woodworking blades to cut any metal except do-it-yourself materials, such as aluminum, that can be worked with ordinary woodworking tools. In a pinch, however, you can use metal-cutting blades to saw wood, hard-boards, and similar materials.

Teflon-coated blades are more expensive. Generally, they reduce friction in any cut, but they are especially practical if you plan to do much work with lumber that is green, damp, or contains much pitch. Whether or not it has a special coating, a blade that has few teeth per inch and lots of set is the best choice for such work. This also applies to any heavy stock. However, in cases when you want a reasonably nice finish, it's not taboo to work with a smoother-cutting blade. Just make the cut more slowly than you would with the recommended blade.

"Toothless" Blades

Relatively new, tungsten carbide blades that came into being for industrial applications, are now available to any power tool user. These blades cut almost anything and have a long-use life. The blades do not have teeth like a regular saw blade; instead, they have countless particles of tungsten carbide granules fused to the blade's cutting edge (Figure 3-23).

Cutting speed is not a strong point of the blades. A group of conventional teeth will chew out more material and do it faster than an edge of grit. Judged under average woodworking conditions, this suggests that the toothless blades do not—and probably aren't meant to—replace regular saw blades. But they do provide a valuable supplement, since no conventional blade can manage to saw through ceramic tile or slate or similar materials—or get through sheet metal that isn't sandwiched between scrap material without excessive burring and edge distortion.

The blades will work on wood, and they leave an impressive, almost sanded edge with minimal feathering, but they don't come close to sawing as speedily as conventional blades. Under test conditions, a medium-grit tungsten carbide saber saw blade took about 50 seconds to make a 10″ cut through ¾″ douglas fir plywood. A 10-tooth-per-inch, taper-back blade made it in about 19 seconds, while a seven-tooth-per-inch blade with set teeth ran the 10″ in about 14 seconds (Figure 3-24).

There was, however, quite a difference in the quality of the cuts. Although the taper-back blade (designed for the purpose) left a respectable edge, much more impressive than that left by the coarser blade, the toothless blade was definitely the cut-quality winner.

Tungsten carbide blades are also a good choice when cutting hard metals. Shop tests showed that it took about 92 seconds to get through a 1¼″ OD, heavy-walled steel tube with a 32-tooth, wave-set blade, but only about 80 seconds with a coarse-grit toothless blade. This was not a great difference in time but the other fact that emerged was the difference in the durability of the blades. The conventional blade was obviously tired after the job, whereas the tungsten carbide blade was ready to repeat the chore many times over.

The durability factor applies to the toothless blades generally. There's no question that they will outlast conventional blades by a good margin. But long life and cut-speed are not the prime considerations. The tungsten carbides are the blades to use when you need to use a saber saw to cut ceramic tile, slate, asbestos cement, clay pipe, brick, and other problem materials that you can't touch with a conventional blade.

The chart in Figure 3-25 suggests a practical grit selection for various materials. All of the grit types leave comparatively smooth edges with a minimum of feathering and chipping. The fine grit works best in thin, hard materials when cut quality is important and when chipping and delamination might be a problem. Medium-grit blades can be used if you wish to cut faster or if you find that the waste from the material you're cutting is packing between the tungsten carbide particles. Coarse-grit blades cut the fastest and, since they form a wider kerf, will move around smaller radii than finer-grit blades. This aspect is comparable to being able to make tighter turns with a wide, heavy-set blade than a no-set, narrow blade. There is simply more room in the kerf for the blade to maneuver.

As with any blade, tool speed can be an efficiency factor when working with the toothless blades. Slower speeds are best on materials such as stainless steel and counter top

MATERIAL TO BE CUT	FINE GRIT	MEDIUM GRIT	COARSE GRIT
Fiber Glass (Polyesters, Epoxies, Malamines, Silicones)	X	X	X
Ceramic Tile, Slate, Cast Stone	X	X	
Asbestos Cement, Nail Embedded Wood, Plaster with Nails			X
Chalkboard, Carbon/Graphite, Clay Pipe, Brick	X	X	
Stainless Steel Trim, Sheet Metal to 18 Ga., Ducting, Counter Top Materials, Tempered Hardboard	X		
Plywood, Hardwood Veneer Plywood	X	X	

Note: Use slower speeds with variable speed saws. Highlighted boxes show most popular grit size.

Select fine grit when a smooth cut is desired in thin, hard materials where precision is important, particularly where splitting, chipping, or delamination is a problem. Use medium-grit blades where faster cutting is needed or when loading of fine-grit blades occurs. The coarse-grit blades cut faster in thick or softer materials where a rougher finish is acceptable. Coarser grit saws will permit up to a 30% smaller radius cut.

Courtesy of Remington Arms Co., Inc.

3-25. Suggestions for selecting the most efficient grit when using toothless blades to saw various materials.

laminates. Testing has indicated that in all cases it's wise to start at a slow speed and increase spm (strokes per minute) to the point where the blade is cutting most efficiently. It's a procedure to follow, at least for the first time, on each new material you work on.

Always be certain that the blade is locked securely in the chuck. Methods of achieving this can vary depending on the tool. With some, it's a question of tightening a single Allen screw with a small wrench (Figure 3-26). Others may have a screw that bears against the back edge of the blade as well as a lock screw. The owner's manual will tell how to set the blade securely.

It's not a bad idea to check the lock screw occasionally as you work since vibration might cause it to loosen. Always remove the blade when storing the tool.

Operational Speeds

The rule of thumb is, slow speeds with coarse blades, high speeds with finer cutters. This is based on the thought that, generally, you'll be using heavy blades to saw through comparatively tough material like construction grade fir, and smoother cutters when working on something like kiln dried pine or fancy hardwoods and plywood.

An advantage of a tool with a variable speed control is that you can adjust the speed as you work. For example, you can slow down a bit when the blade has to get through a particularly dense grain area or a knot.

Of course, efficient sawing depends on the combination of blade, tool speed, and feed speed—how fast you move the tool. How the job is going tells a lot. The more you use the tool, the more you'll realize that excessive vibration, having to force the tool to keep it cutting, excessive blade slowdown, and a blade that does more rubbing than cutting all indicate that you're not working as efficiently as you should. Tool sense is acquired—it's not a secret skill you must be born with.

Tool Handling

The major cause of substandard work, and even blade breakage, is excessive vibration in the tool or the workpiece. The practice of clamping work to a solid surface, especially pieces that aren't large or heavy enough to sit solidly on their own, makes sense, and helps you work more safely. Much saber saw cutting can be done with just one hand on the tool, but if you're using a heavy-duty tool and the work is secure, there's no reason why you can't hold the tool with both hands to keep it firmly on the work and to move it steadily forward. This has to be done when using the blade turning feature of a scroller saw (Figure 3-27). The hand on the control knob controls the direction of the blade while the other hand keeps the tool moving.

To minimize vibration, apply pressure down on the tool as you move it. This can't be overdone, of course, but the combination action should assure firm contact between the tool's baseplate and the work throughout the pass. Keep the blade running free by avoiding sideways pressure. Remember that the blade is chucked at only one end so its free to twist and bend. Lateral forces can result in blade damage or breakage, burning of the blade and the work, and substandard cut quality in general.

Saber-saw blades cut on the "up" stroke so any splintering or feathering will appear on the surface of the work that is in contact with the baseplate. This makes it necessary to keep the good surface of the stock "down" anytime the finish cut is important (Figure 3-28). This isn't always possible. For example, you may need to saw a hole through some wall paneling that is already installed. In such cases the most you can do to minimize the feathering is saw with a smooth-cutting blade.

A trick that may come in handy is to place a strip of transparent tape over the cutline before you saw. This does the job of keeping surface fibers together as the blade saws through. Another help, if the tool is so equipped, is to use the

3-26.   Be sure the blade is securely locked in the tool's chuck. It's good practice to check occasionally to be sure vibration hasn't caused the blade to loosen. Always remove the blade when storing the tool.

3-27.   Many heavy-duty saws have an auxiliary handle so you can use a two-hand grip. When the scroller feature on a saw like this one is used, one hand controls the blade to keep it on line, the other hand moves the tool.

special insert that minimizes the opening around the saw blade. Like the tape, the insert bears down on surface fibers close to the blade.

Keeping the baseplate in firm contact with the workpiece is the general rule, but the rule can be broken in certain situations. An exception might occur when you encounter a knot in the wood. Here, rocking the tool will help the blade get through the hard area more easily (Figure 3-29). The idea is to pivot the tool up using the toe of the baseplate as a fulcrum and thus decrease the contact area between the blade and the work. Pivoting back down does the same thing. In effect, the method concentrates the cutting power on smaller areas.

The saber saw can be used for pad sawing, which simply means that you stack pieces that must have the same shape and cut through all of them at once (Figure 3-30). The limitation is the length and stroke of the blade. Naturally, you can stack more ¼″ pieces than ¾″ pieces, but in any event, work as if you are sawing solid stock, selecting an efficient combination of blade, stroke speed, and feed speed.

Straight Cutting

While it isn't difficult to make straight cuts by guiding the saw along a marked line, you can do the job more accurately and with less strain if you work with a guide. The most common aid in this area is the "edge guide" which is lighter but otherwise very similar to those available for portable circular saws (Figure 3-31). Sometimes, they are supplied with the saw. If not, they will be available as an extra-cost accessory.

The arm of the guide is inserted through slots (or some similar arrangement) in the baseplate and secured with, usually, small thumb screws. When using one, measure from the inside surface of the guide's fence to a tooth on the blade that points toward the guide. The fence bears against the edge of the stock to maintain a uniform cut-width as you move the

3-29.   Rocking the tool a bit when you encounter a knot or a particularly dense grain area, will help sawing go easier. In effect, the method reduces the amount of wood the blade must work on.

3-30.   Pad sawing is simply stacking workpieces so you can produce several similar ones in a single operation. Be sure the pieces are aligned and clamped together.

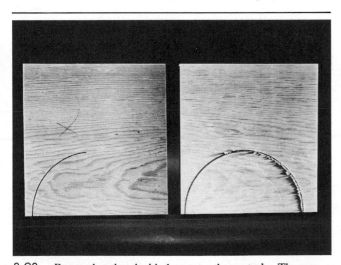

3-28.   Remember that the blade cuts on the upstroke. The samples are top and bottom views of a cut made with the same saw blade. The clean cut on the left, which was the bottom of the workpiece during sawing, proves that material should always be sawed with the good surface down.

3-31.   Edge guides for the saber saw are similar to those supplied for portable circular saws. Remember that it's just a guide. Keeping the saw moving in a straight line, without twisting, is the operator's responsibility.

saw. Remember that the accessory is a guide. Keeping the saw moving without twisting is your responsibility. Some edge guides are dual purpose. When set up as shown in Figure 3-32, they provide a pivoting action that guides the saw through circular cuts.

When the cut you require is too far from the stock's edge to allow using an edge guide, or when you choose to work without one, you can use a straight piece of wood to guide the saw (Figure 3-33). The guide can be tack-nailed or clamped to the workpiece. Always position the guide so you are allowing for the distance from the edge of the base plate to a tooth that is set in its direction. The guide can be secured either to the piece you need or to the part that's being cut off. Making the cut is just a matter of moving the saw so the baseplate bears constantly against the guide.

The same type of guide can be used for any long cut, like sawing across the small dimension of a plywood panel or for

angular cuts. Accessories like the one in Figure 3-34 are available from manufacturers. The advantages are that the guide is a metal extrusion and will have more natural rigidity than a strip of wood, and that it has "built-in" grippers so it's easy to secure without having to resort to tack-nailing or clamps.

Good guides, like the common adjustable square shown in Figure 3-35, for making short, straight cuts can be found right in the shop. For longer cuts, why not use a carpenters square? You can hand-hold the guides as you move the tool along the blade or you can use a clamp.

Any of the guides that were described in the chapter on portable circular saws, including the ones that you can make, can be used with a saber saw for straight or angular sawing.

Extra Thick Cuts

Getting through thick material, say a 4x4 (Figure 3-36), is a matter of working with a longer-than-normal blade. For example, a 6″ blade is long enough to get through 4″ stock. It's assumed, of course, that the tool you have can handle a 6″ blade, but you'll find the answer in the owner's manual.

Most long blades are designed for tough work and so have few, but large teeth with a lot of set—so don't expect perfectly smooth cuts. The general rule is to take it easy. Allow the blade to set its own pace. Forcing the cut won't accomplish anything.

3-32.   Using an edge guide to lead the saw through a circular path. More about this particular technique later on.

3-34.   Guides should also be used for angular cuts. This commercial unit is a strip of extruded metal with its own clamping arrangement. Working with guides minimizes the possibility of human error.

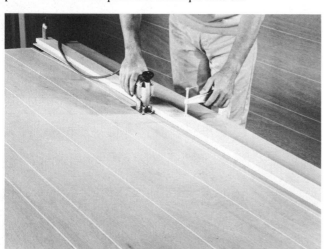

3-33.   When the cut is too wide for an edge guide or you choose not to use one, a tack-nailed or clamped strip of wood will assure a clean, straight cut. Just keep the edge of the baseplate against the strip throughout the pass.

3-35.   An adjustable square is a fine guide for short cuts. A carpenters square, which has a 24″ blade, can be used on wider workpieces.

Freehand Cutting

Freehand cutting is required on scroll-type cuts (Figure 3-37) where it's not possible to work with a guide, and on jobs like forming scalloped edges where it may be more convenient to work without one (Figure 3-38). This type of sawing demonstrates one of the major features of the saber saw—its ability to do cutting that would ordinarily require a jigsaw or that would have to be done by hand with a coping saw.

3-36. "Long" saber-saw blades can get through 4″ material but the saw must have sufficient power. The owners manual should tell you the maximum length of blades you can use as well as the tool's capacity in terms of material thickness.

3-37. Scroll-type cutting calls for narrow blades and very careful tool handling to avoid over-cutting. Scroller-type units are particularly good at this sort of thing since the blade can be controlled independently of the tool's feed direction.

3-38. Planning the route for the saw helps you work more efficiently. Note that the marked cutline bypasses the point where the arcs meet. This area will be cleaned out after the bulk of the waste has been cut away.

Of course, it's not all roses. The saber saw can't turn on itself or manipulate minute radii. But there are ways to compensate; a common one being to drill holes where lines meet at right angles so all that's left for the saw to do is make straight cuts. Actually, when the design permits, it's a good idea to pre-drill the workpiece wherever an arc fits in. Then you won't have to strain the saw around tight turns.

Note, in the illustration that shows a scalloped edge being formed (Figure 3-38), the marked cutline bypasses the point where the arcs meet. The saw is brought back to clean out the corner after the bulk of the waste has been removed. The technique eliminates the need to make a lot of lead-in cuts.

Making tight turns, doing scroll-type work, calls for careful tool-handling. A slow feed, just barely enough to keep the blade working, produces best results. Always anticipate where a straight line flows into a curve and start the turn a fraction before you get there. A common error is to over-cut at this point so back-tracking is needed to get to the point where the curve begins.

Curves and Circles

The general rule is, don't force blades to follow curves or make turns they are obviously struggling to make. There are techniques you can use that allow a blade to follow a curve it couldn't ordinarily do. In some cases, forming preliminary radial cuts or in-cuts, a common practice on bandsaws and stationary jigsaws, can be used with the saber saw (Figure 3-39). For example, if you need to cut a small half circle in the edge of a piece of stock, or wish to round off the end of a narrow board, you can "do the impossible" by making a series of cuts from the edge or end of the workpiece to the cut-line before starting to saw the arc. What happens then, is that pieces of waste fall away as you cut, thereby providing more room for the blade to maneuver. The wider the blade and the tighter the arc, the more in-cutting you must do.

3-39. Sawing preliminary radial cuts or in-cuts will allow a blade to follow a curve it couldn't ordinarily do. The waste pieces fall away and so the blade has more room to turn.

When rounding an end, you can also get around a tight turn by making tangent cuts. Start sawing the arc and when the blade starts to bind, run the cut out to the edge of the stock. Then return to where you left off and repeat the procedure. You'll probably have to do this many times before the arc is complete.

You can saw gentle curves very accurately by letting the saw follow a clamped-on guide strip that you've shaped for the purpose (Figure 3-40). The critical factor is maintaining a constant tangent contact between the bearing surface of the guide and the edge of the baseplate. To put it another way, the distance from the blade's teeth to the guide must be constant throughout the pass.

It's an especially good procedure to follow when you need many similar pieces. You can extend the idea's usefulness by stacking pieces so you can cut several at a time.

Circles, whether you need a disc or are forming an opening through a panel, can be cut freehand, or the tool can be guided using a pivoting arrangement which will assure a uniform cut. Some edge guides are designed so they can also be used for this purpose (Figure 3-41). The fence of the accessory is slotted so a trammel point can be secured to serve as the center of the circle.

When the radius of the circle is beyond the capacity of the edge guide, or if your unit isn't designed for the purpose, you can easily custom design a pivot guide like the one being used in Figure 3-42. The pivot is a piece of thin metal which can be gripped in the slots normally used for the edge guide. The pivot end is bulked out so the hole for the pivot point, which is just a small nail, can be in line with the front of the teeth on the saw blade. The length of the guide is optional. In either case, the guide is adjusted so the distance from the pivot point to a tooth set in its direction is equal to the radius of the circle. This applies if the disc you are cutting is the part you need. When a circular opening in a workpiece is needed, then the dimension must be taken from a tooth on the opposite side of the blade—kerf on the outside of the line for a disc, on the inside for an opening.

To start the sawing you must make an opening for the blade, either by making a plunge cut (Figure 3-43), a technique we'll talk about in a bit, or by drilling a hole through the work. The entrance-hole idea is more convenient since it lets you get the saw established before setting up the pivot guide. When it doesn't interfere with appearance, the center of the entrance hole can be directly on the circumference. This way, positioning the blade directly on the cutline won't be a prob-

3-40.   Guide strips can be used for accurate sawing of gentle curves. The technique is most useful when you need many similar pieces. Stacking workpieces will make the job go faster.

3-42.   You can make pivot guides using thin sheet metal or something similar so you can saw any size circle you wish. One end of the guide is wider so the pivot point, a small nail, can be in line with the front of the teeth on the blade.

3-41.   Edge guides, as we have said, are fine for guiding a saw through a circular cut, but they have limited capacity.

3-43.   The plunge cut is started by resting the tool very firmly at an angle on the forward edge of the baseplate. The angle must be extreme enough so the teeth will start to cut when the tool is switched on.

lem. Since plunge-cutting forms a straight kerf, it's best to use the idea when the disc is the waste piece.

After the saw's position is established, let the pivoting arrangement do the guiding. Move the tool slowly and steadily. Any blade can be used, but narrow ones will do a better job on small circles.

Plunge Cutting

Since one end of the saber-saw blade is free, the tool can be used to do internal cutting without the need of a lead-in cut from an edge of the stock, or the necessity of a starting hole for the blade (Figure 3-43).

The technique works this way. Place the tool at an angle so it rests on the forward edge of the baseplate. The angle must be judged so that some teeth on the blade will make contact with the work. A firm grip on the tool and sure contact between the baseplate and the work are critical. Turn on the motor and very slowly tilt the machine back to start sawing. It's necessary to avoid letting the initial contact be between the point of the blade and the work. If this happens, you'll feel like you're gripping a pogo stick—the tool will do nothing but hop about.

The starting cut is a surface groove. As you continue to tilt the tool back, the groove gets a bit longer and deeper and the blade finally penetrates (Figure 3-44). Keep the contact between the baseplate and the work very firm. If you allow the tool to move back, it will bounce off the back end of the groove. Also, letting the tool jiggle as you're going through the procedure can mar the surface of the work. To eliminate this possibility, start the cut by using a piece of thin scrap material as a buffer between the base plate and the work (Figure 3-45). The buffer can be any material that doesn't have a very slippery surface—even heavy cardboard will do.

Another way to provide firm bracing for the tool, and to keep it from moving about until the blade gets through, is to clamp a piece of scrap material to the work so the base plate can bear against it (Figure 3-46). When you attempt a plunge cut for the first time, do it in a waste area. After some practice you'll be able to accomplish it directly on a cutline.

Before proceeding with sawing, be sure the blade has penetrated sufficiently so the tool can seat solidly in its normal, fully-flat baseplate position (Figure 3-47). If the cutout is circular, then one continuous pass will complete the operation. There are several ways to go when the cutout has square corners. You can cut each side of a rectangle or square

3-44. The blade starts to cut as you very slowly pivot the tool backward, until it finally penetrates the stock. Keep a very firm grip—don't force the blade.

3-46. Another method you can use to get a plunge cut started is to clamp a block to the work to act as a brace for the baseplate. It keeps the tool steady so you can start the cut accurately.

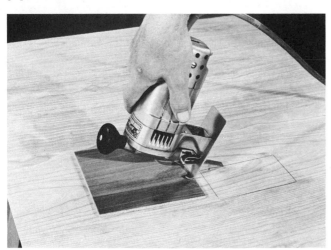

3-45. You can use a scrap of thin material under the edge of the baseplate to avoid the possibility of marring the workpiece.

3-47. After the blade has fully penetrated, sawing proceeds in normal fashion with the tool solidly on the baseplate.

3-48.   You can avoid having to repeat plunge cuts by working this way. Saw to an area where you can veer off and come back to the starting point to clean out the corner. Repeat the procedure for each corner.

3-49.   Guide blocks can be used for more accurate sawing with minimum fuss. The arm of the guide can be the full length of the cutting line. Position the guide to allow for the distance from the blade to the edge of the baseplate.

by starting with a plunge cut for each one. This can be bothersome, so since the piece being removed is usually scrap, it's more practical to procedure as shown in Figure 3-48. Make a partial cut and then veer off so you can circle back to clean out the corner. The job is finished by following a similar procedure for each corner.

When it's necessary to be perfectly accurate, you can use a guide block to control the sawing (Figure 3-49). The arms of the guide block can be longer than the one shown so the saw can be guided for the full length of the cut.

Entrance Holes

While the plunge cutting feature of the saber saw can provide a solution in some woodworking situations, it is not mandatory that you use it for all cutout work. In fact, it's often more practical and convenient to set up for the job by drilling a starting hole for the blade (Figure 3-50). The piece being cut out won't be marred to the point where it must be wasted if you locate the hole carefully, close to a cutline. Also, the diameter of the hole doesn't have to be greater than the width of the blade.

Many times, entrance holes can be part of the design (Figure 3-51). They can be located to provide nicely rounded corners or, in the case of some fancy scrollwork, anyplace in each of the waste areas. The point is, plunge cutting doesn't have to be considered the cure-all. It makes sense to preview cutout work and to use entrance holes where you can, either as part of the design or to make the job easier and faster to do.

Bevel Cuts

Bevel sawing is done by tilting the baseplate so the saw blade will be at the angle you need (Figure 3-52). Handle the tool as if you were doing a square cut but bear in mind that the cut is "thicker" because the blade is angled. This calls for the same feed-speed change you would make when going from, say, ¾" stock to 1½" stock.

Since more of the blade is in the cut and is more subject to twisting and binding, use the widest blade that will do the job. On thick material it pays to use a coarse blade, cutting

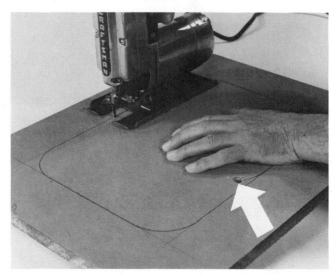

3-50.   It's not mandatory that you use the plunge-cutting technique for all internal cutting. Many times, it's more convenient to drill an entrance hole for the blade (arrow).

3-51.   Entrance holes, when accurately located, can become rounded corners. The system is flexible since the entrance holes can be as large as you wish.

3-52. Bevel cutting doesn't differ too much from square cuts except that the blade, at an angle, has to get through more wood. So adjust feed-speed accordingly.

3-53. A common metal-cutting saber saw blade is designed like a hacksaw blade and so can do any of the cutting that's possible with the hand tool. As with any blade, the cut must not be forced.

just outside the line, and then make the edge more acceptable by sanding.

Bevel cutting can be done freehand but, like crosscutting and ripping, you'll work more accurately, especially on long cuts, if you use guides.

Sawing Metals

With the right metal-cutting blade installed in the tool and using a suitable speed, you can cut any metal that can be cut with a hacksaw blade (Figure 3-53). As we said in the beginning, the right blade is usually a wave-set type except when cutting do-it-yourself material that can be handled with regular wood cutting blades.

The saber lets you work faster than by hand and requires less effort. Capacity is also increased since you are not hindered by the frame on a conventional hacksaw. A point to remember is that as many teeth as possible should bear against the edge of the stock (Figure 3-54), so choose the blade accordingly. This material can sit between the teeth of a coarse blade, and this can result in stripping the teeth, bending or breaking the blade, and generally poor edges on the work. The rule, of course, doesn't apply to toothless, tungsten carbide blades. On thicker materials, you can use coarser blades so long as they are designed and tempered for metal work. Actually, it's good practice not to depend entirely on blades with tiny teeth since, on some materials, they can clog very quickly.

All workpieces must be firmly supported to eliminate vibration and so you can saw smoothly. The best way to cut thin sheet metal is to place it on some scrap wood or sandwich it between covers of thin plywood or hardboard (Figure 3-55). If you work this way, you'll get minimum vibration and the support pieces will prevent the blade from forming jagged edges. When it's not possible to work this way—you may be cutting rain gutters or downspouts—feed the tool very slowly to avoid distorting the metal (Figure 3-56). It's almost impossible to work this way without getting burrs on the cut edges, so some finishing with emery or steel wool is in order.

3-54. The drawing demonstrates the rule of thumb for sawing metals. The thought applies particularly to thin materials.

3-55. The most efficient way to saw sheet metal is to support it as shown or to sandwich it between thin sheets of plywood or hardboard. This keeps the metal firm and eliminates jagged edges.

3-56. When you can't work the ideal way, be sure to hold the work very firmly and cut slowly. Toothless blades help do such work more easily.

3-57. Thicker, more rigid sheet metal, doesn't require the support suggested for thin material, but be sure to use clamps to hold the material firmly. Keep the cut area clean of chips that might scratch the surface of the workpiece.

3-58. Keeping the workpiece firm leads to smoother, more accurate sawing. Gripping the work, especially small pieces, in a vice, is good practice.

You can work on thicker metals without providing support sheets so long as the work itself is suitably clamped (Figure 3-57). Be sure that the underside of the baseplate is smooth and clean to avoid marring the work. Also, keep the cut area clear of waste; chips can collect under the baseplate and cause scratches. Whenever possible, grip workpieces, especially small ones, in a vise (Figure 3-58).

When saber-sawing metals, especially heavy nonferrous materials, it pays to apply a grease stick lubricant to the blade as you work. Sometimes, wax will work. I've seen plumbers rub chalk on hacksaw blades. Anyway, the applications are meant to help the blade run cooler and to prevent the blade's teeth from becoming clogged with waste material.

Sawing Other Materials

Saber-sawing doesn't have to be confined to wood and metal. If something is sawable, this unique tool can perform. Usually, efficient sawing is a matter of the blade you use and how fast you move the tool. Figures 3-59 through 3-62 provide information on sawing other materials you might encounter in the shop or on location.

3-59. The only problem you might encounter when sawing materials like "Plexiglas" is heat build-up that can fuse waste in the kerf. The manufacturer of the material suggests using a blade with at least 14 teeth-per-inch. Keep the protective paper in place until all sawing has been done.

3-61. Fiberglass can be cut with almost any blade, but quick dulling can result. You can use a metal-cutting, wave-set blade or a toothless one when sawing is extensive. Be especially firm with your grip when sawing corrugated material.

3-60. Synthetic marble like "Corian" cuts easily with wood-cutting blades but don't use coarse ones that might cause surface-chipping. Best results are with fine-tooth blades or toothless ones. In either case, the feed-speed should allow the blade to cut at its own pace.

3-62. Not much choice on tile and ceramics but to saw with a toothless blade. Be sure to provide firm support for the workpiece and to grip the tool securely—excessive vibration can cause the material to crack.

4. The Reciprocating Saw

There can be some confusion between the *reciprocating saw* and the *saber saw*, but it's in name only as you can see by comparing the representative tools shown in Figures 4-1 and 4-2. Some of the puzzlement results because of names used by manufacturers. Both tools are often called "Bayonet saws" or even "All-purpose saws", and for the reciprocating saw there are tags like "Tiger saw", "Blitz", "Recipro", "Super saw", "Cut saw", "Sawzall", or simply "Recip".

While there is a degree of overlap in function—each tool can work with rough, fast cutting blades or smoother, slower cutting blades—neither is a justifiable substitute for the other. Mechanically, the reciprocating saw is a more heavy-duty tool that can drive longer and tougher blades than those you can chuck in a saber saw.

The saber saw drives a blade that has a vertical sawing action. The blade on a reciprocating saw moves to and fro horizontally, longitudinally in line with the body of the tool. There are many times when the saber saw can be efficiently controlled with one hand. It will be a rare situation when you might feel free to control a reciprocating saw without both hands gripping firmly—which says something.

Carpenters will use the reciprocating saw for rough remodeling chores like cutting quickly through standing 2x4s or 2x6s, or even completely through an existing wall. A plumber will use it to cut holes or notches for pipes, or to cut through an installed pipe that must be replaced. An electrician finds it useful for shaping notches for wiring or for opening a wall to install an outlet box. All these chores, and others, are, of course, in the work-scope of home craftsmen. Add other chores like pruning heavy branches, cutting small logs for firewood, topping off fence posts, and so on, and you have a realistic view of the heavy-duty concept of a reciprocating saw.

4-1.   Any reciprocating saw is essentially a heavy-duty tool that can handle blades as long as 12″. When used with the correct blade, it will saw anything from soft, panel materials to heavy metals. Its blade, which cuts on the back stroke, moves to and fro in line with the body of the tool.

4-2.   The saber saw, also a versatile machine, is not designed for the very rough work that can be accomplished with a reciprocating saw. There is some overlap in function, but neither is a complete substitute for the other.

An Overview

Reciprocating saws are available in single speed, two speeds, and variable speed models. On the average, a single speed model will operate at about 2000 strokes per minute (spm). With a two speed model you can operate in the areas of 1700 spm or 2400 spm. A variable speed unit has infinite speed settings starting at zero and ranging to about 2600 spm. These are general specifications; you will find some variations depending on the model and the manufacturer.

Having more than one speed is an advantage since you can adjust for compatibility with the blade you are using and the material being cut. For example, a slow speed for metal work and a higher speed for sawing wood and other relatively soft materials. Being able to adjust spm is a plus even when sawing wood since you can slow down a bit when hitting a particularly dense area or a knot.

Some of the tools are shaped so the front area provides for gripping by the left hand, or right hand as the case may be (Figure 4-3); others are equipped with auxiliary handles. Whatever the design, a two-hand grip that minimizes vibration and chatter and keeps the blade on the cutline should be standard practice.

The shoes (or sole plates) on some of the saws have a fixed position while others can swivel (Figure 4-4). Each has an advantage touted either by the manufacturer or a dedicated user. In general, a fixed base provides a firm brace-point for routine cutting, whereas one that swivels can make it easier to do plunge cutting. In either case, to make internal cuts without having to drill a starting hole for the blade, the tool is rested firmly on the shoe so the blade is clear of the work, then the tool is tilted, slowly, so the blade can start penetrating (Figure 4-5). A cautious initial contact is critical since being hasty will cause the tool to jump about. The blade will first form a groove which will deepen as you tilt the tool until the blade gets through the material. Plunge cutting is best done with the shortest, heaviest blade that is suitable for the work at hand.

The blade clamp on most reciprocating saws is adjustable so the blade can be situated to cut up or down, horizontally, or even at an angle. Setting a blade so its side is parallel to the body of the tool makes it possible to cut close to the base of a vertical surface (Figure 4-6)—handy, for example, in some phases of remodeling work.

The length of the blade stroke might be as little as ⅝″ and as much as 1½″ with the average being about 1″. Longer blade strokes do more work more quickly and should be accompanied by greater horsepower.

Other features you can check for include a shoe that is adjustable in and out so you can, in effect, change the area of the blade that is working; thus, you don't have to discard a blade because an inch or two of its teeth are too dull to cut. Also, a guided air flow that helps keep the saw cool and clears waste from the cutting area is an asset.

As you might expect, electronics are affecting the design of modern reciprocating saws. Some have electronic speed controls. The unit shown in Figure 4-7 works with a microprocessor that provides feedback to the motor so that cutting power will be consistent under varying sawing conditions.

4-3.   Some of the units are shaped so the forward area of the casing is a grip area for the hand that is not holding the handle. Others may have an auxiliary handle. Whatever—most jobs call for a firm two-hand grip.

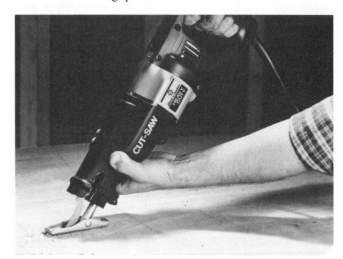

4-4.   The shoe, or sole plate, may have a swiveling action or it may be fixed. Whatever the design, it's there to provide a brace-point for the sawing operation. Keeping it firmly on the work throughout the pass will minimize vibration and chatter.

4-5.   Like the saber saw, the reciprocating saw can do plunge cutting—making internal cutouts without the need of a starting hole or a lead-in cut. It's critical that the initial blade-contact with the work be made very cautiously to avoid blade breakage or having the tool jump about.

Saw Blades

One of the secrets to getting the most out of a reciprocating saw or, for that matter, any sawing tool, is to make a study of the blades that can be used with it. Trying to do all things with one or two blades is like trying to get by with one or two screw-sizes for all wood connections. The chart in Figure 4-8 shows most of the blades that can be used with the saw and suggests the best application for each one. You'll note that even if your activities involve only wood there are particular designs for optimum results whether you are pruning a tree, doing remodeling work where you might encounter nails or plaster and metal lath, forming scroll-type components, and so on. The one, or the several blades that come with the tool are okay to get started with, but collecting an assortment is good practice and economical in the long run since you are not likely to ruin a blade by using it on material it was not designed to cut.

Generally, when there is a choice of blades, it's wise to select the shortest one that will do the job.

Use Hints

Accept that the right way to work is with a firm, two-hand grip. Brace the shoe of the tool tightly against the work as you start to cut. Sometimes, for example, when encountering a tough knot in wood, you'll put less strain on yourself and the tool if you rock it a bit as you make the pass.

Be especially careful to determine in advance what is inside the wall when doing remodeling work that involves cutting through a wall covering or a partition. You don't want the saw to discover a water line or electrical wiring!

4-6. An adjustable blade-clamp mechanism that allows setting the blade on different planes is very handy. This can be a built-in feature or the manufacturer may offer an accessory that provides for the same setup.

4-7. As with all tools, electronic technology is affecting the design of reciprocating saws. A microprocessor "talks" to the motor and assures consistent cutting power regardless of the blade being used and the material being cut.

	LENGTH IN INCHES	TEETH PER INCH	RECOMMENDED USE
WOOD CUTTING			
	6 (Tapered)	6	General roughing-in wood
	9 (Tapered)	6	
	12 (Tapered)	6	
	4 (Scroll)	6	Premium quality scroll cutting hard wood, plywood, plastic, tile, asbestos
	6	6	

(Continued on next page)

	LENGTH IN INCHES	TEETH PER INCH	RECOMMENDED USE
ALL-PURPOSE CUTTING			
	6	6	Wood, plywood, insulation board, asbestos, all-purpose cutting
	6	10	
	6	18	Nail embedded wood, non-ferrous metals, plywood, insulation board, wood siding, all-purpose cutting
	3½	24	
	6	24	
SPECIAL PURPOSE CUTTING			
	6 (Flexible)	6	General roughing-in wood
	4 (Double Edge)	7	General roughing-in wood—thick plywood
	6	10	Plywoods, nail-embedded wood, heavy gauge (non-ferrous) metals
	12	10	Cutting nail-embedded wood in hard to reach areas
	12 (Flexible)	18	Opening crates, removing siding, cutting nail-embedded wood in hard to reach areas
	6	6	Plaster, including plaster with metal lath, plaster board
	4 (Armoredge)	14	Fiberglass and other abrasive materials
	6 (Armoredge)	14	
	4	Wavy Knife	Paper, corrugated cardboard, rubber, cork
	5 (Carbide)	6	Taper back carbide tip blade for cutting asphalt tile, plastics, sheet rock, plaster, and general wood cutting
	12	6	Pruning limbs, cutting green wood
METAL CUTTING HI-SPEED STEEL			
	3¼ (Scroll)	10	Heavy gauge ferrous and non-ferrous metals, cast aluminum, copper, brass, rubber, pressed wood, fiberglass
	6	10	Heavy gauge (non-ferrous) metals, bar and angle stock, cast aluminum, hard rubber, plastic, including laminates, pressed wood

(Continued on next page)

	LENGTH IN INCHES	TEETH PER INCH	RECOMMENDED USE
	3¼ (Scroll)	14	Heavy gauge ferrous and non-ferrous metals, cast aluminum, copper, brass, rubber, pressed wood, fiberglass
	6	14	Heavy gauge (non-ferrous) metals, band and angle stock, cast iron, sheet steel (over 18 ga.) hard rubber, pressed wood, fiberglass
	3¼ (Scroll)	18	Metal scroll, cast iron, bar and angle stock, galvanized pipe, tubing (over 18 ga.)
	4	18	Heavy gauge (non-ferrous) metals, bar and angle stock, galvanized pipe, tubing (over 18 ga.)
	6	18	Heavy gauge (non-ferrous) metals, bar and angle stock, cast iron, sheet aluminum
	3¼ (Scroll)	24	Metal scroll, stainless, cast iron, bar and angle stock, galvanized pipe, tubing (over 18 ga.)
	4	24	Sheet steel (under 18 ga.), galvanized pipe, tubing (under 18 ga.)
	6	24	
	4	32	Sheet steel (under 18 ga.), galvanized pipe, tubing (under 18 ga.)

4-8.   You don't have to own all these blades but an assortment that provides optimum results on the kind of work you do is good practice and a wise investment.

When making long straight cuts, say on plywood, you can work more accurately by moving the tool so its shoe bears against a guide strip clamped to the work. Don't try to turn corners with blades that are too wide for the job. If the narrowest blade you have won't do, use the relief cuts technique demonstrated in the chapter on saber saws.

Figures 4-9 through 4-14 show some typical applications for this versatile sawing tool.

4-9.   Combining a firm two-hand grip with good pressure down on the shoe will minimize vibration and lead to acceptable results. Often, on straight cuts, you can guide the tool along a clamped-on guide strip just as you would with a saber saw.

4-10.   Cutting through a full-thickness partition is no problem
for a reciprocating saw that is equipped with the proper blade. Be
sure you determine what is inside the wall before you start cutting.
Meeting a water line or electrical wiring can be an unpleasant
surprise!

4-11.   Always use the shortest, heaviest blade that is adequate for
the job. If you are just sawing through a facing you don't want to
use a blade that is too long because it will tend to bounce against
the back area of the project. Don't forget to consider the stroke-
length of the tool when selecting a blade length.

4-12.   With the right kind of blade and the correct speed it won't
matter if you encounter an occasional nail. Many industrial firms
use a reciprocating saw to open crates with minimum fuss.

4-14.   Sawing through pipe or, for that matter, steel or aluminum or other metals, is routine. If the tool allows it, start such work at a slow speed and rev up to the point where the blade is cutting consistently. The cut should never be forced. Allow the blade to cut at its own pace.

4-13.   Again, the right blade is the answer for getting easily through this stucco wall. Incidentally, you should not only know what is inside the wall, but also what is on the other side.

5. The Portable Electric Drill

One of the most versatile power tools you can buy—actually a first choice on any list of practical power tool equipment—is the portable electric drill. The name "drill" doesn't tell the story, even though the tool is fantastic for drilling small or large holes accurately and with minimum effort. A more realistic picture, because of modern innovations and the myriad accessories that have become available for it, is of a lightweight, multipurpose shop you can hold in your hands. Alone, like many other electric tools, it can't do anything but spin its chuck, but add a suitable accessory and the unit serves efficiently as a drum or disc sander, grinder, polisher, screwdriver, flex-shaft machine, doweling jig, and more. It can also be used as a power source to drive specially designed units like a bandsaw, belt sander, even a small lathe. Place it in a stand and it will serve as a stationary drill press. The combination of portable drill and accessory isn't meant to be a substitute for the tool it imitates, however, the ideas do work.

Types, Sizes, Speeds

The mechanism of a portable drill is fairly simple (Figure 5-1). A motor drives a chuck which grips a cutting tool. In between motor and chuck is a system of gears that provides the correct torque and speed for what the drill is designed for. While this is the basic concept, there are other factors that are part of the picture; variable speed controls, double insulation, reversing switch, electronic features, and power.

Electric drill sizes you might be interested in are, ¼″, ⅜″, and ½″. The size indicates the maximum tool-shank diameter that can be gripped by the chuck, not necessarily its drilling capacity. There are many cutting tools, like spade bits, that range up to 1½″ and have ¼″ shanks. Hole saws and the like can be used to form holes well over what you can accomplish with a drill bit but many of them have ¼″ shanks and can be gripped in a small capacity drill. But it's not all roses. Complete freedom to use any cutting tool in any drill is another matter. The unit may not have the power or the efficient combination of power and speed to do the job.

The capacity of a drill can usually be judged by the manufacturer's specifications. The ¼″ unit shown in Figure 5-2, with a speed range of 0-2000 rpm, is rated at 2.7 amps and can form ½″ holes in hardwood and ¼″ holes in steel. As the size of the drill increases so does its power, however, its top speed usually decreases. The ⅜″ drill shown in Figure 5-3 is rated at 3.2 amps, has a speed range of 0-1200 rpm, and can drill ¾″ holes in hardwood and ⅜″ holes in steel. Move up to a

MOTOR
GEARED CHUCK
TRIGGER SWITCH
SPEED-REDUCING GEAR TRAIN (USUALLY 2 OR 3 STAGES)

5-1. Basic mechanism of a portable electric drill. Engineering provides for a practical combination of power and speed.

5-2. A ¼″ drill, rated at 2.7 amp, provides speeds of 0-2000 rpm with capacities of ¼″ in steel and ½″ in hardwood. Other features include double insulation and a switch that can be pre-set at a desired speed.

½" tool like the one in Figure 5-4, and you can drill ½" holes in steel and 1" holes in hardwood. This particular drill has an amp rating of 4.5 and a speed range of 0-850. Note that the size of the drill usually tells the maximum size hole it should be used for in steel, and that size doubles in hardwood.

The fact that speed decreases as power goes up tells something about good practice with electric drills. Jobs like drilling ½" holes in steel (Figure 5-5) call for good power and low rpm. Of course, there is always some overlap in functions even among tools that are different sizes. You can occasionally use a "small" drill beyond its capacity for holes in steel by working in steps; start with a small bit and gradually increase bit-size which, by the way, is generally good practice with any drill. On the other hand, there's no reason why you can't use a "large" drill to form very small holes. Over-taxing the tool is what to avoid. If the tool gets too warm, or stalls, or its speed decreases drastically, you are asking too much.

Not too long ago when you selected a drill for its power or chuck capacity you got a single, compatible speed with it. The combination of size-capacity-speed made the unit ideal for a particular category of work. Such tools are still avail-

able, and they may even be a good choice if you require no-fuss performance for a particular application. However, the tool would be a compromise for general-purpose use. For example, it might be too fast for drilling in steel, too slow for small holes in wood.

The trigger-controlled variable speed feature that is available on drills of all sizes does away with the limitation of one speed and makes any drill a more versatile tool. Many times it's good practice to start work at a slow speed and gradually increase rpm until the cutter is working without strain. This variable speed feature also makes any drill an electric screwdriver, since choosing the right speed for such work is critical. Add a reversing feature, also generally available, and you can remove screws as well as drive them.

Electronic technology is making it easier to use a particular speed. The ⅜" drill in Figure 5-6 has electronic analog feedback which maintains the desired speed under loaded conditions.

The ability to work anywhere, even without electricity, and being able to function without the fuss of a dangling cord has made the new cordless drills quite popular (Figure 5-7). I

5-3.   Generally, as the drill-size goes up power increases while top speed decreases. This ⅜" unit has a 3.2 amp. rating and speeds of 0-1200 rpm. Its capacities are ⅜" in steel and ¾" in hardwood.

5-5.   Drill functions, regardless of the tool's speed and power, can overlap, but for heavy-duty work like drilling ½" holes in steel, you can't substitute a small, light model for a husky unit like this ½" model.

5-4.   This ½" drill is reasonably light in weight (about 4½ lbs.), yet has the power to drill ½" in steel and 1" in hardwood. Variable speed ranges from 0-850 rpm. Extra handle allows a firm two-hand grip.

5-6.   New ⅜" electronic drill features analog feedback which maintains desired speed under loaded conditions. Another feature is a powered chuck; no key is needed.

5-7.   Cordless tools are popular because of the freedom they provide; no cord from the tool, no extension line to worry about. Use them anywhere since they carry power with them.

find myself using a cordless drill, even in the shop, for many jobs I used to do with a plug-in portable. Much progress has been made in the design of cordless drills. The unit shown in Figure 5-8 has variable speeds, a reversing switch, a built-in torque control, and its battery can be recharged in a few hours. Most users buy an extra power pack to keep one battery charging while the other is used. That's a good idea.

Another innovation in electric drill design is the "hammer drill", a tool that drills like a drill but is also adjustable to provide an impact action. This adds a new term to electric drill nomenclature; bpm—which means *blows per minute*, an action that can be used alone or in combination with the routine rotary motion. These special concepts are given different names, like the "XTRA-TOOL" shown in Figure 5-9, but they all have similar advantages. Namely, modes that provide for routine drilling or hammer drilling or hammer-chiseling. The selection for the mode you wish to use is made by hand-turning a collar between the chuck and the forward end of the housing (Figure 5-10).

How can they help? Well, for one thing, if you do any kind of carving you can use the hammer mode with a gouge-chisel to do work like hollowing (Figure 5-11), or carving in

5-8.   It's a good idea to have an extra power pack for a cordless tool; keep one charging while using the other. New chargers quickly bring batteries to full capacity.

5-10.   Turning a collar lets you choose the action that is most efficient for the job at hand.

5-9.   You have a choice with a "hammer drill". Use it conventionally, or add an impact action for faster hole-forming in materials like concrete and masonry.

5-11.   Special chisels are available as accessories for the hammer drill. A gouge, used with the hammer mode, makes fast work of hollowing and similar chores.

the round, or bas-relief, much quicker and with less effort than required with the chisel and mallet technique.

Mount a butt chisel and you can use the hammer mode to form hinge mortises, clean out dadoes, or the cavities needed for tenons (Figure 5-12). Also on the practical side is combining the hammer and rotary actions when forming holes in concrete or masonry (Figure 5-13). I found I could drill three to five times faster when I added the impact mode.

Making a Choice

A ¼″ drill is a popular first choice but it may not always be the best one. This size drill may not have the power needed for some relatively heavy-duty work like using large hole saws or drilling in concrete. A ⅜″ unit with variable speeds might be the best *first* choice since it's huskier but can also do most of the lighter work ordinarily done with a smaller tool. Actually, since the price of electric drills is not out of line, you might think of having several if your work-load justifies it.

An adjustable speed control is a good feature. This is usually a small knob set into the trigger and turned in or out to provide a predetermined speed. Thus, you can do any number of similar operations that require a particular rpm without reliance on finger control.

Double insulation makes sense since it provides additional safety barriers against a possible electric shock.

A reversing switch is recommended since it allows loosening fasteners, like screws, as well as driving them. Also, you can work more efficiently with accessories like sanding drums, wire brushes, and buffing wheels when you reverse direction of rotation. Doing this will often help these accessories last longer.

How the tool "feels" in your hand can be a selection factor. Some handles are placed centrally; others are more like a pistol grip. Heavy-duty drills, and even some lighter ones, might have an auxiliary handle that can be attached on either side and sometimes on top of the drill's body. This extra "hold" point is handy for tough drilling jobs.

Weight is a consideration and should be judged in terms of what you will use the tool for. It's logical that a powerful unit with greater capacity will be heavier than a unit with less capacity. Assuming all critical factors among an assortment of tools are similar, it's not illogical to base a choice on how the unit feels when you handle it.

5-12.   A butt chisel is used to clean out drilled mortises, to make cavities for hinges, to clean out dadoes, and so on.

Cutters That Form Holes

A rule to follow when choosing a hole cutter is that it should have a brad-type point, not the type of screw tip that is found on auger bits used in a hand brace (Figure 5-14). The screw tip is designed to pull the cutter into the work which is okay when using a hand tool but would require a specific rpm to match the pitch of the screw if used under power—a factor you can't coordinate when using a portable electric drill.

Twist drills are probably the most frequently used drill bits. This is probably because size-availability is so extreme, ranging from hair-thin bits to better than ½″, any of which can be chucked in a portable drill. Actually, the common twist drill, with a 59° cutting angle, is designed for drilling metal. It's okay to use them on wood, but should you have a

5-13.   Adding the hammer mode to the rotary action lets you drill much faster in masonry products—three to five times faster.

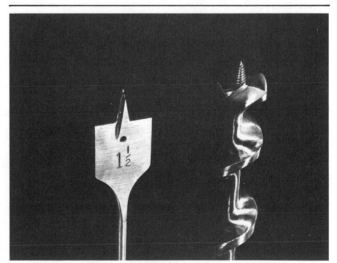

5-14.   Screw-point cutters like the auger on the right should not be used under power. The screw will take over feed-speed, which is something *you* should control.

5-15. Twist drills are used for hole-forming in wood or metal, but they work most efficiently in the materials when the cutting edges have the angles shown here.

NUMBER SIZE DRILLS

NO.	SIZE OF DRILL IN INCHES	NO.	SIZE OF DRILL IN INCHES	NO.	SIZE OF DRILL IN INCHES	NO.	SIZE OF DRILL IN INCHES
1	.2280	21	.1590	41	.0960	61	.0390
2	.2210	22	.1570	42	.0935	62	.0380
3	.2130	23	.1540	43	.0890	63	.0370
4	.2090	24	.1520	44	.0860	64	.0360
5	.2055	25	.1495	45	.0820	65	.0350
6	.2040	26	.1470	46	.0810	66	.0330
7	.2010	27	.1440	47	.0785	67	.0320
8	.1990	28	.1405	48	.0760	68	.0310
9	.1960	29	.1360	49	.0730	69	.0292
10	.1935	30	.1285	50	.0700	70	.0280
11	.1910	31	.1200	51	.0670	71	.0260
12	.1890	32	.1160	52	.0635	72	.0250
13	.1850	33	.1130	53	.0595	73	.0240
14	.1820	34	.1110	54	.0550	74	.0225
15	.1800	35	.1100	55	.0520	75	.0210
16	.1770	36	.1065	56	.0465	76	.0200
17	.1730	37	.1040	57	.0430	77	.0180
18	.1695	38	.1015	58	.0420	78	.0160
19	.1660	39	.0995	59	.0410	79	.0145
20	.1610	40	.0980	60	.0400	80	.0135

LETTER SIZE DRILLS

A	0.234	H	0.266	O	0.316	V	0.377
B	0.238	I	0.272	P	0.323	W	0.386
C	0.242	J	0.277	Q	0.332	X	0.397
D	0.246	K	0.281	R	0.339	Y	0.404
E	0.250	L	0.290	S	0.348	Z	0.413
F	0.257	M	0.295	T	0.358		
G	0.261	N	0.302	U	0.368		

5-16. Decimal equivalents of number and letter size drills.

special wood-drilling chore that you'll repeat very often, it's a good idea to re-grind the point to an angle of 40° to 45° as shown in Figure 5-15.

Twist drills are available individually; however, it's more economical to buy them in sets and also equips you with bits for various jobs. Wire-gauge bits come in sets of sixty and are so numbered—#1 through #60. In a wire-gauge set you'll find bits that come close to drilling hair-size holes. A common set of fractional size bits will contain 29 units, starting at 1/16″ and increasing by a 64th of an inch up to 1/2″. Then there are letter size bits in sets of 26, identified by letters A through Z. The decimal equivalents of number size and letter size twist drills are shown in Figure 5-16.

Common twist drills are available in carbon or high-speed steel. Carbon steel is okay for drilling in wood and even in some soft metals, but for overall, durable performance in many materials, including steel, high-speed steel bits (identified as "H.S." or "H.S.S.") are a better choice even though they cost more.

Titanium-nitrade-coated bits have recently been introduced and are said to provide seven times longer life than conventional bits. The titanium bits can be used on tough materials like cast iron or stainless steel as well as on wood or plastics (Figure 5-17).

Using a nail to form a hole when you don't have exactly the right size drill bit is an idea you might occasionally find helpful (Figure 5-18). A practical application is forming pilot holes when nailing wood that tends to split. "Drill" with a smaller nail than those you will drive. The nail will do more burning than cutting, but it serves the purpose.

Spade Bits

Spade bits (Figure 5-19), sometimes called "wing" or "flat" bits, are available in various designs but all are meant for wood drilling under power. Although they do more scraping than cutting, they form clean, accurate holes when kept sharp and used correctly. An advantage is that they are available in sets that start at 1/8″ or 1/4″ and range up to 1 1/2″. Even if you

5-17. Titanium-nitrade-coated drill bits are newcomers, said to provide seven times longer life than high speed bits. They can be used on tough materials like cast iron and stainless steel in addition to wood and plastics.

5-18. Use a nail as a drill bit? It's a handy improvisation when you don't have the right size drill bit for the job. The nail compresses fibers instead of removing them, and it may burn a bit, but the idea works.

5-19. Good spade bits do a fine job of wood-drilling. Don't buy poor-quality ones, like the cheap sets often found in "bargain" bins.

used them only for drilling oversize holes, they would be worth the cost.

The business end differs on various types. Although all have generous points, some cutting edges are winged while others are flat (Figure 5-20). The flat type produce flat-bottom holes which can be a useful feature in some areas of woodworking.

The long points help provide accuracy when starting a hole and make it easier to get started when drilling at an angle (Figure 5-21). The point, which you can embed by hand-turning the chuck, will set the cutter firmly before the hole starts to form.

Contrary to the good, general rule that advises drilling large holes at slow speeds, spade bits work best at higher rpm. Working at about 1500 rpm, even when drilling a 1½″ hole, is not out of line.

5-20.   All spade bits have nice, long points, but cutting edges may differ. This may not matter too much when drilling through holes, but affects the shape of the bottom when drilling blind holes.

5-21.   The long point on a spade bit is especially useful when drilling at an angle. The point penetrates enough to keep the bit from wandering when the cutting edge starts to work.

Hole Saws

Hole saws are used primarily to form holes larger than you can accomplish with conventional bits. Some, like those in Figure 5-22, have continuous saw teeth on the perimeter of a "cup" and come in specific sizes. Another design offers band-type saws, so it's possible to work with a single mandrel for different size holes (Figure 5-23). A third type, which can be fitted with wood or metal-cutting blades, has an adjust mechanism for setting the blades to a particular diameter (Figure 5-24). Since settings are infinite, you are not limited to specific size holes.

These cutters work hard and should be used with only enough feed pressure to keep them cutting. On the other hand, you'll do more burnishing than sawing if you try to be too gentle. Always start them at a very slow speed. Increase speed only to the point where the saw teeth are working efficiently. Although the tools cut cleanly and with minimum feathering when they break through, it's not a bad idea to use a back-up block (Figure 5-25).

Think of them as dual-purpose cutters; they form holes by removing a disc which, among other things, can be used as wheels for toys—the axle hole is already formed! An offbeat use is shown in Figure 5-26; overlapping, limited depth circles for a decorative effect. The pilot holes can be plugged with a matching or contrasting dowel.

5-22.   Specific-size hole saws are cup-like devices with continuous saw teeth. They mount on a mandrel that is gripped by the drill-chuck.

5-23.   This type of hole saw works with a single mandrel and an assortment of band-type blades. The saws lock into grooves in the mandrel—each saw a specific-size hole.

5-24. Another type hole-saw also has a single mandrel but works with individual metal or wood-cutting blades. Blade-diameter settings are infinite, so you can saw any size hole within the unit's capacity.

5-25. Hole saws cut pretty cleanly but if you wish to eliminate feathering completely when the saw breaks through, clamp a backup block behind the hole.

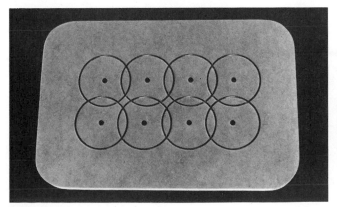

5-26. Drilling to limited depth and overlapping holes lets you use hole saws for some decorative work. Center holes can be plugged with matching or contrasting dowels.

Extension Bits

Conventional bits have limited depth capacity. Even with spade bits, which have long shanks, you can't drill deeper than four or five inches. Extension bits (Figure 5-27), which are made in several sizes, might provide a solution when you need an exceptionally deep hole or are making a project, like a lamp base (Figure 5-28). When doing jobs like this, it's best to drill from both ends. If you try going through completely from one end, the point of the bit might be influenced by grain direction and travel where it shouldn't.

It's also possible to buy extensions that can be used with conventional drilling tools (Figure 5-29). The advantage here is that they can be used with bits of different size so long as the shank on the bit can be gripped in the "chuck" of the extension.

5-27. Extension bits are available in several practical sizes. These are ¼", ⅜" and ½".

5-28. Forming a cord hole through a lamp base is a typical application for an extension bit. You'll work more accurately if you drill from both ends.

5-29. Extensions with a chuck-like device at one end are also available. These provide a long reach for conventional bits.

Always start extensions at a very slow speed and be sure the point is well seated before getting to operational rpm. These long cutters can "whip" if you allow them to run free.

Masonry Bits

Drilling in concrete or masonry calls for bits that have tungsten carbide cutting points and spiral-type flutes that carry waste from the hole (Figure 5-30). Like other bits, they are available individually or in sets; a typical set has ¼", ⁵⁄₁₆", ⅜", and ½" sizes. Good results depend as much on the right combination of drill power and speed as on the bit. A light-duty ¼" drill is a poor choice. A heavy-duty ⅜", especially if it has variable speed is acceptable, but a husky ½" unit is best. As we mentioned before, a drill with an impact feature can make the work easier.

A slow speed and enough feed pressure to keep the bit cutting without overtaxing the tool is good, general practice. Using progressively larger bits helps considerably to get to the size hole you need. Using a small amount of water in the hole will minimize heat buildup. You'll find it easier to drill in materials like brick and cinder block and some flagstones than to drill in concrete, especially when the bit meets a particularly hard piece of aggregate. If the bit starts to do more rubbing than cutting, try cracking the aggregate by hammering with something like a length of drill rod.

Use the Chuck Key!

The key is designed to move the jaws of the chuck so they will bear firmly on the shank of the mounted tool (Figure 5-31). If you don't use the key (try to grip the tool by hand-holding the chuck and spinning the tool) the grip will not be secure enough. The bit may turn when running free but will stay put when working , while the chuck spins. Of course, remove the key before pressing the switch. It can be a harmful projectile. Be sure the shank of the tool is centered in the chuck. It *is* possible to grip it off-center. The jaws of the chuck should bear against any flats that might be on the shank of the bit.

Maybe a sign of things to come is the new portable electric drill shown in Figure 5-32. The tool has a power-driven, automatic chuck and doesn't require a chuck key to lock tools securely.

Operating Techniques

The more powerful the drill, the more torque there will be at the cutting end. Heavy, ½" drills are strong enough to spin you about should the cutting tool jam in the hole. To a lesser extent, this also applies to small units. They may not spin you about, but they can twist your hand. Maintaining a firm grip at all times is the way to avoid these hazards. When the work is small and the drilling chore is light, you might be able to secure the work with one hand and the drill with the other hand, so long as hand pressure is sufficient to keep the workpiece firmly down on a workbench or sawhorse. Holding the job in mid air and then applying the drill is not a good or safe practice. Whenever possible, secure the work to a stable surface with clamps or grip it in a vise. Most of the time, it makes sense to grip the drill with both hands, using any auxiliary handle that may be provided with the tool. This provides a safety factor in addition to helping you work more accurately.

5-31.   Always use the chuck key and then be sure to remove it. Center the bit in the chuck's jaws. If the shank has flats, let the jaws bear against them.

5-32.   New ⅜" drill has a power-driven chuck. You don't need a key to secure cutters.

5-30.   Tungsten-carbide-tipped bits are used for drilling concrete and masonry. Jobs like this are easier if you start with a small hole and enlarge it in stages.

The optimal drilling speed is something you will come to judge. You can control speed but there is no gauge to accurately pinpoint specific speeds through all the available ranges. Also, the free-running speed is not the load speed. Signs that call for an operational change in either rpm or feed pressure are—a cutter that jams, a cutter that spins without removing material, or an overheating tool. All factors assume, of course, that the cutting tool you are using is SHARP!

It's generally a good idea to use a piece of scrap as a backup to minimize the splintering that can occur when a bit breaks through a workpiece. This also applies to sheet metals which can buckle under drill pressure. Also, it's usually good practice, especially on metal, to drill "up" to the hole-size you need. This means starting with a pilot hole and enlarging it by stages.

Most accessories designed to be powered by an electric drill come with literature that, among other things, suggests an appropriate operating speed. Many times, the speed you *can* supply is a compromise. For example, shaping accessories are available for power drills, but conventional shaping is done at rpm of 10,000 and higher. Even so, you can do an acceptable job PROVIDING YOU USE CUTTERS DESIGNED FOR USE IN A PORTABLE DRILL. One way to compensate for lack of speed is to slow up on feed so, in effect, more cutting teeth will pass over a given area of the work. There are also safety considerations that have to do with speed. Turning large cutters at speeds they were not designed for can be dangerous. Always wear safety goggles, and a dust mask when one is needed.

Starting Accurately

A good way to spot a hole location is to use a square and a sharp, hard pencil to mark intersecting lines. To assure that the hole will start where it should, use an awl or a center punch to form an indent where the lines intersect (Figures 5-33, 5-34). A "center punch" has a sharper point than a

"prick punch" (Figure 5-35), and you can use this to advantage when hole locations in metal are critical. Make a slight indent with a center punch and then "broaden" it with a prick punch so the point of the bit will have a seat to start in.

Keep the drill vertical. This is critical if the hole is to be square to the work's surface. You can do this fairly accurately by aligning the drill with a square placed on the work, or you can make a guide block like the one shown in Figure 5-36.

5-34.   A punch can also be used to form the starting indent. Put the point where the lines intersect, then tilt the punch to vertical position and tap it with a hammer.

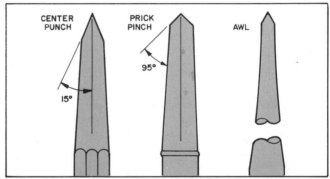

5-35.   Punches and awls have points with different shapes that should be maintained when they are sharpened.

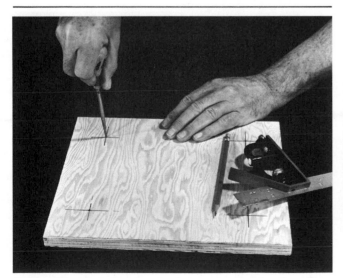

5-33.   Mark hole locations by drawing intersecting lines. Use an awl to form an indent so the bit can get started accurately.

5-36.   A guide block, which is marked for alignment with lines on the workpiece, assures that the hole will be perpendicular to the surface.

The block should be marked like the one in Figure 5-37 so it can be aligned with intersecting marks on the workpiece. Since the block can be used for various jobs, the hole through it shouldn't be more than 1/16″. Thus, it can be used for pilot holes in the work which you later enlarge to the right size.

A handy accessory that makes drilling at a 90° angle very easy when using a portable drill, is the Portalign "Drillguide" (Figure 5-38). This one application doesn't demonstrate the versatility of the attachment so we'll be seeing more of it as we go along.

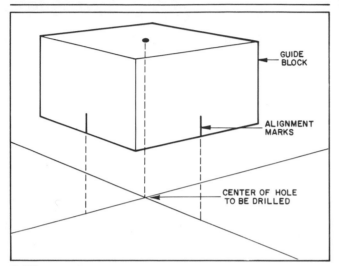

5-37.   Use hardwoods like maple or birch when making guide blocks. The guide-hole should be small to provide pilot holes in the work. Thus, the gauge can be used for various jobs.

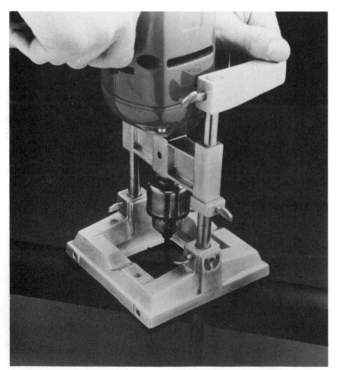

5-38.   The Portalign "Drillguide" is a handy accessory which, among others things, assures vertical-drilling accuracy.

5-39.   You can drill to a specific depth by using a guide block that allows the bit to penetrate just so far.

5-40.   A bushing, drilled and tapped for a set screw, is an adjustable hole-depth gauge that can be used on various drill-sizes. Two, one with a 1/4″ hole and the other with a 1/2″ hole will serve for most work.

5-41.   Some manufacturers offer adjustable, depth-control accessories. Some may be used only on a specific product, so check before buying.

Drilling to a Specific Depth

Drilling to a specific depth, something you will need to do, for example, when forming holes for dowels, can be difficult without some sort of a depth gauge. The one shown in Figure 5-39 is simple but efficient. The gauge is made so its height allows the bit to penetrate just so far.

Another solution is to use a suitably-sized bushing which is drilled and tapped to receive a set screw (Figure 5-40). Since the gauge can be secured at any point on the bit, it can be used for various hole-depths.

A type of adjustable depth gauge which is offered as an accessory by some manufacturers is shown in Figure 5-41. Probably the easiest method of all to gauge drill penetration is simply to wrap several layers of masking tape around the bit so you'll know when to stop feeding.

Angular Drilling

Trying to judge a particular angle by eye is pretty rough. You can get some help by aligning the drill with a protractor, but to be precise it's best to work with a custom-made block that is clamped or tack-nailed to the workpiece (Figure 5-42). To make such a block, follow the steps shown in Figure 5-43. First, drill a hole through a block of wood that has parallel surfaces. Then saw off one end so the body will tilt to the angle you need. If you make the gauge correctly it can also serve to limit the bit's penetration.

The Portalign "Drillguide" may also be used for angular drilling (Figure 5-44). Since its base is vertically adjustable along the posts, the accessory can be braced to allow the drill to work at almost any angle. An adjustable stop, situated on one of the posts, allows you to control how far the bit will penetrate.

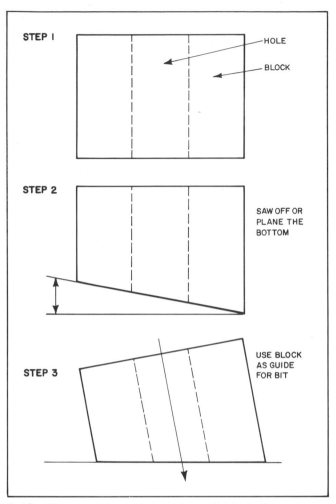

STEP 1 — HOLE / BLOCK

STEP 2 — SAW OFF OR PLANE THE BOTTOM

STEP 3 — USE BLOCK AS GUIDE FOR BIT

5-43.   One way to make an angular guide block. Shape the bottom of the block to the angle you need after drilling the guide-hole.

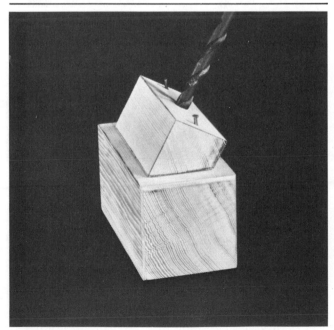

5-42.   For precise angular drilling, it's best to work with a custom-made guide block that can be tack-nailed or clamped to the work.

5-44.   The Portalign "Drillguide" may be used for angular drilling by raising the base so the drill can function in a tilted position. Adjustable stop is used to control hole-depth.

Center Drilling Jig

5-45. A special jig that you make will allow center-drilling on stock edges regardless of the stock's thickness.

5-46. The drilling jig can also be used to drill center holes on surfaces. You can increase the jig's capacity by making an extra, longer bar.

5-47. Details of the center-drilling jig. It's a simple concept but take the time to make it accurately.

A Jig for Center Drilling

The center drilling jig will eliminate layout time while providing accuracy when it's necessary to drill in the center of a board or along its edge (Figures 5-45, 5-46). While it is simple in design, the project does require care in construction (Figure 5-47).

Make the bar first, drilling the holes exactly on the centerline. It's okay to use a bushing that is not the size shown, but be certain it's a press fit in the bar—or take the precaution of seating it with an epoxy. A ⅛″ hole will do for most jobs. The idea is to provide a pilot hole that you can enlarge if necessary. You can turn the guides yourself or make do by cutting sections from a large dowel, but be sure the hole for the bolt is centered. For more flexibility in the guide's placement, you can add additional holes in the hardwood bar.

Guide for Radial Holes

The guide shown in Figure 5-48 assures drilling accurate holes on a circumference. The guide is a strip of ⅛″-thick do-it-yourself aluminum, with ¹⁄₁₆″ holes spaced ½″ apart on a common centerline. A nail, at the center of the circle, is used in one hole so the guide can be pivoted to determine the correct radius at any point. When the holes must be spaced in a particular fashion, which is usual, start the job by marking diameters that indicate how the guide should be placed for each hole. The initial drilling provides pilot holes which can be enlarged to whatever size is needed.

The same guide, as demonstrated in Figure 5-49, can be used to drill equally-spaced holes. The points at each end of the guide are used to align it with a line marked on the work.

Drilling for Mortises and Slots

The major difference between a drilled mortise and one formed on a drill press with special mortising bits and chisels is that the drill-press version has square ends and the drilled version has round ends; there is no difference strength-wise.

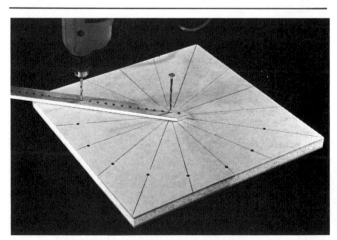

5-48. An aluminum bar with accurately-drilled, equally-spaced holes is fine for drilling a series of holes on a circumference. Points on the bar are guides for aligning it with radial lines on the work.

To drill a mortise, select a bit whose diameter equals the width of the cavity and then drill overlapping holes on a common centerline (Figure 5-50). Drill end-holes first and then those in between, spacing them to remove as much waste as possible. Use brad point bits when you can since they permit more overlapping than twist drills.

When drilling is complete, clean out the remaining waste material with a sharp chisel (Figure 5-51). Note that the ends on the tenon are rounded.

Slots are formed in the same manner (Figure 5-52). If the slot needs to have square ends, use a file to clean out the end corners.

Drilling Holes for Wood Screws

In order for the fastener to have maximum holding power, there are two different diameter holes that should be drilled before driving a screw. One is the *body hole*, which equals the shank diameter of the screw, the other is the *lead hole*, which allows the screw to penetrate while providing enough material for the screw-threads to grip (Figure 5-53).

The holes can be formed individually using drill bits, in which case it's wise to drill the lead hole first and enlarge the top portion to body hole or you can do the work more easily and more accurately by using special cutters like those shown in Figures 5-54 and 5-55. Notice that some offer different features. One provides the essential holes and has the capability of countersinking (Figure 5-56) and, if you went deeper, would also form a counterbore.

Countersinking is needed so flathead screws can be driven flush. Notice in Figure 5-57 that a stop, which is available for the screw-hole forming tool, is used to control the bit's penetration. On hardwoods, countersink to the full depth of the screwhead. On softwoods, stay a bit on the minus side. The screw will pull flush as you finish driving. When you are driving very small screws, especially in softwood, you can simply make a straight starting hole with an awl. You might even find this possible to do on some hardwoods. Make a judgment after testing with one or two screws.

5-50. You can form mortises by drilling a series of overlapping holes. Drill the end holes first. You'll work more accurately if you use brad-point type bits.

5-51. The waste that remains is cleaned out with a sharp chisel. Note that the ends on the tenon have been rounded to conform to the shape of the mortise.

5-49. The same bar can be used for drilling equally spaced holes. Here too, the points on the bar are used to set it to a line on the work.

5-52. The overlapping holes technique also serves to form slots. Finish with a file if the slot must have square ends.

HOLE SIZES FOR WOOD SCREWS

SCREW NO.	SHANK DIAM.	LENGTHS AVAILABLE	LEAD HOLES	
			HARDWOOD	SOFTWOOD
0	.060″	¼″-⅜″	70 (¹⁄₃₂)	75 (¹⁄₆₄)
1	.073″	¼″-½″	66 (¹⁄₃₂)	71 (¹⁄₃₂)
2	.086″	¼″-¾″	56 (³⁄₆₄)	65 (¹⁄₃₂)
3	.099″	¼″-1″	54 (¹⁄₁₆)	58 (³⁄₆₄)
4	.112″	¼″-1½″	52 (¹⁄₁₆)	55 (³⁄₆₄)
5	.125″	⅜″-1½″	49 (⁵⁄₆₄)	53 (¹⁄₁₆)
6	.138″	⅜″-2½″	47 (⁵⁄₆₄)	52 (¹⁄₁₆)
7	.151″	⅜″-2½″	44 (³⁄₃₂)	51 (¹⁄₁₆)
8	.164″	⅜″-3″	40 (³⁄₃₂)	48 (⁵⁄₆₄)
9	.177″	½″-3″	37 (⁷⁄₆₄)	45 (⁵⁄₆₄)
10	.190″	½″-3½″	33 (⁷⁄₆₄)	43 (³⁄₃₂)
11	.203″	⅝″-3½″	29 (⅛)	40 (³⁄₃₂)
12	.216″	⅝″-4″	25 (⅛)	38 (⁷⁄₆₄)
14	.242″	¾″-5″	14 (³⁄₁₆)	32 (⁷⁄₆₄)
16	.268″	1″-5″	10 (³⁄₁₆)	29 (⁹⁄₆₄)
18	.294″	1¼″-5″	6 (¹³⁄₆₄)	26 (⁹⁄₆₄)
20	.320″	1½″-5″	3 (⁷⁄₃₂)	19 (¹¹⁄₆₄)
24	.372″	3″-5″	1 (¼)	15 (³⁄₁₆)

5-53.   Chart tells what size holes are needed when drilling for wood screws. Providing the holes is the right way to go if you wish to drive screws with minimum effort and have them hold with maximum grip.

5-54.   A typical screw-hole former. Whether you countersink and then add a counterbore depends on how deep you drill.

ONE-PIECE BIT

ADJUSTABLE COMBINATION BIT

PLUG CUTTER

5-55.   Other tools that allow accurate drilling of holes for screws with minimum fuss. The bottom cutter is used to make plugs that are used in counterbored holes. They are useful because you can cut plugs from any species of wood you choose.

5-56.   Cross-section of holes drilled for screws shows what a neat job the special cutter can do. The cutters should be purchased in sets, since each is designed for a particular size screw.

5-57.   Some sets come with an adjustable stop, or one can be purchased as an accessory. The stop makes it easy to control hole-depth for either countersinking or counterboring.

Counterboring is required when you wish to set the fastener head below the surface, which is usually done so the fastener can be concealed with a wood plug (Figure 5-58). The counterbore is no more than a shallow hole sized to suit the head of the screw or bolt or whatever. When you wish to use a particular size plug, it's okay to form the counterbore with a conventional drilling tool like a spade bit or brad-point bit and then use a screw-hole forming tool or regular bits to do the shank and pilot holes.

Counterbored holes can be filled with dowels, plugs you cut yourself, or with plugs or buttons that you buy and use as-is (Figure 5-59). Both types are set in place with glue. The plugs are sanded flush—the buttons are used to provide a decorative detail.

When power-driving screws, use the slowest speed that will keep the screw turning and a screwdriver-bit that will fit snugly in the screwhead slot (Figure 5-60). It's wise to have an assortment of screwdriver-bits in various sizes and types on hand.

Drilling for Dowels

A common use for dowels is as reinforcement in wood connections. They are often used in edge-to-edge, end-to-edge joints, miter joints, and so on. Since the dowels must fit into matching holes, accuracy in layout and in drilling is essential. Dowel Centers (Figure 5-61) are often used to mark the location of mating holes after the first ones have been drilled. The centers are placed in holes drilled in one

5-58.   Lengths of dowel are often used to fill counterbored holes, but store-bought dowels are not always accurate and they are not available in many wood species. It's best to make your own by using plug cutters.

5-59.   Plugs and buttons, which you buy ready-made, can be used to fill counterbored holes. The plugs are sanded flush, the buttons are used to provide a decorative detail. Both are glued in place.

5-60.   Use a slow speed when driving or removing screws. The screwdriver bit should fit snugly in the screwhead slot, which is why it's wise to have several sizes on hand.

5-61.   Dowel centers, placed in holes in one piece, mark hole locations in the mating piece when the two parts are pressed together.

piece and then the two pieces are pressed together so the points on the centers mark the spots where the holes are required in the second piece. These items are available in sets that include ¼″, 5/16″, 3/8″, and ½″ sizes.

A doweling jig can be a big help when drilling holes in boards that will be edge-joined to form a wide panel. The one being used in Figure 5-62 can grip material as wide as 4″. Its revolving turret has holes that allow the use of 3/16″ through ½″ drill bits. To work accurately, clamp the boards to be drilled surface-to-surface and mark the hole locations across all edges using a square. Index lines on the turret make it easy to line up the hole with the mark on the work.

An offbeat use for the jig is shown in Figure 5-63. Round or square stock is placed between V-blocks and then secured with the screw-clamp of the jig. The idea can be a big help when you need to drill concentric holes.

A fairly new "how to drill for dowels" idea is the Haddon Wood Joiner Kit which includes the materials shown in Figure 5-64. The tool, actually a very precise template, has 72 holes that are positioned so that one row of holes will center on boards of various width. The joiner, as it's called, is positioned on the edge of one board (Figure 5-65) and holes are drilled, spaced according to the holes you select. Stop collars on the bits, which are supplied, limit the drilling depth. Then the operation is repeated on the second board using the other side of the joiner (Figure 5-66). This is a rather quickie presentation of the jig but it's pretty much how it works. It can also be used to drill holes in mitered edges (Figure 5-67) and for face-doweling work.

Figures 5-68 through 5-71 show how to use dowels to reinforce various wood connections.

5-62.   Doweling jig, clamped to the work's edge, provides a guide for drilling centered, perpendicular holes. Revolving turret has holes for various size bits. The tool can grip stock up to 4″ thick.

5-64.   Hadden Joiner Kit includes materials shown here. You can get started on edge-to-edge joints right off.

5-63.   Using it as a guide for drilling concentric holes is an off-beat use for the doweling jig. Round or square stock is gripped between V-blocks.

5-65.   The joiner is clamped to the edge of one board and holes are drilled with spacing determined by the holes you select.

5-66. The second step is done with the other side of the joiner clamped to the second board. Adjustable stop collars are provided so you can drill all holes to the same depth.

5-67. The Hadden tool can also be used to drill dowel holes in miter cuts. The system is fairly simple and can be used on stock of various thicknesses.

Reinforcing Joints with Dowels

5-68. Miter joints can be reinforced by drilling a through hole and then gluing in a dowel. Use a longer dowel than necessary so you can trim it and sand it flush after the glue dries.

5-70. Dowels can be used to reinforce the joint between a drawer front and its sides. Drill the first hole and then insert a dowel to keep the pieces aligned for the remaining holes.

5-69. A pre-drilled, V-shaped guide will let you drill accurately through the miter joint.

5-71. Use a dowel this way to reinforce a finger lap joint. Drill the hole after the parts have been assembled.

The Drill as a Sander

Among the most practical sanding accessories for the portable drill are sanding drums like the one shown in Figure 5-72. They are available in diameters as small as ½″ and as large as 3″ or more. Most will have ¼″ shanks but oversize ones may have ⅜″ or even ½″ shanks. The tools are rubber cylinders that grip, or release, abrasive sleeves when a nut at the free end of the shank is tightened or loosened. They are available individually or in sets of various diameters. A typical assortment contains four or five sizes ranging from ½″ to 1½″.

The abrasive sleeves come in various grits with common designations being "fine", "medium", and "coarse". The texture of the sandpaper has some bearing on the most efficient speed to use. Generally, 1000 to 1500 rpm is okay for coarse paper, while higher speeds can be used with finer grits.

In all cases, bear in mind that the abrasive particles are cutting tools and you must give them a chance to work. Excessive pressure against the piece being sanded does more harm than good and can even distort the cylinder on which the sleeves are mounted. Other harmful effects are— premature wear of the abrasive, burning the sleeve or the work, and sanded edges that are irregular.

One of the major uses for sanding drums is smoothing curved edges and the inside edges of cutouts (Figures 5-73, 5-74). Good control of the tool is necessary for the sanded edge to be square to surfaces. A light touch and a continuous feed are basic techniques. If you don't keep the drum moving, you'll form indents in the work-edge. The workpiece should be held firmly. It's wise to clamp small parts to a benchtop or to grip them in a vise.

You can arrange to apply the work to the tool rather than the tool to the work by mounting the drill on a stand, which is a common portable drill accessory (Figure 5-75). Secure the stand to a plywood base or, so it will be more portable, attach it to a block of wood so it can be gripped in a vise when needed. Go a bit further by duplicating the setup shown in

Figure 5-76 and you will have more assurance that the sanded edge will be square. The support piece, with a hole through it for the drum, has a base-cleat so it can be clamped in place or attached with screws. Be sure it's a sturdy attachment and that the angle between the support plate and the surface of the drum is 90°.

The drill can also be used like a stationary disc sander when you mount it as shown in Figure 5-77. Discs are usually available in rubber and designed for use while hand-holding the drill. The jig idea works best with a rigid disc. If you can't find a suitable one, or if you prefer, you can make several of your own by following the specifications in Figure 5-78. Be sure you install the table and situate the drill so the angle between the disc and the table is 90°. Always apply the work to the "down" side of the disc (Figure 5-79). If the drill has a reverse mode, you can choose to work on the left- or the right-hand side of the table.

Another practical sanding accessory for the portable drill is the "Sand-O-Flex" product shown in Figure 5-80. The abrasive strips are backed by cushioning brushes which make them conform to various configurations or force them into corners and even small openings. As the abrasive wears,

5-73. Smoothing irregular edges is a job you can do very quickly with a drum sander. Keep the drum moving to avoid indenting the edge. Keep the drill horizontal throughout the pass.

5-74. Drum sanding is especially useful for smoothing internal cutouts. It's best to hold small workpieces in a vise, or to clamp them.

5-72. Drum sanders can be used very efficiently with a portable drill. It's best to buy them in sets and to have a nice supply of sleeves in various grits on hand.

5-75.   Secure the drill to a stand and you can apply the work to the tool instead of the reverse. The stand can be attached to a plywood base or to a block of wood that can be gripped in a vise when needed.

5-76.   Add a support piece that has a hole the drum can pass through and you have more assurance that the sanded edge will be square to surfaces. Be sure the angle between the drum-surface and the support-face is 90°.

5-77.   Use a table like this with a stand-mounted drill and you have a small but efficient disc sander. You can buy discs or make your own by following the suggestions in the next illustration.

5-78.   How to make your own sanding discs. Make several so you can have various sandpaper grits ready to go.

5-79.   Always apply the work to the "down" side of the disc. This would be on the left side of the table if the disc is turning counterclockwise when you face it.

5-80.   "Sand-O-Flex" wheel has brush-backed sanding strips that let you smooth contours or get into tight areas. Worn strips are cut off and "renewed" by turning the tool's index knob.

the ends are cut off and fresh strips are exposed by turning the index knob on the unit. Here too, you can sand by hand-holding the drill or apply the workpiece by securing the drill on a stand (Figure 5-81).

Other Abrading Tools

For heavy stock removal, you can consider various types of rotary rasps, examples of which are pictured in Figure 5-82. The "Surform" product, shown in Figure 5-83, cuts in one direction with hundreds of preset, hardened steel teeth, each of which works like a miniature chisel. The teeth work hard to remove a lot of material but they are spaced so that they resist clogging. Like a sanding drum, the tool should be used with only enough pressure to keep the teeth cutting. A continuous feed is necessary to keep the cutter from indenting a workedge. Unless the project calls for a less-than-smooth edge, rasping should be followed by sanding.

The smaller rotary rasps are available in various shapes and sizes so, with several in stock, you can select one that's just right for the job at hand. I use them to get into corners and areas where other tools won't fit, and for fun jobs like carving in the round (Figure 5-84). These too, are not really "smoothers", so if you need a slick-to-the-touch finish follow rasping with sanding.

A cheese-grater-type disc rasp (Figure 5-85), is a simple concept that does some surprising work. It cuts fast and doesn't clog, but, on the other hand, it doesn't produce a ready-to-stain finish. I use it to round off edges and corners quickly and for preliminary surfacing on rough stock (Figure 5-86). The disc is not as rigid as a steel plate so it must be applied carefully to avoid distorting it. Light pressure is wise; bear down too heavily on the disc and it will tend to stall or try to travel like a wheel.

Wire Brushes

There are many types of wire brushes available. Like other abrasives they are designated as "fine", "medium", and "coarse" which essentially tells the gauge of the wire they are made of. Some are complete units, mounted on a shank that can be gripped in a chuck, others are designed for mounting on a separate arbor (Figure 5-87).

When you mount one, especially a new one, hold it away from you and allow it to run free for a bit to be sure no loose wires are thrown your way. Always wear safety goggles! The speed to use will depend on the type of wheel and the job. Most of the time, the literature that comes with the tool will warn of a maximum operating speed. To be safe, and to work efficiently, start wire-brushing jobs at a slow speed and increase rpm to the point where the unit is doing what you wish.

Coarse brushes do a good job of removing rust or dirt from metals, while fine ones can be used to create a satin finish (Figures 5-88, 5-89). Usually, it's best to make parallel, overlapping strokes, but there are options, especially if you are trying for a decorative effect.

Either a fine or coarse wheel can be used on certain wood to create a sculptured, 3-D effect (Figure 5-90). The

5-81.   This unique sanding tool can also be used with a stand-mounted drill. Be careful when smoothing small pieces; your fingers, as well as the wood can be sanded.

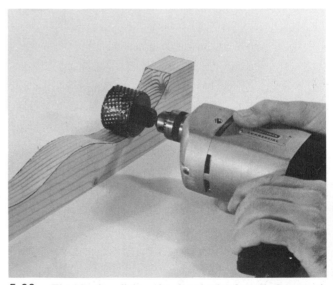

5-82.   Rotary rasps and the "Surform" drum at the right will remove stock quickly but they are not "smoothers".

5-83.   The "Surform" drum has hundreds of small, sharp teeth that work like tiny chisels. It cuts only in one direction. Keep it moving—try to work so you cut *with* the grain of the wood.

5-87. Wire brushes are available as "cups" with built-in shanks, or as wheels with center holes so they can be mounted on arbors. Safety goggles, as always, are a must.

5-84. Rotary rasps are great for getting into tight places and for carving operations. If you want a smooth finish, you'll have to do some sanding after rasping.

5-88. A coarse-grit wire brush can be used to remove rust or dirt from metals. Use overlapping strokes. Move the drill so cutting is done against the wheel's rotation. Keep a firm grip to prevent the wheel from walking.

5-85. Disc rasp has cheese-grater-type teeth that cut fast without clogging.

5-86. The disc rasp is helpful for, among other things, preliminary surfacing of rough stock. Keep a firm grip on the drill and move the disc slowly. Excessive pressure will do more harm than good—the drill may stall and the disc might "walk".

5-89. A fine-grit brush can be used to put a satin finish on soft metals. Strokes can be parallel or haphazard, depending on the effect you want.

5-90.   A wire brush will create a sculptured, 3-D effect on wood. The treatment is especially effective on wood with hard and soft grain areas, like fir. Use a coarse wheel to start with, a fine wheel to finish.

5-91.   Some of the stands that are available for portable drills include a guard that is mounted as shown here. Use it for all abrading operations but don't let it lull you into neglecting safety goggles.

5-92.   Add a table that can function somewhat like the tool rest on a bench grinder. It serves as support for workpieces and also covers more of the wheel.

treatment is more effective on wood that has areas of hard and soft grain, like fir plywood or lumber.

Some holders available as accessories for portable drills include an adjustable guard so a wire brush can be used (Figure 5-91). This is a nice way to work on small pieces that require cleaning or polishing. Be sure you don't abrade your fingers along with the work; a possibility you can help avoid by wearing tight fitting gloves. If what you are working on is very small, grip it with pliers so your fingers can't come close. Figure 5-92 shows an example of a tool-rest table that you can add to the setup.

If the drill has a reversing feature, use it occasionally to reverse a wire wheel's direction of rotation. This will bring new, sharper points on the end of the wires into play, and will prevent the wires from taking a set in one direction.

The Portable Drill as a Drill Press

Many portable drill users who don't care to add a stationary drill press to their shop equipment but want some of the accuracy and convenience such a tool can provide, buy one of the many stands that allow a portable drill to be used in similar fashion. Most manufacturers offer one as an accessory —Skil, Wen, Sears, Black & Decker, Montgomery Ward, Rockwell all have one. Some will take *any* drill, others are designed specifically for one product, so check if you decide to buy one.

Some of the units are basic, being a post and stand combination, with a vertically adjustable drill holder, and a feed handle with a spring-action return (Figure 5-93). Others

5-93.   Most manufacturers who sell drills also offer a stand that allows drill-press functions. Some are designed for a single product, so check before buying.

(Figure 5-94) are a bit more sophisticated and come closer to imitating the functions of a drill press. The addition of a work table and extra features allows operations like those shown in Figures 5-95 and 5-96.

In no way can the portable-and-stand combination downgrade the stationary tool, but for many workshop chores it can serve as a substitute. You'll find that many jobs you've done by hand-holding the drill are easier and more accurate using a stand-mounted drill (Figures 5-97, 5-98). I feel that the portable-and-stand combination should be viewed on its own merits. It can be an asset to any shop regardless of the existing complement of tools. You can use it as-is, or extend its versatility by improvising setups and by dressing it up with some homemade jigs.

5-96.   Being able to turn the drill holder 90° allows a horizontal mode.

5-94.   Some stands are more sophisticated than others. These examples are closer to drill-press design since they include a work table in addition to the base. They might even include a guard (Left).

5-97.   It's more convenient to use accessories like hole cutters when the drill is mounted in a stand. Use a backup block under the work, and a clamp to keep the work secure. This stand is mounted on cleats to provide room under the base for clamping.

5-95.   The table may have a V-slot which is handy when drilling radial holes through round stock or tubing.

5-98.   Use a drill-press vise or another adequate holder when working on small pieces and when drilling or countersinking metal. Often, it's also necessary to clamp the vise. This photo doesn't show it, but stands should be bolted or screwed to a firm surface.

5-99.   The drill/stand combination is completely portable so you can use it like this to drill perfectly square-to-the-surface holes in standing posts, beams, joists, or whatever.

A novel but practical application is demonstrated in Figure 5-99. Say you must drill squarely through a post or column or beam; by clamping the stand to the work, as shown, you will assure that the hole will be perpendicular to the work-surface. The base of the stand can be clamped under the work or, assuming the base has a center hole, on top of it.

You can come closer to a true drill-press mode with stands that do not have a worktable by making a special base like the one in Figure 5-100. This allows the base of the stand to be used as a worktable. You can increase capacity between chuck and table by substituting a length of tubing or pipe that has the same diameter as the original post. If the base—now the table—flexes under drill pressure, brace under its front edge with a block of wood. The drawing in Figure 5-101 suggests how a new base can be made.

Another modification that provides even greater flexibility is shown in Figure 5-102. Here, galvanized pipe and fittings are used in place of the original base and post. Now the unit can be used in horizontal mode and, by adding the table and guides that are detailed in Figure 5-103, it becomes practical for quite a few chores that are normally done on a drill press. Figures 5-104 through 5-108 show how the table and guides can be situated, and demonstrate a few applications for the setup.

5-101.   Construction details of a special base you can make for a drill stand.

5-100.   Make a special base and the original base can be used as a work table. For more capacity, you can substitute some heavy tubing or pipe for the original column.

5-102.   Add even more flexibility by making a completely new column module. Actually, the only original part you use is the drill holder.

FENCE MODULE

¼ WING NUT & WASHER

DADOES ³⁄₈ X ⁵⁄₈

⅝ X 5" X 16"

RABBET ³⁄₈ X ⁵⁄₈

DADOES ³⁄₈ X ⁵⁄₈

WIDE

⅝ X 4¾ X 4¾

EYE BOLT

COLUMN BRACE

COLUMN

BACKING ¾" X 8" X 36"

BASE ¾" X 8" X 11¼"

30¾"

4½"

6½"

COLUMN MODULE

TABLE MODULE

TO SUIT

¾" X 10" X 12"

¾" X 4¾" X 14½"

8"

1" D.

DADOES ½" X ¾"

¼ X 2" CARRIAGE BOLT

FOR NO. 10 X 1¾ F.H. SCREWS

5-103.   How to make a new column module. The drawing also shows guides and tables that are used with it.

5-106.   The fence can be used as a guide when it's necessary to drill a series of holes on a common centerline.

5-107.   Place the unit on its "back" and you have a horizontal boring machine.

5-104.   Stand the unit on end, add the table and you have the drill-press mode.

5-105.   The fence is attached to the table with bolts and wing nuts so it is adjustable in relation to the centerline of the drill.

5-108.   The eye bolt shown in the drawing is there so the drill's cord can be held out of the way.

Drilling Metal

Twist drills are the most common tools used for forming holes in metal. While there are some similarities between drilling wood and drilling metal, there are *major* differences you should be aware of. While it might be possible to drill a good-size hole in wood in one operation, it's not a good idea to do so in metal. The practical procedure, for accuracy *and* safety, is to start with a small hole and get to the size you need by enlarging the hole in stages.

Metal drilling can develop considerable twisting action, and the bit can snag when it starts to break through. Therefore, the work must be securely clamped to a firm surface or gripped in a vise. There are several types of holding devices—usually called "drill-press vises"—that are handy for holding work, especially small pieces, securely (Figure 5-109). The faces of the units are usually V-cut or extra pieces with the same configuration are supplied so you can use them to grip round stock as well as straight pieces. The bases of the units are designed so they can be bolted or clamped to the drill-press table. You can provide the same extra security when working with a portable drill by locking the unit to a bench top or to a hefty block of wood that you can then grip in a bench vise.

Always start the drilling operation by marking the hole location with a punch (Figure 5-110). If you don't do this, the bit will probably move off the mark when you start the drill. Always start at a very low speed; gradually increase speed, but only to the point where the bit consistently cuts away material. A good combination of speed and feed pressure will curl a ribbon of metal out of the hole. Being too gentle won't accomplish anything but dull the bit since it will be doing more rubbing than cutting.

The best way to drill thin, sheet material is to sandwich it between pieces of scrap wood (Figure 5-111) or, at least, clamp or tape it so it lays flat on a backing block. If you work without these precautions, the bit will start to snag right off, the hole will have considerable burrs, and it may be anything but round.

An interesting and practical operation—not a drilling chore—that I use when working with small tubing is shown in Figure 5-112. Instead of turning the cutter, let a stand-mounted drill spin the tubing. The idea, of course, is most useful when you need many pieces. In fact, when many pieces of the same length are required you can use the jig setup shown in Figure 5-113. An L-shaped block clamped to the vise serves as a gauge while the tubing cutter is gripped by the jaws of the vise. In both cases, the knob of the cutter is turned while the drill spins the tubing at a fairly low speed.

5-111.   The best way to drill clean, burr-free holes in sheet metal is to sandwich it between scrap pieces.

5-109.   Vises like these are designed for use on a drill press but they are also very practical for use when working with a portable drill. The V-blocks, with clamps used for holding round stock, are usually sold as separate units.

5-112.   Not a drilling job, but the idea may come in handy, especially when you have many pieces of tubing to cut. The knob of the cutter is turned slowly while the drill rotates the tubing.

5-110.   Always start a metal drilling operation by indenting the hole location with a punch. In this automatic punch, a heavy spring impels the point when the top cap is pressed down.

5-113.   When you need many similar pieces you can clamp the cutter in a vise and use an L-shaped gauge to determine the length of the cutoffs.

A Selection of Special Accessories

The portable electric drill, on its own, isn't more than a power-source. What can be gripped in its chuck, whether for drilling or doing other shop and home chores, is what makes it such a versatile tool. The following illustrations and captions describe some of the accessories I have used with favorable results. They make the portable drill more than a drilling tool.

The Drill as a Lathe
Figures 5-114 through 5-116.

5-114.   A Leichtung "kit" supplies all the necessary components needed to use a drill as a lathe. "Headstock", "tailstock", and tool rest clamp to the edge of a workbench while the drill, through a special bushing, drives the spur center. End parts are situated to accommodate the length of the mounted workpiece.

5-115.   The drill sits at the headstock end and connects to drivers by means of a shaft and ball bearing bushing. What you can do with the lathe depends on the drill you use. A heavy-duty, 3/8″ drill with variable speeds is recommended.

5-116.   A faceplate is included in the kit. Always be sure that components are firmly clamped. Check them while working to be sure that vibration hasn't caused them to loosen.

As a Sander/Grinder
Figure 5-117.

5-117.   With the Hirsh sander/grinder, you use a portable drill to turn a disc to which you can attach conventional or wet-or-dry abrasive sheets. The unit can be used for conventional disc sanding and as a sharpening tool. A water tray and brush assembly, under the table, carries moisture to the disc so sharpening can be done with minimum heat buildup. The unit provides a tilting table and a small miter gauge.

As a Water Pump
Figure 5-118.

5-118.   Hand-size drill pump works impressively. It can be used with any garden hose to move 200 gallons per hour. Results are best when the drill turns at about 2000 rpm. The intake hose should not be longer than ten feet but the outlet hose can be as long as one hundred feet. The unit that is shown is a Black & Decker product. It's a good idea to wear rubber boots and gloves when using electricity near water.

For Right-Angle Drilling
Figure 5-119.

5-119.   Right-angle drilling is a boon when working in tight places. A special accessory that makes such an application easy is generally available. Most of them can be used with any drill.

As a Drill Saw
Figure 5-120.

5-120.   With "drill saws" you drill through to the cutter section of the tool and then cut in any direction you please. Thus you can form odd-shaped holes, do some scroll work, shape curves, and so on. Another typical use is enlarging existing holes. Metal as well as wood-cutting units are available.

For Mixing Paint
Figure 5-121.

5-121.   Tools that make it easy to mix paint to the correct consistency come in various forms. Be sure the mixer is in the paint before you turn on the drill—and—that the drill is stopped before removing the tool. Use a slow speed so you don't churn paint out of the container.

As an Earth Auger
Figure 5-122.

5-122. Jisco earth augers form 1¼″ holes quickly in all kinds of soil. They are available in 18″ long units for use with a ¼″ or larger drill, and in a 24″ long model that should be used with at least a ⅜″ drill. The augers are handy for jobs like deep root fertilizing and watering of trees and shrubs, and for drilling holes near foundations for insecticide treatment.

For Shaping
Figures 5-123 through 5-126.

5-123. Special bits are available that allow some amount of shaping with a portable drill. It's best to move the cutter very slowly and to use the drill's highest speed. The work should be held in a vise or firmly clamped. Keep a good grip on the drill and maintain it in a horizontal position through the pass.

BEADING CUTTER

COVE CUTTER

OGEE CUTTER

5-124. Examples of shapes available for use in a portable drill.

5-125. Portalign offers special, low speed shaper bits which can be used together with their "Drillguide". The guide is mounted under a platform that has been drilled so the cutters can pass through. A clamped, straight strip of wood with a notch in it serves as a fence.

For a Special Kind of Sanding
Figure 5-127.

5-126.   The shaper bits are available in various profiles. Nine cutting edges and a fairly large diameter for higher rpm speed, is what enables the bits to make acceptable cuts at low speeds. They are not meant to be used freehand.

5-127.   Sears kit for sanding or polishing round components includes a special attachment, sandpaper strips, and a polishing strap. It can be used with ¼″ or ⅜″ portable electric drills.

6. The Portable Router

If you associate the saber saw with a jigsaw or bandsaw, a portable drill with a drill press, or a cutoff saw with a table saw or radial arm saw, then you'll view the portable router as a close relative of the stationary shaper. Too often though, the router—and the shaper too—is limited by the user to forming decorative edges on furniture components, which is like using a saw only for crosscutting. The router is as practical a power tool as you can find. Professional woodworkers see it as a first-choice tool for many of the operations required for classic wood joints. It can often make the difference between amateurish and professional projects.

For example, the dovetail joint, a hallmark of well-designed and constructed furniture, is easily within the scope of a beginner when the router is used together with a dovetail jig. With a jig, dovetails can be formed about as quickly and easily as a dado or rabbet joint, and they will be precise. Some of the jigs are for equally spaced, through dovetails, while more sophisticated units allow variable spacing, whether you are forming through or half-blind dovetails. The point is, you don't have to be an expert to use them, but they provide expert results.

With appropriate cutters, the router is used to form spline joints, mortise and tenon connections, rabbets, dadoes, half-laps, the mating shapes needed for a drop-leaf table, and it does them with impressive ease and speed.

The router can be used freehand with accessories you buy, jigs you make, or with templates. Often, template cutting and freehand work are combined. The drawer fronts on the little Spanish chest in Figure 6-1 are an example; outlines were cut using a template, rough texturing was done freehand.

The router is basically a simple tool, consisting of a motor with a cutter-gripping device at one end, and a base that holds the motor erect and allows vertical adjustment to control depth-of-cut (Figure 6-2). Alone, like a portable drill, it can't do anything but whir. However, have an assortment of router bits, jigs, and a selection of accessories (some of which are briefly described in Figure 6-3) on hand and the tool will be one of the most-used in your shop.

6-1.   The router is used for esthetics as well as practical purposes. The carved drawer fronts and all the joints required to put this little Spanish-style chest together were done with a portable router.

6-2.   Basic construction of a router. Features not shown are things like double insulation, placement of switch, and possible electronic controls.

A QUICK LOOK AT PORTABLE ROUTER ACCESSORIES	
ACCESSORY	REMARKS
ROUTER BITS	Many types available either for joinery or decorative work—may be high-speed steel, solid tungsten carbide or carbide-tipped—most designs available with integral or ball bearing pilots.
DOVETAIL TEMPLATES	Devices that allow quick and accurate forming of various types of dovetail joints—some permit user to space joints to suit—used with dovetail bits.
SPECIAL TABLES	For mounting a portable router so it can be like a shaper—usually equipped with adjustable fences and guard.
HINGE MORTISING TEMPLATE KITS	Adjustable templates on a clamp that secures to edge of door—quick and accurate method of routing mortises for hinges.
PLANER ATTACHMENT	Allows the use of a router as a portable plane not available for all makes of portable routers.
EDGE GUIDE	Used when making cuts parallel to an edge—sometimes supplied with the tool.
CIRCLE-CUTTING GUIDE	Used for forming circular grooves or cutting discs—EDGE GUIDE and CIRCLE-CUTTING GUIDE often available as combination tool.
TEMPLATE GUIDES	Attach to router's base—typical application is pattern routing—needed when working with dovetail templates.
LAMINATE TRIMMING BITS	Special cutters for trimming of plastic laminates and wood veneers—usually carbide-tipped—some routers require a special base or attachment for such applications.
BIT SHARPENER	Unit attaches to router base and works with router motor—grinding wheel is secured in router collet—special guides assure accurate work.
LETTER AND NUMBER GUIDES	Special templates for routing house numbers, nameplates, and so on—available in various sizes—usually with template guides.
PANTOGRAPH	Router duplicates illustrations, letters, and numbers that are traced with a stylus—some units allow enlarging or reducing the pattern.
DOOR AND PANEL KITS	Adjustable guides and templates for decorative grooving of doors, panels, and drawer fronts.
EDGE-CRAFTER*	For decorative edging of round or oval frames and piecrust-type table tops—used with a router table.
ROUTER-RECREATOR*	Allows router to duplicate 3-dimensional objects as well as letters or numbers.
ROUTER-CRAFTER*	Lathe-type accessory for forming decorative furniture legs and posts.
WOOD THREADER**	For cutting threads in any species of hard or soft wood—matching taps available.
BOWL CRAFTER*	Used with router for "turning" a variety of projects such as bowls, goblets, plates, and boxes with fitted lids.

*Sears (Craftsman) product   **Beall Tool Company

6-3.   The router is one of the power tools that can perform beyond its basic function because of the host of accessories that are available for it.

Types, Sizes, Speeds

While the basic function of the portable router is fairly standard, manufacturers have specific ideas about how the product should look, where the on-off switch should be placed, and how the handles should be formed. Many times, you'll find a variety of shapes in a single catalog. So there are about as many to choose from as there are designs of automobiles. Those pictured in Figure 6-4 don't begin to tell the story but do show something of the various tool profiles.

All units provide for a two-hand grip. This may be matching knobs, a pair of upright handles, or a combination of knob and pistol grip (Figure 6-5). Some have the switch at the top of the motor, others incorporate it in one of the handles (Figures 6-5, 6-6). An advantage of the latter design is that you can have your hands in place and the tool in position before using the switch. A disadvantage is that there must be an extra length of cord between the motor and the handle.

Routers have split-collet type chucks which tighten around the shank of a bit when a threaded lock nut is turned. This is often accomplished with a pair of wrenches, one used on the motor shaft, the other on the lock nut. Some units have a built-in motor shaft locking mechanism which can be a convenience since you need only one wrench to tighten the collet.

Routers, especially light-duty ones, may be designed for a single collet, say, one that will grip bits with ¼″ shanks. More rugged routers might take a ⅜″ or even a ½″ collet, or be so designed that they can handle collets of different sizes. It's logical to assume that the horsepower of the tool must go up along with increases in collet size. In general, a one-collet router grips only one shank-size. A router with interchangeable collets is more versatile, not only because it will probably have more horsepower and can do more work, faster, but because it can also grip a greater number of cutters, including some that are specialized production units.

The plunge router is a newcomer, in our country anyway, which has some advantages over conventional designs (Figure 6-7). For one thing, you can start internal cuts like those needed for stopped dadoes, mortises, and many types of carving, with the router sitting firmly on the work.

6-5.   D-shaped handle on this 1¼ hp router has a built-in trigger switch, which is a convenience on many operations. The 10 lb. tool turns at 22,000 rpm and can be used with a ⅜″ or ¼″ collet.

6-6.   Weight usually goes up along with horsepower. This 1½ hp unit weighs 14 lbs and turns at 23,000 rpm. Standard collet size is ½″, but it can be used with ¼″ size as well.

6-7.   This 1½ hp plunge router has an electronic depth of cut readout which reads in inches or centimeters. It has a built-in work light and a spindle lock so only one wrench is required to secure bits.

6-4.   Router designs are as varied as the number that are available. Whatever the profile, handle placement, and so on, they all turn at high speeds.

Then you can lower the bit to a depth you read off on a scale or to a depth you have previously established by a control on the tool. Without the plunge capability, the router has to be held at an angle and then slowly tilted downward until the bit has penetrated and the router's base is firmly settled. It works, but it's inconvenient and somewhat more difficult to get the cut started accurately. Regular, straight-shank bits can be used for plunge cutting but when you need to go completely through the work, it's best to work with a plunge-cutting bit which has a cutting point that works something like a drill bit.

All routers operate at high speeds, somewhere between about 15,000 and 30,000 rpm, which is why they cut so smoothly. You might think that horsepower should increase with speed, but it doesn't work that way. Many light routers turn just as fast as heavy ones. More horsepower allows for deeper or heavier cuts.

Generally, among tools of equal horsepower, the faster turning one will cut more smoothly because of a greater percentage of cuts along a given distance. It's just a theory, and it also assumes that the feed-speed—how fast the tool is moved—is exactly the same. Which brings up a point; if the tool with fewer rpm's is moved more slowly than the faster turning one, it can provide just as many cuts per inch.

Router horsepower can start at about ½ and range up to better than 3 (Figures 6-8 and 6-9). One thing that does go up along with horsepower is weight. A ¾ hp model might weigh less than 4 lbs, while a big 3 hp unit can be as heavy as 18 lbs. Weight, along with what you anticipate using the router for, is a factor to consider when deciding which router to purchase. A 1 hp or 1½ hp tool that weighs 7 or 8 lbs will be fine for general woodworking. It's a size and weight that's pretty popular even in commercial woodworking shops. If you need to do really heavy-duty work, like plunging and cutting through a 1½″ pad to get duplicate pieces, then you should think of one of the big fellows. After you know something of what can be done with a router, you may be tempted to have more than one size.

Electronic technology is starting to affect the design of portable routers. The router in Figure 6-10 has many of the good features of conventional routers but also contains an electronic microprocessor which maintains the set speed under loaded conditions. It also monitors how fast you move the tool and signals when you are cutting too fast or too slow. You can preset the unit's speed to be compatible with the hardness of the material and the size of the cutter you are working with. It's nice to know that no matter how sophisticated tools become they will still need a human hand to guide them.

Another type of router is called a "trimmer" or "laminate trimmer" (Figure 6-11). Such units are usually light in weight—4 lbs and under—and turn at top speeds, usually in the area of 30,000 rpm. The units are compact and lack handles since they are designed for one-hand control. Their primary purpose is trimming plastic laminates and similar materials but they are often used for freehand carving and other router chores that require a light touch.

Router Bits

Router bits are what make the router, and you can find exactly the right one for forming anything from classic molding to merely rounding off an edge, and from making complicated joint forms to merely doing a rabbet cut. Some catalogs have page after page of cutters. Those shown in Figure 6-12 are just a sampling, but it's a selection that I feel is very practical for general woodworking.

6-8.   Double insulated, 3 hp tool can be preset for specific-depth plunge cuts. It turns at 23,000 rpm and can be used with ½″, ⅜″, and ¼″ collets.

6-9.   Black & Decker claims that this 3½ hp electronic router is the most powerful unit on the market. It can be used at 20,000 rpm for working in wood and other light materials, or at 16,000 rpm for harder materials like aluminum and plexiglass.

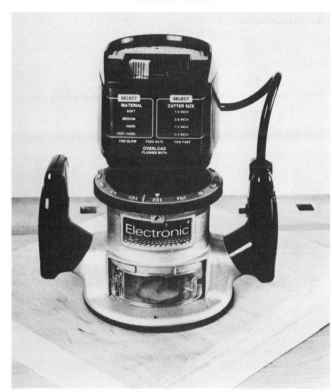

6-10. Router with electronic microprocessor does about everything but guide itself. It maintains the set speed under loaded conditions, monitors the feed rate, and a panel lets you select speed depending on material hardness and cutter size. Speed range is 11,000 to 25,000 rpm.

6-11. Trimmer is compact and light for one-hand control but has the power to do what it must. This unit has an offset drive spindle which allows laminate trimming in-and-out of 90° corners. Flat top, found on many routers, permits "up-right" bit changes.

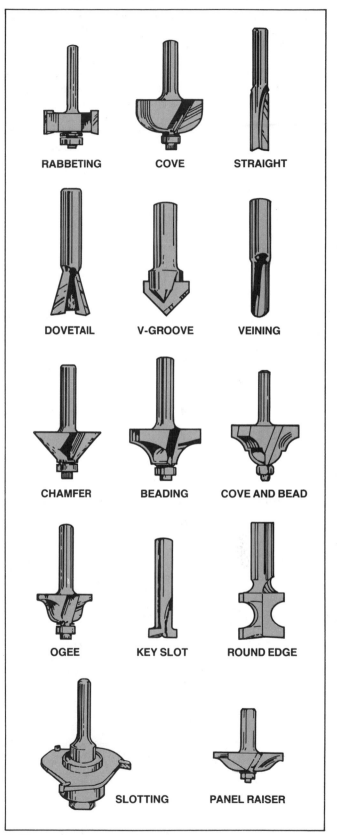

RABBETING   COVE   STRAIGHT

DOVETAIL   V-GROOVE   VEINING

CHAMFER   BEADING   COVE AND BEAD

OGEE   KEY SLOT   ROUND EDGE

SLOTTING   PANEL RAISER

6-12. A sampling of typical router bits. Hundreds of shapes and sizes are available.

CUTTING DIAMETER	NO. OF FLUTES	LENGTH OF CUTTING EDGE	SHANK DIAMETER	OVERALL LENGTH
1/16	1	5/16	1/4	1 1/2
1/8	1	3/8	1/4	1 1/2
1/8	2	3/8	1/4	1 1/2
5/32	1	5/8	1/4	1 1/2
5/32	2	5/8	1/4	1 1/2
3/16	1	1/2	1/4	1 1/2
3/16	2	1/2	1/4	1 1/2
3/16	2	5/8	1/4	2
7/32	1	3/4	1/4	2
7/32	2	3/4	1/4	2
1/4	1	3/4	1/4	2
1/4	2	3/4	1/4	2
1/4	1	1	1/4	2 1/2
1/4	2	1	1/4	2 1/2
1/4	2	1	1/4	3
1/4	1	1	1/4	3
1/4	2	3/4	1/2	3
1/4	2	1	1/2	3
5/16	2	1	1/2	3
5/16	1	1	5/16	2 1/2
5/16	2	1	5/16	2 1/2
3/8	2	1	3/8	2 1/2
3/8	2	1	1/2	3
3/8	2	1 1/4	1/2	3 1/4
1/2	2	1	1/2	3
1/2	2	1 1/4	1/2	3
1/2	2	1 1/2	1/2	3 1/2

6-13.   The number of bits available is affected by sizes in each category as well as different shapes. This chart, from a Freud catalog, illustrates this point.

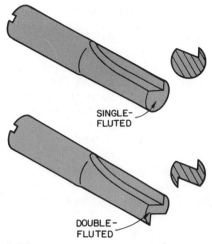

6-14.   The more flutes, or cutting edges, on a bit, the smoother it will perform simply because it makes more cuts per revolution.

6-15.   Examples of bit styles. The two on the left have tungsten-carbide cutters and ball bearing pilots. The next one is an arbor on which various cutters can be mounted. The last is an all-steel unit with integral pilot.

6-16.   Bits like this are designed primarily for laminate trimming. The pointed one is used for plunging. All are designed so the cutting circle matches the diameter of the pilot. The one on the right produces a beveled edge instead of a square one.

Not only are bits offered in an impressive variety of shapes, but in each category you'll find modifications of forms and different sizes. The information about straight bits in Figure 6-13, taken from a Freud catalog, makes the point. It may seem confusing, but it's actually a help, since by careful selection you will have a bit that is right for the tool you have and for the bulk of the work you do. Incidentally, double flute bits will cut smoother than single flute bits (Figure 6-14), simply because they make twice as many cuts per revolution.

Good router bits come in three varieties—high-speed steel, high-speed steel with tungsten-carbide cutting edges, and solid-tungsten carbide (Figures 6-15 and 6-16). Bit styles include one-piece units with integral pilots, units with ball-bearing pilots that are secured with screws so they can be replaced or exchanged for a different diameter, drill-point types that can penetrate through a workpiece, and arbor-type designs that are primarily a shaft and pilot between which you can secure various cutters (Figure 6-17). There are also slotting cutters which need to be mounted on an arbor (Figure 6-18), and which come in sizes to cut kerfs ranging from 1/16" to 1/4". Ball-bearing pilots of various diameters are available for the arbors so you can choose one to provide the kerf-depth you need. Slotting cutters are regularly used to form the groove that is required to install T-molding in the edge of a counter, but there is no reason why they can't also form, for example, grooves for splines when joining boards edge-to-edge.

Tungsten-carbide bits can cost three times as much as their all-steel counterparts, but they are smoother cutters and will stay sharp for much longer periods especially if they are used frequently on tough or abrasive materials (Figure 6-19). For some jobs, like trimming plastic laminates, a tungsten carbide tip is mandatory for optimum results and long cutting life. This doesn't mean you should completely avoid all-steel bits. Those of good quality will do a good job. In general, if you have a constant need for a bit, tungsten carbide is a good idea. If you don't spend all your time with a router in your hands, then high-speed steel will do nicely.

Remember that tungsten carbide, while tough, is also brittle. You can't bang them about or store them carelessly, not if you wish to maintain nick-free cutting edges.

The pilot on a router bit, whether it's an integral, smooth shank or an attached ball bearing, rides against the edge of a workpiece to guide the router and to control the width of the cut. The fixed pilot turns just as fast as the cutting edges of the bit and so can create friction that results in burn marks on the wood. A ball-bearing pilot turns freely, rotating only as you move the tool, so there is no friction to cause burn marks.

Whichever is being used, the pilot must be kept firmly against the work edge throughout the pass, and there must be sufficient bearing surface between pilot and work (Figure 6-20). It's also critical for the work edge to be perfectly smooth and free of imperfections. The pilot will faithfully follow any bump or crevice—and guide the cutter to duplicate it.

Some new cutters, not necessarily with strange profiles but requiring non-conventional router-use methods, have

6-17.   With arbor types, a single shaft is used with a variety of cutters.

6-18.   Slotting cutters are used with arbors. While offered primarily for the grooves needed to install T-moldings on counter edges, they can be used for spline grooves as well.

6-19.   Tungsten-carbide bits do a fine job generally, but they are especially efficient when used on hard, abrasive materials like "Corian". Guide here, is simply a length of rod with a hole for the nail that serves as the pivot.

6-20.   Always be certain that there is sufficient bearing surface between the work edge and the pilot. If the cut is too deep to allow this, clamp a second piece under the work to "thicken" the edge.

been introduced. The Sears "Crown Molding Kit", shown in Figure 6-21, is one of them. The kit includes bits for V-grooves, end coves, beading and chamfering, cove box (which is tungsten carbide), and an arbor with pilots. Each bit forms part of a pattern so that when the sequence of cuts shown in Figure 6-22 is followed, the end result is a standard molding form, or an exclusive profile that you create. The advantage of the kit has to do with the difficulty in finding moldings to match the wood used for a furniture project or a wall paneling installation. With the cutters, you can produce moldings on any wood species.

With a kit of cutters called "The Door Shop", produced by Zac Products, you can use a portable router for the stile, rail, and panel-edge shapes required to make professional paneled doors (Figure 6-23). The illustrations in Figure 6-24 show, briefly, how the cutters are used. The bits have ½" shanks so you know they must be used with a heavy-duty router.

However, there is a catch. The bits are not used in conventional fashion, that is, by hand-holding the router. Instead, the router must be used in stationary shaper fashion. This can be accomplished by mounting the tool under a surface that will serve as a worktable, plus using a clamped-on strip of wood to work as a fence. Many manufacturers offer special stands so the router can be used like a shaper (Figure 6-25). This is much better than a makeshift improvisation, especially since the setup can also be used with conventional router bits. Later in the book, we'll provide construction details so you can make your own router/shaper stand.

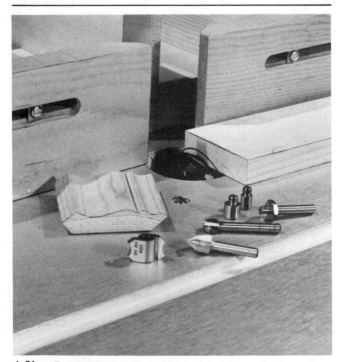

6-21. Crown Molding Kit includes all the bits needed to produce standard molding forms. The advantage is that you can produce moldings on any wood species. Cutters like these *must* be used in a router/shaper setup.

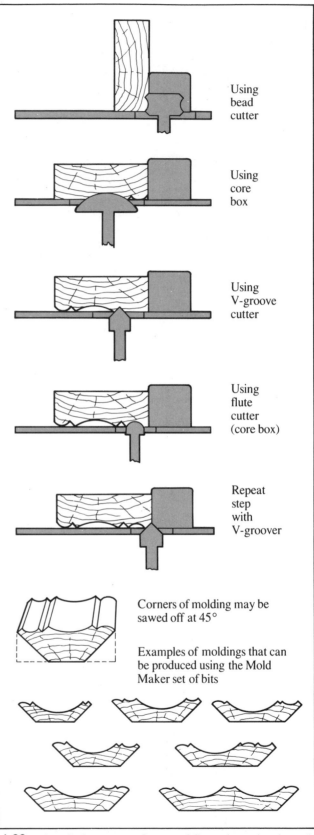

Using bead cutter

Using core box

Using V-groove cutter

Using flute cutter (core box)

Repeat step with V-groover

Corners of molding may be sawed off at 45°

Examples of moldings that can be produced using the Mold Maker set of bits

6-22. A typical sequence of steps to follow when using the mold maker set of bits. Many design variations are possible.

6-23. The router, with special bits and mounted in a stand, can be used to make all the cuts that are required to produce professional, paneled doors.

The Router at Work

If you take a bird's eye view of the router, you will see that the motor rotation, and thus the direction of cut, is in a clockwise direction. Basic practice is to move the router so the cutter tends to pull itself into the work. If, for example, you are shaping an edge, the feed direction, how you move the router, is from left to right. If you reverse this, the bit has the freedom to run along the edge like a wheel. It might occasionally be necessary to reverse the feed direction, but a greater degree of control is needed to keep the router firm and to avoid rough edges. Freehand carving or hollowing a project like a tray or bowl, when the tool is moved in various directions, are examples of reversing feed direction. The answer is to keep a very firm grip on the tool but, actually, this applies to any router operation, even fairly simple ones like shaping a straight edge (Figure 6-26).

You'll get the smoothest cuts when you move the router so the bit is cutting *with* the grain of the wood. When this isn't possible, as is often the case, move the router more slowly than you normally do. When working on four edges of a workpiece, do the end-grain cuts first. This is because some feathering and even some splintering may occur where the cutter leaves the work. The final passes, made parallel to the grain, will remove any imperfections.

Feed speed and depth of cut go hand in hand, although it's not farfetched to say that the slower the feed, the smoother the cut will be regardless of its depth. But you must

The configuration in the face of rails and stiles is shaped with the ogee bit.

The ogee bit is raised, and, after test cuts, is used to form the cope cut on the end of the rails.

The slot-cutting bit forms panel-insert grooves in stiles and rails.

The slot-cutting bit is lowered to complete the shape of cope-cut rail-ends.

The panel-raiser bit shapes the edges of the panel that will be inserted in the frame.

6-24. This is a quick look at how the bits in the set called "The Door Shop" are used. A very detailed instruction booklet comes with the cutters.

6-25.   A table like this sets the router up for stationary shaper operations. This particular one can also be used with a saber saw.

6-26.   Let the router get to full speed before you contact the work. Use a two-hand grip and keep the tool moving steadily. Wear safety goggles even if the router has a chip deflector.

6-27.   It's important to secure workpieces with clamps, or in a vise, or with weights. One way to secure small pieces is to frame them with thinner, tack-nailed strips.

keep the cutter *working*. Generally, the more wood being removed, the slower the feed should be. Feeding too fast or cutting too deep will tax the motor and reduce its efficiency. This will be apparent from the sound of the motor, if nothing else. Feeding too slowly will not accomplish much and may result in burning the wood, even drawing the temper from the cutting tool. At the correct "load", which has to be a combination of feed-speed and cut, the tool will maintain a uniform speed without overheating, the cut will be smooth, and there will be no burn marks.

The more powerful the tool you are using, the faster you can feed and the deeper you can cut. Final judgments, guided by the equipment being used, have to be made by the operator. If it's obvious that the tool is struggling to make a particular cut, decrease the depth of cut for the first pass and then repeat the pass after adjusting the bit to get the full cut you need. You might even do this more than once—it's a way to use a light-duty unit for a heavy-duty operation.

Work security is important. By assuring that the project will remain still, you automatically eliminate one factor that leads to rough cuts and you contribute to your own safety. On large components, say you are shaping the edges of a plywood panel, and on assembled projects, the movement problem is minimized. But many times, routing is required on small parts prior to final assembly. In my own shop I keep a heavy piece of steel on the workbench for just such applications. This is used as a weight to keep the part firm as I apply the router. If this isn't practical, or doesn't do the job, I often use tack-nailed strips of wood around the piece which act as a frame to hold it firm (Figure 6-27). Clamps and a vise are also means of gripping pieces so they can't move when you work on them.

Be prepared for the jolt, caused by the starting torque of the motor, that occurs when you flick the switch. A firm grip will keep the router where it should be. Allow the tool to attain full speed before applying it. Don't have the cutter in contact with the work when you first turn it on. Let the tool come to a full stop after a cut before you set it down on its side. Never hold the machine, or rest it, so that the cutter is pointing toward you.

Follow the instructions concerning bit security that come with the tool. Bits must be tight in the collets. Placing them so the collet grips less of the shank than it should, in order to get more depth of cut, is not a good idea. If you have never used a portable router, be an apprentice for a bit. Make some light cuts on scrap stock. Use wood like pine and maple so you can judge the different cutting characteristics. Get the "feel" of the tool. Always wear safety goggles!

Straight Cuts

Straight cutting can be done by allowing the pilot on the bit to guide the router or by moving the router along a guide-strip that is tack-nailed or clamped to the work (Figure 6-28). The guide strip must have a smooth, straight edge and should be fairly stiff, especially if the cut is a long one. The direction of feed is from left to right, and you may either push or pull the tool—a decision that is based primarily on operational convenience. Whichever way you work, it's necessary to exert some lateral force as well, in order to keep the router base snug against the guide throughout the pass. There are times when a guide strip is good to use even if the bit has a pilot, especially if you are working on hard wood. The guide will allow you to minimize the pressure you must exert to keep the pilot in contact with the work edge, thereby reducing the possibility of friction burns.

Straight cuts on an edge or away from an edge, can also be done with an edge guide, a router accessory which, if not supplied with the tool, can be purchased as an 'extra'. Figure 6-29 shows a typical unit being used to guide the router through a groove-cut, which is actually a dado that is cut parallel to the wood grain. Always be sure that the work edge against which the guide will bear is smooth and straight.

A point to remember when making cuts on work edges is that you can often vary the results you get from a single cutter by using different depth-of-cut and width-of-cut settings. This applies whether you are using a shaped cutter or a straight-shank bit.

Since straight cutting is a routine, often-used router application, it pays to make some clamp guides like those shown in Figure 6-30. Then you won't have to improvise or search for wood-strips that are right for the job. Construction details for some that I use are shown in Figure 6-31. Note that the guide may have a fixed length or can be adjustable if you form a slot in the bar. Use a fairly stiff wood; something like straight-grain fir.

The clamp guide can be used whether you are working on or away from a work edge as demonstrated by the rabbet and dado cuts shown in Figure 6-32. Forming a dado or a rabbet that is wider than the largest diameter bit you have is just a matter of making more passes after the clamp guide has been repositioned (Figure 6-33).

The router is often used to make decorative surface cuts (Figure 6-34). This is just a matter of using a particular bit and controlling the depth of the cut. Straight cuts are accomplished with a guide. Some techniques for guiding the router for curved lines will be shown later.

6-29.   Edge guides that come with the router or are available as accessories are used this way. The cut may be on the edge of the work or away from it. The edge the guide bears against must be smooth and straight.

6-30.   Clamp guides that you can make are very practical for straight router cuts.

6-28.   A tack-nailed or clamped strip of wood is a good guide to use for long, straight cuts. The tool may be pushed or pulled so long as it is moved from left to right.

6-31.   This is how the clamp guides are made. It's a good idea to have one for use on boards of standard, maximum width (11¼"), and another, adjustable one for various stock widths.

6-32.   The clamp guide can be used whether the router is working on an edge or away from it. Here, it has been used to guide the router through a rabbet cut and a dado.

6-33.   Repeat passes produce a rabbet, or a dado, that must be wider than you can form by making one pass with the largest cutter you have.

6-34.   Decorative surface cuts are made by using particular bits and limiting depth of cut. A "veining" bit, which forms round bottom grooves, is often used for this kind of work.

Circles and Curves

Shaping the edge of curved pieces doesn't differ from shaping a straight edge, except that the bit, unless special techniques are employed, must have a pilot. A method that solves the problem of keeping the router flat on the work is demonstrated in Figure 6-35. The scrap piece that remains after the workpiece has been sawed to shape is positioned to provide outboard support for the tool. The idea is practical for straight as well as curved cuts.

The router is a super tool to use for forming perfect circular grooves or for producing uniform discs or rings, providing it is used with a circle guide (Figure 6-36). Most manufacturers have a version of such an accessory; some might even provide one with the router. In a few cases, the edge guide that is available is designed so it can also be used as a circle guide. In any case, the technique is simply a matter

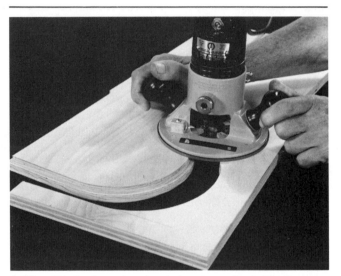

6-35.   Shaping irregular edges is done in routine fashion but always with a piloted bit. Using the cutoff, as shown here, will keep the tool horizontal throughout the pass. Use the same technique on straight cuts.

6-36.   Some edge guides do double duty. They can guide the router through a circular as well as a straight cut.

of moving the router about a pivot point that is established with the guide.

One of the problems with commercial circle guides is that they have a limited capacity. To do more, or simply to avoid having to buy one, you can make your own along the lines shown in Figure 6-37. Yours will be exclusive for the router you own since the holding ring must be just right for the router's base. If you have routers with bases of different diameters, various holding rings can be provided and held in place with short screws.

To use the jig, determine the radius of the circle you need and then drive a nail through a hole in the bar that will provide it. Then, move the router so it is guided by the jig (Figure 6-38). Normal feed direction for the router will be in a clockwise direction. The jig, as I've made it, will form circles up to 36″ in diameter.

Circle guides can be used to form rings or discs (Figure 6-39). An extra precaution is needed here. Since the cutter must pass through the material, clamp or tack-nail the work to a backup piece. If the stock is thick, and the router doesn't have the power for a one-pass operation, get through by adjusting the bit extension for each of any number of passes you must make. Proceed in routine fashion when cutting a disc; for rings, make the inside cut first. When you need many similar pieces, you can pad materials and cut through them all at once.

A "gadget" you can make that will serve as a circle guide and also as a trammel tool is shown in Figure 6-40. One head is mounted when the project is used as a circle guide for the router; two heads are used for layout work. The advantage of such a tool when used as a circle guide is that the distance between the pivot and the bit is infinitely variable.

CIRCLE GUIDE

6-37. A circle guide that you can make. The holding ring must suit the router's base. If you have several routers, you can provide rings with different inside diameters, attaching them to the jig with screws as you need them.

6-39. Forming precise rings or discs is routine when you work with a circle guide. A backup piece is needed since the cutter must penetrate through the workpiece.

6-38. The circle guide that you make will have more capacity than a commercial one. The one I use, which you can duplicate, has a 36″ diameter capacity. A longer bar would increase the capacity.

6-40. How to make a tool that can be used as a trammel for marking arcs and circles, and as a circle guide for the router.

Working with Templates

By using a template—or a "pattern" if you prefer—the router can be guided along fairly complicated lines or used to make as many similar pieces as you need. To be used in this fashion, the router's base must be equipped with template guides like those shown in Figure 6-41. This particular type of guide is not interchangeable with all routers, so be sure you buy those that work with the tool, or tools, you own. The guides provide what is essentially a sleeve through which the cutter passes (Figure 6-42). The router is moved while keeping the sleeve in constant contact with the edge of the template. Since the wall of the sleeve has thickness, the cutter will be held away from the pattern's edge by that distance. This may not be critical on some jobs, but when it is, you simply compensate by making the template larger or smaller, as the case may be. For example, the template for an inside circle would be sized to suit the radius of the circle you need *plus* the thickness of the sleeve's wall. The reverse would be true if you were cutting a disc.

6-43.   Templates can be as simple as this one, which was shaped to guide the router through a hinge mortise.

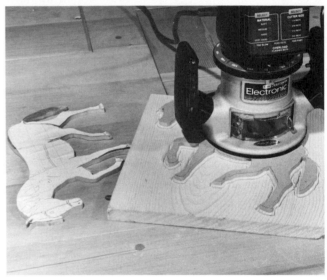

6-44.   Use the smallest straight, or veining bit you have when working with more complicated templates like this horse profile. A tiny bit lets you get into confined areas.

6-41.   Template guides, used in the router's base, are designed for bits of different diameter. One design can't be used with all routers so be sure to buy those that are right for the tool you own.

6-42.   The router bit passes through the sleeve of the template guide. The sleeve, riding against the edge of the template, guides the cutting.

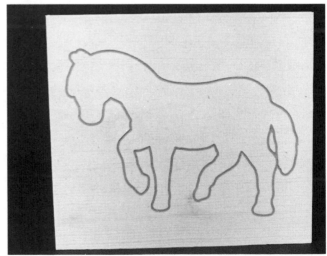

6-45.   The groove for the horse carving was filled with plastic aluminum. There are other ways to go—use the router freehand to recess the figure, or to raise it by cutting away material on the outside.

Templates can be fairly simple, like the one in Figure 6-43 which is used to guide a router through a mortise for a hinge, or they can be quite complicated, involving many twists and turns like the one in Figures 6-44 and 6-45. On jobs like this, you should use the smallest diameter veining or straight-shank bit that the router can handle so you can get as close as possible into tight corners. For jobs like the hinge mortise, you should work with a fairly large straight-shank bit. Some hinges are made so they will fit the round corners left by the bit. If not, the corners can be cleaned out with a chisel.

Commercial router templates, especially those that are designed for incising decorative patterns on doors, are used in many cabinet shops. One of them, the "Wing Router Template", consists of lengths of tubing and special fittings so a guide system for the router can be organized to suit the project. Various templates can be added to the assembly for incising designs like those shown in Figure 6-46.

Such products might not be the kind of tool for every home shop, but by improvising you can achieve similar results. Figure 6-47 demonstrates how guide pieces of various shapes can be tack-nailed to a component and used as a template. The design that results is shown in Figure 6-48. The possible variations are limitless; the end results depend entirely on how you construct the template (Figure 6-49). Often, a single template can be used to create designs that are more advanced than the template itself. The idea is to preview the design you want and then to place the template

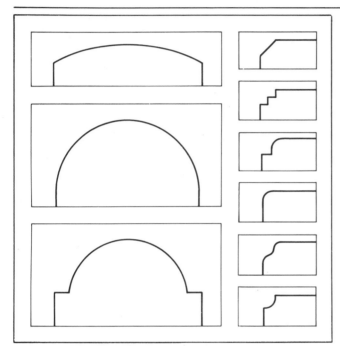

6-46.   Various guide patterns are used with the "Wing Router Template" to produce decorative grooves like these. Work like this is very common on cabinet doors.

6-48.   The template shown in Figure 6-47 was used to produce this grooved decoration.

6-47.   Templates can simply be pieces of specially shaped wood or hardboard that are tack-nailed or clamped to the project. Holes left by tack-nailing can be filled with wood dough.

6-49.   You can create a template to produce just about any kind of design. Once made, the template can be used to produce any number of similar pieces.

appropriately for each of the cuts (Figures 6-50 and 6-51). Tack-nailing does leave small holes in the project but they are easily concealed with wood dough. When possible, of course, use clamps to hold the parts of the template.

Grooves for tambour doors are usually formed with a router (Figure 6-52). Since the grooves must be perfectly aligned in top and bottom case members, it is necessary to work with an accurate template and to be precise when attaching the template to the mating pieces. Note, in Figure 6-53, that the template is designed so the grooves will "run out" at the back edge of the components. This allows the tambours to be inserted from the rear after the case members have been assembled. It's more convenient than having to put the doors in place *during* assembly.

Special Router Bases

The diameter of bases on routers is fine for most work but there are times when it is difficult to keep the router level because the base isn't large enough to span across support areas. Typical situations are hollowing jobs on trays or bowls or boxes. The practical solution is to make a long, auxiliary base that substitutes for the regular one (Figure 6-54). The homemade bases can be any shape or size and they will fit the router as they should if you use the original base as a pattern for drilling the center hole and those needed for the screws

6-52.   The grooves that are required for tambour doors are usually formed with a router.

6-50.   Often, a single template can be used as a multi-form guide. It's just a question of repositioning the template for each of the cuts you need.

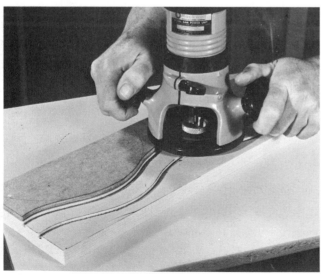

6-51.   The single template idea also works for jobs like forming a series of "parallel" irregular grooves. Accuracy depends on how carefully you set the template for each of the cuts.

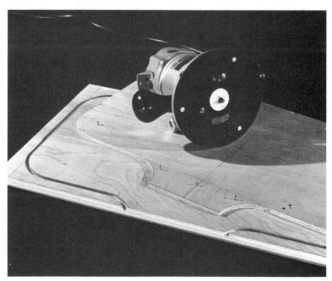

6-53.   A carefully made template is used for the grooves needed for the tambour. Note that the grooves "run out". This is so the doors can be inserted from the rear of the project after it has been assembled.

(Figure 6-55). The screwheads will have to be set flush in counterbored holes.

It's also possible to use a special base when the job requires a template guide. It's just a matter of seating the guide in the auxiliary base so its bottom surface will be flush (Figures 6-56 and 6-57). This calls for a slight counterbore on the perimeter of the through hole. You can accomplish this with the router itself by making a template with a suitably-sized hole. It can also be done with hole saws, using one to go just deep enough for the counterbore, and a second one to form the through hole.

One of the problems with regular router bases and those you might make is that they don't provide as much visibility as you might like. A solution is to make see-through bases using a material like "Lexan", a shatterproof, scratch resistant plastic.

Router Joinery

The more familiar you become with the portable router, the more impressed you will be with its versatility. You will find, for example, that you will use it more and more for precise joint constructions. By using particular bits, sometimes with special techniques or jigs, you can master any of the connections that are shown in Figure 6-58.

6-56. Many hollowing, and similar jobs, are done by working with templates. Any auxiliary base that is used must be fitted with a template guide (Figure 6-57).

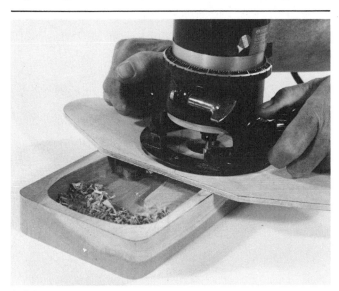

6-54. Auxiliary bases are used for jobs like hollowing when the regular base isn't big enough to span across supporting edges.

6-55. One-quarter-thick hardboard is a good material for auxiliary bases. Use the original base as a pattern for the center hole and for the holes for attachment screws. See-through bases can be made by using "Lexan", a tough, plastic material.

6-57. The template guide must be set flush in the special base. This calls for a slight counterbore on the perimeter of the through hole.

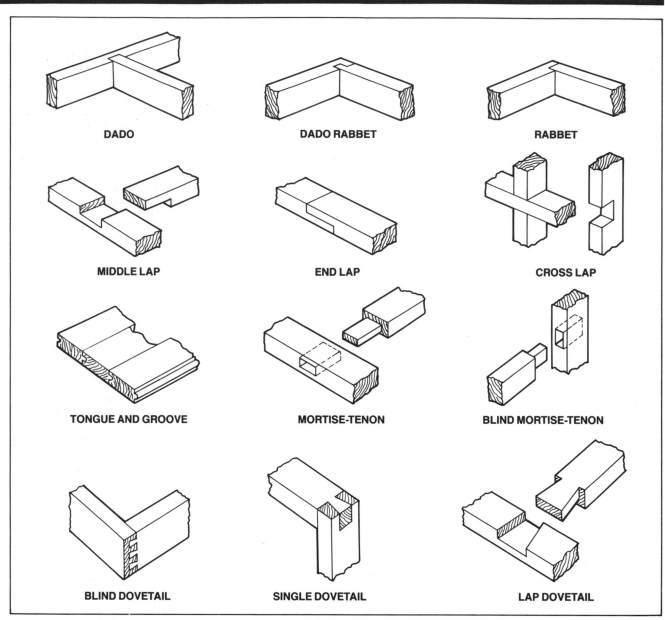

DADO   DADO RABBET   RABBET

MIDDLE LAP   END LAP   CROSS LAP

TONGUE AND GROOVE   MORTISE-TENON   BLIND MORTISE-TENON

BLIND DOVETAIL   SINGLE DOVETAIL   LAP DOVETAIL

6-58.   By using guides and jigs that you make or buy, you can form all these joints with a portable router.

6-59.   Rabbets and dadoes (or grooves) are done best by moving the router along a guide strip. When possible, use a bit with a diameter that matches the thickness of the piece that will be inserted in the cut.

6-60.   "Stopped" dadoes or rabbets are cuts that start and end away from the work edge. Stop blocks, clamped to the guide, control the length of the cut. Plunge routers make jobs like this easier to do.

Dadoes and rabbets, which are used so often in woodworking, are probably the easiest to do, requiring only that you guide the tool accurately along a straight line. This can be accomplished with an edge guide, but for more flexibility in router placement it's best to work with a clamp guide (Figure 6-59). How wide the cut will be depends on the bit you use. Cuts beyond the capacity of a particular bit, can be widened by repositioning the guide and cutting again. How deep you can cut in a single pass depends on the hardness of the material and the power of the tool. Usually, the depth of a rabbet or dado is about one half the thickness of the stock.

The appearance of a rabbet or dado isn't too pretty when viewed from the front after assembly, but you can get around this when the project calls for it, by making "stopped" cuts like those in Figure 6-60. The cut is started away from the edge of the work, and its length is controlled by stop blocks that are secured to the guide with clamps. The cut is started with the router at an angle so the cutter clears the work. Then it is tilted down until it rests fully on its base. This is an operation where you can see the advantage of a plunge router—the cutter can be lowered into the work with the tool firmly seated to begin with.

The router does a fine job of forming both parts of a tongue and groove joint (Figure 6-61). You can clamp the work between scrap pieces when you feel you need extra support for the router. The router, situated so it will cut in the center of the work edge, can be guided with an edge guide (Figure 6-62). To be sure that the groove will be centered, make a second pass with the edge guide bearing against the opposite edge of the work. To form the mating part, use a similar setup and make a pass on each edge of the stock to leave the projection which is the tongue. In this case, you will be cutting into the scrap pieces as well as the work. When making many parts, the one set of scrap pieces can be used for all of them.

One way to form a round-end mortise is shown in Figure 6-63. An L-shaped guide block, situated so the bit will cut along the center of the stock, is secured directly to the router's base. The cut is started with the router tilted like it is in the photograph. Here too, is an example of where a plunge router can be handy. If you form slots in the L-shaped guide instead of just drilling attachment holes, it will have some adjustment capability so you will be able to use it on stock of different thicknesses.

6-62.   Forming a groove by controlling the router with an edge guide. The extra, clamped-on pieces provide more support surface for the tool.

6-61.   On a tongue and groove joint, the groove is formed in a single pass; the tongue requires a pass on each edge of the stock.

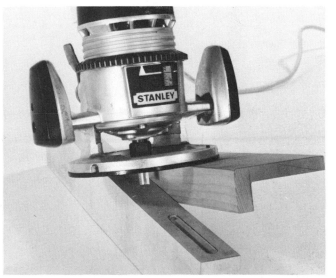

6-63.   Round-end mortises can also be formed with an edge guide, or you can work with an L-shaped guide that you make. When the guide is slotted, it can be adjusted for use on stock of different thicknesses.

2"

$1\frac{1}{2}$" X 6" X 22"

$1\frac{1}{2}$"

$\frac{3}{4}$"

$\frac{1}{2}$" X 8" CARRIAGE BOLT

$\frac{1}{2}$" HOLES

1"

$1\frac{1}{2}$" X 3" X 22"

VISE CLAMP

WASHER

WING NUT

1" X $1\frac{1}{2}$" X $6\frac{1}{2}$"

6-64.   How to make a vise clamp. Use a hardwood like maple or birch.

$1\frac{1}{2}$"

$\frac{1}{4}$" X 6" X 12"

WING NUT

WASHER

2" DIA.

SLOTS =
$\frac{1}{4}$" WIDE X $3\frac{1}{2}$" LONG

$\frac{3}{4}$" X $2\frac{1}{2}$" X 8"
(2 REQ.)

$2\frac{5}{8}$"

**USE FOR MORTISING
FORMING DOVETAIL SLOTS,
EDGE GROOVES, AND
SIMILAR CHORES.**

$\frac{1}{4}$" X $1\frac{1}{2}$" CARRIAGE BOLT
(4 REQ.)

$\frac{5}{8}$"

6-65.   A special, adjustable base lets you guide the router accurately for many types of joint cuts.

In my own shop, I use custom-built jigs for jobs like mortising and forming edge-grooves whether they are simple or dovetailed. One jig is the vise clamp detailed in Figure 6-64, the other is an adjustable, auxiliary base (Figure 6-65). For mortising, the work is gripped between the jaws of the vise clamp and the assembly is then secured in a bench vise. Forming the mortises begins after the work has been marked to show the position and the length of the cuts (Figure 6-66).

The adjustable side-guides of the auxiliary base are secured so that the cut will conform with the layout that is on the workpiece (Figure 6-67). You can form mortises that are centered or off-center, depending on how you situate the left- and right-hand side-guides.

6-66. A mortising operation starts by gripping the work in the vise clamp and marking it so you'll know where to start and end the cuts.

6-67. The slides on the special base can be adjusted so the bit will cut on the center of the edge or, if you choose, away from it.

Tenons to match the mortise can be formed with a router by following the ideas shown in Figures 6-68 and 6-69. First, select a block of wood that is wide enough to supply the number of rails you need. Don't forget to allow for the kerf-waste when the block is sawed into individual pieces. Then, working with a clamp guide and a large straight bit in the router, make as many passes as it takes to establish the length of the tenon. This is done on both sides of the stock, with depth-of-cut established to produce the correct tenon-thickness.

The second step, after individual pieces have been sawed from the block, is to flip them on edge and assemble them in a clamp guide (Figure 6-69), or directly in a bench vise. Then use the router to finish trimming the tenons which, like the first step, requires cutting on both surfaces. Since the mortise has round ends and the tenons have square ends, you will have to dress one or the other. Either use a narrow chisel to square the ends of the mortise, or round off the end of the tenon to suit the mortise.

6-68. First step when forming tenons. Work on a piece of wood that's wide enough to supply the number of rails you need. Use a large, straight bit and make as many passes as it takes to reach the tenon's length. Cuts are made on both edges.

6-69. The pieces ripped from the original block are placed on edge and secured in a clamp guide. Then the router is used to finish forming the tenons. Depth of cut must be precise for both of the operations required to produce tenons.

Mortises for splines that are used to reinforce miter joints can also be formed by using the vise clamp/adjustable base technique (Figure 6-70). It's just a matter of situating the pieces in the vise clamp so the mitered ends will be on a horizontal plane. Be careful with layout and depth of cut. If the mortise is too long or too deep, the cutter will pass through the material. Splines should be a slip-fit, with a length that is a fraction less than two times the depth of the mortise (Figure 6-71). The same also applies to tenons. If they must be forced into the mortise and if they don't allow some room for glue, they can split the mating piece.

Figures 6-72 and 6-73 show how the special jigs are used to guide the router through straight or dovetail grooves in stock edges. The vise clamp is also a practical way to secure narrow pieces for edge-shaping (Figure 6-74).

6-72.   Accurate grooves in stock edges can be cut by gripping the work in the vise clamp. You can be certain that the groove will be centered if you make a second pass after reversing the position of the router.

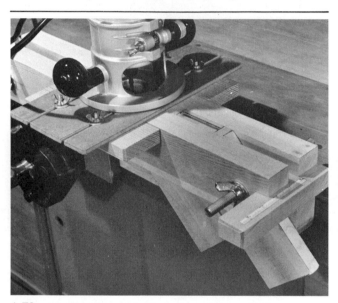

6-70.   Mortises can also be formed in miter cuts. It's just a matter of situating the pieces correctly in the vise clamp.

6-73.   Work the same way to provide dovetail grooves. To shape the tongue for the groove or the pin for the dovetail, grip the work between scrap pieces. Then make cuts on both edges of the material.

6-71.   The spline for the miter joint is shaped to suit the round ends of the mortises. It should slip easily into the cuts and be a bit shorter than the combined depth of the mortises.

6-74.   Another use for the vise clamp is gripping narrow pieces securely. Scrap pieces can be added if you need more support for the router.

Dovetails

The router, turning a dovetail bit, and used with ingenious jigs that you buy, makes you an instant dovetail expert. The application is one of the router operations that impresses everyone. In a short time, even a rank beginner can produce classic, quality joints like the one shown in Figure 6-75. It's just a matter of acquiring the jig—a finger template goes with it—and then being careful about following the instructions. A common jig design, offered by many manufacturers, provides for holding two pieces of wood (for example, the front and side of a drawer) in correct position. The router, fitted with a template guide, follows the shape of the fingers (Figure 6-76). Since the shapes are cut simultaneously in both members, they fit precisely. The only "problem" with this jig design is that you are limited to uniformly spaced dovetails of a particular size and pattern.

The Leigh jigs that are shown in Figures 6-77 and 6-78, are more advanced designs which allow some originality in the appearance of the dovetail joint. They can be used for through or half blind dovetails (Figure 6-79), but the operator has the option of deciding how many connections there should be in the joint and how they should be spaced (Figure 6-80). This is an advantage. While small, equally spaced, hidden dovetails are perfectly fine for drawer joints, it is often more estheticly pleasing to have dovetails that appear larger and which are spaced creatively on case work, or any project where the joint is exposed.

Being able to choose spacing is possible on the Leigh jigs because of individual template fingers which are locked along a slide bar in the position you opt for. Cutting techniques differ in that the parts of the joint are formed separately. Also, pin pieces with the fingers set up as shown in

6-75.   The router, used with special jigs, makes you an almost instant dovetail expert. You do have to learn to use the jigs correctly, but that doesn't require much time.

6-77.   One of the Leigh dovetail jigs lets you work on stock up to 12″ wide.

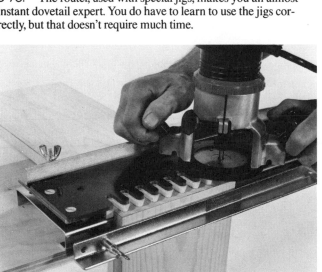

6-76.   A common dovetail jig grips both parts of the joint. The router, moved around a finger template, cuts both parts of the joint. You can't miss if you use the jig correctly.

6-78.   A more advanced model will take stock up to 24″ wide. The advantage with both units is that you are not limited to uniformly spaced dovetails.

Capabilities of Leigh Jigs

6-79.   The Leigh jig can be organized for through or half blind dovetails.

6-80.   Being able to choose dovetail spacing, whether they are through or half blind, can make projects appear more customized.

6-82.   The mating part of the joint is formed with a dovetail bit after the position of the guide fingers has been reversed.

6-81.   The jigs have clamp bars that hold the stock firmly under the adjustable guide fingers. The fingers are adjusted by moving them along a slide bar. Pins are formed with a straight bit.

6-83.   Half blind cutting is done with the work in horizontal position. The Leigh jigs require some study time but the design freedom they provide is worth it. Large jig has an adjustable tube which can be connected to the hose of a vacuum cleaner.

Figure 6-81 are formed with a straight bit, while the tail pieces with the finger assembly flipped over (Figure 6-82) are formed with a dovetail cutting bit. It takes a little getting used to but the system is anything but complicated. Once you have spaced the fingers on the slide bar, the same setup is used to cut both parts of the joint.

Pin pieces for a half blind dovetail are done with the workpiece clamped in horizontal position under the template fingers (Figure 6-83). If you are really into dovetail work and are using a Leigh jig, it pays to work with two routers, one with a dovetail bit, the other a straight bit. A very detailed instruction book comes with the jigs. Read it carefully and then do some experimental dovetailing on scrap stock.

Routing Plastic Laminates

Any router can be used to trim plastic laminates. One way is to substitute a special base for the regular one. The trimmer base is essentially a guidance system, usually with a ball bearing "pilot" that lets you move the router along an edge while the cutter, preferably tungsten carbide, trims the sur-

face laminate flush with the edge of the workpiece. The critical step is adjusting the guide so the cut will be accurate.

Another way to work, which doesn't require a special accessory, is simply to work with router bits that are specifically designed for such cutting (Figure 6-84). Some have integral pilots, others have a ball bearing, but whatever, they are made so the diameters of the pilot and the cutter are exactly alike. Thus, doing perfect trimming is merely a matter of moving the router along the work edge (Figure 6-85). Be careful to hold the router in correct position throughout the pass. Any accidental tilting will mar the work.

For perfect butt joints, improvise a setup like the one shown in Figure 6-86. Both pieces, after they have been carefully aligned and clamped, are cut at the same time. The edges will be smooth and will mate perfectly. Simultaneous cutting can also be done to assure a perfect connection for miter joints (Figure 6-87). The workpieces are taped face-to-face and then clamped at a 45° angle with a strip that also serves to guide the tool. The straight-shank, tungsten-carbide bit passes through a groove in the plywood jig.

6-84. Laminate trimming bits come in a variety of styles. Some are solid carbide, others have blades with tungsten-carbide edges.

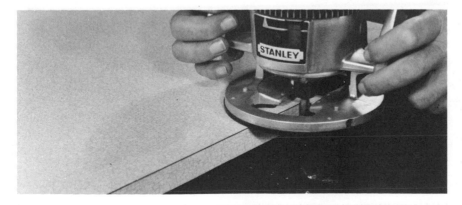

6-85. Trimmer bits are designed so the diameter of the pilot and the cutting circle of the blades are exactly alike. The part being trimmed will be perfectly flush with the work's edge.

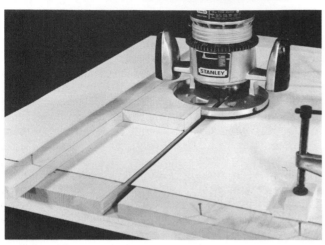

6-86.   A setup like this will let you cut edges so they will form perfect butt joints. The parts must be carefully aligned to begin with.

6-87.   You can use a similar idea to get perfect edges for miter joints. Be sure to situate the pieces at the correct angle.

The Router as a Shaper

The router can provide many of the advantages of a stationary shaper as long as it is mounted, inverted, to the underside of a stand that you buy or make. Many manufacturers offer stands that are similar to the one in Figure 6-88. Some are designed to take most any router, while others can be used only with a specific product. What all of them provide, in addition to the stand, is individually adjustable fences so depth of cut can be controlled and so they can be organized to provide support for workpieces whether you are making a partial cut or one that removes the entire edge of the stock—which is exactly the way a stationary shaper is used. The fences are set in line for a cut like shaping a top edge of a workpiece. When the cut is deeper, in essence one that reduces the width of the work, the outfeed fence is placed forward of the infeed fence an amount equal to the stock that is removed so that the work will have support after it has passed the cutter.

How much you can do with a router/shaper stand depends on the tool you use. A heavy-duty router, especially one that can be used with ½″ shank bits, is recommended, although not essential. Much depends on the kind of work you will demand from the unit.

Making your own shaper table has some advantages. You can decide how large a table you want. When the unit is designed as a floor model you can use it anywhere without having to worry about bolting it down, and you'll have room to install storage drawers.

One that I made for myself, and which gets considerable use in my shop, is shown in Figure 6-89. It has large fences that are individually adjustable to or fro and which can also be moved laterally to minimize the opening around cutters. It is equipped with two guards, one for fence work, the other for freehand shaping against fulcrum pins; a technique that is used when the shape of the work doesn't allow it to be guided by a fence.

6-88.   Stands are available so a portable router can be used like a stationary shaper. The idea makes the router even more versatile.

6-89.   A router/shaper stand that you can make. It features heavy-duty, individually adjustable fences, an aluminum clad work surface, and guards.

6-90. The stand has its own on-off switch so you don't have to keep reaching under the table to use the one on the router. Don't let the router keep running unnecessarily.

The only custom aspect of the stand is the recess on the underside of the table to suit the router's base. You may also have to cut a groove to accommodate a D-shaped router handle. Allow the router to run only when you are cutting. That's why the outside on-off switch is included; it makes turning on and shutting down easy (Figure 6-90). There is little point in letting those tiny ball bearings in the tool run at high speeds unnecessarily. Another point, since the tool is used in an inverted position, it might catch more waste than usual. Check occasionally—remove waste with a blower or small brush.

Figures 6-91 through 6-94 show a few, typical router/shaper stand operations. Construction details and a materials list for a stand you can make are shown in Figures 6-95 through 6-97.

Typical Router/Shaper Operations

6-91. Straight shaping is done by moving the work along the fences in the direction indicated by the arrow. Keep the fences in line for partial cuts—offset the outfeed fence when the entire edge of the stock is removed. Use the guard!

6-93. Work edges that can't be guided with a fence can be shaped freehand. Always use the fulcrum pins for bracing the work. Don't work on narrow pieces. Keep your hands away from the cutting area.

6-92. Always use a miter gauge when edge-shaping narrow pieces. Make the slot in the table to suit a miter gauge you have or one that you buy. (Guard removed for clarity.)

6-94. Freehand work MUST BE DONE WITH PILOTED BITS. Arrow indicates the fulcrum pin against which the work is braced before it is moved to contact the cutter. Use the guard!

DETAIL "A"

TO SUIT BASE OF ROUTER

2½"   ½"

DETAIL "B"

2½"   ½"   1½"   1"   ¼"

DETAIL "C"

⅜"   ⅜" TEENUT

FULCRUM PINS
(MAKE FROM
⅜" BOLT)

20   19   18   16   17

8"   8"   9"   2¾"   1"

SEE DETAIL "A"

SLOT = ⅜" x ¾"
OR TO SUIT MITER GAUGE

SEE DETAIL "C"

SEE DETAIL "B"

OPENING FOR BOX
AND ON-OFF SWITCH

33"   14"   ½"   7"   3½"   1½"   3"

20"   19"   1"

RABBET =
½" x 1½"

3½"   ½"

GROOVE = ½" x ¾"

GROOVE = ¼" x ½"

PULL

BEVEL EDGES

SEE MATERIALS LIST
FOR DIMENSIONS NOT
SHOWN ON DRAWING

6-95.   Construction details of the router/shaper project.

6-96. These details show the parts required for the fence assembly and for the two guards.

KEY	PART	NO. PCS.	SIZE	MATERIAL
			MATERIALS LIST FOR ROUTER-SHAPER TABLE	
1	Leg	4	1½″ x 2½″ x 33″	Fir
2	Rail	6	1½″ x 1½″ x 20″	Fir
3	Side	2	¼″ x 16″ x 20″	Hardboard
4	Brace	2	1¼″ x 1½″ x 14″	Fir
5	Shelf	1	¼″ x 17″ x 19″	Hardboard
6	Guide	4	½″ x ¾″ x 18½″	Fir
7	Table	1	1⅛″ x 21″ x 24″	(See note)
8	Cover	1	.025″ x 21″ x 24″	(See note)

(Continued on next page)

KEY	PART	NO. PCS.	SIZE	MATERIAL
\multicolumn{5}{l}{MATERIALS LIST FOR ROUTER-SHAPER TABLE}				
DRAWER				
9	Front	2	¾″ x 7″ x 18″	Pine
10	Side	4	¾″ x 7″ x 17½″	Pine
11	Bottom	2	¼″ x 16″ x 17½″	Hardboard
12	Back	2	¾″ x 6″ x 15¼″	Pine
13	Pull	2	½″ x ¾″ x 10″	Pine
HARDWARE				
14	Connector	6	½″ x 1½″ x 1½″	Metal angles
15	Screws	24	#8 x 1″	Roundhead
16		4	⅜″	Teenut
17		2	⅜″	Nut
18	Stud	2	⅜″ x 4″	Threaded rod
19		2	⅜″	Fender washer
20		2	⅜″	Wing nut
21	Fulcrum pin	2	⅜″ x 2¾″	Make from bolt
FENCE ASSEMBLY				
22	Base	1	1½″ x 5½″ x 24″	Fir
23	Guide	2	1⅛″ x 1⅛″ x 5½″	Fir
24	Fence support	2	1½″ x 5″ x 10″	Fir
25	Fence	2 (L/R)	1″ x 3½″ x 14″	Fir
26	Guard guide	1	1½″ x 3⅛″ x 8″	Fir
27	Guard support	1	1½″ x 5″ x 10″	Fir
28	Shield	1	½″ x 5″ x 8″	"Lexan"
FREEHAND SHAPING GUARD				
29	Height block	1	1½″ x 5″ x 5″	Fir
30	Shield	1	½″ x 10¼″ x 14½″	"Lexan"
HARDWARE				
31		2	¼″	Teenut
32	Stud	2	¼″ x 4″	Threaded rod
33		4	¼″	Fender washer
34		2	¼″	Wing nut
35		1	⅜″	Teenut
36	Stud	1	⅜″ x 5″	Threaded rod
37		1	⅜″	Fender washer
38		1	⅜″	Wing nut
39		6	#9 x 1½″	Roundhead screw
40		4	½″ x ½″	Sq. washer

Notes: Table (#7) made from ready-made glued-up pine slab.

Cover (#8) Wilsonart's aluminum "decorative metal" or do-it-yourself aluminum.

Hardwood like maple or birch can be substituted for fir.

6-97.   Materials list for the router/shaper stand.

Some Special Accessories

The portable router continues to become more and more versatile. There are a host of practical accessories for it in addition to those already shown, and it's logical to accept that more will be introduced. The following illustrations and captions describe some that have been tested with impressive results. All of them are supplied with detailed use-instructions, so you should have no problem getting the most out of them —unless you choose to just plunge ahead, which isn't a wise thing to do.

As a Power Plane
Figure 6-98.

6-98.   When the router is fitted with a special cutter that may have straight or spirally shaped cutting blades, and mounted in a special holder, it becomes a super tool for smoothing edges or reducing stock widths. Many of the jobs done with a hand plane can be done with a router that is equipped with a planer attachment. Such accessories are not interchangeable. To get a match, always purchase the accessory from the manufacturer of the router.

As a Lathe Tool
Figure 6-99.

6-99.   The router, when used with a special "contraption" called a "Router-Crafter" (Sears), can be used, for one thing, to shape table and chair legs in round or square stock up to 3″ square and 36″ long. It's a unique concept, and getting good results isn't difficult. The uses include lathe-type turning, forming flutes and beads, forming spirals or diamond shapes on round stock, and forming shapes by using templates. Since you can use various bits in the router, the effects you can create in any of the tool's modes is virtually unlimited.

As a Bowl Former
Figures 6-100, 6-101.

6-100.   The "Bowl-Crafter" turns a router into an efficient tool for making an almost unlimited variety of bowl-shaped projects. The accessory has its own motor-driven headstock to turn the mounted workpiece. As the workpiece turns, the router-driven bit does the cutting. The accessory can be used with any router that has a 6″ diameter base.

6-101.   Typical projects that you can "turn out" with the "Bowl-Crafter". The initial preparation of the turning blank has a lot to do with the final appearance of the project.

As a Wood Threader
Figure 6-102.

6-102.   A router, any router, can be used to form threads in
wood when it is used with an accessory called the "Beall Wood
Threader". The router is clamped to a device that can be fitted
with various inserts to suit different size dowels or round stock. A
special cutter in the router cuts the threads as the work, guided by
an indexing device, is turned.

As an Edge Crafter
Figures 6-103, 6-104.

6-103.   To cut, or to edge-shape, uniform or wave-shaped edges,
you can work with a router/shaper stand accessory that is called
an "Edge-Crafter". The system can be used on round or oval solid
parts or frames up to 30″ in diameter.

6-104.   A set of guide templates is provided with the "Edge-
Crafter", but you can also make your own.

As a 3-D Carver
Figures 6-105 through 6-107.

6-105.   With a tool called "Router-Recreator" you can carve
3-D figures up to 8″ tall, and do sign plaques, even do some work
on spindles. The router motor and a stylus are mounted on a carriage that can move laterally and to and fro.

6-106.   The stylus, following the shape and contours of the
model, guides the router bit through the cuts it must make. An
adjustable, counter-balancing weight at the rear of the carriage,
makes it easier to move the router about.

6-107. You can make signs or form house numbers with the "Router-Recreator". The stylus can follow stencils or ready-made letters or numbers, or any shaped piece whose outline you wish to duplicate.

6-109. With the "Mill-Route", the router will duplicate any design that you draw or buy. This is a good way to create templates that you first draw on paper. The 3-D carving is possible since the router can be moved in all three dimensions.

The "Mill-Route"
Figures 6-108, 6-109.

For Sign Making
Figure 6-110.

6-108. The "Mill-Route" combines features ordinarily available with a pantograph and milling machine. The router is mounted on a platform which glides easily in any direction on rails. It is also adjustable vertically about 3½". The router always remains parallel to the working surface.

6-110. A layout kit that can be used to produce letters and numbers 2", 3", and 4" high is offered by Dremel, manufacturer of a hand grinder that is often used for light-duty routing, which we'll talk about in a later chapter. The kit includes templates in Old English, Script, and Block styles.

7. The Portable Belt Sander

Of all woodworking chores, the one we most likely want to get through as quickly and efficiently as possible, is sanding—whether it is getting a new project to the point where finishing coats can be applied, or preparing an existing project for a new look. Portable electric tools like the belt sander and the pad sander provide the means of achieving professional results with minimum fuss and effort.

There are two words that can be used to describe the belt sander—tough and fast. It's a super tool for rapid, heavy stock removal. Getting an even, smooth surface on a slab that you can use as a bench or table is one of the impressive belt-sander applications (Figure 7-1). It is often used to strip old paint or varnish, and with a proper choice of abrasive belt, you can use it on non-wood materials like plaster, slate, plastics, marble, and metals. But it's more than a smoothing tool. For example, you will find yourself using it for jobs like removing a smidgen of material from the edge of a door so it will close properly, forming a bevel on a door's edge, or removing excess material on a wood connection. Many times, a joint is deliberately cut so one part will extend more than it should; a rabbet for example, is often cut wider than necessary and the belt sander is used to sand the projection perfectly flush after the parts have been assembled. Other joints that are treated in similar fashion are the through mortise and dovetails. Dowels used to hide screws or to reinforce joints are quickly sanded flush with a belt sander.

Some manufacturers offer accessories so the portable belt sander can be secured in an upright or horizontal position and used as a stationary unit.

Types, Sizes, Speeds

The belt sander drives a continuous loop of coated abrasive over drums or "pulleys", as they are sometimes called, that are located at each end of the machine. One drum, at the rear of the tool, is powered by the motor, usually through a system of reduction gears. The second drum, spring-loaded so it can provide correct belt tension, runs free and has a slight, adjustable swivel action that is used to keep the belt tracking correctly over the drums (Figure 7-2). This has been a manual operation, but some modern units like the one in Figure 7-3 incorporate a system that automatically keeps the belt tracking correctly. It's quite a nice feature since tracking usually requires some attention while the tool is working.

All of the abrasive belt works, of course, but the area that actually contacts the work is determined by the size of

7-1.   The belt sander is a workhorse. It removes a lot of material quickly so it is a popular choice for preliminary work on slabs and rough lumber, but it should not be discounted as a "smoother."

7-2.   The belt-sander motor powers the rear drum through a reduction drive. The front drum is "free", but is used for tracking the belt and to keep the belt taut.

the platen or "shoe" on the bottom of the tool (Figure 7-4). This is usually 3″ or 4″ wide, but platen width is not the only consideration. A 4″ x 4″ platen doesn't provide much more contact surface than one measuring 3″ x 5″, but many users find that the broader surface makes the tool easier to control, especially on wide, flat surfaces.

The size of the tool may be expressed in terms of belt width or belt width plus length. The physical size, weight, and power of the tool usually increase along with increases in belt size. The 3″ x 18″ belt-size unit in Figure 7-3 weighs 6 lbs and is rated at 3.3 amps. The 4″ x 21¾″ belt-size unit in Figure 7-5 weighs almost 11 lbs and is driven by a 9 amp motor that develops 1⅛ horsepower. Also, notice the difference in grip controls. You might use a one-hand grip for some work with the lighter one, but it's not likely that you would try it with the big fellow. The larger unit is designed so that it can be used in a stationary mode by inverting it and clamping it securely to a bench top (Figure 7-6).

The majority of belt sanders, especially large ones, are equipped with dust collection systems or designed so one can be added (Figures 7-7, 7-8). Even though the systems might do a good job, it is still good practice to use a dust mask for extra protection. Dust collection bags should be emptied frequently since a stuffed one will reduce the efficiency of the

7-3.   Compact tool drives the belt at 700 surface feet per minute (sfpm). It provides an impressive amount of sanding surface despite its small size. Design allows a one-handed operation but an assist knob can be used for extra control.

7-4.   The area of the belt that actually contacts the work is determined by the size of the platen. On most belt sanders the width of the platen is 3″ or 4″.

7-5.   Heavy-duty, 1⅛ hp unit drives a 4″-wide belt 1400 sfpm. The tool comes with a dust collection system and features automatic belt tracking. Figure 7-6 shows how it can be inverted and used as a stationary tool.

7-6.   The tool is turned upside down and secured with clamps. Accessory kits for the clamps and a combination guide are available.

7-7.   This 10 lb sander turns a 3″ x 21″ belt at 1300 sfpm. The tool is rated at 6.5 amps. A vacuum dust pickup system is standard equipment.

7-8.   Many belt sanders, like this 3″ x 21″ example, are double insulated. Operators should wear a dust mask even when the tool has a dust collection system.

tool. Clean the bag whenever you change from wood sanding to metal work. Sparks from metal can cause fires in wood dust.

Belt sander speeds are listed in surface feet per minute (SFPM), with the range starting at about 600 sfpm and going up to better than 1500 sfpm. The faster the speed, the faster you can sand, but the speed itself has nothing to do with the quality of the tool or even its capability. A coarse-grit belt moving at high speed will remove stock fastest especially when working across the grain. A fine-grit abrasive can cause burning and can clog quickly when working at a very high speed, but this can be controlled with light feed pressure and taking the time to clean the belt as you work. Any single speed will be a compromise when you consider the variety of jobs a tool can do, but wise tool-handling provides compensation.

Making a Choice

What you plan to use the belt sander for should be a major determining factor when choosing one to buy. A rugged, heavy-duty machine will speed up chores like evening and smoothing large surfaces (Figure 7-9). It will be easier to keep the tool from tilting and gouging the work if it has a broad platen, but it will be a tiresome handful when you use it on vertical surfaces or, possibly, overhead.

On some jobs it will be convenient if you can work up against a vertical surface. For example, you might be sanding a floor or smoothing a shelf and wish to work flush to the wall (Figure 7-10). Many models are shaped to allow for this application, so, if it's important to you, check for projections on the open side of the machine that might prevent such use.

Check to see what is involved in changing the belt and adjusting the drum for correct tracking. Will it be much of a chore to keep the tool properly lubricated? Does it have or will it take a dust bag? Check the balance, the "feel" of the tool, before deciding. If the features of several meet your standards, the more comfortable one might be for you.

Adjustments

Unless the tool has automatic tracking, the idler drum at the front of the machine is adjusted for both belt tension and belt tracking. Abrasive belts are marked with an arrow on their uncoated sides which indicates correct direction of rotation. This is necessary so the seam in the belt will not snag on workpieces. The rotation is clockwise so, when you mount a belt, be sure the arrow points accordingly.

Decreasing the distance between the drums allows you to slip a belt into place. In most cases, this is accomplished by standing the tool on its front drum and pushing down firmly until the drum is locked firmly in a retracted position. After the belt is slipped over the drums a lever, or some similar device, is used to release the front one (Figure 7-11). This pulls the belt taut between the drums to provide necessary tension.

Correct tracking guides the belt in a perfectly straight line over both drums. Any lateral motion would allow the belt to slip off the free end of the drums or to move in the opposite direction where it would rub against the machine's casing. A

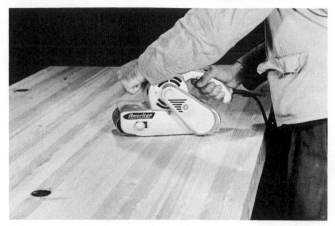

7-9.   A rugged, heavy-duty tool, turning at high speed, makes it easy to even and smooth down large areas. Many operators find that it is easier to keep the tool from tilting when it has a broad platen.

7-10.   Many models are designed so they can be used flush against a vertical surface. Here, even the dust bag doesn't interfere.

7-11.   Belt mounting is accomplished by decreasing the distance between the drums. It's easy to place the belt when the front drum is locked in a retracted position. Spring-pressure causes the drum to snap forward to provide belt tension.

knob on the side of the tool is used to control the angle of the front drum (Figure 7-12). After the belt is mounted and tensioned, turn the tracking knob one way or the other until the front drum appears correct. Then, observe the results as you quickly turn the tool on and off. Make a slight adjustment, if necessary, and turn the tool on and off again. Make a final adjustment with the belt continuing to run.

Tracking is correct when the outboard edge of the belt is in line with the outboard rim on the drums. Tracking may have to be adjusted after you have used the sander a bit and the belt takes a set. This is normal and simply requires an additional touch of the adjustment knob. On the other hand, if tracking requires constant attention return the tool for repair.

Some sanders have a traction block mounted inside the casing at the rear of the idler drum. The block protects the machine against abrasion due to poor tracking. The inboard edge of the belt should parallel to the block. The belt may touch the block, but must not sand into it.

Using the Belt Sander

If you place a belt sander on a surface and then turn it on, the belt will work like the treads on a tractor. The tool will try to get away from you or pull you along with it, but it won't do any sanding. So a primary rule is to grip the tool securely and start it before making contact with the work. Initial contact must be with the platen flat on the work. Only part of the belt will work if the tool is tilted, and the gouges that result will be difficult to remove. Keeping the sander moving is another important rule; hold it in one spot and you'll have a dent the size of the platen.

Generally, the sander should be moved in long strokes run parallel to the wood grain, working to and fro and moving the tool so you overlap the strokes a bit. If the stroke direction is oblique instead of in-line, you will, in effect, be doing cross-grain sanding which is an acceptable technique at times but not to be used when you are sanding to smooth a surface for finishing coats. Cross-grain lines might not be seen under paint, but even slight ones become very apparent after an application of stain.

The major feature of the belt sander is its straight-line action which makes it easy to sand parallel to the wood grain, and this procedure is what always produces best results. It's even advisable to sand *with* the grain whenever possible since working against the grain can raise a nap which requires more sanding to eliminate. This basic rule can be ignored when you wish to remove a lot of material quickly. Then, working against the grain or across it is the way to go.

Keep the platen flat on the work at all times and don't bear down on the tool more than is necessary to keep the sandpaper cutting (Figure 7-13). Most of the time, the weight of the tool alone will provide adequate feed pressure. Forcing won't accomplish much and can interfere with correct belt tracking. Turn the sander off after you have broken contact with the work and don't set it down until the belt has come to a stop.

Keep the sander on the same plane when you come off the end of the work. Allowing it to tilt will form a ramp or will round off the end of the workpiece (Figure 7-14). Another error to avoid is lifting the tool before the stroke is complete.

7-13.   Normally, the weight of the tool is enough for good contact between the abrasive belt and the work. Maintain a firm grip—keep the tool flat and moving.

7-12.   Manual tracking is done by turning a knob on the side of the tool. This alters the angle of the front drum so the belt can move left or right until tracking is correct.

7-14.   Keep the tool level when you come off the work. Letting it tilt, like this, will form a ramp on the work or round off its edge. Turn the machine off after it is free of the workpiece. Let the belt stop before you set the tool down.

Remember that the sander, especially when coarse-grit belts are used, removes material quickly. So be cautious when sanding veneers or plywood (Figure 7-15). It isn't difficult to sand right through surface plies. This is especially important when working on fancy hardwood plywood where surface veneers might be quite thin.

Keeping Work Secure

Just as the belt sander can travel like a tractor and take off on its own unless you hold and guide it with firmness, it can grip pieces of wood and throw them back at the operator. Anytime you are sanding material that is not heavy enough to stay put on its own, or is not attached to something solid, secure the job to a bench top or across sawhorses by using clamps or weights, or even by tack-nailing in waste areas. When the part is small, you can secure it by bracing it against a backup strip that is clamped or tack-nailed to a solid surface (Figure 7-16). The backup, of course, must be thinner than the stock thickness.

7-15.   Sanding veneers of plywood calls for careful handling. It's not difficult for a belt sander to get through a tin ply.

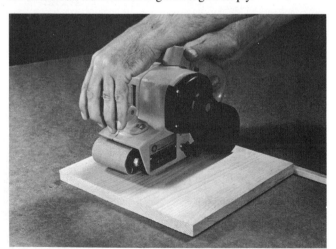

7-16.   Small pieces can be braced securely by backing them against a strip of wood that is tack-nailed or clamped in place. Never try to hand-hold small work.

Some types of clamps, like the "Tru-Grip" model shown in Figure 7-17, do nicely as work holders since they have back-to-back jaws—one set grips a solid surface, the others secure the work. Even very small pieces can be belt-sanded safely if you improvise a means of keeping them secure. A typical jig, designed to hold discs, is shown in Figure 7-18. The hook prevents the sander from throwing the work, while a cleat braces the jig against the edge of a bench.

7-17.   Clamps that have back-to-back jaws are useful for gripping workpieces. With this design, one set of jaws grips a solid surface while the other set holds the work.

V-SHAPED HOOK

7-18.   You can make special holders to secure small or odd-shaped pieces. A V-hook can be used for square as well as round pieces.

Cross-Grain Work

The cross-grain sanding technique is used to remove material quickly. Moving the sander directly across the grain removes material fastest, but you can also use an angular stroke direction. The method is best for jobs like smoothing down edge-to-edge assemblies that you plan to use as a bench or table top, removing the roughness from a tree slab so it can be used as a bench or coffee table, or doing the initial work that removes roughness from unplaned lumber (Figure 7-19). In all cases, the cross-grain work is a preliminary step. Straight-line passes done with finer grits of abrasive must follow in order to eliminate the scratches that will be on the project. Actually, any sanding will leave scratches or grooves. The idea is to reduce them to the point where they can't be felt and are not visible.

Sanding Edges

You can sand edges with a belt sander but the work requires careful handling of the tool in order to keep the platen flat on the work. The narrower the work, the more difficult this is to do. When there are many pieces to do, they can be clamped together as a pad (Figure 7-20). All the edges will be smoothed, with little danger of tilting the tool since the assembly is sanded as if it were a solid block of wood. The method is applicable in other ways. If, for example, you need to sand curved or pointed ends of fence pickets, clamp a dozen or so as a pad and sand them all at the same time.

When it's necessary to sand a single edge and square-ness of the edge is critical, you can try one of the systems shown in Figures 7-21 and 7-22. The idea is to broaden the work edge to provide more bearing surface for the sander.

7-20.   It's easier to sand edges when you have many similar pieces to do. Clamping them in a pad lets you work as if you were sanding a solid block. Note the backup strip.

7-21.   Adding extra pieces to broaden the work surface is one way to go when you must sand a single edge. The extra strips can be clamped in place or secured with ties.

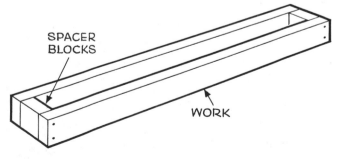

7-22.   Another way to sand a single edge is to make an assembly with an extra support piece. These precautions are necessary only when it is critical for the sanded edge to be square.

7-19.   Cross-grain sanding on rough lumber and the like is usually a preliminary step. In-line sanding with a finer-grit belt is required to bring the piece to acceptable smoothness.

Special Stands

Special stands that allow the belt sander to be used vertically or horizontally in stationary fashion are available as accessories. Most resemble the sketch in Figure 7-23. If you buy one, be sure it is right for the tool you own. Actually, it wouldn't be difficult to make one by imitating the design in the sketch and improvising a means of securing the tool. If you add a groove to the support surface (Figure 7-24), you'll add miter gauge capability to the setup. A later chapter that provides information for constructing a "Sander Shop", shows how you can secure a portable belt sander—and a pad sander—for stationary use.

BELT SANDER

STAND

7-23. Stands, similar to this, are available as accessories—or you can make your own. We'll discuss this use later in the book.

TO SUIT SANDER

MITER GAUGE GROOVE MAY BE INCLUDED

2" STOCK

7-24. Forming a groove in the support surface of an accessory stand that you make will allow the use of a miter gauge. This can be handy when you must sand the ends of narrow pieces.

Removing Old Finishes

Make the first passes with an open-coat abrasive. Select a grit in relation to the thickness of the finish. Thin coatings like lacquer and similar materials don't require very coarse-grit abrasives. You especially want to stay away from coarse grits if the project is made of plywood (Figure 7-25).

Thick coatings of paint, some of which can be softened by the belt's action, will quickly clog even tough, open-coat abrasive belts. In such situations, you can save considerable energy and even some money by removing the bulk of the finish with a heat gun and scrapers or with a solvent that is designed for the purpose. Then, for final touches, you can use a sanding machine.

Generally, it's best to work so you are pulling the sander toward you. Start strokes from the end of the project that is farthest from you, so you will be moving the tool from abraded areas back into painted ones. In most cases, this technique seems to help prevent quick belt clogging. Nevertheless, examine the belt frequently. Keep it as clean as possible by working on it with a stiff brush or an eraser-type product that is made for the purpose. (Further information on abrasives and their use can be found in Appendix 4).

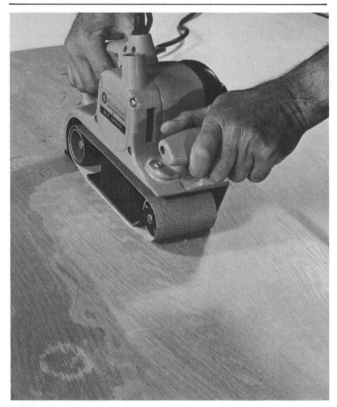

7-25. The belt sander is often used to remove old finishes, but the applications can be overdone. For example, to remove heavy paint coatings, it's best to start with a heat gun and scrapers or a solvent. Then use the sander for the finishing touches.

8. The Portable Pad Sander

The pad sander backs up the abrasive paper with a "soft" material, unlike the belt sander which has a hard platen. It's often called a "finishing sander"; this is a clue to one of the tool's major functions—producing a satin-like surface on many materials before they are coated, and putting a mirror-like gleam on projects after they have been covered with varnish or lacquer or shellac. Often, the sander is used *between* applications of finishing coats, and even to smooth paint jobs.

It might seem that the pad sander is only a light-touch tool, but don't judge it so; it's no sissy. While it should not be used for jobs that can be done better and faster with a belt sander or a hand plane, it does have some heavy-duty capabilities. The kind of hard work you can do with it depends, to some extent, on the type of pad sander you have. A unit that is not much more than palm-size (Figure 8-1) can't be expected to work as fast as a huskier version like the one in Figure 8-2. For one thing, the larger tool has a lot more sanding area.

It's a mistake to assume that the pad sander is just a time saver and a convenient substitute for elbow grease. It's possible to produce fine finishes by hand, but extreme care is required in addition to hard work. The broad, flat pad on the powered sander makes it possible to maintain an even, level, abrasive-to-work contact that is difficult to imitate with fingers.

Types, Sizes, Speeds

Pad sanders operate with the type of mechanism shown in Figure 8-3. The motor, through a unique drive system, causes the pad to move in one of two ways—to and fro in short,

8-1. One-hand, palm-size pad sander is light and easy to handle and can sand flush into corners. It's a super smoothing tool but can be used with many abrasive grits so its use should not be confined merely to finishing chores.

8-2. Larger pad sanders have impressive amounts of sanding area. Units of this type usually have an orbital motion or can be switched from orbital to straight-line action. Being able to work either way is a help on many sanding chores.

CRANK PULLEY

MOTOR

CRANKPIN MOVES SANDING PLATE BACK AND FORTH AS CRANK PULLEY ROTATES

SLIDING BEARING BLOCK MOVES SIDEWAYS

DRIVE BELT

SANDING PLATE

8-3. Mechanism inside a pad sander converts the motor's rotary motion into an orbital or straight-line action. Many modern pad sanders are double insulated.

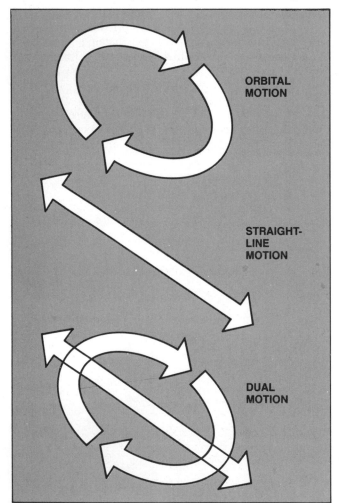

ORBITAL MOTION

STRAIGHT-LINE MOTION

DUAL MOTION

8-4. Typical pad-sander actions. Getting from orbital to straight-line on tools that offer both modes is just a matter of moving a lever.

straight-line strokes, or orbicularly so abrasive grits move in very tiny circles. Some dual-action models offer a choice of both motions—you use a switch or a lever to choose whether the sander will work in an oscillating or orbital mode (Figure 8-4).

In general, orbital sanding works faster and is a little better suited to heavier stock removal because cutting is both 'with' and 'across' the grain. Straight-line sanding is slower, but when done with the grain, produces impressively smooth, swirl-free results. In practice, however, the difference between finishes produced by one action or the other can only be seen with a microscope. One reason is that modern orbital sanders have high speeds and move the sandpaper in tiny circles so that swirl marks are kept to a minimum. In this respect,

8-5. Palm-grip sander delivers 13,000, $\frac{1}{16}$″ orbits per minute. The unit works with quarter-size sheets of sandpaper, which you can buy or cut from standard sheets.

8-6. Unique feature of this sander is that it can be used with 4″ or 5″ square diameter pads. The 1.8 amp, 12,000 orbits per minute tool weighs only 2.4 lbs.

consider the one-handed, palm-grip unit shown in Figure 8-5. It delivers 13,000, $\frac{1}{16}''$ orbits per minute. Actually, most pad sanders available today will be orbital or provide a dual action.

Palm-grip sanders are popular because they are powerful, yet light in weight so they can be handled for long periods of time with less operator fatigue. The sander in Figure 8-6, operates at 12,000 orbits per minute (OPM) with a 1.8 amp motor, yet weighs only 2.4 lbs. A unique feature of this tool is that it can be equipped with 4'' or 5'' diameter pads.

The size of the sanding pad, which is the actual area of contact between the abrasive and the work, is an indication of the amount of work a sander can do. Obviously, the larger the pad the more area it will cover at one time. Pad sizes will vary and, usually, tool weight, size, and horsepower will increase along with greater abrasive area. The double insulated, heavy duty, 4 amp model in Figure 8-7 works with a full half-sheet ($4\frac{1}{2}''$ x $9\frac{1}{4}''$) of standard-size sandpaper.

The size of the sanding sheet the tool can work with is something to consider. If the sheet size is odd, you'll always have to buy directly from the manufacturer or put up with some waste when cutting pieces from standard sheets. Usually though, the tool is designed to eliminate this annoyance.

Some pad sanders are designed to minimize, if not eliminate, the amount of sawdust that escapes into the air. Usually, this is accomplished by enclosing the pad area in a skirt, and providing a collection bag (Figure 8-8).

A new and interesting concept is an air driven, oscillating sander that can be powered by a canister-type vacuum cleaner (Figure 8-9). The unit offers dust-free sanding and, since it doesn't have an electric motor, weighs only about $1\frac{1}{2}$ lbs. The revolutions of the eccentric turbine wheel that creates the movement of the sanding pad can be adjusted with a top-mounted air-flow control. A self-adhesive polishing pad can be used in place of sandpaper so the unit serves as a polisher for automobiles or furniture (Figure 8-10).

8-7. Large pad sanders like this double-insulated unit accept half sheets of standard size sandpaper. Sanding area of about 42 square inches does a lot of work, fast. Levers at each end are for gripping sandpaper.

8-9. Air driven, oscillating sander can be powered by a vacuum cleaner. Unique, eccentric turbine system drives the pad and also collects sawdust. An air-flow control lets the operator control sanding speed.

8-8. Enclosed pad and a collection bag scoop up most of the sawdust. Like all sanders, the trigger switch may be locked in the "on" position, which facilitates using the tool for extended periods.

8-10. By using a special, self-adhesive pad which is supplied with the tool, the air-powered sander can be used for polishing jobs on furniture or automobiles.

Mounting the Sandpaper

In order for a pad sander to work efficiently, abrasive sheets must lie flat and be held taut over the entire area of the pad. If the paper is loose, it won't move with the pad and the amount of sanding it will do, if any, will be minimal. A loose paper is also prone to wrinkles and tearing.

Paper-mounting systems vary from tool to tool. A common method provides spring-loaded clamps at each end of the pad. The paper is gripped by one clamp and then pulled taut and slipped under the second one (Figure 8-11). The paper must be correct in width and length. The paper that comes with the machine will be perfect; it's a good idea to make a matching cardboard template that you can use as a guide when cutting your own replacements. Some manufacturers offer self-adhesive sheets (Figure 8-12). They can be used even though the sander has a clamping system. They are also convenient to have when you need to temporarily change to a different sanding grit. You just stick them on to the paper that is already attached, and then remove them when the current phase of the job is done.

The Pad

All sanders are equipped with a soft pad of felt or some similar material that provides the right flexibility for average work (Figure 8-13). On some materials, like fir with its hard-and-soft-grain characteristics, a soft pad can create depressions between hard-grain areas. In such cases, a hard pad will provide a more efficient backing for the paper since it will span across hard-grain areas. You can provide a hard pad with a piece of thin hardboard that is placed between the original pad and the paper. Slim brads of suitable length can be used to hold the new pad in place, or you can mount the hard pad in place of the original one (Figure 8-14). If you use brads, be sure they are set flush or slightly below the bearing surface of the pad.

8-11.   Abrasive sheets are held, in some way, at both ends of the pad. Be sure to follow manufacturer's instructions. It's critical for the sheet to be flat and taut over the entire pad area.

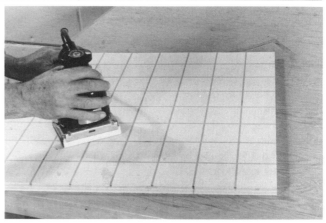

8-13.   The soft pad with which the sander is equipped is fine for general applications. Most of the time, the weight of the sander supplies enough pressure for the tool to work efficiently. Keep the tool moving.

8-12.   Cut-to-size, self-adhesive sandpaper sheets are available. They will adhere directly to the pad or to a sheet that is already mounted. Remove this type of paper once a job is done. The adhesive can take a 'set'.

8-14.   You can make a hard pad by using a piece of ⅛″-thick hardboard. Mount the new pad with short brads directly to the felt, or substitute it for the original pad. In either case, the fasteners must flush or be a bit below the surface of the hardboard.

Conversely, a pad that is thicker (softer) than the one provided can be more efficient when working on curves and cylinders, even on moldings. This type of pad might be offered as an accessory, but you can improvise with pieces cut from an old rug, sponge, or foam rubber. How soft the pad should be will depend on the curves that need sanding. With thicker pads, you must provide longer sheets of sandpaper.

Felt pads can become disfigured and even acquire a smooth patina after extended use. Very bad ones should be replaced, but you can often extend the life of one simply by moving it across a sheet of 60 or 80-grit sandpaper.

A common accessory for pad sanders is a polishing pad. It can be handy to have when you are involved in polishing and waxing chores.

The Pad Sander at Work

How the tool is handled depends to a considerable extent on its design. Palm-grip type sanders are always held with one hand, whereas other types offer options (Figures 8-15—8-17). The extra knob or handle on some units is there mostly so you can provide more control, not so you can 'muscle' the tool to do more work, faster. In some situations, like sanding vertical surfaces, the extra knob provides handling convenience. In most cases, when you are doing routine work on flat, horizontal surfaces, the weight of the tool is about all that's needed for efficient sanding. Too much pressure can harm the tool and leave scratches that you have to remove with more sanding.

Sanding goes faster, but leaves a rougher finish when you move the machine across the grain. Working with the grain is slower, but the work will be smoother (Figure 8-18). It's normal procedure when much sanding is required, to start with cross-grain sanding and then, after changing to a finer grit of sandpaper, finish with with-the-grain strokes. General advice is to start with a coarse-grit paper and work down to the grit that produces the finish you want, but judgments should be made depending on the condition of the work. There is little point in starting with a coarse-grit paper when the work is already reasonably smooth.

8-16.   Larger sanders can also be controlled with one hand, but if you push down, the abrasive sheet will not lay flat on the work surface. Use the hand only for guiding the tool.

8-17.   The extra knob on large sanders permits a two-hand grip, but for more control on rough work, not so you can bear down heavily. It's always best to make several light passes over an area instead of a single heavy one.

ACROSS THE GRAIN—FASTER, BUT ROUGHER FINISH

WITH THE GRAIN—SLOWER, BUT SMOOTHER FINISH

8-18.   Work across the grain only when you wish to remove a lot of material quickly. Always finish the job by making passes that parallel the wood grain.

8-15.   Palm-grip sanders are designed for one-hand operation. They are super tools for producing satin-like finishes, whether working on raw wood or applied finishes.

No matter what the action of the sander, it's usually best to finish sanding jobs by using strokes that parallel the wood grain. If you overlap the strokes by as much as 75%, you'll be sure to get good coverage.

Pad sanders allow working into corners or flush against a vertical surface or edge (Figure 8-19). This applies whether you are sanding a vertical or horizontal surface. It's usually the 'open' side of the sander that you can bring to bear against an obstruction, but the sanding action being used can also affect how you should work. Anyway, you'll know when you are wrong because the contact between the tool and the obstruction will cause excessive vibration and noise.

Sanding Edges

When sanding edges, a two-hand grip helps to keep the tool level so you don't round off corners. If you apply too much pressure, the pad will 'bend' over corners and you'll have a convex edge instead of a square one. Edge sanding isn't difficult to do freehand, but when squareness is critical, you can use some of the ideas that were explained in the chapter on the belt sander. Pieces can be clamped together and sanded as if they were a solid block. Bearing surface for the sander can be increased when sanding a single edge by adding side strips, and so on. The object is to provide enough work surface so it will be easier to keep the sander on a level plane.

Keeping Work Firm

If you are working on a small part, and it is not secured in some way, it will probably move along with the action of the tool and sanding will be nil. Unless the workpiece is substantial enough to stay put on its own it should be secured to something solid with clamps or gripped in a vise (Figure

8-20). A fixed workpiece allows you to concentrate on controlling the sander.

In some situations, especially when odd-shaped parts are involved, it pays to work as shown in Figure 8-21. An extra piece of wood, which can be the waste that remained after the work was shaped, is clamped along with what must be sanded. This technique helps in two ways—it provides good tool support, which is nice especially when using a large machine, and it assures that the work edge will be flat.

8-20.   Keeping the work still is essential for good sanding results. If you don't use very light pressure, and keep the tool level when sanding edges, you may get a convex edge instead of a flat one.

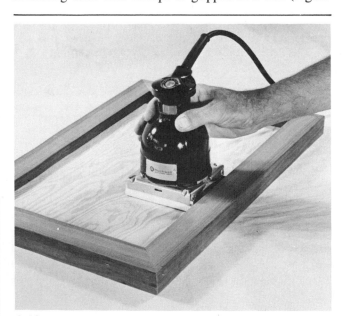

8-19.   Pad sanders can be used in corners and flush to obstructions. It's usually the open side of an oscillating sander that can be used this way. Either side can be used if the sander has a straight-line action.

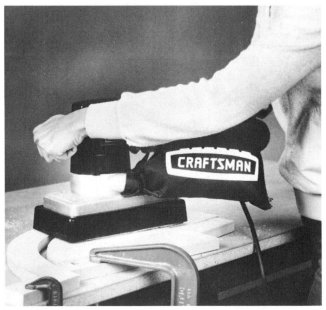

8-21.   Clamping scrap pieces together with the work is a means of keeping a sander on a level plane. It's an especially good way to go when the part being sanded is narrow.

As a Sharpener

A pad sander will never replace an efficient grinder or honing machine, but when it is fitted with a hard pad and a very fine emery paper, it can be used to do touch-up work on butt or lathe chisels, plane blades, knives, and the like (Figure 8-22). This is not a grinding operation—it's not suggested that you use this technique to *renew* edges, but it's a handy way to maintain the keenness of cutting edges. Apply the tool very carefully so you don't cut into the abrasive or the pad.

Sanding Finish Coats

A pad sander is a fine tool to use to smooth surfaces between applications of finishing coats, and to even add a subtle patina to final coats of lacquer, enamel, shellac, varnish, or whatever. How you work on the final application will depend on the material involved and the gloss, or lack of it, you want. A common procedure is to use a ready-made 'rubbing compound'; a standard material that is available in auto-supply stores and many hardware stores.

The compound, which feels like a very fine powder, is sprinkled over the work surface and then gone over with the sander using a piece of carpeting in place of the regular pad and paper. Burlap may also be used, and it is often possible to use the material simply by wrapping it tightly about the base of the machine and gripping it tightly with one hand as you use your other hand to move the tool about.

For a superfine finish on furniture, you can do wet sanding with a silicon-carbide, superfine-grit, waterproof paper mounted on the sander. There are many lubricants you can use for wet sanding, but many professionals still adhere to the clean water and soap combination. The technique involves rubbing the abrasive paper with ordinary hand soap and wetting the work surface with a sponge.

Another mixture often used by professional finishers is a combination of 'pumice' or 'rottenstone' and a light or heavy oil. Often, just a light oil and a very fine emery paper will produce a finish you like. Even though most modern tools are double insulated, it's wise to take extra precautions when work involves electricity and liquids. Wearing tight-fitting rubber gloves and insulated shop shoes is one way to work carefully.

Applying a wax finish is fairly straightforward. Apply the wax by hand, spreading it uniformly in a thin coat. Then make a pad of cheesecloth or some similar material and place the sander in the center of it. Apply just enough pressure on the sander to allow its action to move the cloth pad.

8-22. A sander that is equipped with a hard pad and very fine emery paper can be used to maintain edges on various cutting tools. Don't use this technique to *reshape* edges; that's a job for a grinder.

9. Portable Disc Sanders and Polishers

Portable disc sanders and polishers belong in the category of abrasive tools, but their functions are often misunderstood and unappreciated. While there is overlap in the functions of various sanding machines, those that use a disc to do the work have distinctive features and special applications. They are not substitutes for pad or belt sanders anymore than the latter tools can replace disc-drivers. Overall, as far as use and even appearance are concerned, it is the word 'disc' that supplies the clue to the major distinctions.

There are various types of tools in this category and some confusion can result. For example, one tool that is designed for sanding can have a twin that is best used for polishing. The units shown in Figures 9-1 and 9-2 have the same specifications except for one critical factor. The disc *sander* has a no-load speed of 4000 rpm; the disc *polisher* turns at 2000 rpm. Polishers operate at speeds that are less than sanders require for efficient abrading.

The names of the tools may include 'disc sander', 'disc polisher', 'disc sander/polisher', or 'disc sander/grinder'. A combination sander/polisher (Figure 9-3) may offer a choice of speeds or it may have a single speed, in which case the speed would probably favor the polishing mode. This is logical since too much speed when polishing or buffing can cause burn marks.

Newcomers among disc polishers, simply called 'polishers' or 'buffer/polishers', offer unique work-actions. The one shown in Figure 9-4 has a random orbit action which, in a sense, simulates the motion of hand polishing. Another unit will have an elliptical action, also intended to move the pad about as you would move a cloth with your hand. These tools, which are strictly for polishing, may have two speeds; a low one, in the area of 1700 to 1900 rpm for applying wax, and a high one that might range from 1900 to 2400 rpm, for buffing and polishing.

The sander/grinder (Figure 9-5) is always a heavy-duty tool. Speeds are generally high, running in the area of 5000 to 6000 rpm, and they have workhorse motors—one, two, even three horsepower is not unusual. Accessories for these units, in addition to abrasive discs and grinding wheels, include

9-1.   This 7″ disc sander works at speeds of 4000 rpm and can do a variety of finishing jobs on wood or metal. The size of the tool is stated in terms of the diameter of the backup pad it is equipped with.

9-2.   This 7″ disc *polisher* has the same specifications as the disc *sander,* but there is a critical difference. Its speed is 2000 rpm as opposed to the sander's 4000 rpm. Typically, both tools have built-in lock buttons, which is a convenience for continuous use.

9-3.   This 7″ unit is used as a sander when the backup pad is covered with an abrasive sheet or as a polisher when the pad is covered with a bonnet. Single choice speed is 2400 rpm.

9-4.   This 8″, random-orbit disc polisher is designed to simulate the motion of hand polishing. The ¾ hp motor provides ample power for waxing and polishing tasks. This two-speed tool has a high speed of 2400 rpm and a low speed of 1950 rpm.

9-5.   The disc sander/grinder is always a heavy-duty tool that will stand up under the kind of continuous work that is characteristic of automobile repair shops.

items like cup wheels and wire brushes. This is the kind of tool that is found in welding shops, auto-body repair and remodeling garages, and so on—any place where heavy-duty sanding and grinding are continuing, routine chores (Figure 9-6).

Offset and In-Line Designs

The in-line design looks pretty much like a portable drill. The weight of the motor is near to or directly over the center of the disc. The control handles are in positions that will be familiar to you if you have done any portable drill work at all.

A right-angle bend is the major feature of offset versions. Since these tools usually have a longer body, your hands will be more widely separated; one on the main handle of the tool, the other on an auxiliary knob, or handle, as the case may be. Most of the time one hand will guide the tool while the other exerts as much pressure as is needed for the tool to work. Favoring a light feed pressure is usually much better than forcing the tool. Abrasive discs are cutting tools and, like saw blades, should not be pushed beyond what they were designed for.

Longer tools provide more reach, which can be helpful under certain conditions. For example, it's easier to reach the center of the top of an automobile with an offset polisher.

Choosing a particular design has a lot to do with personal preference. Considering the work these tools are specifically designed to do, the offset is often preferred, even though for average jobs the in-line tool will probably feel more comfortable for most people. It seems easier to let the weight of the tool supply pressure to the pad. With an offset, a lot of the tool's weight is between your right hand and the working end of the machine. This pretty much dictates that your left hand supply any pressure that is needed above what is naturally available simply by resting the abrasive disc on the work. Of course, that's not a good idea with any of the tools. The disc is a wheel and will move in circles unless you keep it where it should be working.

Controlling an offset isn't more difficult than handling an in-line unit. You just adapt to a new handling technique and soon become at ease with the tool.

9-6.   The roughness of this much-used welding table was no match for a sander/grinder. Jobs like this can throw off sparks and a lot of metal particles, so work should be done in a clean area. Safety goggles—with all sanding operations—are a must!

Using a Disc Sander

Like the belt sander, a disc sander is an abrading workhorse. In many situations, like doing preliminary smoothing work on rough lumber, a disc rotating a coarse-grit paper will remove stock faster than a belt sander (Figure 9-7). But there is a catch. Because the sanding action is circular, which means consistent cross-grain cutting, a disc can't do as smooth a job as a belt or pad sander. Of course, it just isn't designed for that purpose. It does star on first-step work on soft or hard woods, 'taking down' and feathering filled dents on automobile bodies, refinishing metal surfaces, removing old paint, and even, with the correct abrasive, smoothing stone or concrete.

To get to a fine finish on rough stock, you can start with a disc sander and then complete the job with a belt or pad sander. Since you can mount sandpaper of various grits on a disc sander, it's often possible to go directly to pad sanding after the disc-tool has done its job. Less critical surface preparation, like exterior paint jobs, may require nothing but the disc, especially if you use one of the new foam backup pads with a fine paper. Overall, it's wise to remember that the disc has a rotary action which is essentially cross-grain sanding.

A particular handling technique is necessary for efficient portable disc sanding. Never place the disc flat on the work and always keep it moving. If you let the disc make full contact and keep it in one place, you will do nothing but cut concentric grooves. Also, since a lot of the waste will not be thrown off, the abrasive paper will clog very quickly (Figure 9-8).

A primary rule is to tilt the machine a bit and to apply just enough pressure to bend the rubber backup pad (Figure 9-9). Quite often just the weight of the tool will be sufficient to do the job. You can judge if additional pressure is required by how the work is going, but never force the tool to the point where the speed of the disc's rotation is drastically reduced.

9-7.   A disc sander is probably the fastest stock remover of all sanding tools, but since the circular cutting action is primarily across the grain, the work will have to be smoothed with a belt or pad sander.

9-9.   Using only part of the disc, and keeping the tool moving, is the most efficient way to use a disc sander. A light touch is always better than a forced one.

9-8.   Working with the abrasive disc flat on the work will create concentric grooves and will clog the paper very quickly, especially if you don't keep the tool moving. This technique is not good practice.

9-10.   The tool must be tilted so only part of the disc will be used, but an extreme angle will limit sanding to the disc's edge and this will result in more 'grooving' than smoothing.

Tilting the tool too much is almost as bad as not tilting it at all since only a small part of the disc will make contact and this will do more circular grooving than sanding (Figure 9-10). In any case, the excess tilt doesn't take maximum advantage of the abrasive disc. The general rule for efficient operation is to keep the machine positioned so that about one quarter to one third of the abrasive surface is in constant contact with the work (Figures 9-11, 9-12).

Other rules to follow are—turn on the motor and let the disc come to full speed before you make contact with the work and keep the tool moving constantly. A haphazard feed pattern might be acceptable at times, but it is generally incorrect. It's best to work with sweeping, straight-line, over-lapping strokes. Even with a disc sander, you'll get optimum results by working parallel to grain lines when you are doing the final strokes.

Open-coat abrasive paper is recommended for general use; it's essential when you are removing an existing finish.

Coarser grades of sandpaper will rough out material very quickly. Finer grades won't cut as fast but will produce smoother finishes. Generally, coarse grades should be used on hardwoods, at least to begin with, whereas finer grades are better when sanding softwoods.

When using a disc sander to clean a metal surface, say the table on a saw (Figure 9-13), always use a tender touch and a very fine emery paper. The tool should just 'whisper' over the material. Finishing the job with a pad sander is a good idea.

Replace the abrasive disc when it is dull or has become clogged and glazed with paint. You can try to renew clogged discs by using one of the methods suggested in the Appendix dealing with abrasives, but if the attempt isn't successful, discard the disc. There are times when you can get more from a worn disc by using it in place of a new disc of finer grit. It's also true that a worn disc, so long as it isn't completely shot, will produce a smoother finish than you can get with a new disc of the same grit number.

When doing extended sanding, use a brush or even a vacuum cleaner to remove loose grit, paint particles, or any waste material. This will lengthen the life of the abrasive and will prevent scratches that can be caused by foreign material that is stuck between grains of abrasive.

When sanding existing finishes you may find that a high sanding speed may soften the material being removed—especially if it is paint—and cause the disc to clog very quickly. When this happens, and assuming the tool allows it, switch to a lower speed; this will reduce heat buildup. If the precautions you take don't lead to an acceptable procedure, it might be best to remove the bulk of the material by working with scrapers or solvents made for the purpose.

9-11.　The correct tool-tilt will allow much of the abrasive disc to work without causing gouging problems.

HOLD AT
SLIGHT ANGLE
FOR SMOOTH CUT

9-12.　Hold the tool so about one quarter to one third of the abrasive will contact the work. Position yourself so waste will be thrown away from you.

9-13.　Nowhere is the tender-touch technique more advisable than when you are smoothing or cleaning a tool's table-surface. Use a very fine emery paper—finish with a pad sander.

Stationary Mounting

Some manufacturers offer a special stand as an accessory so the tool can be secured and used in stationary fashion. If not, or if you choose, you can create the same kind of setup for an offset or in-line tool by making a jig (Figure 9-14).

Another improvisation that can be very handy when using an in-line tool for waxing and buffing floors is shown in Figure 9-15. This idea works best when the tool has auxiliary-handle mounting holes on each side. Then it's easy to mount and secure the yoke.

Polishing

A disc polisher, or disc sander/polisher, can be as handy around the house as it is in the shop. Getting a smooth, glossy surface on a car, walls and floors, and furniture becomes an almost-pleasant chore when you can do it with power.

When polishing, tool handling doesn't differ too much from disc sanding except that, with the tool's backup pad covered with a suitable bonnet, it's okay to rest the bonnet flat on the work surface, at least at the start of the job. You can end with the tool tilted some, using only part of the bonnet in smooth, sweeping stokes. If you have a two-speed tool, you should, of course, switch to the low, polishing speed.

Hold the tool firmly but operate with an easy, free motion. It's never necessary to bear down on the tool; its weight alone will supply as much pressure as is needed for good polishing results.

Keep the tool moving. Use long, sweeping motions in a back-and-forth, overlapping pattern that covers the work. Working with a circular or spiral pattern usually leaves visible swirl marks.

Be sure to read the instructions on the container of wax or polish you use. Some materials must be buffed while in a damp state; others must be allowed to dry. Use polishes, compounds, or wax that are designed for machine application. Some that are intended for application by hand will quickly mat a powered polishing pad and can result in smears and even burn marks on the work.

When working on vertical surfaces, it's more convenient to start at the top and work down. Dust and film from completed sections will be cleaned away as you move downward. On horizontal surfaces, start at the point furthest away from you so you won't be dragging the tool's power cord over finished areas.

Pads and buffs used on a machine polisher will become clogged or gummed up after they have been used a while. They can often be renewed with a thorough wash in soapy water and a rinse in clear water. Shake off as much of the water as possible and then spin them dry by mounting them on the tool. A lamb's wool bonnet can be treated in similar fashion and left to dry completely while still on the rubber backup pad. This will minimize shrinkage of the bonnet.

Don't forget to wear safety goggles. Buffing and polishing chores can spew out small, harmful projectiles just as disc sanding can.

9-14. You can use designs like this to organize an offset tool (top) or an in-line tool (bottom) for stationary use. Plywood can be used for all parts except the split clamp. Make the clamps from 2″-thick solid stock with the holes sized to suit your machine.

9-15. A pivoting yoke, attached to the tool like this, will make it much easier to use a disc polisher on floors. The handle can be a length of aluminum tubing or heavy dowel. The opening in the yoke must be sized to suit the tool. Use bolts through holes in the yoke and into the tool's side-handle holes.

10. Portable Power Planes

Any woodworking chore that can be done with various types of hand planes, including rabbeting planes, can be done faster, even better, with a portable electric plane. Actually, these tools will also accomplish many of the jobs normally done on a jointer (some are called planer/jointers) or with a planer blade that is mounted on a table saw or radial arm saw.

Many of the tools are real huskies, with an impressive depth of cut and the ability to smooth wide swaths in wood (Figure 10-1). Others, like the block plane shown in Figure 10-2, while no less capable, are handled with a more tender touch. Being able to remove as much as ⅛″ of wood in a single pass, as some of the tools can do, *is* impressive, but to me, the products are intriguing because of how easily they can accomplish the *minimum* cut. Planing off see-through shavings is no chore for any of them.

Such control, for example, makes it less likely that you will make a costly or unsightly error when fitting house or cabinet doors. This applies especially at the top or bottom of

the door where you are shaving end grain on the stiles. The minimum cut, plus the high rpm of the tool's cutters, do such jobs with negligible feathering and with far less chance of splitting.

Actually, you have a choice of how you equip yourself for power planing. The *power plane* is a tool in itself. It owns a built-in motor and removable cutter which might have the spiral configuration shown in Figure 10-3, or a cutterhead with replaceable blades, something like the arrangement found in jointers. The tool works in single-purpose fashion. It's a *planer*.

The *plane attachment* is an accessory for a portable router. When the router is fitted in the accessory and equipped with a special cutter, it becomes a portable electric plane. A major difference between the true plane and the router/plane is that the former will usually have (not always) a top-side motor, whereas the power source for the other hangs outboard. This calls for a little more control to keep the tool level when planing edges. A fact to consider when

10-1.   If you have ever used a hand plane you will appreciate how a portable power plane lets you do similar chores much faster and with considerably less effort.

10-2.   Block plane is 'palm size' and can be handled with a more delicate touch than is required with heavier versions, but it's no sissy. Cutting width is 1¹³/₁₆″. Spiral-type cutter turns at 21,000 rpm.

making a choice is this: With a power plane, you can do surfacing beyond the tool's maximum width of cut by making repeat, overlapping passes. You can't work that way with an attachment or, for that matter, with a power plane whose design permits working only on edges.

Types, Sizes, Speeds

One feature all the modern planers have in common is speed: most work in the area of 20,000 rpm. It's interesting, and also makes a point, that while there are differences in how wide a tool can cut, the difference in depth of cut between a "large" tool and a "small" one is rarely extreme. The block plane that was shown in Figure 10-2 has a depth-cut of $1/64''$, whereas the larger, more powerful tool in Figure 10-4 has a maximum cut-depth of $3/32''$.

There are more noticeable differences in width of cut. All the planers can cut across the narrow edge of 2"-thick stock (which actually measures $1\frac{1}{2}''$). Some can plane across the wide edge of a 2x4 (which has a real dimension of $3\frac{1}{2}''$). The average range is about 3" to $3\frac{1}{4}''$. If you plan to use a plane a lot for dressing rough lumber and for reducing stock thickness, then width of cut can be an important factor, since a greater cut-width will require fewer passes to get across wide stock. If your work will be mostly on stock and door edges, and it usually is, then the cut-width factor becomes less important.

Some of the tools have adjustable edge-guides as standard equipment, others do not, but can be equipped the same way with optional accessories (Figures 10-5, 10-6). Adjustable edge guides are important since they allow organizing the tool for accurate beveling and chamfering.

10-3.   Spiral-type cutters are common on many portable electric planes. Some units have jointer-type cutterheads with replaceable knives. It's critical to keep cutting edges keen no matter what the design.

10-5.   This 3" plane is equipped with reversible, double-edged carbide blades. Combination edge and bevel guide can be adjusted up to 45°. Interesting feature is a V-groove in the footplate which makes it easier to do chamfering jobs.

10-4.   "Porta-Plane" is rated at 7 amps and has a cutter speed of 22,000 rpm. It can remove $3/32''$ of material in a single pass on stock up to $2^{13}/32''$ wide. All planers have a depth of cut adjustment so you are not confined to a single cut-depth.

10-6.   This $3\frac{1}{4}''$ product has a maximum depth of cut of $1/64''$ but can cut rabbets up to $9/16''$ deep. The 3 amp motor drives the cutterhead at 20,000 rpm. Like many other models, the unit is double insulated.

The unit shown in Figure 10-7 can be converted into a benchtop jointer by means of a special stand. Most planers can be used for rabbet cutting, but the maximum depth of cut for such work will vary from tool to tool.

Planing with Power

Be sure to strictly follow the alignment procedures that are outlined in the manual that comes with the tool. The horizontal plane of the rear shoe *must* be tangent to the cutting circle. The fence, when one is used, must be at a right angle to the shoe at the zero setting. If these relationships are not provided for correctly, and maintained, you'll get bevels instead of square cuts, and will probably create gouges in the work edge (Figure 10-8).

The secret to good work is controlled, uniform pressure down on the tool throughout the pass. Use both hands; one on the main handle of the tool, the other up front (Figure 10-9). Start cuts by placing the front shoe on the work and applying downward pressure with the hand that's up front. As the cutter engages, apply downward pressure equally with both hands. This can change toward the end of the cut. You can relieve the left-hand pressure and exert more with the right hand. The idea is to keep the tool on an even keel. It's also a good idea to let up a bit on feed-speed as you near the end of the cut to minimize chipping and feathering that can occur as the cutter leaves the work.

Chipping and feathering will occur to a greater degree when planing across end grain and when working on plywood (Figure 10-10). Two methods you can use to completely eliminate these negative possibilities are shown in Figure 10-11. Clamp a scrap piece to the end of the work so it instead of the work will take the abuse, or do the planing on a piece that is slightly oversize, and then saw its end off. You're more likely to get a lot of splintering at the end of the cut when planing across end grain on lumber, but here too, a scrap block clamped to the work as shown in Figure 10-12 will provide a solution.

10-8.   Gouges in the work can be the result of poor tool handling or misalignment. Some feathering or splintering is usual at the end of a cross-grain cut, but can be eliminated by following particular techniques.

10-9.   Secret to good work is controlled pressure down on the tool throughout the pass. Some tools have a thumb indent up front for a comfortable, non-slip grip.

10-7.   Lightweight unit still has a 3¼″ cutting width and a ⁵⁄₁₆″ rabbeting depth. The ⅖ hp motor turns the cutter at 19,000 rpm. It features double-edge throwaway blades that are easy to replace and a stand that converts it into a benchtop 'jointer'.

10-10.   Flaws like this will occur on plywood regardless of whether the planer is moved across or parallel to the grain of the surface veneer. They can be minimized by making extremely light cuts, or eliminated by using one of the methods shown in Figure 10-11.

You can move the tool faster on material like pine than you can on hardwoods. The idea is to adjust the feed speed in relation to the material so the blades will cut consistently but without overloading the motor. On the other hand, you can't be overcautious. Feeding too slowly can cause premature wear on the cutter and can even cause burn marks on lumber or plywood.

The wise general rule is to take it easy with depth of cut. Results are usually better when you accomplish a cut in two passes, even though the tool has the power and the depth of cut to do the chore in a single pass.

If you are working on an uneven edge—one that is slightly wavy—draw a pencil line from end to end on the stock so you can isolate the high spots. Plane this down first before you make full-length passes.

Bevels and chamfers are not more difficult than square cuts. Adjust the guide fence to the angle you need and proceed in normal fashion. A slight chamfer can be accomplished in one pass, but full bevels require multiple passes (Figure 10-13). Full bevels are wider cuts than square ones so it's usually better to slow up a bit on feed-speed.

Always try to feed the tool so it will cut *with* the grain of the wood. When planing four edges, or two adjacent ones, make the cross-grain cuts first. The final with-the-grain cuts will remove any imperfections that occur at the end of the first passes.

Rabbeting

To form a rabbet, you must organize the planer so that only a limited length of the cutter does the work. Some units incorporate a means of accomplishing this. The unit shown in Figure 10-14 has an L-shaped cut machined in the right side of the front shoe. This cut is held firmly against the side of the

10-11.   To eliminate end-flaws, clamp on a scrap block to take the abuse, or work on an oversize piece so you can trim off the bad end.

10-12.   Use the clamped block idea when planing end grain on lumber. The precaution isn't needed when planing with the grain on stock edges.

10-13.   Bevels or chamfers are done by adjusting the fence to the angle you need. Be sure to keep the fence snug against the side of the work. Chamfers can be accomplished in one pass, but full bevels require repeat strokes.

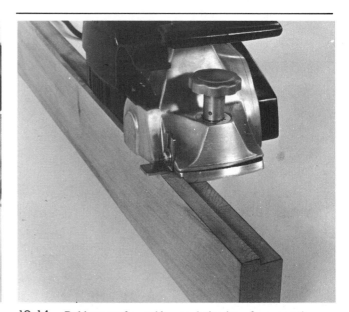

10-14.   Rabbets are formed by regulating how far across the board the cutter will extend. This determines the width of the rabbet. Adjustable angle on this tool is set to gauge the depth of the cut.

board while the rabbet is being formed. The rabbeting plate, which is just a metal angle, is secured at a particular height to judge the depth of the rabbet cut. In any case, and since correct procedures can differ from tool to tool, a wise operator follows the instructions that are supplied by the manufacturer.

You can improvise to some extent, but it's something to do only when the tool isn't equipped for the job. One way is shown in Figure 10-15. A block of wood secured to the tool's fence acts as a width-of-cut control as the planer forms the rabbet (Figure 10-16). The width of the wood block determines the working length of the cutter.

10-15.   Lacking other means, you can do rabbeting by attaching a strip of wood to the tool's fence.

10-16.   The thickness of the wood-strip determines how far across the board the cutter will extend. Keep the strip snug against the side of the work throughout the pass.

Another idea is shown in Figure 10-17. Here, the guide is L-shaped and slotted so it can be moved across the base of the tool. Thus, it is adjustable for rabbets of various widths. It is assumed that the design of the planer will allow this type of guide to be attached securely and without interfering with the tool's mechanism.

Making a Jointer Jig

The jig that is shown in Figure 10-18, and detailed in Figure 10-19, allows a planer to be used somewhat like a stationary jointer. There are too many planers around of different shapes and sizes for one jig to be right for all of them, so a little, or maybe a lot of modification is in order. The jig that was photographed was designed around a Stanley router/plane that's been a friend in my shop for many years. The jig has a block to support the motor and a channel that can be tightened with a C-clamp to secure the plane's handle (Figure 10-20).

A spring-loaded guard lets work pass over the cutter and returns automatically to cover the cutter after the pass is complete—just like a real jointer (Figure 10-21).

Planing Safely

While the openings around cutters are minimal, the cutters are always exposed. So make it a habit to keep your hands topside. Turn the motor off at the end of a cut and allow the cutter to stop turning before you set the tool down. Never touch the cutters for any reason while the tool is plugged in. Always let the motor come to full speed before starting a cut.

Keep the cutters sharp; this contributes to better work and to safety. Most manufacturers offer special sharpening devices. Owning one of these devices, and using it as often as necessary, is a good idea.

10-17.   Whether you can use an adjustable L-shaped guide like this one will depend on the design of the tool. You must be able to attach the guide securely to the base of the tool. Always check the owner's manual to see if, and how, rabbeting can be accomplished without improvising.

Jointer Jig

10-20.   The jointer jig is more adaptable to a planer that has an outboard power source. The wood block supports the motor, while the handle of the tool is gripped in the plywood channel.

10-18.   A jointer jig lets you use a portable planer in stationary fashion. This prototype was made for a Stanley router with a planer attachment.

10-21.   Jointing is done as it would be on a stationary machine. Keep the work snug against the fence and firmly down on the planer's base throughout the pass. The spring-loaded guard moves aside during the pass, then returns to cover the cutter when the pass is complete.

GUARD $\frac{1}{2}$ X 3" X 5$\frac{1}{2}$"

CHANNEL FOR PLANE HANDLE
MAKE 2: $\frac{3}{4}$ X 3$\frac{1}{2}$ X 10"

PIVOT $\frac{1}{4}$ DOWEL

GUARD SUPPORT
$\frac{3}{4}$ X 4$\frac{1}{2}$ X 7"

TO SUIT

2"

1$\frac{3}{4}$

$\frac{3}{8}$

1$\frac{1}{2}$

SPRING

$\frac{7}{8}$

1$\frac{1}{4}$

SCREW EYES

4$\frac{1}{2}$

5$\frac{1}{2}$

3$\frac{1}{2}$

MOTOR SUPPORT
1$\frac{1}{2}$ X 2$\frac{3}{4}$ X 8$\frac{1}{2}$

BASE
$\frac{3}{4}$" X 12" X 20"

10-19.   Construction details of the jointer jig. It's not likely that the dimensions given here will be exactly right for the tool you own, but the concept is simply to provide a sturdy setting for an inverted planer.

11. Hand Grinders and Flexible Shafts

From woodworker to metalsmith, diemaker to auto mechanic, dentist to podiatrist, the handful of speed and power known as the hand grinder can be a most helpful power tool. Quite often, its real capabilities are not appreciated, probably because its small size creates an image of delicate precision and very light-duty applications. Paradoxically, these qualities in themselves are enough justification for rating the hand grinder as an important shop tool. A touch with a hand grinder will often add a customized look to an otherwise routinely finished project. It can take over where other tools leave off, and it can get into places where other tools can't reach.

Like the router, the hand grinder is essentially an encased motor driving a spindle that has a device at its free end for gripping the shaft of various grinding, shaping, sanding, polishing, and sawing tools (Figure 11-1). It's often called a "hobby" tool, but this is misleading. For one thing, those that are available today are much improved in terms of power and durability. For another, there are a wide range of designs available. Not all hand grinders are "palm" size; those that are recommended for use by automobile mechan-ics, for tool and die shops, as tool post grinders, and so on, are comparatively husky fellows. Weights of small ones might be listed in ounces, while the big ones are called out in pounds.

A clue to the tool's power might be found in the size of shanks its chuck can grip, and even in the design of the chuck. A tool that is designed to grip cutters with a ⅛″ shank doesn't need the same power that is required of another tool that can run cutters with ¼″ shanks (Figures 11-2 and 11-3).

In application, the tools should be visualized as high-speed power sources that will drive an endless assortment of abrasive wheels, brushes, buffs, sanding drums, drill bits, saws, and discs. They can be used for machining jobs on most any material, and also drill, cut, smooth, and polish. You can use these tools to shape or sand wood or metal, and they can also be used on plastics, and to mark steel or glass. Often they enter the area of sharpening, engraving, and routing. You can drill holes with them that would be difficult to do with a conventional drill. Therefore, the term "grinder" does not fully describe the tool. What you can accomplish with one depends pretty much on what you lock in the chuck.

You will find that most of the heavy-duty tools are called "die grinders". This doesn't mean that they can't be used with

11-1.   The hand grinder has a simple concept—a motor drives a spindle which has a gripping device at its free end to secure various types of cutting and abrading tools.

11-2.   Power, speed, and chuck designs can differ from tool to tool. This unit has a conventional 3-jaw chuck which is tightened with a key to secure cutters. Speed is 18,000 rpm; chuck capacity is ¼″.

11-3.   Many high-speed grinders employ a collet-style chuck to grip tool shanks. A wrench is used to turn a nut that squeezes the collet about the shank of the tool. This tool has variable speeds of 5,000 to 28,000 rpm. Note the combination router base and edge guide.

11-4.   Heavy-duty tools like this one are often called "die grinders". Speeds on various models can range from 4,500 to 20,000 rpm. Some can develop as much as 2 hp, yet they can weigh under 3 lbs.

11-5.   Die grinders, while being powerful enough to do what they must, can be deceptively slim. This example has a 2 amp rating, a 25,000 rpm speed, and a standard collet size of ¼″. It can also be used with an optional ⅛″ collet.

small-shank cutters. Those shown in Figures 11-4 and 11-5 will work with either a ¼″ or ⅛″ collet chuck. Often various size chucks are supplied with the tool, and chucks other than the standard ones are available as accessories.

Speeds

The one feature that most hand grinders have in common is high speed. Speeds of 20,000, 25,000, or even 30,000 rpm are not rare. This points out an important fact as far as tool-use is concerned. Speed does the job, not feed pressure. This is the reverse of electric drill use, tools with comparatively low speeds but with high torque. For example, feed pressure is required if a drill bit, for example, is to form a hole. Generally, hand grinders are high speed, low torque tools. It's a rare situation when you must apply any kind of pressure to get a job done. High speed, plus the cutter mounted in the chuck, does the job.

While high speed is generally the rule with hand grinder operations, some new models are designed to provide various speeds, or have an infinitely variable speed control. This is usually a small, numbered dial; each number indicating, approximately, a particular speed. With some models, you can add an external speed control like the benchtop unit shown in Figure 11-6. Other types of speed controls can be operated with a convenient foot switch.

Operations you might want to do at lower speeds include polishing, using wire brushes, or maybe even drum sanding.

Cutting Tools

The word "cutters" is used in a general sense to encompass all items that can be locked in the chuck of the tool (Figure 11-7). Generally, any cutter that has a shank that is larger than ⅛″ is meant for bigger, heavier grinders. When making choices there really is no problem though, since the maximum size of the collet, or collets, that can be used with a tool determines maximum shank-size on cutters.

Cutters are either mounted or unmounted. The mounted ones have the cutter permanently attached to the shaft or they are one-piece units. When the cutter is worn, the unit is discarded. Incidentally, dentists use similar tools in their high speed "machines" but accept minimum use, hopefully, in order to save you discomfort. These partially used cutters are not so dull that they can't be used on wood and metal in a home shop. So, you might ask your friendly dentist to pass over his discards. If what he gives you won't cut wood, change to another dentist!

Unmounted cutters are locked on a special fixture that is called a *mandrel*. This is a shaft with a device at one end for gripping the cutter. The lock-on arrangement may be a small nut and bolt, a straight or tapered length of screw thread, or a flathead screw that is turned into a threaded hole in the end of the shaft. Typical accessories that are designed for mounting on a mandrel are felt wheels for polishing, small buffs, rubber polishers, and small, steel saws.

In most cases, brushes are permanently mounted and are available in various sizes and materials. Steel wire, brass wire, nylon, and bristle are very common. Soft brushes are

11-6.   Hand grinders may have a single speed, variable speed with a built-in control, or speeds that can be controlled with a unit placed between the power source and the tool. Controls, like this one, may be benchtop units, or they may be operated with a foot switch.

CUTTERS FOR CARVING, ROUTING, MILLING, ENGRAVING

STEEL AND BRISTLE BRUSHES

GRINDING WHEELS FOR SHAPING AND SHARPENING

SANDING, POLISHING, AND SAW DISKS

DRUM SANDER   MINIATURE DRILL BITS

11-7.   Typical categories of cutters that can be used in a hand grinder pretty much tell the story of the variety of jobs the tool can be used for.

used for cleaning operations on soft materials, while hard ones do similar operations on denser materials. Hard brushes can also be used to produce a decorative brushed effect on soft metal surfaces. Mild abrasive compounds like rotten-stone, very fine emery powder, or even ordinary household scouring powders can be used with the brushes.

Steel saws can be used to cut wood, some soft metals, and plastics. Hard abrasive discs (sometimes called saws) are good for cutting or slotting nonferrous and ferrous metals and for many operations that are required on stones used in lapidary work.

Drum sanders are miniatures of those used in a drill press or with a portable drill. The diameter of a rubber drum is increased or decreased by means of a screw so that abrasive sleeves can be mounted or replaced. Hard, mounted abrasive wheels are available in an endless variety of sizes, shapes, grades, and grains.

As you can tell from the types of cutters available for hand grinders, dust and thrown off waste are part-and-parcel of most operations. So, safety goggles and a dust mask should be a standard uniform.

Most grinders use a collet to grip the shank of the cutting tool, and it's important to use the correct one. If you don't the cutter will not be as secure as it must be. The owner's manual that comes with the tool will tell the range of shank sizes a particular collet will grip. For example, a $\frac{1}{8}''$ collet will grip shank sizes from $\frac{3}{32}''$ up to $\frac{1}{8}''$; a $\frac{1}{16}''$ collet will take shanks from $\frac{1}{64}''$ to $\frac{1}{16}''$. There are also adapter chucks that are used with the standard collet for gripping very tiny (#60—#80) drill bits.

Make a Storage Chest

The hand grinder, or a machine that is specifically designed to drive a flexible shaft, can be considered a small workshop in itself. Because the numerous cutting tools and other accessories that go along with a grinder are usually small, easy to damage, or lose it pays to make a special case to house the equipment.

11-8.   A storage case that is easily moved about is a good way to house and protect a hand grinder "workshop". This one is arranged for a motor/flex shaft combination but its interior can be modified to suit your own equipment.

11-9. Cutters can be stored on shelves in various ways. Drill holes for shafted tools; use blunted nails for wheels that have center holes. Note the provisions made for needle files and abrasive sticks.

The case shown in Figure 11-8 was designed for a flex-shaft tool, but its interior can be easily organized to accommodate just a hand grinder or both types of tools. The important thing is to lay out all the equipment you have and to design the case specifically for each piece, to leave room for items you'll probably add. Making the case as a closed box and then slicing off the lid on a table saw or with a handsaw is a good way to assure an accurate fit.

Note in Figure 11-9 that the cutters are stored on shelves that are drilled to receive the tool shanks. This system works very well for mounted cutters. For unmounted units, drive slim nails up through the bottom of the shelves. Be sure to dull the points on the nails.

The overall size of the case (Figure 11-10) is 7½″ x 17½″ x 22½″. These dimensions can be increased a few inches without making the case unwieldy. Install a handle at the top and a latch to keep it closed; then you can tote it about for any work you must do outside the shop.

11-10. Construction details of the tote-about storage case. Add a screen-door type handle for transportation, and a latch to keep it closed.

The Hand Grinder at Work

Always rely on the speed of the tool to do the work. A tool that is running at 24,000 rpm and is driving a cutter that has sixteen cutting edges, is actually making 384,000 cuts every minute. That kind of cutting speed requires only the slightest feed pressure; just enough to keep the cutter in contact with the work. Folks who aren't familiar with hand grinders will often apply enough feed pressure to stall the tool or to seriously reduce its speed. Then feed pressure is reduced to allow the rpm to build up again and, unfortunately, the procedure is repeated. This is bad practice. It doesn't improve the quality of the work, and it can do considerable harm to the tool.

If the tool gets hot, or if there is excessive decrease in speed, it's almost certain that you are forcing the cut; allowing flutes to become clogged and preventing cutting edges from working as they should. Choose the right style of cutter and the right cutter shape for the job you must do, then use a touch that is just enough pressure to keep the cutter working. This practice leads to maximum tool efficiency, and respectable work quality.

Work that is large enough to stay put on its own, or that can be gripped securely in one hand while the other hand manipulates the tool, can be worked on in a freehand manner. Establish one important rule—don't position a hand that is holding the work so that it is in line with the cutter. Then, if the cutter slips from where it should be, it won't cut more than the work.

It's best to grip small work in a vise or to clamp it to a bench top. A handscrew clamp, with cardboard or some similar protective layer used when necessary between the work and the clamp jaws, makes a good "vise" for holding workpieces.

Most of the time, the hand grinder is gripped in one hand, but there is no law to prevent you from using two hands when the operation makes it advisable. Often, it's possible to work more precisely if you grip at the shaft end of the tool with the fingers of one hand and "palm" the other end of the tool in your other hand.

Cutters are so small and take such tiny bites that it's possible to move against the grain without dire results. Even so, to minimize the sanding chores that might still have to be done, make final strokes *with* the grain of the wood.

Particular cutters are often used to leave a textured surface on projects, especially in-the-round or bas-relief carvings. Finishing such work with a fine, soft brush, will remove sharp ridges and clean away tenacious waste particles. A hard brush, steel or brass, will remove soft wood from between hard grain areas on certain woods and create a sculptured effect.

Tool Holders

Because of the variety of accessory holders that are available commercially, and others that you can make, the grinder does not have to be limited to hand-held use. For example, a swivel-type base to which the grinder can be attached allows positioning the tool in an attitude that is most convenient for the work being done (Figure 11-11).

Some stands allow the grinder to be used in combination with other tools. Team it with a lathe or a drill press, for instance, and it functions as a precision milling, grinding, or routing accessory that can do many jobs normally possible only with larger, more costly machines.

There are stands, including the drill-press version shown in Figure 11-12, that allow a hand grinder to be used like a stationary tool. It may be held vertically, horizontally, tipped at an angle, or even inverted for use as a miniature shaper. With the tool in a rigid position, you can apply the work to the cutter as you would with any stationary tool, and this often guarantees precision that is difficult to duplicate when working freehand. It isn't difficult to create a stand for a hand grinder when a particular one isn't available as an accessory for the tool you own.

11-11.   There are many types of tool holders available for hand grinders. This swivel-type base provides a lot of flexibility.

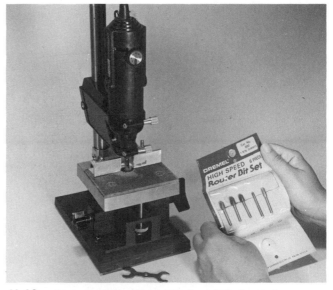

11-12.   Accessories like this one let the grinder be used as a miniature drill press. The table on the drill-press accessory is used for routing operations.

11-13. Special base holds the grinder in vertical position so you can use it for freehand or controlled routing. An adjustable fence is part of this particular unit.

Hand-Grinder Routing

The small hand grinder is not about to rival the big jobs that can be done with a regular portable router, but on a small-job basis it can match a big fellow almost function for function. In fact, for many techniques, particularly in light-cut applications such as inlay or marquetry work, the palm-size tool can be more convenient to use while still doing an exemplary job.

For some hand grinders, especially the Dremel "Moto-Tool", accessories are available that are specially designed so the tool can function as a miniature router-shaper that will do some surprising things in a woodworking shop. The accessories are light and neat, easy to attach and handle, and are used pretty much like conventional router bases. Adjustments are provided for depth of cut, and the accessory may include an edge guide (Figure 11-13).

Routing with the Hand Grinder

11-14. With the grinder mounted in the router base, and the fence (edge guide) attached, the tool can be used for accurate parallel-to-edge cuts.

11-16. A single rod, with a hole through it for a pivot pin, guides the grinder through accurate circular cuts. Accomplish deep cuts by making repeat passes. A slow feed is the answer to quality results.

11-15. The same setup can be used for cuts in stock edges. Always move the router so the cutter moves into the work. This is usually from left to right.

11-17. With just the base, the grinder can be used for free-hand routing. Keep a firm grip since cutting will be done in various directions.

With the grinder mounted in the special base/edge guide combination, you can make straight cuts parallel to an edge like those shown in Figures 11-14 and 11-15. Maximum distance between the fence and the cutter isn't startling, but when it proves limiting you can substitute longer rods for those that are supplied, or you can remove the edge guide and work with a tack-nailed or clamped guide strip as you would with a conventional router.

If you use just one rod, an extra-long one if necessary, you can guide the grinder through perfect circular cuts, again, just as you would with a larger router (Figure 11-16). Work with just the base and you have good control for chores like bas-relief carving (figure 11-17).

The palm-size tool does have limitations. Don't expect to form full-size bead-and-cove or drop-leaf table edges on 1″ stock. Much can be done beyond the full profile shape of the cutter itself, by making repeat passes to deepen or widen cuts, or by using different cutters on the same edge to create an original profile. Some practical applications for the tool when it is fitted with a router base include mortising for hinges and strike plates, raising or incising letters or numbers, inletting for escutcheons, and so on.

How fast you can move the tool and how deep you can cut in a single pass depends on the hardness of the material. In any case, feed must never be so fast or so hard that the tool tends to stall, or that the tool or the cutter get too hot.

As a Shaper

The basic difference between the hand grinder as a router and its use as a shaper, is that in the latter mode the tool is inverted and attached to the underside of a work-support table with flathead screws that thread into holes in the router-base attachment (Figure 11-18). Projects like this can be complicated or as simple as the one shown, but they must be sturdy. Glue blocks, which can't be seen in the photograph and which are not shown in the drawing (Figure 11-19), will reinforce the connection between the top of the project and its legs.

When the grinder is used upside down, its rotation, in a sense, is reversed. Always feed the stock *against* the cutter's direction of rotation. Depth-of-cut, which should never be extreme, is adjusted as it would be normally. Take it easy with feed-speed. As always, don't force the cut. It's bad practice to push hard enough for the tool to slow up excessively.

Other ideas for stands or tables you can make for a hand grinder are illustrated in Figure 11-20 and 11-21.

11-19.   Construction details of a stand that lets the grinder be used as a shaper. Add glue blocks to reinforce the connection between the work surface and the legs.

11-18.   An easy-to-make stand converts the grinder into a shaper. A strip of wood with a true edge is used as a fence. Always move the work *against* the cutters' direction of rotation.

11-20.   A stand like this can be made to hold a grinder in a vertical position.

11-21.   A similar stand will secure the grinder in a horizontal position. Keep the stands secure by clamping them to a solid surface.

Make a Swivel Jig

The unusual fixture that is detailed in Figure 11-22 allows the grinder to be rotated or swung in an arc so it can be used to form decorative cuts like the samples shown in Figure 11-23. The jig is designed so it can be secured to projects that are already assembled, or to components prior to assembly. Take your time when making it; it does require careful work to avoid extra play in either of the actions. The hole in the stand, with a shoulder for the indexer to rest on, can be formed accurately on a drill press, or by using a template-guided router. The indexer plate can be formed in similar fashion. Be sure its outside diameter fits precisely in the hole that is in the stand. Actually, it's best to cut the indexer a bit oversize and then sand it for a perfect fit: it should turn, but without wobble. The swivel collar pivots on pins that pass through the indexing plate (Figure 11-24). Its dimensions, as given in the construction drawing, even its shape, must be checked against the hand grinder you plan to use. Shaping it is a fairly straightforward lathe job, but it also may be made by boring the center hole and then using a coping saw, followed by sanding, to shape its perimeter. Note that two versions of the collar are suggested. One has to be a tight fit for the grinder; the other, which is slotted so it will work something like a split clamp, is tightened with a hose clamp.

Freehand Work

Much work with a hand grinder is done without an attachment or special gadget to guide the tool. Here, more than ever, a wise choice of cutter and a light touch are critical. Keep a firm grip on the tool to keep the cutter working where you want it to. If you are too casual, the cutter will try to move like a wheel. Some typical freehand applications are demonstrated in Figures 11-25 through 11-29.

11-22.   How to make a swivel jig. Careful construction is necessary for the unit to work accurately.

11-23.   A sampling of cuts that were made by using a hand grinder in a swivel jig.

11-24.   The swivel jig allows the grinder to be rotated or swung in an arc. Use repeat passes when you want deep cuts. The jig can be used on components or on projects that are already assembled.

Typical Freehand Applications

11-25.   A light touch and wise cutter selection leads to quality work when carving. Keep a firm grip but allow the cutter to work at its own pace.

11-26.   Often, the shape of the cutter is enough to produce the form you need. Be careful when hand-holding pieces that you don't inadvertently advance to a finger.

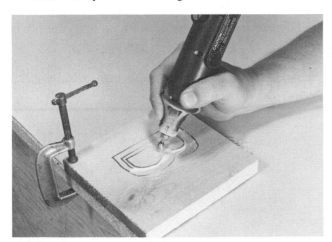

11-27.   It's a good idea to keep small workpieces clamped whenever possible. A light touch doesn't mean that you don't have to grip the tool firmly. If you are too cautious, the cutter will try to move like a wheel.

11-28.   The grinder can be used with very small brushes and abrading units so it is easy to get into crevices and tight corners. A lot of driftwood sculpture is smoothed or textured with a hand grinder.

11-29.   The hand grinder will not replace the portable drill but it can be used to drill small holes. Some hand grinders will take an auxiliary chuck that can grip bits as small as #80.

As a Sharpener

Most any tool in the shop or in the house can be ground or honed with a hand grinder so long as the grinder is fitted with the correct abrasive. Aluminum oxide wheel points are available in many shapes and sizes so it's not difficult to choose one that is right for a particular job. Mostly, the grinder serves best as a touch up tool or as a honer. Removing a lot of metal, necessary when forming a new edge, is best done on a bench grinder.

Many times, the success of a sharpening job depends entirely on the choice of grinding point or wheel. For example, a point with the correct shape will quickly clean out the gullets on a circular saw blade, or redo the teeth of a chain saw. Accessories that guide you through a perfect job when renewing or sharpening the cutting teeth of a chain saw are available (Figures 11-30 and 11-31).

11-30.   Dremel offers a "Chainsaver" chain saw sharpening kit that does such work with speed and precision.

11-31.   The chain saw sharpening kit includes aluminum oxide grinding wheels, spacers, and guides so you can organize to sharpen various types of chain.

Aluminum oxide wheel points will wear and can change shape when they have been used for a while. It's a good idea to touch the turning wheel to a "dressing stone" occasionally to return it to original form. This treatment will also remove grit that tends to clog the pores of abrasive wheels.

Tips on Plastics

Plastics are either *thermosetting* or *thermoplastic*. "Bakelite", "Marblette", and "Plaskon" are trade names of the former type. "Lucite", "Plexiglas", and "Acrylite" are trade names of the latter type. Once the first type has set, it will not become pliable again. The second type becomes pliable when a correct amount of heat is applied.

Thermoplastics will soften if you generate enough heat with the cutter. The gummy result can quickly clog the tool and even cause a drill bit to be cemented in the hole you are trying to drill. The answer is to work with light touches and frequent retractions of drill or cutter to minimize heat build-up. When possible, use coarser fluted cutters than you would use on wood or metal. Check the cutter frequently for signs of gumming and when it occurs stop working long enough for things to cool down. Clean the cutters with a small, stiff brush. Often, plastic chips that have cooled on the cutter can be flicked off with a splinter of wood.

Flexible Shafts

A flexible shaft is a pliant extension between a power source and the cutter, or whatever you are working with. The power source can be a drill press, a motor, a type of hand grinder, a special power unit designed for the purpose (Figure 11-32), or even a portable electric drill (Figure 11-33). With a flexible shaft, assuming that its free end is equipped with a suitable chuck, you can grip any cutter that is operable in a hand grinder, and work as if your fingers were a drill chuck powered by a motor in your shoulder. That is not too unrealistic a picture of what a flexible shaft setup is. The torque and the rpm of whatever power source you choose nestle in the palm of your hand, and the dexterity in your fingers, wrist, and elbow directs the power exactly to where you wish to apply it.

11-32.   Foredom power unit is designed especially to drive flexible shafts. Advantage of a motor-and-shaft combination is that they are tuned to work together for maximum efficiency.

When applicable, a flex shaft allows you to work without the limitations imposed by the rigidity of a solid, straight-line shaft, like when using cutters in a portable drill, a drill press, or even a hand grinder.

A flex shaft can be used with the delicate touch of a surgeon or the muscle of a steel worker. It's not the talents of these people we're talking about, but the fact that they must work with different equipment. To be delicate or tough, efficiently, you must make a wise choice of power source and shaft. The two go together—many high-hp power tools will provide a lot more torque than slim flexible shafts are designed to take.

The Right Core Size

Jobs requiring delicate precision are accomplished more with speed than with power. On the other hand, chores like heavy sanding, weld-grinding, and so on depend more on torque than on high speed. Most of the time, you can judge the type of work a flex shaft can be used for by the size, even the shape, of the end on which chucks are mounted (Figure 11-34). If it can take a heavy, 3-jaw chuck or an arbor on which large buffs, wire brushes, grinding wheels, and the like can be mounted it's certain to be a heavy-duty tool (Figures 11-35 and 11-36). Most of the time, light-duty shafts will have collet-type chucks, but there are exceptions (Figures 11-37 and 11-38).

Overall, small-core shafts are made for high speed (as much as 35,000 rpm) and a light touch; large-core units are designed for jobs that require heavy pressure.

The core size is the diameter of the shaft itself, not its casing. However, it's reasonable to assume that the larger the casing, the larger the core.

A large core can be as much as $5/16''$, or up to $1/2''$ in diameter. Small-core units can start at diameters as small as $1/16''$. A $3/16''$ core is probably the maximum size for chores that require extreme flexibility and control more than power. A $1/4''$ or $5/16''$ core is fine for general, light-duty applications in areas of polishing, buffing, and grinding. For heavy sanding, heavy grinding, and such, a core that is at least $3/8''$ in diameter is not out of line.

11-34.   The tool-holding end of a flex shaft, in addition to its core size, can indicate what it was designed to do. Generally, slim shafts are for high speed and a light touch, whereas others, like the one on the right, will hold up under a lot of power and heavy feed pressure.

11-35.   Some heavy shafts can be fitted with a conventional 3-jaw chuck that can grip tools with $1/2''$ shanks.

11-33.   You can operate a flex shaft with a portable drill but the disadvantages might be—speeds that are too low, and torque that is too high.

11-36.   Some shafts are made like an arbor, or can be fitted with one, so that accessories like grinding wheels and large wire brushes can be placed between washers and secured with a nut.

11-37. Dremel's new "Moto-Flex" tool uses collets to grip cutting tools. It comes with a ⅛" collet, but ¹⁄₃₂", ¹⁄₁₆", and ³⁄₃₂" sizes are available as accessories. The tool has a built-in variable speed control with a range of 7,500 to 25,000 rpm.

11-38. Key-type chuck handpieces are available for some units—this one, for the Foredom line of flex shafts. An adjustable chuck can be more flexible since it can grip any shank size up to its maximum capacity.

All flex shafts are composed of a core, which turns, and a casing, which doesn't. The casing may be a hose-like affair, or a spirally wound steel tube that resembles the type of armored cable often used in electrical work. In quality units, the core, regardless of whether it is large or small, is made of spirally wound, directionally alternating layers of steel wire. The "pitch" of the final layer of wire determines in which direction the shaft should turn.

The most common pitch allows the use of common motors and shop tools as power sources. But since shaft cores are sometimes made with unusual pitches, this feature should be checked before the shaft is used.

The Rotation Rule

Literature that comes with the tool, and , usually, an arrow on the casing, will tell you the shaft's correct direction of rotation. Failure to comply can result in unwinding the core wires, especially under heavy-torque conditions. It's possible to ignore the rule, but to do it safely requires a technical decision that must be based on loading the unit to no more than half its power rating. This type of information may not be available to you and, even if it were, the limits would be difficult to establish in a home shop. Therefore, adhere to the one-direction-of-rotation rule.

Shaft Ends

The coupling end of larger units is usually designed for locking directly to a motor shaft, but the size of the coupling is not always a good indication of the power requirements. For example, a 72" x ½" core shaft may fit ½" or ⅝" motor shafts and be rated for 1 hp. A 50" x ⅜" core shaft may fit the same motor shafts but may have a capacity rating of only ½ hp. These particular specifications are used as examples because both shafts were purchased from the same store. A full load from the more powerful motor applied to the smaller shaft, even though it fits on the motor spindle, can cause problems. The point is—always be sure to check the capacity of the shaft in terms of the horsepower it can handle.

In Use

One of the major rules is not to overload. This is especially important when driving a slim shaft with drill-press, or lathe, or even portable drill power. The available torque may be far beyond the capacity of the shaft. In other words, let the shaft decide the capacity, not the power source.

The tool-mounting end of many large shafts is a straight, threaded spindle fitted with flanges and a lock nut. This spindle design allows mounting of any accessory that has a center hole of suitable size. It's also possible to use conventional chucks that screw onto the threaded spindle so you can mount shafted tools like drill bits, drum sanders, and the like.

Use special care when driving grinding wheels, wire brushes, and similar tools; protect yourself by adding accessory wheel guards. These safety devices cover most of the wheel and some have a handle that lets you grip more firmly. An auxiliary handle is a good idea on all jobs that are done with a heavy-duty shaft (Figure 11-39). Safety goggles, of course, are always a must.

The maximum size of wheels that can be used on a shaft will be listed in the literature that is supplied with the tool. Some ½″ shafts can be used with 6″ wheels, but I think it's better to stay with 4″ wheels on any of the big shafts. When you work with small shafts, say a ⅛″ core, the maximum wheel diameter should be about 1″. Acceptable speeds are determined by efficiency and safety. A safe speed for a 6″ wheel might range from 4,000 to 4,500 rpm, but this is not something you must determine for yourself. Maximum rpms are printed on the flanges of wheels. You need only to read them and obey them.

Very Small Shafts

Slim shafts can be individual units that you operate with various power sources, or they might be sophisticated motor/shaft combinations like the one shown in Figure 11-40. Some units have built-in variable speed controls, which can be handy even though the majority of work done with a slim shaft requires high speed.

When the tool itself is not equipped to provide different speeds, check to see if the manufacturer offers an auxiliary unit—a hand-, or foot-controlled rheostat—that is used between power source and tool to control speed. When high speed and a light touch are required for the job, you may be disappointed if you are powering an individual shaft with a drill press or similar power source—the speed won't be there. It will *always* be available on the coordinated motor/shaft combinations. Some workers make do with a motor salvaged from an old sewing machine or some other high-speed universal motor.

A possible solution when you want more speed than a power source can provide, is to get a special handpiece with a planetary drive which automatically increases the speed at the handpiece to two and one half times the input speed. Thus, for example, if you are driving a shaft 5,000 rpm, you'll get 12,500 rpm at the handpiece. The Foredom unit shown in Figure 11-41 can run as high as 35,000 rpm and can be equipped with collets to take shafts with ¹⁄₁₆″ to ¼″ diameters.

What to Buy

Your interests should, of course, influence your choice of equipment. For example, if your major interests involve work like welding, cleaning, and patching dents in automobiles, applying a satin finish to metals or a sculptured texture to large wood panels, then a heavy-duty shaft, organized with its own motor, is the best way to go. Many such units are available mounted on a roll-around pedestal which makes them more convenient to use. The illustrations in Figures 11-42 to 11-45 show how you can make one.

If most of your work will be in areas like carving in various materials, engraving, glass etching, gunsmithing, model building, jewelry making or polishing, and so on, then a slim shaft or, preferably, a motor/shaft combination is a good choice.

The cutters, wheels, special chucks, and drill bits shown in Figure 11-46 represent what can be done with a slim, flexible shaft.

11-39.   If a heavy-duty flex shaft does not have an integral auxiliary handle, check to see if one is available as an accessory. The extra grip helps you do better work and adds a safety factor.

11-40.   The Foredom power-source-flex shaft combination is a super tool that can be used with any of the handpieces shown here. Some of the handpieces themselves have flexible sections.

11-41.   Foredom's planetary drive handpiece automatically increases the source speed by 2½ times. The unit can run as high as 35,000 rpm and will take shaft sizes from ¹⁄₁₆″ to ¼″.

11-42. Roll-about pedestal that you can make for heavy-duty motor/shaft combinations is always ready to work, anywhere.

11-43. The motor I use with this setup has its own variable speed control. The pedestal adds convenience to many operations since it eliminates motor-placement problems.

11-44. The motor, with a conventional motor-mount base, is secured in a cradle that swivels on bolts that pass through the project's vertical components. The swivel action can be stopped by securing the nuts on the bolts.

11-45. Construction details of the roll-around pedestal. Use heavy-duty casters, preferably those that have a locking lever.

11-46. A slim flexible shaft can be used with all these accessories, and more. Special chucks available for some units let you mount cutters with shanks that are too small to be gripped by a standard collet or chuck.

12. Some Other Interesting Tools

There are more power tools, stationary as well as portable, "than meet the eye". Beyond the assortment that is considered basic for most shops, there are tools that are used infrequently. This is a general statement and will be opposed by those who use a particular tool which they consider a necessity. It certainly doesn't apply to the electric screwdriver or electric stapling gun, tools whose current popularity is justified.

All tools should be considered in the light of your personal needs, and this applies to fundamental equipment as well as borderline tools. The person who is distraught when not playing golf, but might have use for a portable saw once or twice a year, might be better off renting instead of buying one.

The following illustrations show some tools that were not covered in previous chapters, but which are practical and can be considered as permanent acquisitions, or tools to rent when needed.

Electric Screwdrivers

Electric screwdrivers (Figures 12-1 and 12-2) are essentially a low-speed, high-torque tool. They are available in cordless models, which makes them convenient to use anywhere, or as conventional plug-in units. All can be used with slotted or Phillips type bits, and are reversible so screws can be removed as well as driven. Some are more powerful, and the clue is what can be gripped in the chuck. A tool with a 3/8″ chuck has to have more horsepower than one with a 1/4″ chuck.

A built-in clutch is a good feature since it causes the driver to slip once the screw is "home". This prevents damage to the screw or work surface since the bit will not slip off the screwhead. The clutches on some units can be set to provide the correct torque for the fastener being used. Check to see if accessories that can be used to drive or remove nuts and bolts, as well as screws, are available.

12-1.   Cordless screwdriver is neat and easy to use. Low-speed, high-torque tool reverses so it can remove screws as well as drive them.

12-2.   Electric screwdrivers are made with various shapes. This one resembles a pistol-grip type electric drill. They are also available as conventional plug-in units.

Electric Handsaw

The "Wellsaw" (Figure 12-3) looks something like a hand-saw, but it cuts with power. Sawing occurs both coming and going and moves at 8,000 cutting-strokes per minute. The tool can be equipped with 8″ or 16″ blades and there are enough blade designs so working on various materials is not a problem.

The tool is very popular with home builders and remodelers since it can saw heavy or light materials, even through walls. Landscapers use it for pruning and, as examples of its versatility, it's used by butchers, farmers, paper manufacturers, crate builders, and others.

It is not a difficult tool to use and has built-in safety features like a blade that stops in less than 1½ seconds, and a blower that clears chips from the work line.

Portable Bandsaw

This is not a tool you will find in every home workshop but it is a type you will find in rental shops. The portable, metal cutting bandsaw (Figure 12-4) is appreciated by folks who are planning for a house foundation and have a lot of reinforcement bars to cut, and others who are usually or temporarily involved in working with bar stock, angle iron, pipe, and so on. These tools have plenty of power for heavy metal cutting and often offer a choice of speeds (in feet per minute) so an efficient one can be selected for the job at hand. The tools are limited in cut-off length, but it's what they can get through that counts. Capacities can be 3¼″ to 3¾″ in round stock, and 3¼″ by better than 4″ in rectangular material.

The tool has everything needed for efficient operation—planetary gearing system for power directly to the endless blade, adjustable blade guides and tensioning knob, and an assortment of available blades. An accessory is a stand/vise combination so the unit can be used in stationary fashion.

Slim-Belt Sander/Grinder

Black & Decker calls the product shown in Figures 12-5 and 12-6 the "Powerfile". It is a unique tool in that it can drive

12-4.   Portable bandsaw is a metal-cutting tool that gets quickly through round or rectangular stock. Saw blade is a loop, just like those on stationary tools.

12-5.   Unique tool works with narrow, endless belts for sanding, grinding, and polishing. Different size, interchangeable arms are available. Pivoting arm can be locked in any position through a 135° arc.

12-3.   "Wellsaw" works like a handsaw, but is electrically powered to deliver 8,000, 1⅛″ strokes per minute. The replaceable blades are designed to cut on both stroke directions. Blades are available for cutting wood, paper, bone, and other materials.

12-6.   The "Powerfile" can get into tight places and can work on many intricate contours.

endless, abrasive belts as narrow as ¼″ and polishing pads as narrow as ⅛″. Add to this interchangeable arms of various lengths and a sanding head that rotates through a 135° arc, and you can visualize how handy the tool can be for filing, deburring, sanding, and polishing in tight places and on odd-shaped surfaces. In many situations it does jobs that can't be accomplished with a conventional sander or grinder. The tool is less than 17″ long and weighs about 4 lbs.

Slim-Belt Belt Sander

The product shown in Figure 12-7 is a 1⅛″ x 21″ belt sander that is designed for excellent maneuverability when doing close quarter work. The front pulley is exposed so you can even get into tight, inside curves. Its removable side handle can be locked in at various angles so you can place hands in positions that are most suitable for the job. Accessory belts are available in seven grit sizes.

Powered Metal Shears

Cutting a few lengths of sheet metal with a good pair of hand shears is no problem, but when you have a lot more to do you can speed the work and do it more easily and more accurately with electric sheet metal cutters (Figures 12-8 and 12-9). Power, which determines the maximum metal-gauge units can get through, differs from tool to tool, but most are fairly light in weight and are designed for one-hand use. It's easier to get good results with these tools if you provide adequate support for the work near the cutline.

Electric Staplers and Nail Guns

You can appreciate the difference between a hand stapler and an electric one on jobs like installing ceiling tiles (Figure 12-10), vapor barriers, carpeting, and weather stripping. Most can be used with staples of various sizes and designs so the right choice can be made for the material being fastened. Many jobs that are usually done with brads or tacks can be done faster and more efficiently with a powered stapler.

12-8.   Electric shear can get through 10-gauge mild steel and up to 12-gauge stainless steel. The blades have four cutting edges: turning the cutter 90° brings a new, sharp edge into play.

12-9.   This electric shear has a scrap guide to protect the operator's hand. Capacities of the double insulated tool are: up to 16 gauge in mild steel and 18 gauge in stainless steel.

12-7.   Sander works with 1⅛″ x 21″ belts and can be used on a wide variety of surfaces and materials. The compact tool weighs about 4 lbs and has a belt speed of 3,280 feet per minute.

12-10.   The electric staple gun will drive staples cleanly and to full depth as fast as you can pull the trigger. It's a wonder tool for jobs like installing ceiling tiles, but it has other practical uses, like recovering chair seats, attaching weather stripping, and covering valances with fabric.

The electric nail gun (Figure 12-11) looks like a stapling machine, but it drives 1 1/32″ nails with enough power to sink them completely in hard oak. Eliminating having to hold a nail and driving it with a hammer makes installing paneling, assembling picture frames, attaching moldings and edge bandings, and many other chores a lot easier to do. The tool is more accurate than the human hand. Press the trigger with the tool resting solidly on the work and the nail is driven perfectly straight in one quick stroke. It can only drive the nails that are made for it, but when they are suitable, the possibility of whacking a thumb instead of a nail is eliminated, and that's nice.

Vacuum Cleaner

A shop-type vacuum cleaner (Figure 12-12) is as handy in the house or on the patio as it is in the shop. A shop broom and a bench brush, while needed, can't compare with the efficiency of a powered unit. Many portable tools, and stationary ones, are designed to accept the hose of such a unit. Thus, sawdust and wood chips can be collected as the work goes on. Overall, a vacuum cleaner can keep you healthier and safer when you are in a workshop environment.

Power Hone

A power hone (Figure 12-13) is actually a stationary tool but it can help you work better and safer with power tools, and hand tools as well. Many of the units have accessories that hold tools correctly so you are sure to maintain the efficient cutting edge. A power hone is handy for tools used in the house as well as shop tools. It will keep keen edges on knives, scissors, and similar items.

12-11. The electric nail gun drives nails of a particular size with speed and accuracy. You just hold the tool firmly on the work and press the trigger.

12-12. The "prosaic" vacuum cleaner is an important shop tool. Like this one, many are designed to pick up virtually any dry or wet debris.

12-13. With a power hone you can quickly learn to do a professional job of sharpening shop and house tools.

Bench Grinder

The bench grinder (Figure 12-14) is also a stationary tool, but like the power hone, it helps you work better and safer because it lets you maintain keen edges on cutting tools with minimum effort. Actually, the bench grinder and the power hone are good companions. The hone takes over after cutting edges have been reshaped or renewed on the grinder.

Paint Stripper

The electric paint stripper is an effective alternative to caustic chemicals that have unpleasant odors and leave a messy, liquid goo to clean up. The concept of the stripper is simple—

12-14. The bench grinder can be used with different grit wheels so it can be used for sharpening as well as grinding. Tools like this are often used to drive buffs and wire wheels, so having variable speeds can be an asset. This unit has speeds ranging from 0 to 3,800 rpm.

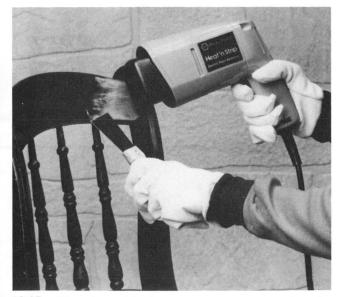

12-15. The nuisance job of removing old paint becomes less of a chore when a heat gun is used to soften the coating enough so it can be scraped off easily.

it blasts out super hot air that heats painted surfaces so the old coating can be quickly removed with a scraper (Figure 12-15). The tool has other uses, like drying surfaces, softening floor tiles and adhesives for easy replacement, and shrinking electrical tubing that is used to cover wire connections.

Glue/Caulker Gun

Electric glue guns (Figure 12-16) are handy because they can be used on wood and non-wood materials like cloth, paper, plastics, and leather. When the correct "stick" is placed in the gun, it becomes an easy-to-use caulking tool. The secret to using the glue gun is to work fast. The stick adhesive is a hot liquid when it leaves the gun but it cools pretty rapidly, so parts should be pressed together as quickly as possible. Use the tools carefully, since the nozzle end of the gun and the glue itself are quite hot.

12-16. An electric "gun" that can be used with different "ammunition" can serve for caulking as well as gluing.

Chain Saw

The chain saw is a super tool for sawing logs (Figure 12-17), so its popularity has grown together with interest in wood burning stoves. It is not a tool to treat lightly even though modern ones have built-in safety features that were lacking in earlier models. Even so, the instructions that come with the tool should be followed to the letter. If you should ever rent one, be sure to ask for the original instruction manual.

Actually, the tool is used for more than cutting firewood. They get through heavy beams, fence posts, and the like quickly. You have probably read articles about chain-saw sculptors. Some manufacturers, like Stihl, provide accessories so the saw can be converted for jobs like hedge trimming and brush removal (Figures 12-18 and 12-19).

Chain saws are available as gasoline-powered or electrically-powered units.

12-18.   Some chain saws have accessories so they can be used for more than sawing. A hedge trimmer is one of them.

12-17.   The chain saw is noted as a fine tool for cutting firewood, but it has other uses. For example, experts can use the front end of the chain to shape mortises in heavy timbers. The wise user wears safety goggles, a hard hat, steel-toed shoes, and ear plugs or some other hearing protector.

12-19.   In addition to the hedge trimmer, the motor of the Stihl chain saw can be attached to a unit that allows cutting heavy grass, weeds, and unwanted shrubbery.

13. How To Make Stationary Work Stations For Portable Tools

Your portable belt and pad sander—and drill—can be harnessed and used as stationary tools if you make the work station described in this chapter. It's not a difficult project and it doesn't limit the tools to a particular mode. Detaching the tools is easy so you can quickly put them back into service as portables. It's like having your cake and eating it too. You can mount all the tools when there are a variety of sanding chores to do, or you can work with just the one that is most suitable for a particular job.

All the sanders are secured to pivoting platforms and thus can be used in a vertical or horizontal position as shown in Figures 13-1 and 13-2. The drill provides rotary-sanding capability. It can be used to drive a variety of sanding drums or a disc that you can make or buy. The saber saw was an

afterthought on my part and is optional. If you include it, be sure to have a blade mounted *only* when doing a sawing job.

I designed the prototype sanding station around good-size tools: a Sears Craftsman 4″ belt sander and a 4½″ x 9⅛″ pad sander. Thus, the pivoting mounting plates on which the tools are secured should be large enough for any brand tool.

The heart of my tool-mounting system is a yoke into which you slip the tool's handgrip, and a pipe strap bent to fit over the grip's projecting top. I lined all straps and yokes with self-adhesive weather stripping but did not allow for its thickness when forming and sizing them. That ensured a snug mounting for the tools and minimum vibration. Tool levelers—blocks of wood sized for the job and weather stripped—complete the mounting system (Figures 13-3 through 13-5).

13-1.   The sander "shop" provides for a belt and pad sander, and a drill that is used to drive disc or drums sanders. The saber saw is optional, but including it involves little extra work.

13-2.   The belt and pad sanders are mounted on hinged plates so they can be used in vertical or horizontal positions. In either case, locking-bolts hold the tools securely and minimize vibration. The drawers provide storage for accessories used with the shop and for abrasive materials.

13-3. This is the system used for mounting the pad sander. The arrow indicates a support block that is sized so the sander will be held in a level position.

13-4. Pipe clamps, lined with self-adhesive weather stripping, grip the sander securely. Weather stripping is also used to line the top edges of yokes and other support pieces.

13-5. Mounting arrangement for the belt sander is similar to the one used for the pad sander. In both cases, some customizing is necessary to suit the handle arrangement and the shape of the tools you will use.

Constructing the Shop

Construction details for the body of the shop, mounting plates, accessories, and guides are shown in Figures 13-6 through 13-8. Saw the legs (# 1 in Figure 13-6) to size, then form the 2¼″ x 10¾″ notch that is required in the top rear of each leg. Be sure the legs are perfect triplets, then begin the assembly by adding the two frame pieces and the back brace. Cut the tool supports and the short leg to size and secure them in place with glue and #10 x 1½″ flathead wood screws. Also, nail through the back brace into the front edges of the tool supports. The drawings don't show them, but there are many areas where you can add some glue blocks for additional rigidity.

Add the drawer guides and then construct the drawers. The materials list (Figure 13-6) calls out exact sizes so you might wish to reduce the width of the drawers by 1/16″ or so to avoid binding. Anyway, doing this part of the job before the top is added makes it easier to be sure the drawers will work smoothly. Bore 1½″-diameter finger holes through the drawer fronts instead of adding knobs.

Make the Top

Cut the piece to overall size and, before forming the openings for the sanders, use a table saw or a portable router to shape the miter-gauge groove and the drill-accessory positioning groove. Use a saber saw to form the relief for the drill's handle, the opening for the junction box, and the open areas for the sanders.

If you decide to include a saber saw, use a router to form the recess for it in the underside of the bench top. The recess is included so the saw blade will have more projection when the saber saw is mounted. Drill a ¼″ or 5/16″ hole for the saw blade, then use the saw to form the blade's access slot. The saw clamps should work for most any saber saw, but check the dimensions against the tool you own just to be sure. The idea is to allow the saw to slip into place merely by loosening the clamp locking screws.

Add the top by coating the top edges of the base assembly with glue and then driving 6d finishing nails, spaced three to four inches apart. Set the nailheads, and fill the cavities with wood dough.

Tilting Mounts for Sanders

Cut the sander-mounting plates and then mark them for the hinge positions. Clamp a strip of wood on the marked line so you can position the hinges accurately, then attach them to the plate. Put the plate on the tool support, then drive the screws for the second leaf of the hinge. Work carefully to be sure the plate is parallel with the shop's work surface. Add the height strip, which should be just thick enough to compensate for the hinge thickness (Figure 13-9).

Swing the plate to the vertical position and drill the two holes for the locking bolts that thread into T-Nuts in the underside of the tool supports. Follow this procedure for all locking bolts and T-Nuts. Drill a ⅛″ pilot hole and then enlarge it to ¼″. Enlarge the end of the hole into which the T-Nut is pressed to 5/16″. The T-Nuts do not have to be set flush, but be sure to use the pronged type. Drill the hole for the

JUNCTION-BOX OPENING

MITER-GAUGE GROOVE
1/4 DEEP x 5/8 WIDE

PAD-SANDER OPENING

3 1/4
1 1/2

16 3/4   2 1/2

BELT-SANDER
OPENING

19"

4 1/2

10"

DRILL-HANDLE
OPENING

17 1/2

DRILL-ACCESSORY GROOVE
1/4 DEEP x 5/8 WIDE

3"

5"   6 1/2"

13

TOP

SABER-SAW
CLAMPS

15

NO.10 x 1 1/2 FLATHEAD
WOOD SCREWS

6

6 3/4

5   14

2 3/4

2

4

7

8   3

9 1/4

10 3/4

17 3/4

BASE
ASSEMBLY

DRAWERS

10   11   12

10

12

11

9

A

10

A

9

FRONT ROUTED ON
ALL FOUR EDGES

3/8 DEEP x
3/4 WIDE

9   3/8

10

5/16

9

TOP VIEW

SEC. A-A

5/16

11

SIDE VIEW

1/4 x 1 1/2
F.H. STOVE BOLTS
(4 REQ.)

2 1/4

1 1/4

1/4 T-NUT
(4 REQ.)

3/8

2 1/2

SABER-SAW CLAMP

MATERIALS LIST

KEY	QTY.	NAME AND SIZE
1	3	Legs 3/4" x 9" x 24"
2	1	Frame 3/4" x 3" x 9 1/4"
3	1	Frame 3/4" x 3" x 17 3/4"
4	1	Brace 3/4" x 2 1/4" x 37 1/4"
5	1	Tool Support 3/4" x 10" x 12 1/4"
6	1	Tool Support 3/4" x 10" x 16"
7	1	Leg 3/4" x 6 3/4" x 10"
8	4	Guides 3/8" x 3/4" x 13"
9	1	Large Drawer Front 3/4" x 6 1/2" x 18 3/8"
9	1	Small Drawer Front 3/4" x 6 1/2" x 9 7/8"
10	4	Large/Small Drawer Sides 3/4" x 5 9/16" x 12 3/4"
11	1	Large Drawer Bottom 1/4" x 12 3/4" x 17 3/4"
11	1	Small Drawer Bottom 1/4" x 9 1/4" x 12 3/4"
12	1	Large Drawer Back 3/4" x 5 1/2" x 16 1/4"
12	1	Small Drawer Back 3/4" x 5 1/2" x 7 3/4"
13	1	Top 3/4" x 24" x 42"
14	2	Height Block 5/16" x 1 1/2" x 10"
15	2	Saw Clamps 3/4" x 2 1/2" x 8"

13-6.   Construction details for the base cabinet of the sander shop. The key in the materials list is the number that identifies the part.

13-7. Details of hinged tool-plates and a typical system for securing the sanders.

13-8. These are accessories and guides that are used with the sander shop. Upper left detail shows one way to secure a portable drill.

bolt that secures the plate in horizontal position *after* the sander has been mounted.

Mounting the Sanders

Check the detail in Figure 13-7 that shows a typical mounting arrangement. It is very important for the tool to be level and positioned so most of its abrasive surface is above the bench top and perpendicular to it.

Make the yoke first, cutting it longer than necessary and then reducing its height to suit the tool. After the yoke is set, cut the support for the tool's main handle and place it to suit the tool. Pipe straps do a good job of securing the tools but they will have to be modified to fit. Most of the time, it's just a question of tapping them with a hammer to flatten the arc a bit. The straps should bear down enough to keep the tools secure. Be especially careful with the pad sander since it will cause more vibration than the belt sander.

The final step is to secure the tool and then to size the tool leveler so its height and position will be exactly right for the tool. Be sure the tool's vent holes will not be covered.

Adding the Drill

The simplest way to add the drill is to buy and bolt on a commercial accessory to hold it. I prefer the yoke-mounting method because it holds the drill more securely (Figure 13-10). It will be easy to draw the patterns for the yokes if you work with a contour gauge. Otherwise, fold a sheet of heavy paper and, by snip-and-see, work out a half-contour. Be sure that the yokes will hold the drill so the horizontal centerline of the chuck will be parallel to the project's work surface. The oversize holes for the locking bolts allow for lateral adjustment.

Accessories

The accessories, detailed in Figure 13-8, are mostly for sanding jobs done with the drill. Adjust the height of the disc-sander table so its surface will be on or slightly above the centerline of the sanding disc. The centerline of the hole in the drum-sander support must match with the centerline of the chuck.

Use a ¼″ or ⅜″ bolt as an arbor for the sanding disc. Cut the bolt to leave a threaded portion that is exactly the right length for the item to be mounted. Peen the free end heavily to secure the nut so the disc can safely rotate in either direction (with reversible drill). Attach the aluminum sheet-metal cover with contact cement.

The miter gauge is used with the sanders and can be used to guide pieces that have square or miter-cut ends.

In General

It is important to work carefully through all phases of construction, especially when mounting the tools. Taking ten minutes to do a five minute job will pay off.

Use a good, cabinet-grade birch or maple plywood. Sand all parts smooth before doing assembly work, then sand once more when the job is complete. Finish with two or three coats of sanding sealer, sanding between applications, and after the final one. Apply paste wax, rubbed to a polish, to all work surfaces.

I used a single combination switch/outlet, and I think it's a good idea for you to do the same. You will be able to plug in just one tool at a time. Thus, you won't accidentally or forgetfully, start a tool while another is running.

Some typical chores that can be done on the sanding station are shown in Figures 13-11 through 13-22.

13-9.   The thickness of the height strip—on the right—should equal the thickness of the hinge when it is in closed position.

13-10.   The yoke-mounting method for the drill provides good security. The bearing areas of the yokes, and the pipe clamps should be lined with weather stripping. Holes for the screws that secure the yokes are oversize so there is some freedom for lateral adjustment of the drill.

Typical Chores on the Sander Shop

13-11.   Edge sanding on the belt sander is done by moving the work against the belt's direction of rotation, as indicated by the arrow. The belt will tend to move the work back, so keep a firm grip. Don't stand in line with the workpiece.

13-12.   You can do end-sanding on some good-size workpieces when the belt sander is locked in vertical position. You can sand miter cuts the same way.

13-13.   When using the belt sander in horizontal position to smooth miter cuts, keep the miter gauge on the right side of the tool. Hold or clamp it securely to counter the belt's tendency to move the work.

13-14.   Use the open end of the belt sander to smooth inside curves.

13-15.   Stationary pad sander is especially useful when you want a super-smooth finish on stock that is too small to hand-hold safely. Move the work slowly across the abrasive. Note the combination switch/outlet that is used for all tools.

13-16.   Use the pad sander in vertical position to smooth the rounded end of a workpiece. Being able to apply the work to the tool, in this fashion, ensures a square edge.

Typical Chores on the Sander Shop (cont'd.)

13-17. Miter-cut pieces can also be smoothed on the pad sander. The miter gauge, that you make, is reversible, so it can be used for left- or right-hand cuts.

13-20. Custom-made, 6″-diameter sanding disc works well with a variable-speed, reversing drill and the accessory sanding table. Always apply the work to the "down" side of the disc.

13-18. The drill can be used to drive drum sanders, or buffers and polishers. DON'T use it to turn a grinding wheel. Always wear safety goggles and a dust mask.

13-21. The sanding table can also be used with drum sanders. This is one of 3M's new drum types. The surface of the table should be at or a bit above the centerline of the drill chuck.

13-19. The advantage of working with the drum-sander support is that it ensures that sanded edges will be square to workpiece's surfaces.

13-22. The saber saw is not a replacement for a jigsaw, but it can be quite handy for many sawing jobs. Don't leave a saw blade in the tool when it is not being used. With a scroller-type saw, turn the control handle 180°; with a conventional saw, mount the blade backwards.

An All-Purpose Table for Portable Tools

You can't beat the convenience of using portable tools in work situations where it's more practical to apply the tool to the job, but the reverse is also true. Quite often it is easier to work more precisely when the tool is stationary and the work is brought to it. With a multipurpose table, that you can build, you can quickly convert portable tools to stationary-tool use (Figure 13-23).

Even though I included a portable saw in the unit, it is an *optional feature* because the guard on the saw will move to the underside of the table during crosscutting and ripping operations and return to cover the blade when the pass is complete, but there will be no over-guard *during* the cut. If you eliminate the cutoff saw, the project can still be used for drilling, sanding, saber sawing, and shaping. If you include the saw, always work so your hands never come near the blade. Adjust the projection of the saw blade so it barely pokes through the surface of the stock.

Picture the project as a sturdy box with a hinged top that has a cutout in it to receive "plates" to which portable tools are secured (Figures 13-24 and 13-25). The large 23″ x 23½″ surface provides a lot of work-support area. The project itself can be considered portable since it can be placed on a workbench, or even on a pair of sawhorses that are spanned with a sheet of thick plywood. It can also be supported on a stand that you make or buy. The system of interchangeable inserts provides the mounting arrangement for each of the portable tools.

Construction details for the main table and the accessories that are used with it, are shown in Figures 13-26 through 13-31. Most of the work involved in making the project can be accomplished with portable tools. Form dadoes with a cutoff saw by setting the blade projection to the required depth and then making a series of overlapping passes to achieve the width of the dado. A straightedge, clamped to the work, will guide the saw to assure parallel cuts. It's best to make the shoulder cuts first and then clean out the waste that remains between them. If you prefer, a chisel instead of a saw can be used for the last step.

For slots, drill a series of overlapping holes and then remove waste with a file or chisel. Another method is to drill end-holes for the slot and then cut between them with a saber saw. Large, internal cutouts can be done by just using the saber saw.

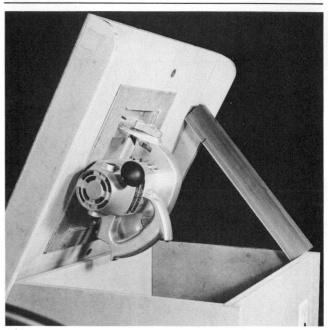

13-24.   The top of the table pivots on two ¼″ bolts so it's easy to mount any tool that won't fit through the table opening from above. The strip of wood is just a prop to hold the table top up.

13-23.   The all-purpose table I made is mounted on its own steel stand. The outlet is wired so it's controlled by the on-off switch. Tool switches are locked in the "on" position, and the cords are plugged into the outlet. Thus, tool activity is controlled with the switch in the table.

13-25.   Tool mounting-plates can be secured with flathead screws. Be sure to set them flush so they don't interfere with workpieces.

TYPICAL INSERT
$\frac{1}{4}$ X 8" X 13"

$\frac{5}{8}$ X 23" X 23 $\frac{1}{2}$

SEE DETAIL A

5"

A

A

2 $\frac{1}{2}$

$\frac{1}{4}$

7"

2 $\frac{1}{2}$

7 $\frac{3}{4}$

8 $\frac{3}{4}$

6"

$\frac{5}{8}$ X 2 $\frac{1}{2}$ X 23"
(2 REQ.)

$\frac{5}{8}$ X 9" X 14"

SECTION A-A

$\frac{3}{4}$

$\frac{3}{8}$

$\frac{3}{8}$

$\frac{1}{2}$

$\frac{1}{2}$

$\frac{1}{4}$

$\frac{5}{8}$ X 11" X 21 $\frac{3}{4}$

2"

$\frac{1}{4}$ TEE-NUT

DETAIL A

$\frac{5}{8}$ X 11" X 19"
(2 REQ.)

$\frac{1}{2}$

$\frac{5}{8}$ X 9" X 21 $\frac{3}{4}$

$\frac{1}{4}$ HOLE

$\frac{3}{4}$

$\frac{3}{4}$

2"

13-26.   Construction details of the basic table. A hardboard veneered plywood is a good choice for material since it can take abuse and will hold up for a long time.

4"

1"

$\frac{5}{8}$ X 3" X 23"

$\frac{5}{8}$ X 2 $\frac{1}{2}$ X 22"

$\frac{1}{2}$

WINGNUT

4 $\frac{1}{2}$

3 $\frac{1}{2}$

$\frac{1}{4}$ X 1 $\frac{3}{8}$
DRILL ROD
(PRESS FIT)

1 $\frac{1}{4}$ X 4 $\frac{1}{2}$ X 8"

$\frac{1}{4}$ X 3"
THREADED ROD

$\frac{3}{8}$ X $\frac{3}{4}$ X 16"

2"

4"

13-27.   An easy-to-make rip fence is held in place with clamps during use.

13-28.   You can make a miter gauge like this or use one that is already on hand.

13-29.   The belt sander has a mounting of its own, but an insert can be attached to the underside so the assembly can be fitted easily to the table. The raised work surface follows the belt's contour for sanding curves. The steel angle and the L-shaped hold-down, which you can make from a ¼″ bolt, will work with belt sanders that have a removable front knob. You may have to modify the arrangement a bit to suit the tool you own.

Work carefully to be sure that the dadoes in the table top will be parallel to the table opening and to the sides of the table. These grooves will be guides for the miter gauge. The accuracy of the finished project relates strongly to the care you use when making it. Since the end result can be a lifetime tool, it pays to take extra time to make it correctly.

First, make and assemble all parts for the main table, then go on to the accessories and the inserts required for the tools. Make a separate insert (mounting plate) for each tool you plan to use, adapting it to accommodate the specific tool. Except for the drill, tools are mounted on the underside of the inserts with holes through their baseplates.

Sand all surfaces before and after assembly, then apply several coats of sanding sealer, sanding between coats and after the last one. The last finishing step is an application of paste wax, rubbed to a polish.

Typical applications of the tools and some construction hints are shown in Figures 13-32 through 13-44.

13-30.   Construction details of the drill press. If you can't find a U-bolt that will work with the portable drill you use, you can make a special one by bending a length of threaded rod. Make the hole in the mounting block so the column fits it tightly. If you wish to avoid making this unit, you can probably substitute a ready-made stand.

13-31.   How to make the adjustable fences that are needed for the router/shaper setup.

Typical Applications and Construction Tips

13-32.   The rip fence, if you have installed a saw, is used by setting it parallel to the saw blade and clamping it in place. Keep hands well away from the blade. For clarity, the projection of the saw blade is higher than it should be. In practice, the blade should barely poke through the surface of the material.

13-33.   Crosscutting is done by using the miter gauge. Note that the guard on the saw is pushed below the table as the pass is made. It will return to cover the blade when the pass is complete. Obey the safety rules if you decide to include a saw in the project.

13-34.   The table on the project supplies ample work-support area. Since saber-saw blades are chucked only at one end, you must feed the work slowly to avoid twisting the blade off the cut-line.

13-35.   If the belt sander is shaped somewhat like this one, you can rest the main handle on a height block and secure it with an L-shaped bolt. Install a T-Nut in the underside of the height block for the bolt.

13-36.   A belt sander that has a removable auxiliary knob can be secured at the front end by using a metal angle. You can make the angle by bending a length of ⅛″ strap steel.

13-37.   The "stationary" belt sander makes it easy to do end-sanding on narrow pieces. The backup holds the workpiece in correct position and keeps it from moving. When sanding edges, move the work against the belt's direction of rotation. Hold the work firmly, since the belt's rotation will oppose the direction in which you move the workpiece.

(Continued on next page)

Typical Applications and Construction Tips (cont'd.)

13-38.   The forward end of the sander is open, so it can be used like a drum sander to smooth inside curves.

13-40.   The outfeed fence of the router/shaper arrangement is adjusted so its bearing surface is on the same plane as the infeed fence, or ahead of it. Its position depends on the kind of cut being performed. In any case, its place is secured by means of a wing nut on a stud that screws into a T-Nut that is in the underside of the table.

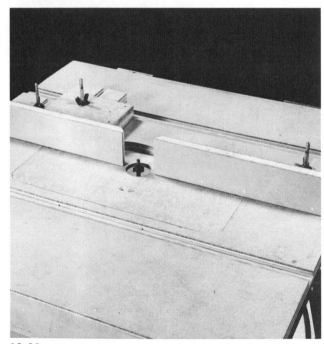

13-39.   Router/shaper setup, with individually adjustable fences, imitates a conventional shaper. Depth-of-cut adjustments are made by moving the router vertically as is normally done. The width of the cut is controlled with fence adjustments. The router is attached to the underside of a mounting plate which has an opening for the bit.

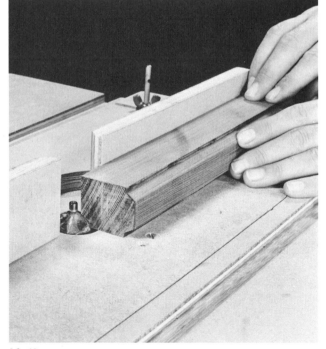

13-41.   When only part of the workedge is removed, the bearing surfaces of the infeed and outfeed fences are set on the same plane. The cutter, because the router is in inverted position, is rotating counterclockwise—so the work must be fed from right to left.

Typical Applications and Construction Tips (cont'd.)

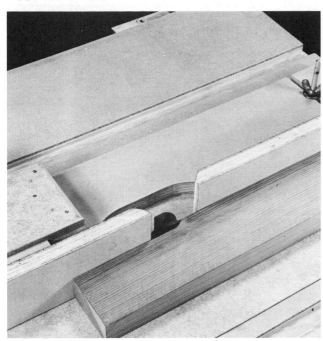

13-42.   When the cut removes the entire edge of the stock, the outfeed fence is set forward of the infeed fence to provide support for the workpiece after it has passed the cutter. The outfeed fence is positioned forward of the infeed fence a distance that equals the mount of material that is removed.

13-44.   The drill press design may have to be modified in some details to fit your drill, but the basic concept will work for most models. Shape the front end of the drill mounting block to fit the case of your particular tool. Use a U-bolt that you buy or make to secure the drill to the mounting block. Careful construction will assure that the drill bits will travel parallel to the column. If necessary, use shims between the drill case and the mounting block. The bolts in the linkage should be just tight enough to keep the drill from sliding down under its own weight.

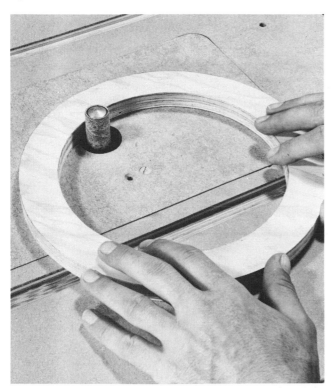

13-43.   You can mount a small drum sander in the router when it is used in the router/shaper mode, but feed pressure must be *very* light since router speed is excessive for this application.

APPENDIX

1. Lumber

Lumber is the staple of almost every handyman, woodworker, or craftsman. The term refers to 'solid' wood—boards cut from a tree, dried, and perhaps planed or treated chemically, but not processed in any other way. You might think that this would be a simple subject, but it's not. There are a wide variety of woods, several different ways to saw a tree, and dozens of variations in grain, density, and strength. Because of this, it takes a bit of study to 'know your lumber'.

The information in this section will help you to select the type of lumber you need for a job. First, there is a list of terms that apply to lumber—this will help you understand the many details you must consider when working with lumber. There is a brief description of the hardwoods and softwoods that are commonly available. You may never have the need to work with many of these woods, but you'll find the information useful in making a selection. There is a simple description of how lumber is graded, how to calculate the 'board feet' in a board, and the common methods for sawing a log. If you do much carpentry, there's information on how to choose lumber for the various parts of a job. Finally, there are instructions on how to interpret the 'lumber marks' you find on most boards.

Lumber Terms to Know

ACTUAL SIZE   As opposed to "nominal size"—the size of a piece of wood after it is reduced by surfacing. For example, a 2 x 4 will be 1½″ thick and 3½″ wide—length will be what you order.

AIR-DRIED   Moisture content is reduced to a specific percentage by stacking wood so air can circulate around it. When the work is done correctly and sufficient time is allowed, air-dried wood is as good as material that has been kiln-dried.

BATTEN   Usually, a slim, narrow strip of wood used to cover a vertical joint between boards. Often used synonymously with "cleat."

BIRD'S-EYE   A small figure resembling the eye of a bird. Can be found on various woods but usually associated with maple. Sugar maple has more of it than other species.

BLEEDING   When soluble salts or resins cause blemishes in or on a painted surface. Resinous woods like pine should be sealed before finishing, especially over knots.

BLEMISH   Has to do with the appearance of wood. Imperfections that are not attractive but do not affect the utility of the material.

BLUE STAIN   A blemish that can be caused by fungi in lumber that has yet to be seasoned. Stains can be grayish or bluish. Blue stain does not affect the strength of the material.

BOW   A type of warp. A board will describe an arc, lengthwise, instead of being flat.

BS   Means "both sides."

BURL   Actually an abnormality. A growth, often dome-shaped, which can be sliced to make beautiful veneer. Large but slabs are often used as table tops.

CLEAT   A strip of wood that is used to support a shelf or similar project. A strip attached to an existing wall to provide a base for hooks. Used across the back of several pieces of lumber to hold them on a similar plane and to help prevent warping.

CLEAR HEART   A fine grade of wood cut from the heart of the tree. In redwood, clear heart means there will be no visible defects on one face of the wood.

CLOSE GRAIN   Wood that has very small and closely spaced pores. Usually, such wood does not require a filler before finishing. "Fine textured" is also used to describe the condition.

CROOK   A distortion that combines a bowed surface and a bowed edge. Also, the distortion might simply be a bowed edge.

CUP   A distortion across the width of a board. Surface is concave instead of flat.

DEFECT   An imperfection in wood that can affect its strength or durability.

DELAMINATE   A separation of plies in a laminated material like plywood—this can happen if an interior grade of plywood is used outdoors or in areas high in moisture.

DRY ROT   Wood-rotting fungi require considerable moisture for growth so the term is used loosely. Wood contaminated by dry rot can be crushed to a powder.

FAS   Means first and seconds.

FIGURE   Patterns produced by annual growth rings and by irregular coloration. Deviations from normal grain structure such as knots and rays contribute to figure design.

FLITCH   A term applied to a log that has been sawed on two or four sides. It is ready for additional cutting, but can be used as is as rough timber.

GRAIN   Generally, the pattern described by the fibers in wood. Affected by how a log is sawed into lumber.

GREEN   Lumber which has not gone through a drying schedule.

GROWTH RINGS   A layer of wood, sometimes bark, which occurs during one growing season. Counting the rings can tell the age of the tree. Close-grained woods and stronger woods come from trees that have narrow growth rings.

HARDBOARD   A man-made material composed of compressed wood fibers. Standard panels are brownish and have one textured surface. Panels with embossed surfaces or with tough, baked-on finishes are available. Uses include furniture components, siding, and inside wall covers.

HARDWOOD   Botanically, wood produced by deciduous trees. Usually, but not always, harder and denser than "softwoods."

HEARTWOOD   From central areas of trees. Usually darker than other areas and in some species more decay and insect resistant than sapwood.

HONEYCOMB   A condition caused by a fungus that leaves small, white pockets in the wood. It does not affect the strength of the material.

KILN-DRIED   Lumber whose moisture content has been reduced to a specific percentage by placing it in a heated chamber for a particular length of time. Temperature and humidity are closely controlled during the procedure.

KERF   The cut made by a saw blade. When the blade has set teeth, the kerf will be wider than the gauge of the blade.

KNOT   Caused (mainly) by the connections between the trunk and branches of a tree. "Tight" knots are firmly fixed and can add to the appearance of wood. For example, knotty pine is used effectively in furniture and for wall paneling.

LATH   A slim, narrow strip of lumber, usually rough, that was widely used as the base for plaster walls. Today, steel mesh and special sheets of gypsum are used instead. These materials are also called "lath."

LINEAR FOOT   Actual length of lumber and wood products regardless of thickness or width.

LOUVER   One or a set of strips set at an angle, usually in horizontal fashion. Used in doors, shutters, and similar projects. A louvered fence will have larger boards set vertically.

LUMBER   The material cut from logs to a size and shape that is usable by woodworkers.

MEDULLARY RAYS   Bands of cells that radiate from the center of the tree. They are most prominent in lumber cut from trees like oak and beech.

MILLWORK   Covers lumber and wood materials that have been fabricated to a particular shape or assembly; for example, doors and windows.

MOLDING   Shaped pieces that can be decorative or structural. There are many varieties: quarter and half round, cove, crown, picture, cornice, and base-cap. Often, its use identifies the shape.

NOMINAL SIZE   The size of lumber before it is surfaced. The nominal size of a 2 x 4 would be 2″ by 4″ or more. After surfacing it would be 1½″ x 3½″.

OPEN-GRAIN   Wood that has rather large, open pores that usually require filling before finishing. Oak is an example.

ORDERING SEQUENCE   How to list dimensions when ordering lumber—thickness in inches by width in inches by length in feet. Use nominal size for thickness and width.

PANELING   Usually, wall coverings that can be plywood or composition material. Solid lumber used as a wall covering is often called paneling.

PARTICLEBOARD   Panels made of wood chips, flakes, or particles that are bonded together under pressure. Available in 4′ x 8′ sheets and in various thicknesses. Can be used for furniture components, substructure for plastic laminates, and floor underlayment.

PATINA   The color and the feel that wood can acquire with age.

PECK   Can be a pitted area or a channel in wood. Usually found in cedar ("pecky cedar").

PITCH STREAK   An accumulation of resin that forms a very obvious streak.

PITH   A soft core that can be found in the center of a tree or limb. Lumber that contains much of it should not be used for structural purposes.

PLAIN-SAWED   An economical method of sawing a log into lumber. Cuts are made tangent to the growth rings. Surface grain pattern displays conspicuous growth rings.

PLY   A layer in an assembly composed of laminated pieces.

PLYWOOD   A material made by bonding together an odd number of veneers with the grain of adjoining plies running at right angles. Grain direction of surface veneers usually follows the long dimension of the panel. Sometimes made by bonding surface veneers to a solid core. Fancy plywood panels are made of the most rare, exotic woods.

POCKET   Actually a crack that appears between growth rings. Often contains pitch.

PRESSURE TREATED   Lumber subjected to a vacuum process that forces preservatives deep into the cells of the wood. The material withstands attack by rot and insects and has become very popular for decks, porches, or any project that will be exposed to the elements. Also used in soil-contact situations.

QUARTERS   A thickness term often used when ordering hardwoods—4/4 means four quarters or one inch, 5/4 means one and one quarter inches, and so on.

QUARTER-SAWED   Lumber sawed from a log that was first cut into quarter sections. The line of cut runs from the center toward the bark, and is parallel to the radius of the quarter section. Grain pattern generally runs in straight lines.

RANDOM LENGTH   Quantity of lumber made up of pieces of various lengths.

RWL   Quantity of lumber made up of pieces of no specific width or length.

SAPWOOD   Those areas of wood that are next to the bark and which are actively involved in the life processes of the tree. Usually lighter in color than heartwood. It can be just as strong as heartwood but can be more susceptible to decay.

SELECT   Lumber that has been carefully selected for appearance.

SHEATHING   An underlayment placed over framework of walls and roofs before finish material is added. Can be plywood or composition material.

SIDING   The final material that covers exterior walls of buildings. Many varieties including plywood, boards, hardboard, and shaped pieces such as "bevel siding."

SLABS   The first pieces cut from a log. Usually processed for use other than lumber.

SOFTWOOD   Botanically, lumber that is cut from evergreen trees. For example, wood from pine or spruce is softwood. The term should not always be taken literally; yellow pine (a softwood) is much harder than basswood (a hardwood).

SQUARE   A quantity of material. A square of shakes will cover 100 square feet of a roof.

STUD   A piece of wood of standard dimensions that is the vertical component in wall structures.

SUBFLOOR   The base for finish flooring. Various types of plywood are made for the purpose.

SUMMERWOOD   A part of annual growth rings that form during the latter part of the growth period. This part of the wood is usually denser and stronger than springwood.

S1S   Surfaced one side.

S2S   Surfaced two sides.

S3S   Surfaced three sides.

S4S   Surfaced four sides.

VENEER   Thin sheets of wood that can run from 1/100 to ¼" thick. "Rotary cut" veneer is formed in a special lathe by rotating a log against the edge of a knife. "Sawed" veneer is produced by simple sawing. "Sliced" veneer is made by moving a log or flitch against a knife.

WIND   A distortion, actually an obvious twist that runs from end to end in a board. A board in wind is difficult to salvage.

WHITE POCKET   A blemish caused by a fungus disease. Sometimes called "white speck." It detracts from the wood's appearance but doesn't affect its strength.

Notes on Popular Woods

AFRICAN CHERRY (MAKORI)   African hardwood which is generally pale red with darker red lines. Often used in furniture, it's strong and easy to work.

AFRICAN MAHOGANY   A hardwood with tones that range from reddish brown to pink. It can be found as the surface veneer of fancy plywood and is a respectable furniture material. Not a true mahogany.

AFRICAN TEAK (IROKO)   A brown wood with yellow bands that follow a zigzag pattern. It has a fine texture and can be found in paneling and furniture. Africans often use it for carving and for making bowls.

AFRORMOSIA   A heavy hardwood somewhat like teak. Generally brownish with streaks that are yellowish-brown. Tough enough to be used for ship decking, but is also used for paneling and furniture.

AGBA   The wood is easy to work, has a pale brown tone, and is very close in appearance to African mahogany. Source is West Africa.

ALDER (RED)   Its use is generally limited to plywood and to reinforcement components in furniture. Tones range from brown to white. Source is the Pacific Northwest.

AMARANTH (PURPLEHEART)   A hardwood of Central America that changes from brown to purple after it is cut. Available in boards and veneers.

AMBOYNA   Interesting wood from the East Indies that is generally rosy red with tiny knots that resemble bird's eyes. Often used for inlay work.

ASH   A tough, heavy wood with a prominent figure. Sapwood is white, other areas can be brown with a grayish tone. Popular for furniture. Takes abuse so it is often used for handles and projects like baseball bats.

ASPEN (POPLAR)   Aspen used in furniture is usually cut from the crotch of the tree. The wood from the cottonwood (an aspen) is used to make boxes. Most species in this category produce wood that is considered inferior and weak.

AVODIRE (AFRICAN SATINWOOD)   A strong, lightweight wood with a clean grain and a golden yellow color.

Can be surfaced to a high polish. Available as lumber and veneers. Very popular for marquetry.

BASSWOOD   One of the hardwoods that is actually quite soft and light. The wood is white, has little grain, is very easy to work but is weak. It's used for crates and boxes, general millwork, and as a core in panels. The "linden", a basswood, is popular for landscaping and shade.

BEECH   A heavy wood that is strong and durable. One of the woods easily bent by steaming. Often used for food containers and woodenware since it doesn't impart odor or taste. Available as lumber or veneer.

BIRCH   Many species, most common being the yellow birch and the sweet birch. The woods have a close grain and are hard and heavy. There are many applications, among them, cabinetmaking, millwork, furniture, and paneling. Available as lumber or veneer.

BOXWOOD   A heavy, hard wood that is not too difficult to work. Uses include tool handles, small combs, backs of bushes, and similar items. Popular for lathe turning, carving, and for inlay and marquetry. The color is generally a yellowish white.

BUTTERNUT   Characteristics are so similar to the American black walnut that it is often called "white walnut;" the difference is in the latter's lighter color. The wood is soft, close grained, and easy to work with all types of tools. Used for paneling, cabinetwork, and furniture.

CEDAR (RED)   This is the aromatic wood that is often used in closets and chests. Generally red in color with a thin layer of white sapwood. Today, manufacturers use material with many knots simply because clear stock is hard to come by. The wood from other varieties of cedars is suitable for fences, poles, shingles and shakes, and furniture. Heartwood is resistant to decay.

CHERRY   A naturally beautiful hardwood that takes a fine polish. Can be worked fairly well with all types of tools and is a popular choice for furniture, cabinets, and paneling. Available as lumber or veneer.

CHESTNUT   Difficult to find today because of chestnut blight which has almost entirely exterminated the species. Might find some as "wormy chestnut," the result of insects eating the tree after it has been killed by the blight.

COCOBOLO   An oily wood that doesn't take to gluing, but colors are intriguing and the wood is often used for turnings. One must be careful about dust from this wood; it can produce an effect similar to ivy poisoning.

EBONY   Most varieties produce wood that is heavy, black, and very durable. Takes a good polish and can be used in cabinetwork, inlaying, and turning. Piano keys and tool handles are often made of it.

ELM (ENGLISH)   The wood is used in cabinetry and for decorative touches. Hard to find except as a manufactured veneer. Importing of logs no longer allowed because of elm disease.

FIR (DOUGLAS)   A "hard" softwood used extensively as structural components in house building and as veneers in plywood. Works easily with power tools but not so with hand tools. Has areas of hard and soft grain; not the best wood for painting.

GUM   Color runs from brown to gray. Often called "spotted" gum because whitish bark contains differently colored spots. Sometimes used as a substitute for satinwood. Grain is erratic; occasionally, highly figured areas are sought after for paneling.

HEMLOCK   An important commercial wood used extensively in construction. Much of western hemlock is used for quality paper and newsprint.

HICKORY   Color is generally brownish. Combination of strength, hardness, toughness, and stiffness make it very suitable for tool handles, agricultural implements, and lawn furniture.

HOLLY (AMERICAN)   Wood is white, light, and practically grainless. Small amounts are made into veneers and lumber. Leaves and berries are important to industries that manufacture holiday sprays and wreaths.

KOA   Hawaiian Islands exclusive; dugout canoes were made from large trees. Resonant qualities of the wood make it exceptional for musical instruments. Has interesting fiddleback figure and takes a fine finish. Can be used in furniture and paneling.

LACEWOOD   Wood has striking figures with colors that range from pink to reddish-brown. Craftspeople like it for cabinetwork when they seek an unusual appearance. An import, often sold here as "silk oak" or "selena."

LARCH   A soft wood that is hard and strong and that has generally straight, uniform grain. It is used in construction, sometimes in the manufacture of lesser quality furniture. Other uses are poles, railroad ties, pulp for fiberboard, and paper.

LAUREL (CALIFORNIA)   Noted for highly figured veneers that take an excellent polish. Used in panels and furniture. Much prized for turning into bowls, trays, candlesticks, and the like.

MAHOGANY   Many species available. Much admired and used for cabinetwork, furniture, paneling, and boat building. Generally reddish brown with nice figuring; is reasonably close grained and easy to work with power or hand tools.

MAPLE   Hard maple is valuable for paneling, flooring, furniture, cabinetwork, veneers, and more. Wood is strong, close grained with generally straight grain, but can be highly figured. Figures sought after for cabinetwork and furniture are "curly," "bird's eye," and "wavy."

MYRTLE   Wood is hard and strong with interesting colors ranging from golden brown to yellowish green. Burls are often used for veneers. A fine wood for lathe enthusiasts.

OAK   Many varieties. Both white oak and red oak produce strong, tough woods, but the white, having a better appearance, is used more for furniture, paneling, trim, and flooring.

Red oak is often found in flooring but it's not completely ignored for other uses.

PADOUK   Some of its wood has a brilliant red color so it is often called "vermilion." Many craftspeople enjoy using it for furniture, musical instruments, and for turnings.

PEAR WOOD   Generally pink in color with light cream background shadings. A good deal of it is used in marquetry for reproducing flesh colors. European pear wood is used for veneers.

PECAN   A species of hickory with reddish brown wood with occasional dark streaks. Wood is hard and heavy. Some of it is made into veneers for furniture. The tree is more popular for its nuts than its wood.

PINE (YELLOW)   Many species; in the "yellow" category which covers "longleaf," "shortleaf," "loblolly," and slash, the wood is yellowish, heavy, and hard. It has good strength and is used in construction and plywoods. Not the easiest wood to work with.

PINE (WHITE)   Generally, this category covers "ponderosa," "sugar," "eastern white," and "western white." There are very slight differences, although the eastern white is often the choice for cabinetry and general carpentry. It is light in color and has a straight, close grain. Easy to work and can be stained or painted without problems.

REDWOOD   The magic wood, growing in a limited area along the pacific coast of the U.S., thought by indians to be immortal because of their long life. Grows to great size; one tree produced 344,000 board feet of lumber. The wood is soft, light, and generally reddish brown. Heartwood is decay and insect resistant. Burls are much sought after for table tops and veneers. Popular material for outdoor projects like planters, decks, and furniture. More than half the redwood lumber is in the form of planks, joists, and beams used in house construction. It is also used for siding and paneling.

ROSEWOOD (BRAZILIAN)   Colors range from cream to brown to black streaks. Once used in the production of superior pianos. Takes a smooth and high polish. Veneers are often for decorative touches and inlays in cabinetwork.

SPRUCE   Many varieties. Much of the wood is valued as pulp for paper. The commercial value of the blue spruce is in landscaping. Most of the wood has a lot of strength in relation to its weight and is used extensively in construction. White spruce is used for interior finishing, for furniture, and for oars and canoe paddles.

SYCAMORE   A moderately heavy hardwood, reddish brown in color. Available as lumber or veneers. It's tough enough to be used in butcher blocks. Much of it goes into railroad ties and fence posts.

TEAK   A very durable wood used extensively for paneling, furniture, shipbuilding, and flooring. Available as lumber or veneers. Dimensional stability is excellent. The wood can vary in color from straw-like tones to deep browns, sometimes with black streaks. It can have an oily surface and may feel sticky when first cut.

WALNUT (BLACK)   One of the most desirable native U.S. woods. Many excellent working qualities in addition to its inherent beauty. Butts, crotches, burls, fiddleback, leaf, and stripes are some of the forms available in veneers. The tree is also appreciated for its food value, the black walnuts we eat.

Pointers on Wood Grading

Softwood

Select Grades

A   Flaws are difficult to find; suitable for natural finishes and staining.

B   This grade is also suitable for natural finishes but it does contain a few, small, visible defects.

C   Contains defects but they will be hidden if the project is to be painted.

D   Will contain defects similar to those in grade "C" but more of them. Another grade that can be selected for painted projects.

Common Grades

1   A sound material that will contain tight knots and limited number of blemishes. It should be free of decay, checks, and splits.

2   Can have defects such as end-checks, loose knots, and some blemishes and discoloration. It should not have splits or distortions like warp.

3   Usually used as a construction lumber of medium quality. Can contain various types of defects some of which should be cut out before the material is used.

4   A construction lumber of low quality. Can contain many defects, even open knot holes.

5   Lowest quality material. It can be used as a filler but much of it will be waste.

Structural Grades

CONSTRUCTION   This is the best quality structural material.

STANDARD   Very similar to "construction" but will have defects.

UTILITY   Structural material but of poor quality. Useable, but should be reinforced with additional components or by increasing number of pieces used.

ECONOMY   The lowest quality structural material.

(Continued on next page)

Pointers on Wood Grading (cont'd.)

Grades for Hardwood Lumber

FIRSTS   The top of the line for super cabinet making. Should be over 90% clear on both sides.

SECONDS   A good choice for most cabinetwork. Should be at least 80% clear on both sides.

FIRSTS AND SECONDS   Combines "firsts" and "seconds" but should contain a minimum of 20% "firsts."

SELECTS   A good material for cabinetwork but some culling may have to be done. One side is ungraded but the other should be at least 90% clear.

1 COMMON   Often used for interior and less demanding cabinetwork. One side should be at least 65% clear.

2 COMMON   Often used for paneling and flooring. One side should be about 50% clear. Sometimes used for painted projects.

EXAMPLES OF A BOARD FOOT

A   1″ x 12″ x 12″ = 1 board foot
B   2″ x 6″ x 12″ = 1 board foot
C   1″ x 6″ x 24″ = 1 board foot

To Find Number of Board Feet in Any Piece of Wood, Use Following Formula:

$$\frac{T \times W \times L}{12} = \text{board feet}$$

T = thickness in inches
W = width in inches
L = length in feet

Examples:

(A   4″ x 24″ x 12′)

$$\frac{4 \times 24 \times 12}{12} = 96 \text{ board feet}$$

(A   1″ x 12″ x 18′)

$$\frac{1 \times 12 \times 18}{12} = 18 \text{ board feet}$$

Cross Section of a Tree

You can learn much about wood by studying a cross section of a tree. The size of the inner cores (pith and heartwood) increase each year as the tree's diameter grows. There is a lot of difference between heartwood lumber and material cut from outer areas of summer and spring growth. For one thing, heartwood is generally closer grained and harder. In some species, like redwood, it is the section of the tree that is resistant to insect damage. How and from what areas boards are cut determines such things as grain pattern and warpage characteristics.

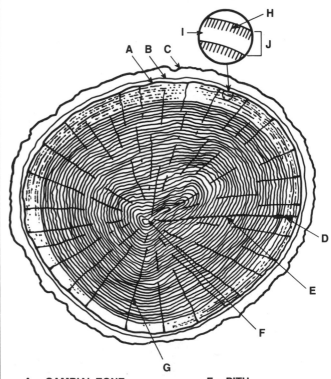

A.	CAMBIAL ZONE	F. PITH
B.	INNER BARK	G. VASCULAR RAY
C.	OUTER BARK	H. LATEWOOD
D.	SAP WOOD	I. EARLYWOOD
E.	HEARTWOOD	J. ANNUAL RING

Common Methods of Sawing Logs

Economical method called "plain-sawed" for hardwoods; "flat-grained" for softwoods. Sawing is done lengthwise, tangent to the growth rings. This method results in the greatest amount of lumber with minimum waste. The grain pattern on the surface of the sawed material is the common "U" or "V" shape; annual rings are very apparent.

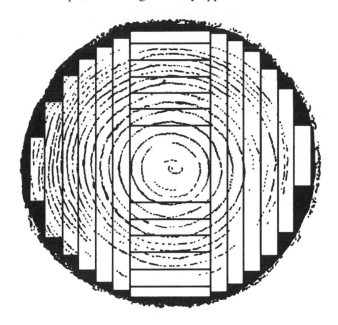

This method is called "quarter-sawed" for hardwood; "edge-grained" for softwood. Boards are sliced from quarter sections of a log with cuts running parallel to the radius of the sections. Advantages include figure beauty and less danger of warping. Grain pattern is generally straight lines running parallel to the long dimension. Lumber produced this way is more costly.

Various areas of a tree lend themselves to particular applications. Lumber, of course, comes from the bulk of the tree. Because of exotic configurations, the burl, butt, and crotch areas are usually formed into veneers.

One method of plain sawing that produces flat-grain lumber. Cuts are made on four sides of the log leaving a solid, center timber for a particular purpose, or which can be reduced further as shown.

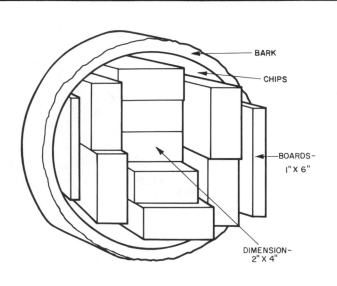

A typical method of sawing lumber from small logs.

Shrinkage factors are determined by the area from which the material is cut. This affects the warpage characteristics of the boards.

FLAT SAWING   **QUARTER SAWING**   **RIFT SAWING**

Grain patterns that result from different kinds of sawing.

WOOD DISTORTIONS (WARPAGE)

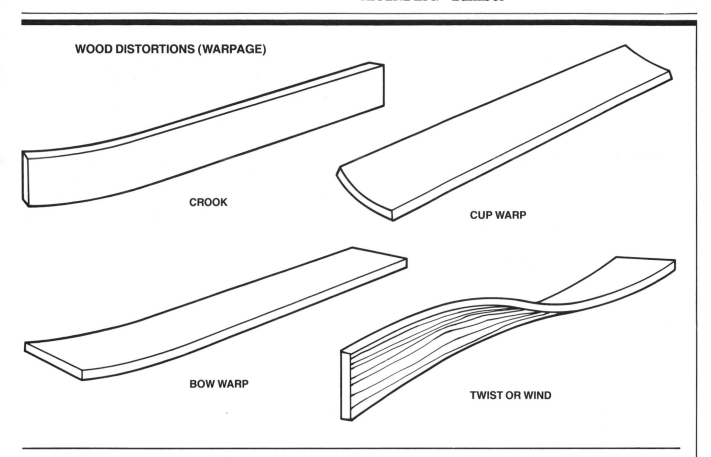

CROOK

CUP WARP

BOW WARP

TWIST OR WIND

TYPICAL LUMBER PRODUCT CLASSIFICATIONS		
MATERIAL	**THICKNESS**	**WIDTH**
Board lumber	1″	2″ or more
Light framing	2″- 4″	2″- 4″
Studs	2″- 4″	2″- 6″
Structural light framing	2″- 4″	2″- 4″
Beams and stringers	5″ and more	More than 2″ greater than thickness
Posts and timbers	5″ and more	Not more than 2″ greater than thickness
Decking	2″- 4″	4″ and more
Siding	Shaped pieces—precut pieces—dimension at butt edge = thickness	
Moldings	Shaped pieces—purchased by linear foot	

Note: Lumber lengths usually start at 6 feet—increase in multiples of 2 feet.
Lumber materials ordered in sequence of thickness, width, and length.

Examples: 1″ x 6″ x 8′   ;   2″ x 8″ x 10′

Lumber Marks

These marks are applicable to all western lumber species graded under the supervision of the Western Wood Products Association.

A WWPA grade stamp on a piece of lumber indicates its assigned grade, species or species combination, moisture condition at time of surfacing, the mill of origin and may also give other useful information. At buyers' request, mills authorized to use WWPA grade stamps will grademark the lumber they ship. Included are nearly a dozen commercially important western lumber species.

This is the official Association certification mark. It denotes that the product was graded under WWPA supervision. The symbol is registered with the U.S. Patent Office and may be used only when authorized by the Western Wood Products Association.

12

Each mill is assigned a permanent number. Some mills are identified by mill name or abbreviation instead of by mill number.

2 COM

This is an example of an official grade name abbreviation, in this case 2 Common Boards as described in the

S-DRY
MC 15
S-GRN

WWPA 1970 Grading Rules. Its appearance in a grade mark identifies the grade of a piece of lumber.

This is a species mark identifying the tree species from which the lumber is sawn, in this case Douglas Fir.

These marks denote the moisture content of the lumber when manufactured. "S-DRY" indicates a moisture content not exceeding 19 percent. "MC 15" indicates a moisture content not exceeding 15 percent. "S-GRN" indicates that the moisture content exceeded 19 percent.

When an Inspection Certificate issued by the Western Wood Products Association is required on a shipment of lumber and specific grade marks are not used, the stock is identified by an imprint of the Association mark and the number of the shipping mill or inspector.

Note: All of the above components may appear in various combinations in the official grade stamps.

Courtesy of Western Wood Products Association.

How to Read Lumber Marks

12	Identifies mill
3 COM	Identifies grade
LP	Identifies species (lodgepole pine)
S-DRY	Moisture content not over 19%

12	Identifies mill
C&BTR SEL	Grade—selects and finish
SP	Sugar pine
MC 15	Moisture content not over 15%

RELATIVE CHARACTERISTICS OF SOME POPULAR WOODS						
SPECIES	HARDNESS	WEIGHT	STRENGTH	GRAIN	GLUING QUALITY	NAILING QUALITY
Ash	High	High	Medium	Open	Medium	Medium
Basswood	Low	Low	Low	Medium	High	High
Beech	High	High	Medium	Medium	Low	Low
Birch	High	High	High	Close	Medium	Low
Cherry	High	Medium	Medium	Medium	High	Medium
Gum	Medium	Medium	Medium	Medium	High	High
Hickory	High	High	High	Open	High	Low
Mahogany	Medium	High	Medium	Open	High	Medium
Maple	High	High	High	Close	Medium	Low
Oak	High	High	High	Open	High	High
Pine	Low	Low	Low	Close	High	High
Poplar	Low	Low	Low	Open	High	High
Redwood	Low	Low	Medium	Medium	High	Medium
Walnut	High	Medium	Medium	Medium	High	Medium

LUMBER SIZES			
WHAT YOU ASK FOR	ACTUAL SIZE	WHAT YOU ASK FOR	ACTUAL SIZE
1 x 2	¾ x 1½	2 x 4	1½ x 3½
1 x 3	¾ x 2½	2 x 6	1½ x 5½
1 x 4	¾ x 3½	2 x 8	1½ x 7¼
1 x 5	¾ x 4½	2 x 10	1½ x 9¼
1 x 6	¾ x 5½	2 x 12	1½ x 11¼
1 x 8	¾ x 7¼	3 x 4	2½ x 3½
1 x 10	¾ x 9¼	4 x 4	3½ x 3½
1 x 12	¾ x 11¼	4 x 6	3½ x 5½
2 x 2	1½ x 1½	6 x 6	5½ x 5½
2 x 3	1½ x 2½	8 x 8	7½ x 7½

| BOARD FOOT CONTENT IN COMMON LUMBER SIZES | | | | | | | | | |
| IN INCHES | | BOARD LENGTH (IN FEET) | | | | | | | |
THICK	WIDTH	10	12	14	16	18	20	22	24
1	2	1.666	2	2.333	2.666	3.0	3.333	3.666	4
1	3	2.5	3	3.5	4.0	4.5	5.0	5.5	6
1	4	3.333	4	4.666	5.333	6.0	6.666	7.333	8
1	5	4.167	5	5.833	6.666	7.5	8.333	9.167	10
1	6	5.0	6	7.0	8.0	9.0	10.0	11.0	12
1	7	5.833	7	8.167	9.333	10.5	11.666	12.833	14
1	8	6.666	8	9.333	10.666	12.0	13.333	14.666	16
1	9	7.5	9	10.5	12.0	13.5	15.0	16.5	18
1	10	8.333	10	11.666	13.333	15.0	16.666	18.333	20
1	12	10.0	12	14.0	16.0	18.0	20.0	22.0	24
1	14	11.666	14	16.333	18.666	21.0	23.333	25.666	28
1	16	13.333	16	18.666	21.333	24.0	26.666	29.333	32
2	2	3.333	4	4.666	5.333	6.0	6.666	7.333	8
2	3	5.0	6	7.0	8.0	9.0	10.0	11.0	12
2	4	6.666	8	9.333	10.666	12.0	13.333	14.666	16
2	6	10.0	12	14.0	16.0	18.0	20.0	22.0	24
2	8	13.333	16	18.666	21.333	24.0	26.666	29.333	32
2	9	15.0	18	21.0	24.0	27.0	30.0	33.0	36
2	10	16.666	20	23.333	26.666	30.0	33.333	36.666	40
2	12	20.0	24	28.0	32.0	36.0	40.0	44.0	48

APPENDIX
2.
Panel Materials

The first panel materials—plywood—began to appear in the last half of the nineteenth century. The manufacture of plywood was made possible by the development of new wood saws, glues, and processing equipment. With continued development, manufacturers introduced more and better varieties of panel materials—hardboard, particleboard, waferboard, strand board, and plywood for many different purposes.

The information in this section will help you to understand the different panel materials that are commonly available and how to best use them. You'll find that although the materials here are grouped under the same general heading, they are very different. With most of the materials, there are a list of terms that apply to just a single material. Materials differ in relative strength, durability, how they take paints, stains, and finishes, and how they may be worked and joined—all of this is discussed. Materials are also graded and classed and specified differently. With each type of panel material, there may be many variations for different applications—interior and exterior, underlayment, fire-retardant, etc. All the common variations are explained, and there are instructions for how to tell one variation from the next.

Waferboard

Waferboard was designed as a structural-use panel, but because it is easy to work with and has a distinctive appearance, its applications have been broadened to include a host of home craft projects. The material has become popular for wall paneling and other uses that include doors or door paneling, fencing, outdoor sheds and farm structures, and decorative inside projects.

Standard panel size is 4' x 8'—thicknesses range from ¼" through ¾".

The panels are made by compressing wafer-like pieces of wood that are bonded with phenolic resin. The wafers can differ in size and thickness, and they can be assembled randomly or in a particular direction. Sometimes the wafers are arranged in layers that relate to their size and thickness.

The panels can be stained, painted, or finished in natural fashion. Semi-transparent stains will provide color while allowing wafer grain and other natural characteristics to show through. When light colors are used, it's recommended that the stain be an oil-based type to guard against discoloration that can happen because of water-soluble compounds (extractives) in the wood.

The material can be covered with either oil- or water-base paints. Most times it's best to use a primer or undercoat before the final finish, but do a test on a scrap piece if the color you wish to apply is very dark. It's possible that a single coat may do.

Varnishes and oils may be used for a natural finish. Two coats of clear, penetrating sealer with a light sanding between coats and after the final coat will produce an attractive finish that is easily maintained. Use a sealer before applying a varnish finish.

The attractive wood texture of Waferwood adapts to "non-structural" applications such as these kitchen cabinets. Other uses include wall paneling, basic furniture, shelving, and storage projects.

Various wood species are used in the manufacture of Waferboard, but aspen (a soft-grain hardwood), is used most often. Logs are debarked and then cut into lengths that are easy to handle.

Large, generally paper-thin wafers are produced by moving the log against a set of razor-like knives that are attached to a rotating surface. The wafers are then dried, separated from waste, and sorted by size.

After wafers are mixed with phenolic resin and assembled on mats, they are fed into a hydraulic press where heat and pressure forms them into solid wood panels.

Particleboard

Particleboard is a man-made panel that may be composed of various wood materials such as flakes, chips, splinters, various selected mill wastes, or even sawdust. The materials are combined with a bonding agent and put through the same type of heat and pressure procedure as waferboard. This results in hard-surfaced panels that may be used as is or as core material for various types of surface veneers. The bonding agent that is used and the particular manufacturing procedures determine the density of the panel and whether it is suitable for exterior applications.

Common panel six is 4' x 8'—readily available thicknesses range from ¼" to ¾". In addition to paneling, the material is available as, for example, bull-nosed stair treads ready for covering with carpeting, or resilient flooring. It is often used as a core for doors and as vinyl-wrapped jambs and molding. The fact that it is flat, smooth, and stable makes it an ideal substrate for countertops and similar projects. Kitchen cabinet manufacturers use particleboard for backs, sides, shelves, and front panels. The construction industry finds it a good material for floor underlayment.

Particleboard is very abrasive, so sawing should be done with a tungsten carbide-toothed blade; a metal-cutting blade when saber sawing. Use tungsten carbide bits when shaping the material with a router.

The material can be finished in various ways—left natural, stained, painted, or varnished. Painting, unless you are using panels that were factory-prepared for the purpose, calls for application of sanding sealer with special attention paid to edges, before final coats. Filling can be eliminated if you wish to achieve a textured effect.

Use oil-based instead of water-based material for staining. Stains can be overcoated with finish like varnish, or such materials can be used alone for a natural finish.

Edges are usually more absorbent and "rougher" than surfaces and need more attention. They can be made smooth with applications of wood paste or, as is common, covered with strips of wood, veneer, or molding. Edges are often covered with special metal moldings when the material is used as a substrate for countertops.

Particleboard Terms

DENSITY   This tells the weight of a panel per cubic foot and has an influence on its strength. Lightweight projects can be constructed with low-density particleboard. Panel strength is also affected by board composition and construction.

TYPE 1   Interior-use panel made with a urea-formaldehyde binder.

TYPE 2   Phenolic resin is used as a binder. Panels are *resistant* to moisture and heat.

CLASS   The product's overall specifications.

MODULUS OF ELASTICITY   Measure of resistance to deflection under load. Generally, it indicates the stiffness of a panel.

MODULUS OF RUPTURE   The measure of a load that is needed to cause a break in a panel. PSI = pounds of load pressure per square inch.

INTERNAL BOND   A measure of the strength of the bond between the individual particles that compose the pane. Tested by measuring the force panel faces will withstand before failure occurs.

SCREW HOLDING   How well does a screw hold? Tests indicate the force required to pull out a No. 10, type A sheet metal screw from the face and edge of a panel.

LINEAR EXPANSION   A measurement of average dimensional changes that can be caused by atmospheric or environmental humidity.

Note: Specifications are stamped on panels, usually in three letter/number symbols. Examples: 1-B-1, 1-A-2. The first symbol (a number) tells the *type*, which bonding adhesive was used. The second symbol indicates density. The third symbol is an overall classification and, in a sense, indicates the actual strength of the panel.

Panels with lower internal bonds are more flexible. This is important when considering the length of span between supports. Generally, denser particleboard is more rigid and can support greater loads without failure. When in doubt it is wise to test, use what the shelf must hold as the test load. This will reveal whether intermediate supports are necessary.

PARTICLEBOARD SPECIFICATIONS

TYPE	DENSITY	CLASS	MODULUS OF RUPTURE (PSI)	MODULUS OF ELASTICITY (PSI)	INTERNAL BOND (PSI)	LINEAR EXPANSION (%)	SCREW FACE LBS.	HOLDING EDGE LBS.
1*	A	1	2,400	350,000	200	.55	450	
1*	A	2	3,400	350,000	140	.55		
1*	B	1	1,600	250,000	70	.35	225	160
1*	B	2	2,400	400,000	60	.30	225	200
1*	C	1	800	150,000	20	.30	125	
1*	C	2	1,400	250,000	30	.30	175	
2**	A	1	2,400	350,000	125	.55	450	
2**	A	2	3,400	500,000	400	.55	500	350
2**	B	1	1,800	250,000	65	.35	225	160
2**	B	2	2,500	450,000	60	.25	250	200

*Interior applications—generally bonded with urea-formaldehyde resin.
**Interior and exterior applications—moisture and heat-resistant binders, generally phenolic resin.

A = High density (at least 50 lbs./cu. ft.).
B = Medium density (between 37 and 50 lbs./cu. ft.).
C = Low density (37 lbs./cu. ft. and under).

Courtesy of National Particleboard Association

PARTICULAR TYPES OF PARTICLEBOARD		
TYPE	**DESCRIPTION**	**TYPICAL USES**
CORE	Basic material of various densities and properties	Laminated components, furniture, case-work, doors, paneling
VENEERED	Corestock overlaid with wood veneer or other material. Ready for use.	Cabinetwork, panels, furniture, dividers, wainscots
OVERLAID	Veneered with fiber sheets or material like hardboard and plastic laminates	Paneling, countertops, furniture, doors, cabinetwork
FILLED	Material that has been sur-face filled and sanded	For projects to be painted
EXTERIOR	Treated with special bond-ing materials	Exterior applications but material is not waterproof
UNDERCOATED OR PRIMED	Painted base coat applied by manufacturer. Available in exterior or interior types	For products that will be painted
UNDERLAYMENT	Panels that are specifically engineered as a substrate	Common application is underlay-ment for carpeting and other finish flooring
FIRE-RETARDANT	Particles are treated with special fire-retardant materials	Used where required by building codes
TOXIC-TREATED	Insect and mold resistant chemicals added to particles	Applications requiring protection against insects and decay

Even the "roughest" particleboard can be brought to paintable condition by applications of thin wood-paste. Sand smooth between coats. Pay special attention to edges. You can eliminate the procedure if you obtain panels that have been factory-prepared for painting.

A unique application for particleboard—preparing edge-beveled pieces for arrangement in an ashlar pattern. I used the idea to cover walls in a hallway. It was a great way to make use of a quantity of scrap I obtained from a local lumberyard.

Terms That Apply to Plywood and Some Other Panel Materials

APA Abbreviation for AMERICAN PLYWOOD ASSOCIATION. Organization representing most of the structural wood panel manufacturers in the nation.

BACK-PRIMING Priming the back of a panel. For example, back-priming the back of cabinet doors will prevent them from warping.

BACKSTAMP Identification stamp on the back of some panels.

BATTEN A plywood or lumber strip that conceals and protects the joint between panels. Often used decoratively.

BEVEL (JOINT) Makes a smooth joint when edges or ends of panels are butted.

BLOW A localized delamination of plies that can be caused by a buildup of steam pressure during the pressing procedure. Can be caused by moisture or excessive glue spread.

BOND Veneers are *bonded* to form a panel of plywood. Heat or pressure, sometimes both, are used so the glue will cure properly.

BOW A distortion. The lengthwise plane of the panel isn't flat.

BRUSHED A surface treatment that accents the grain pattern to create an interesting and attractive texture.

CAULK A sealant, usually waterproof, that is used to fill joints or seams. Available as a putty, in rope form, and as cartridge-contained compounds.

CENTER The inner piece of a panel that has five or more plies. The grain of the center runs parallel with the grain of the face and back.

CHECKING Exposure to changing conditions of dryness and moisture can cause cracks or "checks." Eliminate or minimize by sealing edges and priming, or sealing surfaces before installation.

COMPOSITE PANEL A panel with veneer surfaces but a reconstituted wood core.

CORE The inner plies of conventional plywood. The constituted wood in composite panels.

CORE GAP Open veneer joint that results when core sections are not butted together during manufacturing. Sizes of gaps is controlled by product standards.

CROSSBAND Core plies placed so grain is at right angles to surface veneers.

CUP A distortion. The panel is concave across its small dimension.

DELAMINATION Bond failure that causes separation between plies or within reconstituted wood cores.

EDGE SEALING Coating edges of panels with a sealant (paint or similar product) to reduce possibility of water absorption.

EDGE VOID A gap in the edge of a plywood panel. A defect caused by inner plies splitting or breaking away.

EMBOSSED Special treatment that provides textured effects in the surface of the panel. Usually done by heat and pressure against a master pattern.

EXTERIOR TYPE Plywood designed for outdoor or marine use. Bonding is 100% waterproof.

FACE GRAIN Grain direction of a panel's outer plies. Greatest strength is parallel to the face grain.

GRADES (VENEER)

A Smooth and can be painted. Permissible repairs must be neat. Can take a natural finish when project is not critical.

B Solid surface veneer. Can obtain tight knots and circular repair plugs.

C Can contain knotholes but totals within a specified area are limited by standards. The minimum veneer grade used in exterior type plywood.

C (plugged) An improved C veneer manufactured to standards that limit sizes of splits and knotholes.

D Can contain knots and knotholes up to 2½" and sometimes larger. Some splits are also permitted.

N Selected heartwood or sapwood. Some repairs permitted but no open defects. Usually a special order, natural finish material.

HDO (HIGH DENSITY OVERLAY) Exterior plywood with resin-impregnated fiber overlay. Surface is hard and smooth, and resistant to chemicals and abrasion. Stands up to punishing applications.

INTERIOR TYPE Plywood manufactured for indoor use or construction subjected to temporary moisture. Interior types are often bonded with exterior glue.

LUMBER CORE Plywood with a core of lumber strips. Face and back plies are veneer.

MDO (MEDIUM DENSITY OVERLAY) Exterior plywood with an opaque resin-treated fiber overlay. Surface is smooth and excellent as a base for paint.

NON-VENEERED PANELS Panels of reconstituted wood such as "waferboard", "oriented strand board", or "particleboard." Panels manufactured without veneer plies.

ORIENTED STRAND BOARD Panels of reconstituted, mechanically-oriented wood strands that are bonded with resins under heat and pressure. The material may also be used as a center layer in composite panels.

PARTICLEBOARD Panels of reconstituted wood *particles* that are bonded with resins under heat and pressure.

PEELER LOG Selected log, debarked, and then turned against a long knife to produce thin, continuous sheets of veneer which are then sized, dried, and graded.

REPAIR One of several methods of covering defects. A "patch" is a sound wood insert. "Boat" patches are ovals with pointed or rounded ends. "Router" patches have parallel

(Continued on next page)

sides and rounded ends. "Sled" patches are rectangles with feathered ends. A "plug" may be a circle of wood or a synthetic filler. A "Shim" is a long, narrow repair that can be wood or a synthetic material. There are standards for repairs in particular veneer grades.

TEXTURED   Panels with surface textures. Available in exterior and interior types. Examples are: "brushed", "rough-sawn", "kerfed", "channel groove" and "reverse board & batten".

TOUCH SANDED   Light surface sanding during manufacture brings panels to a uniform thickness but sander "skips" are admissable.

TYPES—EXTERIOR

A-A   Sanded panels with A-grade face and back and C-grade inner plies. Used where appearance on both sides is important. Typical applications include built-ins, cabinets, signs, boats, and fences.

A-B   Sanded panels with A-grade face and B-grade back. Often used in place of A-A when appearance of one side is not critical.

A-C   Panels with A-grade face and C-grade back; inner plies usually C-grade. Use when appearance of only one surface is important. Typical applications include fences, soffits, and building exteriors (farm).

B-B   Panels with B-grade veneer on both surfaces. Utility panel that is paintable.

B-C   Face is B-grade, back is C-grade. Utilitarian material that is often used as a base for exterior coatings.

C-C (plugged)   Face is C-plugged grade; back and inner plies are C-grade. Panels are touch sanded. Often used for severe moisture conditions.

TYPES—INTERIOR

A-A   Panels with A-grade veneers on face and back, with D-grade inner plies. Used when appearance of both sides is important. Often bonded with exterior glue. Applications include built-ins, furniture, cabinets, and partitions.

A-B   A reasonable substitute for A-A when the appearance of one side is not critical. A-grade face, B-grade back, D-grade inner plies.

A-D   A-grade face, D-grade back. Used on projects where smoothness and appearance of only one side is important.

B-B   Utility panel with B-grade veneer on face and back.

B-D   B-grade face, D-grade back. A utility panel often used as a backing material or shelving when appearance is not critical.

C-D (plugged)   Face veneer is C-plugged grade; back is D-grade. Surface is touch sanded. Often used in hidden areas.

UNSANDED   Interior or exterior sheathing grade panels. Made for utility applications.

WAFERBOARD   Non-veneered panels composed of reconstituted wood *wafers* as opposed to *particles* or *strands*. The wafers are bonded under heat and pressure with resins.

Wood Species Used in Plywood Manufactured Under Specific Product Standards

Many wood species can be used in the manufacture of plywood. These species are divided into groups according to relative strength and stiffness. The species in Group 1 are the strongest and stiffest; Group 2 is next and so on. Each group is designated by number in the APA trademark stamped on the back of the panel and tells, generally, the species used for the *face* and *back* veneers. The consumer should check local availability if a particular species is desired.

Group 1

Apitong; American beech; sweet and yellow birch; Douglas fir (A); kapur; keruing; western larch; sugar maple; caribbean and ocote pine; loblolly, longleaf, shortleaf, and slash pine; tanoak.

Group 2

Port Orford cedar; cypress; Douglas fir (B); balsam, California red, grand, noble, pacific silver, and white fir; western hemlock; almond, bagikan, mayapis, red, tangile, and white lauan; black maple; mengkulang; red mereanti(C); mer-wawa; pond, red, Virginia, and western white pine; black, red, and sitka spruce; sweetgum; tamarack; yellow poplar.

Group 3

Red alder; paper birch; Alaska cedar; subalpine fir; eastern hemlock; bigleaf maple; jack, lodgepole, ponderosa, and spruce pine; redwood; englemann and white spruce.

Group 4

Bigtooth and quaking aspen; cativo; incense and western red cedar; eastern and black cottonwood; eastern white and sugar pine.

Group 5

Basswood; balsam poplar.

Notes:

A   Douglas fir trees from Washington, Oregon, California, Idaho, Montana, Wyoming, and provinces of Alberta and British Columbia.

B   Douglas fir trees from Nevada, Utah, Colorado, Arizona, and New Mexico.

C   This species (red meranti) is limited to those with a specific gravity of .41 or more based on green volume and oven dry weight.

Courtesy of APA

SANDED GRADES

APA

Grade of veneer on panel back ——————
Grade of veneer on panel face —————— **A-C** GROUP 2
Species Group Number ——————
Designates the type of plywood —————— **EXTERIOR**

Mill number —————— 000
Product Standard governing —————— PS 1-83
manufacture

(Also available in Groups 1, 3, and 4)

UNSANDED GRADES

APA

Panel grade —————— RATED SHEATHING
Span Rating —————— **32/16** 1/2 INCH
Thickness —————— SIZED FOR SPACING
Exposure durability classification —————— **EXPOSURE 1**
—————— 000
Product Standard governing —————— PS 1-83 C-D NRB-108
manufacture

National Research Board report ——————
number

CONCRETE FORM

APA

Registered trademark of
American Plywood Association
for B-B (Concrete Form) —————— PLYFORM
Grade of veneer on panel back ——————
Grade of veneer on panel face —————— **B-B** CLASS I
Class of production
Designates the type of plywood —————— EXTERIOR
Mill number —————— 000
Product Standard governing —————— PS 1-83
manufacture

(Also available in Class II and HDO)

SPECIALTY PANELS

APA

Siding face grade —————— 303 SIDING 6-S/W
Span Rating —————— **16** OC 19/32 INCH
Species Group number —————— GROUP 1
Designates the type of plywood —————— EXTERIOR
Mill number —————— 000
Product Standard governing —————— PS 1-83 FHA-UM-64
manufacture

FHA Use of Materials
Bulletin number

Grade of veneer on panel face ——————
Grade of veneer on panel back ——————

Designates the type of plywood Product Standard governing
Exterior or Interior manufacture

A-B · G-1 · EXT-APA · PS1-83 · 000

Species Group number Mill number

Examples of trademarks established by APA and how to read them. Shown are four types of trademarks and one typical edge mark. Notations tell the meaning of each of the elements.

A·A·G-1·EXPOSURE1-APA·PS1-83·000

APA A-A

Use where appearance of both sides is important for interior applications such as built-ins, cabinets, furniture, partitions; and exterior applications such as fences, signs, boats, shipping containers, tanks, ducts, etc. Smooth surfaces suitable for painting. EXPOSURE DURABILITY CLASSIFICATIONS: Interior, Exposure 1, Exterior. COMMON THICKNESSES: 1/4, 11/32, 3/8, 15/32, 1/2, 19/32, 5/8, 23/32, 3/4.

A·B·G-1·EXPOSURE1-APA·PS1-83·000

APA A-B

For use where appearance of one side is less important but where two solid surfaces are necessary. EXPOSURE DURABILITY CLASSIFICATIONS: Interior, Exposure 1, Exterior. COMMON THICKNESSES: 1/4, 11/32, 3/8, 15/32, 1/2, 19/32, 5/8, 23/32, 3/4.

B·B·G-2·EXPOSURE1-APA·PS1-83·000

APA B-B

Utility panels with two solid sides. EXPOSURE DURABILITY CLASSIFICATIONS: Interior, Exposure 1, Exterior. COMMON THICKNESSES: 1/4, 11/32, 3/8, 15/32, 1/2, 19/32, 5/8, 23/32, 3/4.

APA

UNDERLAYMENT

GROUP 1

EXPOSURE 1

000

PS 1-83

APA UNDERLAYMENT

For application over structural subfloor. Provides smooth surface for application of carpet and possesses high concentrated and impact load resistance. Touch-sanded. For areas to be covered with thin resilient flooring, specify panels with fully sanded face. EXPOSURE DURABILITY CLASSIFICATIONS: Interior, Exposure 1. COMMON THICKNESSES: 3/8, 1/2, 19/32, 5/8, 23/32, 3/4.

APA

A-C   GROUP 1

EXTERIOR

000

PS 1-83

APA A-C

For use where appearance of only side is important in exterior applications such as soffits, fences, structural uses, boxcar and truck linings, farm buildings, tanks, trays, commercial refrigerators, etc. EXPOSURE DURABILITY CLASSIFICATION: Exterior. COMMON THICKNESSES: 1/4, 11/32, 3/8, 15/32, 1/2, 19/32, 5/8, 23/32, 3/4.

APA

B-C   GROUP 1

EXTERIOR

000

PS 1-83

APA B-C

Utility panel for farm service and work buildings, boxcar and truck linings, containers, tanks, agricultural equipment, as a base for exterior coatings and other exterior uses or applications subject to high or continuous moisture. EXPOSURE DURABILITY CLASSIFICATION: Exterior. COMMON THICKNESSES: 1/4, 11/32, 3/8, 15/32, 1/2, 19/32, 5/8, 23/32, 3/4.

APA

C-C PLUGGED

GROUP 2

EXTERIOR

000

PS 1-83

APA C-C PLUGGED

For use as an underlayment over structural subfloor, refrigerated or controlled atmosphere storage rooms, pallet fruit bins, tanks, boxcar and truck floors and linings, open soffits, and other similar applications where continuous or severe moisture may be present. Provides smooth surface for application of carpet and possesses high concentrated and impact load resistance. Touch-sanded. EXPOSURE DURABILITY CLASSIFICATION: Exterior. COMMON THICKNESSES: 3/8, 1/2, 19/32, 5/8, 23/32, 3/4.

APA

A-D   GROUP 1

EXPOSURE 1

000

PS 1-83

APA A-D

For use where appearance of only one side is important in interior applications, such as paneling, built-ins, shelving, partitions, flow racks, etc. EXPOSURE DURABILITY CLASSIFICATIONS: Interior, Exposure 1. COMMON THICKNESSES: 1/4, 11/32, 3/8, 15/32, 1/2, 19/32, 5/8, 23/32, 3/4.

APA

B-D   GROUP 2

INTERIOR

000

PS 1-83

APA B-D

Utility panel for backing, sides of built-ins, industry shelving, slip sheets, separator boards, bins and other interior or protected applications. EXPOSURE DURABILITY CLASSIFICATIONS: Interior, Exposure 1. COMMON THICKNESSES: 1/4, 11/32, 3/8, 15/32, 1/2, 19/32, 5/8, 23/32, 3/4.

APA

C-D PLUGGED

GROUP 2

EXPOSURE 1

000

PS 1-83

APA C-D PLUGGED

For built-ins, cable reels, walkways, separator boards and other interior or protected applications. Not a substitute for Underlayment or APA Rated Sturd-I-Floor as it lacks their puncture resistance. Touch-sanded. EXPOSURE DURABILITY CLASSIFICATIONS: Interior, Exposure 1. COMMON THICKNESSES: 3/8, 1/2, 19/32, 5/8, 23/32, 3/4.

A guide to sanded and touch-sanded plywood. The trademarks shown here are typical facsimiles. (APA standards)

Continuous, thin sheets of veneer are sliced from a selected log that has been debarked and mounted on a lathe. The veneer is then sized, dried, and graded.

Composite panels are faced with veneers but have cores of reconstituted wood as opposed to conventional plywoods that have veneer cores.

BOW DISTORTION

CUP DISTORTION

The panel is not flat lengthwise.

The panel is not flat crosswise.

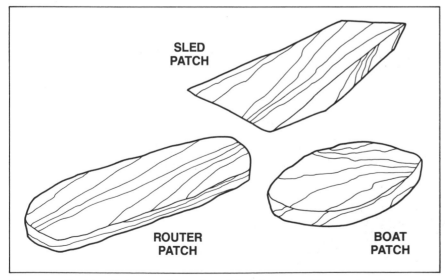

SLED PATCH

ROUTER PATCH

BOAT PATCH

Examples of patches that are used to replace defects in veneers. The sizes, numbers, and shapes of repair pieces in given veneer grades are subject to established standards.

BEVEL JOINT

The connection between panels that are joined edge-to-edge or end-to-end is smoother when a bevel joint is used.

Available Panel Material

A. STANDARD PLYWOOD   Panels are all veneer, usually an odd number placed so the grain in each ply is at right angles to the next one. Grain of front and back veneers runs parallel to panel's long dimension.

B. COMPOSITE PANELS   Face and back veneers are bonded to a reconstituted wood core. Another design has a core of solid wood.

C. WAFERBOARD   Thin, wafer-like wood flakes are mixed with phenolic resin and treated with heat and pressure to form a solid material. Flakes can be randomly or directionally oriented.

D. ORIENTED STRAND BOARD   Panels consisting of small particles; usually arranged in layers by particular size. Particles are usually randomly oriented.

E. PARTICLEBOARD   Panels consisting of small particles; usually arranged in layers by particle size. Particles are usually randomly oriented.

How house-siding plywood can be used to make an attractive project. Kerfed, rough-sawn plywood was used on this patio barbecue stand.

Textured panels. Plywood is available with surface textures and patterns. While essentially a house siding material, the panels can be used effectively for many home craft projects. The photo shows a "rough-sawn" texture. "Brushed", "kerfed", and "channel groove" are among other available designs.

Hardboard

Hardboard is a man-made product manufactured from natural wood materials (sometimes waste) that are reduced to basic fibers by special processes. One involves steaming and grinding; another places wood chips in a high-pressure enclosure into which steam is introduced in a manner that causes an explosion and reduces the chips to fibers.

The fibers are bonded with adhesive lignin, also a wood by-product, and then arranged in thick blankets on mats which carry them through a heat and pressure procedure that forms the fibers into solid, very dense, smooth panels. Particular materials may be added during the panel-forming steps that affect, among other things, the rigidity and the density of the final product.

Hardboard is available in various sizes and thicknesses. Those most likely to be available in local lumberyards, aside from decorative hardboards used as paneling, are 4′ x 8′ panels in thicknesses of ⅛″ and ¼″. Perforated hardboard (pegboard) comes in ¼″ and sometimes ⅜″ thicknesses.

Although hardboard is not as tough on cutting tools as particleboard, it is still a good idea to use carbide-toothed saw blades. Use a plywood blade or something similar if you use an all-steel blade. A combination blade will work but edges will be rougher than you might like. Because of the material's density, it is a good idea to drill pilot holes for nails. Casing nails are preferable to finishing nails when the fasteners must be concealed.

Always use a backup block when drilling. You'll find that hardboard has a greater tear-out problem when the bit breaks through than other materials.

The easiest way to achieve a successful finish on hardboard is to work with a *primed* or *sealed* type. Surface density makes it difficult to apply paint, so un-primed panels must be sanded to provide some "tooth". A fine sandpaper, about #380, wrapped around a wood block will do. You're not trying to renew the surface, just roughing it a bit, so heavy pressure isn't necessary.

Always use an undercoat that is compatible with the finish coat. It's good procedure to sand the undercoat before applying the final one.

Of course, hardboard can be used as the "core" for veneering materials such as plastic laminates, vinyls, and contact papers or plastics.

Types of Hardboard

TEMPERED   Hardboards with moisture inhibitors and other materials that were added before the manufacturing procedure to increase surface hardness, resistance to abrasion, and stiffness. These panels can take more punishment than untreated panels.

STANDARD   Do not resist moisture as well as tempered panels.

SERVICE-TEMPERED   Much the same as tempered hardboard but with a lower percentage of the additives.

SERVICE   Made without additives. Panels will have less tensile strength and resistance to moisture than other types.

INDUSTRIALITE   Special hardboards that are of medium density and lighter than others.

PRIMED   Panels with a base coat that makes them easier to paint. Sometimes the word "coated" is used in place of "primed".

SEALED OR FILLED   Panels with a special manufacturing treatment that allows them to take paint more easily.

PERFORATED   Panels with uniform holes that are used with special hooks and other types of hardware to form storage walls. Often called "pegboard".

EMBOSSED   Panels with a pattern that has been pressed in during manufacture. The embossing can resemble materials like basketweave, woodgrain, and leather.

FILIGREE   Panels that have through geometric or other types of designs. Typical applications are room dividers and cornices—wherever a light, airy feeling is desirable.

PATTERNED   Panels with pressed or machined surface patterns. Used to provide decorative touches. Applications include wainscots and dividers. Available as house siding.

STRAITED   Surface of panel has shallow, randomly-spaced grooves that run the long dimension. Some plywoods are also treated in this fashion.

GROOVED   Panels with grooves that run lengthwise. A siding material that can be used imaginatively elsewhere.

Hardboard Terms to Know

SURFACE   The condition of the face and back of the panel.

S1S   Means the panel has one smooth surface. The opposite side will have a mesh pattern or other rough texture.

S2S   Panels that are smooth on face and back.

WATER RESISTANCE   The amount of swelling that can occur when panels are subjected to extreme exposure. Standards testing requires that panels be fully submerged in water for a specific period of time.

MODULUS OF RUPTURE   What it takes to break a panel across its face. Tested in terms of number of pounds per square inch required to cause failure.

TENSILE STRENGTH   Tested by the force in pounds per square inch of pull that is needed to rupture internal bonding.

Perforated hardboard (pegboard) makes a good storage wall or cabinet back for placing tools. A paper silhouette helps keep things neat and organized—also lets you know when a tool is not in its proper place.

One example of many types of prefinished hardboard—Masonite's "Woodfield". Although created as wall paneling, the products can be used on other projects or merely to supply decorative accents. The panels are available in 4' x 8' sheets, ¼" thick and can be applied with nails or adhesive. Other panel finishes include various wood species and surface grains, even brick and stone. Some of the panels are available perforated.

DRAWER BOTTOMS

CABINET BACKS

"DISPOSABLE" BENCH TOPS

DIVIDERS

Some typical, practical applications for hardboard. S1S material is okay for drawer bottoms, cabinet backs, and bench tops. Use S2S for dividers or partitions. Use tempered material, tacked down with nails for easy removal, for bench tops.

ALL HARDBOARD =
$\frac{1}{8}$" TEMPERED

ADD CENTERS
IF REQUIRED

ALL FRAMING = I" X I"

FRAME FOR SHELVES

NAIL

CORRUGATED
NAILS

HARDBOARD
VENEER

LEG

SHELVES ARE
HARDBOARD VENEER

One way to make a project using hardboard. The frame assembly should be strong even though attaching the covering will stiffen it. Decorative hardboards can be used on projects like this.

Make panels by constructing a sturdy frame then covering with thin hardboard. The hardboard can be attached with contact cement or glue.

HARDBOARD SPECIFICATIONS*									
TYPE	SURFACE	THICKNESS IN INCHES	WATER RESISTANCE				MODULUS OF RUPTURE (PSI)	TENSILE STRENGTH	
			ABSORPTION (%)		SWELLING (%)			PARALLEL TO SURFACE (PSI)	PERPENDICULAR TO SURFACE (PSI)
			S1S	S2S	S1S	S2S			
TEMPERED (1)	S1S	1/12	30		25		7000	3500	150
	S1S and S2S	1/10	20	25	16	20			
		1/8	15	20	11	16			
		3/16	12	18	10	15			
		1/4	10	12	8	11			
		5/16	8	11	8	10			
		3/8	8	10	8	9			
STANDARD (2)	S1S and S2S	1/12	40	40	30	30	5000	2500	100
		1/10	25	30	22	25			
		1/8	20	25	16	18			
		3/16	18	25	14	18			
		1/4	16	20	12	14			
		5/16	14	15	10	12			
		3/8	12	12	10	10			
SERVICE TEMPERED (3)	S1S and S2S	1/8	20	25	15	22	4500	2000	100
		3/16	18	20	13	18			
		1/4	15	20	13	14			
		3/8	14	18	11	14			
SERVICE (4)	S1S and S2S	1/8	30	30	25	25	3000	1500	75
		3/16	25	27	15	22			
		1/4	25	27	15	22			
		3/8	25	27	15	22			
		7/16	25	27	15	22			
		1/2	25	18	15	14			

*Most readily available types.

Oriented Strand Board (OSB)

OSB is a manufactured panel with a composition of strand-like particles of wood that are placed in layers and then compressed and bonded with phenolic resin. While the material was designed specifically for construction applications, its appearance and the fact that the panels are good on both sides have prompted its use in areas that range from wall paneling to shelving. Common panel size is 4' x 8'—thickness range is ⅜" to ¾".

The panels will take stain or paint and can be finished in natural tones. Semi-transparent stain will allow grain and other natural characteristics to show through, but oil-base types are recommended to prevent discoloration that can be caused by water-soluble compounds in the wood.

Oil-base or water-base (latex) paints can be used but a primer should be applied before the finish coat. Light-colored latex stains should be applied over a stain resistant undercoat.

Varnish or oils can be used for a natural finish. A popular treatment is two coats of penetrating sealer with a light sanding between applications and after the final one—then wax.

A variety of wood species can be used in the manufacture of OSB, but a soft-grain hardwood, usually aspen, is most often used. Logs are debarked and cut into short "bolts" which then go to the "flaker". Waste material is removed, and the flakes are sorted by size and then dried.

When dry, the flakes are combined with a phenolic resin, placed on mats, and then passed through a hydraulic press where heat and pressure transform them into solid wood panels. The panels are then trimmed to size and, if made to a particular standard, are sanded.

APPENDIX 3.

Other Wood Products

In addition to lumber, plywood, and common building materials, there are many other wood products that you may want to use. Of these, the most common are ready-made turnings and moldings. Both of these can save you an enormous amount of work. They can also expand your woodworking capabilities if you have limited tools.

Although this section only covers turnings and moldings, it should be noted that there are many more wood products available. They aren't discussed here because they are normally used for very specific types of projects. For example, several companies manufacture wooden 'people', wheels, and axle pegs for toymakers. Some make wooden drawer pulls and other furniture parts for cabinetmakers. There are also overlays and inlays for chess and backgammon boards, wooden wheels for carts, 'Shaker' pegs for closets and hallways—the list goes on and on. Should you wish to locate a supply of a particular wood product, consult a local building center or check the advertisements in various woodworking magazines.

Ready-Made Turnings

Of the many relatively new products available to woodworkers, one of the most practical and intriguing is the variety of ready-made turnings that are available at lumberyards and handyman supply centers. The products are especially useful to folks who work mostly with portable power tools, since such equipment doesn't include a lathe. Even stationary tool users who don't care much for lathe work find the materials practical. The point is, you don't have to be limited to straight lines when designing. Turned legs, lamp bases, posts, railings, finials, and other components can be part of your output when you use the ready-made, turned materials.

Most of the items are designed for specific purposes. For example, legs for tables and chests, newel posts and balustrades for stairways, sets of spacers and finials for shelves, similar sets for two-tiered tables, and so on. However, all can be used imaginatively as individual projects or parts of a major assembly merely by modifying or by culling out sections that suit the purpose.

The illustrations show typical items that are available. Your best bet is to visit local sources to see what fits your needs or suits your imagination. You can also send for catalogues.

Ready-made spindles like those used on the doors of this project increase the design scope of folks who work mostly with portable power tools.

Examples of ready-made turnings. They can be used as-is or sections can be culled out. Slicing items like these in half, longitudinally, provides two half-round moldings.

A   Combination leg; spacer and cap can be used for tables or shelves.
B   Tapered legs equipped with a ferrule and leveler can be mounted vertically or slanted.
C   Early American style version of B.
D   Screw-top, round tapered leg with leveler for slanted mounting.
E   Screw-top, square leg.
F   Screw-top, round leg.
G   Square, tapered leg with ferrule and mounting plate.

Note: Metal plate which is screwed to underside of structure is used with items E and F.

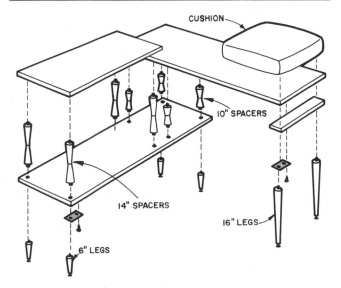

Sets of legs, spacers, and finials can be used to construct tables, shelves, bookcases, and other projects. Such items are available in different lengths and styles.

Turnings designed for stairway constructions can be adapted to other uses. Such components are available in many sizes and styles.

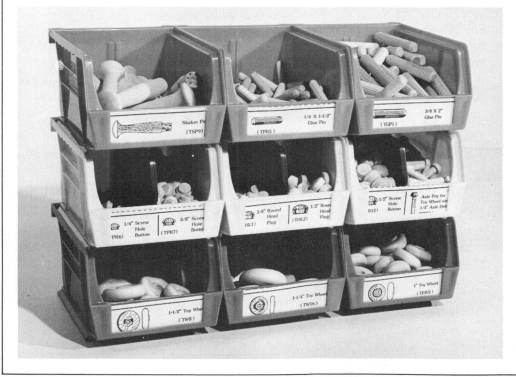

Kit of ready-made turnings includes wheels, hole buttons and plugs, Shaker pegs, even grooved dowels for edge-to-edge joints.

Facts About Molding

Ready-made moldings are available in a great variety of shapes and sizes. Generally, they can be classified as "decorative" or "structural" but the names describe applications more than they do the shape or appearance of the product. For example, **cove** molding was designed for use at the joint between a wall and a ceiling, but many craftspeople, by modifying it with a glass rabbet, use it as picture framing. The same is true for **picture** molding, a design created for use on a wall.

In practical applications, moldings are used to hide and to seal the normal gaps between door jambs and walls and those around window installations, or to finish in good fashion the joint between walls and floors or walls and ceilings. Esthetically, they are used to transform a flush door, add detail to cabinets and chests, or make a blank wall appear paneled. What is obvious is that even when molding is used for architectural purposes, it adds to the appearance of the construction.

Always cut molding with a fine-tooth saw blade. In fact, for the best possible job, it's wise to saw a fraction oversize and to finish to the line by sanding. General rules call for using miters on outside corners but coped joints on inside corners (see sketch). The coped joint requires a little more attention than a straight forward miter but it's good practice to use this joint where, for example, baseboards abut at an inside corner since shrinkage won't result in an obvious gap. A coped joint is one where the end of one piece is shaped to match the cross-sectional shape of the piece it must join with.

Moldings are attached with either finishing or casing nails depending on the size of the material and the application. For example, use casing nails to secure trim around doors and windows, finishing nails if you are adding to furniture or flush doors. Both types of nails are set below the surface of the wood and concealed with wood dough. Don't use nails if you are embellishing a hollow-core door since the plywood surfaces are too thin for any kind of nail to grip. Instead, attach the molding with contact cement or regular glue. If you are working on an outside door, which will probably be solid-core, use finishing nails and a water-proof glue like resorcinol.

Molding can be painted, but you get better results if an undercoat is applied first, followed by a light sanding before finish applications.

For clear finishes, do a light sanding first and then apply the end material. If using more than one coat, do a light sanding between them and after the final one.

Molding can be stained to match or contrast paneling. It's a good idea to cut the piece to size and do a test installation without nailing for all the pieces you need. Then stain before final attachment. This system will also work with clear finishes and even with painted projects, especially if the molding will be a contrasting color.

Here are some molding installation rules that are generally applicable:

- Use a common miter joint on outside corners.
- Use a cope joint on inside corners.
- For tight joints, use glue as well as nails.
- When attaching moldings to walls and in similar situations, locate nails so they will penetrate solid backing members like studs and plates. Use only glue when attaching to thin materials.
- When the backing has slight irregularities, use nails at those points to pull the molding in tightly.
- Driving nails into corners of profiles will help to conceal them. Stain wood dough with the same material used to finish the molding. Colored wax sticks are available for filling nail holes after the finish has been applied.
- At least one of the moldings should be symmetrical when the pattern has an intersection. A "butt block" may be used at an intersection when the moldings are not similar or symmetrical.
- Try to use moldings in one-piece runs. When this isn't possible, use a "scarf" joint at the connection instead of a butt joint.

Standard Moldings and Typical Uses

CROWN Usually used at the joint between walls and ceilings, also under exterior eaves. Does a good job of eliminating sharp lines where two planes meet.

BED Serves functions similar to CROWN. The term usually applies to specific shapes. For example, a combination of cove and bead.

COVE Applications are similar to those of CROWN and BED. The face of the molding has a concave shape.

CASING Provides decorative trim around doors and windows. This type of molding is "relieved" with a shallow back groove. It is used for interior and exterior work.

CASING and BASE These moldings resemble CASING and can be used around doors and windows or as the finishing strip where a wall meets the floor. The edge that rests on the floor is usually beveled a few degrees in the direction of the back face.

STOOL Most common use is as part of a window sill to provide a snug joint with the sash.

CASING and BASE (ROUND EDGE) When the molding has two rounded edges it serves as casing for doors and windows and other trim applications. When it has one square and one rounded edge it serves as a baseboard.

CAP Used to top off wainscots and other horizontal installations.

BRICK Used as an attractive finish where brick or stucco butts against wood in exterior walls.

ROUNDS AND FULL-ROUNDS   Used as closet poles, curtain rods, bannisters, and so on. HALF-ROUNDS can be used to cover joints or for creative embellishments. QUARTER-ROUNDS are generally used at inside corners. They can provide a "shaped" connection where a panel is set into or abuts a square edge.

BALUSTERS   Square stock in various sizes designed as uprights in railings but which are handy for many other uses.

BANDS   Shaped material that is often used to top off baseboards and wainscotting. BANDS make good, ready-made cleats for shelves.

SHINGLE   Provides a decorative joint where siding or shingles butt against eaves or window sills. Can be used as BAND molding or as shelf cleats.

BATTEN   Decorative pieces that can be used to cover joints in flat surfaces. Often used with interior paneling and exterior siding.

LATTICE   Strips with a rectangular cross-section. Can be used as BATTEN but will serve any other decorative or practical purpose.

BEADS (GLASS)   Used to secure glass, wood, or other materials in frames.

STOPS   Make snug joints and keep doors and window sash in correct position. A closed door should be snug against the STOPS.

CASING (MULLION)   Generally used between windows when there is more than one in an installation. Provides a decorative break.

BASE SHOE   Was designed for the joint where the baseboard meets the floor but can be used for many trimming chores.

DRIP CAP   A typical structural molding. Usually used over the exterior side of windows and doors to guard against moisture seeping inside walls.

CORNER GUARD   Used to cover interior or exterior outside corners. Provides a neat finish and protects the corner construction.

BACK BAND   Can be used as caps on some types of BASEBOARD and CASING. Also, as a CORNER GUARD when only one edge of the construction is exposed.

PICTURE   Designed to be used on walls some distance below the ceiling so pictures can be hung. Not in wide use in modern construction.

SCREEN STOCK   Pieces of various sizes with a rectangular cross-section. Can be viewed as a ready-made material for constructing door or window screens. Also useful for various cabinetmaking applications.

SCREEN   Slim strips, usually with a shaped top surface, that are used over screen edges to hold the screen firmly and neatly.

Miter joints are not difficult but accuracy and smooth cuts are essential for parts to mate correctly and form a 90° corner.

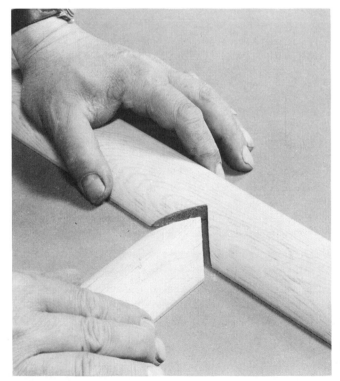

Some moldings that meet at right angles can be joined like this: a V-cut in one piece and a matching pointed shape on the other. Any sharp edges that might remain can be blended with fine sandpaper.

In a coped joint, one piece is shaped to match the cross-sectional profile of the other piece. The shape that must be cut can often be traced by using a compass as shown here.

Driving nails into the corners of profiles helps to conceal them.

Always try to run moldings in continuous strips. If you must join pieces, use a *scarf* joint instead of butting the ends. It's less likely that the joint will separate, especially if you use glue and drive a finishing nail at an angle through the mating ends.

INTERSECTIONS

If possible, it's a good idea to let one of the strips be continuous. Another system involves a "butt block". It can be used with similar or dissimilar moldings and provides an additional decorative detail.

Various Types of Standard Moldings

GLASS BEAD

BASE SHOE

INSIDE CORNER

CORNER GUARD

CHAMFER STRIP

SCREEN MOLDING/ SHELF EDGE

QUARTER ROUND

HALF ROUND

BATTEN

ROUND

SQUARE AND S4S

BACK BAND

PLY CAP

LATTICE

STOP

BASE CAP

DRIP CAP

STOOL

PICTURE MOLD

ASTRAGAL

MULLION

WAINSCOT CAP

CASING

BED

SHINGLE

BASE

CHAIR RAIL

BRICK MOLDING

COVE

CROWN

Most moldings are available in different sizes—many in different configurations.

Ceiling Molding

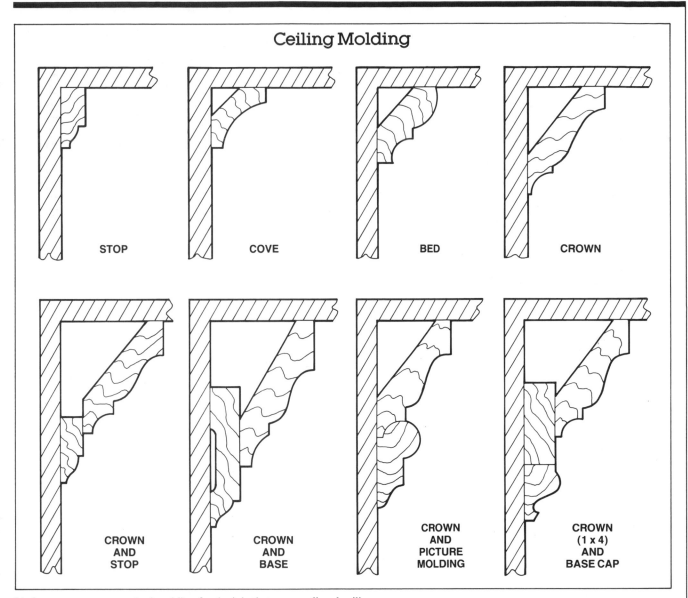

STOP

COVE

BED

CROWN

CROWN
AND
STOP

CROWN
AND
BASE

CROWN
AND
PICTURE
MOLDING

CROWN
(1 x 4)
AND
BASE CAP

Various ways to use standard molding for the joint between wall and ceiling.

Molding Measurements

Molding is measured by its thickness, width, and length. Measurements are listed in that order just as with lumber. A typical order might be ¾″ x 3⅝″ crown molding x 10′. Of course, standard moldings are of specific thicknesses and widths. Your best bet is to check availability at a local source or to work from a chart that illustrates types and sizes (see Glossary for charts available from various sources).

Generally, molding lengths run from 6′ to 16′. Always order to the next rounded foot that suits your needs. It's better to be left with a short cutoff than have to form splices to complete a run. Don't forget to add the extra length required for miters when doing outside corners. For example, when framing a 36″ square window and the molding is 3″ wide, each frame piece needs to be 42″.

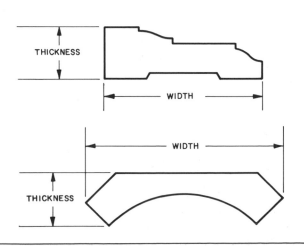

Structural (Practical) Uses for Molding

Around windows.

At the base of a wall.

Decorative Uses for Molding

On flush doors.

On cabinets.

APPENDIX

4.

Abrasives

We conveniently use the words "sanding" and "sandpaper", but sandpaper isn't really "sand" paper at all. The off-white color and somewhat sandy texture of flint, (actually the natural mineral "Quartz") which was one of the first abrasives applied to paper, probably led to the terms we now accept. Even the word "paper" is often erroneous since the abrasives in common use, for power sanding anyway, are bonded to a cloth backing for durability (Figure A4-1).

Flint is not impressive as an abrasive because it dulls and wears rapidly. But because it is one of the cheapest materials, it is often used for chores like the removal of existing finishes, especially paint, that clog the paper very quickly.

More efficient abrasives are natural ones like garnet and emery, and artificial ones like aluminum oxide and silicon carbide. The natural abrasives are mined like any mineral, whereas the artificial abrasives are essentially products of an electric furnace. Aluminum oxide is fused bauxite; silicon carbide results from a sand-coke fusion.

Each type of abrasive is especially good for a particular application, but in practice overlaps do exist. A particular grit in one abrasive will often do the job when the recommended abrasive is not available. It's a good idea to know something about the various types and what they do best.

A4-1.   Coated abrasives may have a paper or cloth backing. Those used on power tools, like the portable or stationary belt sander, should be the cloth types for durability.

Types of Abrasives

Aluminum oxide is available with either cloth or paper backing. The cloth backing is always stronger and more flexible. It can be used dry or with a lubricant and is excellent for machine sanding wood, plastics, and metal. The material is hard and tough and can take a lot of abuse. Paper-backed aluminum oxide can be used on machines—sheets for pad sanders are often made this way—but is generally recommended for hand work. Aluminum oxide is one of the most popular abrasives available today for all-around shop use.

Garnet is another popular woodworker's abrasive. It's a hard, natural material which is mined from the same source that holds the semi-precious jewel bearing the same name. Garnet may be used with machines or by hand, but it does fracture easily and its use is often limited to soft materials. It is a respectable, all-purpose shop abrasive, even though aluminum oxide is favored for power tool use.

Silicon carbide is widely available on waterproof backings and is excellent for wet sanding either by hand or machine. In finer grades, it is commonly used for smoothing finish coats of varnish, lacquer, or enamel on furniture and on automobiles. In most cases you'll find that it is the better abrasive to use on metals.

Emery, which is a combination of iron oxide and corundum, is frequently used for metal finishing but is comparatively dull and tends to wear quickly. It shouldn't be shunned for metal-polishing jobs. In fact, it's often found in powder or stick form so it can be applied to cloth discs for buffing applications.

Tungsten carbide, which has made its mark as hard-working, long-lived cutting edges on saw blades and router bits, is appearing on abrasive products. You'll find that the backing for the abrasive is usually a thin sheet of metal (Figure A4-2). The products don't have the flexibility of paper- or cloth-backed abrasives and their use is confined mostly to flat surfaces.

Flint is the least durable of all abrasives. It's also the cheapest and, therefore, often chosen for preliminary work that is bound to clog the paper very quickly. It's not made for power sanding but, in a pinch, no law says you can't cut up a sheet for use in a pad sander.

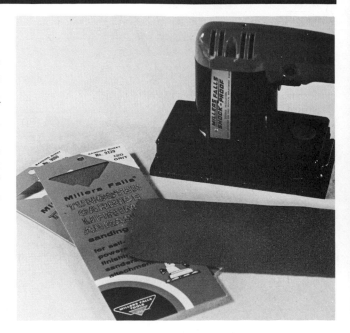

A4-2.   New tungsten carbide sheets are very durable, but since the abrasive particles are bonded to thin sheets of metal they are not as flexible as regular materials and are best used on flat surfaces.

Grit Sizes

The grit number of an abrasive is actually a *mesh number* that indicates the particular wire or silk screen that was used to filter the abrasive particles during the manufacturing process. For example, particles that pass through a number twelve screen would total twelve to the inch if they were placed in a line. When the screen-control method becomes impractical, because of the size of the particles, then a fairly complex flotation system is used to accomplish the same thing. Grit sizes can range from the coarsest, Number 12, to the finest, Number 600.

How smooth a project will be depends on the grit you use. Number twelve would produce results similar to what you would get by rubbing wood with tiny, sharp stones. Using the finest grit is almost like rubbing with flour (Figures A4-3 and A4-4).

The usual recommendation of working through progressively finer grits of abrasive until you achieve the smoothness you want is okay, but only to a point. A critical factor is the grit you *start* with, and this can be judged by the original condition of the surface you must work on. There is little point in routinely working from "very coarse" to "very fine", with a half dozen steps between, if the project is in respectable condition to begin with. It certainly isn't necessary on the plywood and most of the yard lumber that is available today.

The charts shown in Figures A4-5 and A4-6 are offered as guides to help you select the type of abrasive and the grit best suited for a particular application on various materials. The emphasis is on the word "guides", since in each of the steps there is a range of grit sizes.

Remember that abrasives are cutting tools. They do their job by removing material almost like tiny chisels. The "chisel" you start with will leave ridges and grooves that, if necessary, can be made into smaller ridges and grooves by working with smaller "chisels". There will always be striations; you work to the point where you can't feel them, or see them without magnification.

Imperfections will be most obvious after cross-grain sanding that hasn't been followed with sufficient with-the-grain sanding. In the extreme, flaws will appear as cross-grain swirls. Use a cross-grain pattern, regardless of the grit of the abrasive, only when you wish to remove a lot of material quickly. Orbital pad sanders do a lot of cross-grain sanding, but orbits are so tiny and such fine abrasive particles can be used, that imperfections are virtually non-existent.

Abrasive Coatings

"Closed coat" is the term used to describe coated abrasives that are densely covered with cutting particles. The result is a fast-cutting surface, but one that can clog quickly under certain conditions. When the abrasive particles are applied with spaces between them so that only about 50 to 70% of the backing material is covered, the product is called "open coat". Open-coat products won't cut as fast as closed-coat products simply because there aren't as many abrasive particles per given area. On the other hand, there is less tendency for open-coat products to clog; facts to consider when determining the type that is best for a particular job. Closed coats cut faster, usually stand up longer, and do a smoother job. Open coats are best for soft materials, gummy materials, and for removing existing finishes.

TYPE	VERY FINE	FINE	MEDIUM	COARSE	VERY COARSE
Flint	4/0	2/0 - 3/0	0 - ½	1 - 2	2½ - 3½
Garnet	6/0 - 10/0	3/0 - 5/0	0 - 2/0	½ - 1½	2 - 3
Aluminum oxide and silicon carbide	220 - 360	120 - 180	80 - 100	40 - 60	24 - 36

8/0 = 280	3/0 = 120	1½ = 40
7/0 = 240	2/0 = 100	2 = 36
6/0 = 220	0 = 80	2½ = 30
5/0 = 180	½ = 60	3 = 24
4/0 = 150	1 = 50	

A4-3.   This chart groups different abrasives into five classes of word/grit descriptions and indicates the number of the grits that fall in each. Quite often, the word description is enough on which to base a choice.

A4-4.   Here are the number equivalents of the various grit sizes.

ABRASIVE	USE	GRIT			REMARKS
		ROUGH	MEDIUM	FINE	
Aluminum oxide	Hardwood	2½ - 1½	½ - 0	2/0 - 3/0	Manufactured, brown color, bauxite base, more costly than garnet but usually cheaper to use per unit of work.
	Aluminum	40	60 - 80	100	
	Copper	40 - 50	80 - 100	100 - 120	
	Steel	24 - 30	60 - 80	100	
	Ivory	60 - 80	100 - 120	120 - 280	
	Plastic	50 - 80	120 - 180	240	
Garnet	Hardwood	2½ - 1½	½ - 0	2/0 - 3/0	Natural mineral, red color, harder and sharper than flint.
	Softwood	1½ - 1	0	2/0	
	Composition board	1½ - 1	½	0	
	Plastic	50 - 80	120 - 180	240	
	Horn	1½	½ - 0	2/0-3/0	
Silicon carbide	Glass	50 - 60	100 - 120	12-320	Manufactured, harder but more brittle than aluminum oxide, very fast cutting.
	Cast iron	24 - 30	60 - 80	100	
Flint	Removing paint, old finishes	3 - 1½	½ - 0		Natural hard form of quartz, low cost, use on jobs that clog the paper quickly.

A4-5.   This chart is offered as a guide to help you select a type and grit of abrasive for a particular material and finish. Which grit you start with has much to do with the original state of the surface you work on.

MATERIAL	FIRST STEP	SECOND STEP	FINAL
Oak	2½ - 1½	½ - 0	2/0 - 4/0
Maple	2½ - 1	½ - 0	2/0 - 4/0
Maple (curly)	2½ - 1½	½ - 0	2/0 - 4/0
Birch	2½ - 1	½ - 0	2/0 - 4/0
Mahogany	2½ - 1½	½ - 0	2/0 - 3/0
Walnut	2½ - 1½	½ - 0	2/0 - 4/0
Fir	1½ - 1	½ - 0	2/0
Pine	1½ - 1	0	2/0
Gum	2½ - 1½	½ - 0	2/0 - 3/0
Willow	2	½ - 0	2/0
Cypress	2½ - 1½	½ - 0	2/0
Plaster			5/0 - 8/0
Hardboard		3/0 - 4/0	5/0 - 7/0

A4-6.   This chart suggests grit sizes to choose for progressive steps on various materials. Again, it's a "guide". If the material is in reasonable condition to begin with, it's usually okay to skip step number one.

Care of Coated Abrasives

The cost of coated abrasives can add up if you are too casual with how you use them and neglect some simple maintenance chores. When the paper is worn enough so it just doesn't cut, the only choice you have is to discard it. However, a coarse-grit paper used to the point where it no longer does the job it was designed for can be used further as a finer grit.

Dry cleaning with a brush will slow the accumulation of stubborn waste on an abrasive surface. When the accumulation is powdery and loose, a bristle brush will do. When the accumulation is thick and sticky, a wire brush may be used. Work the brush in all directions to uncover particles that might still be sharp enough to work. When you are doing such work on a power tool, don't have the machine running or you will soon have a "brushless" brush; brush over the abrasive surface while the tool is still. You can rotate a belt sander, drum sander, or disc sander by hand as you apply the brush.

A new product from the Granlund Engineering Co. provides a practical and very efficient way to keep abrasives clean and to prolong their life. The units, which resemble oversize gum erasers as much as anything else, are available mounted on handles so they can be applied to the tool, or with a backing so they can be held to a solid surface while the coated abrasive is moved against them (Figures A4-7 and

A4-8). I have found them to do an impressive job even on drum sanders, whether they are powered by a portable drill or a drill press (Figure A4-9). The idea is to use the cleaners frequently to prevent the waste buildup that clogs paper and covers the cutting points of the abrasive particles.

There are times when a smoothing job can't be done with a power tool, or is more convenient to do by hand. The ideas that are shown in Figures A4-10 through A4-14 are some that I have used and which you may find helpful.

A4-7.   Gum-eraser type cleaners for coated abrasives are efficient and easy to use. Those with handles are designed to be applied to the abrasive.

A4-8.   Other "sanding insurance" products, as they are called by the manufacturer, can be secured to a solid surface. The abrasive, in motion, is held against the cleaner.

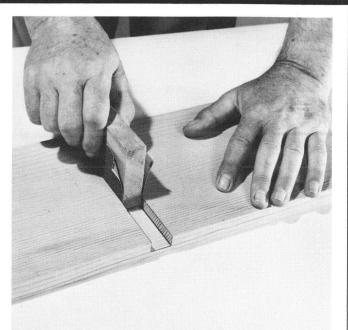

A4-9. The gum-type cleaners can be used on drum sanders regardless of how they are powered. Use the cleaners frequently as you work to keep waste from clogging the cutting particles. Operations like this, as well as sanding, throw off particles, so always wear safety goggles and a dust mask.

A4-11. Use fine sandpaper wrapped around a block of wood to increase the width of a dado that would otherwise be too tight for the insert piece. If you use a very fine sandpaper, the wood block can have the same thickness as the part that must fit the dado. Don't overdo this—what you want is a slip fit.

A4-10. By using a hacksaw blade as a guide, you can cut pieces from regular sheets of sandpaper accurately to use with a pad sander. The teeth on the blade help to produce a clean cut. A strip of wood can also be used, but there will be a greater tendency for the paper to tear unevenly.

A4-12. A piece of molding that must be sanded can be used as a sanding block with matching contours. In this case, the edges of the block have been sawed off so it will conform to major contours.

A4-13.   To smooth tight radii or sharp corners, you can wrap sandpaper around a sharpened, thin piece of wood, or a piece of thin carpeting. It's easier to smooth hard-to-reach areas when the abrasive "carrier" is shaped to suit the job.

A4-14.   A line of abrasive cords and tapes, introduced by E. C. Mitchell Co., lets you get into spots that might be inaccessible with other means. The cords and tapes are available in various diameters and widths, and with coatings that include silicon carbide, aluminum oxide, and crocus. Thus, they can be used on metal as well as wood, and for polishing.

APPENDIX

5. Hardware

There is an old woodworker's saying that the reason early American furniture has such complicated joinery is that hardware was hard to come by. It was cheaper to make a dovetail than use a screw. Whether or not that's true is open to debate. But what is true is that since the beginning of this country, the availability and the variety of hardware has grown steadily. Today, there is a bewildering array of hardware on the market, and most of it at reasonable prices.

This section will help you sort out some of the more common types of nails, screws, and other fasteners. You'll find that within each type of fastener, there is an amazing variety. There are nails for common construction, finishing, concrete work, flooring, paneling, siding, and upholstery, just to name a few. There are also special decorative 'cut' nails available for antique restoration and reproduction. Under the heading of screws, there are not only the usual flathead and roundhead screws, but also hanger bolts, dowel screws, security screws, tapping screws, and the new 'square drive' screws. All of these have different applications. Finally, there are many types of ingenious fasteners that you can use instead of the usual assortment of nails and screws—corrugated nails, 'Skotch' jointers, 'Tite Joint' fasteners, 'Molly' bolts, 'Tee' nuts, and on and on. Some of these are permanent fasteners; you have to destroy the wood to disassemble the project. Others are 'knock-down' fasteners; they are made especially so that you can assemble and disassemble the project for easy storage or shipping. With a good working knowledge of what's out there on the market, you can use the best fastener for the particular job you have to do.

There is a lot of hardware that wasn't included in this section. This isn't an oversight. Hinges, drawer and door pulls, drawer slides, latches, shelving supports, and the like are often specific to a particular project. By contrast, the hardware that was included in this section is more general in its application. You can use each of the fasteners listed here on many different kinds of projects. However, should you need a specific type of hardware, your local hardware store will usually have catalogues that you can look through to find and order what you need.

Basic Nailing Techniques

- Choose a nail that is three times longer than the piece being secured—this is a general rule that can't always apply, but stay close to it when you can.
- Start nails with light taps and get your fingers out of the danger zone as soon as possible—don't drive nails as if you were trying for a prize in a carnival. Nails driven "calmly" will hold better because they cause minimum distortion in wood fibers.
- Let up on the force of hammer blows when the nail head nears the surface of the wood—this is the way to avoid marring wood surfaces.
- Drive finishing and similar nails to within 1/8″ of the work surface—use a nail set to complete driving the nail below the work surface (1/16″ to 1/8″). Use a set that is compatible with the nail-head diameter.
- You may be able to straighten a bent nail by tapping it gently upright with the hammer but it's usually better to remove it and start a new one. A nail bent in the wood where you can't see it can cause problems.
- There is nothing wrong with using a small drill to form pilot holes for nails—this is very useful when nailing hardwoods and when nailing near edges.
- Use a staggered pattern when driving many nails in a confined area—nails driven on the same line are likely to cause splits.
- Nails driven at a slight angle grip better than nails driven straight.
- When clinching, bend the nail *across* the grain of the wood rather than *with* it.
- You can help avoid splitting if you tap the point of the nail with the hammer to dull it slightly.
- A fine way to hide a nail is to use a sharp chisel to lift a thin sliver of wood, then drive the nail in the depression and glue down the sliver.

COMMON NAILS

SIZES OF COMMON AND BOX NAILS						
SIZE d= "penny"	COMMON			BOX		
	GAUGE	LENGTH	# - LB.*	GAUGE	LENGTH	# - LB.*
2	15	1	845	15½	1	1010
3	14	1¼	540	14½	1¼	635
4	12½	1½	290	14	1½	473
5	12½	1¾	250	14	1¾	406
6	11½	2	165	12½	2	236
7	11½	2¼	150	12½	2¼	210
8	10¼	2½	100	11½	2½	145
9	10¼	2¾	90	11½	2¾	132
10	9	3	65	10½	3	94
12	9	3¼	60	10½	3	88
16	8	3½	45	10	3½	71
20	6	4	30	9	4	52
30	5	4½	20	9	4½	46
40	4	5	17	8	5	35
50	3	5½	13	—	—	—
60	2	6	10	—	—	—

*Approximate length in inches.

GAUGE EQUIVALENTS (NAIL SIZES)			
GAUGE	INCHES (IN DECIMALS)	GAUGE	INCHES (IN DECIMALS)
2	.2625	9	.1483
3	.2437	10	.1350
4	.2253	11	.1205
5	.2070	12	.0985
6	.1920	13	.0915
7	.1770	14	.0800
8	.1620	15	.0673

TYPES OF POINTS ON NAILS

	KEY	NAME	COMMENTS
	A	Diamond (regular)	A most common point design that is good for general purpose use but which can cause splitting in dense woods.
	B	Diamond (long)	Easier to drive because of long, tapering point—often found on nails for drywall construction—sharp point penetrates easily and cleanly.
	C	Diamond (blunt)	Especially good for dense wood since blunt point is less likely to cause splitting than a sharp point.
	D	Chisel (or wedge)	Found on large nails, especially spikes—point makes it easier to drive nails into timbers—also found on gutter spikes.
	E	Needle (short)	Similar to diamond but points have circular cross section—easy to start—often used to avoid tearing of fibrous material; carpeting, and fiberboard.
	F	Needle (long)	

SOME COMMON NAILS

DUPLEX

BRADS

ANNUAL RING

UPHOLSTERY

ROOFING

SPIRAL

TACKS

CONCRETE (SQUARE)

CUT

CORRUGATED

"OLD FASHIONED" CUT NAILS			
SIZE	**KEY**	**NAME**	**COMMENTS**
8d (2½)	3	Clinch rose head	Often used for face nailing of wide-board flooring.
8d (2½)	2	Hinge	
8d (2½)	7	Common rose head	
4d (1½)	3	Clinch rose head	For antique decorative effects on paneling, cabinet, doors.
6d (2)	3	Clinch rose head	
8d (2½)	3	Clinch rose head	
¾″	1	Clout	Works well when making or restoring early American furniture.
4d (1½)	5	Fine finish	
7d (2¼)	5	Fine finish	
4d (1½)	2	Hinge	For attachment of antique hinges and similar jobs.
8d (2½)	2	Hinge	
10d (3)	2	Hinge	
6d (2)	3	Clinch rose head	For decorative touches on exterior work such as siding and fences—available zinc plated.
7d (2¼)	6	Common	

Note: Supply source for cut nails: Tremont Nail Co., Wareham, MA 02571

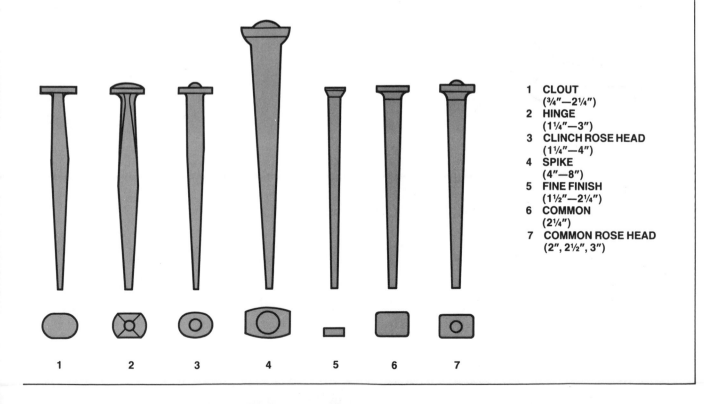

1 **CLOUT**
  (¾″—2¼″)
2 **HINGE**
  (1¼″—3″)
3 **CLINCH ROSE HEAD**
  (1¼″—4″)
4 **SPIKE**
  (4″—8″)
5 **FINE FINISH**
  (1½″—2¼″)
6 **COMMON**
  (2¼″)
7 **COMMON ROSE HEAD**
  (2″, 2½″, 3″)

FINISHING NAILS

	SIZE d= "penny"	GAUGE	LENGTH IN INCHES	APPROX. NO. PER POUND
	2	16½	1	1350
	3	15½	1¼	880
	4	15	1½	630
	6	13	2	290
	8	12½	2½	196
	10	11½	3	125

CASING NAILS

	SIZE d= "penny"	GAUGE	LENGTH IN INCHES	APPROX. NO. PER POUND
	3	14½	1¼	630
	4	14	1½	490
	6	12½	2	245
	8	11½	2½	149
	10	10½	3	94
	16	10	3½	75

WIRE BRADS (SMALL)

	LENGTH IN INCHES	GAUGES		LENGTH IN INCHES	GAUGES
	³/₁₆	20-24		¾	13-21
	¼	19-24		⅞	13-20
	⅜	18-24		1	12-20
	½	14-23		1⅛	12-20
	⅝	13-22			

TACKS							
SIZE (NUMBER)	LENGTH (INCHES)	SIZE (NUMBER)	LENGTH (INCHES)	SIZE (NUMBER)	LENGTH (INCHES)	SIZE (NUMBER)	LENGTH (INCHES)
2	¼	4	7/16	10	5/8	16	13/16
2½	5/16	6	½	12	11/16	18	7/8
3	3/8	8	9/16	14	¾	22	1

VARIOUS NAIL TYPES AND TYPICAL APPLICATIONS	
IDENTIFIED AS	TYPICAL USE
COMMON	A general purpose nail used extensively in house framing and general carpentry. BOX nail (slimmer) is often substituted when splitting is a problem.
DUPLEX OR DOUBLE-HEADED	For temporary structures such as scaffolding—second head projects so fastener can be removed easily.
CONCRETE	Specially hardened for driving into concrete or masonry—also for attachment of furring strips and sole plates.
ROOFING	Special heads, usually larger than normal for securing roofing materials; some with washers attached for waterproof seal.
FINISHING	For cabinetmaking, attachment of trim, and so on—usually driven below the surface and hidden with wood dough.
CASING	Used like a finishing nail but has more holding power—attachment of casing or trim around doors and windows.
CUT (FLOORING)	For edge, blind nailing of flooring—thin, rectangular shape guards against splitting.
SPIRAL	Threaded shank so nail turns like a screw—more holding power—often used in place of CUT nails for flooring.
PANELING	Hard and thin and often ribbed—available in colors to match the paneling.
SIDING	Often in aluminum to guard against rusting—available in colors.
CAPPED	Attachment of insulation sheathing—has large plastic or metal cap—usually with spiral shank.
BRAD	Slim nails resembling finishing nails—usually light duty applications such as attachment of moldings—set and hidden with wood dough.
UPHOLSTERY	Used in upholstery work where nails are not hidden—have large, decorative heads.
TACK	Common for attachment for carpeting and upholstery—used in hidden areas—differ from THUMB TACKS which are not driven with a hammer.
STAPLE	U-shaped fastener for attachment of screening, wire fencing, and so on—also for electrical wiring, some with insulated shoulders.

General Screw Driving Techniques

- Drill shank and pilot holes especially in hardwoods and when using large screws (see chart)—you might get by without these holes when using very small screws in softwood; forming a starting hole with an awl might do the trick.
- Use a screwdriver with a blade-tip that seats snugly the full width of the slot in the screw head—a blade tip that is *too* wide will damage the material.
- You can apply greater leverage by using the longest, suitable screwdriver.
- Keep the screwdriver at right angles to the work surface.
- Use one hand to guide the screw until it is firmly started.

- Be careful when it becomes necessary to exert excessive pressure; you might break the screw—solve the problem by using "threading screw" (see sketch)—sometimes, the solution is as simple as coating the threads of the screw with soap or wax (don't use oil)—enlarge the pilot hole only as a last resort—it's rarely necessary to enlarge the shank hole.
- Countersink to full depth in hardwoods—in softwoods driving the screw will sink it flush.
- Once the screw is started, concentrate on the torque needed to turn it—it's no longer necessary to bear *down* on the screw—it will pull itself into the wood.

Screw Types

A. FLATHEAD
Screw is driven until head is flush with surface of work. Most sizes, especially in hardwoods, require countersunk holes. Can be driven in counterbored holes when hiding with wood plug is desirable.

B. PHILLIPS HEAD
Similar to flathead screws except for cross slots which minimize screwdriver slippage. Special Phillips screwdriver is needed.

C. SQUARE HEAD
New design with fast spiral thread for quicker penetration in soft or hard woods. Square head minimizes driver slippage. Require square-tipped screwdriver.

D. SECURITY (ONE-WAY)
Special slot allows driving screw but screwdriver slips to prevent removal.

E. ROUNDHEAD
General utility screws. Can be used alone or with washers. Often used to secure material that is too thin for countersinking.

F. OVAL HEAD
Combine oval head and flathead configurations. More attractive than flathead screws. Require some countersinking. Often used with raised or flush countersunk washers.

G. DOME HEAD
Flathead screw with threaded hole for attachment of decorative dome. Not common. Usually available on special order.

H. LAG SCREW (BOLT)
For heavy-duty applications. Available with square or hex heads. Usually used with a washer. Driven with a wrench or socket.

I. HANGER SCREW (BOLT)
One end drives like a screw, the other is threaded so a nut can be used to secure the attachment. Can be used in wood and in expansion shields in masonry.

J. DOWEL SCREW
Useful for some end-to-end joints and similar applications.

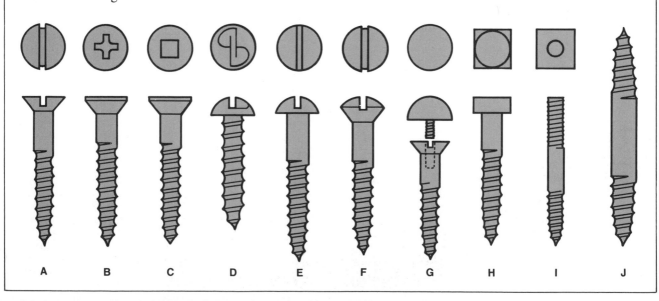

A   B   C   D   E   F   G   H   I   J

SCREW GAUGES (ACTUAL SIZE)

2

3

4

5

6

7

8

9

10

12

14

16

18

Common Head Styles on Wood Screws

A.   FLATHEAD
Can be set flush to surface of work when hole is counter-sunk or can be hidden with a wood plug when hole is *counterbored*.

B.   ROUNDHEAD
Head is left exposed—often used with a flat washer.

C.   OVAL HEAD
Left exposed—requires a partial countersink.

D.   FILLISTER
Left exposed—often used with a flat washer.

E.   PHILLIPS HEAD
Used with Phillips head screwdriver—design is available on all wood screws.

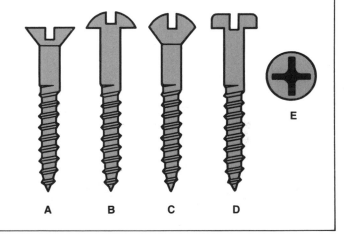

A   B   C   D   E

New screw design has a square recess and is driven with square-tipped drivers which are available for manual or power driving. An advantage of the screw is that the driver is less likely to slip and damage adjacent surfaces. At this writing the screws are available in gauges and lengths that run from #3 x ⅜ to #14 x 3.

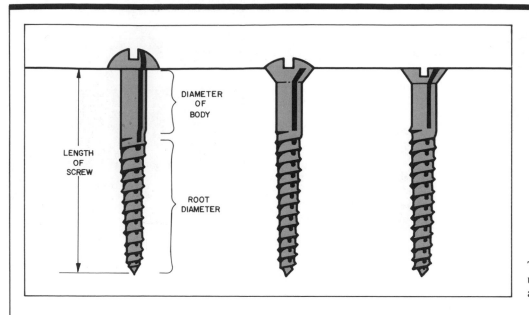

The length of a screw is measured from where the head bears against the work.

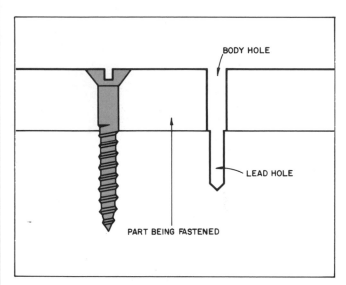

General Recommendations for Screw Holes

Ideally, the length of a screw should be ⅛″ to ¼″ less than total thickness of materials being joined. The pilot or lead hole should be about one half the length of the threaded portion of the screw. The shank or body hole may penetrate the part being fastened.

Washers

A.   COUNTERSUNK
Can be used with flathead or oval head screws.

B.   FLUSH (COUNTERSUNK)
Use with flathead or oval head screws to reduce projection of fastener above surface of work.

C.   FLAT (OR PLAIN)
Can be used with flathead or fillister head screws.

Note: Washers are used to improve appearance or to add to the bearing area of the screw so strength is increased.

Screws Can Be Concealed by Counterboring the Screw Hole

- The counterbore is filled with a *plug* which is sanded flush to adjacent surfaces, or with a *button* that provides a decorative detail.
- Plugs and buttons can be purchased in various sizes.
- Also, you can make plugs with cutting tools called "plug cutters".

COUNTERBORE **PLUG CUTTER**

WOOD PLUG   **WOOD BUTTON**

Special Portable Drill Bits for Drilling Screw Holes

A. Forms shank hole, pilot hole, and countersink.
B. Forms shank hole, pilot hole, and counterbore.

Note: Both cutters are available in sizes to suit various screws.

1¼ × 10

A   B

Try coating threads with soap when a screw is difficult to drive. Don't use oil or other materials that might stain wood.

A "Threading Screw" Can Be Useful

Sometimes it can be difficult to drive a screw even when shank and pilot holes have been drilled correctly. This can happen in hardwoods like birch or maple. Before you try to solve the problem by enlarging the holes, file one of the screws to the shape shown in the sketch and turn it into each of the holes. It will act somewhat like a tap, pre-forming threads so the regular screws will be easier to drive.

Save the "threading screw" as you would any tool; you may have use for it at a later date.

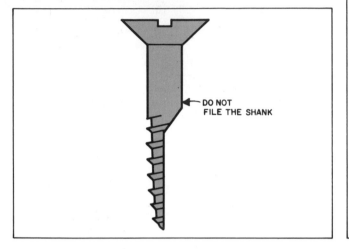

Two Ways to "Lock" a Screw

■ Drill a hole at about a 45° angle and drive a brad through the hole and into the wood.
■ Use a staple that fits the slot in the screw.

Hanger screw (or bolt) can be used in wood or, with a correct shield, in masonry. The fastener allows attachments by means of a conventional nut.

Secure corner blocks or braces on leg and rail assemblies to apply a hanger screw or bolt.

Dowel screws have screw-type threads at both ends. Common applications include joining spindles or squares end-to-end, attaching posts to bases, and reinforcing leg joints. A single one can be used in an edge-to-edge joint.

| LAG SCREWS (LAG BOLTS) ||
DIAMETER IN INCHES	LENGTH IN INCHES
¼	1 to 10
5/16	
3/8	1 to 12
7/16	
½	1 to 12
5/8	1¾ to 16
¾	1½ to 16
7/8	2 to 16
1	2 to 16

Note: Lag screws have square or hex heads and are used for heavy duty connections—are driven with a wrench—usually with flat washers—often used with expansion shields for attaching items to masonry.

CUP HOOK

SCREW HOOK

L-HOOK OR SQUARE BEND

SCREW EYE

SCREW RING OR HITCHING RING

All these special "screw" items are available in various sizes.

Sheet Metal Screws ("Tapping Screws")

Screws that cut or form their own threads. Especially useful for joining thin sheet metal, but can provide greater gripping power than nails or conventional screws when used in plywood, hardboard, particleboard, and even some plastics. Most require a pilot hole sized to suit the screw's diameter (see charts). Gripping strength in very soft materials can be increased by reducing the size of the pilot hole.

Most useful types, "A" and "AB", have gimlet points and are available in lengths up to about 2″. The threads on AB are finer than those on A.

Type "B" is similar to A but has a blunt point and finer threads. It's designed for adequate gripping power when working on thicker sheet metals. Sizes are similar to those available for A.

Another useful type is the "Drive Screw". It works something like a blind rivet, being tapped into place for permanent attachment of thin materials to heavier components. A typical application—nameplate on a tool. Available in lengths from ⅛″ to ¾″.

TYPE A   TYPE AB   TYPE B   DRIVE SCREW

MULTIPLE THREAD

STARTING PILOT

NUMBER AND EQUIV.	METAL THICKNESS		HOLE REQUIRED	
	GAUGE	EQUIVALENT	DRILL	EQUIVALENT
4	28	.0156	44	.0860
	26	.0188		
.112	24	.0250	42	.0935
	22	.0313		
	20	.0375	40	.0980
6	28	.0156	39	.0995
	26	.0188		
	24	.0250		
.138	22	.0313	38	.1015
	20	.0375	36	.1065
7	28	.0156	37	.1040
	26	.0188		
	24	.0250	35	.1100
	22	.0313	33	.1130
.155	20	.0375	32	.1160
	18	.0500	31	.1200
8	26	.0188	33	.1130
	24	.0250		
	22	.0313	32	.1160
.165	20	.0375	31	.1200
	18	.0500	30	.1280
10	26	.0188	30	.1285
	24	.0250		
	22	.0313		
.191	20	.0375	29	.1360
	18	.0500	25	.1495
12	24	.0250	26	.1470
	22	.0313	25	.1495
.218	20	.0375	24	.1520
	18	.0500	22	.1570
14	24	.0250	15	.1800
	22	.0313	12	.1890
.251	20	.0375	11	.1910
	18	.0500	9	.1960

HOLE SIZES RECOMMENDED FOR SHEET METAL SCREWS (TYPES A & AB)

HOLE SIZES RECOMMENDED FOR SHEET METAL SCREWS (TYPE B)				
NUMBER AND EQUIV.	METAL THICKNESS		HOLE REQUIRED	
	GAUGE	EQUIVALENT	DRILL	EQUIVALENT
4	28	.0156	44	.0860
	26	.0188		
	24	.0250	43	.0890
.112	22	.0313	42	.0935
	20	.0375		
6	28	.0156	37	.1040
	26	.0188		
	24	.0250	36	.1065
.137	22	.0313		
	20	.0375	35	.1100
7	26	.0188	32	.1160
	24	.0250		
	22	.0313		
.151	20	.0375		
	18	.0500	31	.1200
	16	.0625	30	.1285
8	26	.0188	32	.1160
	24	.0250		
	22	.0313		
.163	20	.0375		
	18	.0500	30	.1285
10	26	.0188	27	.1440
	24	.0250		
	22	.0313		
.186	20	.0375		
	18	.0500		
12	24	.0250	19	.1660
	22	.0313		
	20	.0375		
.212	18	.0500	18	.1695
14	22	.0313	13	.1850
	20	.0375		
	18	.0500	11	.1910
.243	16	.0625	8	.1990

SCREW LENGTHS THAT ARE AVAILABLE

SCREW	¼	⅜	½	⅝	¾	⅞	1	1¼	1½	1¾	2	2¼	2½	2¾	3	3½	4
0	X																
1	X																
2	X	X	X														
3	X	X	X	X													
4		X	X	X	X												
5		X	X	X	X												
6		X	X	X	X	X	X	X	X								
7		X	X	X	X	X	X	X	X								
8			X	X	X	X	X	X	X	X	X						
9				X	X	X	X	X	X	X	X	X					
10				X	X	X	X	X	X	X	X	X					
11					X	X	X	X	X	X	X	X					
12						X	X	X	X	X	X	X	X				
14							X	X	X	X	X	X	X	X			
16								X	X	X	X	X	X	X	X		
18									X	X	X	X	X	X	X	X	X
20										X	X	X	X	X	X	X	X
24																X	X

LENGTH IN INCHES

SCREW	DRILL TO USE FOR PILOT HOLE				DRILL TO USE FOR SHANK HOLE	
	HARDWOOD		SOFTWOOD		FRACTION SIZE	NUMBER OR LETTER
	FRAC. SIZE	NO. OR LETTER	FRAC. SIZE	NO. OR LETTER		
0	1/32	66	1/64	75	1/16	52
1		57	1/32	71	5/64	47
2		54	1/32	65	3/32	42
3	1/16	53	3/64	58	7/64	37
4	1/16	51	3/64	55	7/64	32
5	5/64	47	1/16	53	1/8	30
6		44	1/16	52	9/64	27
7		39	1/16	51	5/32	22
8	7/64	35	5/64	48	11/64	18
9	7/64	33	5/64	45	3/16	14
10	1/8	31	3/32	43	3/16	10
11		29	3/32	40	13/64	4
12		25	7/64	38	7/32	2
14	3/16	14	7/64	32	1/4	D
16		10	9/64	29	17/64	I
18	13/64	6	9/64	26	19/64	N
20	7/32	3	11/64	19	21/64	P
24	1/4	D	3/16	15	3/8	V

RECOMMENDED HOLE SIZES FOR WOOD SCREWS

Note: Recommended hole sizes are for easiest driving and maximum holding power, especially in hardwoods.

MACHINE BOLTS	
DIAMETER IN INCHES	LENGTH IN INCHES
¼	½—8
⁵⁄₁₆	½—10
⅜	¾—12
⁷⁄₁₆	1—12
½	1—25

HEX HEAD   **COUNTERSUNK HEAD**   **OVAL OR BUTTON HEAD**

STOVE BOLTS	
DIAMETER IN INCHES	LENGTH IN INCHES
⅛ & ⁵⁄₃₂	⅜—2
³⁄₁₆	⅜—6
¼	½—6
⁵⁄₁₆ & ⅜	¾—6
½	1—4

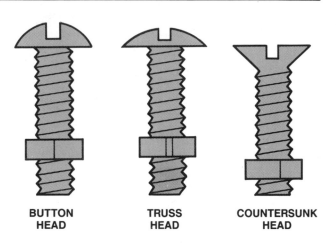

BUTTON HEAD   **TRUSS HEAD**   **COUNTERSUNK HEAD**

CARRIAGE BOLTS	
DIAMETER IN INCHES	LENGTH IN INCHES
³⁄₁₆	½ to 4
¼	½ to 8
⁵⁄₁₆	¾ to 10
⅜	¾ to 12
⁷⁄₁₆	1 to 12
½	1 to 20

Carriage Bolts

Carriage bolts, which were frequently used in the assembly of carriages, are ideal for woodworking projects because of the shoulders under the oval head. They sink into the wood and keep the nut from turning while the nut is fastened. Secure them before tightening the nut by tapping them with a hammer until the shoulders are seated.

Washers

Washers are used to spread the gripping power of the bolt and to prevent damage to the work surface. It's especially important to use washers when bolts are used to secure wood components.

Lock washers are designed to prevent a bolt from loosening. Use a flat washer under a spring-lock washer when bolting wood components.

COMMON FLAT WASHER

SPRING LOCK

EXTERNAL SERRATION LOCK

INTERNAL SERRATION LOCK

EXTERNAL/ INTERNAL SERRATION LOCK

SERRATED COUNTERSUNK LOCK

Types of Nuts

Wing Nuts are used when a project might require disassembly or when a component must be tightened or loosened frequently.

Cap nuts or "acorn nuts" are used when appearance is important.

Castellated nuts are kept from turning through the use of a cotter pin. The pin passes through a hole in the shank of the bolt.

Note: Nuts used most often are the square or the hexagon.

SQUARE

WING NUT

REGULAR HEXAGON

KNURLED

CAP NUT

CASTELLATED

INSTALLATION INFORMATION FOR MACHINE SCREWS

DIAMETER (GAUGE)	THREADS PER INCH	NC	NF	THROUGH HOLE		HOLE FOR TAPPING	
				BIT	DIA.	BIT	DIA.
2	56	X		43	.089	50	.070
3	48	X		37	.104	47	.079
4	40	X		32	.116	44	.086
6	32	X		27	.144	36	.107
8	32	X		18	.170	29	.136
10	24	X		9	.196	25	.150
10	32		X	9	.196	21	.160
12	24	X		2	.221	16	.177
12	28		X	2	.221	13	.185
¼	20	X		F	.257	7	.201
¼	28		X	F	.257	3	.213
5/16	18	X		P	.323	F	.257
5/16	24		X	P	.323	I	.272
3/8	16	X		W	.386	5/16	.313
3/8	24		X	W	.386	Q	.332

NC = National Coarse Threads
NF = National Fine Threads
Note: Screws and bolts with national fine threads (more threads per inch) have greater holding power.

Corrugated Nails

Popular use is to reinforce miter joints but they can be used on edge-to-edge and similar connections. Special "nail sets" are available so the fasteners can be driven below the surface of the wood and concealed with wood dough.

Common sizes are:
3/8" high x 1 1/8" long
1/2" high x 1 1/8" long
5/8" high x 1 1/8" long

Skotch Wood Jointers

A strong "staple" with eight prongs that penetrate easily and spread in the wood to provide a firm grip. Used on butt joints and miters.

Available in various sizes by number:
#0 = 3/8" x 1"
#1 = 3/8" x 1 5/16"
#2 = 1/2" x 1 11/16"
#3 = 1/2" x 1 1/8"

Special Dowels for Miter Joints

These 90° degree angle plastic dowels are specially designed for miter joints. Depressions on all sides of the units allow generous glue spread. Can be used with available adhesives.

Overall size is 1⅜″ and they come in diameters of ¼″ and ⅜″. Drill holes to match diameters but a fraction deeper than the length of one leg of the dowel.

Clamp Nails

Clamp nails are specially shaped steel splines with divergent flanges that grip and pull together the parts of the joint. They are popular with manufacturers who use them on miter, bevel, butt, and other joint designs. The Clamp Nails are driven into matching 22-gauge kerfs that are required in each part of the joint. When the fasteners are installed correctly it is virtually impossible to separate the joint without destroying the wood.

The items are about ⅝″ wide and available in lengths from ½″ to 2″. They can be used in wood thicknesses from ⅝″ to 1″.

Tite Joint Fasteners

A mechanical means of pulling mating edges together with controlled pressure so parts have less tendency to twist or buckle. Can be used on panel edge-to-edge joints; often used on workbench leg-to-rail assemblies and similar projects where vibration may make retightening necessary. In such cases the fasteners are used without glue.

Installation requires two holes for the tubular "nuts" and a horizontal hole between them for the threaded rod. A drill guide is available so the holes can be drilled accurately.

They cost about $1.75 when purchased in single units.

Right Angle Connector

Consists of a ¼″-20, 2″-long steel bolt with flat head, and hex socket and a steel "dowel" with a threaded hole. Installation requires accurately sized and positioned holes for the dowel and the bolt.

Can be used with glue or alone for assemblies you may wish to break down. Very good for joints that may have to be retightened occasionally.

Cost about $.50 when purchased in units; about $4.50 for sets of ten.

JACK NUTS			
NUT (NUMBER)	DUTY	USE ON MATERIAL THICKNESS	USE MACHINE SCREW
4S	Light	To $^3/_{16}$"	6-32
4L	Light	To $^3/_8$"	6-32
6S	Medium	To $^3/_{16}$"	10-24
6L	Medium	To $^3/_8$"	10-24
8S	Heavy	To $^3/_{16}$"	$^1/_4$-20
8L	Heavy	To $^3/_8$"	$^1/_4$-20

Note: Jack nuts pull together to grip the material when the screw is tightened. They provide metal threads in thin materials, hollow walls, and hollow-core doors.

TEE NUTS	
SIZE (INTERNAL THREADS)	INSTALLATION HOLE REQUIRED
6-32	$^3/_{16}$"
8-32	$^7/_{32}$"
10-24	$^1/_4$"
10-32	$^1/_4$"
$^1/_4$-20	$^5/_{16}$"
$^5/_{16}$-18	$^{25}/_{64}$"
$^3/_8$-16	$^{29}/_{64}$"

Note: A tee nut is a fastener that permits the installation of machine screws in wood and similar materials. To install, drill hole and then hammer tee nut into place so the prongs penetrate.

THREADED INSERTS	
SIZE (INTERNAL THREADS)	INSTALLATION HOLE REQUIRED
6-32	$^{11}/_{64}$"
8-32	$^{13}/_{64}$"
10-24	$^7/_{32}$"
10-32	$^7/_{32}$"
$^1/_4$-20	$^5/_{16}$"
$^5/_{16}$-18	$^3/_8$"
$^3/_8$-16	$^{15}/_{32}$"

Note: Use these to install permanent machine threads in wood and similar materials. The inserts have slots so they can be turned into a hole with a screwdriver.

Molly® Bolts (Hollow-Wall Anchors)

The item is passed through a hole and tapped to imbed the gripping prongs. The screw is tightened to spread the anchor so it grips the wall. Then the screw is removed and reinserted after it is passed through the fixture. The screw can be removed without losing the anchor.

Available for wall thicknesses from ¼″ to 1¼″.

Toggle Bolts

Toggle bolts are used to secure items to hollow structures such as tile walls and concrete block. The hole must be large enough to allow passage of the spring-activated wings on the bolt. The wings spread and grip so the screw can be tightened. The screw cannot be removed without loosening the wings which in effect, act as a nut.

Available in diameters from ⅛″ to ½″, and in lengths from 2″ to 10″.

To use, pass the bolt (or screw) through the item to be fastened and then add the wings. Pass the wings through the hole and add the wings. Pass the wings through the hole and tighten the bolt.

Fiber Anchors

Fiber anchors allow wood screws to be used in masonry. They are available for No. 6 to No. 20 screws, in lengths ranging from ⅝″ to 2″. For maximum strength only the threaded portion of the screw should enter the anchor.

Expansion Shields

Expansion shields, used with lag screws, are driven into holes drilled in masonry. Driving the screw spreads the shield to provide a firm grip.

Short shields are okay in hard masonry but use longer ones when the material is porous.

The hole required equals the diameter of the shield.

Available in diameters of ¼″ to 1¼″ and in lengths from 1″ to 8″.

JOIST
HANGERS

FRAMING
ANCHORS

FRAMING
ANGLES

NAIL-ON
PLATES

POST ANCHORS
AND CAPS

Examples of special wood fasteners used extensively in house construction, but also very practical for assembling framework for projects like cold frames, shelters, decks, patio covers, wood storage racks, fences, and retaining walls. The fasteners, which are galvanized metal, can be made more attractive when necessary by painting them and using decorative screws instead of nails.

This special tool makes it easy to drive corrugated fasteners accurately. The fastener is held in a sleeve and set by tapping the ram.

APPENDIX 6.

Shop Math

Don't let the title of this section scare you off. There isn't so much figuring in 'shop math' as there is common sense and a few unique tricks.

In order to plan a project, you have to manipulate and manufacture simple geometric shapes; this is what most woodworking is all about. The boards you purchase at the lumberyard are simple squares and rectangles. Depending on how you machine these boards, you may turn them into triangles, circles, or—most likely—smaller squares and rectangles. These geometric shapes are joined in a way that somehow becomes a finished project, such as a storage shed (rectangles and triangles), a table (rectangles and circles), or a built-in cabinet (just rectangles). Shop math is a collection of methods to accurately measure and draw the geometric shapes you want to reproduce.

There are four indispensable measuring tools that you'll need to do this 'math'—a straightedge, a compass, a protractor, and a square. Don't skimp when you purchase these tools. You'll quickly find that a good straightedge is every bit as important (if not more so) than a good saw. What's the use of being able to cut a straight line if you can't scribe one? Once you have good measuring tools, always use the same tool to measure when laying out a project. Don't measure some parts with one straightedge, and other parts with another.

You may also want to invest in an awl for marking. It's hard to get used to an awl, but you'll quickly find that it offers two advantages over a pencil. First, the scribed line is always crisp and even; it doesn't broaden like a pencil line. This makes it easier to make accurate cuts. Second, an awl scores the wood grain before you cut it, helping to prevent tear-out.

The Circle

The Triangle

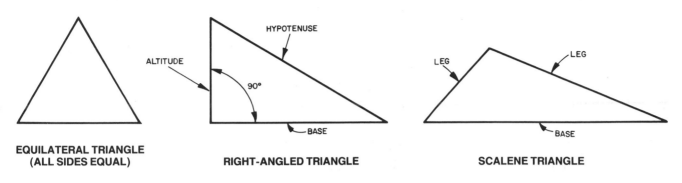

EQUILATERAL TRIANGLE
(ALL SIDES EQUAL)

RIGHT-ANGLED TRIANGLE

SCALENE TRIANGLE

Figures

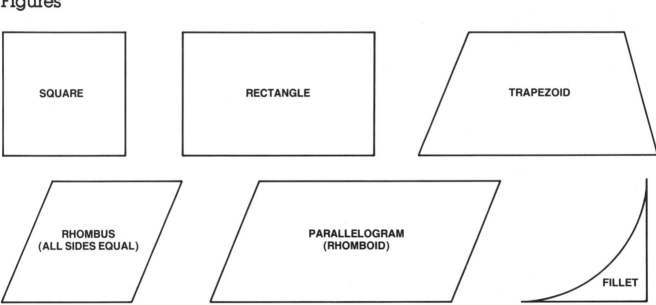

SQUARE

RECTANGLE

TRAPEZOID

RHOMBUS
(ALL SIDES EQUAL)

PARALLELOGRAM
(RHOMBOID)

FILLET

How to Find the Center of a Circle

- Draw two lines AB and CB from a common point on the circumference of the circle—direction of the lines is not critical.
- Construct a perpendicular bisector (D and E) for lines AB and CB.
- Point F, where lines D and E intersect, is the center of the circle.

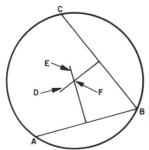

How to Construct a Square in a Circle

- Draw lines to connect the ends of perpendicular diameters.

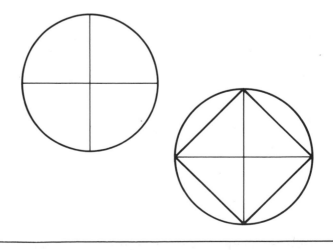

How to Construct a Circle in a Square

- Draw intersecting lines from opposite corners.
- Set the compass to equal the distance from the intersection of the lines to one side of the square.
- Use the intersection as the center of the circle.

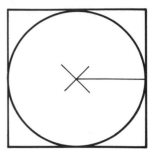

How to Construct a Hexagon (Six Sides)

- Set the compass so it equals the radius of the circle.
- Strike six arcs on the circumference using each intersection as the center point of the following arc.
- Draw lines to connect points where the arcs cross the circumference.

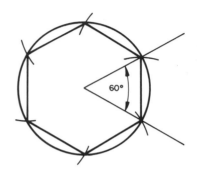

How to Construct a Pentagon (Five Sides)

- Form perpendicular diameters and then bisect a radius (AB).
- Form a line from point C to point D.
- Using the line CD as a radius and point C as a center, strike the arc E.
- Set the compass to equal the distance from point D to where arc E crosses the diameter.
- Use the settings to strike arcs on the circumference of the circle—each arc is the center of the following one.
- Draw lines to connect points where arcs cross the circumference.
- H is equal to the distance from D to where arc E crosses the diameter.

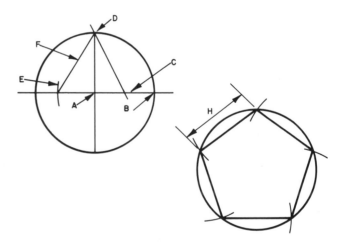

How to Construct a Five-Point Star

- Scribe a circle that represents the overall size of the star.
- Divide the circumference into five equal parts—360 divided by 5 = 72°.
- Connect the points as shown.

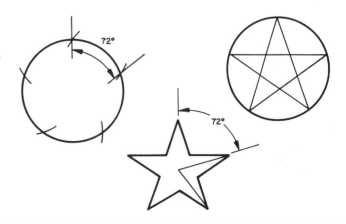

How to Form an Inside Corner (Concave)

- First, bisect the angle of the corner (line D).
- Establish a point on line D (E) and use it as the radius (F) for the arc.

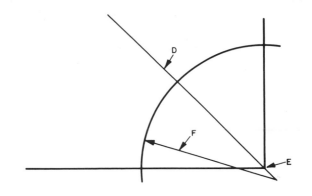

How to Round Off a Corner

- First, bisect the angle of the corner (line A).
- Select a point on line A (B) and set the compass to equal the distance from B to a side of the corner (C).
- Strike the arc using B as a center.

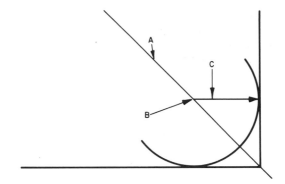

How to Construct Tangent Arcs

- Find the centers of the existing arcs (or circles) and draw a line through them (A).
- Establish point B by bisecting line A between the existing arcs.
- Use the distance between point B and one arc as a radius (C).
- Use point B as the center to strike the new arc or circle (D).

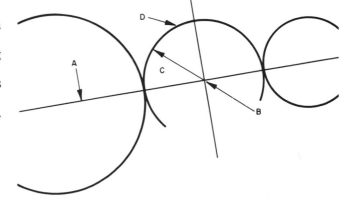

How to Construct an Equilateral Triangle

- Draw base line AB (equals one side of triangle).
- Set compass to equal distance between A and B.
- Use A as a center to strike arc D.
- Use B as a center to strike arc C.
- Draw lines from A and B to the intersection of arcs C and D (E).

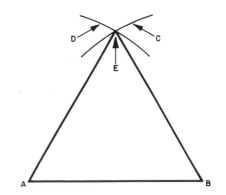

How to Bisect an Angle

- Set the compass arbitrarily and using A as a center strike arcs B and C.
- Set the compass arbitrarily and using points D and E as centers, strike arcs F and G.
- A line (H) drawn from A and through the intersection of arcs F and G will bisect the angle.

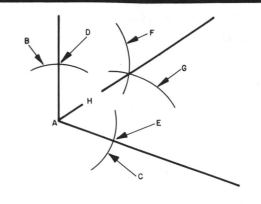

How to Find the Correct Cut Angle for Segmented Forms

The Formula: Divide 360 by the number of segments, and divide the result by 2.

- The example shows a 12-sided figure:
  360 divided by 12 = 30
  30 divided by 2 = 15
  15° is the correct *cut* angle.
- The cut angle is always ½ of the joint or included angle.

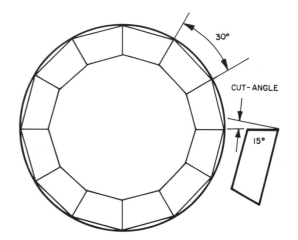

How to Bisect a Line

- Set the compass arbitrarily and using each end of the line as a center point, strike arcs C and D.
- A line (E) drawn through the intersection of arcs C and D will bisect the existing line.
- The new line will also be perpendicular to the existing line.

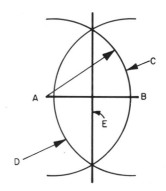

How to Construct a Perpendicular Line

- Mark the base-point of the perpendicular (A).
- Set compass arbitrarily and use A as a center to strike arcs B and C.
- Set compass arbitrarily and use points E and D as centers to strike arcs F and G.
- The perpendicular (H) will be a line drawn from A through the intersection of arcs F and G.

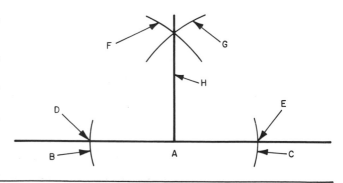

How to Draw a Line Parallel to an Existing Line

- Set the compass to equal the distance that is required between the lines.
- At arbitrary points A and B, strike arcs C and D.
- A line drawn tangent to the arcs (E) will be parallel to the existing line.

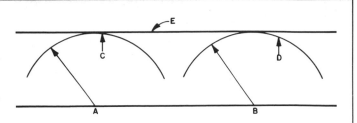

How to Make a Pattern for an Arbitrary Ellipse

- Draw a rectangle using lines A and B as the major and minor axes of the ellipse—length of rectangle = major axis—width of rectangle = minor axis.
- Fold the paper on the minor axis and again on the major axis.
- Draw a smooth curve or use a slim, flexible strip of wood as a guide—then cut off the waste.
- Unfold the paper to have the pattern for the ellipse.

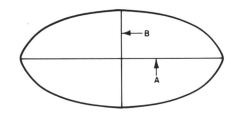

How to Use the String Method to Form an Accurate Ellipse

- Draw a rectangle with length and width to equal the major and minor axes of the ellipse.
- Divide the rectangle into four equal parts—lines AB and DE.
- Set compass to equal AC and use E as center to strike arcs F.
- Drive brads at point D and where arcs F cross line AB.
- Tie string tightly around the three brads and then substitute a pencil for the brad at D.
- Allow the pencil to be guided by the string as you move it to mark the ellipse.

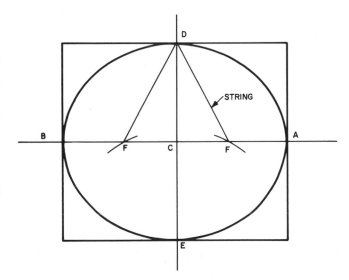

Decimal Equivalents

To find the decimal equivalent of a fraction, divide the numerator by the denominator.

$$\frac{\text{NUMERATOR}}{\text{DENOMINATOR}} = \text{DECIMAL EQUIVALENT}$$

Examples: ¾   3.000 divided by 4 = .750
           ³⁄₆₄   3.000 divided by 64 = .046875
           ⅝   5.000 divided by 8 = .625

A Quick Look at Metrics

Most Common Prefixes

Milli = .001   (one thousandth)
Centi = .01   (one hundredth)
Kilo = 1000   (one thousand)

CONVERSIONS

mm x .03937 = inches
mm divided by 25.4 = inches
cm x .3937 = inches
cm divided by 2.54 = inches
m x 39.37 = inches
m x 3.2809 = feet
m x 1.094 = yards
Km x .621377 = miles

SYMBOLS AND RELATIONSHIPS

NAME	SYMBOL	RELATIONSHIP
Millimeter	mm	10mm = 1cm
Centimeter	cm	10cm = 1dm
Decimeter	dm	10dm = 1m
Meter	m	10m = 1Dm
Decameter	Dm	10Dm = 1Hm
Hectometer	Hm	10Hm = 1Km

EQUIVALENTS

1mm = .03937 inches	1Km = .62137 miles
1cm = .3937 inches	1 inch = 2.54cm
1dm = 3.937 inches	1 foot = 30.48cm or .3048m
1m = 39.37 inches (also 3.281 feet or 1.094 yards)	1 yard = 91.44cm or .9144m
	1 mile = 1.6093Km

Using a Carpenter's Square as a Protractor

If you draw a line from the 12″ mark on the tool's tongue to a point on its blade you will have the hypotenuse of a right triangle. The idea is to use the correct dimension point on the blade to get the angle you need.

The drawing shows dimension points for some commonly used angles. The angles formed by the line you draw are complementary. If, for example, the line forms a 30 degree angle with the horizontal plane, then the angle between the line and the vertical plane will be 60 degrees.

As shown in one of the charts, the same system can be used to discover correct joint angles for multi-sided figures.

FOUR SIDES   **NINE SIDES**   **TWELVE SIDES**

DIMENSIONS TO USE FOR NUMBER OF SIDES IN PROJECT		
NO. OF SIDES	DIMENSION ON TONGUE	DIMENSION ON BLADE
3	12″	20⅞″
4	12″	12″
5	12″	8²⁵/₃₂″
6	12″	6¹⁵/₁₆″
7	12″	5²⁵/₃₂″
8	12″	3³¹/₃₂″
9	12″	4⅜″
10	12″	3⅞″
11	12″	3¹⁷/₃₂″
12	12″	3⁷/₃₂″
14	12″	2¾″
16	12″	2¹³/₃₂″
18	12″	2⅛″
20	12″	1²⁹/₃₂″

EXAMPLES OF DIMENSIONS TO USE FOR PARTICULAR ANGLES		
ANGLE REQUIRED	DIMENSION ON TONGUE	DIMENSION ON BLADE
30°	12″	20⅞″
45°	12″	12″
60°	12″	6¹⁵/₁₆″
70°	12″	4⅜″
72°	12″	3⅞″
75°	12″	3⁷/₃₂″
80°	12″	2⅛″
81°	12″	1²⁹/₃₂″

DECIMAL EQUIVALENTS OF COMMON FRACTIONS

FRACTION					DECIMAL	FRACTION						DECIMAL
1/64					.015625	33/64						.515625
2/64	1/32				.03125	34/64	17/32					.53125
3/64					.046875	35/64						.546875
4/64	2/32	1/16			.0625	36/64	18/32	9/16				.5625
5/64					.078125	37/64						.578125
6/64	3/32				.09375	38/64	19/32					.59375
7/64					.109375	39/64						.609375
8/64	4/32	2/16	1/8		.1250	40/64	20/32	10/16	5/8			.6250
9/64					.140625	41/64						.649625
10/64	5/32				.15625	42/64	21/32					.65625
11/64					.171875	43/64						.671875
12/64	6/32	3/16			.1875	44/64	22/32	11/16				.6875
13/64					.203125	45/64						.703125
14/64	7/32				.21875	46/64	23/32					.71875
15/64					.234375	47/64						.734375
16/64	8/32	4/16	2/8	1/4	.2500	48/64	24/32	12/16	6/8	3/4		.7500
17/64					.265625	49/64						.765625
18/64	9/32				.28125	50/64	25/32					.78125
19/64					.296875	51/64						.796875
20/64	10/32	5/16			.3125	52/64	26/32	13/16				.8125
21/64					.328125	53/64						.828125
22/64	11/32				.34375	54/64	27/32					.84375
23/64					.359375	55/64						.859375
24/64	12/32	6/16	3/8		.3750	56/64	28/32	14/16	7/8			.8750
25/64					.390625	57/64						.890625
26/64	13/32				.40625	58/64	29/32					.90625
27/64					.421875	59/64						.921875
28/64	14/32	7/16			.4375	60/64	30/32	15/16				.9375
29/64					.453125	61/64						.953125
30/64	15/32				.46875	62/64	31/32					.96875
31/64					.484375	63/64						.984375
32/64	16/32	8/16	4/8	2/4 1/2	.5000	64/64	32/32	16/16	8/8	4/4	2/2 1	1.0000

Index

Illustrations are marked by book (I or II) and figure number and are in bold.